# Giorgio Vasari

By the same author:

*SELF-PORTRAITS BY WOMEN PAINTERS*,
Liana De Girolami Cheney, Alicia Craig Faxon
and Kathleen Russo
(New Academia Publishing 2009)

*VASARI'S LIFE AND LIVES: The First Art Historian*,
by Einar Rud.
Editor and Preface by Liana De Girolami Cheney
(New Academia Publishing 2011)

Read an excerpt at www.newacademia.com

# Giorgio Vasari

## Artistic and Emblematic Manifestations

Liana De Girolami Cheney

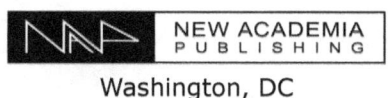

NEW ACADEMIA
PUBLISHING

Washington, DC

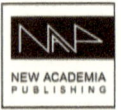

New Academia Publishing
P.O. Box 24720, Washington, DC 20038-7420
info@newacademia.com - www.newacademia.com

To Paola Barocchi, Wolfram Prinz and Richard Wallace

In recognition and with gratitude for their inspiration
in my studies on Giorgio Vasari (1511-1574).

# Contents

All photographs were taken by the author if not otherwise indicated in the captions.

# Acknowledgments

This writer is thankful for the permission to reproduce her articles published in *Exploration in Renaissance Culture, Papers in Art History,* The Pennsylvania State University, *Fifteenth Century Studies Journal, Sixteenth Century Journal, Italian Culture, The Journal of the Italian Astronomical Society* and Peter Lang Publishers.

The author is grateful for the access and assistance to consult in Europe and United States archives, libraries and art historical centers for the visual and textual research of this book, such as in Europe, the Archivio di Stato of Arezzo, Bologna, Florence, Naples, Rome and Venice and Archivio Vaticano, Rome; the British Library in London, Kunsthistorisches in Florence; and Bibliotheka Hertziana in Rome; the Cabinet des Dessins at the Musée du in Paris, the Gabinetto Disegni e Stampe degli Uffizi in Florence; the Gabinetto di Stampe e Disegni at the Villa Farnesina, in Rome; and the Albertina Drawing Collection in Vienna. And in United States, the Harvard University Libraries in Cambridge, the Boston University Library, the Avery Library at Columbia University in New York, the New York City Public Library, and the Library of Congress in Washington, DC.

The author is appreciative to these various private and public collections, museums, libraries, galleries and publishing companies that have given me permission to consult and publish reproduction of certain works in their collections on Giorgio Vasari and other artists included in this book, such as to the Ministero per i Beni Culturali e Ambientale of Arezzo, Florence, Rome and Naples, the Gabinetto dei Disegni e delle Stampe and the Galleria delgi Uffizi in Italy; Cabinet des Dessins at the Musée du Louvre, The Collection F. Lugt, Istitute Neerlandais and the Bibliothèque Natonale in France; Museo del Prado in Spain; Wallace Collection and the British Museum Library in England, the Los Angeles County Museum of Art, Saint Louis Museum of Art, the Minneapolis Institute of Arts, the Boston Museum of Fine Arts, the Art Institute of Chicago, the Philadelphia Art Museum, the Library of Congress, Washington, DC, and the National Gallery of Art, Washington, DC in USA and, in particular, Art Resource in New York.

My gratitude is also extended to the University of Massachusetts Lowell for supporting my research throughout the years with traveling grants and sabbatical leaves. However, it is to Giorgio Vasari, most of all, that my appreciation is directed since he is my teacher and a constant source of bewilderment, inspiration and wonderment for my understanding of art and theory. *Vasari, Adiuta Lianam!*

Liana De Girolami Cheney
Boston 2011

# Preface

## By Wolfram Prinz

Liana De Girolami Cheney's *Giorgio Vasari's Artistic and Emblematic Manifestations* provides an extensive survey of the content and meaning of Giorgio Vasari's art and symbolism. Cheney's considers Vasari's intellectual ability, observing his erudition, his knowledge of ancient literature and philosophy, and his relationship with the humanists of his time. This book successfully demonstrates how Vasari is a master of visual culture in the sixteenth century.

The book examines Giorgio Vasari's paintings and writings, including his impact in the emblematic tradition. Cheney postulates a unique notion on Vasari's conception of *history painting,* which evolves in the development of religious and secular decorative cycles in the sixteenth century. Following his classical education, his love for collecting art and his quest for artistic expression through *disegno* (drawing), Vasari reveals his humanistic culture. He fuses the classical artistic, literary and philosophical traditions with Renaissance literary and visual conventions, thus formulating a practical and theoretical artistic language as well as an historical visual and emblematic repertoire of images with their signification.

The essays, here presented, examine Vasari's extraordinary artistic and intellectual talents. In them, the emphasis on the cultural and emblematic tradition provides one more layered in the understanding of the motives of patrons, as well as of the didactic purpose and intent of many of Vasari's pictorial inventions. His approach links his artistic conceptions to the humanistic literary and philosophical traditions.

It is difficult to imagine where the history of Italian Renaissance art would be without the writings of Giorgio Vasari's *The Lives of the Most Excellent Architects, Painters and Sculptors* (*Le vite de' più eccellenti architetti, pittori, et scultori*, 1550 and 1568 editions). It is the first book on the history of art that designs within an historical frame an interwoven chain of cultural patterns, anecdotal stories, and visual imagery, which are embodied in the biographies of the artist; and also articulates the intent and aesthetic quests of art, which is contained in the prefaces.

*Giorgio Vasari's Artistic and Emblematic Manifestations* will interest not only those who are initiating their study of Italian art, but in general, all those who are interested in Italian culture. In addition, it will be of value to scholars of art history.

Wolfram Prinz, Professor of Art History, Johann Wolfgang Goethe Universität, Frankfurt am Main, and former President of the *Classe Storia dell'Arte* of the Accademia delle Arti del Disegno, Florence

April 2011

# Giorgio Vasari
## Artistic and Emblematic Manifestations

# Introduction

# Giorgio Vasari: Artistic and Emblematic Manifestations

*It is undeniably true that if the artists of our own time were justly rewarded they would produce even greater works of art, far superior to those of the ancient world.*

—Giorgio Vasari, *Vite* (Preface III).[1]

Giorgio Vasari (1511-1574) is one of the most important cultural figures in Italy during the middle of the sixteenth century, having achieved prominence as an art critic, historian, architect, aesthetician, painter and impresario. His accomplishments in all these capacities have long been the subject of extensive study, including his work as an iconographer, a precursor of the emblematic tradition, and promoter of the classical tradition in art, theory of art, philosophy and literature.

In many respects, he is an exemplary case of what Baldassare Castiglione called *renaissance man*,[2] as noted in the writings of Paola Barocchi, T. S. R. Boas, Paul Barolsky, Patricia Rubin, Wolfram Prinz, and, in particular Einar Rud.

Vasari's artistic training and studies with Rosso Fiorentino, Baccio Bandinelli and Michelangelo, and early humanistic learning in the classics with Giovanni Pollastra provide a dynamic interdependence of conceits, which are manifested in his early works and directly relate to the fruitful maturity of his late decorative cycles and his other art forms. His passion for deciphering mystery has much to do with the efforts of mythographers and antiquarians (Andrea Alciato, Pierio Valeriano, Vincenzo Cartari, Paolo Giovio, Cosimo Bartoli and Cesare Ripa), who study the manifestation of the visual arts in ancient and Christian art, as represented in ancient coins, reliefs sculpture, works of art, and music, as well as the commentaries of classical and Christian scholars (Pliny the Elder, Vitruvius and Church Fathers). The philosophical revival of classical text and figures (Plato, Plotinus and Hermes Trismegistus) by Renaissance Neoplatonists (Marsilio Ficino and Giovanni Pico della Mirandola) facilitate the quest for composing conceits. Artists and humanists of sixteenth century who, in turn, are also fascinated by the exploration, collection and expression of the innovations and discoveries in their century assimilate this intellectual ardor. And Vasari is an exponent of such zeal.

This impetus or *furor poeticus* for ancient hieroglyphs, symbols and emblems is prompted and promulgated by Quattrocento and Cinquecento or Renaissance Neoplatonists. These philosophers (Ficino and Pico della Mirandola) encourage the search for alternatives to language in visual symbols, which could offer an image for the immediacy of experience with verbal language could not offer. As Ernest Gombrich explains, the visual image for these humanists is based on conventional or private traditions.[3] The image contains three distinct levels of meaning. First, a painting may represent an object of the visible world, such as a woman holding a balance or a snake. Second, the image may also symbolize an idea, such as Justice—a traditional allusion of a woman with the balance—or Envy—a depiction of an elderly woman holding a snake. Both of these meanings rely on conventional understandings incorporated into the cultural milieu of the time. The third meaning expresses the artist's conscious or unconscious mind. It is a personal reference to the representation of the image, e.g., the image of a snake may symbolize the sin of pride (original sin) in Christian symbolism or wisdom in ancient mythology. The balance may allude to the virtue of Temperance in Renaissance iconography or the judgment of souls in Egyptian symbolism.

Vasari's art and theory is conceived from the classical and Cinquecento artistic traditions where the essence of creativity is imparted by God and manifested in the conception of *disegno* (drawing). Under the influence of Renaissance Neoplatonism and Christian Renaissance religious conventions, Vasari's artistic notion is conceived by God and then projected into the artist's soul. From the artist's mind/soul, the artistic conception is then visualized into a practical form, a drawing of the idea or an imagery. From the imagery, the artistic notion expands into the conception of a *history painting*, a single narrative, a  program or a decorative cycle. Thus, God (artistic notion) and artist *(disegno)* are an artistic conception, which is manifested through the elaboration of the history of cultural imagery and the association of humanistic and philosophical ideals.

In his art, Vasari constructs an elaboration based on Leon Battista Alberti's concept of *istoria* (dramatic narrative), a *history painting*. I coin this term "history painting" to mean the depiction of painted scenes with narrative content from classical history, Christian history, and mythology, as well as depicting the historical events of the far or near past. These include paintings with religious, mythological, historical, literary and allegorical subjects. Vasari's history paintings may embody some interpretation of life or convey a moral or intellectual message. Thus, a *history painting* is a single visual narrative or a decorative cycle with cultural, emblematic and humanistic implications. These implications are interconnected with didactic and moral messages as well as with a literary and philosophical conceits. Vasari is proud to come from an artistic Florentine tradition that produced creative individuals such as Alberti, Leonardo, Michelangelo Dante, and Ficino. Thus, Vasari's imagery and writings attest to his Florentine artistic and intellectual lineage.

With the assistance of his teachers, humanists and patrons of the time, Vasari carefully studies classical writings on art by Pliny and Vitruvius. In his decorative cycles and imagery, Vasari projects an assimilation of their artistic descriptions and theories. From Pliny, he learns to recall the ancient artists and to record their lives; from Vitruvius, he extracts his theory of art in terms of five principles (*disegno* or drawing, rule, proportion, order, and *maniera* or style). From  Alberti, Vasari conceives the concept of beauty, which he transforms into a theory of Mannerism in relation to Neoplatonic notions of Beauty and Good.

Vasari emphasizes in his writings, particularly in the prefaces of the *Vite,* that an allegory or symbol must assimilate, visually and verbally, its ancient sources. Such emblematic sources provide him with an extensive repertoire of images, which he collects and uses in the iconography of his paintings. Vasari's symbols embody aesthetic theories and philosophical concerns of the cultural milieu of his time. His legacy to the humanistic endeavors and the emblematic tradition produces a symbolic heritage in art, literature and music during the Cinquecento. His significance for the humanistic and emblematic traditions relies on defining and explaining artistic concepts such invention, imagination and judgment. His questioning of the use and meaning of terms in the visual depiction influences the art of the sixteenth century, and this method of artistic inquiry continues beyond his time.

Other issues considered by Vasari in the manifestation of art are the interpretation of classical myth, interconnecting with Christian attributes and non-Christian symbols known in the sixteenth century. This mythical tradition is assimilated and incorporated in art, in particular, in the sacred and profane decorative cycles of the Cinquecento. The visual tradition of symbols assists the artist in creating conceits for humanists, enlightened individuals,  and artists themselves.  With the intellectual assistance of the literati, artists could compose conceits with elusive meaning of myth, allegory and personification. Thus transforming the role of an artist from mere laborer into mythmaker and validating the intellectual potentials of the artist, who could conceive and unravel these conceits. Vasari is able to provide this new ground for the Cinquecento artist because he has assimilated and learned from the ancient and modern masters, their instructions about inventing art, imitating art, and judging the merits of creating art.

As Vasari learns about the formulation of inventions of image from his teachers, he also creates a new vocabulary in art—an encyclopedia of images and symbols—by using emblematic sources for his paintings. This visual repertoire becomes an educational instrument for artists and humanists, offering instructional guidance to the mystery of images. Vasari's method of systematized images for the use of the artist paves the way for Cesare Ripa's *Iconologia* (1593) and demonstrates the assimilation of the classical, humanistic and emblematic traditions in Italian paintings of the sixteenth century.

The learner, Vasari, becomes the teacher of composing images, enlightening his fellow artists as well as those for centuries to come.

The purpose of this collection is to celebrate the 500 year anniversary of Vasari's birth (1511-1574). To honor this historical event, I selected articles in this book: some published, some revised and expanded, some never published. These articles demonstrate the immense contribution that Vasari makes in the history of art. His extraordinary impact in the culture of sixteenth century art and art theory is still stimulating and intellectually challenging, is his influence in later imagery, art theories, and formulations on approaches to the study of art history.

Another aim of this book is to reveal the many important artistic and art historical issues associated with the paintings and writings of Vasari. These include his artistic achievements as an emblematist, with an emphasis on his decorative paintings, and more specifically his role in the redefinition of *history painting;* his work in the development of new formal conventions for decorative cycles; his augmentation of the classical and emblematic traditions; and, his formulation of the foundations of art history as an academic discipline and a humanist pursuit in the sixteenth century.

As a leading artist of his day, Vasari reveals his notions about art from his early works, the imagery focuses on the most significant artistic, intellectual, cultural, and political forces, affecting the origins and development of his mature iconography programs, decorative style, and history of art. The essays consist of two elements: the first group of six essays focuses on the early decorative and secular cycles, while the second groups of five essays address moral and religious issues.

These essays emphasize how Vasari's humanist milieu influences the formal characteristics and visual imagery of his early works, as well as his written commentaries on art theory. The impact of his emblematic training with Pierio Valeriano and Andrea Alciato contribute to his artistic emblematic formation. Vasari employs the artistic and intellectual strategies of his early period in working through a concept of *history painting.*

Vasari emerges as an artist with a profound humanistic interest. This particularly holds true in the analysis of his early decorative cycles, namely, the Bolognese paintings of San Michele in Bosco,

1539-40; the Venetian paintings, 1541; Case Vasari in Arezzo and Florence 1542-1555; the Neapolitan paintings for the Refectory of Monteoliveto, 1545; and the Roman paintings for the Palazzo della Cancelleria, Sala dei Cento Giorni, 1546. The studies of these early decorative cycles are included in the first part of the book. These early decorative cycles represent a prelude to Vasari's later works, for example, the decorative cycles for the Palazzo Vecchio in Florence, the fresco paintings for the Dome of Santa Maria del Fiore in Florence and for the Sala Regia in Rome, because Vasari repeats and elaborates his earlier emblematic, iconographical, and artistic inventions. In addition, he applies these artistic inventions to his religious paintings as well, which are essays in the second part of the book.

The essays introduce Vasari to the reader of the many strengths of this peripatetic wall-painter whose decorative cycles are found in cities throughout Italy. His theory of art (rebirth, nature, classical and beauty) and criteria for art (imitation, invention, and judgment) are clearly articulated in these imageries as well as in the prefaces of Vasari's *Vite*. The frescoes located in Bologna, Venice, Arezzo, Florence, Naples and Rome, clearly indicate Vasari's understanding of the cultural taste of sixteenth-century patrons. Vasari collects and appropriates antique sources and he incorporates emblematic sources, such as the writings of Andrea Alciato, Vincenzo Cartari, and Pierio Valeriano, in these decorative cycles. Perhaps of greater importance, Vasari's pictorial imagery and personifications anticipates the influential emblematic encyclopedia of a later time, most notably Cesare Ripa's *Iconologia* of 1603.

Beyond my consideration of iconography and iconographical issues, Vasari's artistic achievements must be considered in light of his profound knowledge of antiquity and exposure to the ideas and ideals of Neoplatonism as well as his religious Christian tradition. The second set of articles in the second chapter address these manifestations. Finally, the influence of the intellectual and philosophical world of Renaissance humanism on Vasari, the demands of his patrons, his refined skill as a connoisseur, and his achievement in the making of pictures is revealed in these collection, not only with respect to how all these elements feed into the theoretical framing of his famous *Vite* of 1550 and 1568, but also in terms of a long-standing dialogue existing between the verbal and the visual which characterized Vasari's work from its germinal period.

The essays also shed light on Vasari in several new aspects. For example, philosophically, they reflect on Vasari's interpretation of humanist concepts such as Neoplatonism and Idealism, notions that are manifested in his writings, namely, *Le vite dei più eccellenti pittori, scultori ed architettori*, 1550 and 1568, *I Ragionamenti* (1568-70), diaries and letters, as well as in his early decorative cycles of 1539-1554. Historically, these essays show how Vasari, in his *Vite*, prefaces the formulation of art history and provides an art historical framework for the first time since antiquity (Pliny, Vitruvius). Vasari achieves this goal by classifying and documenting artists' works and lives from antiquity to the present.

Aesthetically, these essays reveal the contribution of Vasari to the theory of art in establishing criteria for assessing art as well as founding an academy of art to teach the principles of art. Iconographically, the essays analyze the nature of interpreting images. These images maybe depicted as allegories or personifications in relation to emblematic sources (Alciato, Cartari, Valeriano). Thus, the visual imagery of Vasari establishes a pictorial emblematic tradition in the Cinquecento. His pictorial emblemata anticipates the emblematic encyclopedia of Cesare Ripa's *Iconologia* (1603). Also, artistically, these essays reveal how Vasari fuses the ancient pictorial tradition (Pliny, Vitruvius) with Cinquecento's imagery (for example, Michelangelo's Sistine Ceiling, Raphael's Stanze, Perino del Vaga's Castel St'Angelo, Bronzino's Villa Imperiale; and Francesco Salviati's Sale Farnese), establishing a convention for decorative cycles in the sixteenth century

The essays manifest Vasari's extraordinary artistic and intellectual talents. In them, the emphasis on the cultural and emblematic tradition provides one more layered in the understanding of the motives of patrons, as well as of the didactic purpose and intent of many of Vasari's pictorial inventions. His approach links his artistic conceptions to the humanistic literary and philosophical traditions.

In view of the celebrated position of Vasari as a leading artist of his day, it is important to honor the 500 year anniversary of his birth (1511) and to consider his works by focusing with some care on the most significant artistic, intellectual, cultural, and political forces that affected the development of his religious and secular decorative program, and impacted the course of history of art, art theory and art criticism.

With these essays, the goal is to provide for the student of fine art, art history, classics, history and the humanities, and interested readers of European history, literature, decorative arts, and Italian visual culture, an insight and understanding of sixteenth-century art, artistic theories, and assimilation of the classics in Italy through the eyes and mind of a Renaissance accomplished artist and writer–Giorgio Vasari. Thus, this collection of essays contributes to the scholarship of sixteenth-century patronage, theories of art and criticism, and to the understanding of Giorgio Vasari's paintings.

## Notes

1. Vasari continues, "Instead, the artist today struggles to ward off famine rather than to win fame, and this crushes and buries his talent and obscures his name. This is a shame and disgrace to those who could come to his help but refuse to do so." *Le vite dei più eccellenti pittori, scultori ed architettori*, ed. Gaetano Milanesi (Florence: G. C. Sansoni, 1970-74) , Preface III.

2. Baldassare Castiglione, *Il Cortegiano* (Venice: Aldus, 1528), 5.

3. Ernest Gombrich, *Simbolicae Questione* (London: Phaidon Press, 1972), 172.

# Part One

## Decorative Religious and Secular Cycles

# 1

# The Paintings of the Casa Vasari in Arezzo

*Giorgio Vasari non visse da pittore ma da principe.*[1]

One indication of the artist's professional status in the Cinquecento was the freedom he enjoyed to purchase, design, and decorate his own house. By the 1540's Giorgio Vasari had established himself as a painter and writer, and he begun work on a small house in Arezzo. This house located in Borgo San Vito still stands (fig. 1). Vasari is a prime example of the artist as householder, and the paintings of his Casa Vasari abundantly demonstrate this new situation. Perhaps more important, Vasari's intellectual curiosity, enthusiasm, and artistic ability enabled him to develop a new attitude towards artistic patronage. The collection of works created for the Casa Vasari expresses in personal terms this artist's love for his masters, his fascination with antiquity, and his delight in virtuosity. Vasari's aim in building and decorating his house was to establish an artistic monument to his own accomplishments, and in this endeavor he manifestly succeeded.

Vasari's autobiography and his letters and *ricordi* remain the best and most complete source for the dating and description of the paintings in the Casa Vasari.[2] At times, however, Vasari is vague, and his comments about the iconography are sketchy; they may even seem willfully cryptic. Vasari's program for the decoration of his house is not philosophically, theologically, or mythologically systematic. He was its sole inventor, depicting in the four decorated rooms his own ideas about a variety of subjects  - Art, Fame, Fortune, History, and Religion - by means of allegorical themes and personifications. The allegorical themes contain biblical and antique stories, which are depicted in a Cinquecento setting.

Yet, for all his originality, Vasari drew upon a decorative scheme characteristic of the Cinquecento. He paid special attention to the Sistine Ceiling, Roman Stanze, and Giovio's Museum. And Vasari borrowed conceits from his own work: those used in the apparatus for *La Talanta* (Venice), the decorations from the Cornaro Palace (Venice), the Refectory of Monteoliveto (Naples) and the Sala dei Cento Giomi (Rome).[3]

The Casa Vasari is a unique Cinquecento museum. It immortalizes the Cinquecento man as artist, historian, and patron. The message conveyed in the Casa Vasari, for all its reliance on the past, is both original and intimate.

Off and on Vasari spent approximately twelve years, from 1542 to 1554, painting the four rooms of the *piano nobile* of the Casa Vasari (fig. 2).[4] The rooms are identified for the subjects depicted on their respective ceilings, namely Fame, Abraham, Apollo, and Fortune. The ceilings of these rooms are painted in various media: the Chamber of Abraham is painted in tempera, the Chamber of Fortune in oil, and the other two ceilings are painted al *fresco*. The only chamber that has paintings on both ceilings and walls (the latter *al fresco)* is the Chamber of Fortune.

In the Chamber of Fame, Vasari continued a Quattrocento and Cinquecento tradition of immortalizing the artist's house by painting allegories of the Fine Arts and portraits of artists, or *uomini famosi.* The allegories of the Fine Arts - Painting, Sculpture, Architecture, and Poetry - are governed by the Allegory of Fame, which is located in the center of the ceiling.[5] In the lunette of the Allegory of Fame are eight portraits of famous artists, as well as teachers and ancestors of Vasari: these include Andrea del Sarto, Bartolomeo della Gatta, Luca Signorelli, Masaccio, Michelangelo and Lazzaro Vasari. Vasari's own portrait appears among these *uomini famosi,* to be sure; most significantly is the fact that - influenced by the writings of Antonio Filarete,[6] the Quattrocento architect - Vasari is the very first painter of the Cinquecento to adorn his own home with portraits of other artists.

The inclusion of the Allegory of Poetry in the realm of the Fine Arts is most revealing for its allusion to two concepts: *ut pictura poesis* and *furor poeticus*. The idea of *ut pictura poesis* (as is painting, so is poetry) comprehends the complementary natures of poetry and painting, equating the inspiration of the poet with the imagination of the painter. Both are concerned with imitating nature - the poet with words, the painter with visual elements.[7] In the Chamber of Fame the Renaissance Neoplatonic concept of *furor poeticus* (frenzy of the poet, or intellectual creative force) is manifested not only by the depiction of the Allegory of Poetry but by showing all the allegories of the Fine Art in the act of creating art.

In discussing the theory of painting, Vasari stresses the relation of *furor poeticus* to the creation of an art work. He considers two alternatives for achieving artistic creativity: one may either achieve by imitation-that is to say, a method of learning - or else by invention, an autonomous means of conceiving artistic ideas.

At the center of the ceiling, the Allegory of Fame blows her golden trumpet in the direction of the Allegory of Painting, as if to acknowledge the importance of painting and of Vasari's importance as a painter. It is important in this context to recall that this room is the entrance to the house. As such, as in view of its pictorial composition, it serves both as a memorial to Vasari's activity and as a greeting hall to entering visitors and friends.

Among the ceilings of the Casa Vasari only the Chamber of Abraham deals with religious subject matter. According to Vasari the Chamber of Abraham was the second ceiling he painted. He writes that he began work in May of 1548 and finished it by the end of July; and he painted this ceiling in tempera because, "as I always worshipped the memory and works of the ancients and observed that the method of coloring in tempera was going out, I tried to revive it and did the whole work in that manner, which certainly ought not to be entirely condemned or abandoned."[8] As its name implies, the theme of this ceiling draws upon the story of Abraham and Isaac. In contrast to Quattrocento and Cinquecento traditions of depicting the sacrifice of Isaac, however, Vasari presents a most inventive *istoria*: God the Father blessing the seed of Abraham. This blessing, which occurred after the attempted sacrifice of Isaac by Abraham, is described in Genesis 22:17: "I [Lord] will bless you

[Abraham) abundantly and greatly multiply your descendants until they are numerous as the stars in the sky and the grains of sand
on the seashore."[9] Surrounding the tondo of Abraham and Isaac
in rectangular settings are four personifications of virtue (Peace,
Concord, Chastity, and Modesty), and at the corners of the square
ceiling the four cardinal virtues (Prudence, Temperance, Chastity,
and Fortitude).

Socrates and Cicero held that certain cardinal virtues were essential to the life of the perfected human being. Later, Ambrose and
Alcuin held similar views.[10] The cardinal virtues were considered
the foundation of a Christian life; also, special benefits of grace were
bestowed upon man by God through the sacred banquet.

In the ceiling of the Chamber of Abraham the four virtues Modesty, Chastity, Peace, and Concord convey a Christian message as
well. But this meaning derives in part from a pagan iconography;
it is transformed into a Christian language encapsulated in the Latin inscription *Modestia vestra nota sit omnibus hominubus* (Let your
modesty be known to all human beings). This motto is taken from
a passage in Paul's letter to the Philippians; the importance of living a model life by imitating Christ is stressed, and Christians are
exhorted to bear gifts and to receive greetings and benediction.[11]

The tondo image of God blessing the seed of Abraham suggests
that this room was the nuptial chamber of the house. Moreover, because the cardinal virtues are gifts of grace, they can be related logically as well to God's blessing of Abraham. The figure of Abraham
is associated with the moral virtue of obedience, as well as the willingness to live by the other Christian virtues. To Vasari, Abraham is
the exemplary figure of a Christian husband, and in the tondo he is
shown surrounded by all the virtues necessary for a good marriage.

The ceiling of the Chamber of Apollo, painted *al fresco* in 1550,
depicts Apollo with the court of the muses and reveals Vasari's erudition in the arts and music.

In the Chamber of Apollo, Vasari symbolized the god's dual nature. His divine nature is manifested in a portrayal of Apollo as a
personification of human intellect that governs the arts and sciences, which are represented by the surrounding muses. And Apollo's
human nature and role as earthy hero are indicated by his attributes - the bow, quiver, and *lira da braccio* - and by the fact that he is

crowned with laurel by a pair of cupids. The actions of flying and crowning executed by the cupids also recall the love myth of Eros and Anteros (love and Counterlove).[12]

Vasari places Apollo alone on a mountain top - probably an allusion to Mount Parnassus - in an arid and rocky landscape which includes only a small tree trunk with laurel branches. According to Ovid, when Apollo witnessed the metamorphosis of Daphne into a laurel tree, he began to kiss the tree, which shrank from his kisses. Apollo vowed to adopt the laurel tree as his emblem and to adorn his hair, lyre, and quiver with its leaves. It is this myth of which Vasari reminds us.

That Vasari's interpretation of the nine muses is very personal is evidenced by the inclusion of his wife's likeness among the muses. Two important changes had occurred in Vasari's life by the time he completed this room. The first was his marriage, commemorated by the portrait of his wife Nicolosa in 1550. The other was publication in 1550 of the first edition of *The Life* of the *Artists*. Vasari was henceforth considered a writer as well as an artist.

Nicolosa's prominent position as the muse Erato suggests that she is special and presides over the other muses. This emphasis, along with her similarities in physiognomy and Cinquecento attire to those of the other muses, stresses that this is a courtly gathering. Thus the lady of the house is surrounded by her attendants while Apollo with his music and poetry inspires their activities and harmonizes the intellectual pursuits of the Vasari family.

In relating the design of the ceiling of the Chamber of Apollo to the other ceilings in the Casa Vasari, one notices that in the tondo of the Chamber of Abraham the blessing event also symbolizes the religious protection that the household of the Casa Vasari enjoys. Likewise, in the Chamber of Apollo the god of wisdom illuminates and protects the intellect of the Vasari family.

Strong iconographical relationships are found in a comparison of the ceiling of the Chamber of Apollo with that of the adjacent room, the Chamber of Fame. In each room a central figure reigns over the other figures of the ceiling. In the Chamber of Fame, the arts and artists are honored by Fame; and in the Chamber of Apollo, inspiration and harmony rule humanistic learning. Vasari's paintings indicate that in the house of an artist homage is paid to artistic and humanistic endeavors.

The last room to be described is Vasari's studio or library, the Chamber of Fortune. This room illustrates the Casa Vasari's richest iconographical program; it also exemplifies the Renaissance *camera picta*.[13] Vasari painted the ceiling in oils and the walls *a1* fresco in 1548.

Vasari's decorative and thematic cycle is divided between ceiling and walls. The program of the ceiling is further subdivided into three themes - the allegorical figures of Fortune, Envy, and Virtue are viewed in the *palco*; around them are the four seasons or ages of man; and surrounding them are eight planetary gods with the signs of the zodiac (fig. 6). Putti holding Vasari's coat of arms are found in the corners of the ceiling.

As Vasari noted in the description of this chamber, when walking around the room, one may see the images on the *palco* changing; at times one sees Fortune above Virtue and Envy, and on other occasions Virtue is above Fortune and Envy. The placement of the allegory of Fortune between the allegories of Virtue and Envy (Vice) is most significant because it exemplifies the Cinquecento concept of the challenge or contest between good and bad forces in nature: "Fortuna comes Virtutis."[14] And it relates specifically to the rest of the theme on the ceiling. Fortune and her vicissitudes are dependent on the dispositions of the planetary gods and the signs of the zodiac because they both control the destiny of human beings through life.

In the ceiling one notices that the stars are favoring good fortune for Vasari, a fact symbolized by the full-blown sail that Fortune holds. Vasari was aware that, although good fortune is indispensable to an artist's success, this condition is not constant in the life of human beings - hence the ambiguity in the images of the *palco*. The scheme of the wall decoration is divided into two parts (figs. 7-10): the upper part deals with two types of personifications and the lower part with classical *istorie*. The two types of personifications of the upper part have to do with the dimensions of human existence and guidance of the good life for an artist. While the classical *istorie* of the lower part do certainly convey didactic messages to the painter, their primary function is to provide commentary on the history and methods of art. In the upper pan the seated personifications display the moral virtues essential for living, (Honor, Prosperity, Fortitude, Liberality, Justice, Peace, Prudence and Wisdom) while the standing personifications symbolize Religion, Abundance, Art, and Nature (figs. 7_10).[15]

It is no accident that Vasari arranged for the statue of Aphrodite (fig. 9) to face the painting of Artemis of Ephesus (fig. 10). The strong contrast between the attributes, elements, and composition of these two figures gives added cogency to their identification as personifications of art and nature respectively.[16] An artist experiences nature but creates art. Vasari thought that painting, more so than sculpture, could surpass nature because it may contain a greater number of variations, impressions, and *istorie* from nature.

The classical *istorie* of the lower part are all painted in a monochromatic reddish tonality, thereby simulating antique paintings. The *istorie* relate to three general ideas: the invention and methods of painting (Gydes of Lydia and Protogenes), the criticism and competition among artists (Parrhassius and Zeuxis), and the content and expression found in paintings (Apelles and Timanthes).[17]

In the Chamber of Fortune there is a general underlying philosophy that gives unity and meaning to the various personifications and *istorie*, but this philosophy is a set of personal convictions rather than a result of systematic thought. Thus there is a relationship between the ceilings' and walls' decorations. In the ceiling the planetary gods control and grant benefits to Vasari through time. These benefits are personified by four simulated sculptures of nature, art, religion, and abundance and eight seated figures representing the qualities to which a virtuous man as Vasari must aspire in order to live a prudent, honorable, and successful life. The *palco* scene on the ceiling and the classical *istorie* on the lower part of the walls together imply that Vasari has achieved good fortune and fame through his accomplishments as a painter by imitating and inventing as the ancient masters had done.

Reviewing the program of the Casa Vasari as a whole, one discovers that in the ceiling of each chamber the central figure provides the due to the underlying philosophy of the artist. In the Chamber of Fame the viewer is instructed on the arts and the artists and gently reminded that this is the house of an important painter whose portrait is included in the decorative scheme: Fame blows her trumpet towards the Allegory of Painting, this celebrating one aspect of Vasari's talents. As the viewer enters the next room, the Chamber of Apollo, he is greeted by Apollo and a court of Muses. There is a corridor adjacent to a garden. The guest enters the *orto*. Returning from the garden, the viewer reenters the house through the Chamber of Abraham. Moved by the blessing scene, he is reminded of the Christian and cardinal virtues bestowed upon his people by God. After a moment of silence, he walks into the Chamber of Fortune to encounter a delightful exposition of various capricci: landscape scenes, classical *istorie*, portraits, simulated and actual sculptures, mottoes, and *all'antica* ornamentation. The latter attest to Vasari's conception of art, nature, and history. The planetary gods confront the viewer from the ceiling. They control the destiny of the individual as well as the seasons and Fortune. As the guest continues around the chamber looking at the ceiling, he may notice that the *palco* scene has shifted emphasis and that now Virtue is controlling human destiny. This note of humor teases one's fancy and is an invitation to linger and to learn more of the complexity of this chamber.

As guests depart, they are reminded of the unique nature of the residence they have just visited: on the doorway is a marble bust of Vasari flanked by two frescoes allegories of painting and architecture. In this *piano nobile*, an artist once lived (fig. 11).

## Notes

This article is a reprint from "Giorgio Vasari's Paintings of the Casa Vasari Arezzo," *Exploration in Renaissance Culture* (Spring 1985), 53-73.

1. I am borrowing Vasari's description of Raphael's role, which I think can be applied to Vasari. See Giorgio Vasari, *Le Vite de' più eccellenti pittori, scultori, et architettorie*, 1550, 1568, ed. Gaetano Milanesi (Florence, 1970-74), IV, 384-85. All succeeding references to this text will be noted as Vasari-Milanesi. For literature containing bibliography on the houses of Quattrocento and Cinquttento artists, see W. Bombe, "Giorgio Vasari Hauser in Florenz und Arezzo." *Belvedere*, 13 (1928), 58f.; Wolfram Prinz, "Vasaris Sammlung von Künstlerbildnissen," *Mitteilungen des Kunsthistorischten Institutes in Florenz*, 12 (1966), 10-11. 20-22; L Cheney. 'The Paintings of the Casa Vasari," Diss. Boston Univ., 1978; K. W. Forster and R.J.

Tuttle, "The Casa Pippi: Giulio Romano's House in Mantua," *Architectura*, 2 (1973), 104-30; A. Cecchi, "Vasari e le case degli artisti." *Cat. Mostra di Giorgio Vasari: Principi, letterati e artisti nelle carte di Giorgio Vasari*, ed. Laura Corti et al. (Arezzo, 1981), pp. 35-7; and Vol. 3, Pio Peccai, *Giorgio Vasari. Vite*, (Milan, 1930) for the houses of A. San Gallo, Correggio and Palladio.

2. See Vasari-Milanesi; K. Frey, ed., *Der literarische Nachlass Giorgio Vasaris*, 2 vols. (Munich, 1923, 1930); W. Kallab, *Vasaristudien*, (Vienna, 1908); A. del Vita, *Il Carteggio di Giorgio Vasari* (Arezzo: Tipographia Zelli, 1923, 1941); *Le Ricordanze di Giorgio Vasari* (Rome: R. Istituto Archeologico e Storia dell'Arte, 1938); *Lo Zibaldone di Giorgio Vasari* (Rome: R. Istituto Archeologiro e Storia dell'Arte. 1938); and J. Draper, "Vasari's Decoration in the Palazzo Veocchio: The Ragionamenti," tr. and intro. J. Draper, Diss. Univ. of North Carolina, 1973.

3. Called to Venice in 1541 by Pietro Aretina, a close friend of Paolo Giovio, Vasari was requested to do a series of scenographic: paintings for an *apparato* commissioned by the Compagnia della Calza, named the Sempiterni. In this *apparato* Aretino's comedy, *La Talanta*, was to be performed. For a complete description of these paintings, see Vasari-Milanesi, VI, 222-23, 670; Frey, II, 111-19; and L Landuacci, "Giorgio Vasari a Venezia," *Atti del Reale Instituto Veneto di Scienze, Lettere ed Arti* (Venezia, 1911), pp. 168-76. See J. Schulz, "Vasari at Venice," *Burlington Magazine,* 103 (1961), 500-11; J. Schulz, *Venetian Painted Ceilings of the Renaissance* (Berkeley: Univ. of Calif. Press, 1968), pp, 11, 15-16, fig. 6; and David McTavish, "Giorgio Vasari," *Cat Mostra da Tiziano al Greco* (Venice, 1981), p. 86. Unfortunately, the ceiling of the Refectory of Monteoliveto has not been studied iconographically. It displays many interesting ideas of Vasari's which need to be investigated. The most recent article by Pierluigi Leone DeCastris, "Napoli 1544: Vasari e Monteoliveto," *Bollettino d'Arte,* 12 (1981), 59-88, discusses only the stylistic sources for the Refectory.

4. See Cheney, Chap. 2, for descriptions and diagrams of each chamber.

5. Alciati, *Emblematum Libellus cum Commentariis*, 1531, ed. Claude Mignault (Antwerp, 1577), p. 449; Cesare Ripa, *Iconologia*, ed. Erna Mandowsky (New York, 1970), p. 302.

6. Filarete described an ideal city called Sforzinda in his architectural treatise (1451-1464). In this city, there is an architect's house decorated with wall paintings, architectural views and portraits of inventors, heroes and artists. See John Spencer, *Filarete's Treatise on Archirecture* (New Haven: Yale Univ. Press, 1965). According to Wolfram Prinz, Vasari had no knowledge of Filarete's treatise until the time of the publication of the second edition of the *Vite*, where it is first mentioned by him. However, Vasari was familiar with Filarete's ideas through other humanistic sources. See Prinz, p. 11; and J. Rouchette, *La Renaissance que nous a leguée Vasari* (Paris: Société d'Edition, 1959), pp. 115-27.

7. M. Roskill's *Dolce Aretino and Venetian Art Theory of the Cinquecento* (New York, 1968), pp. 97, 239, and G. P. Lomazzo's *Tratto dell'arte della pictura,* secultura et *architettura* (Milan, 1585) summarize Leonardo's and Dolce's conceptions of the relationships between poetry and painting. See also, R. Lee, *Ut Pictura Poesis: Humanist Theory* of *Painting* (New York, 1967), p. 1, n. 2; G. B. Armenini in *De'* veri *precetti della pittura* (1587), p. 23, commented on this fashion: "Per cio si chiama la pittura, Poetica che tace, et la Poetica, Pittura che parla, et questa l'anima dover esser, et quella il corpo, dissimile pero quin questo si tengono, perchè, l'una imita con i colori, l'altra con le parole. Ma certamente che qui quanto all'inventione predetta et quin quanto alla Verità sono d'una stessa proprietà, el d'uno effetto medesimo." Torquato Tasso referred to the poet as a *pittore parlante* (speaking painter) in *Del Poema Eroico.* And in a letter to Vasari (May 10, 1548), Annibale Caro refers to the: artist as a poet and painter: "...l'inventione mi rimetto a voi, ricordandomi d'un altra somiglianza, che la poesia ha con la pittura, et di piu, che voi siete così poeta come pittore, et che ne l'una et ne l'altra con più affettione et con più studio s'esprimono i concetti et le idee sue proprie che d'altrui..." (Frey, I, 220). See K. Borinski, *Die Antike in Poetik und Kunsttheorie* (Leipzig, 1914-24), I, 30, 97ff., 175, 183, 238; II, 106, 125-27, on the history of the dispute about *ut pictura poesis* and L. Mendelsohn, *Paragoni: Belledetto Varchi Due Lezzioni and Cinquecento Art Theory* (Ann Arbor: Univ. of Michigan Press, 1982), pp. 109-42.

8. Vasari-Milanesi, VII, 686: "Feci ancora nel *palco* d'una camera di legname intagliato Abram in un gran tondo...e la feci tutta a tempera...." See also, del Vita, *Le Ricordanze di Giorgio Vasari,* p. 50, letter 68; "Ricordo come adi 9 di maggio 1548 resto finita di dipingere la camera che in casa mia in Arezzo avevo fatta et ci lavorai il palco a tempera fatto da Marsilio legnaiuolo che è quella che risponde sulla via."

9. *Biblia Sacra: Juxta Vullgatum Clementinam* (Rome: Typis Societatis S. Joannis Evang., 1956), 4:215.

10. Usually, the predominant iconographic symbol for Temperance is the water vessel (a reminder of diluting water with wine); for Prudence, the serpent or a book (signifying wisdom) and a cornucopia (signifying richness): for Fortitude, a sword or the depiction of a figure with a Herculean body (signifying strength); and for Justice, a pair of scales or a measuring rod (signifying impartiality). These tetrads refer to Pythagorean cosmology. The four basic qualities of hotness, dryness, coldness and moistness are related to fire, earth, water and air. See S. K. Heninger, Jr., *Touches of Sweet Harmony* (San Marino: The Huntington Library, 1974), pp. 153-54,160-76, for a discussion of Pythagorean cosmology.

11. Paul's Epistle to the Philippians in *Biblia Sacra: Justa Vulgatum Clementinam* (1956), 4:215.

12. For Vasari the representation of the two cupids could connect the Apollo scene with the portrait of his wife in the same ceiling. See E. Panofsky, *Problems in Titan* (New York: New York Univ. Press, 1969), 13033): J. R. Manin, *The Farnese Gallery* (Princeton: Princeton Univ. Press, 1965), pp. 87ff.; and E. Verheyen, "Eros et Anteros," *Gazette des Beaux-Arts*, 65 (1965), 321-40. For further information on this love myth also see Alciati, Emblemata CIX, *Anteros Amor Virtutis.*

13. G. Pacchioni, *La Camera Picta da Andrea Mantegna* (Milan: Edizione del Milione, 1960), explains the concept of *camera picta* in the Camera degli Sposi (Ducal Palace, Mantua) painted by Mantegna in the 1470's. In the Casa Vasari, Vasari also captures this idea, particularly in the Chamber of Fortune.

14. R. Wittkower, "Chance, Time and Virtue," *Journal of the Warburg and Courtauld Institutes* 1 (1937-38), 313-21; E. Cassirer, *The Individual and the Cosmos in Renaissance Philosophy* (New York: Harper and Row, 1963), p. 73ff.: A. Doren, "Fortuna in Mittelater und in der Renaissance," *Vortrage der Bibliothek Warburg,* 1 (1922), 71-144: H. R. Patch, *The Tradition of the Goddess of Fortune in Medieval Philosophy and Literature* (Northampton: Smith College Studies in Medieval Languages, 1922); M. Tanner, "Chance and Coincidence in Titian's Diana and Actaeon," *Art Bulletin,* 56 (1974), 535-50; A. Warburg, *Die Ernewrung der beidnischem Antike* (Leipzig, 1932); E. Wind, "Platonic Tyranny and the Renaissance Fortuna," *Essays in Honor of Erwin Panofsky* (London, 1961), pp. 491-96, and *Giorgione's Tempesta* (Oxford: Clarendon Press, 1969); E. Panofsky, *The Iconography of Correggio's Camera di San Paolo* (London: The Warburg Institute, 1961) and *Studies in Iconology* (New York.: Harper and Row, 1962), p. 225; and N. G. L Hammond and H. H. Scullard, The *Oxford Classical Dictionary* (New York: Oxford Univ. Press, 1970), p. 445. The fickleness of Fortune was sometimes contrasted with the personification of Virtue with the explanation: *Sedes Fortunae Rotunda; Sedes Virtutis quadrata.* See Alciati, Emblemata XCVIII, p. 338ff. Also, see figs. 317 and 318 in this text.

15. See Cheney, Chap. 5, for an extensive discussion of the iconography.

16. M. Winner, "Die Quellen der Pictura - Allegorien in gemalten Bildergalerien des 17 Jahrhunderts zu Antwerpen," Diss. Univ. of Cologne, 1957, pp. 26-27 and 47-49, discusses the distinctions between art, nature, and drawing portrayed in Vasari's Chamber of Fortune and Florentine Sala. See also L. Corti et al., *Giorgio Vasari: Principal, letterati e artisti nelle Carte di Giorgio Vasari* (Florence: Edam Editrice, 1981), pp. 37-40, and F. H. Jacobs, "Vasari's Vision of the History of Painting: Frescoes in the Casa Vasari, Florence," *Art Bulletin* 66 (1984), 399-416.

17. Pliny, (Plinius Secundus, C.), *Naturlis Historiae,* tr. H. Rackham (Cambridge: Harvard Univ. Press, 1938-62), XXXV, 36, and Hammond and Scullard for depictions of the ancient painters.

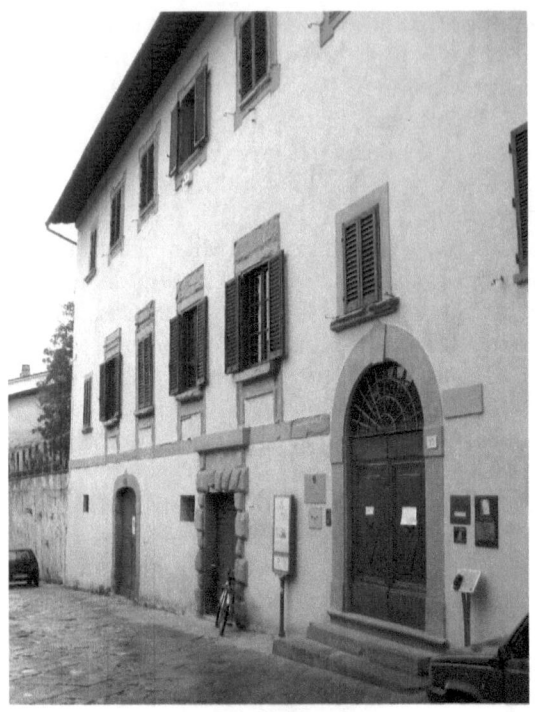

Fig. 1A.  Giorgio Vasari, Casa Vasari,  Arezzo, 1542, exterior.

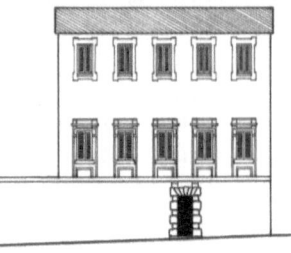

Fig. 1B.  Cheney's reconstruction of Giorgio Vasari, Casa Vasari, 1542.

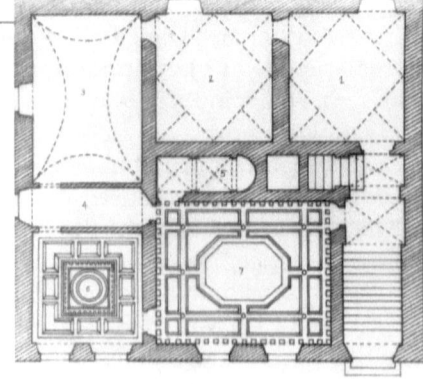

Fig. 2.  Cheney's reconstruction of the *piano nobile*, Casa Vasari Rooms' Allocation: 1-Fame, 2-Apollo, 3-Kitchen, 4-Corridor, 5-Chapel, 6-Abraham and 7-Fortune.

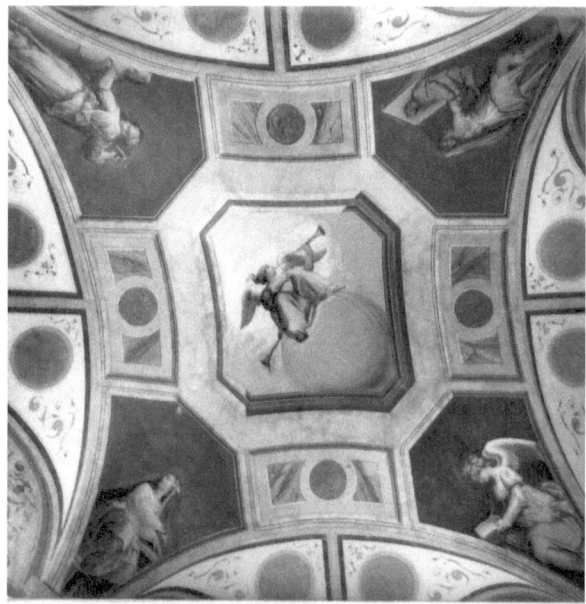

Fig. 3.  Giorgio Vasari, Chamber of Fame, 1542. View of the ceiling, Casa Vasari, Arezzo.

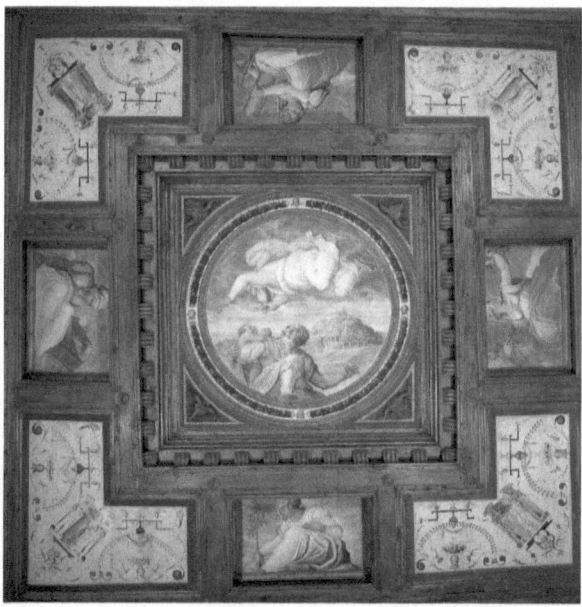

Fig. 4.  Giorgio Vasari, Chamber of Abraham, 1548. View of the ceiling, Casa Vasari, Arezzo.

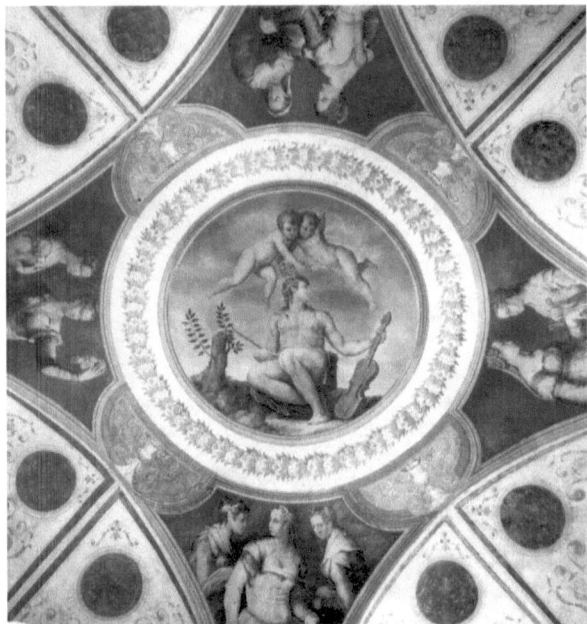

Fig. 5.  Giorgio Vasari, Chamber of Apollo, 1550-54. View of the ceiling, Casa Vasari, Arezzo.

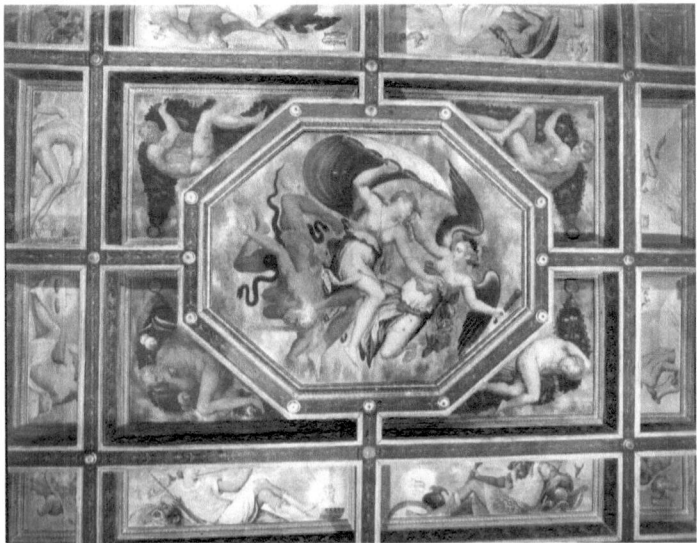

Fig. 6.  Giorgio Vasari, Chamber of Fortune, 1548. View of the ceiling, Casa Vasari, Arezzo.

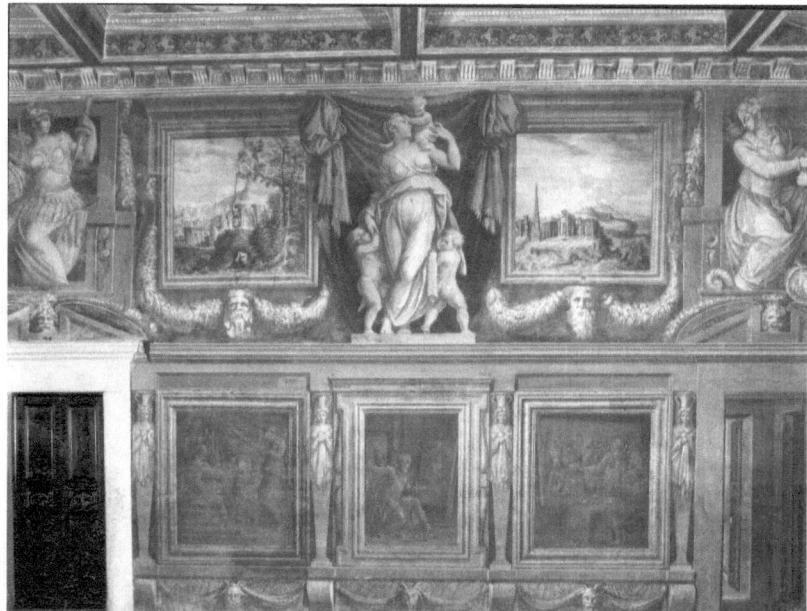

Fig. 7.  Giorgio Vasari, *Charity/Religion*, 1548. Chamber of Fortune, west wall. Casa Vasari, Arezzo.

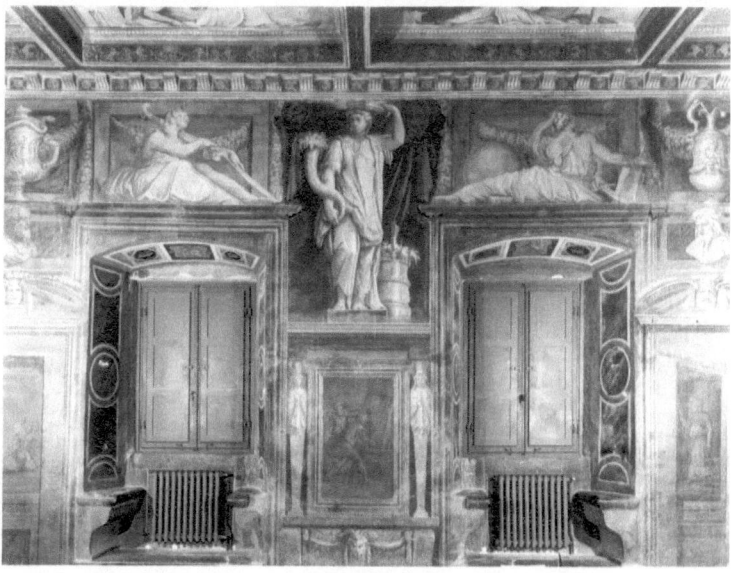

Fig. 8. Giorgio Vasari, *Abundance/Earth*, 1548. Chamber of Fortune, east wall. Casa Vasari, Arezzo.

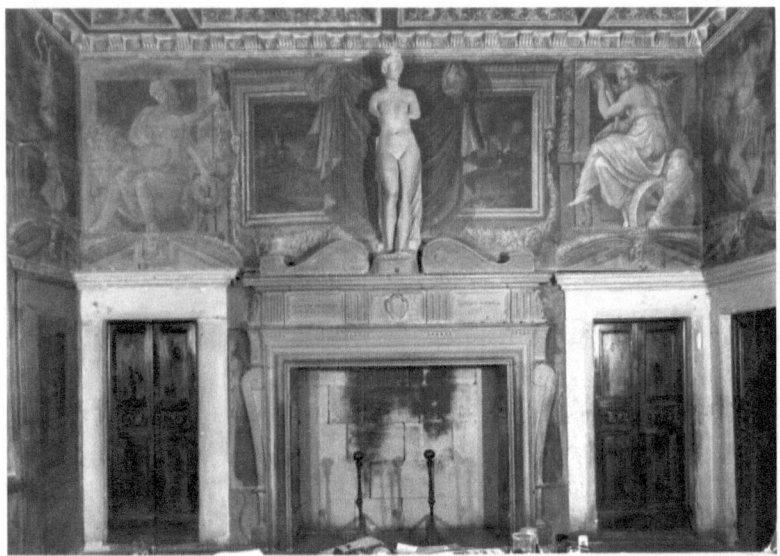

Fig. 9. Giorgio Vasari, *Venus/Art*, 1548. Chamber of Fortune, south wall. Casa Vasari, Arezzo.

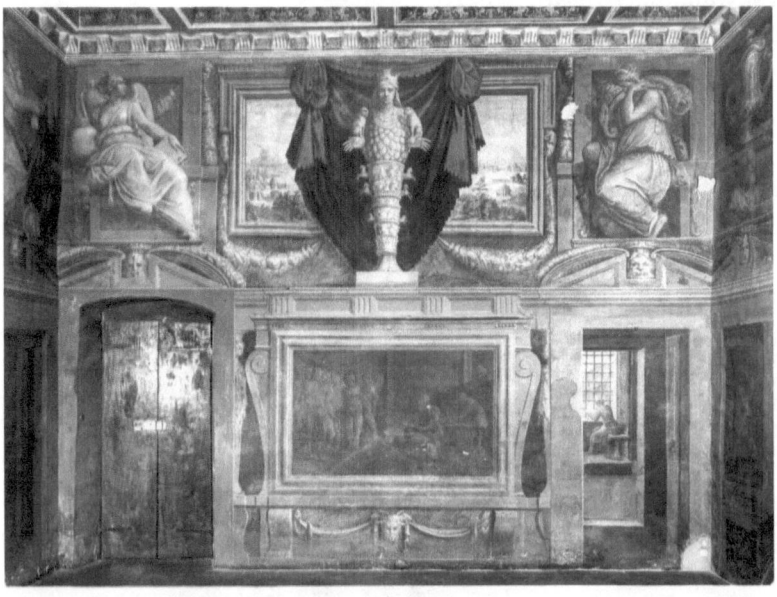

Fig. 10. Giorgio Vasari, *Diana/Nature*, 1548. Chamber of Fortune, north wall, Casa Vasari, Arezzo.

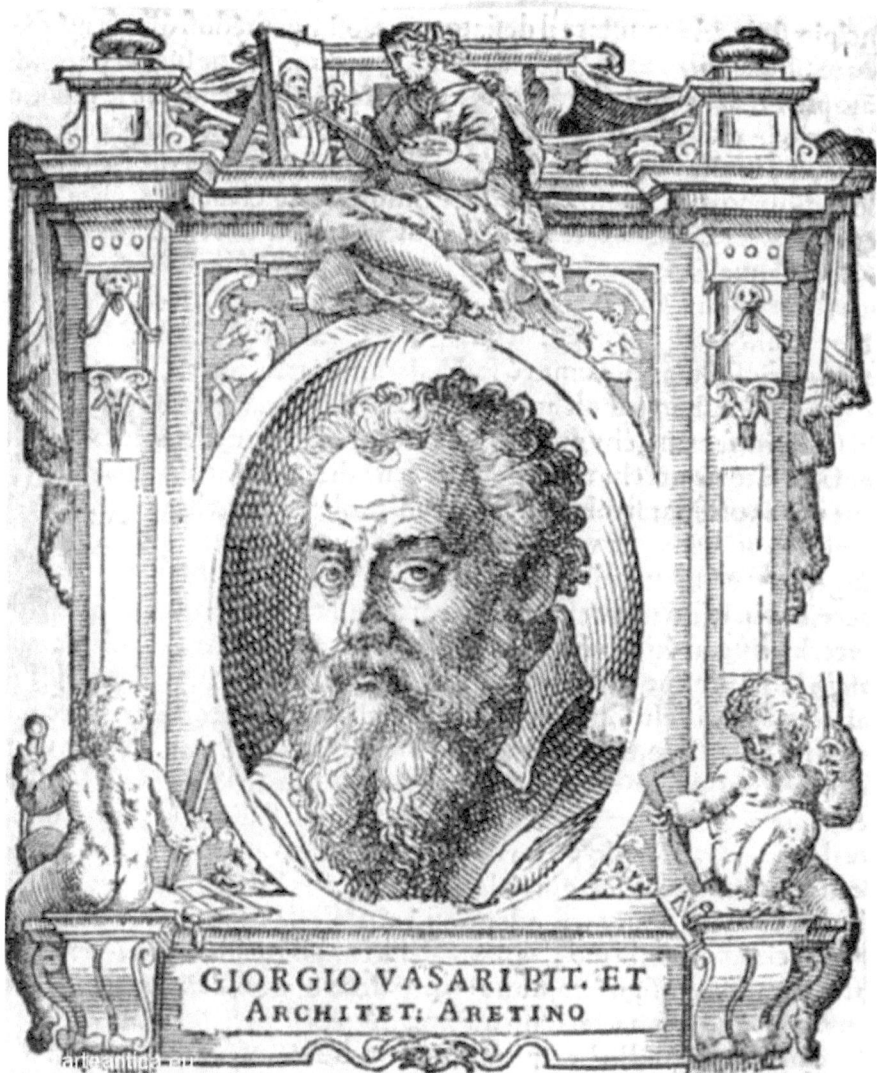

Fig. 11. Giorgio Vasari, Self-portrait, 1547, woodcut from the *Vite*.

# 2

# Vasari's Depiction of Pliny's Histories

One indication of an artist's professional status in the Cinquecento was the freedom he enjoyed to purchase, design, and decorate his own house. By the 1540's, Giorgio Vasari had established himself as a painter and writer, and he began work on a small house in Arezzo. This house, located in Borgo San Vito, still stands. Vasari is a prime example of the artist as householder, and the paintings of his Casa Vasari abundantly demonstrate this new situation. Perhaps more important, Vasari's intellectual curiosity, enthusiasm, and artistic ability enabled him to develop a new attitude towards artistic patronage. The collection of works created for the Casa Vasari expresses in personal terms this artist's love for his masters, his fascination with antiquity, and his delight in virtuosity. Vasari's aim in building and decorating his house was to establish an artistic monument to his own accomplishments, and in this endeavor he manifestly succeeded.

Vasari's autobiography and his letters and *ricordi* remain the best and most complete source for the dating and description of the paintings in the Casa Vasari.[1] At times, however, Vasari is vague, and his comments about the iconography are sketchy; they may even seem will-fully cryptic. Vasari's program for the decoration of his house is not philosophically, theologically, or mythologically systematic. He was its sole inventor, depicting in the four decorated rooms his own ideas about a variety of subjects - Art, Fame, Fortune, History, and Religion - by means of allegorical themes and personifications. The allegorical themes contain biblical and antique stories of classical *istorie* which are depicted in a Cinquecento setting.

Off and on, Vasari spent approximately twelve years, from 1542 to 1554, painting the four rooms of the *piano nobile* of the Casa Vasari.[2] The rooms are identified for the subjects depicted on their respective ceilings, namely Fame, Abraham, Apollo, and Fortune. The ceilings of these rooms are painted in various media: the Chamber of Abraham is painted in tempera, the Chamber of Fortune in oil, and the other two ceilings are painted *al fresco*. The only chamber that has paintings on both ceilings and walls (the latter *al fresco*) is the Chamber of Fortune.

The decoration in the Chamber of Fortune consists of two parts: (1) a painted oil ceiling with a projecting *palco* representing the personifications of Fortune, Virtue, and Envy which are surrounded by the four ages of man and the planetary god; and (2) the frescoed walls depicting the personifications of Charity (west wall), Abundance (east wall), Art (south wall), and Nature (north wall) (figs. 4-7). These personifications are located in the upper section of the walls, while in the lower sections the classical *istorie* contribute to the decoration of the Chamber of Fortune.

In the Chamber of Fortune, Vasari introduced the concept of artistic creativity as an integral part of painting as exemplified in the classical *istorie* or antique stories. In the *Lives of the Artists*, Vasari expressed his artistic ideas about portraiture as follows:

> And to tell the truth, he who executes portraits must contrive, without thinking of what is looked for in a perfect figure, to make them like those for whom they are intended. When portraits are alike and beautiful, they may be called rare works, and their authors truly excellent craftsmen.[3]

Vasari's interest in portraiture was stimulated by his writings of the *Lives of the Artists* and by Paolo Giovio's collection of portraits for his Museum.[4] In Giovio's correspondence with Vasari, he frequently described the portraits he had received from different artists. As well, he noted his efforts to secure additional portraits from artists and requested Vasari's assistance in the matter.

Giovio's delight in portraits extended to the point of soliciting drawings of Vasari's self-portrait for the decoration of his Museum in Como, and a sketch of Vasari's bride-to-be, Nicolosa Baci.[5]

Vasari's desire to decorate his house with portraits of famous artists represents a fusion of Roman and Quattrocento custom. It was common in ancient Rome to decorate a house with portraits of kinsfolk and notables, and in the Quattrocento this tradition was continued.[6] Portraits of *uomini famosi* were portrayed on the walls of secular and religious buildings. The interest of Quattrocento artists in painting portraits of famous men derives from the Italian humanists (Dante, Petrarch and Boccaccio), who in turn were influenced by the Roman writers, especially Cicero and Virgil.

Likewise, in the Cinquecento, humanists, such as Paolo Giovio, provided in their thematic programs portraits of both ancient Romans and contemporary famous people (*Sala dei Cento Giorni* in Rome) and decorated their homes as well with portraits of *uomini famosi* (Giovio Museum). Vasari's familiarity with Giovio's plans to decorate his house with portraits of humanists, princes, soldiers and prelates must have had a strong influence on the artist.

Under the spell of Giovio, Vasari began collecting portraits of the artist to be used in the illustrations for the *Lives of the Artist*[8] and decorated the Chamber of Fortune with portraits of Pliny and Michelangelo.

On the east wall of the Chamber of Fortune of the Casa Vasari, Giorgio Vasari in 1548 painted two bust portraits: one portraying Pliny the Elder, the ancient historian and author of *Historia naturalis*, the other depicting Michelangelo, a Cinquecento artist and Vasari's mentor (figs. 1 and 2).[9]

The selection of these two personages is significant as they are inspirations for Vasari's accomplishments as an artist, historian, and writer. In writing his *Lives of the Artists*, Vasari glorified and emulated Pliny, the classical historian, who first wrote about art and artists; and in his painting. Vasari followed Michelangelo, who immortalized art.

Vasari illustrates Pliny's art historical narratives or the classical *istorie* painted *al fresco* by Vasari in the lower section of the Chamber of Fortune (1548). These narrative scenes of classical *istorie* convey a didactic message and comment on the history and methods of art (figs. 4-6).

The classical *istorie* are all painted in a monochromatic reddish tonality, simulating antique paintings. The classical *istorie* or narrative scenes relate to three general ideas: the invention and methods of painting, the criticism and competition among artists, and the content and expressions found in paintings.

In the lower section of the east wall, below the personification of Abundance, a man is portrayed before a fireplace outlining his shadow (fig. 8). This image, which probably represents the origin of painting, introduces a highly debatable subject: Where and how did painting begin? Who was the inventor of painting? Which originated first, painting or drawing? These were questions that had been raised since classical times. According to Pliny, the origin of painting is obscure and is the subject of many different legends. But common to every story is the idea that "painting began with the outlining of a man's shadow; then a single color was employed, and afterwards this style received the name of monochrome,"[10] Pliny distinguished the invention of painting from that of drawing and identified the inventor of each. "The invention of linear drawing is attributed to Philokles of Egypt, or to Kleanthes of Corinth ... and the invention of painting with color made . . . from powdered potsherds is due to Ekphantos of Corinth."[11]

After Pliny, Quintilian stated that painting in classical times was restricted to tracing a line around a shadow cast by the sunlight.[12] During the Renaissance, the quest for the origin of painting continued with Alberti[13] and Leonardo,[14] who based their theories on the speculations of Pliny and Quintilian. In the preface to the *Lives of the Artists*, Vasari pursued his interest in the origin of painting.[15] After repeating Pliny's theory, he went on to identify Gyges of Lydia in Egypt as having invented drawing by tracing on the wall of his studio the shadows cast in the light from a fireplace.

In the fresco painting on the east wall of the Casa Vasari, *Man Outlining His Shadow*, the artist depicted resembles Vasari, while the outline of his shadow looks like an easel painting. Since no painting tools appear in the picture, Vasari appears to suggest that drawing originated before painting, and that drawing and painting are mutually dependent.[16] Vasari must have liked this theme, since he repeated it years later in his Florentine Sala of his house in Florence (1564) (fig. 9).

If we connect the *istoria* of a *Man Outlining His Shadow* (Gyges of Lydia) in the lower section with the upper section representation of a classical bust, we can surmise that the portrait is of Pliny, who having written about the origin of painting, ancient artists, and art in general, may be considered the first art historian.

In this instance, Vasari creates two parallels: one historical and the other artistic. The historical comparison relates to Pliny, as the first art historian of the *Historia naturalis*, with Vasari, as the first Italian Renaissance art historian, of the *Lives of the Artists*. The artistic parallel is with the depiction of his self-portrait in the rendering of Gyges of Lydia, the first artist in the *Man Outlining His Shadow* (compare figs. 3 and 8).

On the north wall, below the personification of Nature, is Vasari's representation of Pliny's account of Zeuxis' *Story of Helen* (fig. 10). Zeuxis executed this painting, his most famous, for the Heraion of Croton by selecting for the model of Helen the most flawless parts of the bodies of Croton's most beautiful women.[17] Thus, Helen was celebrated as the embodiment of perfect female loveliness. Vasari illustrated this event by depicting Zeuxis in his studio, drawing a figure from the nude models standing before him. Here, Vasari has stressed the professional position of the artist, working in his own studio, and assisted by young artists (behind the figure of Zeuxis an apprentice grinds pigments). Vasari has also emphasized the idea of selection and observation from nature (Zeuxis based his figure on his models) and the importance of creating a figure with *grazia* and *bella maniera* (creation of the perfect figure from the best parts of the most beautiful bodies).[18] By depicting an onlooker in the painting, Vasari differentiates between the viewer's and the artist's appreciation of nature and art. The onlooker is a passive observer, whereas the artist is the active observer.

It is no coincidence that Vasari place the painting of Zeuxis' *Story of Helen* below the personification of Nature (Diana of Ephesus) (fig. 6) for by doing so, Vasari expressed his ideas about imitation and invention in art and the difference between nature and art. In the Florentine Sala, Vasari recreated the *Story of Helen*, substituting the artist Apelles for Zeuxis. In the Sala, Apelles is painting a life-sized figure of Diana of Ephesus by selecting the most beautiful parts of his models (figs. 15-16). According to Vasari, the artist

(Zeuxis or himself) imitates nature in the creation of a perfect form. But even though the artist draws upon nature for his creations, imitation is based on observation, study, and selection from nature. For Vasari, the work of art is initially based upon nature, but surpasses it through the artist's process of selectivity and invention. Vasari's portrait of Zeuxis' *Story of Helen* manifests his belief that the artist learns the process whereby art surpasses nature by studying the masters. Thus, Vasari considered art superior to nature.

Giorgio Vasari's discussion on the principles of art derives from his explanation of artistic creativity which is based fundamentally on the Italian Renaissance tradition which considered creativity as a faculty present in all humans' activities.[19]

Vasari's conception of artistic creativity is related to his theory of painting. He considered two alternatives in developing or achieving artistic creativity for a painter: by imitation (*imitazione*) and by invention (*invenzione*).[20] Imitation is the exercise of copying art as a method of learning, whereas invention is autonomous from imitation and is the means for conceiving artistic ideas.[21] Imitation guides and teaches the artist in composing and creating perfection. For Vasari, imitation draws upon three different sources: copying from nature (*copia dal vero*), selecting from artistic works (*giudizio*) and selecting from one's work (*imitare se stessi*).[22] He emphasized that copying from nature is important for the artist in order to learn to create forms that are alive.[23] This mental activity also helps the artist to learn how to draw so that eventually he may draw anything from memory without the need of a model.[24] Vasari's idea of *giudizio* is also related to selection from and improvement on nature. Thus, the artist has to study antiquity and the masters so that he may learn how others have acquired the experience of imitating nature.[25]

The third aspect of imitation, when the artist copies or quotes from his own work, demonstrates the manner in which art surpasses nature. Vasari found examples of this achievement, particularly in the works of Michelangelo.[26] This is the reason for the depiction of the bust portrait of Michelangelo in the Chamber of Fortune (fig. 2).

On the west wall, a classical *istoria* painted by Protogenes is portrayed beneath the personification of Charity (fig. 4). According to Pliny, Protogenes' reputation was established when he visited Apelles in Rhodes and made the people recognize the merits of the city.[27] Because of the intensive labor and minute care he devoted to his work, he produced few paintings. Vasari depicts the scene of Protogenes' painting the representation of *Ialysus with His Dog*. This was Protogenes' most famous painting and exemplified the artist's methods. Pliny explained that Protogenes gave four coats of color to this painting to preserve it for posterity. It is said that Protogenes, frustrated at his inability to depict the dog foaming, took a wet sponge and threw it on the portion of the canvas where he had painted the dog's mouth, thus achieving realism in the painting.[28]

In the Vasari painting, the ancient artist is seated at an easel in his studio. The picture in the easel is of a hunter with his dog (*Ialysus with His Dog*): Vasari's familiarity with Pliny's account of Protogenes is clear from the fact that he has painted Protogenes in the process of throwing the sponge. In his depiction of this classical *istoria*, Vasari commented on the methodology of the artist and the relation of art to nature. For Vasari, Protogenes exemplified the artist's concern with the careful execution of his work and the realism of his painting (fig. 11), but at the same time, acknowledged the happy accidents in the painting process.

Vasari's ideas on the competition among artists and on the artist's virtuosity are illustrated in the *istoria* located in the center of the east wall, below the figure of Abundance. This painting depicts the contest between Zeuxis and Parrhasius (fig. 12). Pliny relates that Zeuxis, having entered into a pictorial contest with Parrhasius, painted some grapes so naturally that birds were attracted to them. Elated with his success, Zeuxis demanded that a curtain be drawn over his painting so that his opponent, Parrhasius, not see it. Days later, Zeuxis was obliged to admit defeat when he learned that the curtain drawn over his painting had been painted by Parrhasius.[29]

For Vasari, the quality of virtuosity in an artist was very important. It expressed not only the imagination and wit of the artist, but also his rapidity and skill in executing a work of art. In painting a classical *istoria* concerning Parrhasius, Vasari also emphasized the importance of drawing in painting. According to Pliny and Quintilian, Parrhasius made great contributions to the development and understanding of art through the linear and expressive qualities of his forms and the precision of his drawings.[30]

On the west wall, framing Protogenes' *Ialysus with His Dog,* are two classical *istorie*: the *Sacrifice of Iphigenia* painted by Timanthes, and *Alexander* and *Campaspe* by Apelles (figs. 13 and 14). The narrative content of Timanthes painting, based on Ovid's *Metamorphoses* (12:25-28) appears below the personification of Liberality. Iphigenia was the daughter of Agamemnon, King of Mycenae, who led the Greek forces against Troy. The success of the expedition was jeopardized because Agamemnon had killed a stag sacred to Diana, the goddess of the hunt. Diana demanded the sacrifice of Iphigenia as punishment. But when Iphigenia patriotically accepted her destiny, Diana took pity on Iphigenia, and in her place provided a stag with her features. Diana then carried Iphigenia away to be her priestess. In illustrating Ovid's story, Timanthes focuses on the tragic quality of the narrative, the sacrificial event, and the parent's grief. The dramatic impact of Timanthes' painting is known to us through Pliny's description of the picture. "(Timanthes)...depicted Iphigenia standing by the altar ready for death. Having presented all the onlookers and especially her father's brother as plunged in sorrow and having thus exhausted every presentiment of grief, Timanthes has veiled the face of her father for which he had reserved no adequate expression."[31]

Vasari's painting dearly resembles Pliny's description of Timanthes' *Sacrifice of Iphigenia* (fig. 13). In the Vasari rendering, Timanthes portrays the sacrifice. The picture shows Diana, in the clouds, observing the sacrifice. Blindfolded, Iphigenia sits on an altar awaiting her fate. Among the lamenting figures that surround her is her father, who is veiled because his grief is beyond expression. With the representation of this classical *istoria,* Vasari appears to express several ideas about artists and their paintings. In addition to being familiar with artistic technique, the artist must be able to represent and interpret a narrative event. Timanthes skillfully executes the painting of the *Sacrifice of Iphigenia* and classical writers consider this work is one of the most famous in ancient painting.[32] For Vasari, it also is important for a painter to express dignity and grief in a tragic scene, as exemplified by the depiction of Iphigenia and Agamemnon. Perhaps Vasari also is stating that in an historical painting, the artist must present a moral interpretation of the narrative.

Finally, on the west wall under the personification of Fortitude, one finds the representation of *Alexander and Campaspe* (fig. 14). The story was painted originally by Apelles, who was renowned for his portraits and his paintings of the female nude. In his own house, Vasari portrayed Alexander the Great surrounded by his officers in a camp, Apelles has entered the tent with Campaspe. According to Pliny, Apelles fell in love with Campaspe while painting her portrait. On learning this, Alexander magnanimously gave his mistress to Apelles.[33] This dramatic moment is expressed in Vasari's painting as Campaspe and Apelles with her painted portrait appear in front of Alexander the Great. The ruler's gesture of extending his arm grants Apelles the gift of Campaspe, Vasari's painting of the narrative story on Campaspe varies from Apelles' in that the Aretine artist represents her clothed in front of Alexander and Apelles holding a portrait of her, whereas, in Pliny's writings, Apelles painter portrayed Campaspe in the nude for Alexander the Great. The drama revolves around a story of love and renunciation. The courage and virtue of a man is being tested. In the scene of *Alexander and Campaspe*, unlike the *Sacrifice of Iphigenia*, the Campaspeun like the *Sacrifice of Iphigenia*, the Campaspe Apelles story narrates an event in the life of an artist. In this case, the painter, Apelles, is not merely depicting a significant event but experiencing it.

In the classical *istorie* of painters, inspired by Pliny's *Natural History*, Vasari pays tribute to the art of painting, to famous antique masters, and to himself as a successful Cinquecento artist. These *istorie* illustrate the criteria for judging painting: selection from nature (Zeuxis' *Story of Helen*), virtuosity (contest of Zeuxis with Parrhasius), inventiveness (Gyges of Lydia's *The Artist Outlining His Shadow*), imitation and realism (Protogenes' *Ialysus and His Dog*), portraiture (Apelles' *Alexander and Campaspe*), and narrative (Timanthes' *Sacrifice of Iphigenia*). In his classical *istorie* Vasari also demonstrated the ancient painters' interpretation of art in relation to nature: first to imitate nature (Gyges of Lydia, Parrhasius, and Protogenes), and then to surpass it (Zeuxis, Apelles, and Timanthes).

Inspired by Pliny, Vasari is the first Renaissance artist to launch a program with such illustrations. Therefore, the classical *istorie* in the Chamber of Fortune immortalize Vasari as a sixteenth-century artist, historian, and theoretician. The message conveyed in the Chamber of Fortune, for all its reliance on the past, is both original and personal. Vasari as the first Renaissance art historian recreates what he thought an original representation of a classical painting to be; he tries to imagine the painting as it was seen and understood in the past. In doing so, he went back to the original sources, Pliny's description of the classical painters in *Historia naturalis*, as well as interpreting contemporary accounts (Paolo Giovio's writings) for the visual interpretation and recreation of the art of the past. In the classical *istorie*, Vasari combined historical sources with art theories, thus explaining and comparing visually artistic views of ancient paintings with the art of the sixteenth century.

## Notes

This articles is a reprint from "Vasari's Depiction of Pliny's Histories," *Exploration in Renaissance Culture*, Vol XV (December 1989), 97-120.

1. Giorgio Vasari, *Le vite de' più eccellenti Pittori, Scultori, et Architettori* (Florence, 1550 and 1568), ed. Gaetano Milanesi (Florence, 1970-74). All succeeding references will be noted as Vasari-Milanesi.

2. Liana Cheney, *The Paintings of the Casa Vasari* (New York: Garland Publishing, 1986).

3. Vasari-Milanesi, IV, 280.

4. In a letter, Giovio expressed hope that Vasari would visit the "Museum" on his way to Milan. See Paolo Giovio, *Opere*, 8 vols. (Rome: Instituto Poligrafico della Stato, 1858), II, 120. Letter 290, dated Rome, March 31, 1548. In numerous passages throughout the Lives, Vasari mentions Giovio's delight in collecting portraits. See Giovio, *Opere*, VIII, 1-10. At this point, a few comments on the Giovio Museum are in order. Paolo Giovio built and furnished a villa on Lake Como (on the very site of Pliny's Villa) where he collected portraits of illustrious men. Some of these portraits were originals, and some were copied from statues, busts or paintings. The Giovio Museum derives its name from the portrait gallery and a dining hall in the villa where Apollo Cithaerodus and the nine muses with their musical instruments were represented. See F. A. Gragg, *An Italian Portrait Gallery* (Boston: Chapman and Grimes Publishers, 1935), pp. 25-26. This museum was described by Anton Francesco Doni to the Count Agostino Landi in a letter dated July 20, 1543. See Giovio, *Opere*, VIII, 1-2.

n.1, and Gragg, *An Italian Portrait Gallery*, pp. 17-22. For further interest in Paolo Giovio's concept of portraiture, see L. Rovelli, *L'opera storica ed artistica di Paolo Giovio - il suo museo dei ritratti* (Como: Azienda Autonoma Soggiorno Turismo, 1928); L. Rovelli, *Paolo Giovio nella storia e nell'arte* (Como: Azienda Autonoma Soggiorno Turismo, 1952); and E. Müntz, *Le musée des portraits de Paul Jove* (Paris: Imprimerie Nationale. 1901).

5. Giovio, *Opere*, II, 114. Letter 283, dated Rome, November 5, 1547, and Letter 252, dated Rome, March 19, 1547, pp. 75-76.

6. The Roman tradition of honoring one's lineage is illustrated in the sculpture of the *Roman Patrician with Busts of his Ancestors* (Capitoline Museum in Rome). See H. W. Janson, *The History of Art* (Englewood Cliffs: Prentice Hall, 1972), p. 141; and I. Lavin, "Sources of and Meaning of Renaissance Portrait Bust," *Art Quarterly*, 3-4 (1971), 207-15.

7. The Ducal Palace in Urbino by Justus van Ghent and assistants and S. Apollonia in Florence by Andrea Castagno. See A. Chastel, *The Golden Age of Renaissance. 1460-1500* (London: Thames and Hudson, 1965), pp. 280-83, Figs. 281 and 282, and J. Burckhardt, *The Civilization of the Renaissance in Italy* (New York: Harper and Row Publishers, 1958), p. 158, Fig.72.

8. Giovio, *Opere*, II, 55, Letter 240, dated Rome, November 27.

9. Pliny the Elder, *Historia naturalis*, Book XXXV (Parma: Biblioteca Palatina, MS Parma 1278). See Lilian Armstrong, "The Illustration of Pliny's *Historia naturalis*: Manuscripts before 1430," *Journal of the Warburg and Courtauld Institutes*, 46 (1983), 19-39, and K. Jex-Blake and E. Sellers, *The Elder Pliny's Chapters on the History of Art*, (New York: Macmillan, 1968).

10. Pliny, *Historia naturalis*, 35: 101.

11. Pliny, *Historia naturalis*, 35: 101-102.

12 Quintilian, *De institutio oratoria* X.ii.7, "... non esset pictura, ni si quae lineas modo extremas umbrae, quam corpora in sole fecissent, circumscriberet," quoted from R. Rosemblum, "The Origin of Painting: A Problem in the Iconography of Romantic Classicism," *Art Bulletin*, 19 (1957), 199, n.3.

13. *On Painting*, trans. J. R. Spencer (New Haven: Yale Univ. Press, 1956), pp. 64 and 118 on Alberti.

14. Erwin Panofsky, *Codex Huygens* (London: Thames and Hudson, 1940), p. 61 on Leonardo.

15. Vasari-Milanesi, I, 218: "Ma secondo che scrive Plinio quest'arte venne in Egitto da Gige Lidio il quale, essendo al fuoco e l'ombra di se medesimo riguardando subito cor un carbone in mano contorno se stesso nel muro...." There has been much discussion of Vasari's interpretation of Pliny's test and his attribution of the invention of painting of Gyges of Lydia. See Rosenblum, "The Origin of Painting...," p. 199; E. Combrich. "Vasari's *Lives* and Cicero's *Brutus*," *Journal of the Warburg and Courtauld Institutes*, 23 (1960) 309-1 J; and M. Winner, "Die Quellen der Pictura-Al-

legorien in gemalten Bildergalerien des 17 Jahrhunderts zu Antwerpen,"
Ph.D. diss., Univ. of Cologne, 1957.

16. Throughout his *Lives* Vasari constantly stressed the importance of drawing (disegno) in painting.

17. Pliny, *Historia naturalis*, 35:64: "Zeuxis bestowed such minute pains upon his work that before painting for the people of Agrigentum a picture to be dedicated in the temple of Hera on the Lakinian promontory, he inspected the maidens of the city naked and chose out five whose peculiar beauties he proposed to reproduce in his picture." See Cicero, *De inventione*, II, p. 13; F. R. Dati, *Vile dei Pittori Antichi* (Padua: Tipografia della Minerva. 1821); and G. Turnbull, *A Treatise on Ancient Painting* (Chicago: Alder Publishers, 1975).

18. Vasari-Milanesi, IV, pp. 5-7; and Quintilian, *De institutio oratoria*, XII, X, pp. 4-5: "Zeuxis was concerned in his art to emphasize the links of the human body and had discovered the method of representing light and shade."

19. R. Klein, *La Forme el l'intelligible* (Paris: Gallimard Editions, 1970), and V. de Ruvo, "La concezione estetica di Giorgio Vasari," *Studi Vasariani* (Florence: G. S. Sansoni, 1952), pp. 47-56.

20. Yasari–Milanesi, II, 95-96; and Pliny, *Historia naturalis*, 35:84.

21. de Ruvo, "La concezione estetica di Giorgio Vasari," pp. 47-56; A. Blunt, *Artistic Theory in Italy, 1450-1600* (New York: Oxford Univ. Press. 1968); and W. Prinz, "I ragionamenti del Vasari sullo sviluppo e declino delle ani," *Il Vasari: Storiografo e Artista* (Florence: Leo S. Olschki, 1976).

22. *Ibid*

23. Vasari-Milanesi, I, 99; A. Blunt, *Artistic Theory in Italy*, and L Maclehose and G. B. Brown, *Vasari on Technique* (New York: Dover Publications, Inc.1960), p. 210.

24 .A. Blunt, *Artistic Theory in Italy*, p. 90.

25. C. H. Smyth. *Mannerism and Maniera* (New York: J. G. Augustin, 1963).

26. Vasari-Milanesi, IX, I, 18; IV, 84; and IV, 83.

27. Pliny, *Historia naturalis*, 35:36.

28. *Ibid.*, 35: 102-103. "He gave this picture four coats of color to preserve it from the approach of injury and age, so that if the first coal peeled off the one below might take its place. The dog in this picture is the outcome as it were of miracle, since chance, and not art alone, went into the painting or it. The artist felt that he had not perfectly rendered the foam of the panting animal, although he had satisfied himself - a difficult task - in the rest of the painting. It was the very skill which displeased him and which could not be concealed, but obtruded itself too much, thus making the effect unnatural; it was foam painted with the brush not frothing from

the mouth. Chafing with anxiety, for he aimed at absolute truth in his painting and not at a makeshift, he had wiped it out again and again, and changed his brush without finding any satisfaction. At last, enraged with the art which was too evident, he threw his sponge at the hateful spot, and the sponge left on the picture the colors it had wiped off, giving the exact effect he had intended, and chance thus became the mirror of nature."

29. Pliny, *Historia naturalis*, 35:64, "The story ran that Parrhasius and Zeuxis entered into competition, Zeuxis exhibiting a picture of some grapes, so true to nature that the birds flew up to the wall of the stage. Parrhasius then displayed a picture of a linen curtain, realistic to such a degree that Zeuxis, elated by the verdict of the birds, cried out that now at last his rival must draw the curtain and show his picture. On discovering his mistake he surrendered the prize to Parrhasius, admitting candidly that he had deceived the birds, while Parrhasius had delded himself, a painter."

30. Pliny, *Historia naturalis*, 35:36, and Quintilian, *De institutio oratoria*, ed. F. H. Colson (Cambridge, England: The University Press, 1924), XII; X, 5.

31. Pliny, *Historia naturalis*, 35:73.

32. M. T. Cicero, *De oratore*, trans. E. W. Sutton (Cambridge. Mass.: Harvard Univ. Press, 1942), p. 22; Quintilian, *De institutio oratoria*, ii, p. 3; and Valerius Maximus, *Memorabilia* (Venice, 1534), vii, 4, ext. 6.

33. Pliny, *Historia naturalis*, 35:86, "Alexander commissioned Apelles to paint a nude figure of his favorite mistress Campaspe, so much did he admire her wondrous form, but perceiving that Apelles had fallen in love with her, with great magnanimity and still greater self-control he gave her to him as a present, winning by the action as great a glory as by any of his victories. He conquered himself and sacrificed to the artist not only his mistress but his love, and was not even restrained by consideration for the woman he loved, who, once a king's mistress, was now a painter's."

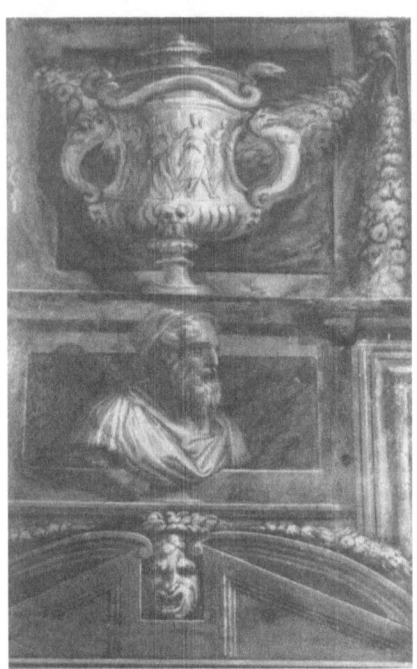

Fig. 1. Giorgio Vasari, Pliny, 1548, east wall, Chamber of Fortune, Casa Vasari, Arezzo.

Fig. 2. Giorgio Vasari, Michelangelo, 1548, east wall, Chamber of Fortune, Casa Vasari, Arezzo.

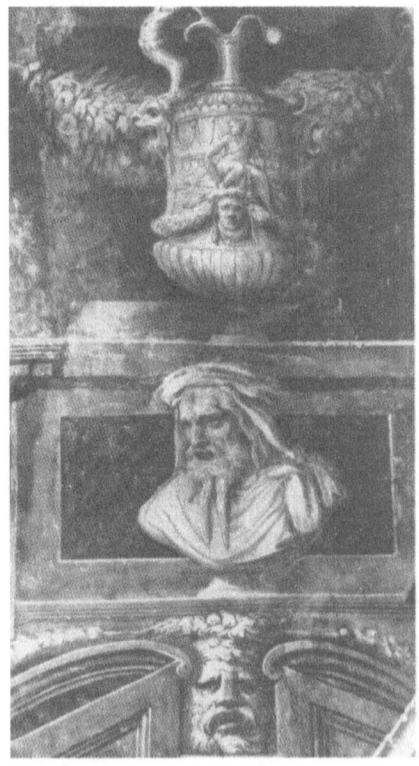

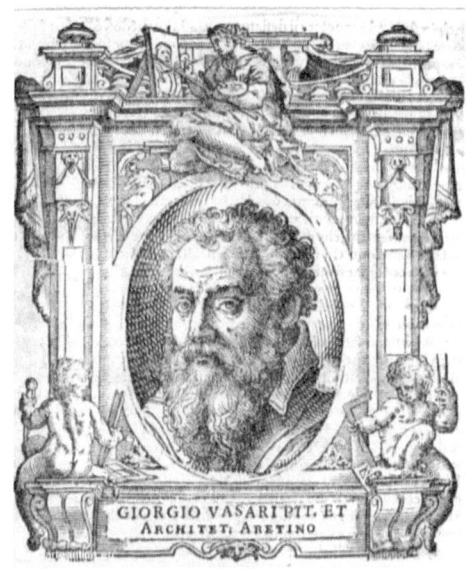

Fig. 3. Giorgio Vasari, Self-portrait, 1547, woodcut from the *Vite...* Courtesy of the Kunsthistorisches Institut Library, Florence.

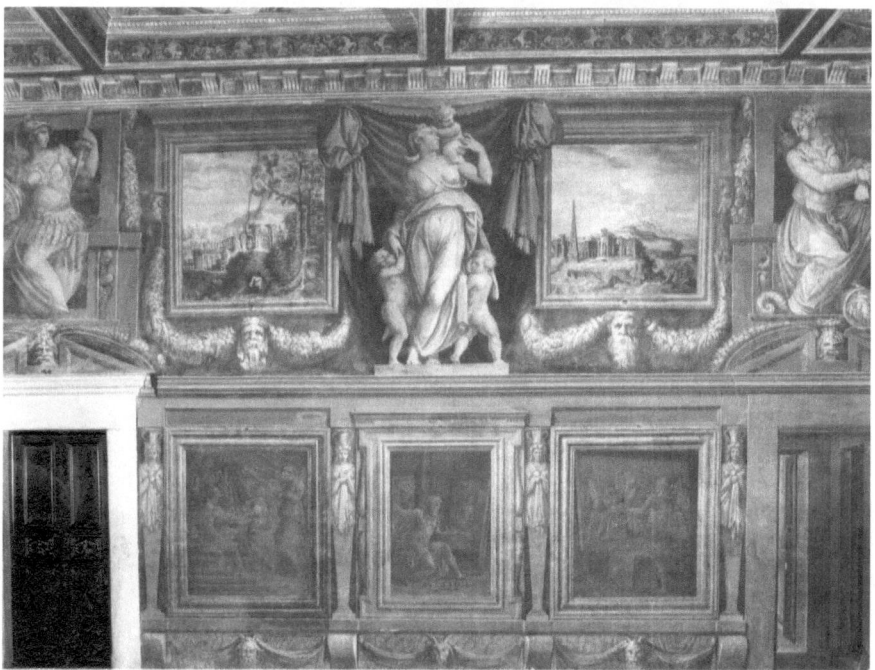

Fig. 4. Giorgio Vasari, Charity, 1548,  west wall, Chamber of Fortune, Casa Vasari, Arezzo.

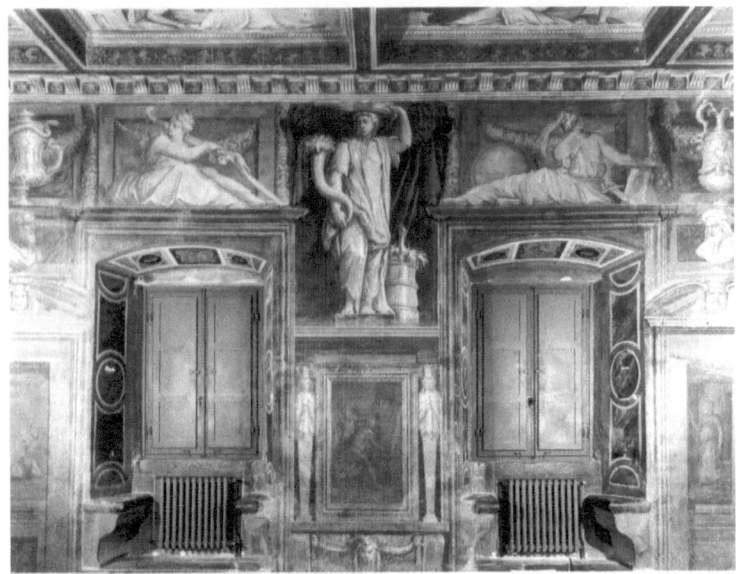

Fig. 5. Giorgio Vasari, *Abundance*, 1548, east wall, Chamber of Fortune, Casa Vasari, Arezzo.

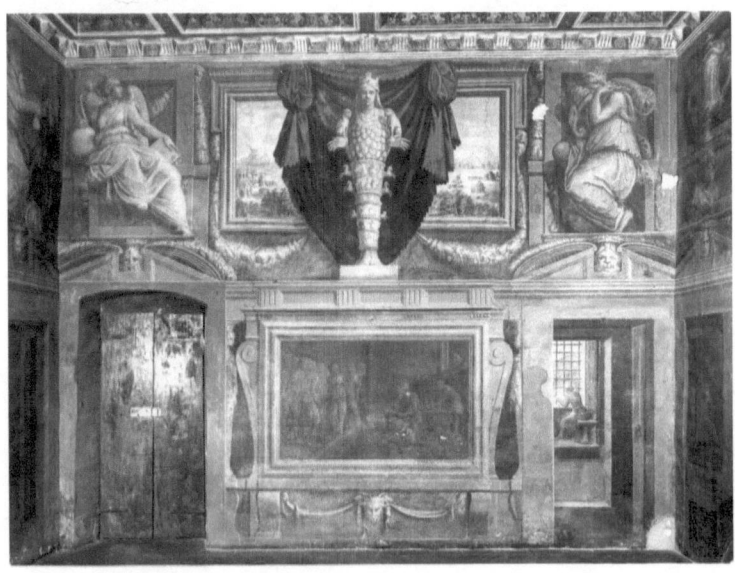

Fig. 6. Giorgio Vasari, *Nature*, north wall, Chamber of Fortune, Casa Vasari, Arezzo.

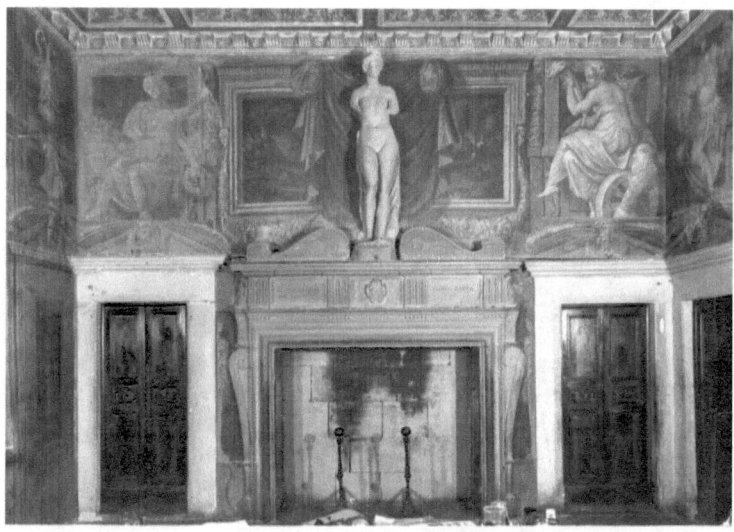

Fig. 7. Giorgio Vasari, Art, south wall, Chamber of Fortune, Casa Vasari, Arezzo.

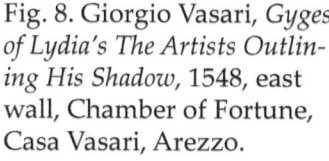

Fig. 8. Giorgio Vasari, *Gyges of Lydia's The Artists Outlining His Shadow*, 1548, east wall, Chamber of Fortune, Casa Vasari, Arezzo.

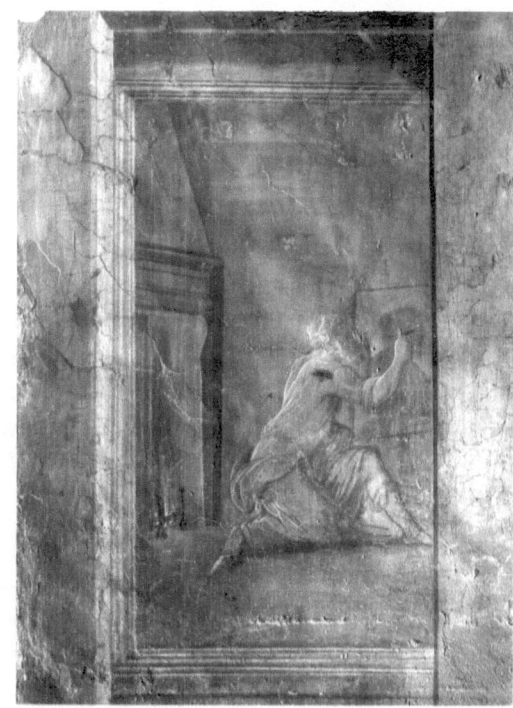

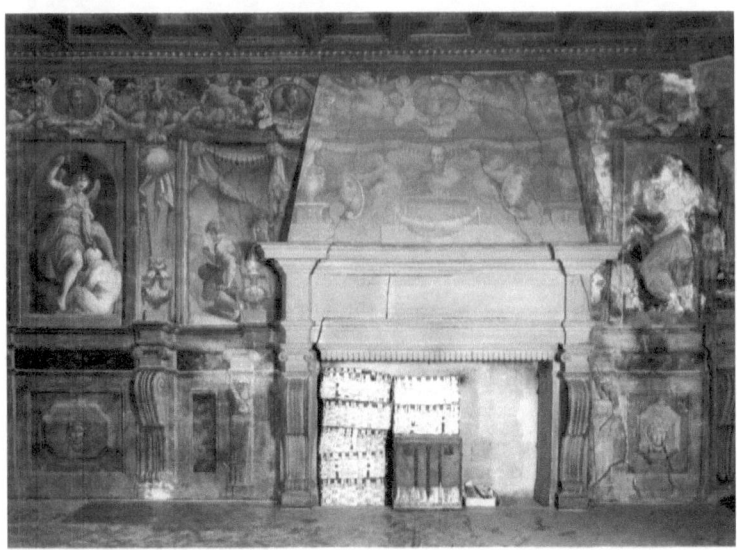

Fig. 9. Giorgio Vasari, *Apelles' Drawing His Shadow*, 1555-1561, Sala, south wall, Casa Vasari, Florence.

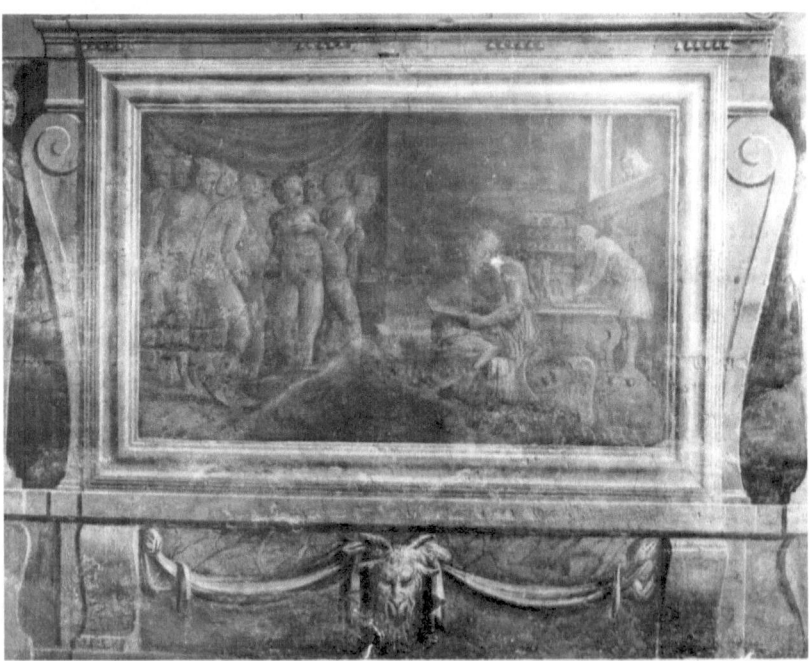

Fig. 10. Giorgio Vasari, *Zeuxis' Story of Helen*, 1548, north wall Chamber of Fortune, Casa Vasari, Arezzo.

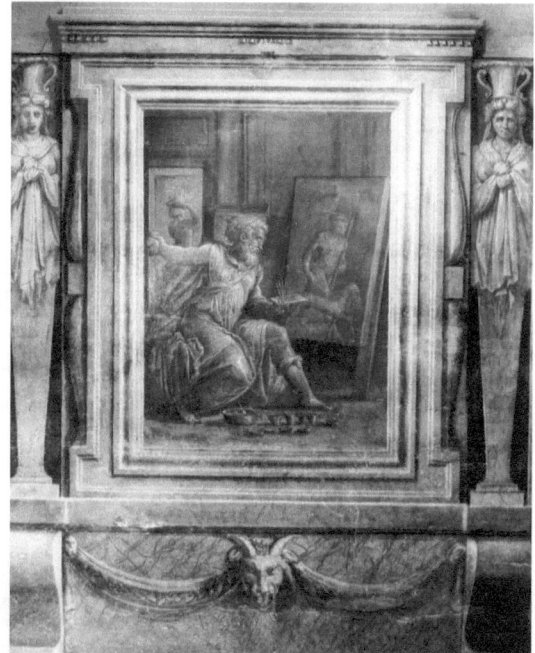

Fig. 11. Giorgio Vasari, *Protogenes' Ialysus with his Dog*, 1548, west wall, Chamber of Fortune, Casa Vasari, Arezzo.

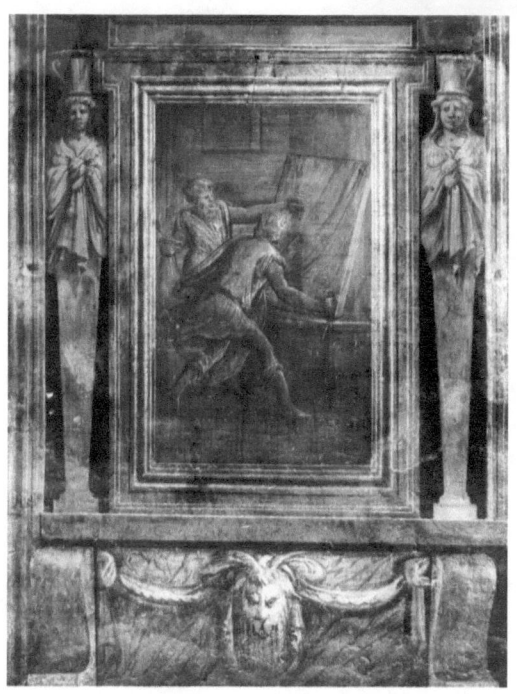

Fig. 12. Giorgio Vasari, *Parrhasius' The Contest with Zeuxis*, 1548, west wall, Chamber of Fortune, Casa Vasari, Arezzo.

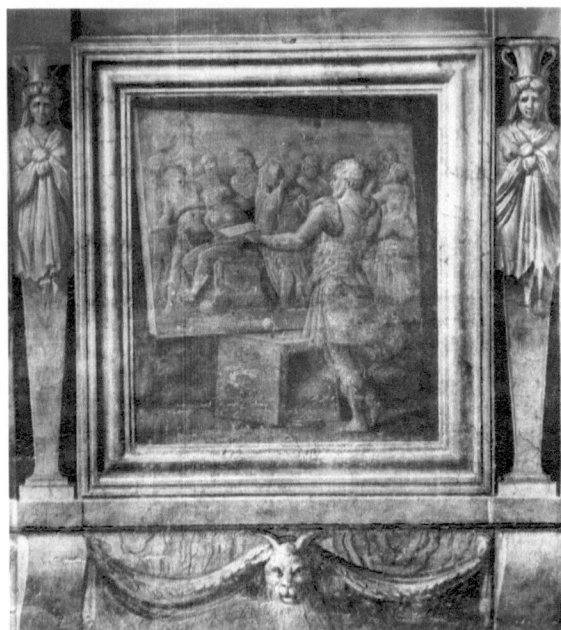

Fig. 13. Giorgio Vasari, *Timantes' The Sacrifice of Iphigenia*, 1548, west wall,  Chamber of Fortune, Casa Vasari, Arezzo.

Fig. 14. Giorgio Vasari, *Apelles' Alexander and Campaspe,* 1548, west wall, Chamber of Fortune, Casa Vasari, Arezzo.

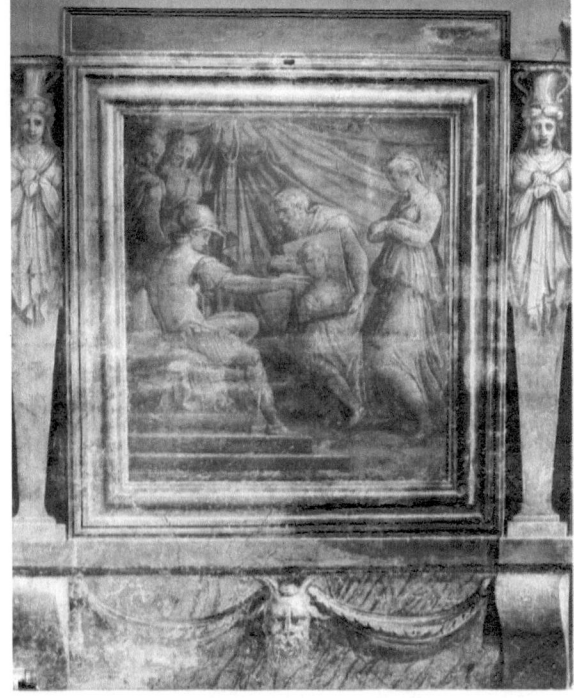

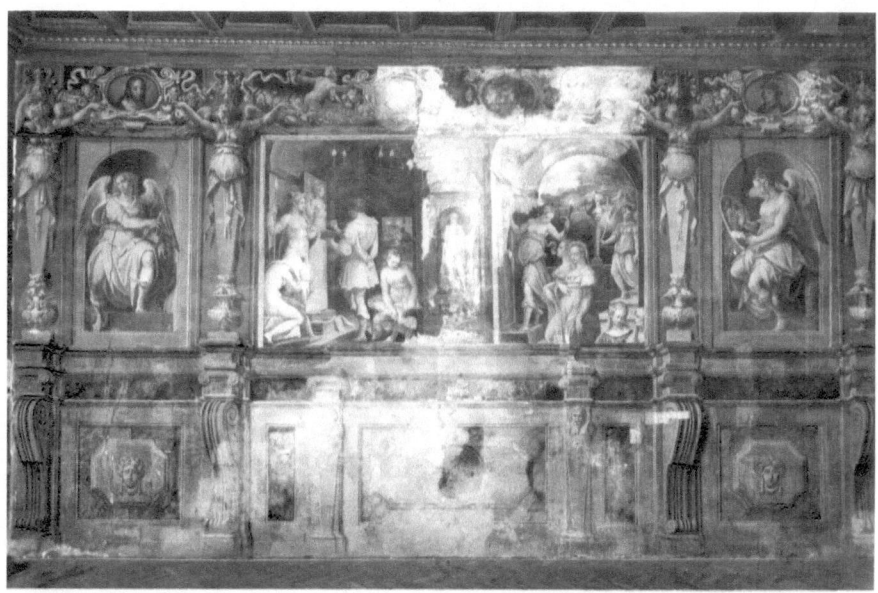

Fig. 15. Giorgio Vasari, *Apelles' Studio*, 1555-1561, east wall, Sala, Casa Vasari, Florence.

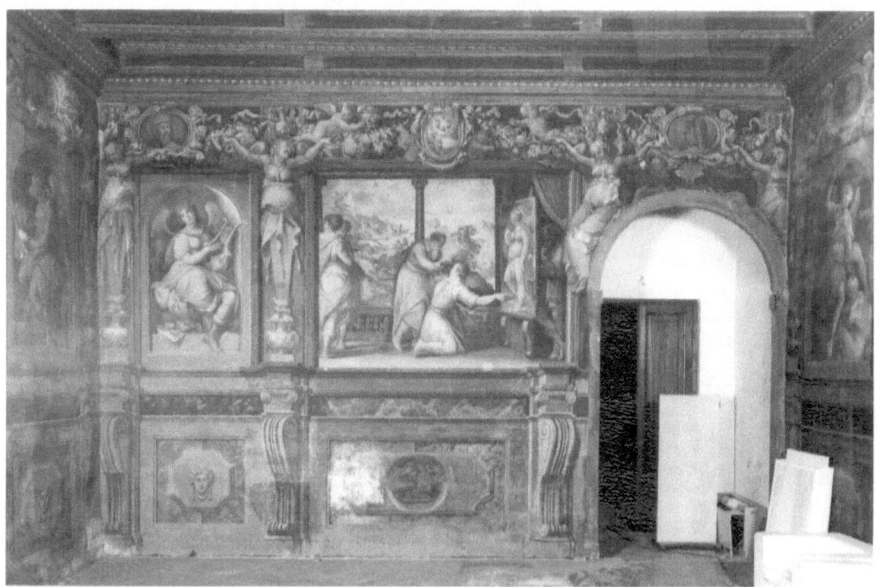

Fig. 16. Giorgio Vasari, *Apelles and the Shoemaker*, 1555-1561, south wall, Sala, Casa Vasari, Florence..

# 3

# Vasari's Early Decorative Cycles:
# The Venetian Commissions Part I

*In memory of Veda Cobb-Stevens*

"Setestorico, poeta, filosofo e pittore" ("You are a historian, poet, philosopher, as well as painter") (Aretino, Lmere 1: 79): in this manner, Pietro Aretina. Cavalier di Radi, praises his compatriot painter, Giorgio Vasari, and invites him to visit Venice.[1] This study considers two commissions that Vasari executed in Venice in 1541-42 - one secular (the *apparato* or stage settings for Aretino's comedy *La Talanta*) and the other religious (the ceiling decoration of Giovanni Cornaro's nuptial cbamber). Unfortunately, these two decorative structures have been dismantled or destroyed. Their reconstruction rests mostly on Vasari's descriptions, along with a few surviving drawings and paintings. Examination of these two Venetian commissions, however, reveals Vasari's formation of a repertoire of personifications and a new artistic formula, or *quadro riportato*, for decorative cycles.[2] Vasari's adroit inventiveness in the creation of a new type of decorative design and his resourceful imagination in the embellishment of emblematic imagery contribute to the artistic richness of sixteenth-century art.

A temporary decoration, the Venetian stage designs or *apparato* were demolished after the carnival in 1542. Vasari explains how he attempted to reproduce and save the *apparato*'s drawings, but he was stopped by the members of I Sempiterni ("ni fu tolta di mano da costoro" - "they removed them from my hands"), who felt that the honors he had already received for its creation were sufficient

(Frey and Frey 1: 118).[3] Regrettably, only a few drawings and engravings of the *apparato* decorations have survived - some drawings from sections of the ceiling and the walls, but none from the entrance and background portals. In the first part of this study, I will reconstruct a version of what the *apparato* may have been and will argue its iconographic meaning, relying in great part on Vasari's documentation (here cited in full), on Juergen Schulz's suggested reconstruction for the apparato design (505), as well as on a series of drawings attributed to this commission. After a brief discussion of the historical background between Pietro Aretino and Giorgio Vasari, Vasari's descriptions of the *apparato* for this first Venetian commission will be examined, followed by an analysis of the existing drawings for the *apparato* and the compositional arrangement, and an interpretative view of the symbolism in the *apparato*.

### The *Apparato* for Aretino's *La Talanta*

The connection between Pietro Aretino and Giorgio Vasari elucidates Vasari's commissions in Venice. The first recorded communication between Pietro Aretino and Vasari comes from a letter written in 1533 or 1534 by Vasari in Florence to Aretino residing in Venice. In this letter, Vasari honors and thanks Aretina for his literary *invenzioni*: "Sete [sic] come Febo mi avete illuminato l'animo... come la venuta dell' Aurora" ("You are like Phoebus; you have illuminated my spirit ... like the arrival of Aurora") (Frey and Frey 1: 3-4; Vasari 8: 244 and 252; Bertaux 329-33). The correspondence between the two friends continued throughout their lives. Their letters were exchanges of artistic and literary ideas and anecdotes, as well as vehicles for business transactions to commission and collect works of art. Vasari even visited Aretino in Venice (Landucci 168-76; Schulz 500-11).

Pietro Aretino likely moved from Rome to Venice in 1526 after the death of his dear Florentine friend, Giovanni delle Bande Nere.[4] Also, Aretino's inability to remain in Rome was due to his *lingua malefica* (malicious tongue), which antagonized and mocked the Roman nobility and their political views. In fact, his irornc and satirical comments provoked a Roman patrician from the Volta family to make an attempt on his life, prompting Aretino's flight to Venice.

In the Venetian Republic, Aretino was free to speak his mind (p. Luzio 109-11; A. Luzio 11; Cairns 13-31). During his long stay in Venice until his death in 1556, he wrote religious and secular poetry, short stories, and plays - in particular the comedies *Il Marescalco* (1531), *La Cortegiana* (1534), *Il Filosofo*, *Lo lpocrito*, and *La Talanta* (all published between 1542 and 1546), and the tragedy *L'Orazia* (1542-46). As illustrated in tbe five-act comedy of *La Talanta*, published by Francesco Marcolini and dedicated to the Duke of Florence,[5] the playwright's inventiveness moved away from the canon and the rules of the classical tradition to write with daring and erotic innuendo in a vernacular language. *La Talanta* tells the story of Talanta, a beautiful courtesan loved by four men who represent different types of love -true love, jealous love, possessive love, and deceptive love. Aretino follows the Roman -Tuscan tradition for illustrating a comedy by providing a *scena* made up of ancient Roman buildings and houses with balconies and *loggie*.[6] The action takes place in the *piazza* of the Pantheon, in the streets and houses where Talanta and her four lovers reside. The play unfolds with comical vignettes showing these men, from young to old, eagerly striving to win Talanta's heart.

In 1541, I Sempiterni – a new Compagnia della Calza, composed of twelve noblemen – commissioned *La Talanta* for the 1542 carnival[7] The Compagnia della Calza (so called because its youthful members wore fancy stockings at the Venetian festivals, parties, and plays) was renowned for its spectacular receptions honoring distinguished visitors to Venice. *La Talanta* was enacted in the Palazzo Gonnella, later known as Palazzo Valier at San Giobbe or Palazzo Gonnella-Valier at Canal Regio, designed and constructed by Antonio Scarpagnino before 1540 for a Paduan family (Kurneta 110-19).[8] ln 1541, however, the edifice was still an "unfinished palazzo on the Canaregio, containing fourteen windows facing the Canal Regio" (Vasari 6:223). Even though the Palazzo Gonnella was destroyed in 1795, a few engravings from the Venetian sites by Jacopo de' Barbari executed in 1500 and by Lucas Carlevarijs in 1703 (Figs. 1-3) assist in recapturing the location and spaciousness of the fatcade.[9]

The sixteenth-cemury Italian theater was not exclusively a coun phenomenon.[10] Religious and civic organizations commissioned in religious or secular edifices (Muir 116, 289)[11] many comic and tragic plays as well as festivals, *trionifi*,[12] and *apparati*. These performances were conceived as temporary decorations combined with a rich interplay of architectural and sculptural ornamentation and elaborate pageantry. In addition to religious organizations that performed sacred dramas, companies of high-spirited youths also performed, among the most notable being the Venetian Companies of the Stocking, *della Calza*, whose excellent performances and luxurious costumes are described by many Venetian diarists and historians.[13] The court spectacles took place in the palace courtyard, great hall, or garden (see Fig. 4).[14] From the few remaining records on the Palazzo Gonnella, it may be concluded that the performance of *La Talanta* took place in the great hall, with its fourteen windows, or *piano nobile*.

On 15 December 1540, with the site and the commission in place, Aretino wrote a lengthy letter to Vasari, inviting his friend to design the *apparato* for *La Talanta*:

> Il desiderio che io ebbi sempre circa il conoscere un buon dipintore de la mia patria, e stato, o figlioulo, adempiuto da la bontà di Dio, onde lo ringrazio, e ringraziaodolo, supplico la sua misericordia che dia vita prospera a voi che sete l'uomo che io cercava.

> It has been my desire to know a fine painter from my homeland and state; dear son, I thank God for His goodness, and in thanking Him, I also appeal to His mercifulness in granting you a prosperous life because you were the man that I was looking for.
>
> (Lettere 2: 24; my translation)

Aretino's choice of Vasari is not surprising. For two years (1535 and 1536), their correspondence consisted in great part of Vasari's description of his involvement in the decorations for the entries of dignitaries in Rome and Florence, such as the *apparato* for the reception of Charles V in Rome after the first African campaign,[15] the *apparato* for the triumphal entrance of Charles V in Florence,[16] and the decorations for the Medici villas (Letter of 11 or 18 March 1536, Frey and Frey 1: 40-46). In 1534, Vasari also decorated the *ap-*

*parato* for a comedy by Pollastra (Giovanni Lappoli), his tutor in the classics.[17] Since the fourteenth century, Florence had been the originator of festal decorations with traveling *festaiuoli* about Italy.[18] Aretino hoped that Vasari's decorative style, evolving from such a tradition as it had, would influence and challenge the Venetian artists.

Vasari arrived in Venice in December 1541. By February 1542 he had completed the decorations for the *apparato* with the aid of three assistants, Cristofaro Gherardi, Battista Cungi, and Bastiano Fiori of Arezzo (Borghini 1:7).[19] In act one, scene three of the *commedia*, Messer Vergolo (a Venetian who is visiting Rome) instructs Scrocca (a Venetian villain) about Roman antiquities; in particular, he points out the Arch of Septimius Severus and praises Florentine painters such as Vasari:

> Certo mi s'avvisa, mi si scrive e mi si notifica, che un Messer Giorgio d'Arezzo, di etade dun XXXV anni, ha fatto una scena et un apparato che il Sansovino, e'l Tiziano, spiriti mirabili, ne ammirano. Or torniarno al amica (Talanta) [sic], che sono sazio di vagheggiar marmi e stuatue.

> Of course, I am advised, I am instructed, and I am notified that a Mister Giorgio of Arezzo, of 35 years of age, has composed a scene and an *apparato* that is admired by both kindred spirits, Sansovino and Titian.
>                   (Aretino, *La Talanta* 39, 1.1; my translation)

Thus Aretino cleverly underscores Titian's and Sansovino's admiration of Vasari's settings.[20]

The performance of *La Talanta* took place along the wall of the loggia, one of the largest in Venice (Kurneta 110-19). The theatrical *apparato* was 143 feet long and 32 feet wide and consisted of a series of paintings. Vasari describes the *apparato* in four different documents – briefly in autobiography[21] and *ricordanze*,[22] elaborately in a letter to Ottavio de' Medici in Florence (Vasari 8: 283-87; Frey and Frey 1: 111-19, Letter 47 and in his biographical description of Cristofaro Gherardi (Vasari 6: 222-23). These four documents do correlate with one another in content; however, some slight variations differentiate them – such as elaborations or omissions, inclusions of personifications, and descriptions of some of the scenes. The two latter documents are most useful in recreating Vasari's iconography in the *apparato*.

Along the walls, platforms were erected for seating the ladies of the aristocracy; these platforms were broken by niches containing antique portrait busts. The walls and ceiling were decorated with pictures: the ceiling contained four large paintings, oils on canvas depicting the four stages of time in a day and the twenty-four hours. The walls presented in chiaroscuro (monochromatic color) landscape settings eight stories of the Veneto and personifications of the Virtues - Charity, Fortitude, Concord, Compassion, Liberality, Prudence, Justice, Religion, Fame, Fortune, and Peace - surrounded by elaborate ornamentation. The *messa in scena* was an architectural design in perspective representing the major monuments from Rome. Lighting was created by making a highly realistic sun that moved across the scene during the performance, giving out an exceedingly bright light reflected in glass vessels filled with water and lit by lamps. This lighting effect demonstrated Vasari's incorporation into his Florentine stage decoration the new Venetian technology in theatrical illumination.[23] Proudly, Vasari observed how the *apparato* was highly praised by everyone who saw it, and accordingly, he expressed his perplexity at its dismantling (Fletcher 130; Vasari 7: 670).[24]

In the *Vita of Cristofaro Gherardi*, Vasari further elaborated on the description of the *apparato*. To capture the true flavor of Vasari's description, the complete passage is included here:

Now the said gentlemen of the Calza had taken at the end of the Canaregio a large house that was not finished - it had nothing, indeed, save the main walls and the roof - and, in a space forming an apartment seventy braccia long and sixteen braccia wide, Giorgio caused to be made two ranges of wooden steps, four braccia in height from the floor, on which the ladies were to be seated. The walls at the sides he divided each into four square spaces of ten braccia, separated by niches each four braccia in breadth, within which were figures. And these niches had each on either side a terminal figure in relief, nine braccia high; inasmuch as the niches on either side were five and the terminal figures ten, in the whole apartment there were altogether ten niches, twenty terminal figures, and eight square pictures with scenes. In the first of these pictures [which were all in chiaroscuro], on the right hand, next to the stage, there was, representing Venice, a most beautiful figure of Adria, seated upon a rock in the midst of the sea with a branch of coral in her hand. Around her stood Neptune, Thetis, Proteus, Nereus, Glaucus, Palaemon, and other sea gods and nymphs, who were presenting to her jewels, pearls, gold, and other riches of the sea; and besides this, there were sortie Loves that were shooting arrows, and others that were flying through the air and scattering flowers, and the rest of the field of the picture was all most beautiful palms.

In the second picture were the Rivers Drava and Sava naked, with their vases. In the third was the Po, conceived as large and corpulent, with seven sons, representing the seven branches that, issuing from the Po, pour into the sea as if each of them was a kingly river. In the fourth was the Brenta with other rivers of Friuli. On the other wall, opposite to the Adria, was the Island of Candia, wherein was to be seen Jupiter, being suckled by the Goat, with many Nymphs around. Beside this, and opposite to the Drava, were the River Tagliamento and the Mountains of Cadore. Beyond this, opposite to the Po, were Lake Benacus and the Mincio, which were pouring their waters into the Po; and beside them, opposite to the Brenta, were the Adige and the Tesino, falling into the sea.

The pictures on the right-hand side were divided by these Virtues, placed in the niches: Liberality, Concord, Compassion, Peace, and Religion; and opposite to these, on the other wall, were Fortitude, Civic Wisdom (Prudence), Justice, a Victory with War beneath her, and. lastly, a Charity. Above all, then, were a large cornice and architrave, and a frieze full of lights and of glass globes filled with distilled waters, to the end that these, having lights behind them, might illuminate the whole area.

Next, the ceiling was divided into four quadrangular compartments, each ten braccia wide in one direction and eight braccia in the other; and, with a width equal to that of the niches of four braccia, there was a frieze that ran right round the cornice, while in a line with the niches there came in the middle of all the spaces a square compartment of three braccia. These compartments were in all twenty-three, without counting one of double size that was above the stage, which brought the number up to twenty-four; and in them were the Hours, twelve of the night, namely, and twelve of the day.

In the first of the compartments ten braccia in length, which was above the stage, was Time, who was arranging the Hours in their places, accompanied by Aeolus, God of the Winds, by Juno, and by Iris. In another compartment, at the door of entrance, was the Chariot of Aurora, who, rising from the arms of Tithonus, was scattering roses, while the Chariot itself was being drawn by some Cocks. In the third was the Chariot of the Sun; and in the fourth was the Chariot of Night, drawn by Owls, and Night had the Moon upon her head, sortie Bats in front of her, and all around her darkness.

Of these pictures Cristofano executed the greater part, and he acquitted himself so well that everyone stood marveling at them, particularly the Chariot of Night, wherein he created by way of oil-sketches that which was, in a manner of speaking, not possible. And in the picture of Adria, likewise, he painted those monsters of the sea with such beauty and variety that whoever looked at them was struck with astonishment that a craftsman of his rank should have shown such knowledge. In short, in all this work he bore himself beyond all expectation as an able and well-practiced painter, particularly in the foliage and grotesques.

The stage chiefly showed views of Rome: a great many specimens of ancient and recent buildings - The Pantheon (La Rotonda), the Coliseum, the Temple of Fortune, Trajan's Column, etc.- together with beautiful palaces, houses, and churches containing a great many picturesque details of Doric, Ionian, Corinthian, Tuscan architecture, and a sun that, moving across the stage during the performance, produced an immense light by means of glass globes.

(Vasari 6: 222-25; my translation)[25]

Vasari offered discussion of the *apparato* in a letter to Ottavio de' Medici tbat is morc complex and precise in its description, probably because it was written in the same year that the *apparato* was created, 1542. To capture the true flavor of the passage, it has also been cited here its entirety:

### To The Great M. Ottaviano De' Medici

Description of the Decoration of I Sempiterni, Made in Venice for the Performance of Pietro Aretino's La Talanta

Greetings, Great Lord. After much suffering, as well as worrying, I am at peace. I must write you this letter that will be testimony to the end of the many difficulties with the play tbat you know. I have done this play for the holiday and for the ornament, entitled as you know by our M. Pietro, and I have managed to do him this honor so that he might call upon me another time. I leave up to him the task of sending you the play, because he has written it; I will give you a description of the decoration. I leave to him also the trouble of telling you about the praise given to him, both in public and private, because wanting to praise myself to you would be superfluous, knowing how much I am worth in similar situations. Therefore, what I want to tell you is this: the decoration was such that every person who looks at it becomes amazed and thinks that it is a big mistake to destroy it, as though it could be preserved in memory.

I have not encountered so many troubles in a long while, though I have had some minor household problems, but these personal problems were not known, so envy could not have been the reason for my current situation. But, in order to share with you what I have done, I will tell you, about the invention of the thing, short and simple, because if I let the pen write, a notebook would be needed. The room where the decoration was done was very large. Likewise, the stage, that is to say the perspective illustrating Rome, was big. In it were the Septimius Arch, the Temple of Pacis, the Pantheon, the Coliseum, the Pace, Santa Maria Nuova, the Temple of Fortune, tbe Trajan Column, the Palazzo Maggiore, the Seven Stairs, the Conti's Tower, tbe Militia Tower, and finally Maestro Pasquino, more handsome than ever; there were also beautiful buildings, houses, churches, and a variety of things in Doric, Ionic. Corinthian, and Tuscan Architecture - wild but neat; and I wanted a sun that moved across the stage during the performance to illuminate the stage greatly, for which I used big glass globes.

The play was performed by these Great Men, young men of the noblest class. There were in attendance a great many people, so much so that one could not linger because of the heat generated by the lights and the closeness of bodies suffocating one another. The invention was this: the ceiling of the whole room was made of carved wood and was divided into four large paintings. Night was in the first painting, Dawn was in the second, Day in the third, and Evening in the last. In Night there was an Endymion sleeping with his love. Bats, parrots, and owls were pulling a beautiful wagon filled with witches, visions, and dreams.

The wagon was filled with stars and Diana who had a moon on her forehead and tbe cornucopia beneath her. Diana's clothing was turned inside out from the waist down. Painted with oil, it had wood figures and decorations all around it.

Each painting displayed six hours around it, with several fictitious females in various poses with wings in their heads, and to show how many they were, each one had a shield with a number written on it. In the Dawn painting, there was a half-naked female dressed in iridescent red and blue, with golden, swept-up hair adorned with many roses. She was embraced by Tithonus who did not want her to go away. Roosters were pulling the wagon, and one could see the air, blazing in red, remaining purified where she appeared, above the inscription .... The third painting, Day, depicted a Phaeton falling down rapidly with no brakes, burning through the air over us and seeming to collapse on the viewers, with an inscription.... In Evening, the fourth painting showed Icarus learning to fly from his father Deadalus's instruction, but moved by too much desire and reluctance to obey him, he approached the Sun's rays; his wings melted and he fell. This would indicate that sometimes it is important to do things the way knowledgeable people tell you. The painting bore an inscription....

As I said, in the four paintings the Hours were represented, divided by Time into twenty-four; each one indicated its time, and each had different hair, winged-heads, and several orioles telling the time indicated, so that the Twelfth Hour was embracing it with the desire of being consumed.

Under the four paintings, there were in the facades four squares per area, and each one was partitioned by measures of six arms long; in this way the stories were each seven arms long, and the measures were double with a niche in the middle where there were shown certain virtues and then the stories. These measures were holding up a doorhead, a frieze, and a very beautiful cornice; in the first niche there was Prudence with two faces, one old and the other young, with a sphere inside it that bore words of an inscription....

Opposite to Prudence was Justice with a sword and open panders, with dress tucked up and untied as is customary.... For decoration, there were several circles that were holding up a doorhead, frieze, and cornice that was highlighted inside above the niche where the said figures were. And in the prominence above every marker there was a weapon in relief, round, in stucco, of the I Sempiterni Company, and between the weapons in the space of the niche was Saint Marcus, three arms long, that is, a lion with his paws in the water. And between the spaces of the frieze, where the stories were, there were big stucco festoons and masks, which made partitions with excessive ornamentation in golden relief. The height of the frieze was two arms long, having a cornice in relief all made of carved wood with a big console between which there were sevenl stucco rosettes, all of them golden in color and very beautiful.

Under Justice was Religion in another niche, having at her feet the Old Testament and in one hand the New Testament open to St. Peter's letters, showing the chronicle of St. Jacob, who was pointing to a cross that was in the Pope's Kingdom and an inscription....

Opposite to Religion was Fame, with one foot on earth and the other one in the air, the former foot lying on top of a world in motion. Fame played two trumpets at the same time; fire representing evil was coming out of one trumpet, and the other trumpet was throwing out splendor for the good of all, with an inscription....

Under Fame was Fortune with a fixed look, half naked, having a scepter in her right hand and in the other hand an inflated sail, with her hair hmging loosely in the air ahead. She was sitting on a wheel which was resting on top of a Dolphin, with words inscribed....

Opposite to Fortune was Peace adorned with various scanty clothes, who, raising her head, was giving thanks to heaven; underneath her she burned with a torch many weapons and trophies and the words of an inscription....

In the large paintings, between the niches and the markers, representing Venice was Adria, daughter of the Sea, a completely naked, lascivious young girl, holding a palm in her right hand and raising her left arm in the air. She had a branch of corals on her back; her hair, soft and hanging loosely, was becoming blonde under the sun that was drying it with blazing rockets. She was sitting on a rock in the water with one leg in the sea and the other one on shore; in the ocean some marine gods crowned with rush presented some niches full of corals and baskets covered with turtles and full of pearls and happiness - these were Glaucus, Nereus, and Galatea with her head full of palms, showing the peacefulness of the place - and an inscription....

In the second one a very big figure represented the Po, sitting on a glass and surrounded by six other glasses all throwing water, representing his seven branches. On his back was a horn of abundance full of various fruits, and on his head was a tree wreath and words of an inscription....

In the third, there were two rivers and a mountain; the mountain was a very dry, rough, muscular figure that was resting an arm on a rock; the legs were turning into stone, the head was made of branches of oak tree and of thorns, and the beard was frozen. With one hand he was overturning an urn held by Brenta, a very ugly old woman, crowned with reeds and rushes, under whom there was a very large river that was leaning with one arm on top of an urn, while the other arm held a horn of abundance. The: face of the river was downward and was flooding the earth, and there was an inscription....

Under this third painting was a fourth, in which there was the Tagliamento, the river of this village, that comes from the Swiss mountains; from its mouth it spewed an abundance of water, showing that it took its name from the top of the mountain. Timavo, a big river in Friuli, turned its head toward another river, bigger than these two rivers, and showed them a horn full of beautiful fruit, declaring itself to be Livenza, river of these lords. Underneath, there was an inscription....

Opposite to this painting on the other side was our Arno, which had a wreath made of panicles, millet, and sorghum, and a horn full of fruit with an open glass of water, which was resting on a lion; he had a fleur-de-lys on his hand, and his head was turned toward the Tiber. He was shown reclining with open legs, holding a branch, and leaning on a very large glass of water that was spilling out. This gave way to a figure of a she-wolf that was nursing the beautiful children, Romulus and Remus. In the middle was an old man representing the Apennine, who had a beard made of mountain feathers and who by embracing both of the children indicated that they were his....

Opposite to the Tagliamento and above it, there was Benaco, a Garda lake that was lying down with his hands on his hair, which, when he squeezed it, made a lake and became the river Tesino, young and foreshortening because it lasts briefly. He held an urn toward Benaco in order to retain everything that Benaco was pouring, to give it to the Po as a present. In the meantime Tesino, with an angry attitude, was pouring waters into the sea, not wanting to be seen to be inferior to the others, and it bore this inscription....

Above this one, and opposite to the Po, was the Island of Candia, where Jupiter, with lighming in his hand and an eagle beneath him, sat with an old lady. The lady embraced a goat that was nursing Jupiter, and she was indicating that she did not want to miss the happiness of the festivities offered by the other Gods and rivers but was obligated to provide milk to the country of Candia for the existence of this Highness Republic Venice. Underneath were the verses of the inscription....

Opposite to Adria's painting and above Candia was the Island of Cyprus, who was pictured as a lascivious Venus with Cupid in the forest of Adonis, where, resting on top of some Dolphins, were spreading roses, along with an arch, quivers, arrows, torch, bandages, myrtle, doves, all the symbols of love, and inscribed verses.... The door was fashioned in a beautiful architectural design in the shape of a triumphal arch, and it displayed verses in a bizarre epitaph....

I will let M. Pietro, the inventor of all these things, give your Honor more detailed information, as I am sure he will. It is enough for me to refer to what I have done, so that you know what I have accomplished in two month's time; and I offer myself to your service.

Venice, 1542.

(Frey and Frey 1: 111-19 [Letter 47], and 8: 283-87; my translation)

Although other journals recording a Venetian carnival are now lost and surviving evidence of such decoration by established artists is difficult to uncover, Vasari's artistic contribution rests not only in the artistic enterprise but in the literary and historical contribution of having recorded a folkloric event (Fletcher 130).26 To Vasari's great disappointment, the Venetian *apparato* was treated as a temporary decoration and, as such, was dismantled and destroyed after the carnival. Vasari felt that the honors he had received for its creation were destroyed along with the decorations.27 Unfortunately, only a few drawings and engravings of the designs for the ceiling, walls, and panel decorations have survived (Schulz 505), but a brief discussion of them will assist in reconstructing the *apparato*. The discussion consists of a listing of the present location of *apparato*. The discussion consists of a listing of the present location of these drawings, as well a comparative analysis of the drawings with emblematic images for symbolic identification.

No drawings are known to have survived of the entrance and background portals of the apparato, but some drawings of sections of ceiling and the walls exist, depicting the Hours of Time and the Chariots of Time in the ceiling and personifications of Water and moral virtues on the walls. Some drawings of the personification of the Hours are preserved at tbe Staatiliche Kunstsammlungen in Kassel; one of them depicts the Third Hour as a figure holding in one hand a mirror in which she views the hourglass on her head, and in the other hand a triangle implying the third hour, though all of these attributes allude to the passing of time (Cecchi, "Nuove acquisizioni" 51-52 Fig. 1). Another drawing, at the Kunstmuseum in Düsseldorf (FP6422), represents the Fourth Hour (Schaar 21-22 n 14 Fig. 11). The drawing for the Nineteenth Hour appeared on the London art market in 1975 (Clifford 319-21 Fig. 52). In the fourth drawing, which was auctioned in Milan, the hour is unidentifiable (*Asta di disegni* Lot 44. attributed to Taddeo Zuccaro). But Vasari-Stradano's *Study for a Ceiling* of 1560 (see Fig. 5) for the *Ceiling of Saturn* in the Palazzo Vecchio (Barocchi, *Mostra* 191 Fig. 64), representing the twenty-four hours of the day, can assist in visualizing Vasari's Hours.

The drawings of the ceiling associated with the Chariots of Time are few, as well; there are only four of them. A drawing for the car of Aurora or Dawn to Midday (*Il Giorno*) (see Fig. 6) is located at the Staatliche Graphische Sammlung in Munich.28 Vasari was inspired by the image of Vincenzo Cartari's Aurora (see Cartari 53): riding with a cock in a chariot pulled by Pegasus, Aurora holds a flaming torch in one hand and discards roses with the other (see Fig. 7). A second drawing (see Fig. 8), found at the Instituto Nazionale per la Grafica in Rome, depicts the car of Phaeton as the time of Midday to Dusk (*Il Mezzogiorno*) and was undoubtedly inspired by Andrea Alciato's Emblem 56, *Temerity* (see Fig. 9), where Phaeton is falling from his chariot.29 Another drawing (see Fig. 10), located at the Cabinet des Dessins in the Louvre, portrays the car of Icarus as the time of Dusk to Midnight (*La Sera*). For the imagery of this drawing, Vasari also appropriated Alciato's Emblem 104, *Against Astrologers* (see Fig. 11), which displays a composition similar to Vasari's description of the falling winged figure.30 A drawing of Midnight (*La Notte*) (see Fig. 12), located the Metropolitan Museum of Art, depicts a dormant Endymion. In front of him rests his faithful companion, while in the distance witches and demons are in flight, casting their spells.31

Dispersed among European collections are several drawings for the walls of the *apparato* consisting of aquatic deities, such as the scene of Adria (see Fig. 13), the symbol of Venice, seated on a rock and surrounded by four marine deities, which is located at the Cabinet des Dessins of the Louvre (Schulz 505 - 06; Monbeig-Goguel, *Vasari et Son Temps* 166 Fig. 216). Although Barocchi attributes the drawing to Cristofaro Gherardi, il Doceno (*Vasari Pittore* 127 Fig. 19b; Vasari 7: 8), resemblances in composition and figure positioning to an Amsterdam drawing at the Prentenkabinett in the Rijksmuseum (see Fig. 14) are so strong that one wonders if Vasari, rather than Gherardi, may not have actually executed the Louvre drawing. Vasari attributed the sea monsters to Gherardi, but not the design of the figure of Adria: "In the picture of Adria, Gherardi depicted marine monsters with such a virtuosity and beauty that it stupefied those who admired them" (Barocchi, *Vasari Pittore* 13; Vasari 7: 653-54). The design of Adria is reminiscent of Vasari's careful study of Michelangelo's Sistine Ceiling. Vasari's masculine and sculptural treatment of the body of Adria, along with her outstretched arm, are similar to that of Michelangelo's Eve in the Temptation scene in the Sistine Ceiling. Although the seated position of Adria is somewhat different from Eve's, Vasari's stylistic dependence on the stance of Michelangelo's figure is obvious. He repeated Adria's composition in another Venetian commission, the personification of Faith in the ceiling of the Cornaro Palace in 1542, and he reapplied the design of Adria in a later depiction of Calliope, the muse of Music and the Arts, in the Palazzo Vecchio in 1566 (L. Cheney, "Giorgio Vasari's Scrittorio" 160-75).

The Amsterdam drawing (see Fig. 14) illustrates one complete bay of the design. In the center of the main scene, Adria is accompanied with four marine deities: Glaucus, Nereus, Thetis, and Galatea. On each side, a flanking herm and niche frame the scene. The niches contain two allegorical figures - Fame on the left, Pallas Athena on the right (Schulz 501; Vasari 7; 651-52). The Berlin drawing at the Kupferstichkabinett in the Dahlem, Ehem. Staatliche Museen (see Fig. 15), identified by Hermann Voss (267 n 1), depicts three seated sea deities or personifications of rivers: Tagliamento, who spouts water from his mouth; Livenza, who holds a cornucopia; and Timavo, who rests his hand on a Greek vase.

To visualize tbe wall decoration of the *apparato*, further assistance is provided by recently discovered drawings, such as *The Mincio, Timano and Po* (Cecchi, "Nuove acquisizioni" 51-52 Fig. 4) in the Collection of Colonel J. Weld at Lutworth Manor (see Fig. 16), and *The Arno and Tiber Rivers Embraced by the Apennine Mountain* in the Worcester Art Museum (see Fig. 17). Alessandro Cecchi correctly attributes another version of tbe latter drawing (Uffizi. Inv. n. 92184) to a design for the *apparato* (Cecchi, "Qualche contributo" 143-61). The river god motif of reclining figures depicted in these drawings is a Vasarian appropriation from antiquity, similar to those of the ancient reclining statues representing the personifications of the Nile and Tiber located in the Capitoline and Vatican museums in Rome. Vasari repeats this motif in many of his paintings, such as in tbe Sala dei Cento Giorni of 1546, in the Palazzo della Cancelleria, as well as in the frontispiece for Leon Battista Alberti's *De architectura*, published in 1550.

The only known engraving after a Vasari drawing for a section of the wall of the *apparato* is illustrated as a lithograph facsimile and is identified by D. Vivant-Denon (3: 115, Pl. 185) as a *Study for a Festival Decoration* (see Fig. 18). The overall format of this engraving constitutes a facsimile of the Amsterdam drawing to the extent that a principal scene with Adria and marine deities is framed by flanking herms (compare Figs. 14 and 18). In the engraving, however, this scene differs in the number of figures and their artistic designs - Adria, pouring water from an urn, is encircled by three marine deities.

The other set of drawings for the walls of the *apparato* is associated with the personifications of Virtues. Although there are few drawings from this group, tbese drawings compliment the visual reconstruction of the *apparato* decoration. These images of Virtues frame the narrative stories of the aquatic deities. Drawings from other Vasarian decorative cycles assist in reconstructing the *apparato*'s setting and the design of the Virtues. For example, Vasari's *Project for a Ceiling*, at the Uffizi Gabinetto Disegni e Stampe (see Fig. 19), depicts the virtues of Fortitude, Justice, Prudence, Temperance, Charity, Faith, and Hope in separate niches (Barocchi, *Mostra* 19 Fig. 16), while other drawings depicting a single Virtue - Prudence, Peace, and Concord - provide an insightful record on the figure-type and iconography of the Virtues. Several drawings of Prudence are located at the Gabinetto Disegni e Stampe in the Uffizi (see Fig. 20).32 A drawing of *Peace* is found at the Graphische Sammlung Albertina in Vienna (see Fig. 21)33 and a drawing of Concord is housed at the Staatliche Kunstsammlungen in Kassel (see Fig. 22).34

The style and composition of these drawings for the *apparato* illustrate Vasari's interest in, and familiarity with, the mural decorations of central Italy, especially with the *dadi* decorations from the Vatican *stanze*.35 The compositional design of the wall decoration, which is segmented into squares and rectangles, is a Bramantesque and a Cinquecento innovation. It is in the *apparato* for *La Talanta* where the beginning of Vasari's decorative formula - a design marked by squares depicting an *istoria* (dramatic scene) with a classical literary theme and by rectangles that contain either a niche with allegorical figures or personifications of virtues or are flanked by architectural herms - can be seen.

Vasari's training and travels gave him a thorough acquaintance with the diverse types of ceiling and wall decorations prevalent in Cinquecento art. On his arrival in Venice, he was able to manifest this artistic assimilation of festive decorations. The *apparato*'s rectangular design, composed of wall and ceiling decorations, can be viewed as an architectural parallel and metaphor for Vasari's visualization of a visitor's experience entering Venice - the boat's crossing of the Grand Canal, framed on both sides by Venetian *palazzi* and above by the heavenly blue tapestry of the sky.36

The *apparato*'s fanciful ceiling decorations were echoed in the wall decorations (see my reconstructions, Figs. 23 and 24 here). A total of twenty-seven images faced the fourteen windows, containing a corresponding tripartite articulation carried over into tbe ceiling composed of a central scene depicted in a square and circular format, with monochromatic personifications of rivers and Venetian territories. The square format was elaborately framed on each side by chiaroscuro Virtues residing in rectangular niches protected by stucco herms. In 1539, Vasari first utilized this type of frieze decoration in one of his earliest decorative commissions for the Refectory of San Michele in Bosco in Bologna (L. Cheney, "Vasari and Naples" 48-126).

Under the guidance of Aretino, Vasari created an inventive program of iconography infusing the Venetian artistic repertoire with Roman and Tuscan emblematic and visual traditions. From the narration ofthe play, for example, it can be visualized that the *messa in scena* of the *apparato* consists of a *veduta* of Rome,37 a comic stage format showing houses surrounding the Pantheon. Vasari made the setting more elaborate by including numerous classical buildings, such as the Arch of Septimius, the Temple of Peace (now Biblioteca Pacis), the Coliseum, the Temple of Fortune, the Trajan Column, the Santa Maria della Pace, tbe Santa Maria Nuova (now San Francesca Romana), the Palazzo Maggiore, the Avenue of the Seven Hills (near the Esquiline Hill), tbe Torre dei Conti, the Tower of the Milizie, and the statue of Master Pasquino. Unfortunately, none of these depictions survived.38

The thematic program of the *apparato* was not accidental or merely fictive, but it was actual and representative of Venetian environs - for example, the River Tagliamento set against the mountains of Cadore (Titian's birthplace) and the representation of Adria as a personification of Water and of Venice, "Adria" being a loose Italian translation of *hydra*, the Greek word for water. It was also the name of Aretino's favorite daughter, who represented to him the essence of a Venetian beauty (Fletche, 130).

The *apparato*'s imagery, unprecedented in *apparati* decoration, proclaimed the supremacy of Venice through the personification of Air and Water that presented the cosmological relation between the elements of Air and Water through Time. In the ceiling decoration, tbe imagery of the sky or celestial tapestry opens up with the lunar control of Juno,39 Goddess of the Moon, Air, and Sky, who orders Iris,40 the Rainbow Goddess, to irradiate the sky with colors. Its reflections in pools, rivers, and lakes represent the panoramic changes through Time and the Hours. The sky goddesses, who are symbolic of the life forces of energy, mind, and light, are closely related to the processes of time. The images in the ceiling show the transformations of light and life through the cycle of tune.

This cycle, which was designed in four circular shapes, can be seen as symbolic of the four stages of time, metaphorically represented in riding chariots or *trionfi*: Dawn to Midday (*Il Giorno*) as Aurora; Midday to Dusk (*Il Mezzogiorno*) as Phaeton; Dusk to Midnight (*La Sera*) as Icarus; and Midnight to Dawn (*La Notte*) as Endymion. The further subdivision of time into temporal facets of twenty-four Hours alludes to recalling, consuming, and keeping daily time. In the *Illiad* (5.749; 8.393 and 21.450), the Hours are personifications of the atmospheric moisture, as they open and close the gates of Olympus. They form and disperse the clouds and govern the seasons and changes in life. Ranged around the chariots of Time, the Hours constitute the retinue of the sky and repre-sent the cosmic forces in nature and their cosmic moments of influence upon human actions.

The celestial energy of light and air that controls the motion of the body of water on earth was illustrated in the decorations of the north and south walls. The body of water was personified with mythological aquatic deities interacting with one another and protecting and controlling the flow of the authentic rivers. The aquatic deities included Adria, Neptune, Thetis,41 Proteus,42 Nereus,43 Glaucus,44 Galatea,45 and Palaemon.46 The rivers shown were, from the Veneto region, the Drava, Sava, Po, Brenta, Tagliamento, Tesino, Timavo, Livenza, and Adige, plus, from the central region of Italy, the Arno and Tiber. The fictive realm created by the mythic sea gods and goddesses alludes to divine intervention in the natural world in the same manner that Juno, Iris, and Time rule the celestial realm in the ceiling's program. The temporal realm is forged by the rivers, with their continuous mutation and movement, paralleling the changes of the Hours shown in tbe ceiling. Traditionally, rivers such as tbe Nile, tbe Tigris, and the Euphrates are seen as symbolic of the cradle of civilization. Their function is dynamic, influenced by the changes of tbe moon and cosmic heavenly forces. In addition, Aretino and Vasari visually transformed the natural elements of air and water into personifications. The river Brenta, for example, is described as "old woman, very ugly, crowned with canes and reeds" (Vasari 8: 286). Also included are lakes (Garda, Benacus, and Mincio), islands (Candia and Cyprus), and mountains (Cadore and Apennines), from which the rivers orignate.

The relationship of the celestial energy of light to the natural energy of water found a parallel in the simulated sculptures in the niches representing the cardinal and Christian virtues (Prudence, Justice, Fortitude, Charity, Religion, Peace, Concord, Liberality, Fame, and Fortune). The virtues are beneficent, given to humankind by divinity, and can be seen metaphorically here as symbols of the good deeds offered in Venice to its inhabitants. Vasari noted that he painted the virtues in chiaroscuro so as to simulate sculpture and to contrast with the *istorie* (dramatic scenes) in monochromatic colors depicting landscapes.47 Unlike tbe sky realm symbolically illuminated by the deities, the water realm is "full of candles, and in front of these, large glass globes, filled with distilled water, [which] caught the rays and so lit up the whole room" (Vasari 6: 223-25).

Vasari thus displayed the four elements in the *apparato*: Fire, through the rotating sun design, candles, and glass bowls; Earth, through the simulated sculptural figures depicting Virtues; Air, through the pictured chariots pulling personifications of Day, Night, Dusk, and Dawn; and Water, through depictions of rivers and lake. For Aretino, Water personified Venice, and his comedy was performed at carnival time, in anticipation of Spring, because cosmically Water is the first conception of the power of Nature in Spring.

In the *apparato* design, Vasari created cosmic time in suspension for the audience. Having arrived at the palace in their gondolas, the audience would have entered a theatrical arena, a space that symbolically represented Venice, so as to behold a beautiful, imaginary world. Passing through a triumphal arch decorated with the *imprese* of the I Sempiterni, the patrons and the guests crossed the large hall adorned with representations of Venetian spiritual richness (the Virtues) and Veneto natural richness (the landscape). In the seating area, they found not only the perspectival *messa in scena* of Rome, with its classical marvels, but also the imagery of Juno,

Iris, and Time, suspended in the heavens with the Hours and the Chariots of Time. These co-present metaphorical references to the fictive and the real, the celestial and the natural, the eternal and the temporal, created a paradox and provided contrapuntal interest for the audience. The design of the *apparato* created the elliptical shape of the cosmic axis, composed by vertical and horizontal lines, uniting what is above with what is below and suspending space and time.

Evidently, Vasari developed here a new decorative formula that would form the basis for his cycle paintings, a formula that can be traced to his early work in Venice. With this *apparato*, Vasari began to prepare a pictorial dictionary of personifications that he would continue to apply in all his decorative cycles; he also visualized an early concept of *quadro riportato*, which would be later popularized in the seventeenth century by Annibale Carracci in the Galleria Farnese in Rome (see Wittkower 65-68). Vasari's elements of the new decorative cycle revolutionized ceiling decorations in the sixteenth century: the central concept based on the *quadro riportato*, where scenes representing an *istoria* in a landscape or architectural setting are framed by flanking herms and niches (tabernacles) that contain allegorical figures or personifications symbolizing moral or aesthetic virtues and then are ornamented overall with *all'antica* and grotesque motifs.

The other of Vasari's significant innovations in decorative cycles was the application of Venetian ecclesiastical ceiling decoration to secular buildings. In Venetian ecclesiastical ceiling decoration of the sixteenth century, it was common to decorate flat ceilings with applied wood or stucco, so structured as to create not the illusion of space but a rhythm that continues throughout the composition. The flat wooden beams intersect, creating recessed compartments of modified geometric patterns that contain histories or figurative images, as in Pordenone's Venetian ceilings of Stanza Terrena in the Scuola di San Francesco and in the Sala del Pregadi (now the Sala dello Scrutinio) in the Ducal Palace. Encountering this northern tradition on his trip to Venice in 1541, Vasari was the first artist to apply the ecclesiastical ceiling structure to a secular building, the ceiling of the nuptial chamber in Giovanni Cornaro Palace, his second commission in Venice.48 The examination of this ceiling will comprise tbe second part of this study, which will continue in the next Issue.

## Notes

I wish to express my gratitude to Professors J. Héli Hernandez of UMASS Lowell, Mary Ann Winkleman of Harvard University, and Anthony Kurneta of the Wentworth Institute, for their comments and *amicizia*. This research was made possible by the generosity of the University of Massachusetts Lowell.

1. Pietro Aretino praises Giorgio Vasari in a letter dated December 15, 1540. See also Vasari 8; 244, 252, and 262-65. In these writings, Vasari promotes himelf for his own speed and skill when working, in particular on the Florentine entry of Charles V.

2. I think that the motif of the *quadro riportato* derives from the wedding feasts, royal entries, and in particular, *apparati* decorations or portable theatrical settings. This form of artistic illusionism subsequently was expanded by tbe Carracci brothers in the ceiling decoration of tbe Galleria Faroese of 1595 in Rome, where the *quadro riportato* illusionism is transformed into framed pictures on a painted frescoed ceiling. The temporary multimedia effect of tbe *apparati* here becomes a permanent visual experience. See Wittkower 65-68.

3. Vasari likely felt that, since Aretino's comedy was dedicated to tbe Duke of Tuscany and the Medici family, in particular Ottavio de' Medici, his dear patron, sbould have a copy of the *apparato* designs, which he executed in eight days.

4. See Del Vita, *L'Aretino* 5 for the political impact on Venice by Giovanni delle Bande Nere and Charles V. Pietro Aretino arrived in Venice on 25 March 1527 and met Titian.

5. See Villani, *L'Aretino* 3: 113; and Epstein 14-15 for discussions on the friendship among these three men who founded the Accademia Pellegrina (where Doni was the president and secretary, Mucolini the printer, and Aretino the writer), as well as for an explanation of the devices of *Fortuna virtutis* used by Marcolini and Aretino's *Veritas Filia Temporis*, Figs. 15 and 16. See also Symonds 370; Doni; and McTavish, "Apparato" 116 Fig. 13, for Aretino's *Veritas Filia Temporis* of 1542 drawing (Biblioteca Nazionale Centrale, Palat. E.6.6.135), and McTavish, "Speculations" 20-27.

6. In the *Vita di Peruzzi*, Vasari recalls Baldassare Peruzzi's depiction of a comic scene using richly decorated houses for the celebration in Rome

of the appointment of Giuliano de' Medici, brother of Leo X, to General of the Church in 1515 (Vasari

4: 595). Perhaps Peruzzi's drawing, *Allegory of Mercury* of 1515 (Inv. 1419 at the Cabinet des Dessins in the Musèe du Louvre), was a study for this comic scene.

7. I Sempiterni drew up a contract on 22 December 1541 (Frey and Frey 2: 859). See also Venturi 15-16; Schulz 500-11; and Fletcher 129-53.

8. See also Tassini 152-55; and Zorzi 10 for a recount of how Palace Valier (now demolished) is the former Gonnella Palace at San Giobbe. In addition, see Sansovino, who comments, "No city in Europe has more places spread over such a broad area, both on the Grand Canal and in other parts of the town, than does Venice" (Zorzi 10). On the patronage of Venice as the new Rome, see Hollingsworth 145-53.

9. Vasari 6: 223. According to Foscari 273, the palace was totally demolished in 1805. The final records of the palace come from a collection of engravings by Luca Carlevarijs entitled *Le fabriche e vedute di Venetia* (Venice, 1703) and engravings by Francesco Zucchi after the watercolors of Luca Carlevarijs for *Icongrafica rappresentazione della città di Venezia* in 1729. See also Concina 135, Plate 87.

10. See Bertelli, Cardini, and Zorzi 136-37; Newton 37-60 on the structure of Renaissance Theatre, and 193-216 on costume in the Italian theater of the sixteenth century; d'Ancona; the excellent study of the magnificent festivities, both secular and religious, in Europe during the Renaissance and Baroque periods by Wisch and Munshower; Brown 136-88 for a discussion of the relationship between Venetian civic ceremonial art and paintings of the late fifteeenth and early sixteenth centuries; and also Muir.

11. According to Newton 37-60, the chariot of *trionfi* evolved from *edifici*. They first developed from candles carried in the hand; later the candlesticks grew to immense proportions that needed to be carried in enormous wooden structures. Some of these edifices held statues or paintings of the *festeggiato* (honored person) and expanded to the point of becoming platforms for the enactment of plays. See also Guasti 20.

12. Under the court of Lorenzo de' Medici the *trionfi* (triumphal cars) in Florence contained *all'antica* (classical) costumes, references, and decorations. See Newton 152-53; and Cambiagi 65. The *trionfi* rolled in processions outdoors around the city square and indoors around the grand hall as a parade. The concept of *trionfi* originated in literature with Petrarch's *Triumphs* or dramatic representations on processional cars depicting personifications of virtues. For examples, see the paintings of Pesellino -*Triumphs of Petrarch: Triumphs of Love, Chastity and Death; Triumphs of Fame, Time, and Eternity* - at the Isabella Stewart Gardner Museum in Boston. See also Eisenbichler and Iannucci. Another example of depicted *trionfi*

is Andrea Mantegna's narrative fresco of the *Triumph of Caesar*, now in Hampton Court. For studies on Mantegna's cycle, see Hope 297-316; and Martindale.

13. See, for example, Sanudo's diaries in the Marciana Library in Venice. Cl, vii, cod, CDXIX-XDLXXVII, which were published in fifty-eight volumes in Venice between 1879-1903; see also Newton 52-53 and 281. The Compagnia della Calza's costumes were so rich and elabonne that the sumptuary regulations allowed them to dress in their splendor only when important foreign visitors came to Venice. Throughout Italy there were also other Companies of the Stockings, such as the *Compagnia della Gatta* in Florence.

14. In 1556, Vasari constructed a temporary theater (*apparato*) in the Salone dei Cinquecento of the Palazzo Vecchio for the nuptial festivity in honor of Johanna of Austria with Francesco de' Medici in 1566 (see Fig. 4 in this essay). See Pallen 103-14; Satkowski Fig. 223 gives a view of the reconstructed model.

15. See Aretino *Lettere* 1: 79; Vasari 4: 545, 5: 329, 7: 652; P. Luzio 109-11; and Frey and Frey 1: 40-46, for a letter dated 12 November 1535 from Vasari in Florence to Aretino in Venice. For fifteenth-century Florentine artists' involvement with entries, festivities, and spectacles, see Minor and Mitchell; Testaverde Matteini 323-52; Shearman 36-54; Strong; Tofani and Testaverde 298-331; and Pacciavi. And for the sixteenth-century, Vasari's art and recording in the Vite, in particular Tribolo, San Gallo, and Rustici are the most important sources for the *feste* decorations.

16. In a letter to Pietro Aretino, Vasari meticulously describes the magnificence of this festivity. See Vasari 8: 252, 254; Guazzo 201-04. Aretino requested a copy of Vasari's letter on the "apparati e trionfi" (Aretino, *Lettere* 84-86 n 69 and 252 n 202. For a reconstruction of this triumphal entry, consult Testaverde Matteini 33; L. Corti 185-86. See also Mitchell, "Firenze" 995-1004, regarding the *apparati* for Henry II into Lyons and Philip II into Antwerp; P. Corti; and for an excellent study on the culmination of Florentine festivals, see Saslow.

17. See Kallab and Schlosser 69; Vasari 6: 13; Schulz 503 n 27; and McTavish, "Apparato" 112-13, for a listing of Vasari's involvement in *apparati*, entries, and wedding decorations since 1533. Discussions of his assistants (including Bronzino) in the *apparato* for a comedy performed by the Compagnia dei Negromanti in Antonio Antinori's house are found in Frey and Frey 2: 852 n 58. In 1536 he decorated the *apparato* for the performance of Lorenzo de' Medici's Alidosio at the marriage of Duke Alessandro and Margaret of Austria, continuing in 1539 with the enactment of Antonio Landini's *Commodo* at the marriage of Cosimo I and Eleanor of Toledo, and culminating with the *apparato* for Aretino's *La Talanta* in Venice in 1542 (Vasari 6: 439-40).

18. Villani *Chronicle* 8: 70; and Borghini 1: 56:

> The only truth lies in wood and painted canvas in the shape of
> arches, facades and other buildings; greenery and tapestries
> may, if need be, do for merry-makings or even church festi-
> vals; living figure, Virtues, etc., are a *magra invenzione*; the most
> desirable aim should surely be to be able to have something
> permanent built of stone, for example, the growing *grandezza*
> can no longer tolerate the jolly village-fair style.

19. Vasari must have been very honored by Titian's praise. His admiration for Titian is well known, as it is recorded in letters written to Aretino
in 1536 and 1536. See Vasari's letters from Florence to Aretino in Venice in
Frey and Frey 1: 36-37 (Letter of 9 July 1535) and 1: 40-46 (Letter of 11 or
18 March 1536). See also Vasari 6: 223-24, 7: 670-72; Kallab and Schlosser
59-61; and Frey and Frey 1: 104-06 and 2: 858-61.

20. Dazzi 27 discusses the carnival festivities at the Fondaco. Titian's
frescoes for the Fondaco had given publicity for the *Compagnia della Calza's* merrymaking. See Wethey 3: 155 and Figs. 15-16.

21. Vasari 7: 670:

> I was summoned to Venice by M. Pietro Aretino, then a poet of
> renown and my fast friend. As he greatly desired to see me I was
> obliged to go. Reaching Venice I did the decorations for the festi-
> val of the Signors of the Calza, assisted by Battista Cangi, Cristo-
> faro Gherardi of Borgo San Sepolcro and Bastiano Flori of Arezzo,
> men of great skill, of which enough has been said elsewhere. I also
> did the nine pictures for the ceiling of a chamber of the palace of
> M. Giovanni Coronaro at San Benedetto. (my translation)

See Frey and Frey 2: 111-19 for a complete description of these paintings.
See also McTavish, "Apparato"112-13.

22. Del Vita, *Il Libro* 37-38:

> Ricordo come adi primo di dicembre 1541, Io arrivai a Venetia
> et mi messi in casa di Francesco Lioni." ("I remember that on I
> December 1541 I arrived in Venice and I sojourned in the house of
> Francesco Lioni") (Carta 34; my translation); and

> Ricordo come adi 22 di dicembre 1541, Io presi a fare in Venetia
> da ecompagni di Calza Gentiluomini Venetiani un apparato duna
> commedia la quale avea composta Messer Pietro Aretino la quala
> si debbe recitare in Canal Regio et con questio patti conditioni
> cioè che io sai obligato farviun soffitato de quattro quadri grandi
> di tela bozati a olio drentovi in uno l'aurora col carro et Titone,
> nell'altro il giorno col carro di Fetone quando ecade in Po; et nel
> teno icaro quando dedalo glinsegnia a volare et nel quarto il carro
> della Notte et di più in 24 quadri le XXIIII ore. Sotto nelle pariete

di detto aparato dodici virtù et otto storie grandi con tutti e fiumi e i monti figurati di quel paese tutti lavorni di chiaro et scuro; et di più chio dovessi fare la prospettiva di detta Commedia osiena tutta e spese loro e che io avessi cura della architettura di detta sciena et aparto et perciò dovessi disegniare et lavorare di mia mano fino a che la fussi condotta come più apertamente mostra una scritta fatta lore di mia mano di tale obbligazione: Et loro mi promettono per detta opera pagare fina che sia finita scudi 300 doro di moneta vinitiana et perciò mi derono per il primo pagamento scude cento contanti. Apresso pagarono il restante che sono a conto mio entnta allibro di Fnncesco Lioni, scudi 300.

I remember that on 22 December 1541, for the gentlemen of the Gaiza, I created an *apparato* of a comedy composed by Pietro Aretino in Venice. The comedy was to be recited in Canal Regio. Agreeing to the commissioned conditions, I painted four large pictures with oils on canvas for the ceiling, depicting in one the Chariot of Aurora and Tithonus, in another Phaeton falling in Po, in the third one Icarus when Deadalus teaches him how to fly, and in the fourth one the Chariot of Night, and in addition twenty-four paintings of the twenty-four hours. Below, in the walls of the *apparato*, I painted twelve virtues and eight large stories depicting rivers and mountains from the region, all painted in chiaroscuro. In addition, I was to execute the scenery for the comedy at their expense. I would be responsible for the architecture of the scenery and *apparato* as well as for the design and labor until completion, as stated in the written document I composed that defined my obligations. They promised to pay for the completed work 300 golden Venetian scudi, and they advanced as first payment 100 scudi. Eventually, they paid me the rest. The 300 scudi are recorded as my entry in Francesco Lioni's book.

(Carta 35; my translation)

23. For example, a rotating large glass ball filled with water received light from behind and represented the sun. See Fletcher 130.

24. Vasari 7: 670: "questo apparato è stato tale, che ogni persona che la guarda viene in confusione, e stima grandissima errore che ciò si guasti." (my translation: "This *apparato* was so impressive because of its great merit; every person that saw it remained bewildered that it had to be dismantled.")

25. See also Frey and Frey 1: 111-19, Letter 47, for a complete description of these paintings; and Vasari 8: 283-87. See also McTavish, "Apparato" 112-13, and "Speculations" 28 n 41, where he considers Vasari's change in the lighting arrangement for the *apparato* when viewing the Amsterdam

drawing in relation to the Louvre (No. 13411 F) design.

26. Fletcher remarks that the Florentine Sansovino, an expert in *apparati*, did not produce any *apparati* when he resided in Venice, except for a processional umbrella for Sultan Suleiman.

27. Frey and Frey 1: 118, Letter to Magnifico Duca dated from Venice 1543.

28. Another similar example is the *Study of the Car of Juno Pulled by Peacocks* (Inv. 1975.47) at Yale University, New Haven, CT, illustrated in "Giorgio Vasari: Study for a Ceiling" 46-47.

29. The admiration between Vasari and Alciato is well documented, in particular, Alciato's honorable citation on Vasari's artistic activity in decorating the Bolognese Refectory of San Michele in Bosco in 1539. See L. Cheney, "Vasari and Naples" 48-126. Alciato explains the meaning of Emblem 56 by identifying the motto's inscription, *Temerità* and illustrating the picture with an epigram's description: "In vain does the charioteer (Phaeton) hold the bridle, for the bolting horse carries him headlong down a precipice. Do not trust yourself to a man who is half-crazy, in whom there is no reason at all, since he is governed by his will." See Alciato's *Emblematum liber* and Daly, Callaghan, and Cuttler Emblem 56. For the attribution of these two drawings for the ceiling of the *apparato*, see Monbeig-Goguel, "A propos" 273-76 n 28; and for the description of the cars of Aurora and Phaeton, see Vasari 8: 284.

30. Alciato's motto reads: *Against Astrologers* (On Astrologers), and the picture illustrates the epigram's description: "Icarus wanting to fly to the sublime heaven, fell into the sea. Thus, great ruin overwhelms the wise man, who thinks of flying to the heavens into the bosom of God; while he who does not attain our esteem, has the secrets of known desire. The higher is the persos vain, the greater is his fall." See Emblem 104 in Alciato's *Emblematum liber* and Daly, Callaghan, and Cuttler. For the discovery and attribution of the Icarus drawing, see Monbeig-Goguel, "Giulio Roman et Giorgio Vasar" 273-76.

31. Following Vasari's description of Midnight, I think that one of the two drawings, *Allegorical Designs*, from the Rogers Fund of the Metropolitan Museum of Art, is associated with the Venetian *apparato*.

32. Barocchi, *Mostra* Figs. 24 and 25; McTavish, "Apparato" 114; McTavish, "Speculations" 20-28, Figs. 5 and 7, depicts a drawing of Prudence (Inv. 17917).

33. For a discussion on the earlier attribution of this drawing to other artists, Perino del Vaga and Salviati, see McTavish, "Apparato" 115; and McTavish, "Speculations" 20-28 Fig. 8. A copy of this drawing is found in a private collection in the United States. See Monbeig-Gougel, "Giorgio Vasari et son temps" 105-06, Plate 25. Another drawing of Peau (Inv. n.

1618E) is located at the Gabinetto Disegni e Stampe, Uffizi.

34. Cecchi, "Nuove acquisizioni" 52-51 and 54 Fig. 1. For other speculations on drawings for the Venetian *apparato*, see Clifford 319 and 321 Fig. 52; *Galleria Evangelista*, Lucca, 5, 6, 8 (December 1980), D. 24; and Asta di disegni, lot no. 44, attributed to Taddeo Zuccaro. Vasari repeats the image of Concord in his decorative ceilings of the Chamber of Abraham in the Casa Vasari at Arezzo and the Refectory of Monteoliveto in Naples. See L. Cheney, "Vasari and Naples" 48-126.

35. See L. Cheney 359-74 for a significant discussion on ceiling ornamentation; and L. Cheney, Paintings 83-109.

36. The conception of creating a heaven in a dramatic scene, *trionfo*, or *intermezzo* was known to Vasari through the art of Andrea Mantegna's *Triumphs of Caesar*. Mantegna constructed a heaven (*cielo*) as a canopy of stretched-out cloths, extended along the street to protect the heads of the *magnifici* from the sun's rays and birds' droppings. See Newton 118-19, for example; the *Paradiso apparto* presented at the Este court in Ferrara was described as "la festa de Amphitrione...con un paradiso con stelle et altre rode che fu una bella cosa" ("the feast of Amphitrite...depicting a paradise with stars and other [astral bodies] was a beautiful thing") (*Diario Ferrarese*, R.I.S., 24.7: 122; and Mitchell, *1598, A Year of Pageantry* 3-11, my translation). Leonardo da Vinci was familiar with this *apparato* and created in *La Festa del Paradiso* a spectacular heaven for the wedding ceremony of Ludovico il Moro with Beatrice d' Este. See Solmi.

37. Vasari was familiar with this type of scenic design through the architectural designs of Baldassare Peruzzi See Satkowski, Plate 8.

38. Baladassare Peruzzi's drawing of 1525-30, *Allegory of Mercury* at the Cabinet des Dessins in Musèe du Louvre (Inv. 1419), shows a theatrical scene with ancient Roman and Cinquecento edifices, which assists us in visualizing Vasari's architectural design.

39 Cartari explains how Juno is associated with the Hours and Iris in the writings of Pausanius who describes Polycleitus's *Juno*, a statue of ivory in Corinth, in which the goddess wore a beautiful colored crown containing the representations of the Hours (Cartari 152-53 and 160).

40. Iris forms a celestial ard! as a force of divine benevolence and conveys tbe good wishes of the gods by creating a rainbow of clotbed iridescent dew in tbe sky (Canari 157-58).

41. She was of the Nereids and was fated to bear a son, Achilles, mightier than his father, Peleus. She came up from the sea with her fellow Nereids to comfort him after the death of Patroclus.

42. A minor sea god, shepherd of the flocks of sea-creatures, endowed by Neptune with tbe gift of prophecy and also tbe power to change his shape until firmly held.

43. A primitive sea god known to Homer and Hesiod, said to be endowed with wisdom and the gift of prophecy like Proteus. He was the father of fifty or more Nereids, including Amphitrite.

44. The name of several Greek mythological figures, in particular a fisherman of Boetia who pursued Scylla and was changed into a God of the Sea after eating a magic herb.

45. A Greek sea nymph in love with the Sicilian shepherd Acis and pursued by the Cyclops Polyphemus. She fled into the sea off the coast of Sicily and turned Acis into a river.

46 Also known as Melicertes, son of Athamas and Juno. Wben Juno leaped into the sea in her madness, carrying Melicertes in her arms, both were transformed into sea deities. He was honored under this name, Palaemon, as the presiding hero of the Isthmian games.

47. The Cinquecento debate over the relative superiority of painting and sculpture appears to be indicated. As demonstrated, Vasari is stating that painting is superior to sculpture, since his simulated sculptures are painted.

48. Vasari was to fuse the Central Italian and Venetian traditions in such later decorative commissions as the Palazzo Vecchio.

## Works Cited

Alciato, Andreas. *Emblematum liber*. Lyon, 1549.

Aretino, Pietro. *Il primo [secondo] libro della lettere*. Ed. Fausto Nicolini. 2 vols.

Scrittori d'Italia. P. Aretina. Corrispondenza. 1-2. Bari: Laterza, 1913-1916.

_____. *La Talanta*. Ed. Carla Cremonesi. Biblioteca universale Rizzoli. 1047-1049. Milan: Rizzoli, 1922.

*Asta di disegni dal XVI al XIX secolo*. Milan, Finarte 204 (1975): lot no. 44.

Barocchi, Paola. *Mostra di disegni del Vasari e della sua Cerchia*. Florence: Leo S. Olschki. 1964.

-- *Vasari pittore*. Milan: Edizioni per Il Club del Libro, 1964.

Bertaux, Emile. Mélanges Bertaux: recueil de travaux: dédié a la mémoire d'Émile

Bertaux. Paris: E. De Boccard, 1924.

Bertelli, Sergio, Franco Cardini, and Elvira Garbero Zorzi. ed. *The Courts of the Italian Renaissance*. Trans. of *Le corti italiane Rinascimento*. New York: Facts on File, 1986.

Borghini, Vincenzo. *Lettere pittoriche. Carteggio arrtistico innedito*. By A. Lorenzoni. Florence, 1912.

Brown, Patricia Fortini. "Measured Friendship, Calculated. Pomp: The Ceremonial Welcomes of the Venetian Republic." Wisch and Munshower 1: 136-88.

Cairns, Christopher. *Pierto Aretino and the Republic of Venice: Researches on Aretino and his Circle in Venice, 1527-1556.* Biblioteca dell' "Archivum Romanicum." Serie I, Storia, letteratura, paleografica. 194. Florence: Leo S. Olschki, 1985.

Cambiagi, Gaetano. *Memorie istoriche, riguardanti le feste solite farsi in Firenze per la natività di San Gio. Batista, prottetore della città e dominio fiorentino, raccolte e con annotazioni illustrate da Gaetano Cambiagi.* Florence: Stamperia granducale. 1766.

Carlevarijs, Luca. *Le fabriche e vedute di Venetia.* Venice, 1703.

Cartari, Vincenzo. *Imagini delli Dei de gl'Antichi.* Venice, 1556. Ed. Walter Kosachtzky. Graz: Akademische Druck, 1963.

Cecchi, Alessandro. "Nouve acquisizioni per catalogo dei disegni di Giorgio Vasari." *Antichià viva* 1 (1978): 51-52.

_____. "Qualche contributo aI corpus grafico del Vasari e del suo ambiente." *Il Vasari storiografo e artista: arti del Congresso internazionale nel IV centenario della morte, Arezzo-Firenze, 2-8 settembre 1974.* Florence: Instituto nazionale di studi sul Rinascimento, 1976: 143-61.

Cheney, Iris. "Francesco Salviati (1510-1563)." Diss. New York U, 1963.

Cheney, Liana De Girolami. "Emblematic Approaches in the Paintings of Giorgio Vasari: *Justice and Patience.*" International Conf. On Ages of Life and Learning. University of Minnesota, Minneapolis. 26-28 April 1995.

_____. "Giorgio Vasari's *Astrea*: A Symbol of Justice." *Word and Image.* Forthcoming.

_____. "Giorgio Vasari's Chamber of Abraham: A Religious Ceiling in the Aretine House." *Sixteenth Century Journal* (Fall 1987): 355-80.

_____. "Giorgio Vasari's Scrittorio of Calliope: ut pictura poesis and ut pictura musica." Neoplatonism and the Arts. Ed. Liana De Girolami Cheney and John Hendrix. New York: Edwin Mellen, 2002. 160-75.

_____. *The Paintings of the Casa Vasari.* New York: Garland, 1985.

_____. "Vasari and Naples: The Monteoliveto Order." *Papers in Art History* 5 (1994); 48-126.

Clifford, T. "Old Master Drawing in Albermarle Street." *Burlington Magazine* 117 (1975); 319-21.

Concina, Ennio, ed. *Luca Carlevarijs Le Fabriche, e Vedute di Venetia.* Venice: Marsilio, 1995.

Corti, Laura, et al., ed. Giorgio Vasari: principi, letterati e artisti nelle carte di Giorgio Vasari, Casa Vasari, pittura vasariana dal 1532 al 1554, Sottochiesa di S. Francesco: [catologo della mostre] Arezzo, 26 settembre-29 novembre 1981. Florence: Edam, 1981.

Corti, Piero Ginori. *L'apparato per le nozze di Francesco de' Medici e di Giovanna d'Austria: Narrati da Vincenzo Borghini e Giorgio Vasari.* Florence: Leo S. Olschki, 1936.

D'Ancona, Alessandro. *Origini del teatro in Italia, libre tre; con due appendici sulla rappresentazione drammatica del contado toscano e sul teatro mantovano nel sec. XVI.* 2 vol Turin: E. Loescher, 1891.

Daly, Peter M., Virginia W. Callahan, and Simon H. Cuttler, ed. *Andreas Alciatus.* 2 vols. Toronto: U of Toronto P, 1985.

Dazzi, Manlio Torquato, ed. *Il fondaco nostro dei tedeschi.* Venice: n. p., 1941.

Del Vita, Alessandro. *Il libro ricordanze di Giorgio Vasari.* Rome: Istituto d'archeologia e storia dell'arte, 1938.

_____. *L'Aretino: le cause della sua potenza e della sua fortuna.* Arezzo: Edizioni della casa Vasari, 1939.

*Diario Ferrarese.* Ed. Giuseppe Pardi. *Rerum italicarum scriptores* 24.7: 122.

Doni, Anton Francesco. *La vita dello infame Aretino; lettera CI et ultima.* Ed. Constantino Arlìa. Città di Castello: Editore S. Lapi, 1901.

Eisenbichler, Konrad, and Amilcare A. Iannucci, ed. *Petrarch's* Triumphs: *Allegory and Spectacle.* University of Toronto Italian Studies. 4. Ottowa: Dovehouse, 1990.

Epstein, Marion K. *Francesco Marcolini, Antonfrancesco Doni, and Pietro Aretino: Facts, Figures, and Fancies.* Ts.23. New York: n. p., 1969.

*Firenze e la Toscana dei Medici nell'Europa del '500.* 3 vol. Biblioteca di storia toscana moderna e contemporanea. 26. Florence: Leo S. Olschki, 1983.

Fletcher, Jennifer M. "Fine Art and Festivity in Renaissance Venice: The Artist's Part." Onians 129-53.

Foscari, T. *Catalogo e Mostra Archittetura et Utopia.* Milan: Electa, 1980.

Frey, Karl, and Herman Walther Frey, ed. Der literariche Nachlass Giorgio Vasaris. 2 vols. Munich: Georg Müller, 1923-1930.

"Giorgio Vasari: Study for a Ceiling: *Juno and the Peacocks.*" *Yale University Art Gallery Bulletin* 1 (1976): 46-47.

*Galleria Evangelista.* Lucca, December, 1980. D.24.

Guasti, Cesare. *Le feste di S. Giovanni Batista in Firenze, descritte in prosa e in rima da contemporanei.* Florence: G. Cirri, 1884.

Guazzo, Marco. *Historie di M. Marco Gvazzo di tvtti i fatti degni di memoria nel mondo svccessi dell'anno M. D. XIII: sino a qvesto presente con molte cose novamente giunte in piu luoghi del'opera, & nel fine, chene l'altre non crano nouamente & con diligenza ristampate.* Venice: Gabriel Giolito de Ferrari, 1546.

Hollingsworth, Mary. *Patronage in Sixteenth-Century Italy.* London: J.

Murray, 1996.

Hope, Charles. "The Chronology of Mantegna's Triumphs." Morrough 297-316.

*Icongrafica rappresentazione della città di Venezia consacrata al Reggio Serenissimo Dominio Veneto.*Venice, 1729.

*Il potere e lo spazio. La scena del principe.* Florence: Leo S. Olschki, 1983.

Kallab, Wolfgang, and Julius Schlosser, ed. *Vasaristudien.* Vienna: W. Grasser & Kie, 1908.

Kurneta, Anthony Edward. "The Palazzo Loredan in the Campo Santo Stefano: Counter-Currents in 16th Century Venetian Architecture." Diss. Boston U, 1976.

Landucci, Lando. "Giorgio Vasari a Venezia." *Atti del Reale Instituto Veneto di Scienze, Lettere ed Arte* 71.2 (1911-12): 168-76.

Luzio, Alessandro. *Pietro Aretino: La corte dei Gonzaga.* Florence: E. Loescher, 1888.

Luzio, P. *Amino nei primi suoi anni a Venezia.* Turin,1868.

Martindale, Andrew. *The Triumphs of Caesar by Andrea Mantegna in the Collection of Her Majesty the Queen at Hampton Court.* London: Harvey Miller, 1979.

McTavish, David. "Apparato dei Sempiterni." L. Corti 112-16.

-- "Speculations on Two Drawings Attributed to Giorgio Vasari." *Bulletin of the National Gallery of Canada* 28 (1976): 20-28.

Minor, Andrew Collier, and Bonner Mitchell, comp. *A Renaissance Entertainment; Festivities for the Marriage of Cosimo I, Duke of Florence, in 1539. An Edition of the Music, Poetry, Comedy, and Descriptive Account, with Commentary.* Columbia, MO: U of Missouri P, 1968.

Mitchell, Bonner. *1598, A Year of Pageantry in Late Renaissance Ferrara. Renaissance Triumphs and Magnificences* 4. Binghamton, NY: Medieval & Renaissance Texts and Studies, 1990.

_____. "Firenze illustrissima: l'immagine della patria negli apparati delle Nazioni fiorentine per le feste di Lione del 1548 e di Anversa del 1549." *Firenze e la Toscana dei Medici nell'Europa del '500.* 995-1004.

Monbeig-Goguel, Catherine. "A propos de Vasari historien et collectionneur." *Revue du Louvre et des Musées de France* 29 (1979): 273-76.

_____. "Giorgio Vasari et son temps." *Revue de l'art* 14 (1971): 105-106.

_____. "Guilio Roman et Giorgio Vasari: Le dessin de *La chute d'Icare* retrouvé." *Revue du Louvre et des Musées de France* 29 (1979): 274-75.

_____. *Vasari et Son Temps.* Vol. 1 of *Musée National du Louvre. Paris. Cabinet des dessins: Inventaire général des dessins italiens.* Dir. Roseline Bacou. Ed. Catherine Monbeig-Goguel, and Françoise Viatte. Paris: Ed des Musées nationaux, 1972.

Morrough, Andrew, et al., ed. *Renaissance Studies in Honor of Craig Hugh*

*Smith.* 2 vol. Villa i Tatti. 7. Florence: Giunti Barbèra, 1985.

Muir, Edward. *Civil Ritual in Renaissance Venice.* Princeton: Princeton UP, 1981.

Newton, Stella Mary. *Renaissance Theatre Costume, and the Sense of the Historic Past.* New York: Theatre Arts Books, 1975.

Onians, John, ed. *Sight and Insight: Essays on Art and Culture in Honour of E. H. Gombrich at 85.* London: Phaidon, 1994.

Pacciavi, R. "Immagini Arti e Archietture nelle Feste di Età Laurenziana." Ventrone 21-54.

Pallen, Thomas A. *Vasari on Theatre.* Carbondale, IL: Southern Illinois UP, 1999.

Sansovino, Francesco. *Venetia, citta nobilissima et singolare.* Venice, 1581.

Sanudo, Marino. *I diarii di Marino Sanuto.* 58 vols. Venice: F. Visentini, 1879-1903.

Saslow, James M. *The Medici Wedding of 1589: Florentine Festival as "theatrum mundi".* New Haven, CT: Yale UP, 1996.

Satkowski, Leon George. *Giorgio Vasari: Architect and Courtier.* Princeton: Princeton UP, 1993.

Schaar, Eckhard. "Giorgio Vasari." *Meisterzeichnungen der Sammlung Lambert Krahe: Ausstellung 14. November, 1969-11. Januar, 1970, Kunstmuseum Dusseldorf.* Dusseldorf: Kunstmuseum, 1969.21-22.

Schulz, Juergen. "Vasari at Venice." *Burlington Magazine* 103 (1961): 500-11.

Shearman, John. "The Florentine Encrata of Leo X." *Journal of the Warburg and Courtauld Institutes* 38 (1975): 36-54.

Solmi, Edmondo. *La Festa del Paradiso di Leonardo da Vinci e Bernardino Bellincione 13 gennaio 1490* (Extract from Archivio storico lonbardo, fasc. 1). Milan, 1904. Este Library, cod. ita. h. 521 segnatura J.4.21.

Strong, Roy C. *Art and Power: Renaissance Festivals, 1450-1650.* Berkeley; U of California P, 1984.

Symonds, John Addington. *Renaissance in Italy.* London, 1888.

Tassini, Guiseppe. *Edificia di Venezia; Distrutti o vòlti ad uso diverso da quello a cui furono in origine destinati.* Venice: Filippi, 1969.

Testaverde Mantini, Anna Maria. "La decorazione festiva e l'itinerario di 'rifondazione' della città negli ingressi trionfale a Firenze tra XV e XVI secolo." *Mittelungen des Kunsthistorichen Instituts in Florenz* 32.2 (1988): 323-52.

Tofani, Anna Maria Petrioloe, and Anna Maria Testaverde Matteini. "Gli ingressi trionfali." *Il potere e lo spazio.* 298-331.

Vasari, Giorgio. *Le vite de' più eccellenti pittori, scultori ed architettori.* Ed. Gaetano Milanesi. 9 vols. Florence: G. C. Sansoni. 1906.

Ventrone, Paola. *Le Temps revient: Il Tempo si rinuova: feste e spettacoli nella*

*Firenze di Lorenzo il Magnifico: Firenze, Pallazzo Medici Riccardi, 8 april-30 giugno 1992.* Florence: Silvania, 1992.

Venturi, Lionello. *Le Compagnie della Calza in Nuovo Archivio Veneto.* Ms. 1909, Sec 15-16. Venice, 1909. Extracted from the Nuovo Archivio Veneto, Nuova Serie. 16.2: 1-157.

Villani, Giovanni. *Croniche.* Venice: Bartholomeo Zanetti Casterzagense, 1537.

_____. *L'Aretino in Roma: Studi del XVI secolo...* Palermo: Stabilimento operai tipografi, 1869.

Vivant-Denon, D., and Amaury Duval. *Monuments des arts du dessin chez les peuples tant anciens que modernes, recueillis par le baron Vivant Drnon... pour servir à l'histoire des arts; lithographiés par ses soins et sous ses yeux.* 4 vols. Paris: B. Denon, 1829.

Voss, Hermann. *Die Malerei der Spätrenaissance in Rom und Florenz.* 2 vol. Berlin: G. Grote, 1920.

Wethey, Harold Edwin. *The Paintings of Titian.* Volume 3: *The Mythological and Historical Paintings.* London: Phaidon, 1975.

Wisch, Barbara, and Susan Scott Munshower, ed. *Art and Pagentry in the Renaissance and Baroque.* 2 vols. Papers in Art History from the Pennsylvania State University. University Park, PA: Department of Art History, Pennsylvania State U. 1990.

Wittkower, Rudolf. *Art and Architecture in Italy, 1600 to 1750.* 3rd rev. ed. The Pelican History of Art. Harmondsworth, Middlesex; New York: Penguin, 1982.

Zorzi, Alvise. *Venetian Palaces.* New York: Rizzoli, 1989.

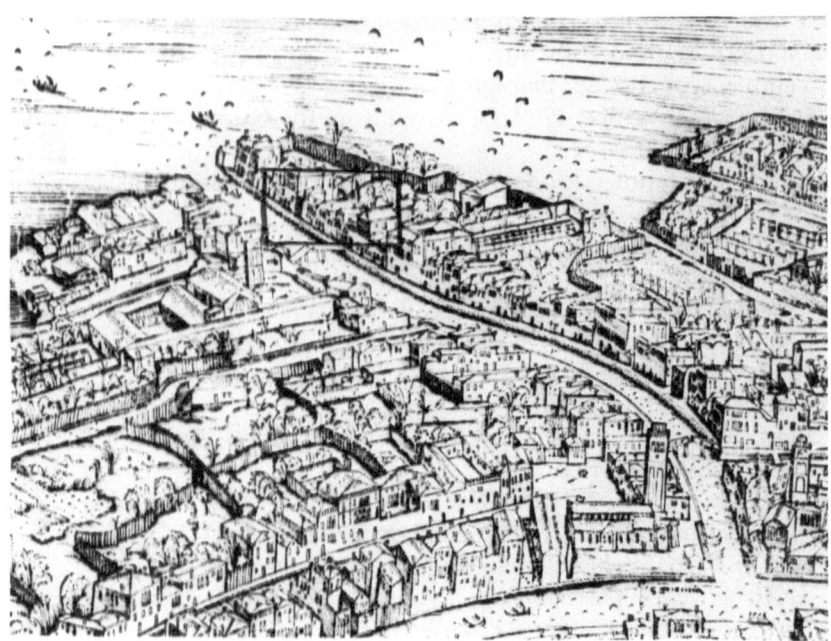

Fig. 1.  Jacopo de Barbari, *View of Palazzo Valier in Canal Regio*, Venice, 1500, engraving.

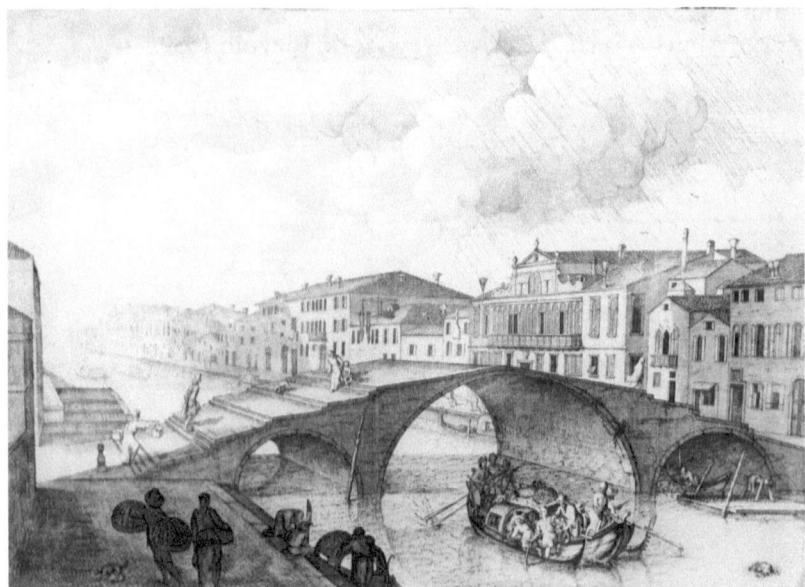

Fig. 2.  Antonio Scarpagnino, *View of  Palazzo Valier in Canal Regio*, Venice, 1540, engraving by Lucas Carlevarijs, 1703.

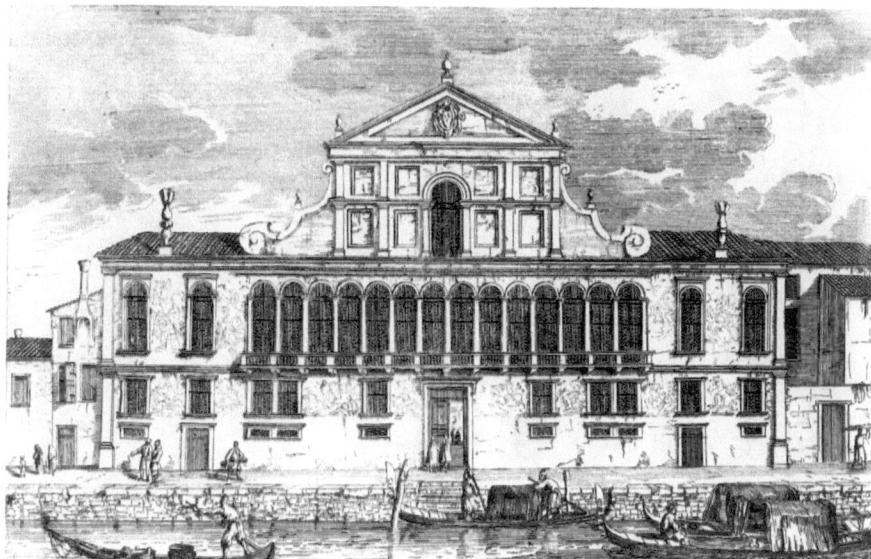

Fig. 3. Antonio Scarpagnino, *Palazzo Valier in Canal Regio*, Venice, 1540, engraving by Lucas Carlevarijs, 1703.

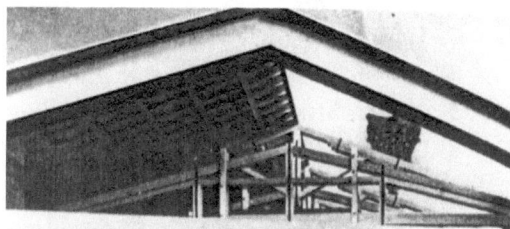

Fig. 4. Model of a Temporary Cinquecento Theater, Florence. Soprintendenza beni architettetonici.

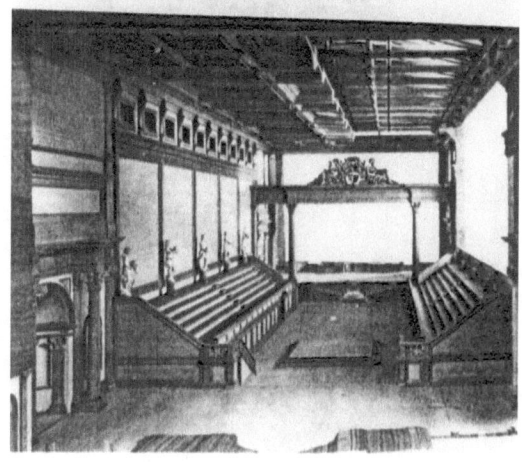

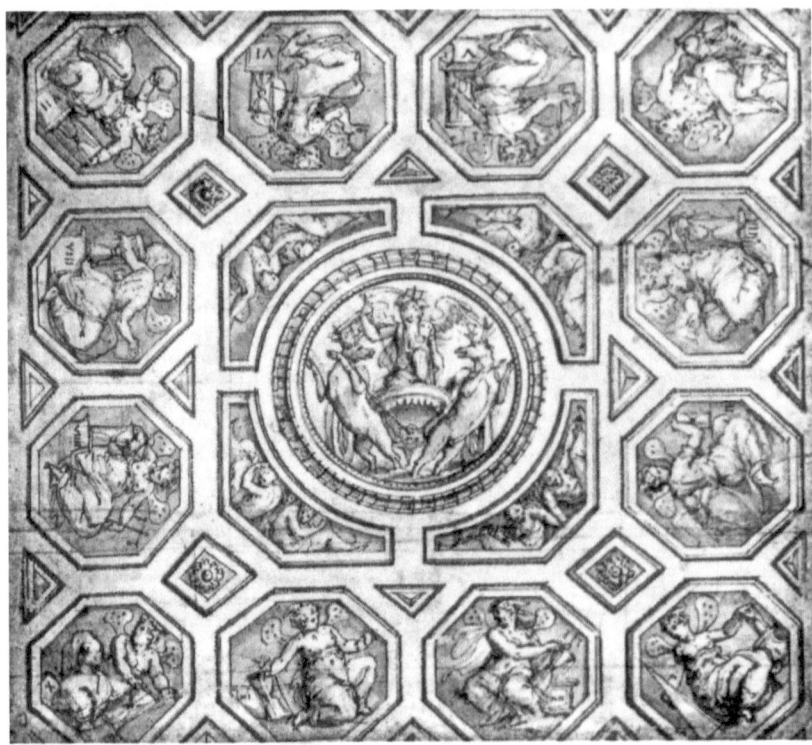

Fig. 5.  Vasari-Stradano, *Study for a Ceiling*, 1560, drawing  for the Room of Saturn, Palazzo Vecchio, Florence), Uffizi, Gabinetto Disegni e Stampe (Inv. n. 7 Orn). Photo: Gabinetto Disegni e Stampe, Uffizi.

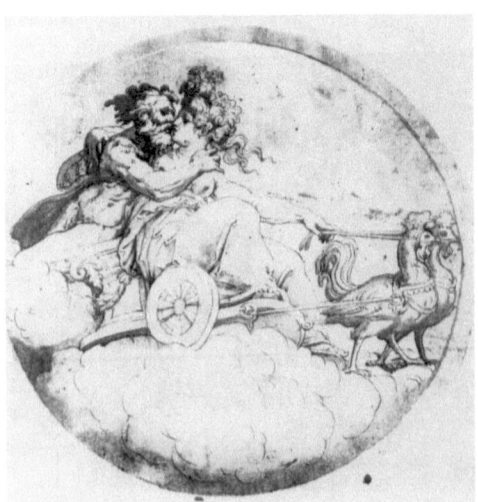

Fig. 6.  Giorgio Vasari, *Aurora*, 1542, drawing. Munich, Staatliche Graphische Sammlung (Inv. 8825).
Photo: Staatliche Graphische Sammlung, Munich.

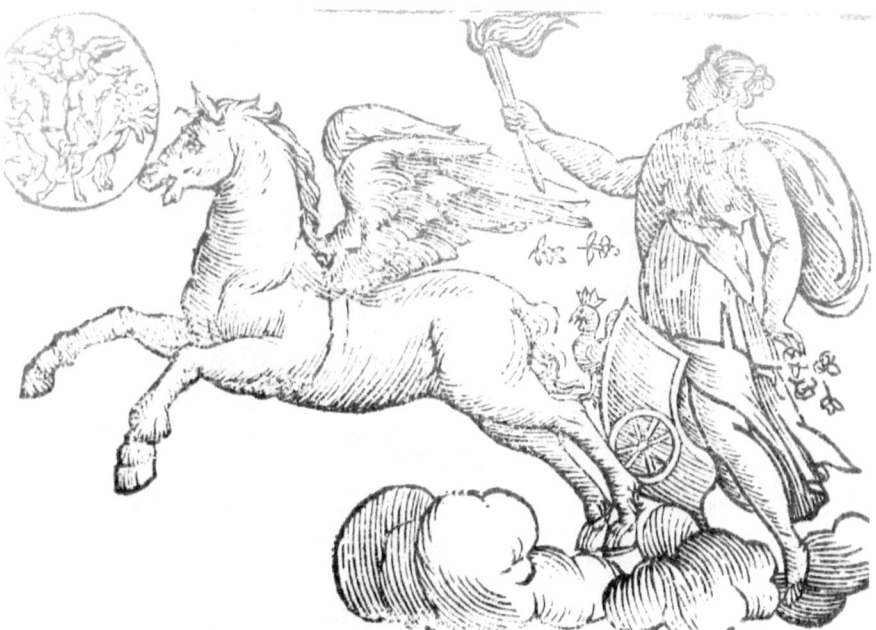

Fig. 7. Vincenzo Cartari, *Aurora*, engraving. *Imagine...* (Venice 1547).

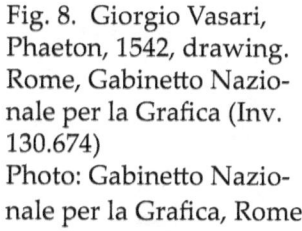
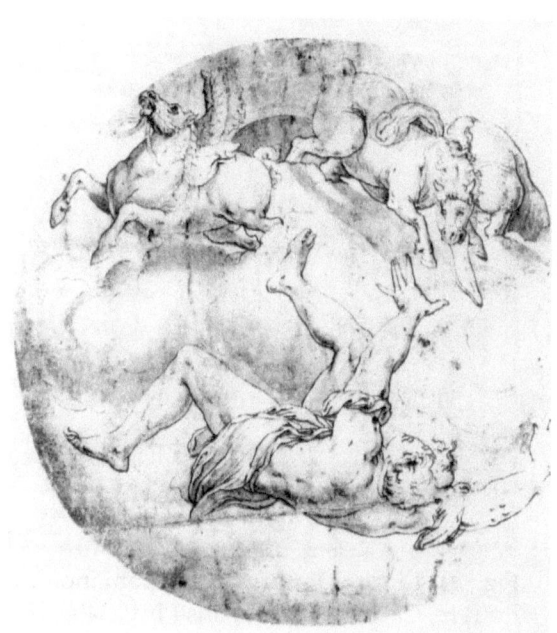

Fig. 8. Giorgio Vasari,
Phaeton, 1542, drawing.
Rome, Gabinetto Nazio-
nale per la Grafica (Inv.
130.674)
Photo: Gabinetto Nazio-
nale per la Grafica, Rome

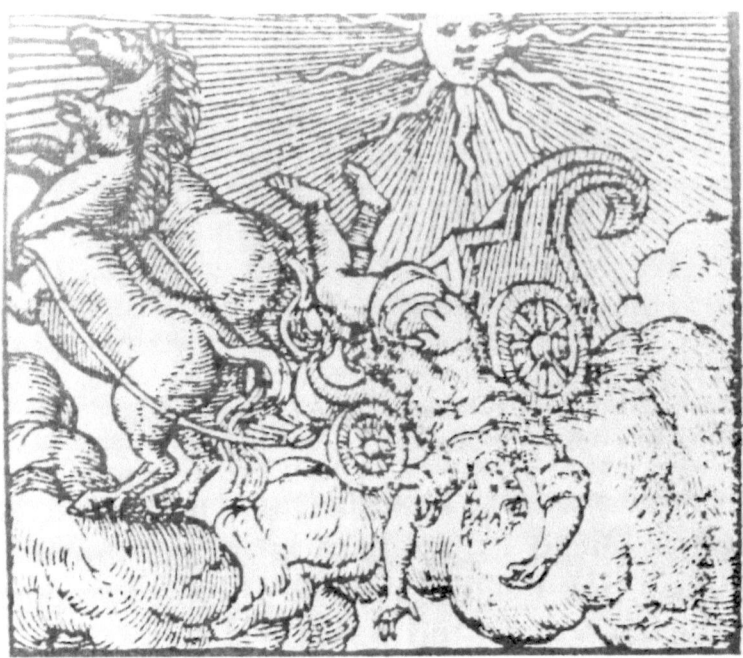

Fig. 9.  Andrea Alciato, Emblem 56, *Temerity,*  in *Emblematum liber,* engraving (Lyon 1549).

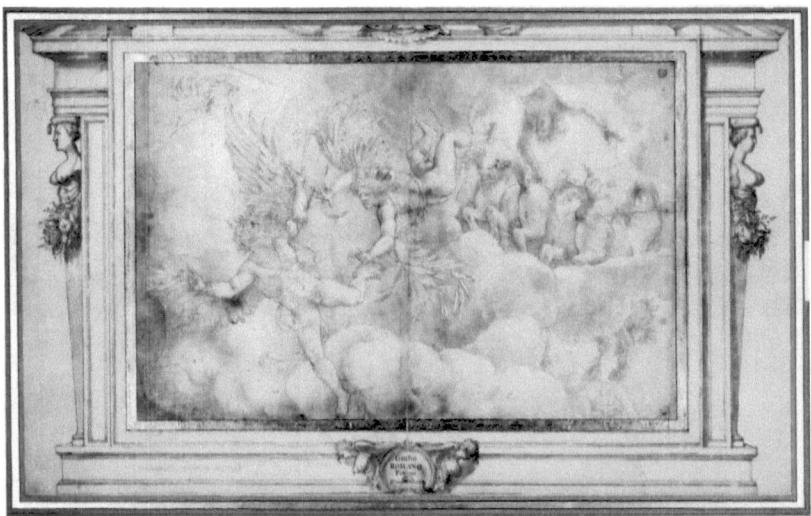

Fig. 10. Giorgio Vasari-Giulio Romano, *Icarus,* 1542, drawing. Paris, Louvre, Cabinet des Dessins ( Inv. 3499). Photo: Reunion des Musées Nationaux, Paris.

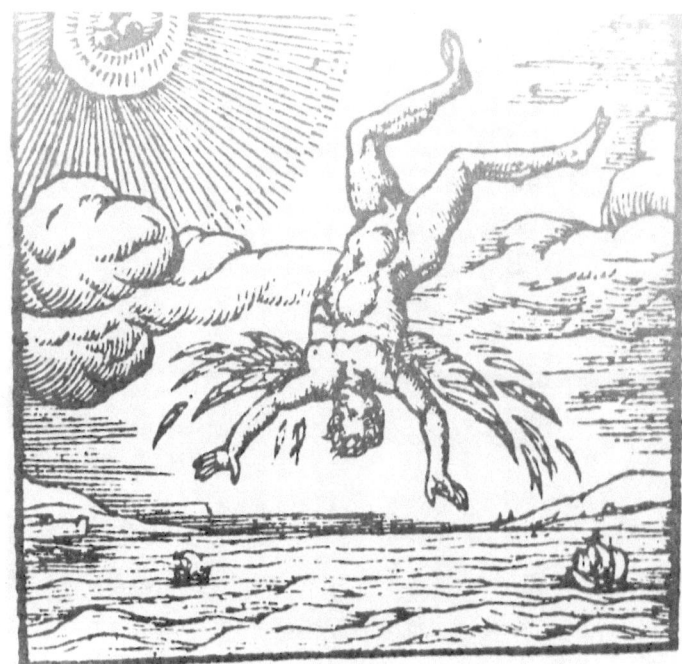

Fig. 11. Andrea Alciato, Emblem 104, *Against Astrologers,* in *Emblematum liber,* engraving (Lyon 1549).

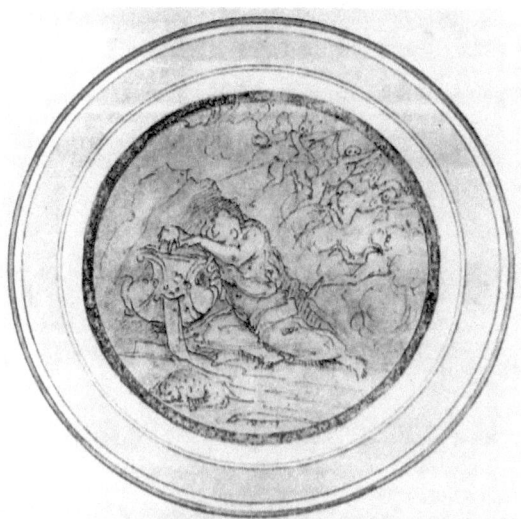

Fig. 12. Giorgio Vasari, *Ednymion,* 1542, drawing. New York, Metropolitan Museum of Art, Rogers Fund. Photo: Metropolitan Museum of Art, New York.

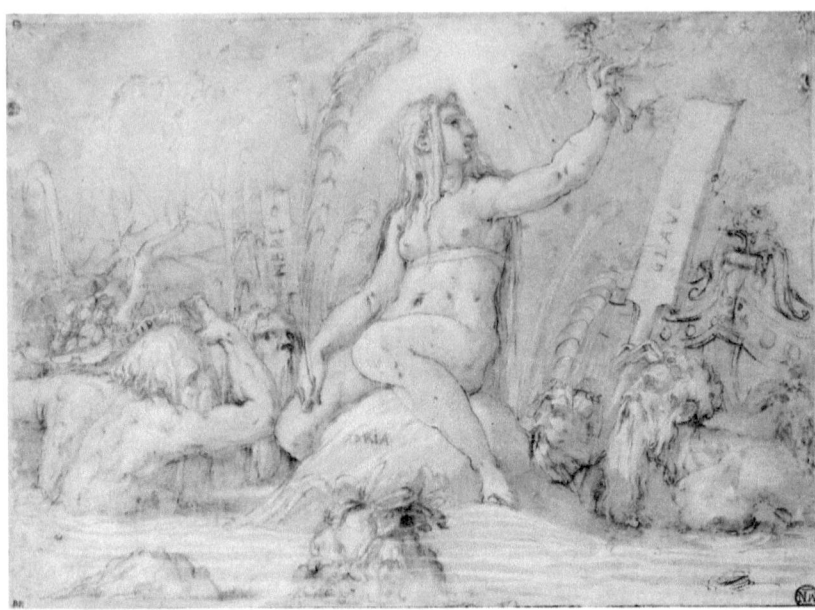

Fig. 13. Giorgio Vasari, *Adria*, 1542, drawing. Paris, Louvre, Cabinet des Dessins (Inv. n. 2168). Photo: Reunion des Musées Nationaux, Paris.

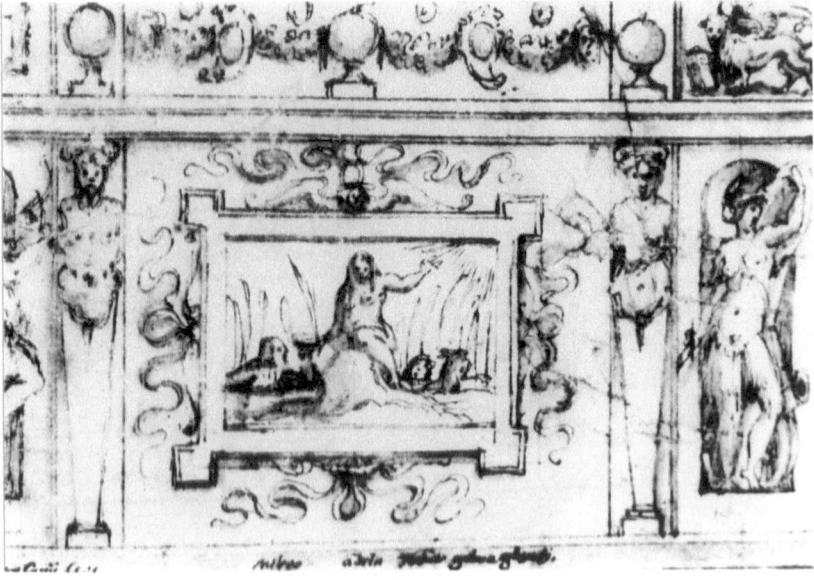

Fig. 14. Giorgio Vasari, *Adria*, 1542 drawing. Amsterdam, Rijksmuseum, Prentenkabinett (N1958:42). Photo: Rijksmuseum, Prentenkabinett, Amsterdam.

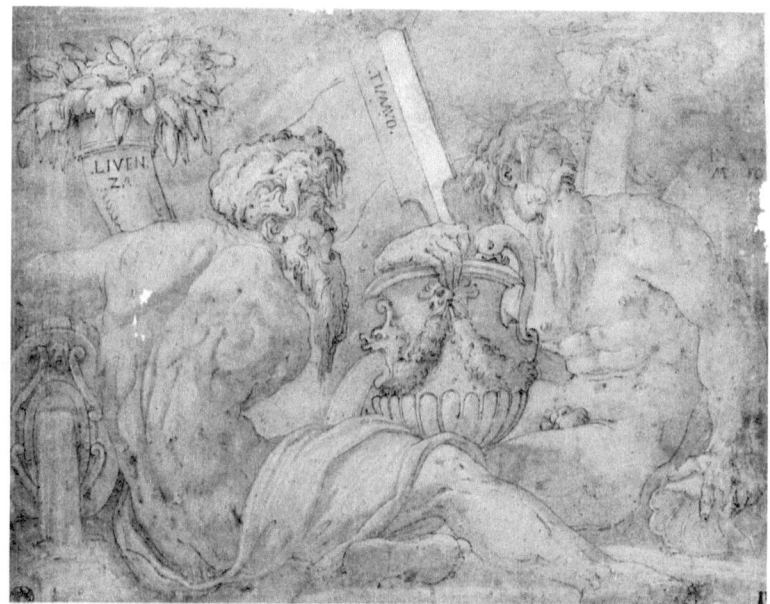

Fig. 15. Giorgio Vasari, *River Gods*, 1542, drawing. Berlin, Ehem. Staatliche Museen (N15260:251). Photo: Ehem. Staatliche Museen, Berlin.

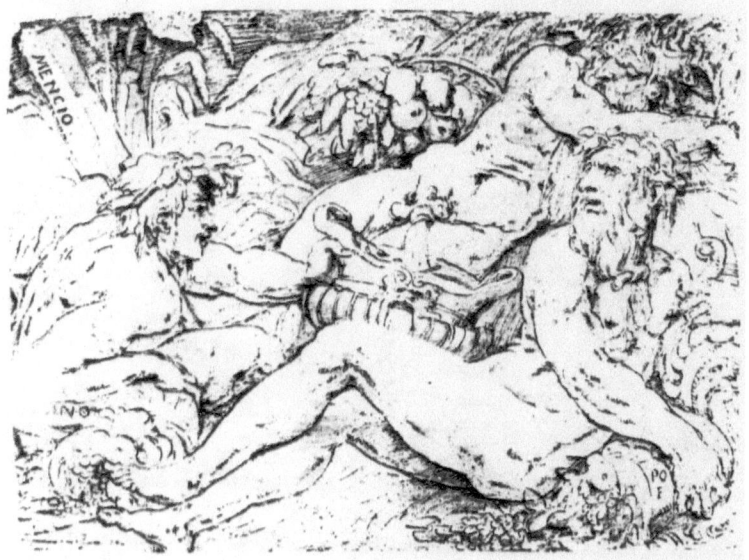

Fig. 16. Giorgio Vasari, *River Gods: Mincio and Po*, 1542, drawing. Lutworth Manor, Collection Colonel J. Weld

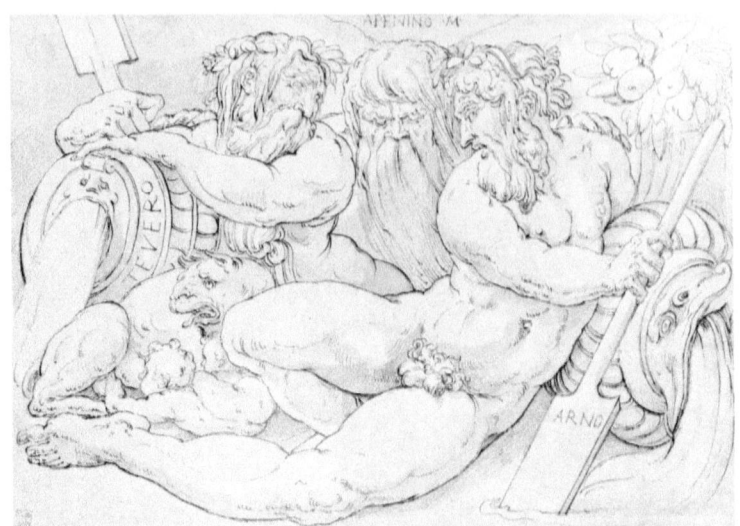

Fig. 17.  Giorgio Vasari, *River Gods: Arno and Tiber*, 1542 drawing. Worcester Art Museum. Photo: Worcester Art Museum, Worcester.

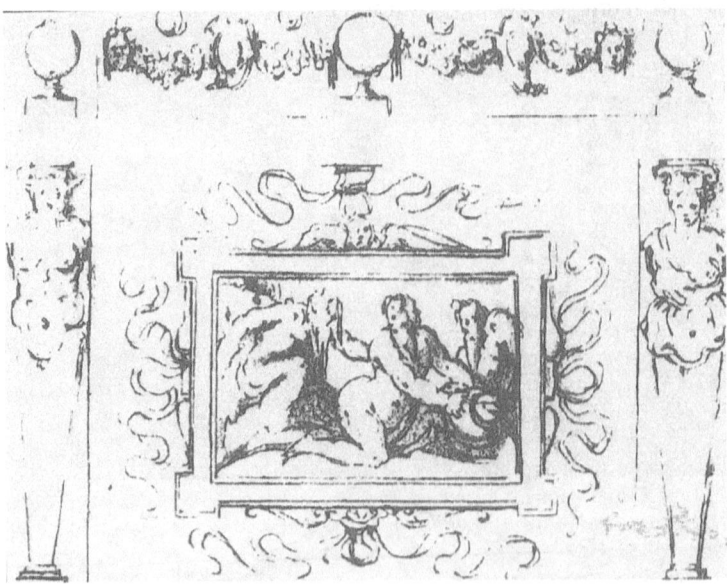

Fig. 18. Study for a Festival Decoration, lithograph facsimile of a drawing by Giorgio Vasari  in *Vivant-Denon, Monuments des arts du dessin*, III, 185.

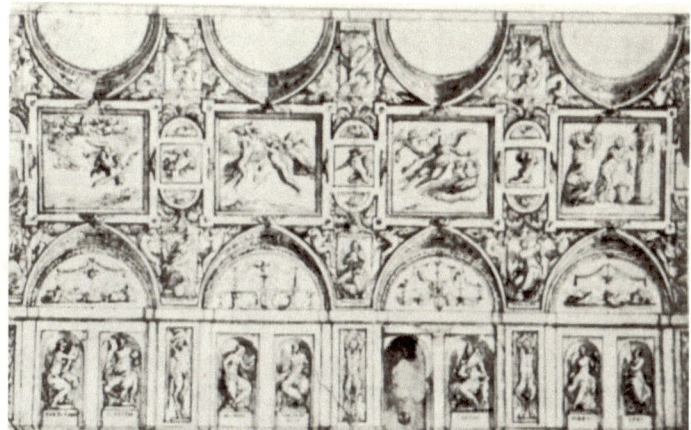

Fig. 19. Giorgio Vasari, Decorative
Project, 1542, drawing. Uffizi, Gabinetto
Disegni e Stampe (Inv. no. 1618E). Photo:
Gabinetto  Disegni e Stampe, Uffizi.

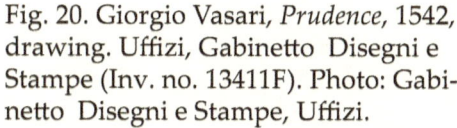

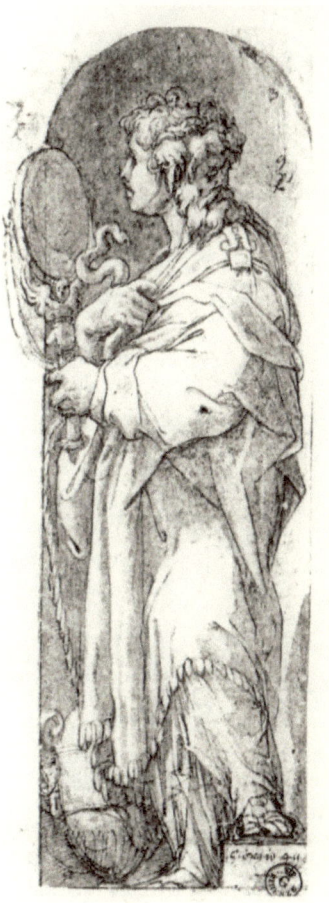

Fig. 20. Giorgio Vasari, *Prudence*, 1542,
drawing. Uffizi, Gabinetto  Disegni e
Stampe (Inv. no. 13411F). Photo: Gabinetto  Disegni e Stampe, Uffizi.

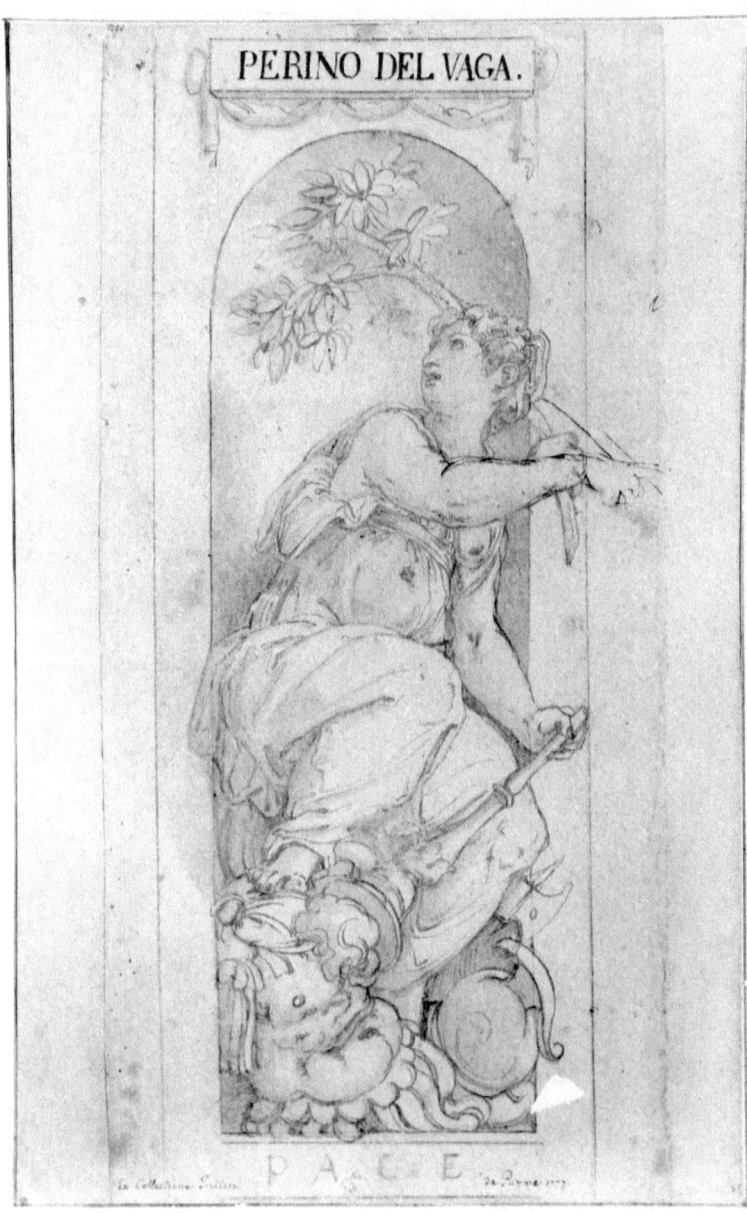

Fig. 21. Giorgio Vasari, *Peace*, 1542, drawing. Vienna, Albertina, Graphische Sammlung (Inv. 462). Photo: Albertina, Graphische Sammlung, Vienna.

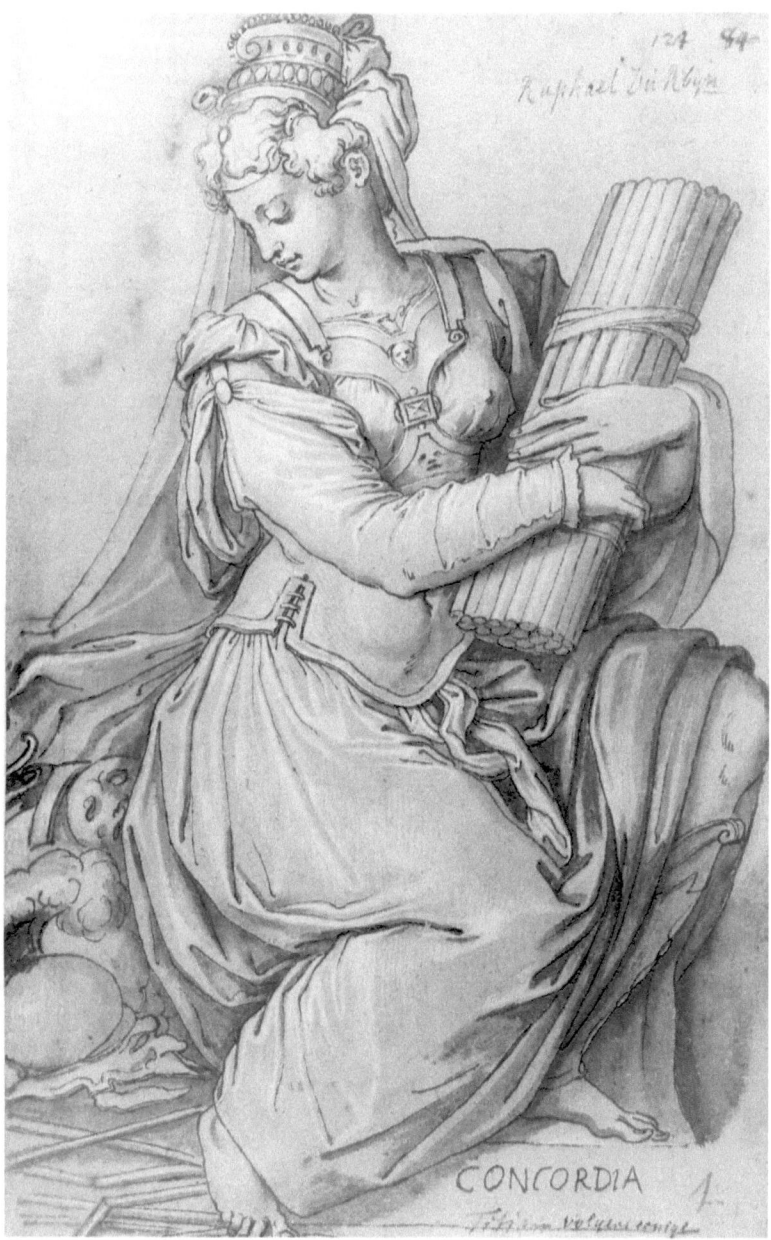

Fig. 22. Giorgio Vasari, *Concord*, 1542, drawing Kassel, Staatliche Kuinstsammlungen. Photo: Staatliche Kuinstsammlunge, Kassel.

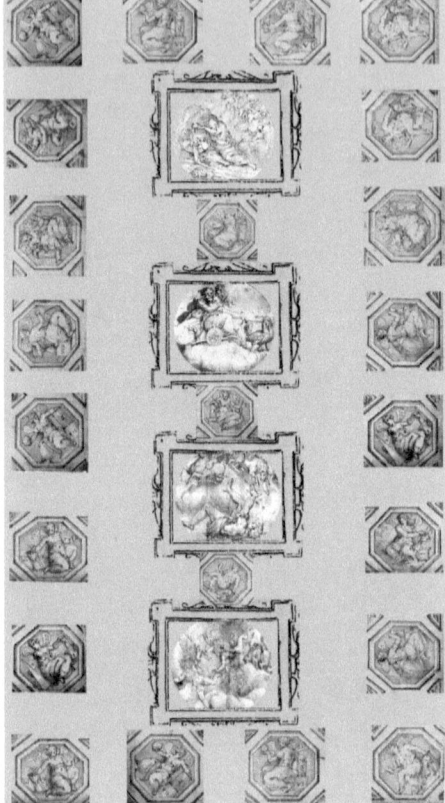

Fig. 23.  Cheney's ceiling reconstruction of the apparato for La Talanta.

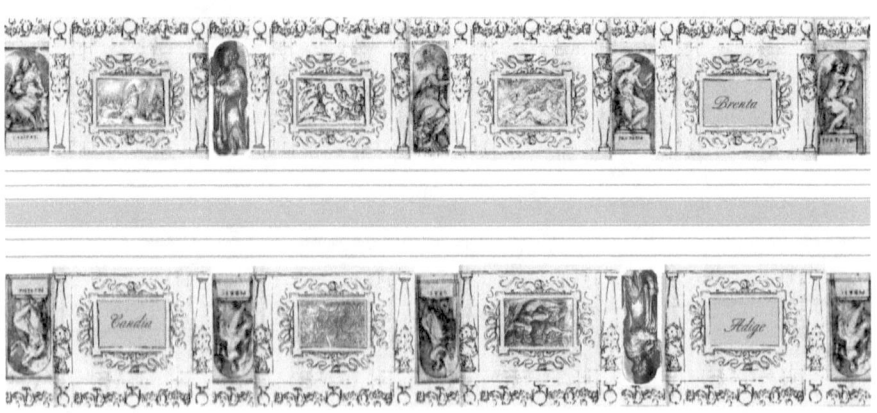

Fig. 24.  Cheney's walls reconstruction of the apparato for La Talanta.

# 4

# Vasari's Early Decorative Cycles: The Venetian Commissions Part II

*For my father, Ettore De Girolami, MD*

This study considers two commissions that Giorgio Vasari executed in Venice in 1541-42 - one secular (the *apparato* or stage settings for Aretino's comedy *La Talanta*, which I have examined in "Part I" published in the previous issue of this journal) and the other religious (the ceiling decoration of Giovanni Cornaro's nuptial chamber, to be examined here in "Part II"). Unfortunately, these two decorative structures have been dismantled or destroyed. Their reconstruction rests mostly on Vasari's descriptions, along with a few surviving drawings and paintings. Examination of these two Venetian commissions, however, reveals Vasari's formation of a repertoire of personifications and a new artistic formula, or *quadro riportato*, for decorative cycles, revolutionizing ceiling decorations in the sixteenth century: the central concept based on the *quadro riportato*, where scenes representing an *istoria* in a landscape or architectural setting are framed by flanking herms and niches (tabernacles) that contain allegorical figures or personifications symbolizing moral or aesthetic virtues and then are ornamented overall with *all'antica* and grotesque motifs. Here, the analysis of the second Venetian commission, the ceiling decoration of Giovanni Cornaro's nuptial chamber, will consist of three sections. The first section cites Vasari's descriptions of the ceiling assignment. Since the ceiling was dismantled some time after the sixteenth century, the second section discusses a possible reconstruction of the ceiling design based on the present remaining drawings and paintings. And the last section offers an interpretative view of the imagery in the ceiling, demonstrating how Vasari's humanistic learning and literary contacts provided him with literary descriptions and emblematic sources, which he then integrated into the construct of his personifications (Vasari 8: 244, 252, 262-65; Gombrich 172).

### The Ceiling of Giovanni Cornaro Palace

In January 1542, Giovanni Cornaro[1] purchased a late fifteenth-century palazzo, the Cornero-Spinelli Palace, on the Grand Canal (Fig. 1). He then commissioned Michele Sanmichele to enlarge and renovate the original palace designed by Mauro Cadusso (Zorzi 158). Sanmichele designed and constructed the framework for one of the palace's ceilings in which a series of nine paintings was to be encased. Vasari assisted in obtaining the painting commission from the Cornaro family. At an unknown date, the ceiling paintings were dismantled and dispersed throughout various European collections.[2] Providentially, some paintings have recently been unearthed, for example, *Charity*, originally attributed to Jacopo Zucchi (Fig. 2).[3] The others (Figs. 3-6) are housed in various European collections, but two of the corner putti are still missing. A few drawings have also survived that assist in reconstructing the Cornaro commission: the drawing of Charity from the Uffizi (Inv. 107 1S; Fig. 7),[4] and a well-known drawing of the personification of Justice from Haarlem (Teylerstiching, N K94; Fig. 8).[5]

Vasari describes his paintings in the *Ricordanze*:

> On April 8, 1542, the Honorable Sir Giovanni Cornaro, Venetian Gentleman, under the recommendation of Sir Michele da Sanmichele, Veronese Architect of Saint Mark, commissioned a *palco* or wooden ceiling, painted with oils, depicting nine large pictures. In its center is Charity encircled by her putti who crown the four paintings depicting Faith, Hope, Justice, and Patience. Each of the paintings is accompanied by diverse figures corresponding to their appropriate designs. In addition to these four paintings, four other paintings with putti are to be placed in

the corners. I promised to complete this work as early as the first of August of same year.

(del Vita 39-40, Carte 37; my translation)[6]

Although the function of this room is not exactly known, its religious and moral imagery of love - with the inclusion of Charity or Divine Love, in particular, surrounded by Justice, Patience, Hope, and Religion or Faith - suggests that it was a nuptial chamber. Furthermore, some of the attributes associated with these virtues indicate marriage symbolism (Chevalier and Gheerbrandt 307; Biedermann 11): in particular, the overall celebratory mood of the flying putti, who honor the virtues with garlands shaped like rings, alludes specifically to a marriage ceremony; the pelican feeding its young held by Charity is a symbol of love, parental nurturing, and sacrifice; and the dove, an attribute of Hope, connotes fidelity in marriage, as well as sacred vows in marriage. In fact, for his own bedroom in 1558, in the Chamber of Abraham at his house in Arezzo, Vasari, under the Venetian spell, painted a religious ceiling alluding to love and sacrifice by depicting Abraham's sacrifice surrounded by the personifications of Concord, Modesty, Peace, and Virtue (compare Fig. 9 with Figs. 12 and 13; see Cheney, "Giorgio Vasari's Chamber of Abraham" 355-80).

The iconography for the Cornaro nuptial chamber can be decoded in light of Vasari's visual and emblematic repertoire, as well as the humanist and classical tradition of sixteenth-century art. Schulz posits a possible reconstruction of the setting for the virtues in which Justice faces Hope, Faith, and Patience. Lacking visual evidence, he omits from his study the discussion of the central panel in the ceiling (Fig. 10; Schulz, *Venetian Painted* 120 Plate 6), Fortunately for Florian Härb, the painting from the central panel recently surfaced in the art market, providing her with a total reconstruction of the ceiling, with the exception of two corner panels with putti that are still missing. Even with the addition of the central panel, Härb supporrs Schulz's arrangement of the virtues (106, her Fig. 31; see Fig. 11 here). I present here another possible design, in view of the new discovery as well as through further analysis of the symbolic interconnection of the virtues (Figs. 12 and 13).

It is known from Vasari's description of his commission that he placed Charity, a personification of Divine Love, in the center of the ceiling, surrounding her with the other virtues Faith, Hope, Justice, and Patience. With this frame of reference, the ceiling can be seen in the shape of a *crux dissimulata* ("disguised cross") or Greek cross, with Charity in the center encircled by the virtues. Bur it remains unclear from Vasari's description how these virtues related to each other, as well as how they were set in the ceiling. But the symbolism of the virtues in connection to the function of the chamber assist in reconstructing a likely decorative design.

The panels in the ceiling are connected both iconographically and stylistically. The compositional arrangement of the architectural balustrade and rope devised in each panel creates an illusion of continuous space from panel to panel in the ceiling. He further unified the composition of the scenes by designing the virtues with the reclining and contra-puntal turning of their bodies. Although the virtues are set in a limited space - inside rectangular frames - the backgrounds of their settings reveal illusionistic depictions of the natural world, where, in extended skyscapes, the times of day and seasons are visible. In contrast, the center panel depicts flying figures existing in a celestial space, whose circular movements and actions extend outside their realm in order to connect with the virtues in the natural realm. In this manner, Vasari invites the viewer to look around and visually participate with both the spiritual and natural worlds.

Thematically, Vasari depicts five virtues from the Christian tradition: Hope, Faith, and Charity are the theological virtues associated with the love of God. These virtues assist the individual in achieving spiritual love as well as sustaining this love in a Christian household, particularly in a good Christian marriage. In contrast, Patience and Justice are associated with human or secular love. Both of these virtues - which are connected with the cardinal virtues of Fortitude, Prudence, and Temperance, and are necessary for achieving harmony in a good marriage, family life, and friendships - portray a microcosm of a good society.

By reconstructing the ceiling as a Greek cross and connecting the symbolisms among the virtues, we find that two possible configurations emerge. One possible arrangement is that Hope and Faith are placed from right to left on a horizontal axis, flanking Charity in the center, interacting with her and with each other, while Patience and Justice are set at the top and bottom, respectively, of the vertical axis (Fig. 12). In another possible arrangement, the theological virtues of Hope and Faith stand above and below Charity on the vertical axis, with Patience and Justice to the right and left of Charity on the horizontal axis (Fig. 13). In either scenario, all four virtues rotate around Charity, the pivotal image.

An examination of the symbolism and interaction of the virtues provides a further rationale for these two configurations. The shape of a Greek cross (Chevalier and Gheerbrandt 253)[7] alludes to the victory of the union of two natures, human and divine, as manifested by the personification of Charity and the virtues. Moreover, the cross, because of its shape's connection with the cardinal points, is a symbol of orientation for human existence - spatial in relation to the terrestrial world and temporal in relation to the celestial world (Champeaux and Sterckx 27). Spatial orientation connects the individual with the east-west axis - representing the rising and setting of the sun - while the temporal orientation ties the individual with the north-south axis - representing thee rotary movement of the world. The individual achieves physical and spiritual well-being when there is harmony, with both the spatial and the temporal orientations. When this harmony is achieved through the grace of God, the Christian believer can transcend from the terrestrial realm (spatial orientation) into the celestial realm (temporal orientation). The theological (Faith, Hope, and Charity) and cardinal (Fortitude, Justice, Prudence, and Temperance) virtues guide the faithful in achieving this Christian goal. And specific to the symbolism of the ceiling of the chamber, the virtues assist in providing a Christian union between the spouses and among the spouses and God.

For example, proceeding from the center of the *palco* or wooden ceiling, one observes radiant Charity in flight, guided by a celestial putto (Figs. 2 and 7.) Charity continues to move across the heaven with her six celestial putti, four of whom are encircling her while offering crowns of laurel to the virtues in the adjacent panels. Their rotating movement creates a *mandorla* or elliptical shape within the rectangular frame of the painting, alluding to the potency of the nimbus, which reveals the impregnation of divine power. Behind

Charity, a sixth putto, holding a vase with flames, follows Charity's gaze. The shape of the vessel, the fire, and the flame typify the heart, with symbols of Charity's dual aspects of love, spiritual and natural (Cooper 66-67).[8] Charity's cherished object is a pelican, who was fabled to feed its own blood to its young (Cooper 128). She holds this symbol of love with her raised left hand as if it were a miraculous trophy.

The signification of Charity as a symbol of love derives from the translation of the Latin word *caritas* (Greek *agape*). The Greeks considered two kinds of love, *eros* and *agape*. According to Plato, *eros* means the love or desire of the individual for the Divine, while agape refers to contemplation for the attainment of the Good (Plato, *Symposium* 210A-E). In the New Testament, the two Platonic aspects of love are fused into one, *agape*, which means God's generous love (1 John 4.8). Charity is the greatest of the three theological virtues - Faith, Hope, and Charity - and her spiritual connection with them is complex for many scholars. For St. Paul, charity represented the highest virtue to be attained, a Christian attitude toward one's neighbor, and, rarely, love toward God (Rom. 8.28 and 1 Cor. 2.9, 8.3): "And now together faith, hope, charity, these three: but the greatest of these is charity" (1 Cor. 13.13 KJV). From the time of St. Augustine, however, Charity has signified God's love of human beings as well as human love for God. The Church ultimately teaches that charity is both love of God, *amor dei*, and love of neighbor, *amor proximi*, which was of no real worth without *amor dei*. When the symbolism of Charity is directly associated with marriage, it takes on the meaning of brotherly love, alms giving, and nursing, as illustrated in Christian art, where Charity becomes a symbol of *Virgo lactans*, such as a woman suckling or nursing two infants or a woman embracing and surrounded by children (Figs. 14 and 15).[9]

Although stylistically, the Venetian *Charity* represents a visual source for his depiction of *Fortune* in the Chamber of Fortune in Arezzo, Vasari's Venetian *Charity* contrasts with his visual depiction and meaning of charity. The Venetian *Charity*, with her attributes of purification and divine love - a vase with burning flames, a pelican feeding the young, and putti carrying laurel crowns - depicts a holy Charity. She personifies Religion, because she symbolizes the three theological virtues that are given to human beings by the love of God (*amor dei*), as well as qualities of generosity and love for humankind, which are emulated by good Christians (*amor proximi*).

In the thirteenth century, Bonaventura associated metaphorically ardent love with a burning flame or Charity's love. In a drawing of *Charity with Saints* of 1570 (Uffizi, Inv. 1187E; Fig, 16) for the ceiling of the Cappella of San Pietro Martire in Rome, Vasari appropriated Bonaventura's metaphor by portraying Charity's love as a nursing mother surrounded by flaming vases. This drawing in the shape of a tondo (birth salver)[10] reveals a different type of symbolism, one more in tune with later examples of Charity as a personification of God's love for humankind. For example, Cesare Ripa assimilated Vasari's image into an emblem of Chariry as *Virgo lactans* and transformed the strands of her hair into a flaming fire symbolizing Christ's love, recalling the Christian saying, "*Ignem veni mittere in terram, et quid volo, nisi ut ardeat*" ("I came to put fire onto the earth, and I wish that it should burn") (Ripa. Praz ed. 49). Moreover, Ripa employed the image of flaming fire for his representation of Religion's emblem, where a veiled woman holds in her left hand flames of fire, symbolic of ardent and continuous love.

The images of Charity that Vasari depicted in subsequent years followed the stylistic traditions of the Renaissance, focusing on Charity's love for humankind by portraying her as a nursing mother. For instance, in 1545, Vasari composed a fine preparatory drawing of Charity for the Refectory of Monteoliveto in Naples, now located in the Pinacoteca of Bologna (Cheney, "Vasari and Naples" 48-126; Fig. 14). Here, Vasari depicted a figure of Charity, bare-breasted and statuesque, standing and holding a nursing child in one arm, while two other children are shown at her side. The three children symbolize the three aspects of faith, hope, and love (charity).[11] Vasari repeated a similar image in 1548 for the Chamber of Fortune (his study) in his house in Arezzo (Fig. 15). And thematically, in 1546, he used a similar image in the Sala dei Cento Giorni in the Palazzo della Cancelleria in Rome.

The other virtues depicted in the Cornaro ceiling follow the Christian iconography, as well. For example, in Renaissance art, Justice is often blindfolded, an allusion to her fairness and honesty. But Vasari's *Justice* turns her back to the viewer and gazes toward the heavens for divine inspiration (Figs. 3 and 8). Vasari may be distancing his Justice from any association with human blindness, thereby connecting her with divine light, emphasizing the Christian virtue of truth and its connection with charity or love. Vasari's Justice reclines, holding a book and a sword, while a terrestrial globe lies at her unshod feet. The book in her hand displays a round medallion that sketchily portrays a standing figure, perhaps Minerva, Goddess of Wisdom and Reason. The sword is a symbol of power and impartiality; the book signifies the codes on which her judgments are made; and the globe represents the universality of her judgments (Valeriano 566; Cartari 242-43; Wind 95-96). Perhaps by depicting Justice with her back to the viewer, Vasari is suggesting that, since the judgment of Justice is assisted by God, it is essentially impartial. Two figures carrying Roman fasces with their heads bowed likely represent the two aspects of human justice, civil and military. In contrast, the crowned, regal figure on their extreme left, perhaps King Solomon or Emperor Trajan, holds a scepter. Like Justice, he looks up at the heavens for wisdom and divine judgment.

Vasari's interpretation of justice as a symbol of right or law derives from the classical tradition; the writings of Plato and Aristotle best explain the meaning and implication of this concept. Plato held that justice is of two types: natural and conventional. In an ideal city, justice regulates the actions of the citizens with the other cardinal virtues (*Republic* 4.427). Likewise, Aristotle also identified two kinds of justice: distributive and retributive. During the Middle Ages, Aquinas also considered there to be two aspects of justice: natural and rational, both discernible through the exercise of reason.[12]

Justice, the leader of the cardinal virtues, was often represented in Medieval and Renaissance public buildings wherever the law was administered (as seen in the Palazzo Publico, Siena). However, Vasari designed a simplified version of Justice for either a private palace or secular commission. In addition to the blindfold and sword, the scales were another traditional emblem associated with Justice.[13] The scales of Justice represent balance, equality, and harmony, as also seen in the Tarot card of Justice and the zodiacal sign of Libra, where the scales symbolize equity. The symbol of the scales is ancient in its origin: Themis used it to represent law, order, and truth, while the Romans employed it as a symbol of impartiality. In his composition, Vasari substitutes a book for the scales; set square, compasses, and other traditional symbols of impartiality are also omitted.

The compositional motif of Justice found in the ceiling of the Cornaro Palace is repeated in the east wall of the Chamber of Fortune (1548) at Vasari's house in Arezzo (Fig. 17). Vasari was fascinated with this imagery, also presenting Justice in the Refectory of Monteoliveto in Naples in 1545 (Fig. 18) and in the Sala dei Cento Giorni in Rome, preferring to depict a standing, militant Justice (Cheney, *Paintings* 170-82). In his *Vita*, Vasari describes yet another *invenzione* of *Justice* of 1543 for Cardinal Alessandro Farnese (Frey and Frey 1221-22; Cheney, "Giorgio Vasari's *Astraea*"). Here, Justice is seated and rules in judgment over the vices that surround the figure. In this imagery, Vasari focuses on the ancient representation of Justice (as discussed by both Plato and Aristotle), contrasting in both symbolism and composition with the Cornaro *Justice*.

If my reconstruction of the ceiling is indeed correct, the personification of Justice faced Patience in a contrapuntal design of back and from views of the reclining figure. Although looking away, barefoot Patience faces the viewer and carries a yoke (Fig. 4). Vasari depicts Patience resting quietly with her yoke: "il giogho al collo et il capo basso" ("the yoke placed on her neck and bending her head") (qtd. in del Vita 25). The yoke, a symbol of obedience and servitude (Ripa, Mandowski ed. 363, 450), plus Patience's humble and austere appearance, emphasize her endurance. The yoke, the reins, and the rope all refer to Patience's selfless willingness to surrender autonomy and to devote herself to a goal that demands great self-abnegation. The word patience derives from the Latin *patiens*, meaning "enduring." In Christian iconography, Patience is viewed as a virtue or gift given by the Holy Spirit.[14] Familiar with this tradition, the emblematist Andrea Alciato composed an emblem with this moral intention. For example, Emblem 34 contains the motto "Bear and Forbear," which describes the attitude of the bull in the emblem of Patience (Fig. 19), where a bull is separated from three cows by a man wielding a club. The epigram explains the image:

Sad fortune must be endured by the man suffering it, and a too happy fortune is often to be feared. Epictetus used to say *bear and forbear*. It is fitting to endure much, and to keep one's hands from illicit things. Thus the bull with its right knee tethered suffers the command of its master; thus it abstains from the pregnant cows.[15]

Years later, Ripa visualized Patience (*Patientia*) seated, holding a yoke on her shoulder, alluding to suffering and tolerance. In another emblem, Ripa represented Patience standing, holding a yoke and a scroll, with the motto *Suave* (Fig. 20), deriving from Virgil (appropriated by Piero Valeriano for his emblem in *Hieroglyphica*, consisting simply of a yoke and the motto).[16] Moreover, for Valeriano the yoke was a symbol of matrimonial bond and servitude ("legame matrimoniale e servitù").[17] Vasari, a pupil of Valeriano, appropriated this meaning for his personification of Patience.

Vasari's Patience looks over her shoulder, gazing at the yoke's ring, recalling its meaning from antiquity, when rings were used by individuals as a sign of freedom (Ronchetti 62) as well as a sign of bond, union, or matrimony.[18] Patience's bowed head probably implies that, through the virtue of patience, a person can tolerate and even venture with tranquility through the adversities of life and through marriage in particular.

Vasari repeated this image of Patience in many of his decorative cycles commissions. For example, in 1548, on the east wall of the Chamber of Fortune at his house in Arezzo he depicted a simplified, reclining figure of a barefoot Patience embracing a yoke and bending her head to the right, while the medallion of her dress showed a snail, a symbol of time and of perseverance (compare Fig. 21 with Fig. 4).[19] The Venetian Patience may also be looking at a snail on her medallion, but it is difficult to decipher from the picture. Because of the shape of its body, with a shell of the pattern of a ram's horn, as well as the snail's association with moisture, the snail also alludes to conception, pregnancy, and birth: as a symbol of the cycle of rebirth, the snail is associated with lunar changes and fertility cycles (Chevalier and Gheerbrandt 890).[20]

In 1545, Vasari portrayed Patience again in the frescoed ceiling of the Refectory of Monteoliveto in Naples, but here she is seated rather than reclining. Her attributes continue to contain traditional emblems such as the yoke and reins. However, in the Venetian Patience, Vasari employs the rope as a symbolic substitute for the yoke and reins, because, in Christian iconography, its knot formation and chain decoration associate the rope with endurance and the rites of passages of life (Hall 268; Cooper 92, 14), thereby possibly symbolizing salvation and access to heaven. The difficulty in loosening the rope's knots or overcoming life's vicissitudes is only achieved through Patience and Faith. This traditional symbolism explains the presence of Patience in Vasari's depiction of two men who are bound with rope on Patience's right. A pensive Michelanglesque Jeremiah sits at her left, with a rope around his neck. Perhaps this biblical man is Saint Mark, evangelist and patron saint of Venice, who miraculously saved a Christian slave from being dragged through the streets with a rope around his neck (as seen in the painting of Tintoretto, *Saint Mark Rescuing a Slave* of 1540, in the Accademia, Venice).

In the reconstructed Cornaro ceiling, next to *Patience* is *Hope* (Fig. 5). Vasari portrays Hope (Latin *spes*, a theological virtue) praying and gazing up to the heavens, pleading for divine attention and intervention. She is surrounded by her attributes of love and peace - the anchor and the dove.[21] These attributes are alluded to in the scriptures of both the Old and the New Testaments. God promises an anchor of protection and security to the faithful soul (Heb. 6. 18-19). In Latin, the anchor is called *crux dissimulata* ("disguised cross"). Being of similar shape to the cross, the anchor alludes to Christ's suffering and endurance at the crucifixion. In the Old Testament, Noah's action of embracing the grapevine, also in the shape of a cross, foreshadows Christ's acceptance of His cross and destiny. And in the New Testament, the apostle Paul refers to Hope as the anchor of our life in the spiritual journey of Christian life (Heb. 6. 19).

In Vasari's painting, the anchor is seen grounded on the parapet, implying the moral attributes of endurance and safety, as well as referring to the Christian meaning of the crucifixion-redemption and salvation. Above the anchor is a white dove - representing the soul and innocence - carrying an olive branch, the symbol of peace. Like the anchor, the dove carries symbolic significance in the Old and New Testaments. According to the Hebraic tradition, white doves are sacrificed at the Temple for purification, and in the Old Testament, a dove is sent forth from Noah's Ark on the seventh day after the deluge to announce a new life and peace. The dove represents hope for the obedient Noah, whose trust in the God provides safety for his people. The dove becomes, then, the symbol of the Holy Spirit, the Announcer of God or the Third Person of the Trinity. In the New Testament, the dove is a symbol of purification, as well as a witness to Christ's baptism (Matt. 3.16). And most significantly, a dove appears at Mary's conception to reaffirm her purity and to announce the Incarnation of Christ, as illustrated in the Annunciation scenes. Thus the old man, likely Noah, next to Hope in the painting could also represent Saint James the Great, who testified to the incarnation of Christ (Ferguson 124). In the painting, Vasari portrays Noah embracing a pole laden with fruitful grapes and looking at the flying dove nearing him, recalling Noah's drunkenness after the dove's return that showed they had reached land. In the depiction of Noah's trust and hope, Vasari constructs an image of reverence.

Associating the function of the room with the placement of the personification of Hope provides significant revelations. The depiction of Hope's attributes in the bedroom chamber allude to marriage and fecundity. For example, the anchor refers to stability, trust, and faith in marriage, while the dove symbolizes fruitfulness. In antiquity, the dove, a symbol of fecundity and maternity, is sacred to all Great Mothers (Isis and Aphrodite). Furthermore, in Christianity, the dove is associated with the Mother of God, as she embodies the flesh in the incarnation depicted in scene of the annunciation. With the depiction of Hope's attributes (anchor, dove, olive branch, and grapes), Vasari visually interconnects the Old Testament symbolism as pre-figurations of New Testament affirmations.

Opposite *Hope*, Vasari portrays another aspect of trust, *Faith* (Fig. 6). Gazing into the heavens, *Faith* offers baptism, as she pours water on the head of a young child who sits on what may be books or an urn. The neophyte piously embraces the new faith as he joins his hands in a praying gesture of reception and acceptance. According to St. Paul (1 Cor. 13.13), who extolled the theological virtues, the two primary elements of Christian faith are the beliefs in Christ crucified and in the miracle of the sacraments, which are symbolized by the cross and the chalice.

In the Cornaro *Faith*, Vasari substituted a kylix, containing water used for baptism, for a chalice. Faith is holding in her free hand a Latin cross surrounded by a rope tied in a love knot. Two elderly men are behind the cross and the extended rope. Although the men have close access to the instruments of the Faith, they are spiritually distinct, contrasting with the immediate leap of Faith of the young child. Vasari unites the imagery in this ceiling, not only compositionally but iconographically as well. The hand gesture of the child is paralleled on the opposite side with the figure of Hope, whose presence is a spiritual necessity for having faith. The lighted background alludes to the illumination of the mind brought about by Faith. Thus are represented the theological virtues of Faith (Greek *pistis* and Latin *fides* – "to trust") and Hope (the third is Charity), as distinct from the natural or cardinal virtues of Prudence, Temperance, Fortitude, and Justice. In 1546, Vasari repeated this bond between Hope and Faith in the Sala dei Cento Giorni (compare Fig. 22 with Figs. 5 and 6).

Faith is typically represented as a woman, associated with such objects as a chalice, a cross, a candle, and a baptismal font, sometimes wearing a helmet and displaying the *Decalogue* at her feet. The open book of the Decalogue represents the Old and New Testaments, the source of learning and maintenance of the faith. The helmet protects Faith's mind against the injuries and dangers of false doctrines. In Vasari's imagery, she is not wearing a helmet, bur she is shown in a cuirass instead. Moreover, Vasari reveals Faith's ascending and descending love - and alludes to the third theological virtue, Charity - through the depiction of a rope, a symbol of cosmic unity (Chevalier and Gheerbrandt 811 -12; Cooper 22-23). First he creates a lover's knot with the rope that decorates the Latin cross held by Faith. Then he incorporates segments of the rope in other panels in order to extend outwardly and unite all panels with the message of spiritual love and ascension. As with the symbolism and compositional construction of the Greek cross, Vasari connects the Neoplatonic symbolism of ascending and descending love in two ways: in the natural realm, by the depiction of the rope in the virtues panels, and in the celestial realm, by the depiction of the putti crowning the virtues with laurel wreaths. Thus the pursuit of Faith reflects Charity's message of love.

In traditional sixteenth-century fashion, Faith's attributes combine the personifications of Religion and Faith - the cross, the chalice, and the Host. Redemption and salvation can be achieved through acts of faith. Vasari employed them all in his decorative cycles, in particular, the ceiling of the Cornaro Palace (Venice, 1540-42); the Chambers of Abraham and Fortune in his own house (Arezzo, 1542-48); the Refectory of Monteoliveto (Naples, 1545); the Sala dei Cento Giorni in the Palazzo della Cancelleria (Rome, 1546); and the rooms of the Palazzo Vecchio (Florence, 1565-72). He frequently depicted the emblem or the image of Faith with all the pertinent attributes, as in the Cornaro Palace and Refectory of Monteoliveto. At other times, he represented the expression of having faith, as seen in the Chamber of Abraham (Fig. 9).[22]

It is not by mere serendipity that Vasari combined the classical connection with the Christian tradition. In the biblical writings of both the Old and New Testaments, the concept of faith is interrelated with hope and charity, focusing on the Platonic concept of love (*Symposium* 210A-E). These virtues are interconnected and complementary according to classical and Judeo-Christian legends. Also according to second-century tradition, Faith, Hope, and Charity were the daughters of Sophia (Greek for wisdom) and had the Greek names of *Pistis* (Faith), *Elpis* (Hope), and *Agape* (Charity). All four of the women were said to have been put to death during the reign of the Emperor Hadrian (117-38 CE) and buried on the Aurelian Way. Paralleling this myth, four Roman martyrs with Latin names *Sapientia* (Wisdom), *Spes* (Hope), *Fides* (Faith), and *Caritas* (Charity) are buried on the Appian Way in the catacomb of Saint Callistus. Recognizing this fusion, St. Paul explains the concept of faith in terms of the individual's response to God (Rom. 8.28; 1 Cor. 2.9, 8.3; and Eph. 6.24).

In the writings of the Church Fathers in the Middle Ages (Ambrose 2.2; Augustine Ch. 117, 3; and Aquinas 2.2, q.2, a. 1), faith is the will to believe in God - a principle codified by Augustine as Credo *ut intelligam* ("I believe in order to understand") and then accepted by Saint Anselm. Faith is a virtue of the intellect given as a gift of grace by God to individuals who respond to God. This will to believe is essential for eternal salvation. In the Cornaro ceiling, Vasari reveals this attitude by painting next to the personification of Religion as an innocent young boy holding Moses's tablets (alluding to Old Testament law) and keys (symbolizing the New Testament as well as the Four Evangelists). The entire composition stresses divine intervention through the Holy Spirit, or Religion intertwined with Charity, Faith, and Hope.

Following the Christian tradition,[23] Vasari's mentor Andrea Alciato also placed great importance on the virtue of faith. But, in doing so, he moved away from the Medieval discussion of the theological and cardinal virtues to focus instead on the classical interpretation of *arete* or *virtus*. Emblematist Alciato interpreted faith in the spirit of Renaissance Humanism (Alciato Emblem 9; see also Daly, Callaghan, and Cuttler). For him, faith is the first virtue and a symbol of fidelity, as seen in Emblem 9, *Fidei symbolum* (Fig. 23). The epigram explains the *pictura* (image):

> Let Honor, dressed in purple cloak, hold hands with naked Truth [*Veritas*], while Eros [*Amor*], holy and sincere, crowned with garland of roses, stands between us. This faith [Fidelity] sustains Honor, gives birth to Truth, and nurtures Love.[24]

This conceit of fidelity is easily associated with marital fidelity, relating it to the function of Cornaro's nuptial chamber.[25] The unity of the iconographical Vasarian program depends on the image of Faith or Religion representing the Christianization of the classical tradition: "dividitur autem religio in has species: in fidem, spem et caritate" ("Religion, however, is divided into these categories: into Faith, Hope and Charity") (Ripa, *Religione* in *Iconologia*, Mandowski ed. 378). Familiar with Christian symbolism, Vasari applied it to his religious program by including in a bedroom the imagery of human and divine love, a sentiment to be emulated and sustained in a devoted and faithful marriage.

Moreover, in the ceiling of the Cornaro Palace, Vasari revealed iconographically two connections with the personifications of Faith, Hope, and Charity that are affiliated with the civic aims of the Venetian Republic, *La Serenissima*. The first refers to a private and intimate symbolism of marriage and family virtues to be emulated in a Venetian patrician household. The second alludes to a good public and civic Venetian society, where socioeconomic, political, and religious ties are personified by the images of Faith, Hope, and Charity in churches, guilds edifices, and the doge's palaces.[26] In the ceiling of the Cornaro Palace, Vasari created private symbolism that reflected a public state, a Venetian microcosm and macrocosm.

### Epilogue

Vasari's stylistic contributions in Venice are as significant as any other of his works. There he established the beginnings of the decorative formula in the apparato for *La Talanta*. Although it is difficult to determine the stylistic sources for the apparato, the few drawings available provide a rich and complex program for secular theatrical performance. Of Vasari's Venetian commissions, the Cornaro Palace offers new insight into the stylistic assimilation and innovation in his art. The ceiling of the Cornaro Palace reveals further development of the Vasarian decorative formula used in the apparato for *La Talanta*. Here, Vasari introduced the notion of *quadro riportato* (a placement of a panel painting on a ceiling), with an *istoria* (dramatic narrative) consisting of allegorical figures or personifications of the virtues that embody a moralizing message. The ceiling of the Cornaro Palace clearly illustrates Vasari's stylistic dependencies on the initial development of his formula for decorative cycle,[27] including motifs borrowed from the classical tradition, Roman and Tuscan style,[28] and Venetian illusionism - a *di sotto in su* perspective.[29] The type of illusion that Vasari employed in the ceiling of the Cornaro Palace fuses both traditions, the Venetian type of ceiling decorations (flat, beamed ceilings filled with rich carvings and encased paintings) and the classical type (illusionistic architectural scenes and narrative stories). Thus the Vasarian decorative formula was conceived in a simple manner in the apparato for *La Talanta*, orchestrated in the ceiling of the Cornaro Palace, personalized in the Casa Vasari, fancifully displayed the Sala dei Cento Giorni of the Palazzo della Cancelleria, and beautifully aggrandized in the *sale* of the Palazzo Vecchio.

Although disappointed by the dismantling of his *gran fatica*, the *apparato*, Vasari extended his stay in Venice in order successfully to complete a religious commission that would permanently remain and honor his artistic merits in Venice. In addition to working on Cornaro's commission, Vasari wished to meet the renowned Titian, whom he highly praised in the *Vite* (7: 425-71), and Francesco Marcolini, the Venetian printer who subsequently assisted him in the publication of his biographies. The trip to Venice was most rewarding artistically and professionally for Vasari, allowing him to embellish and expand the content of the biographies of the *Vite*. It brought him in contact with the Venetian painters and humanists, as well as with his compatriot, Pietro Aretino. With Aretino, Vasari had the opportunity to exchange critical ideas about writing and theories about art and artists (Bertaux 329-33).[30] Although the literary influence of Aretino on Vasari is not apparent in the first edition of the *Vite* (1550), it does become evident in the second edition (1568). The contact with Francesco Marcolini afforded Vasari the opportunity to have access to a printing press for producing the second edition of his *Vite* with woodcut portraits of the artists. And most of all, the Venetian sojourn provided Vasari with a knowledge of Venetian illusionism that he fused with the central Italian tradition of ceiling and wall decorations, thus creating a new pictorial imagery for decorative cycles in the sixteenth century in Italy and throughout Europe.

## Notes

I would like co express my gratitude to the University of Massachusetts Lowell for its support of this research.

1. The Cornaro's descendants were a distinguished Venetian family. Many of their members were naval captains, cardinals, and senators, as well as rulers of the Adriatic, among them Caterina Cornaro (1454-1510), known as the Queen of the Adriatic, Cyprus, and Asolo. See Clement 226-41.
2. Presently the location of these paintings is as follows: two corner putti, *Justice* and *Patience*, previously owned by Prince Giovanelli of Venice, then acquired by the Letizia Amendola di Capua collection in Rome, are now secured in the Accademia of Venice (see *Arte Veneta* [1987] 41: 244). *Hope* has been preserved in the George Weidenfeld

collection in London. *Faith*, previously located in the R. Scholz-Forni collection in Hamburg, then acquired by the H. Trainé collection in Zurich, is now in a private collection in London. *Charity*, residing in the Castello Sforzesco of Milan, was acquired by the Museo della Società Gallarantese per gli Studi Patri (lnv. 586).

3. Earlier, Paola Barocchi attributed Vasari's painting and drawing of *Charity* to Jacopo Zucchi. See Barocchi, *Complementi al Vasari Pittore* 288, Figs. 115 and 116; Colasanti 406-43; and Barocchi, "II Vasari Pittore" n 2. Recently, however, Florian Härb has attributed the Zucchi's painting and drawing to Vasari (104 n 59: 272 n 61; and Figs. 31 and 32).

4. Another drawing for a ceiling decoration, in the Courtauld Institute Galleries in London, contains an image of Charity in flight, surrounded by putti holding laurel wreaths. This latter drawing is similar, but smaller in scale to the Uffizi drawing (Inv. 1071S). Other drawings, found in the Louvre (Inv. 218) and the Uffizi (lnv. 1187E), are studies of Charity. See Monbeig-Gougel 52; and Barocchi, *Complementi al Vasari Pittore*, 282 Fig. 30. Obviously, the Vasari's *tondo* design is influenced by Michelangelo's *Doni Tondo*.

5. Vasari 7: 13,653-54. Juergen Schulz attributes the drawing to Vasari and advances it persuasively as a *modello* for the panel of Justice ("Vasari at Venice" 505).

6. Ricordo come adi otto di aprile 1542 il Magnifico Messer Giovanni Cornaro Gentiluomo Venetiano mi alloga per ordine di Messer Michele da Sanmichele Veronese Architetto di San Marcho un palcho o soffitato di legniame a dipingiere a olio con nove quadri grandi in uno di mezzo la Carità che con li suoi putti atorno che coronano i quattro quadri la Fede la Speranza et la Giustitia et la Patientia che tutte sono accompagniate da figure diverse secondo un disegnio fattoli perciò e di più 4 quadri dentrovi quatro putti ne canti: la quale opera promessi darla finita perfino a di primo dagosto prossimo. See also Vasari 6: 365 and 7: 444-46.

7. For an explanation of the highly complex symbolism of the shape of cross as symbol of the external and internal world, earth and heaven, and cardinal points, see Chevalier and Gheerbrandt 248-57.

8. The light and heat of the fire alludes to the fecundity of the intellect as well as to the power of emotions.

9. During the Middle Ages, *amor proximi* was often depicted as a woman receiving or nursing children. In Gothic art, in particular, it is represented by the figure of a woman performing the six works of mercy (Matt. 25.35-37): tending the hungry, the thirsty, the stranger, the naked, the sick and the imprisoned. These became abbreviated into the representation of one act only: clothing the naked (for example, a beggar

putting a shirt over his head beside the figure of Charity who perhaps holds a bundle of clothes). Henceforth, in Italian Renaissance art, the figure of Charity came to be represented with a flame, customarily emerging from some form of vase that she holds in her hand.

From the fourteenth century, Charity was depicted holding a flaming heart as if she were offering it to God. This sometimes came to be combined with attributes suggesting earthly charity, such as the cornucopia or bowl of fruit. For example, in Giotto's fresco cycle at Padua, 1305, the cardinal and theological virtues face their vices on the opposite wall of the Scrovegni or Arena Chapel. There, Giotto's representation of Charity as a young, garlanded woman demonstrates the twofold nature of her love - the love of God and the love of her neighbors: she offers up her heart, while she holds a basket or bowl of fruit and flowers, with a sack of corn and coins depicted at her feet, ready for distribution to the needy. The vice opposed to Charity in the Middle Ages was Avarice, depicted with money bags, a purse, or filled coffer.

Charity possibly derives from the earlier image of the *Virgo lactans*, a woman nursing two infants (see the marble *Charity* of Tino da Camaino, 1320, in the Museo Bardini, Florence). Combined with the older motifs of the flaming heart (suggesting the utmost religious fervor) and the candle, it predominated until the sixteenth century, when it becomes the standard type of representation in European art. In subsequent versions, clustered around the mother figure, are three or four infants, one of whom is customarily at the breast, paralleling the motif of the pelican feeding its young with its own blood. These various aspects of Charity are frequently portrayed in art. Sec Levin 119-200, for an excellent discussion on this topic.

10. See Olson for a discussion of the *tondo* as a spiritual and familial symbol.

11. The female figure represents the union of these three virtues, as illustrated many years later in Ripa's *Iconologia*, Praz ed. 49.

12. Aquinas, *Summa Theologica* (2a., 2ae, q. 33a.5), Macrobius's *Commentary* on Cicero's *Somnium scipionis,* and Petrarch's *Africa* are texts concerned with the concept of justice as a primary virtue that ought to accompany the life of a hero.

13. See Cooper 145: and Hall 183. The scales as an attribute of impartiality are also the emblems of the Archangel Michael. In representations of the Last Judgment, Justice may have an angel in each scale-pan, one crowning the virtuous, the other executing a malefactor. In the sixteenth century, artists replaced the scales with fasces, the Roman symbol of authority.

14. See Schiffhorst, an excellent study on the iconography of Patience. See also Cheney, "Emblematic Approaches"; and Cheney, "Vasari's *Patience*: The Measure of Time" 13-23.

15. See Alciato Emblem 34. In the Old Testament, Job is viewed as an example of Patience because he bore his troubles with fortitude.

16. See Valeriano 45-46. Giovio associates the mono *Suave* with the impresa for Pope Leo X de Medici: "jugum meum suave est, et onus meum leve" ("My yoke is sweet and my weight light"). See also Florentii 184-86, Emblem LXII, *Patientia*.

17. See Valeriano 648. In Chapter 40, Valeriano dedicates his essay to Giovanni Cornaro in honor of his recent marriage. This action reveals the continuous connection between the Cornaro family and the literati and artists of the time, such as Valeriano and Vasari.

18. See Ripa, Mandowski ed. 363, 450. Moreover, to honor a legal document, the seal of a ring is required to witness the contract as an act of good faith, and, of course, this contractual association is also related to marriage.

19. In *Iconologia*, Praz ed. 339, Ripa also associates the snail with the personification of Patience, since the snail stays inside her conch or house for long periods. Obviously, Vasari's representation anticipates Ripa's emblem. See also Wittkower 171-77.

20. See also Florentii 156, Emblem LII, "sapiens in omnibus providus," mentioned by Seneca as a symbol of Prudence.

21. See Biedermann 10-11 for the anchor's symbolism; see Biedermann 100-02 for the dove's.

22. Cheney, "Giorgio Vasari's Chamber of Abraham" 355-80. In 1545, on the ceiling near the altar of the Refectory of Monteoliveto in Naples, Vasari painted another personification of Religion, who floats on a bundle of wheat and displays her attributes - the keys of St. Peter, the four gospels, and the veil. Religion dramatically turns her head to receive divine inspiration from the Holy Spirit. A rose bush with thorns behind her recalls the sacrificial redemption. See Cheney, "Vasari and Naples: The Monteoliveto Order" 48-126.

23. During the Middle Ages. Faith is represented in a place of honor next to Christ. According to Thomas Aquinas (2.2, q. 77, art. 7 and q. 84, art. 2), Religion is that moral virtue in which the Christian dedicates all his honor to God with all his heart, soul, and body. Aristotle differentiates humans from beasts for their ability to reason and, in this manner, to reach and comprehend the divine. Cesare Ripa's *figurazione* or image of Religion is veiled, reflecting St. Paul's statement *per speculum in aenigmate* ("in a glass darkly"), alluding to the mysteriousness of rites, ceremonies, and religious events. Other attributes accompany Reli-

gion: a book, fire, and a cross. The book alludes to the Holy Scriptures, revelations, and religious conventions. The fire that Religion holds in her hand suggests pure and sincere devotion to God. The cross symbolizes Christ and His Christian doctrine.

Sometimes, an elephant guards Religion, alluding to Pliny's explanation about the good nature of this animal (*Natural History* 7: 1). Pliny observes that this animal is prudent, charitable, and a lover of equanimity. In *Hieroglyphica* (Venice, 1556) 20-21, Piero Valeriano recounts how the elephant is depicted in the Egyptian hieroglyphics, and for this reason, Pliny explains the elephant worships the sun and the stars and kneels in front of the moon for reverence. On a full moon, the elephant seeks water to bathe his body in preparation to worship the moon, alluding to his symbolic qualities of prudence, justice, and humility. See Ripa, *Iconologica*, Praz ed. 378.

Other illustrations of Religion in Ripa's *Iconologia* focus on her clothing, with white linen alluding to Religion's purity and chastity. According to Plutarch's book on Isis and Osiris, the religious customs of the Egyptian decreed that no wool object could be found inside the temples or tombs, which is the reason that the deceased was mummified in linen garments. In addition, the personification portrays Religion as a woman covered by a veil and accompanied by a dove, a symbol of the Holy Spirit. The woman sits on a square, stone bench, a symbol of a sacrificial altar as well as the foundation of the church by Christ in Peter (from *pietra*, meaning stone).

24. For Alciato, Honor is that quality acquired freely and voluntarily; an individual received this merit by his virtue. Alciatio's presentation of naked Truth as *nuda veritas* derives from his readings of Horace (*Odes* 1.24.7) on the subject as a symbol of simplicity, sincerity, and the essence of life. See Alciato and Valeriano 788: both humanists combine Faith with Honor, Love, and Truth.

25. In contrast to Alciato, Ripa focuses on the symbolism of Faith as a divine gift rather than as a human attainment. In *Religione* in his *Iconologia*, he differentiates several types of Faith: Christian Faith, Catholic Faith, Friendship Faith, and Marital Faith. The first two types, Christian and Catholic, are religious and are represented with similar attributes - a young woman dressed in white, who wears a helmet and carries a heart or a candle and a book or *Decalogue*. Ripa refers to Pythagoras's and Virgil's comments regarding the contrast between Faith and Blindness, which symbolizes unfaithfulness and lack of illumination. As to the other types of Faith, which are secular and associated with Fidelity, Friendship Faith is usually depicted by a veiled, old woman with extended arms, and Marital Faith is represented by a

young woman dressed in white who holds a ring, a symbol of matrimony. See also Ronchetti 62.

26. Sagredo discusses how the guilds of the arts placed their protection under Justice.

27. This early version of the formula found application in the paintings of the Casa Vasari, as earlier demonstrated in a discussion of the Chamber of Abraham (the house's second painted ceiling) and the east wall of the Chamber of Fortune (third painted room) in Cheney, *The Paintings of the Casa Vasari* 83-86 and 98-106. See also Cheney, "Giorgio Vasari's Chamber of Abraham" 355-80.

28. Vasari studied and sketched Michelangelo's sculpture in the Medici Chapel, learning how to represent semi-reclining personifications, as in the ceiling of the Cornaro Palace. This reclining motif is also present in the Chamber of Fortune of the Casa Vasari, where Vasari repeats the compositional motif of Justice and Patience.

29. Though simplified, the composition and positioning of the figures here are closely related to the personifications in the ceiling of the Cornaro Palace and the Sala dei Cento Giorni. This becomes most evident when one compares the designs of *Faith* (Cornaro Palace) and *Religion* (Sala dei Cento Giorni). Each seated figure inclines her head to the left, extending arms that carry the appropriate attribute. Also, they are similarly attired. Another close association exists between the designs of *Hope* (Cornaro Palace) and *Hope* (Sala dei Cento Giorni). See Cheney, "Giorgio Vasari's Sala dei Cento Giorni" 121-51.

30. In this pioneering article on Aretino's and Vasari's literary ideas, Bertaux clearly postulated this idea at the beginning of the twentieth century.

## Works Cited

Alciato, Andrea. *Emblematum liber*. Lyon, 1549.

Ambrose. Abraham. *Ambrosii opera omnia*. Ed. J. P. Migne. *Patrologia Latina*. Paris, 1844-64.

Aquinas, Thomas. *Summa Theologica*. Ed. P. Caramello. Rome: Marietti, 1948. *Arte Veneta* (1987) 41: 244.

Augustine. *Enchiridion*. Ed. J. P. Migne. *Patrologia Latina*. Paris, 1844-64

Barocchi, Paola. *Complementi al Vasari Pittore*. Florence: Olschki, 1968.

———. "Il Vasari Pittore." *Rinascimento* 7.2 (Dec. 1956): 187-212.

Bertaux, Émile. *Mélanges Bertaux: recueil de travaux: dédié a la mémoire d'Émile Bertaux*. Paris: E. De Boccard, 1924.

Biedermann, Hans. *Dictionary of Symbolism: Cultural Icons and the Meanings Behind Them*. New York: Meridian, 1994.

Cartari, Vincenzo. *Imagine delli Dei de gl'Antichi*. Venice,1556. Ed. Walter Kosachtzky. Graz: Akademische Druck, 1963.

Champeaux, Gérard de., and Dam Sébastien Sterckx. *Introduction au monde des symboles*. Saint-Léger-Vauban, Yonne: Zodiaque. 1966.

Cheney, Liana De Girolami. "Emblematic Approaches in the Paintings of Giorgio Vasari: Justice and Patience." International Conf. On Ages of Life and Learning. University of Minnesota, Minneapolis. 26-28 April 1995.

_____. "Giorgio Vasari's *Astraea*: A Symbol of Justice." *Word and Image*. Forthcoming.

_____. "Giorgio Vasari's Chamber of Abraham: A Religious Ceiling in the Aretine House." *Sixteenth Century Journal* (Fall1987): 355-80.

_____. "Giorgio Vasari's Sala dei Cento Giorni: A Farnese Celebration." *Explorations in Renaissance Culture* 21 (1995): 121-51.

_____. *The Paintings of the Casa Vasari*. New York: Garland. 1985.

_____. "Vasari and Naples: The Monteoliveto Order." *Papers in Art History* 5 (1994): 48-126.

_____. "Vasari's *Patience*: The Measure of Time." *The Inspiration of Astronomical Phenomena*. Raymond E. White, ed. Sarasota, FLA: OTS Foundation P, 2000. 13-23.

Chevalier, Jean, and Alain Gheerbrant. *A Dictionary of Symbols*. Trans. John Buchanan-Brown. Oxford; Cambridge, MA: Blackwell, 1994.

Clement, Clara Erskine. *The Queen of the Adriatic*. Boston: Erstes and Lauriat, 1893.

Colasanti, Arduino. "Il memoriale de Baccio Bandinelli." *Repertorium für Kumstwissenschaft* 28 (1905): 406-43.

Cooper, Jean C. *An Illustrated Encyclopaedia of Traditional Symbols*. New York: Thames and Hudson, 1987.

Daly, Peter M., Virginia W. Callahan, and Simon H. Cuttler, ed. *Andreas Alciatus*. 2 vol. Toronto: U of Toronto P. 1985.

del Vita, Alessandro, ed. *Lo Zibaldone di Giorgio Vasari*. Opere inedite o rare di storia

dell'arte. Rome: Istituto d'archeologica e storia dell'arte, 1938.

Ferguson, George. *Signs and Symbols in Christian Art*. New York: Oxford UP, 1966.

Florentii (Florentius Schoonhovius). *Emblemata Florentii Schoonhovii I. C. Goudani:*

*Partim moralia, partim etiam civilia. Cum latiori eorundem ejusdem auctoris interetatione*. Goudæ, Apud Andream Burier, 1618.

Frey, Karl, and Herman Walther Frey, ed. *Der literariche Nachlass Giorgio*

*Vasaris.* 2 vol. Munich: Georg Müller, 1923-1930.

Gombrich, Ernest H. "Icones Symbolicae. Philosophies of Symbolism and their Bearing on Art." *Symbolic Images: Studies in the Art of the Renaissance.* London: Phaidon, 1978. 123-99.

Hall, James. *Dictionary of Subjects and Symbols in Art.* Icon editions. New York: Harper and Row, 1974.

Härb, Florian. "Modes and Models in Vasari's Early Drawing Oeuvre." *Vasari's Florence: Artists and Literati at the Medicean Court.* Ed. Phillip Joshua. Cambridge: Cambridge Up, 1998. 83-110.

Horace. *Odes.* Baltimore: Penguin Classics, 1970.

Levin, William R. "The Iconography of Charity Redux: The Origins of Two Little-Known Symbols for *Amor proximi* in Fifteenth-Century Italian Art." *Fifteenth Century Studies* 20 (1993), 118-25.

Macrobius. *Commentary on the Dream of Scipio.* Ed. W. H. Stahl. New York: Columbia UP, 1990.

Monbeig-Goguel, Catherine. *Vasari et Son Temps.* Vol. 1 of *Musée National du Louvre, Paris.* Cabinet des dessins: Inventaire général des dessins italiens. Dir. Roseline Bacou. Ed. Catherine Monbeig-Goguel and Françoise Viatte. Paris: Ed des Musées nationaux, 1972.

Olson, Roberta. "The Perfection of the Circle: Florentine Tondi and Neoplatonism." *Neoplatonism in the Arts.* Liana De Girolami, ed. New York/London: The Edwin Mellen Press, 2003.

Petrarch (Francesca Petrarca). *Africa.* Ed. N. Festa. Florence: Sansoni, 1926.

Plato. *Republic.* Oxford: Oxford UP, 1998.

_____. *Symposium.* Oxford: Oxford UP, 1999.

Pliny. *Natural History.* Ed. Jex-Blake Sellers. *The Elder Pliny's Chapters on the History of Art.* Chicago: Ares P, 1976.

Ripa, Cesare. *Icologia, overo descittione d'imagini delle virtv', vitij, affetti, passioni humane, corpi celesti, mondo e sue parti.* Padua: P. P. Tozzi, 1611. Ed. Mario Praz. Milan: Thea, 1992.

_____. *Iconologia: overo descrittione di diverse imagini cavate dall'antichità, e di propia inventione.* Rome, 1603. Ed. Erna Mandowski. Hildesheim; New York: G. Olms, 1970.

Ronchetti, Giuseppe. *Dizionario ilustrato dei simbloi: simboili, emblemi, atriburi, imagini degli Dei, ecc.* Manuali Hoepli. Milan: Ulrico Hoepli, 1922.

Sagredo. Agostino. *Sulle consorterie delle arte edificative in Venezia: studi storici con documenti inediti.* Venice: P. Naratovich, 1856.

Schiffhorst, Gerald J., ed. *The Triumph of Patience: Medieval and Renaissance Studies.* Orlando, FL: U Presses of Florida, 1978.

Schulz, Juergen. "Vasari at Venice." *Burlington Magazine* 103 (1961): 500-11.

_____. *Venetian Painted Ceiling of the Renaissance.* Berkeley: U of California P. 1968.

Valeriano, Giovanni Pierio. *Hieroglyphica, sive De sacris Aegyptiorum literis commentarii.* Basileæ, 1556.

Vasari, Giorgio. *Le vite de' più eccellenti pittori, scultori ed architettori.* Ed. Gaetano Milanesi. 9 vols. Florence: G. C. Sansoni, 1906.

Wind, Edgar. "Platonic Tyranny and the Renaissance Fortuna." *The Eloquence of Symbols: Studies in Humanist Art.* Ed. Jaynie Anderson. Rev. ed. Oxford: Clarendon, 1993. 86-96.

Wittkower, Rudolf. "Patience and Change: The Story of a Political Emblem." *Journal of the Warburg and Courtauld Institutes* (1937-38): 171-77.

Zorzi, Alvise. *Venetian Palaces.* New York: Rizzoli, 1989.

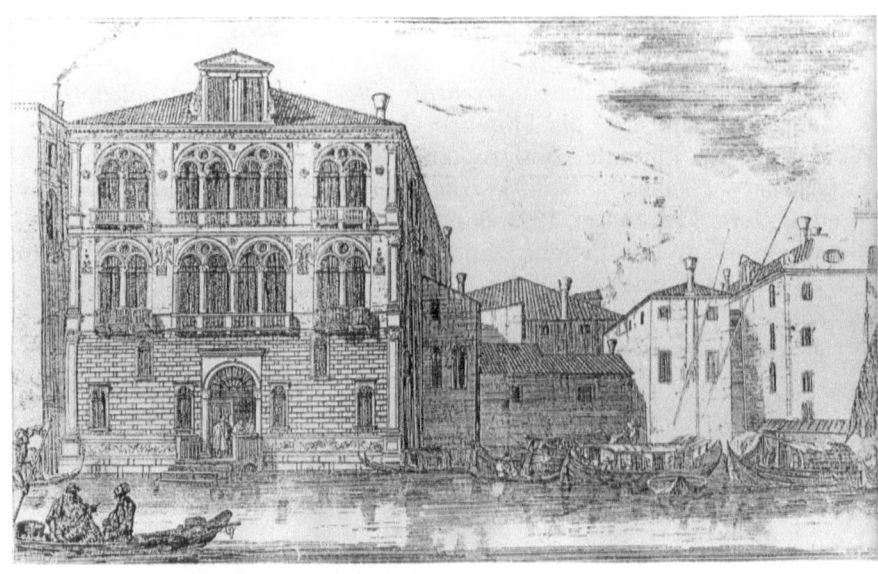

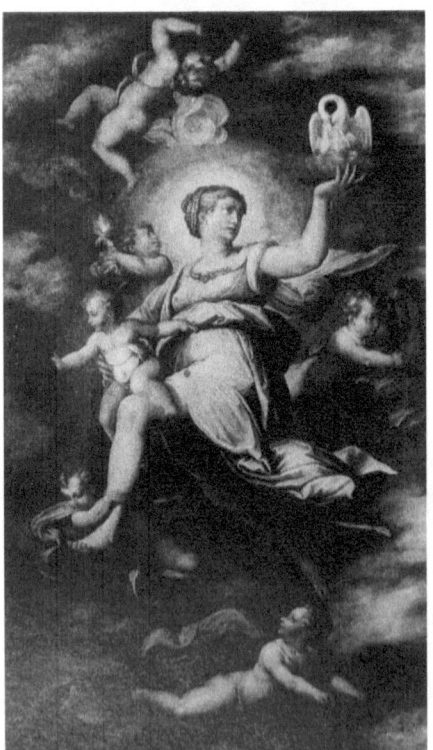

Fig. 1.  Michele Sanmichele and Mauro Cadusso, *Palazzo Cornaro*, 1540. Canal Grande, Venice, engraving by Lucas Carlevarijs, 1703.

Fig. 2. Giorgio Vasari, *Charity*, 1542, oil. Museo della Società Gallarantese per gli Studi Patri (Inv. 586). Photo: Museo della Società Gallarantese.

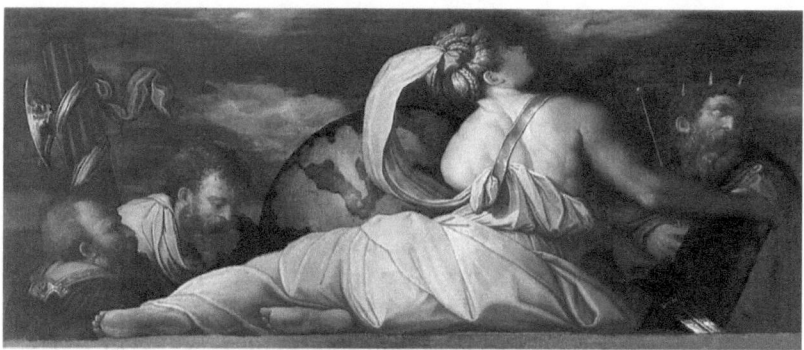

Fig. 3. Giorgio Vasari, *Justice*, 1542, (det of ceiling), oil. Venice, Corner-Spinelli Palace . Present Location: Accademia, Venice.

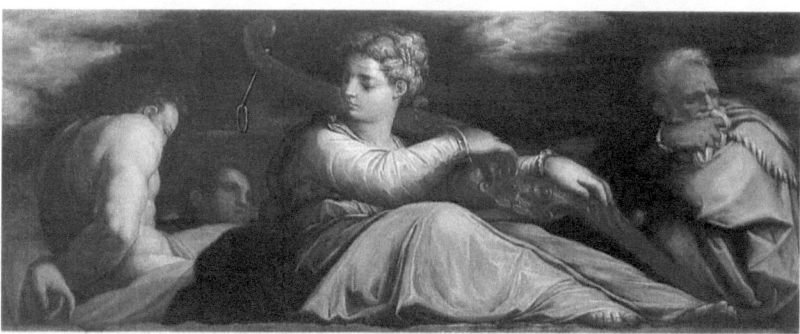

Fig. 4. Giorgio Vasari, *Patience*, 1542, (det of ceiling), oil. Venice, Corner-Spinelli Palace. Present Location: Accademia, Venice.

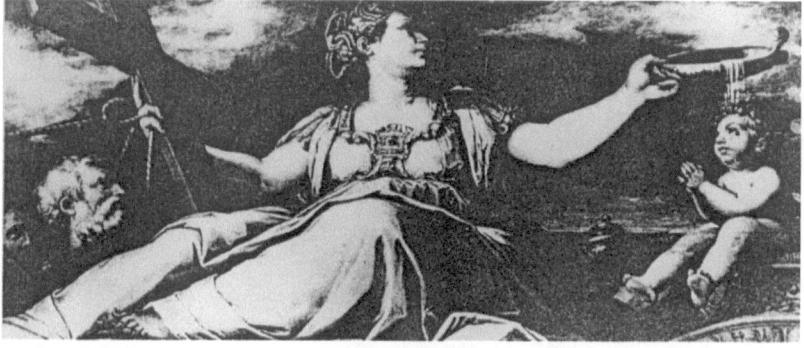

Fig. 5. Giorgio Vasari, *Faith*, 1542, (det of ceiling), oil. Venice, Corner-Spinelli Palace. Present Location: Private Collection, London.

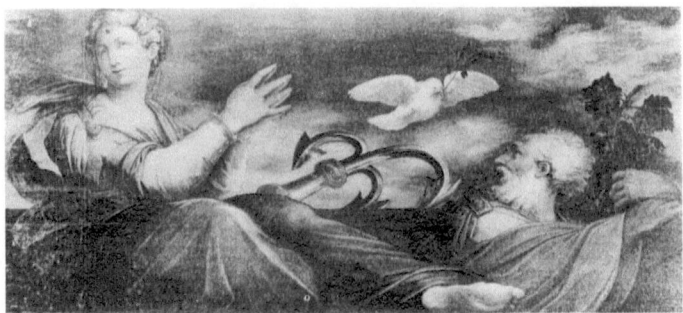

Fig. 6. Giorgio Vasari, *Hope*, 1542, (det of ceiling), oil. Venice, Corner-Spinelli Palace. Present Location: Collection of G. Weidenfeld, London.

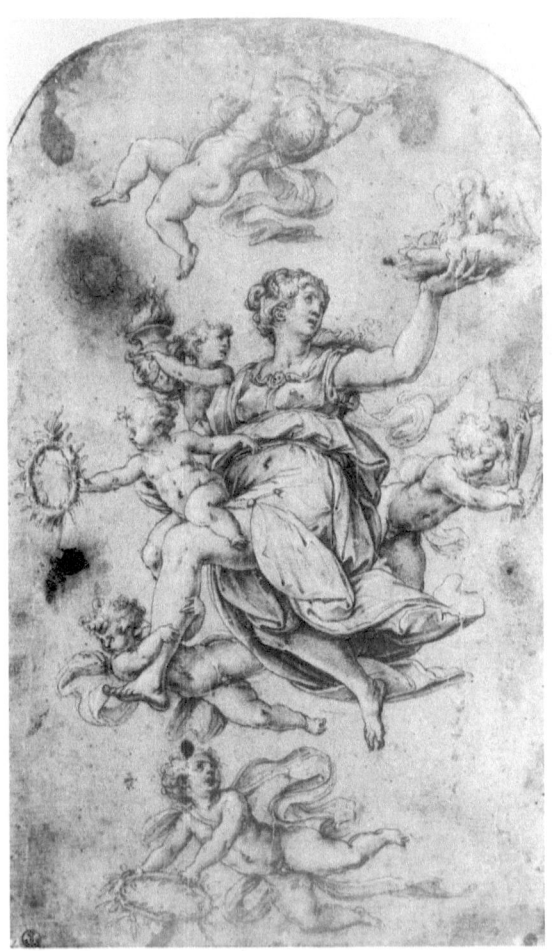

Fig. 7. Giorgio Vasari, *Charity*, 1542, drawing. Florence, Uffizi, Gabinetto Disegni e Stampe (Inv. 1071S). Photo: Gabinetto Disegni e Stampe della Galleria degli Uffizi, Florence.

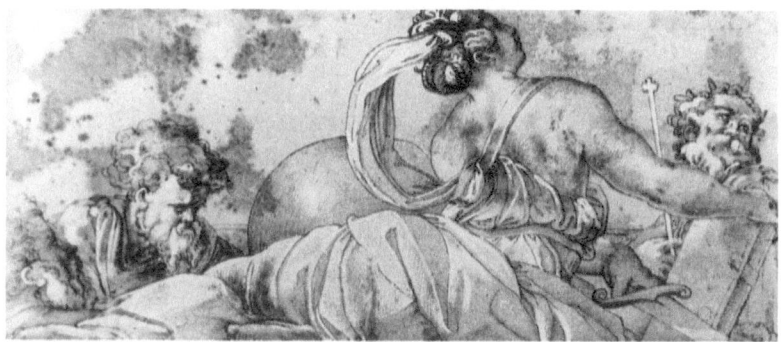

Fig. 8.   Giorgio Vasari, *Justice*, 1542, drawing. Haarlem Teylerstiching (N K94). Photo: Teylerstiching, Haarlem.

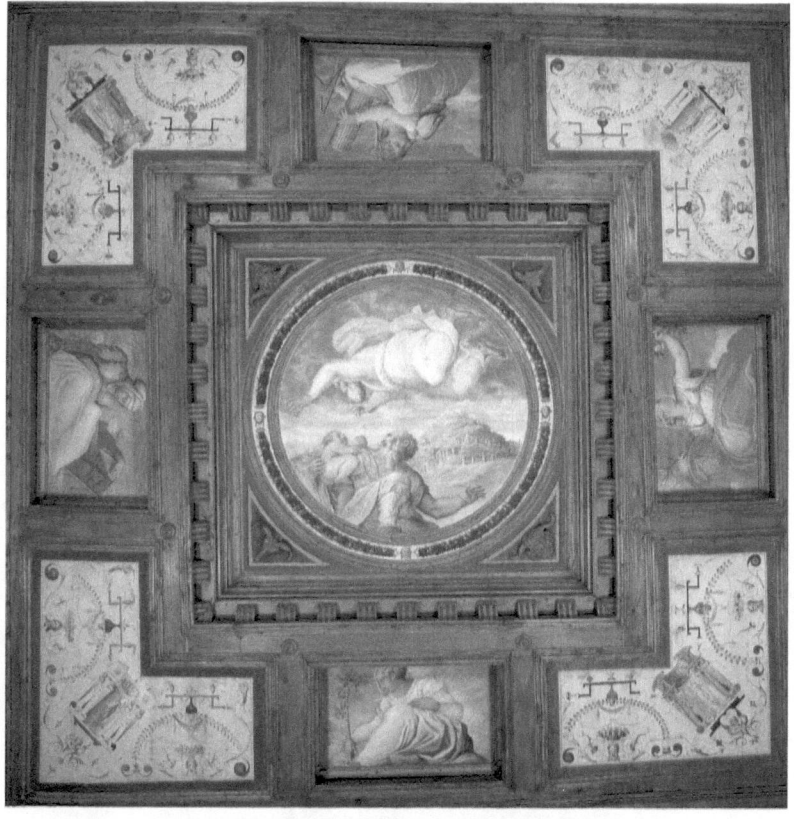

Fig. 9. Giorgio Vasari, Ceiling of Abraham, 1548, tempera. Arezzo, Casa Vasari. Chamber of Abraham.

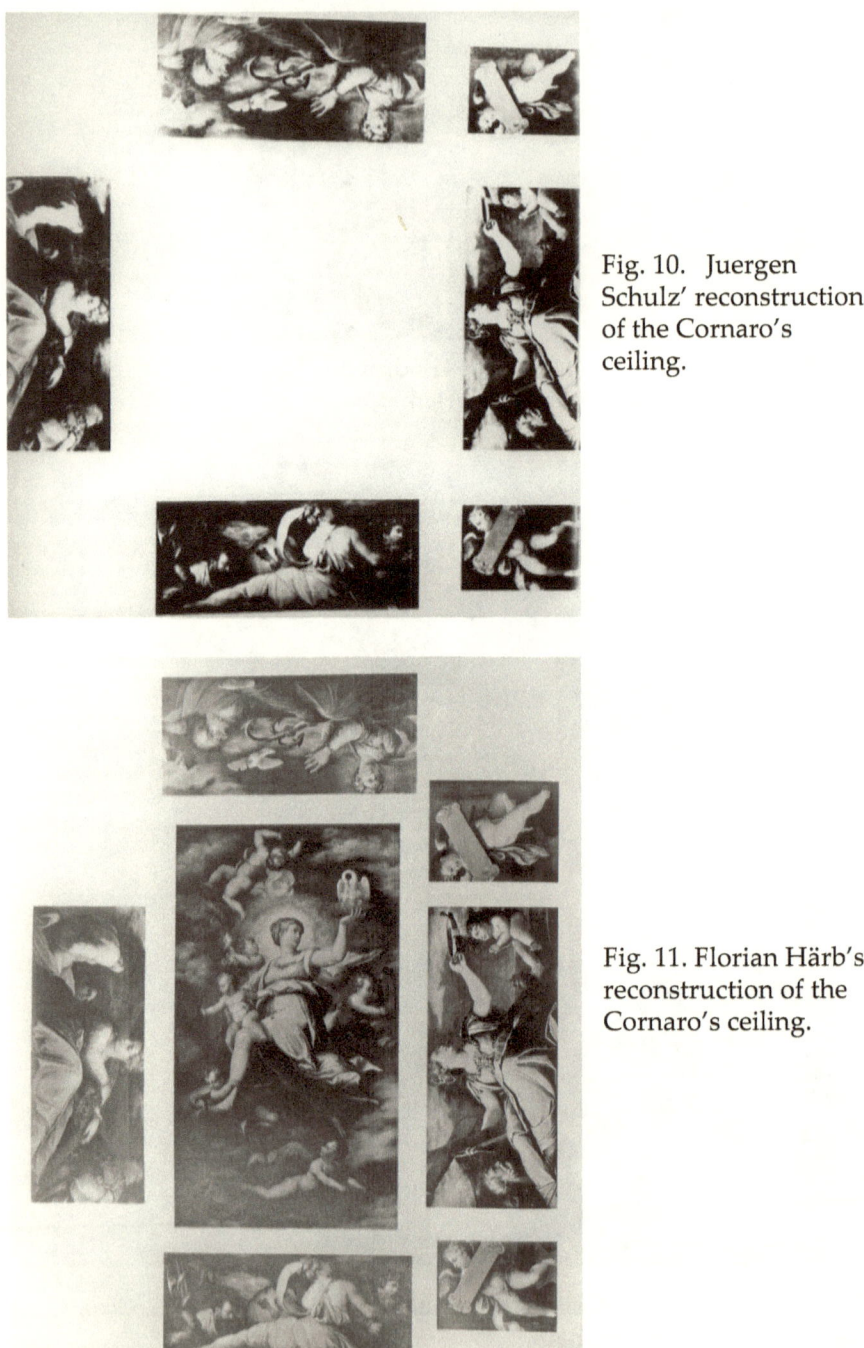

Fig. 10.   Juergen Schulz' reconstruction of the Cornaro's ceiling.

Fig. 11. Florian Härb's reconstruction of the Cornaro's ceiling.

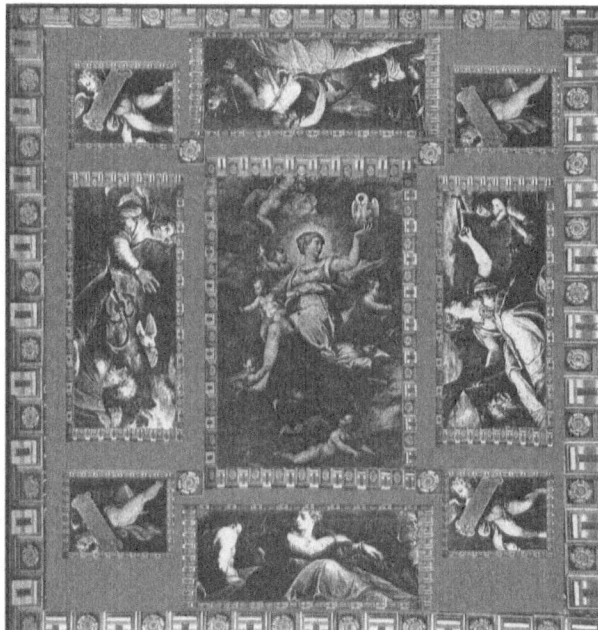

Fig. 12. Cheney's reconstruction A of the Cornaro's ceiling.

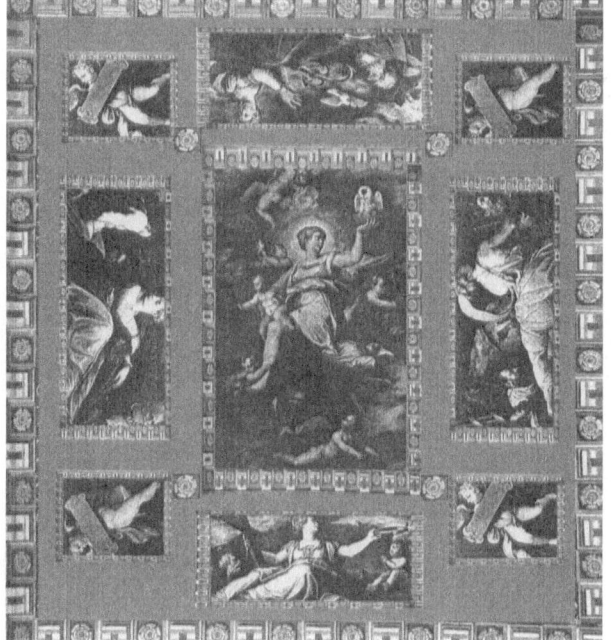

Fig. 13. Cheney's reconstruction B of the Cornaro's ceiling.

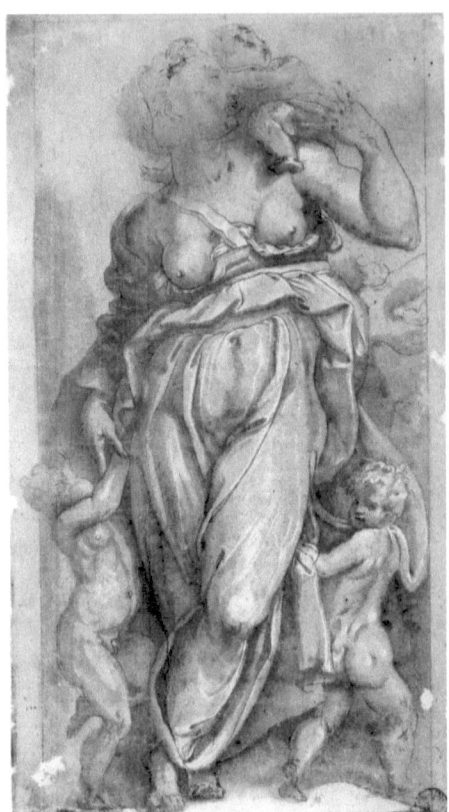

Fig. 14. Giorgio Vasari, *Charity*, 1545, drawing. Bologna, Gabinetto dei Disegni e delle Stampe (Inv. 1613). Photo: Gabinetto dei Disegni e delle Stampe, Bologna.

Fig. 15. Giorgio Vasari, *Charity*, 1545, fresco. Arezzo, Casa Vasari, Chamber of Fortune.

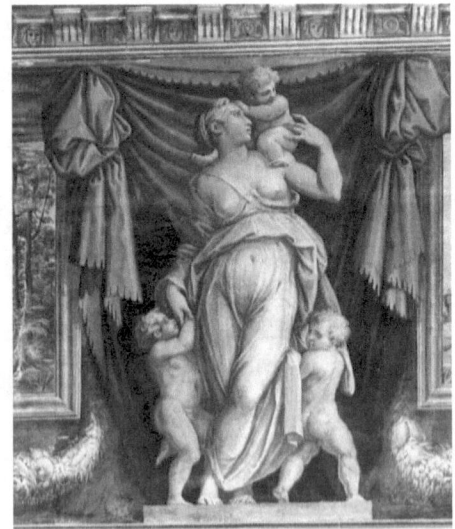

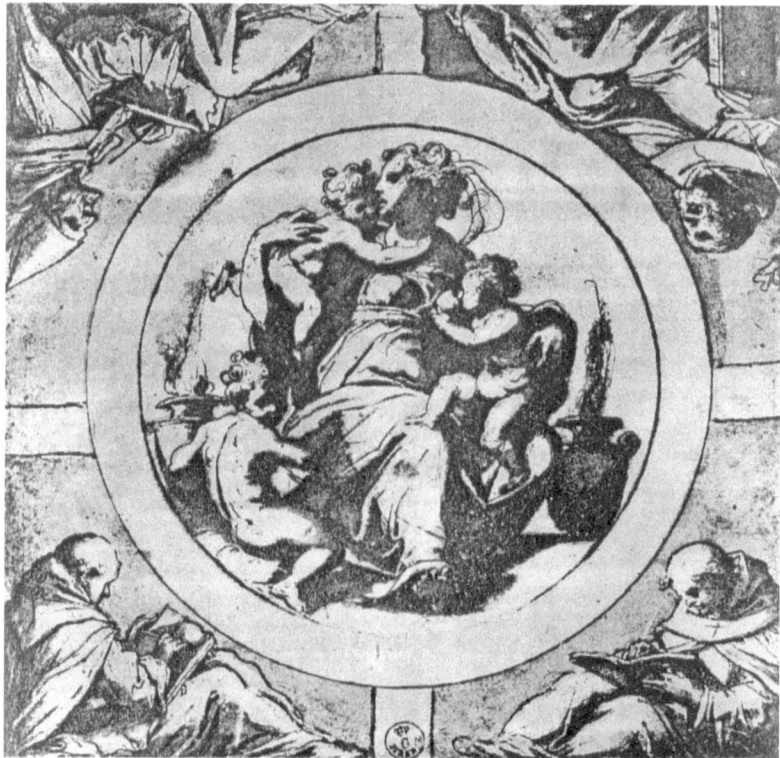

Fig. 16.Giorgio Vasari, *Charity*, 1570, drawing. Florence, Uffizi, Gabinetto Disegni e Stampe (Inv. 1187E). Photo: Gabinetto Disegni e Stampe della Galleria degli Uffizi, Florence.

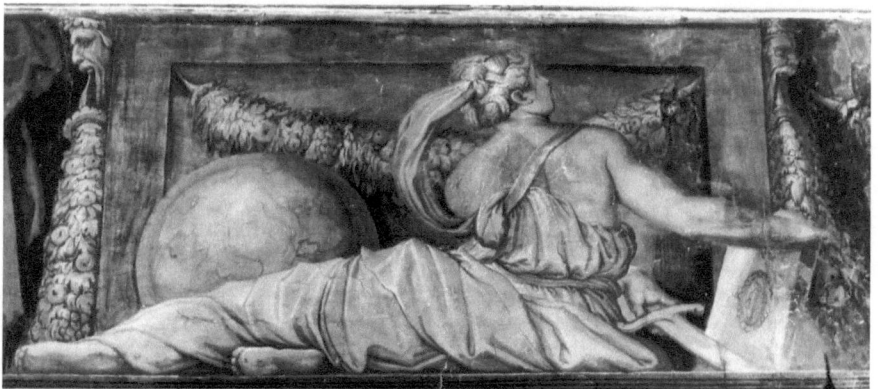

Fig. 17. Giorgio Vasari, *Justice*, 1548, fresco. Arezzo, Casa Vasari, Chamber of Fortune.

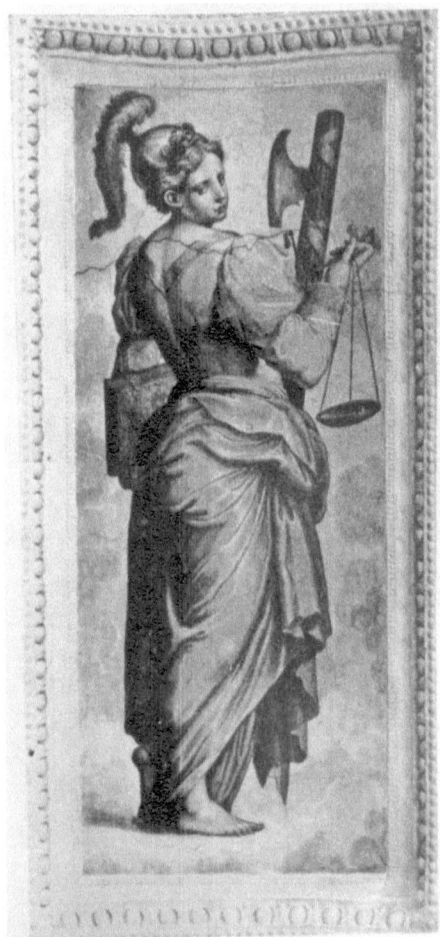

Fig. 18. Giorgio Vasari, *Justice*, 1545, fresco. Refectory of Monteoliveto, Naples.

Fig. 19. Andrea Alciato, *Emblem IX*, engraving, *Emblematum liber* (Lyon 1549).

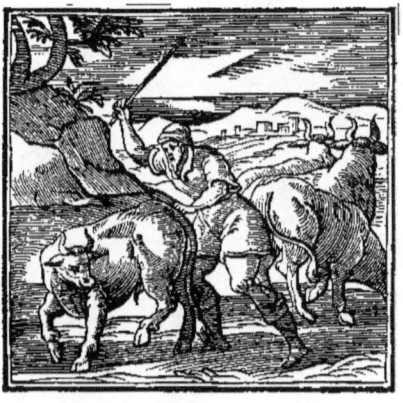

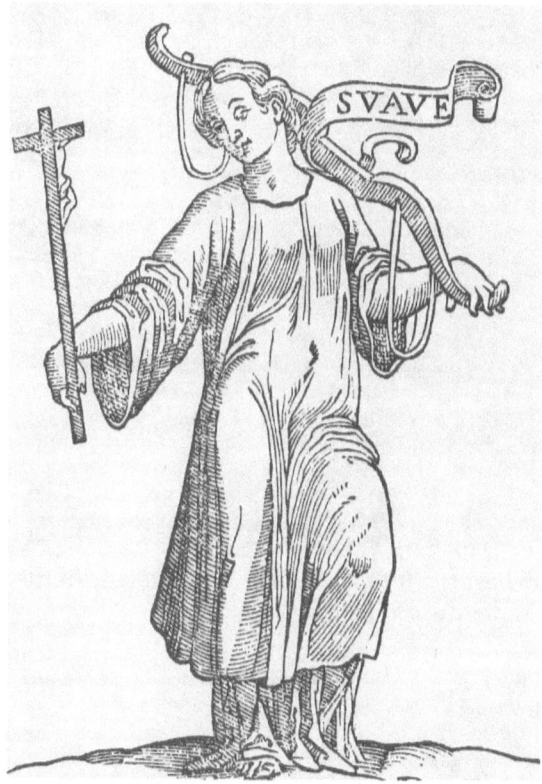

Fig. 20. Cesare Ripa, *Patience,* engraving, Iconologia (Rome, 1603).

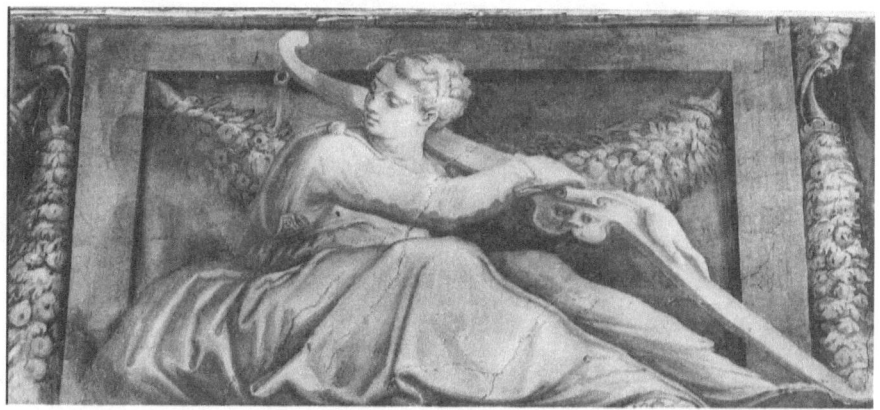

Fig. 21. Giorgio Vasari, *Patience,* 1548, fresco. Arezzo, Casa Vasari, Chamber of Fortune.

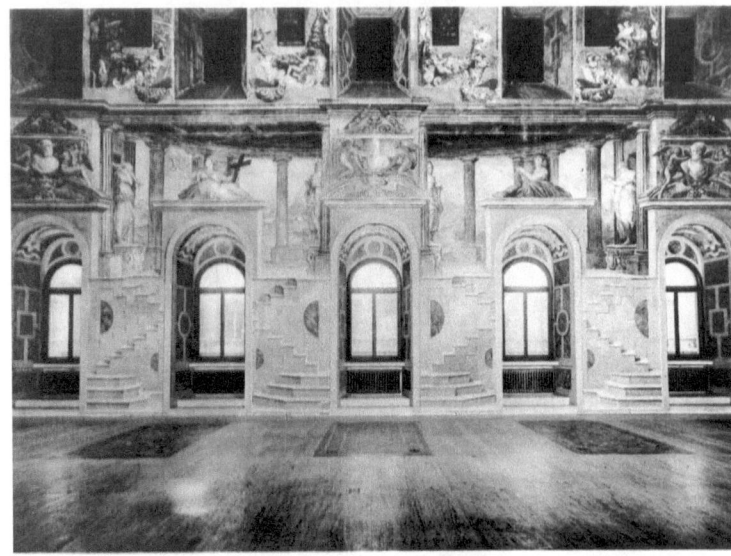

Fig. 22. Giorgio Vasari, *Hope and Faith*, 1546, fresco. Rome, Palazzo della Cancelleria, Sala dei Cento Giorni.

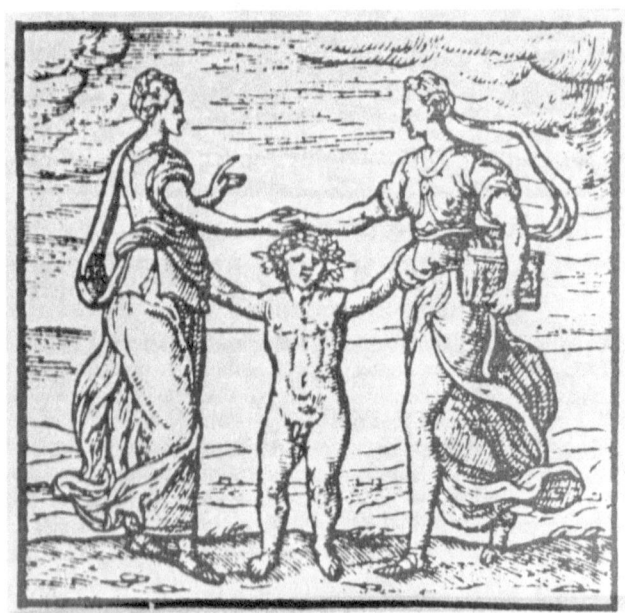

Fig. 23. Andrea Alciato, *Emblem XXXIV*, engraving, *Emblematum liber* (Lyon 1549).

# 5

# Vasari and Naples:
# The Monteolivetan Order*

Giorgio Vasari (1511-1574), Florentine painter, architect, and writer, is best known for his *Lives of the Most Excellent Painters, Sculptors and Architects*, which was first published in 1550 and again, in an enlarged edition in 1568, illustrated with woodcuts of artists' portraits (Fig. 1-1).[1] By virtue of this work, he is known as "the first art historian." Vasari wrote with a definite philosophy of art and art history. He believed that art is in the first instance, an imitation of nature and that progress in painting consists of perfecting the means of such representation. At the same time, Vasari accepted the belief of Italian Humanism that these means had been taken to a high level of perfection in classical antiquity, that art had passed through a period of decline in the Middle Ages, and that it had been revived and set once more on its true path by Giotto. The main theme of *The Lives* sets forth the revival of the true art in Tuscany by Giono and Cimabue, records its steady progress in the hands of such artists as Ghiberti, Brunelleschi, and Donatello, and examines its culmination with Michelangelo, Leonardo, and Raphael, living artists in whom this progress had finally reached its "summit of perfection."[2] In the first edition, the apex was reached in Michelangelo, whose biography represented the only life of a living artist. Although Vasari 's accuracy has often been refuted on particular points, *The Lives* remains one of the most important sources for the period it covers and is also an invaluable document for the outlook on aesthetics and art history that prevailed in the sixteenth century.

Vasari's book is the first comprehensive work on art history, in that its introduction discusses the techniques of art, its prefaces explain the theories of art from the antique to the contemporary, and the biographies illustrate the historical development of the individual artists' accomplishments. Vasari's purpose was to provide for his fellow artist historical perspective and artistic guidance. These two significant issues are evident in Vasari's explanation of the concept of *rebirth* which combines the idea of progress with that of moral intention. His idea of progress is manifested in his examination of the inevitable pattern of change from imperfection to perfection in the arts - an artistic canon. And his concept of moral intention is reflected in his religious paintings and is related to the Cinquecento idea of the spirit of history, which fulfills its real purpose by inspiring individuals to be prudent and showing them how to live.

By focusing on one aspect of Vasari' s artistic career - the refectories - we can best understand the impact of his art in the sixteenth century. Giorgia Vasari's refectories provide an interesting insight, in general, into the sixteenth-century taste for the decoration of the dining hall, or *cenacoli* and, in particular, into the patronage of the Monteolivetan order, which commissioned the Bolognese and Neapolitan refectories. Numerous studies discuss the importance of the *cenacoli* in the fourteenth and fifteenth centuries,[3] and usually these investigations center on the painted scene of the Last Supper. For the sixteenth century, however, no studies exist specifically addressing the structure and subject of the rcfectories.[4]

The refectory or *cenacolo* serves as a dining hall. Members of a religious order meet at certain times of the day to share their meals. Previous to the commissions of Vasari, the dining hall was decorated with fresco paintings of the Last Supper or Crucifixion such as the well-known Milanese refectory of S. Maria delle Grazie by Leonardo, and the S. Croce *Cenacolo* in Florence.[5]

This study centers on Vasari's artistic endeavors for the refectories of the Monteolivetan order in Bologna (1539-1541) and in particular, in Naples (1544-1545). The salience of these religious commissions for the Monteolivetan order is expressed by the way Vasari applies his art historical, philosophical, and critical ideas to painting: first, by his discussion and explanation, in his writing for the commissions, the role of their patronage, the participation of other artists in the completion of the refectories, and his revelation of what were his own contributions to the successful completion of their commissions. Second, by his commentary on the condilion and renovation intended for the refectories, as well as his judgment of their artistic merit. Moreover, as an architect and painter, Vasari contributes to the investigation and expansion of his own artistic quest and avant-garde style – *maniera*.[6] According to Sydney Freedberg, Vasari's "mature style helped to shape the major course of art historical events in Rome and Florence, and in lesser artistic places [*as in Bologna and Naples*] changed the history of the local school."[7] Recent studies on the development of Neapolitan art in the Cinquecento clearly demonstrate the impact of Vasari's refinement and inventiveness in painting, as well as the spread of the *maniera* in southern Italy.[8]

With Giorgio Vasari we are fortunate in the examination of this topic, since he was commissioned to decorate several refectories during his early mature artistic period (1540s-1550s), in several Italian cities: S. Michele in Bosco in Bologna (1539-1541; Fig. 1-2), S. Anna di Monteoliveto (S. Anna del Lombardi) in Naples (1544-1545; Fig. 1-3), the Monastery of the Murate in Florence (1546; Figs. 1-4 and 1-5), the Badia of SS. Flora and Lucilla in Arezzo (1548; Figs. 1-6 to I-8), and the Serristori Hospital in Figline (1550s).

As varied as the commissions of Giorgio Vasari's refectories are, so are the religious representations depicted on the supper themes. The traditional theme of the Last Supper appears in the Refectory of the Monastery of the Mutate of 1546 in Florence[9] and in the Refectory of the Serristori Hospital of the 1550s in Figline. In both of these examples, the refectories functioned as dining halls for nuns. As to be expected in these *cenacoli*, a more conventional imagery was selected, probably due to its type of patronage - a female and poor religious order having limited funds and an imposed religious structure. In these *cenacoli*, Vasari follows stylistically the *maniera* treatment of figures, interior space, and overall compositional decoration. Similar observations can be made from his representations of the Last Supper in predella panels for large altarpieces, such as the *Last Supper* for the Camaldoli Pala of 1539, or for small devotional panels such as that of the *Last Supper* at the Troyes Musee de

Beaux-Arts et d'Archeologie (Fig. 1-9), and the one at the Walters Art Gallery in Baltimore, both probably executed in the early 1540s (Fig. 1-10). Further analysis of the depiction of these examples of the Last Supper shows some interesting common changes. For example, in the small devotional panels the composition consists of a simple domestic interior displaying only a few culinary objects (wine jugs and large plates) primarily dominated by a circular table where the apostles and Christ sit in close proximity around it. In this depiction, Vasari intentionally conveys a strong sense of intimacy in the scene. In contrast, the *cenacoli* for the Murate represents a monumental evocation of the event. In a palatial interior, Christ and the apostles dine comfortably seated along a rectangular table which has been lavishly garnished with an elaborate meal. Vasari's composition, here, obviously illustrates the post-Leonardesque impact on Italy. For his last refectory commission on the subject of a supper, Vasari painted his most lavish representation of a biblical feast, *The Marriage of Esther and Ahasuerus* (signed and dated *Georgius Vasarius Aretinus Faciebat A. D. MDXLIX*).[10] This majestic picture for the refectory of the Badia SS. Flora e Lucilla in Arezzo was executed on site because of its impressive physical size (289 x 745 cm; Figs. 1-6 to 1-8)). Unfortunately, it was moved several times from the refectory, and at present the painting is located in the Museo Statale di Arte Medievale e Moderna in Arezzo. Vasari executed numerous drawings for this painting which can be found in Frankfurt and the Gabinetto dei Disegni e delle Stampe at the Uffizi (numbers 719E. 647F aod 649F).[11] The banquet scene takes place in a luxurious interior where magnificently dressed figures participate in the wedding celebration. For the architectural setting, grouping of figures, figure types, *maniera* treatment of the figures, and display of ornamental objects (vases), Vasari quotes and borrows from his previous paintings on this theme, such as *Christ in the House of Martha and Mary* (1539) and *The Feast of St. Gregory* (1539), both painted for the refectory of S. Michele in Bosco in Bologna, and *The Fall of the Manna* (1544) and *Christ in the House of Simon* (1544), both painted for the refectory of S. Anna di Monteoliveto in Naples. In the *The Marriage of Esther and Ahasuerus*, Vasari culminates his quest for the creation of a supper theme with *maniera* conceits.

In contrast Vasari's refectories for the Monteolivetan order challenged this conventional thematic tradition by decorating the walls and the ceiling with religious themes not based on the Crucifixion and the Last Supper but on such prototypes for the Last Supper theme as *Abraham ond the Three Angels* or *Abraham's Feast, Christ in the House of Martha and Mary, The Feast of St. Gregory, The Fall of the Manna, Christ in the House of Simon,* and *The Marriage of Esther and Ahasuerus.*

Luckily Vasari designed not one refectory for the Monteolivetan order, but two. The first, dated 1539, is located in the convent of S. Michele in Bosco (now Instituto Ortopedico Rizzoli) in Bologna;[12] the other, executed in 1545, is in the church of S. Anna di Monteo-livelo (or S. Anna dei Lombardi) in Naples.[13]

In these refectories Vasari visualized an iconography predicated on the instructions of the Monteolivetan order.[14] The artist rendered tangibly and visually the order's concept of monastic living, that is to say, the "monks seek to be like Christ an icon or an image of God's beauty, and the monastery is that quiet place where the work can be perfected - a kind of *atelier* of the soul."[15]

A few comments on the Monteolivetan order will guide us to an understanding of the iconography of the refectories as well as to Giorgio Vasari's *invenzioni* and resolutions for the commissions. The Monteolivetan order was founded in 1319 in the *contando* of Montalcino, diocese of Arezzo, by Bernardo Tolomei, senator of Siena, Ambrogio Piccolomini, and Patrizio Patrizzi.[16] They called themselves *I Bianchi* (The White Ones) because of the white cloaks they wore as a symbol of monastic life.[17] The Monteolivetan order was part of the Benedictine order. St. Benedict of Norcia (Umbria, c. 480 - c. 547), founder of the Benedictine order, wrote the *Holy Rule* (Rule of the Monks), published in Venice in 1505, as *Speculum Monachorum.*[18] This book provides an understanding of the monastic vows of chastity, obedience, and poverty as well as the purpose of the Monteolivetan refectories. It compares "the cloister's life to an artist's workshop, concerning the whole life of monks as a creative process."[19]

The *Holy Rule* further informs us what types of meals should be served during different times on the church calendar - during lent, and on days of fasting as well as regular days. It discusses what kind of food should be eaten; namely, bread, fresh vegetables and fruits (figs, pears, apples), as well as limited amounts of meat and wine. The chapter on temperance advises that wine should be consumed in moderation: "Il vino fa traviare anche ai saggi, non bere fino la sazieta (wine makes even the wise fall away, then drink sparingly and only to satiety)."[20]

In 1535, Don Miniato Pitti became abbot of the Monteolivetan order in Pistoia, and Vasari's palron.[21] It was he who was responsible for Vasari's receiving the commission to decorate both refectories, and who provided the iconography for S. Michele in Bosco.[22] Together with Filippo Serragli, abbot of S. Michele, Don Miniato encouraged patronage for Giorgio Vasari.

According to Francesco Malaguzzi·Valeri, Cardinal Androvino della Torre of Bologna gave to the (Monte) Olivetan order the Church of S. Michele in Bosco in 1364.[23] "Originally," Albana Sorbelli slates, "the Church of San Michele in *bosco* (so called because it was surrounded by a forest), was built on top of the ruins of a pagan deity by S. Basilio, bishop of Bologna in 1368."[24]

Pasquale Carbonara, in *Archittetura Pratica*, discusses the architecture of monasteries in the Cinquecento. He explains that the refectory was always located opposite the church, was usually of rectangular shape, and was situated parallel to the church.[25] The kitchen was placed close to the refectory, but away from the church, in order to keep the odors from disturbing the monks at their religious functions. The *lavabo* was also located close to the refectory in an ædicule of the cloister, which in turn was placed at the south end of the church, for protection from cold weather.[26] Usually two refectories were recommended in the design of a monastery: one for the abbot, and the other for the monks. If a guest was invited he ate with the abbot; if there was not a guest, the abbot would invite one or two monks to share his meal.[27]

The Monteolivetan monasteries present a good example of Carbonara's description of sixteenth century monastic architecture. The Bolognese Monteolivetan monastery was enlarged several times between 1398 and 1523. Cristoforo Tibaldo (Tibaldo Tibaldi) designed the architecture for the dormitory and refectory in 1523. The *Libri delle Fabbriche degli Olivetani di San Michele in Bosco* reports: "In December of 1540 also the work on the refectory is completed by Cristoforo Tibaldo who had plastered and painted it... Now the refectory, next to the dormitory, the most spacious of the building (*convent*) awaits only the decoration of Vasari and his assistants."[28]

Johann Fichard, a sixteenth-century writer describing Bologna and its surroundings, comments upon "the beauty of the location of San Michele in Bosco as well as the magnificent library and refectory where we see the beautiful paintings done by Vasari."[29]

Vasari received the commission in 1539, which consisted of painting (biblical and religious) subjects for three large oil paintings (located at the end of the refectory), a frescoed frieze (along the walls) with *grotteschi* decoration in each lunette consisting of a story from the Apocalypse (framed with landscape scenes from the monasteries of the Monteolivetan order), and (further to paint) the borders of eight large windows in tempera with festoons and fruits.[30] With his assistants, he began painting in the spring of 1541, and continued through the fall of 1541, completing it before December, when he went to Venice. In his autobiography Vasari writes that he had completed the Bolognese commission of three oil paintings and frescoed frieze decoration in eight months, "being employed in 1539 to do three panels in oils, with a frieze, and twenty subjects of the Apocalypse in small figures, the monasteries of the order, grotesques and festoons for the monks of Monteolivetan, in their monastery of San Michele in Bosco, outside Bologna, at the end of a refectory."[31] His assistants were Stefano Veltroni (Vasari's cousin), Giambattista Cungi, and Cristofano Gherardi.[32] Amusingly, we observe that some of the grotesque masks supporting the elegant festoons, in the lower decorative section of window frames, have been purposely replaced with male heads. Could these male heads be the portraits of Vasari's assistants, and could the Uffizi sketch of a mask (no. 93727) by Gherardi be a self-portrait? (cf. Figs. 1-19 and 1-20).[33]

The refectory of S. Michele in Bosco is rectangular, approximately 500 feet long by 160 feet across, with a barrel vaulted ceiling. Tbe south and north walls contain four large windows, and below them is a broken frieze of approximately three feet in height with nine rectangles. Each rectangle contains an *ovato* painted *al fresco* with scenes of the Apocalypse, flanked by two square *vedute* of the Monteolivetan monasteries throughout Italy. *Grotteschi* decorate the scenes and frame of the rectangular frieze. The west wall contains three oil paintings - *Abraham and The Three Angels, Christ in the House of Martha and Mary,* and *The Feast of St. Gregory* - and below them are two friezes. The entrance is on the east wall, and two friezes frame the door. Above the doorway Andrea Alciatio's inscription honors Vasari and his work:

> Octonis mensibus opus ab Aretino Georgio
> pictum, non yam
> praecio, quam amicorum obsequio et honoris
> voto, anno 1539
> Philippus Serralius pon. curavit.[34]

The commission called for three oil paintings and a frescoed frieze for the decoration of the refectory.[35] The three paintings were (1) *Abraham and the Three Angels* or *The Feast of Abraham*, which is no longer there.[36] Vasari designed several preparatory drawings for this subject which are now located in the Gabinetto dei Disegni e delle Stamfe at the Uffizi in Florence (no. l192E; Fig. 1-11),[37] and in the Musée Wicar at Lille (no. 47; Fig. l-12).[38] And most recently, I found another drawing, probably the first design for this commission with a simplified rendition of the theme in a Boston private collection (Fig. 1-13).[39] (2) *Christ in the House of Martha and Mary* is *in situ* (Fig. 1-14).[40] A drawing for this painting can be found in the Cabinet des Dessins at the Louvre (RF92; Fig. 1-15).[41] The drawing differs from the painting in its conception of space, substituting a flat area for the background scene. The influence of Andrea del Sarto and Pontormo is obvious in Vasari's treatment of figures - gestures, movement of the body and idealized expressions. (3) *The Feast of St. Gregory* signed *Giorgio Aretino Faceva MDXXXX* (the only signed work for this commission) was moved in 1805 to the Pinacoleca of Bologna where it slill hangs today (Fig. 1-16).[42] Only a small drawing at the Uffizi, probably sketched by Vasari for his assistants to follow can be connected with this painting (Fig. 1-17).[43] This drawing is the only one known for this painting; however, more significantly, it partially illustrates the frieze's elaborate decorations that frame the scenes with festoons, masks, and theatrical curtains seen rhythmically repeated along the wall frieze of the refectory. The painting of *The Feast of St. Gregory* reflects the influence of Raphael's *Pope Leo with his Nephews* of 1515 in the Pitti Palace. Vasari's St. Gregory is portrayed in the likeness of Pope Clement VII, and Duke Alessandro's portrait can be seen in the man standing behind St. Gregory. In *The Life of Cristofano Gherardi*, Vasari describes how Gherardi painted the still-life objects on the table with lively naturalism.[44] Vasari writes in his autobiography that these three paintings hung side by side on the top wall of the refectory (west wall), where *Christ in the House of Martha and Mary* is presenlly located.

The frescoed frieze contains a background of *grotteschi* decorations, probably executed by Vasari's assistants, but mainly by Cristofano Gherardi.[45] In its center *ovati* illustrate scenes from the Apocalypse: *The Angel with the Key of the Bouomless Pit, The Vision of the Heavenly Jerusalem. St. John before God and the Elders, St. John Devouring the Book (10: 1-2), The Apocalyptic Whore (12: 1), The Babylonian Whore (18: 21), The Beast with Two Horns Like a Lamb (XIII. 11), The Avenging Angels (9: 15-16), Four Angels holding the Winds (7: I), The Vision of the Seven Candlesticks (1: 8; 18), The Shower of Flames, Angel with the Stone (18: 21), The Beast Rising from the Earth (13: 11), The Beast Rising from the Sea (12: 1),* and *The Four Horsemen.* The stylistic source for these prophetic images is, of course, Albrecht Dürer, whose Apocalypse series of 1498 was well disseminated in Italy. Kristina Hermann-Fiore discusses convincingly the relationship between Vasari and Dürer[46] - which can be clearly observed when we compare the respective images of the *Vision of lhe Candlesticks* and *St. John before God and the Elders* (Figs. 1-18 and 1-19).

Complementing the decoration of the frieze are the *vedute* which frame the *ovati*. In the *vedute* we notice how Vasari developed his twofold concept of landscape painting: (1) in part it derives from the actual observation of nature or imitation of nature - the design is true to nature, *dol vero*; that is to say, the landscape is an accurate representation of a scene or a depiction of a topographical view, and (2) by contrast, the design is created by the mind or invented - is fanciful - *ull capriccio*, portraying, tbe landscape in a sketchy and imaginary manner.[47] The *vedute* represent the most important Olivetan monasteries in Italy, namely S. Stefano di Genova (1530), S. Maria di Monte Oliveto, Piemontore di Milano (1400), S. Ponziano di Lucca (1378), S. Maria Nova di Roma (1352), S. Maria di Gradara in Mantova (1454), S. Benedetlo Novello di Padova (1443),

S. Maria Annunziata di Rimini (1422), S. Bartolomeo di Fiorenza (1342), S. Bernardo di Arez.zo (1333), S. Benedetto di Siena (1322), Monteoliveto Maggiore di Siena (1319), 5. Girolamo Agnano di Pisa (1360), S. Maria della Riviera in Padova (1349), S. Bartolomeo di Prato (1342), S. Miniato di Fiorenza (1373), 5. Michele in Bosco di Bologna (1364), S. Elena di Venezia (1407), S. Maria di Castione di Parma (1488), S. Andrea di Volterra (1339), and S. Anna in Camprena (1334).[48] Some of these monasteries Vasari would have seen, and in these instances he portrays *dal vero*: for example, S. Miniato al Monte in Florence, S. Maria di Rimini, and S. Bartolomeo di Prato. Others he probably depicted from his imagination, inspired, peIhaps, by oral descriptions of the Olivetan monks; for example, S. Stefano di Genova and Piemomore di Milano. Vasari had not traveled that far north by this time.

It is not by accident that Vasari was commissioned to depict these monasteries since during the Cinquecento the Monteolivetan order began to expand and open new centers. Indeed, over the course of several decades, approximately thirty new monasteries were built, *oltre l' Appennino*, in the Lombardian and Venetian provinces, as well as *di qua d'Appennino*, in the Neapolitan and Sicilian province and by the end of the Cinquecento, the Monteolivetan chronicles record that there were seventy-six monasteries housing 1,044 monks and oblates.[49]

The *vedute* are sketchy, spontaneous, and illusionistically portrayed as Vasari recalled in his Roman educational experience.[50] Their uniqueness resides in the fact that - unlike the *ovati* scenes, which are carefully rendered and illustrate specific religious events - they are portraits of actual settings, unprecedented in Vasari's style and represent an early comment on landscape as a theme in its own right.

In the refectory of S. Michele in Bosco, Vasari revolutionizes the decorative scheme of *cenacoli*. He combines pagan ornamentation wilh prophetic images. Furthermore, he replaces the conventional singular representation of lhe Last Supper with a triptych composition of three separate paintings portraying themes of suppers from the Old Testament (*Abraham and the Three Angels*) to the New Testament (*Christ in the House of Martha and Mary*) and then, present-day Christian life by adding a contemporary meal celebration where the participants are members of the Monteolivetan order (*The Feast of St. Gregory*). Although the inclusion of this latter scene appears to be out of place, historically and thematically, on deeper scrutiny we discover that it closely relates to the history and patronage of the Monteolivetan order. During 593 and 594, Pope Gregory the Great (540-604) wrote *The Dialogues*,[51] the significance of which is not only literary but historical. The second book of *The Dialogues*, in particular, compiles for the first time a documented biography on St. Benedict of Norcia (c. 480-c. 547), the founder of the Monteolivetan order. It provides as well the only literary source lhat affords visual guidance to artists for the portrayal of St. Benedict's life.[52]

St. Gregory the Great regarded himself as *servus servorum Dei*, and his life is exemplified by humility and charitable actions as well as by his strong dedication to monasticism. In Italy he founded seven monasteries - six in Sicily and one in Rome. Probably the inclusion of the representation of St. Gregory in the refectory was prompted by Filippo Serragli, abbot of the Monteolivetan order in S. Michele in Bosco, who saw strong parallels between the lives of St. Benedict and St. Gregory in terms of their charitable accomplishments and monastic commitment, and himself, as the abbot of S. Michele in Bosco.[53]

It is not certain how Vasari had arranged these paintings on the wall. By considering the source of light in the paintings, the architectural design in each composition, and thematic meaning, we could propose that *The Feast of St. Gregory* was in the center, *Christ in the House of Martha and Mary* on the left and *Abraham and the Three Angels* was on the right or perhaps vice versa. By further analyzing the treatment of the figures and architectural layout in these three paintings, we observe how Vasari deliberately structured different habitats in each of them in order to establish a historical context in each painted scene. For example, in drawings for *Abraham and the Three Angels* Vasari illustrates a background with a rustic, wooden house and the supper takes place outdoors. The figures, dressed in simple garments, gesticulate in a profound manner. The faithful Abraham immediately responds to the miraculous intervention by kneeling and receiving with open arms the divine messengers; however, Sarah, seated against the door, skeptically observes the visitors, while Hagar, carrying Ishmael in her arms, curiously rush-

es with the other servants out of the house to see the divine apparition.[54] In contrast, in the composition of *Christ in the House of Martha
and Mary*, he portrays figures dressed in stylish attire actively preparing a meal in an elegant, indoor, Mannerist-architectural style
household. (Even the preparatory drawings for this painting show
a more complex and elaborate environment than that of the former.) The inclusion of this theme in the refectory is not accidental
since the house of Lazarus, Mary and Mary Magdalene was located
in Bethany on the Mount of Olives, obviously a historical connection between the New Testament and the order's name - Monte
Oliveto.[55]

Vasari illustrates the biblical passage according to Luke (10: 38-
42) where an apron-clad Martha, preparing food, surrounded by
her domestic paraphenalia and pointing with both hands towards
the kitchen, reprimands Christ by saying: "Lord, doth thou not care
that thy sister hath left me to serve alone?" And the seated Christ,
with a gesture of the hand, replies: "Mary hath chosen that good
part, which shall not be taken away from her."[56] Vasari depicts
Mary, seated at the feet of Christ, enthralled by His words - hence
Mary Magdalene's ascription *Optimam partem elegit*.

*The Feast of St. Gregory* is celebrated in a majestic early Christian
loggia or atrium where figures are actually seated at a table; however, they are dressed in modern clothes and numerous Olivetan
monks partake of the banquet; identifiable portraits add to the ve-
racity of the time; for example, St. Gregory as Pope Clement VII;[57]
standing behind his chair is Duke Alessandro de' Medici, an important patron for Vasari, and Cardinal Ippolito de' Medici, a distinguished member of the Monteolivetan order.

In studying the thematic composition of these three suppers,
we further realize why Vasari would have placed *The Feast of St.
Gregory* in the center since it is the only scene that includes members of the order in the festivity. Moreover, when the three supper
scenes are viewed together, *The Feast of St. Gregory*'s triumphal arch
motif becomes the pivotal point, stylistically and iconographically,
because it is decorated with the personifications of the theological
virtues (Charity seated on the plinth flanked by Faith and Hope)
which represent the basis of Christian life and address also the aims
of the Monteolivetan order.[58] The presence of divine intervention is

experienced in the Old Testament scene with the apparition of the Angels to Abraham, and Abraham's forthright response alludes to the acceptance of the covenant made with God at Mamre and the theological virtue of Faith, while the painting of *Christ in the House of Martha and Mary* refers to the New Testament, and the presence of Christ alludes to His granting benefits to the house of Lazarus. The prosperous offering of Christ is further signified by the representation of the statue of Abundance, located at the top of the staircase on a vertical axis with the seated figure of Mary in the foreground. Her trust in the giving and teaching of Christ as well as His presence in her house are both manifestations of Hope. In the painting of *The Feast of St. Gregory* we see the elemosynary actions on the part of the Monteolivetan monks in providing a banquet not only for dignitaries but also for poor people. This charitable meal also alludes to the effective and philanthropic administration of St. Gregory the Great during his papacy where great sums of money were spent in humanitarian endeavors. Thus the intervention and manifestations of Charity can be experienced in *The Feast of St. Gregory*.

Even though we have interpreted for each painting the singular intervention of the theological virtues (Faith, Hope and Charity), all the paintings incorporate individually the divine blessings of the theological virtues as well as the human response in the acceptance of these divine gifts. For example, Abraham's faith implies a hope to achieve a covenant with God, and it is by virtue of Abraham's charitable offering of a meal to the three angels that God grants the covenant to Abraham and his people. Mary Magdalene's hope for forgiveness signifies also her trust and faith in the teachings of Christ as well as her love (Charity) for Christ. She thus finds salvation through her gift of love to Christ and becomes a symbol for Christian hope.[59] St. Gregory's Christian faith is indicated by the role of his papal ministry and the hope for divine guidance to successfully perform such a task. Obviously the three paintings are united by thc underlying message of the greatest of the theological virtues Charity (*caritas*) and its three aspects (*amor dei, amor proximi, and amor sui*).[60] Henceforth, Abraham embodies *amor dei*, Mary Magdalene *amor sui* and St. Gregory, *amor proximi*. Therefore, when the Monteolivetan monks partook of a meal in this refectory and

saw these three paintings they were reminded of the manifestations of charity as well as of the necessity and benefits of charitable
behavior, which are fundamental ingredients in Christian religion
and, of course, *sine qua non* necessities to be integrated in their spiritual and monastic life.

Moreover, these Old and New Testament scenes were regarded as prefigurations of Christ's Last Supper, and it was during the
papacy of St. Gregory the Great that the book of illumination on
the Passion cycle of the Gospels of St. Augustine was written and
included the earliest depiction of a Last Supper scene.[61] In addition, throughout the Renaissance a plethora of Gregorian legends
circulated about the various miracles of the Host and the Mass of
St. Gregory, in which Christ appears as the Eucharistic Man of Sor-
rows, because St. Gregory had played a significant role in the development of the Roman doctrine of the Mass and liturgy.[62] Thus
the inclusion of the The Feast of St. Gugory in the group of supper
themes, wholly accords with this emergent tradition.

In interpreting the meaning of these representations as the prefiguration of the last supper another explanation can be found for
their configuration. During the early church period, the Messianic
meal of bread and wine was called meal *eukharistia* (from the Greek
word meaning thanksgiving) because the prayer pronounced before eating expressed gratitude toward God for the gifts about to be
received. The three suppers represented in the Bolognese Monteolivelan refectory symbolize an *eukharistia*.

Furthermore, the presence of the Holy Spirit in *The Feast of St.
Gregory* strengthens the connection between the theological virtues
and the *eukharistia* meaning for the Monteolivetan order. According
to both the Old and New Testaments, the Holy Spirit was an instrument of divine action, both in nature and in the human heart. In the
writings of St. Paul (I Cor. 3: 16; 6: 17. and Gal. 5: 22) the Holy Spirit
occupies a central place in Christian life because through the granting of fruits and gifts, moral purity and holiness can be achieved.
From the sixth century until the end of the sixteenth century, there
was in the Roman rite, only one eucharistic prayer which was
known as the Canon of the Mass where an *epiclesis* (Greek term for
invocation) of the Holy Spirit was recited before and after consecra-
tion. This invocation or petition asked the Father to send the Holy

Spirit upon the bread and wine to transform them into the Body and Blood of Christ.[63] If we consider the participation of the Holy Trinity in the eucharistic prayer, yet another obvious bond is established between the three paintings, since they each manifest individually and as a triad the presence and intervention of the Holy Trinity. When one views the three paintings together it is apparent that the scene of *Abraham and the Three Angels* portrays the presence of God the Father. *Christ in the House of Martha and Mary* illustrates the presence of Christ the Son, and *The Feast of St. Gregory* reveals the presence of the Holy Spirit. Additionally, in *Abraham and the Three Angels*, the presence of the Holy Trinity is manifested by the figure of Abraham who welcomes three angels at Mamre (Genesis 18: 1-19). Abraham's visitors are depicted without wings, in accordance with the Jewish tradition. Nevertheless they were considered by the Church Fathers to be the prefiguration of the Holy Trinity.[64]

Understanding the iconography of the three oil paintings on the west wall of the refectory, we may now inquire how the rest of the decorations relate to them. Thus, how do the *vedute* of the Monteolivetan monasteries, the apocalyptic scenes depicted in the *ovati* and. of course, the supper scenes relate to each other? Did Filippo Serragli, abbot of the Bolognese Momeolivetan refectory, design an iconographical program for Vasari? Although no document of such an iconographical program can be located, I submit that Vasari's imagery in itself guides us to the understanding of the meaning and purpose of this unusual commission. Indeed, several connections can be drawn when we look at the whole program together in terms of social, psychological, and spiritual affiliations. Remembering that this is a hall in which the Monteolivetan monks gathered for meals and, as customary, the recitation of thankful prayers before the meal for the offering received, we can see that the *vedute* of lhe Monteolivetan monasteries provided a social and psychologlcal bond between the Bolognese Monteolivetan and lhe other monks of the order.

The Apocalyptic scenes dealt with the supremacy of the Law or Divine Will to be followed by Christians in the same manner as the Benedictine rule provided the Monteolivetan monks with the guidance to follow the Divine Will. For Christian theologians, God discloses certain truths about Himself, in the Revelation of St.

John. Some truths can be known through the human being's natural endowments, such as Charity, while others, like the Doctrine of the Holy Trinity, can only be known through Faith.[65] These three scenes of the suppers allude to the various levels of acceptance of the Divine Will (for example, Faith and recognition in the case of Abraham; Hope and learning for Mary; and Charity through revelation and guidance for St. Gregory the Great). They also represent the hope of salvation through the eucharistic meal from the past (Old and New Testament scenes - *Abraham and the Three Angels*, and *Christ in the House of Martha and Mary*, respectively), through the present (*St .Gregory's Feast*), and into the future (Apocalyptic stories). Thus Vasari painted both a physical and spiritual banquet for the Bolognese Monteolivetan monks.

In 1544, Giorgio Vasari received another contract from the Monteolivetan order. This commission entailed the decoration of the walls and ceiling of the refectory of the Neapolitan Monteolivetan monastery (Fig. 1-3).[66] Once again. Don Miniato Pitti was responsible for obtaining this commission for Vasari, together with Don Ippolito of Milan, who was also a member of the Olivetan order. Both guests of the order at that time, they convinced the abbot general of the Monteolivetan order in Naples. Don Giammateo d' Anversa, to have Vasari decorate the refectory built by King Alfonso I.

The correspondence between Vasari, Don Miniato, and Don Ippolito on this commission is extensive. Vasari was again assisted by Giambattista (Bagnacavallo of Bologna) Cungi and Stefano Veltroni, joined by Raffællo delle Colle, who arrived in Naples in January 1545. Gherardi did not join them on this commission because, as so often, he was ill. The work was completed by the end of June 1545.[67] In addition to these assistants, Vasari employed two Spanish artists who resided in Naples, Pedro Ruviale (Roviale) and Bizzera.[68]

In 1408 Guarello Origlia, from the Durazzeschi legacy, had arranged with the abbot of the Olivetan order for the donation of a convent and a church in honor of the Blessed Virgin of Monteoliveto to be located in Ampurro, a region with rich vegetable gardens (Fig. 1-21).[69] In 1412 Pope Boniface IX allowed the construction of the church of S. Maria di Monteoliveto.[70] In 1581, the name was changed to S. Anna dei Lombardi.[71]

In the *Notizie del bello dell' antico e del curiose della città di Napoli*,

Carlo Celano explains that part of the third cloister (called "little cloister") was the refectory of Giorgio Vasari, located next to the sacristy.[72] Abbot Chioccia of the Monteolivetan order was in charge of completing the renovation and decoration of the refectory. In his autobiography, Vasari clearly describes what he had to do:

> When I arrived I felt inclined 10 refuse the work, as the building is Gothic, low and dark, so that I feared the work could bring me little credit considering it hopeless without a great profusion of ornament, as numerous figures would confuse the spectator, I decided to cover the vaulting with stucco, and gel rid of the old-fashioned awkward sections by making rich compartmenLS in the modem style ... I was able to carve my squares, ovals and octagons ... This stucco-work was the first in the modern style to be made in Naples ... The vaulting was divided into three parts: one for Faith, the second for Religion and the third for Eternity. Each of these is accompanied by eight Virtues, to show the monks eating there what is required of them, I enriched the spaces of the vaulting with grotesques, forming a framework for the forty-eight celestial images ... Having thus improved the proponions of the refectory I did six oil paintings, three of each at the end of the room.[73]

When Vasari mentioned six oil paintings executed at each end of the refectory, he was referring to two triptychs designed to be placed on the end walls of the refectory. The misfortunes experienced by these two triptychs are evidenced by the fact that they have been dismantled over the years and are no longer *in situ*. Only the wings of both triptychs have survived (currently in two different museums in Palermo and Naples), and they are both in desperate need of restoration. Both central panels have been lost, but luckily a drawing and an engraving have survived to help us reconstruct the composition of both triptychs. Their subjects are *The Fall of Manna with Moses and Aaron* (located above the altar wall of the refectory; Figs. 1-22 and 1-23) and *Christ in the House of Simon* (located above the door· way; Figs. 1-24 and 1-25). Vasari does not abide by the traditional structure of a triptych composition where there is a thematic separation between the wing panels and central panel; that is to say, where the wing panels contain a differem type of subject, although their subjects are still related to the central panel. Vasari, as always. creative and Mannerist, prefers to focus the whole narrative in the central panel and to use the winged panels for the purpose of expanding and elaborating lhe overall composition. The triptych over the altar, indeed, depicts the scene of a meal from the Old Testament, *The Fall of Manna with Moses and Aaron.*[74] The center scene has been lost. Fortunately through a facsimile lithograph of a lost drawing by Vasari, found in D. Vivant-Denon (*Monuments des arts du dessin chez les peuples tant anciens que modernes*), we can reconstruct Vasari's painting (cf. Figs. 1-26 and 1-27 with Figs. 1-22 and 1-23).[75] The two winged panels which survived, now located in Palermo at the Museo Arcivescolive, continue the action of the center scene. The triptych on the opposite wall over the doorway represents a New Testament scene, *Christ in the House of Simon.* A drawing survives in the Rijksmuseum in Amsterdam Cor the center part (Fig. 1-24, center). Not only have the winged panels of this painting survived, now in the Museo di Capodimonte in Naples, but also, recently, a drawing for these panels was auctioned at Sotheby's and is now part of the collection in Philadelphia (Figs. 1-24 and 1-25).[76]

In the depictions of the Old and New Testament scenes in the Neapolitan refectory Vasari continued with the iconography of the eucharistic meal represented in the refectory of S. Michele in Bosco. However, in the Old Testament scene Vasari focuses on the figure of Moses rather than upon Abraham.[77] The biblical passages from Exodus 16: 11-36 and Numbers 11: 7-9 describe the moment when the Israelites began to murmur against Moses and Aaron for fear of starvation. In response, God provides for their nourishment by a rain of manna (in Hebrew, the phrase for what is it?). In fact manna is believed to have been wafers made of honey or edible lichen having deliciously sweet taste. Following Moses' instructions, the Israelites gather it in large quantities in various baskets. Vasari has clearly illustrated this passage in *The Fall of the Manna with Moses and Aaron*, and specifically, Vasari quotes visually from Exodus 16: 4-5: "Then said the Lord unto Moses, Behold, I will rain bread from heaven for you; and the people shall go out and gather a cetain rate every day, that I may prove them, whether they will walk in my way, or no." In the center scene of the lithograph, after Vasari's lost drawing for the painting (also lost), we see the Israelites gathered together in the desert with Aaron and Moses collecting the manna sent by God in large receptacles. The lithograph also shows several nomad-like tents in the background probably signifying a foreign land and alluding to the exodus of Moses from Egypt in search of God's promised land. The agitation and excitement of the Israelites is visually translated by Vasari in his Mannerist twisting and turning of their bodies, and in the beautiful and exaggerated action and proportions of human figures as well as in the inanimate objects, especially the vases.

Iconographical parallels, obviously, can be drawn between the miracle of the manna in the desert and the *bread of life* or the bread *of heaven* (John 6: 31ff, and I Corinthians 10: 1-4) and the episode of the three angels visiting Abraham (in the refectory of S. Michele in Bosco) and Abraham and Melchisedek (predelle of Camaldoli and Walters Art Gallery) in the Old Testament. In turn, these Old Testament themes are the *ante legem* or prefiguration of the Last Supper themes in the New Testamenl (Christ in the House of Martha and Mary, Christ in the House or Simon, Christ at Cana, The Last Supper); that is to say, the Old Testamenl's food gathering and blessings represelll the prefiguration of the New Testament's eucharistic meal.

The scene above the doorway of the Neapolitan refectory, *Christ in the House of Simon*, is a story from the New Testament which derives from several passages according to the gospels of Mark (14: 3-9), Luke (7: 33-50), but in particular, John (12: 1-8) and Matthew (26: 6-13).[78] These gospels tell us that a penitent harlot (whom we identify with Mary Magdalene) came to the house of Simon the Leper or the Pharisee at Bethany, in the village on the Mount of Olives, bringing oil of spikenard in an alabaster box,[79] while Christ and his apostles were having supper. She knelt in front of Christ and began to weep, her tears wet his feet which she wiped with her hair, and then kissed and anointed them. Simon the Leper or Judas Iscariot protested at the waste of the precious ointment. And Christ reprimanded Simon (or Judas) by saying: "Why trouble ye the woman? for she hath wrought a good work upon me. For that she hath poured this ointment on my body, she did it for my burial (Mauhew 26: 6-13)."[80]

In Vasari's drawing we see Christ dining in the house of Simon the Leper at Bethany in the village on the Mount of Olives - where he and his disciples often stayed.[81] During the meal, Mary Magdalene begins to wash his feet with her tears, dry them with her hair, and anoints them with a precious oinlment.[82] However, according to John 12: 1-8 and 16: 4-6: "Christ and his disciples arrived at Lazarus's house and, while Martha served at table, Mary anointed Christ's feet and wiped them with her hair while Judas Iscariot protested at the waste of the expensive ointment." If It is interesting to observe that Vasari has represented in the drawings for this commission (Amsterdam and Philadelphia) the passages according to John's Gospel of the banquet event and has followed Matthew's Gospel in the description of the anointing event, which took place before Judas Iscariot offered himself to the high priests as Christ's betrayer.[83] Vasari's drawings for this triptych illustrate an elaborate Mannerist loggia where Solomonic columns not only support a Venetian sunken ceiling, but also become the unifying motif from center to side panels.[84] A Mannerist composition is created by compressing the space in the loggia with massive and decorative columns and with a large crowd of actively engaged figures. Simon's guests are gathered around the table or are seated at the table with Christ and his disciples, who are enjoying the banquet being prepared by Simon. He can be seen in the background ordering his servants to fill jugs and cups with wine and to distribute the newly prepared food to his guests. Simon's friends are busy conversing among themselves or focusing on Christ and Mary Magdalene, the "intruder" - as she is often referred to in the Bible.[85] Judas, who protests Mary Magdalene's action, sits across rrom Christ, wnile desperately holding on to his money bag or purse, and expresses his anger and scorn against the penitent sinner. Moreover, in the upper left hand corner of Vasari's composition, a landscape can be seen with a *tempietto* at a distance, and a man preventing a woman from entering the loggia, at the entrance -probably an earlier moment in the narrative of the penitent Magdalene.

In the oil paintings and their preparatory drawings for the Monteolivetan refectories at Bologna and Naples, Vasari created a compositional contrast of exterior and interior space for the narrative representations of the biblical stories - illustrating the Old Testament with open space and the New Testament with interior space. At the same time, he establishes an iconographical parallel between the Old Testament and New Testament prefiguration of the eucharistic meal. In addition, he unifies the functions of the refectory in his use of religious imagery since he is aware of the Early Christian tradition of agape, the communal meal, which can be compared with daily meals received in the refectory by the Monteolivelan monks, as well as with their *eukharistia* or sacramental meal which they also receive daily at Mass, and combines them as prefigurations of the Eternal banquet.

One of the major compositional differences between Vasari's work in the Bolognese and the Neapolitan refectories occurs in the frescoed decoration. As discussed earlier, in S. Michele in Bosco, the decoration appears in a frieze format along the walls - with repetitive rectangular shapes containing *ovati* and *vedute* whereas in the S. Anna di Monteoliveto (S. Anna dei Lombardi) the frescoed decoration is painted on the groined vault ceiling.

Although Vasari describes the design and the program of this ceiling, he never elaborates on the explanation of the iconography for the program, perhaps because he knew that the monks who saw it would have comprehended the symbolism and the impact of the meaning of the imagery on their spiritual life. And those people who merely read about this commission would also have understood, at that time, the symbolism of the Monteolivetan order. As we know from reading Vasari's writings and other archival documentation, the program was composed by the abbot of the Monteoliveto monastery, Don Giammateo d'Anversa (d' Aversa; Fig. 1-28) and probably was assisted by the insightful suggestions of Don Miniato Pitti, an important member of the order as well as Vasari's patron and particular friend.

The structure of the ceiling in the Neapolitan refectory consists of a groined vault divided in three sections which have been covered, in a *horror vacuii* manner, with a background of celestial images of *grotteschi* decorations, zodiac signs, and constellations, and a foreground of populated religious personifications of virtues - a Vasarian *tour de force* decoration or a collection of *maniera* conceits

(Fig. 1-3). In the center of each section an octagon contains a dominant religious personification: Religion (next to the altar wall), Eternity (in the center); and Faith (next to the doorway; Figs. 1-29,1-30, 1-31). These central religious personifications are surrounded by eight personifications of virtues, which are arranged compositionally to create two types of crosses: one set of virtues is contained in four rectangles arranged to form the shape of the first cross - a Greek cross-and the other set of virtues is placed in four *ovali* forming the second - St. Andrew's cross.

Religion is surrounded by four rectangles, creating a Greek cross, containing the Christian personification of Charity, Silence, Science (scientific knowledge), and Reflection (spiritual knowledge). In the *ovati* the personifications, creating a St. Andrew's cross, are Poverty, Goodness, Concord, and Instruction. In the center of the ceiling, Eternity oversees the personifications of Justice, Liberality, Audacity, and Vigilance in the rectangles, forming the Greek cross; and of Wisdom, Fortitude, Providence, and Hope in the *ovati*, shaping the St. Andrew's cross. Leaving Ihe refectory we see, in the cenler of the groined vault, the figure of Faith, who rules Peace, Obedience, Modesty, and Abundance in the rectangles designing the Greek cross; and Prudence, Patience, Chastity, and Hope in the *ovati*, establishing the St. Andrew's cross.

When analyzing the overall program of the ceiling and, in particular, each individual section we observe symbolic geometrical designs that correlate with the meaning of the virtues and their placement. For example, the dominant religious personification, residing in the octagonal shape in the center of the section, is in a pivotal position because it creates a radius which forms a Greek cross and a St. Andrew's cross. Moreover, this dominant religious personification, being at the center of the intersections of these crosses, creates a rotating radius which in turn forms a circle or a wheel.[86] From these geometrical designs - a circle or wheel and two crosses - and their symbolic connections through radial, axial and diagonal movements, three significant manifestations can be implied: first, the dominant religious personifications in the center oversee and bestow four gifts; second, these four gifts are represented in the personifications of the virtues in the rectangular shapes creating the Greek cross; and third, the personifications of virtues in the *ova-*

*ti,* forming the St. Andrew's cross, are qualities required in order to obtain the four gifts granted by the dominant religious image. Bearing in mind these geometrical and programmatic schemes, then, it becomes clear how the selection of these virtues correlate and interrelate with each other in the section and with the program of the ceiling. Vasari has created in the overall design and iconography a macrocosm as well as, in each section, a microcosm of the Monteoliveto monastic aspiration of ways to achieve the good life on earth and eternal salvation in heaven.[87]

The complex symbolism of the crosses alludes to the Tree of Life.[88] The crosses represent the worldaxis, the center of that axis relates to the center of the cosmos; that is to say, the crosses function as the primary bridge between the celestial and the earthly worlds. The Greek cross signifies the primordial direction for reaching the celestial world. St. Andrew's cross or saltire cross represents the unity between the two worlds.[89] Thus the crosses are the way or the bridge whereby the soul achieves the Divine.

Now, returning to the specific stylistic and iconographical sources for the imagery in the ceiling, we notice how Vasari has repeated many of the personfications he had employed previously in his earlier decorative cycles; in particular, the ceiling of the Cornaro Palace in Venice (1540-1542), which depicts the personifications of Justice, Patience, Hope and Faith, and the Chambers of Abraham and Fortune in his house at Arezzo (1542-1548), where we find the personifications of Modesty (Humility), Concord, Chastity (Virginity), and Peace in the Chamber of Abraham; and Honor (Virtue), Felicity (Prosperity), Fortitude (Strength), Liberality, Charity, Abundance, Prudence, Wisdom. Patience, and Justice in the Chamber of Fortune.[90]

In analyzing the iconography of the Neapolitan ceiling, we unveil the *clavis interpretandi* when we consider the following constituents: (1) specific religious symbolism, such as that professed by the Monteolivetan order combined with the writings of St. Gregory the Great and St. Benedict as well as the adoption of the Judeo-Christian literature from the Middle Ages to the present, in particular Prudentius, *Psychomachia;*[91] (2) the philosophical ideas of the time, such as Neoplatonism-Marsilio Ficino's *Corpus Hermeticum* and *De vita coelitus comparanda*[92] and the publication of Greek manuscripts, such as Niliacus Horapollo, *Hieroglyphica*[93] and Francesco Colonna, *Hypnerotomachia Poliphili* (Dream of Poliphilo);[94] (3) the popularization of Claudius Ptolemaeus's *Almagest* and the impact of the scientific discoveries and studies, such as astrological and cosmological investigations Pico della Mirandola's *Disputationes adversus astrologiam divinatricen*[95] and Nicolaus Copernicus' *De revolutionibus orbium coelestium* (1543);[96] and (4) the cultural milieu of the Neapolitan courts.[97] The Aragonese royal court sponsored several humanists, in particular, Giovanni Gioviano Pontano, a Greek scholar and writer, who was sufficiently well known in the humanists' circle to dedicate sections of his last book *De rebus coelestibu* (1503) to Pietro Bembo. In this astrological book Pontano discusses Marsilio Ficino's ideas on astrology, as well as its limitations and its applications to agriculture, geography, and medicine, and the influence on the planets on the arts and labors.[98]

The Humanists found in the literary or rhetorical learning of antiquity an educational ideal that met the cultural aspirations of their society. For the Humanists the discovery of ancient mythology and astrology, with their concealed morality, added a new dimension to Christian teaching.[99] According to Seznec, the translation and interpretation of ancient texts made it possible for the Humanist to grasp the central relationship between practical wisdom (Aristotle's *phronesis*) and the wisdom of the Bible (Aristotle's *sophia*).[100] Obviously Vasari's Neapolitan ceiling illustrates the assimilation and fusion of all these practical, spiritual, and intellectual pursuits, since he was fortunate to have been commissioned by enlightened patrons who promoted these humanistic ideas.[101]

Returning to the interpretation of the symbolism in the Neapolitan ceiling, we observe that the personifications of virtues represented in each section make reference to the theological virtues (Charity, Hope and Faith), the cardinal virtues (Justice, Fortitude, Temperance, and Prudence), the gifts of the Holy Spirit (Counsel, Fear of God, Knowledge, Piety, Strength, Understanding, and Wisdom)[102] as well as the twelve fruits of the Holy Spirit or the gifts of virtues (Benignity or Mercy, Chastity, Continence or Poverty, Faith, Goodness, Joy or Abundance, Longanimity or Patience, Love or Charity, Meekness or Obedience Modesty or Pudicity, Peace or Concord, and Temperance.[103] In the Neapolitan refectory, Vasari combines at random these personifications in the three sections of the ceiling, without separating or distinguishing between their iconographical order, biblical classification or classical tradition.[104] In this fashion, Vasari unites the function of the theological and cardinal virtues with the gifts of the Holy Spirit and their manifestations in a virtuous person (the Monteolivetan monk).

We observe in the first section, near the allar, Religion, floating on a sheaf of wheat, depicted with her attributes - the keys of St. Peter, the four Gospels, and the veil (Fig. 1-29). She dramatically turns her head to receive divine inspiration from the Holy Spirit. A rose bush with thorns behind her recalls the sacrificial redemption. Religion represents the Cbristianization of the classical tradition: *dividitur autem religio in has species: in fidem, spem el caritatem.*[105] Religion, as a symbol of the Monteolivetan order, governs the Christian personification of Charity (Figs. 1-32 and 133),[106] Silence,[107] Science (scientific or terrestrial knowledge,)[108] and Reflection or Piety (spiritual knowledge);[109] framed in four rectangles of the Greek cross, these are the attributes which explain the meaning of tbe order. Curiously enough, perpendicular to Religion, we see in a roundel the emblem of the Monteolivetan order - a cross resting on three mounds with two olive branches. In the *ovati*, the personifications, creating a St. Andrew's cross, are Continence or Poverty, (*Parcitas*),[110] Goodness,[111] Concord (Figs. 1-34 and 1-35),[112] and Instruction (Fig. 1-36).[113]

In the center of the ceiling Eternity (Fig. 1-30)[114] oversees the personifications of Justice (Fig. 1-31),[115] Liberality (Figs. 1-38 and 1-39),[116] Courage (Strength),[117] and Vigilance (Fig. 1-40)[118] in the rectangles forming the Greek cross; and of Wisdom,[119] Fortitude (Fig. 1-41),[120] Providence,[121] and Fear of God (Fig. 1-42)[122] in the *ovati*, shaping the St. Andrew's cross.

Before leaving the refectory, we see in the center of the groined vault the figure of Faith,[123] who rules Peace (Figs. 1-43 and 1-44),[124] Obedience or Meekness (Fig. 1-45),[125] Modesty or Pudicity (Fig. 1-46),[126] and Abundance or Joy (Figs. 1-47 and 1-48)[127] in the rectangles designing the Greek cross; and Prudence (Figs. 1-49 and 1-50),[128] Patience (Fig. I-51; frontispiece),[129] Chastity,[130] and Hope[131] in the *ovati* creating the St. Andrew's cross.

Vasari's Neapolitan ceiling, in part, includes an encyclopedic il-

lustration of the virtues to be emulated by the members of the Monteolivetan order as well as a series of virtues representing how divine guidance can assist the monks to obtain their eternal salvation.
However, in the rest of the ceiling, Vasari illustrated another aspect
of divine intervention not through the personifications of virtues
but rather through the planetary actions in the cosmos. Vasari's inventive fusion of *maniera* style and iconography contributed to the
development of his own art and the art of the time; that is to say,
his style and iconography created an impact on Neapolitan art in
the sixteenth century.

Vasari writes in his autobiography that he had "enriched the
spaces of the vaulting with grotesques, forming a framework for
the forty-eight celestial images."[132] The *grotteschi* decorations create
the background for the personification of virtues in the rectangles
and *ovati* and the "framework" for twenty-four circles and twenty-
four hex.agons. These "forty-eight celestial images" contain planetary constellations and zodiac signs. Although when looking at the
celestial images in the ceiling it appears that Vasari haphazardly
displayed them in each section, after careful scrutiny, we observe
that he laid out a complex program: (1) two wheels, formed by the
celestial images in the circles and the hexagons, surround each central figure in the octagon (Religion, Elernity and Faith; Figs. 1-29 to
1-31); (2) each wheel contains a particular grouping of planetary
constellations and zodiac signs; (3) the planetary constellations and
zodiac signs included in each wheel relate in meaning to the central figure; (4) it appears that the pictures in the two wheels do not
relate iconographically to the personifications of virtue adjacent or
opposite to them; and, (5) it is clear that the celestial images in the
wheels -in circles and hexagons-and the personifications of virtues
in rectangles and *ovati* - associate directly with the central figure
in the octagon. In this manner, Vasari's depiction of forty-eight celestial images in a compositional design of rotating wheels alludes
to the Ptolemiac system of the diurnal movement of the spheres
as well as to the definition of the spherical cosmos bound by fixed
stars, which are catalogued in forty-eight constellations (twelve zodiac, twenty-one northern, and fifteen southern; Fig. 1-52).[133]

When viewing the Vasarian ceiling, in the section near the altar where Religion governs we observe (Fig. 1-29): the first wheel,

created by the celestial images in the circles, rotates immediately around Religion; in a clockwise movement we see the constellations of Perseus, Cynus, Hercules, Crown, Heniochus, Ophiuchus, Cassiopeia, and Cepheus (Fig. 1-53); in the second wheel, formed by the celestial images in the hexagons encircling the first, again in a clockwise movement, we see the constellations of Tetum or Sagitta (Fig. 1-54), Aquila, Lyra, Ursa major, Ursa minor, Anguis, Murana, and Drago. It is interesting to note that no zodiac signs appear in this section of the ceiling.

In the central section Eternity rules (Fig. 1-30); we see in the two wheels a combination of zodiac signs and constellations, for example: the first wheel created by the encircled celestial images contains (in clockwise movement) the zodiac signs of Gemini (Fig. 1-55), Leo, Taurus, the constellations of Andromeda and Pegasus (Fig. 1-56), and the zodiac signs of Aries, Virgo, and Scorpio; the second wheel composed of hexagons shows the signs of Capricorn, Cancer, Sagittarius, the constellations of Equical, Delphinus, Delthoton (Fig. 151), and the signs of Libra and Aquarius. The zodiac sign of Pisces does not appear in this area.

Faith administers the last section of the ceiling (Fig. 1-31). Two wheels also surround her, the first wheel with the circles shows (again clockwise) the constellalions of Anticanis, Amphora. Lepus, Canis, Orion (Fig. 1-58), Argus, Bootes, and Crown (royal; Fig. I-59), and the second wheel with the hexagons includes the constellations of Hydra, Canis major, the zodiac sign of Pisces (Fig. 1-60), and the constellations of Ara, Nothius, Eridanus, Corvus or Avis, and Cetus.

The Cinquecento Humanists and theologians saw no contradiction between astrology and science; as part of Divine law, God created and ruled the universe, which was controlled by heavenly bodies that in tum affected all earthly things as part or the Natural law. The idea of physical causality between the unjverse and the individual, between macrocosm and microcosm was accepted by many as a scientific fact. According to Eugenio Garin in L' eta nuova, the Renaissance viewed astrology as the study of the moving of the spheres, between heaven and earth, between a person and the cosmos, where the powers of the here and now and beyond created the forms.[134]

Vasari's celestial images represent a *maniera* iconography derived from the assimilation of ancient and recent scientific developments (Manilius, Ptolemy, and Copernicus), reprinted editions of Agrippa, *De occulta philosophia* (1530) and Angelus' *Astrolabium planum* (1488),[135] and new printed books on astrology and celestial maps or constellation configurations, such as the *Farnese Globe* of Pope Paul III,[136] Albrecht Dürer's *Celestial Map* for Emperor Maximilian (1515; Fig. 1-52). Hyginus, *Astronomy* (1517), and Luca Gauricus, *Tractatus astrologicus* (1525).[137] Of course, Vassri's awareness of these sources depended on his contact with the theologians of the Monteolivetan order (Don Miniato Pitti, Don Ippolito of Milan, Don Giammateo d' Anversa) and his Humanist friends (Aretino, Borghini, Caro, and Giovio). Moreover, Vasari knew about or had seen many of the significant decorative cycles in Italy, particularly in Florence, depicting constellations and zodiac signs, such as the exterior and pavement of S. Miniato al Monte in Florence (1207; another Monleolivetan monastery), the floor of the Baptistery of St. John in Florence (ninth-eleventh centuries) containing that masterful palindrome: *engi rolor te sol cicloes el rolor inge* (the sun runs in a circle without beginning or end), and Brunelleschi's cupolas of the Old Sacristy in S. Lorenzo for the Medici family (1426) and Pazzi Chapel (1430s) containing the natal horoscope of the patrons.[138] Moreover, outside Florence, Vasari probably saw Niccolo Mireto and Stefano di Ferrara 's *Salone* in the Palazzo della Ragione at Padua (1420): Cosimo Tura and Francesco Cosss's *Salone dei Mesi* in Palazzo Schifanoia at Ferrara (c. 1470s); Peruzzi's and Agostino Chigi's horoscope ceiling at the Villa Farnesina in Rome (1511) and, Raphael's planets in the Chigi funerary chapel at S. Maria del Popelo in Rome (c. 1515). Furthermore, during his travels Vasari probably studied the zodiac *horologia* in most of the important Italian cities, such as Bergamo, Bologna, Cremona, Modena, Padua, and Venice.

Vasari created this unified vision of the universe in his Neapolitan ceiling as a manifestation of God's will to the monks of the monastery through the intermediation of the celestial bodies and the personification of virtues.[139] The constellations, zodiac signs, and planetary symbols in each section of the ceiling do not integrate with the personificalions of virtue in any specific manner.

These cosmological representations portray the influence of the stars on Nature. The zodiac signs and constellations alluded to relationships in the universe and to cyclical and seasonal transformations - the wheel of life - and the archetype of the universe. The movements of the heavenly bodies had the power to directly influence the course of events on earth, all human activities, from affairs of the state to bodily health. The monks saw how to subordinate themselves to the laws of Nature as well as to the Law of God.

When analyzing the celestial images in each compartment of the ceiling some interesting observations can be made. In the section of Religion the constellations allude to mythological or ancient planetary structures, worshiped in the past in other religions, and adumbrate the Judeo-Christian religion; for example, the constellation of Cassiopeia prefigures Eve, Cepheus foreshadows Adam, and Perseus hints at Logos.[140] We should also recall that originally the painting of *The Fall of Manna with Moses and Aaron* hung below the section of Religion, prefiguring Christ's Last Supper as well as God's omnipotence. The absence of zodiac signs in this compartment implies that God created the universe before humanity.[141]

The compartment dedicated to Eternity, placed in the center, contains all the zodiac signs with the exception of Pisces. Vasari illustrates a Neoplatonic view of the harmony of the spheres or heavens created by God since eternity (Genesis 1: 1-8).[142] After composing a macrocosm God created a microcosm in a human form.[143] The microcosm was controlled by the zodiac signs. According to Ficino's Neoptatonic philosophy these zodiac signs determined the potentials of individuais.[144] Since they were associated with the constellations, a correlation was created between the heavens and the individual which was both anatomical and psychological. Thus the zodiac signs acted upon the humorous, spirits, labors, and personalities of individuals, and each sign also ruled over some part of the human body or *melothesia*.[145]

Faith's area contains the most complex symbolism. The zodiac sign of Pisces has been exclusively assigned to this section accompanied by numerous water constellations (Fig. 1-60). The picture of Pisces depicts two fishes swimming in opposite directions, implying that the spirits of heaven and earth desire opposite things; however, they are united by a *nodus* (a silver cord) which creates the connection between human aspirations and heavenly pursuits. According to the acrostic verse of St. Augustine in the *City of God*, the Piscean symbol refers to Christ or *IXTHEUS* in Greek (I I esous X I isthos TH I eou EU I ios S I oter) which means Jesus Christ, Son of God, the Saviour. The constellation of Pisces corresponds to the Age of Christ, since He was born under this astrological sign, thus He contains a dual nature - human and divine - and the *nodus* connects Him with the earthly realm and the heavenly realm. The inclusion of the water constellations probably refers to the traditional and contemporary philosophical issues on the cosmic fall, the deluge, and the origin of baptism.[146] In 1524 there was a long debate concerning the influence of the astral virtues and the positions of the stars as well as the planets and the zodiac signs. One particular aspect of this debate dealt with the astral inflictions of Pisces on the heavens which were believed to have caused the deluge.[147]

Purposefully, Vasari depicted aquatic constellations in the compartment of Faith because they relate to Pisces, the sign of Christ, and allude to the baptism of the world (the flood). These constellations under the control of Pisces pave the way on earth (or the coming of the Saviour and the advent of Christianity. Furthermore, Faith governs the constellation of Pisces indicating to the Monteolivetan monks that through baptism, charitable actions, and spiritual instruction redemption can be obtained as well as eternal salvation. Hence, the overall view of the ceiling gave a message of hope, faith, and love to the Monteolivetan monks: the realm of Religion manifests for them the confidence and guidance in their Christian faith, Eternity offers them a choice between their destiny and free will; and, Faith guides them to achieve redemption through baptism and attain eternal salvation through Christ. The message is exemplified by Mary Magdalene's action of love in the painting, located above the doorway and below the section of Faith, in *Christ in the House of Simon*.

The central figures of Faith and Religion are necessary elements to achieve Eternity -eternal salvation for the lay Christian as well as for the Monteolivetan monk. The personifications in the rectangles and *ovati* symbolize means by which Faith, Religion, and Eternity can be obtained. The integration of the imagery of the ceiling with that of the wall is dependent upon the closest painting and its ceiling section. For example, the *Rain of the Manna with Moses and Aaron* is next to Religion, and the attributes that surround her allude to virtues to be emulated. Similarly, on the opposite wall, over the doorway, is *Christ in the House of Simon* and in the ceiling above it Faith rules. It is Mary Magdalene's faith in Chdst that inspires the Monteolivetan monks. Through their vows of chastity, obedience, and poverty and their daily charitable works, they can obtain this faith as well as peace and the hope for eternal salvation.

In summary, in each section of the ceiling Vasari has created four concentric wheels which originate from the octagon (Religion, Eternity and Faith): two wheels are shaped with the personifications of virtues formed in each Greek cross (Charity, Silence, Science, Reflection, Justice, Courage, Liberality, Vigilance, Peace, Obedience, Modesty, and Abundance), and in each St. Andrew's cross (Poverty, Goodness, Concord, Instruction, Wisdom, Providence, Fortitude, Fear of God, Prudence, Chastity, Hope, and Patience); the second set of two wheels is formed by the celestial images in the circles: Perseus, Cynus, Hercules, Crown, Heniochus, Ophiuchus, Cassiopeia, and Cepheus; zodiac signs of Gemini, Leo, Taurus, the constellations of Andromeda and Pegasus, and the zodiac signs of Aries, Virgo, and Scorpio; and the constellations of Anticanis, Amphora, Lepus, Canis, Orion, Argus, Bootes, and Crown (royal), and in the hexagon (the constellations of Tetum or Sagitta, Aquila, Lyra, Ursa major, Ursa minor, Anguis, Murana, and Drago; zodiac signs of Capricorn, Cancer, Sagittarius, the constellations of Equical, Delphinus, Delthoton, the zodiac signs of Libra and Aquarius; and Hydra, Canis major, the sign of Pisces, and the constellations of Ara, Nothius, Eridanus, Corvus or Avis and Cetus); hence each section in the ceiling is a microcosm of the macrocosm. In the ceiling of the Neapolitan refectory Vasari painted a pictorial universe designed by God so that the Monteolivetan monlcs could meditate upon God's creation, gifts, and guidance.

In conclusion, we have seen that Vasari's *invenzioni* include the merging of religious imagery with secular representations. His refectories decorated in the *maniera* style represent a departure from the traditional depiction of *cenacoli* in three major ways: (1) stylistically, by having decoration on walls and ceiling (Neapolitan refectory); (2) compositionally, by the formation of continuous concentric movements with Greek crosses, St. Andrew's crosses (Neapolitan refectory); (3) iconographically, by including unusual religious themes: in the Last Suppers from the Old and the New Testaments (Bolognese and Neapolitan refectories); in the apocalyptic revelations (Bolognese refectory) and in the personifications of virtues; as well as, by composing inventive secular themes, such as the astrological representations of zodiac signs and constellations (Neapolitan refectory), landscape (*vedute*) scenes (Bolognese refectory); and, *grotteschi* ornamentation (both refectories).

The treatment of the theme traditionally depicted in the Last Suppers of earlier *cenacoli* is the simple and austere blessing of a meal. In the *cenacoli* for the Monteolivetan monasteries, Vasari transforms the last supper theme into an *eukharestia* from the Old Testament prefigurations of waiting for the *holy meal* with Moses and Abraham, to the New Testament participation of the *holy meal* with Christ. Believers and unbelievers convert through faith (Mary Magdalene). Giorgio Vasari's refectories represent a new religious iconography for the *cenacoli* of the Monteolivetan monasteries where the ambience of a shared meal elevates the souls of the monks toward a glorious Eternal banquet.

## Notes

* I want to express my gratitude to the people who graciously assisted me in the undertaking of this study: Professors Jeanne Porter and Susan Scott Munshower, The Pennsylvania State University, for their patience and invaluable comments. Professors Iris Cheney, University of Massachusetts Amherst; Virginia W. Callahan, Howard University, Emerita; Barbara Miliaras, University of Massachusetts Lowell; and Wolfram Prinz, Accademia del Disegno (Florence) for their insightful observations. Further thanks are extended to the assistants of the Archivio di Stato in Naples, the Bibliotheca Hertziana in Rome, and the Monteoliveto order in Bologna and Naples. The awards received from the University of Massachuselts Lowell and the National Endowment for the Humanities Travel Grant made it possible to sustain and complete this research.

1. Giorgio Vasari, *Le vite de' più eccellenti pittori, scultori el architertori con nuove annotazioni e commenti di* Gaetano Milanesi, Florence, 1973. This edition will be used throughout the essay as Vasari-Milanesi. See

R. Beltarini and P. Barocchi, *Le vite de' più eccellenti pittori, scultori et architettori*, Florence, 1966, for an exceptional comparative study of the two editions, 1550 and 1568.

2. In the third preface of *The Lives*, Vasari states that *maniera* is that artistic element by which a perfect form is created; the total configuration of a beautiful figure or perfect form is the result of comparing and copying parts from other beautiful or perfect figures (Vasari-Milanesi, IV, pp.7-15). Perhaps it is no accident that Vasari's quest for life centered upon the achievement of beauty and excellence in art, since he was born and raised in Arezzo, a village originally founded by the Etruscans in seventh century B.C. whose inhabitants strove for the highest endeavors, as their town's name implies. The name Alezzo derives from the Greek word *areté* (virtue), or from the Latin term *arretium* (altar), and/or from the Hebraic word *arez* (far fertile land).

3. G. Gilbert, "Last Suppers and their Refectories," in Charles Trinkaus, ed., *The Pursuit of Holiness in Late Medieval and Renaissance Religion*, Leiden, E. J. Brill, 1974, pp. 371-402. See C. Colds, "Queries on Last Suppers and their Refectories," in Charles Trinkaus, ed., *The Pursuit of Holiness*, pp. 403-407. And. L. Venova, *I Cenacoli Fiorentini*, Turin, Edizione Radiotelevisione Italiana, 1965.

4. A few studies by Philipp Fehl provide insights into Venetian paintings of 'suppers,' particularly Veronese's Last Suppers; for example. "Veronese's Decorum: Notes on *The Marriage at Cana*," in Mosche Barash, *et al*, ed., *Art the Ape of Nature*. New York, 1981, pp. 341-65, and Philipp Fehl and Marilyn Perry, "Painting and the Inquisition at Venice: Three Forgouen Files," in *Interpretazioni veneziane: studi di storia dell' arte in onore di Michelangelo Murano*, Venice, 1989. Fehl also discusses Francesco Salviati, *Marriage at Cana* (1554) for the refectory in the convent of S. Salvatore in Lauro in Rome. For another study on Venetian refectories in the sixteenth century, see Ferdinando Forlati, *San Giorgio Maggiore*, Padua, 1977, on Palladia's refectory (1562) and Veronese 's *Marriage at Cana*.

5. During the Florentine Quattracento, numerous refectories depicted the scene of the Last Supper; for example: Fra Angelico, in S. Marco, Andrea Castagno, S. Appolania, Domenico Ghirlandaio, the Ognissanti, Pietro Perigino, S. Onofrio (Foligno), to name but a few. Also in the Aorentine Cinquecento representations appear, but less frequently; for example, that of Andrea del Sarto in the *cenacolo di S. Salvi*, and Alessandro Allori, in *cenacoli* for S. Maria Novella (ex-refectory) and S. Maria del Carmine (ex-refectory).

6. I am employing Vasari's definition of *maniera* from the third preface of *The Lives*, where he states that "*maniera* is one of the five stylistic quali-

ties that compose a good work of the Cinquecento. These five stylistic qualities are *regola* (unit of measurement) *ordine* (order), *misura* (proportion), *disegno* (design), and *maniera* (style). Vasari goes on to say that *"maniera* is more than an element of art, it is a technique (a method or style) by which a perfect form is created...when this method is used for all the figures in an art work it is called *bella maniera,"* (Vasari-Milanesi, IV, pp. 7-15; I presented a paper on "Vasari's Position as an Exponent of the Maniera Style: Maniera / Rebirth," at the Sixteenth Century Studies Conference in Philadelphia in October, 1991. Furthermore, I am using Smyth's dates (1520-1585) to define the period (see Craig Hugh Smyth, *Mannerism and Maniera*, Vienna, 1993; and John Shearman's definition of the term *maniera* "as an aesthetic ideal." (See John Shearman, "Maniera as an Aesthetic Ideal," *Studies in Wesurn Art: Acts of the Twentieth International Congress of the History of Art*, Princeton, pp. 200-221, reprinted in *Renaissance Art*, Creighton Gilbert, ed., New York, 1970, pp. 181-221).

7. S. J. Freedberg, *Painting in Italy: 1500-1600*, Baltimore, 1971, p. 308.
8. The ideas for this study originated many years ago when I began my research on Giorgio Vasari; see *The Paintings of the Casa Vasari* (unpublished Ph.D. dissertation, Boston University, 1978), where I discuss the *lacunae* in the understanding of Vasari's paintings, particularly in Naples. Subsequently, I corrected some of these gaps in my second study on Vasari, *The Paintings of the Casa Vasari*, New York, 1985, and fortunately I influenced other writers to join in this effort. For a specific study on Vasari in Naples, see Pieriuigi Leone de Castris, "Napoli 1544: Vasari e Monteoliveto," *Bolletino d'Arte*, October-December, 1981, pp. 59-88. Other significant studies are Paola Giusti and Pierluigi Leone de Castris, *Pittura del Cinquecento a Napoli: 1510-1540 forastrieri e regnicoli*, Naples, 1988, pp. 60-76; 86-111; and pp. 132-186 discuss the impact of the Raphael school (Pedro Machuca, Polidoro da Caravaggio and Giovan Francesco Penni), and the Roman school (Cesare da Sesto) on Andrea da Salerno Sabatini, as well as the formation of the Mannerist style in Andrea Sabatini (see Giovanni Previtali, *Andrea do Salerno Nel Rinascimento Meridionale*, Florence, 1986). Pierluigi Leone de Castris, *Pittura del Cinquecento a Napoli: 1573-1606 l' ultima maniera*, Naples, 1991, p. 75, discusses how several artists residing in Naples were influenced by Vasari's style; for example, Francesco Curia (pp, 109-110), the Greek Belisario Corenzio's paintings of *The Last Supper* in the refectory of S. Andrea delle Dame in Naples (1595), and in the Church of SS. Annunziata in Nola (1590s). Obviously, these examples of the Last Supper were compositionally and thematically dependent on Vasari's Last Supper paintings (pp. 212 and 215). Furthermore, de Castris describes

how Vasari, during his sojourn in Naples, met non-Italian painters who were working there, such as the Flemish Giovanni di Calker, and how Vasari wrote about them in *The Lives* (see Vasari-Milanesi, VII, 1568 edition, p, 58). Giovanni Previtali, "La pittura napoletana dalla venuta del Vasari (1544)," in *Storia di Napoli*, vol 2, Naples, 1972, pp, 874 -911, clearly demonstrates the importance of Vasari 's Neapolitan sojourn in the formation of the *maniera* style in Naples. For an opposite view and critical appraisal of Vasari's *maniera* style and Mannerism in Naples, see Anna Ariemma Capriglione, *Giorgio Vasari Pittore: e la sua influenza sulla piltura napoletana*, Naples, 1970, pp. 9-13 and 35: "II Vasari fu artists mediocre o quanto meno freddo interprete del manierismo, passivo esecutore della 'moda' del suo tempo." And Capriglione continues that "Giorgio Vasari fu il piu criticato ed attaccato per i giudizi negative sinceramente espessi sul valore dell'arte napoletana di quel periodo."

9. The Staaliche Graphische Sammlung in Munich owns a drawing of Vasari's *Last Supper* (no. 2271) for the Murate refectory. The drawings help to reconstruct the composition of the original painting, now in segments, to be restored by the Florentine Commission for Restoration See E. Viviani Della Robbia, "Note e notizie sul *Cenacolo* del Vasari per il monastero delle Murate di Fiorenza," in *Studi Vasariani*, Florence, 1952, pp. 220ff. See also K. Frey, *Der Lilerarische Nachlass Giorgio Vasaris*, Munich, 1923, II, p. 865, Ricardo no. 167 dated 13. XI.1546 (with a notation by Giustina Niccolini of 1597). The ricordo states that in 1546 Sister Faustina di Vitello Vitelli, in order to enter the monastery, donated to the convent a *Last Supper*, which today hangs in the refectory, executed by the excellent painter  "Maestro Giorgino Aretina," one of the most renowned and famous masters from that city." The ricordo continues to describe how the painting was praised for its originality and beauty, thus creating a moving devotional image. It also illuminates Vasari's charitable action of charging only 134 scudi for his services in this respect instead of the customary 300.

10. Frey, *Der Literarische Nachlass Giorgio Vasaris*, II, Ricardo 182, p. 867; Corti, Vasari, p. 76; de Castris, "Napoli 1544: Vasari e Monteoliveto." p. 63; and Barocchi, *Vasari Pittore*, pp. 120 and 131. Vasari illustrates the biblical passage from the book of Esther 4 and 5, and the Apocryphal book of Esther, 15.

11. Ibid., and E. Parma Armani, "Fonti per il 'Convito per le nozze di Ester e Assuero' di Giorgia Vasari in Arezzo," *Studi di storia delle arti*, III, 1980, pp. 61-75.

12. Vasari-Milanesi, VII, p. 664. "Being employed in 1539 to do three panels in oils, with a frieze, and twenty subjects of the Apocalypse in small figures, with grotesques and festoons for the monks of Monteo-

liveto, in their monastery of San Michele in Bosco, outside Bologna, at the end of a refectory." See I. B. Supino, *L' arte nelle chiese di Bologna, Secoli XV-XVI*, Bologna, 1938; L. Arze, *Indicazione storico-artistico nelle cose spettanti alla villa legatizia di San Michele in Bosco*, Bologna, 1850; Archivio di Stato di Bologna, Libri delle Fabbriche: Olivetani in San Michele in Bosco, Book 4; Carte 5:38; 5:39; and Umberto Beseghi, *Introduzione alle chiese di Bologna*, Bologna, 1956. p. 281.

13. Vasari-Milanesi, VII, pp. 674-675. "When I arrived I felt inclined to refuse the work, as the building is Gothic, low and dark, so that I feared the work could bring me little credit...Considering it hopeless without a great profusion of ornament, as numerous figures would confuse the spectator, I decided to cover the vaulting with stucco, and get rid of the old-fashioned awkward sections by making rich compartments in the modern style... I was able to carve my squares, ovals and octagons...This stucco-work was divided into three parts: one for Faith, the second for Religion and the third for Eternity. Each of these is accompanied by eight Virtues, to show the monks eating there what is required of them. I enriched the spaces of the vaulting with grotesques, forming a framework for the forty-eight celestial images." See A. del Vita, *Il Libro delle Ricordanze di Giorgio Vasari*, Arezzo, 1938, pp. 41-61; Mario Rotili, *L'arte del Cinquecento nel Regno di Napoli*, Naples, 1972, p. 186; Ottavio Morisani, *Storia di Napoli*, vol.5. Naples, 1967; Archivio di Slato di Napoli, "Monasterio di Monteoliveto," vols. 5504; 5529; 5532; 6033; and 6035; and de Castris, "Napoli 1544: Vasari e Monteolivelo," pp. 59-88.

14. F. Strazzullo, "La fondazione di Monteoliveto in Napoli," in *Napoli nobilissima*, Naples, 1963-1964, pp. 103-111.

15. T. G. Verdon, *Monasticism and the Arts*, Syracuse, 1984, p. 2. See G. Ferrari. *Early Roman Monasteries*, Rome: Pontificio Istituto di Archeologia Christiana, 1957; and P. Helgot and M. Bullot, *Ordini Religiosi*, Lucca, 1737-1739, vol. 8 on Naples.

16. See Fran Antonio da Barga, *Chronicon Montis Oliveti* (1451-1452), for the first book written on the Monteolivetan history, and Don Modesto Scarpini di Asciano, *I Monaci Benedettini di Monte Oliveto*, Bologna, 1952, for the history of the Montiveolivetan order to the present.

17. Benedetto Croce, *et al*, *Napoli nobilissima*, Naples, 1961, p. 186.

18. Carlo de Frede, "Santa Maria di Monteoliveto," *Storia di Napoli*, vol. 3, Naples, 1967, p. 516. The literature on the Rule of St. Benedict is extensive. See *I. Cassioni, De institutis coenobiorum*, M. Petschenig, ed., Vindabonae, 1888, p. 525, P. 1, 49.; E. C. Butler, *The Rule of St. Benedict*, critical edition, Freiburg, 1912-1935 with full bibliography; A. de Vogüe, *La Régle de S. Benôit*, Paris, 1971-1977; A. de Vogüe, *La comunu-*

*ate et l' abbe dans La Régle de S. Benôit*, Paris, 1961; G. Le Bras, *Les ordres religieux*, Paris, 1979, pp. 78-338; and Leonard J. Doyle, *St. Benedict's Rule for Monastaries*, Collegeville, Minnesota, The Liturgical Press, 1990. The only source ror the life of St. Benedict is the *Dialogues of St Gregory* in J.P. Migne, *Patrologia latina*, vol. 77, Paris, 1844-1864, pp. 149-430. There is a strong possibility that Vasari knew about the *Holy Rule* not only because he had visited Venice in 1541 (almost forty years after its publication) to see his friend and countryman, Petro Aretino, who resided in Venice at this time; but also because Vasari's patronage by members of the Menteoliveto would certainly have offered him the opportunity to familiarize himself with the rules of the order.

19. Verdon, *Monaticism and the Arts*, p. 2.

20. *Ibid.*, pp. 354 – 375. See also Enzo Carli, *Le Storie di San Benedetto: A Monteoliveto Maggiore*, Siena, 1980, pp. 162 – 180.

21. A. del Vita, *Il Cartegio di Giorgio Vasari*, Arezzo, 1938, Carta 7, *verso*; A. del Vita, *Libro delle Ricordanze di Giorgio Vasari*, Arrezzo, 1938, Ricordo 47, p. 46.

22. Frey, *Der Literarische Nachlass Giorgio Vasaris*, I, Letter 38, pp. 100 – 102.

23. Francesco Malaguzzi-Valeri, *La chiesa e il convento di San Michele in Bosco*, Bologna, 1893, and *L'archittetura di Bologna*, pp. 160 – 169. See R. Pane, *Archittetura del Rinascimento di Napoli*, vol. II, Milan, 1977, and R. Renzi, *San Michele in Bosco*, Bologna, 1971.

24. Albano Sorbelli, *Bologna negli Scrittori Stranieri*, vol. IV, Bologna: Nicola Zanichelle, 1930, p. 306.

25. Pasquale Carbonara, *Archittetura Pratica*, vol. I, Turin, 1964, pp. 812 – 816. See Francesco Malaguzzi-Valeri, *L'archittetura a Bologna nel Rinascimento*, Bologna, 1890, pp. 160 – 169. For studies on earlier Benedictine architecture consult Christopher Brooke, *Die grosse Zeit Kloster: 1000 – 1300*, London, 1974 and Basel, 1976, pp. 33 – 40. Brooke observes that throughout the Middle Ages (1000 – 1300) the development of the refectory was paralleled and closely connected with the cloister as seen in reconstructed architectural diagrams of Benedictine, Augustine and Cisterian monastaries and churches (see Tables 3, 8, 12, 13, 17, 20, 23, 28, and 31 for the architectural reconstruction which record the placement of refectories having a rectangular shape, close to the kitchen and opposite the church in these monateries).

26. Carbonara, *Archittetura Practica*, pp. 812 – 816.

27. Amselmo Lentini, *San Benedetto; La Regola*, Montecassino, 1980, pp. 497 – 501.

28. Archivio di Stato di Bologna, Libro delle Fabricche: San Michele in Bosco, Book 1, Carte 38, 29, Fab. 5, p. 165 (1437 – 1492).

29. Sorbelli, *Bologna negli Scittori Stranieri*, vol. IV, p. 51.

30. Vasari –Milanesi, VII, p. 664. For a complete bibliography on the literature of this commission see also Corti, *et al, Principi, letterari e artisti nelle carte di Giorgio Vasari*, Florence, 1981, p. 56.

31. According to Frey the first letter regarding this commission was written by Don Miniato Pitti to Vasari (Letter of 20 January 1939); subsequent to this letter a contract was drawn by Don Filippo Serragli, abbot of S. Michele in Bosco, and close friend of Don Miniato Pitti. The detailed contract of 2 February 1539 stated at the beginning in parenthesis that "it was written with the same specification as the letter of Don Miniato," ... "I soggetti delle tre grandi tavole a olio (nella testata di quell refettorio), un fregio dipinto ad affresco di grottesche con storie della Apocalisse lungo il perimetro del refettorio, e a otto grandi finestre, bordi di festoni lavorati a tempera di frutte." Ricordo 98, Frey, *Der Literarische Nachlass Giorgio Vasaris*, II, p. 856.

32. Vasari-Milanesi, VII, p. 664. Vasari wrote to ask Cristofano to come to Bologna with Giambattista Cungi.

33. With this playful action Vasari is consistent with Italian Renaissance practices of artists to include themselves in their work; for example Gheberti's self-portrait on the East Doors of the Baptistery of Florence. The Uffizi houses several studies and sketches done by Gherardi for the decorations of the wall frieze in the refectory of S. Michele in Bosco.

34. Vasari on the life of Cristofano Gherardi, describes his commission as follows: "I tre Angeli...in una luce celeste, che mostra partirsi da loro, mentre I raggi d'un sole gli circondano di una nuvola...il vecchio Abramo adora...mentre Sara si sta ridendo...e Agar, con Ismael in braccio, si parte dall'ospizio." Vasari-Milanesi, VI, p. 222; VII, pp. 265-266: and, Vasari-Barocchi, *Autobiografia*, VI, p. 379.

35. The contract stated: "debba fare di piu un fregio di grottesche et sono ogni lunetta una storia della Apocalisse et paesi contafatto i munisteri loro tutto a fresco." See Frey, *Der Literarische Nachlass Giorgio Vasaris*, II, Ricordo 98: 2 Febbraio, 1539, p. 856.

36. This painting has disappeared. On 6 June 1798, the French government forced the monastery of S. Michele in Bosco to close. As a consequence of this act of folly, the three paintings and the frescoed frieze in the refectory were disassembled during the Napoleonic invasion. The frescoed frieze was removed from the wall. In 1892, when the wall frieze was restored and relocated in the refectory, five *vedute* and four stories from the Apocalypse were destroyed. The oil paintings suffered different types of misfortunes (see Laura Corti, *Vasari: Calalogo completo*, Florence. 1989, p. 24). In 1805 the painting of *Abraham and the Three Angels* was sent to Milan to be placed in the new Italian

National Museum at Brera as part of the major masterpiece collection. After remaining in the warehouse for twenty-two years, the painting was transfered in 1827 to the Milanese Church of S. Maria Incoronata. Years later, it was learned through a warehouse-released receipt, that the *Abraham and the Three Angels* was moved to the Oratory of S. Sempliciano under the title of *The Annunciation to the Birth of Christ* (see Barocchi, *Vasari Pittore*, p. 126). Unfortunately, today there are no traces of the whereabouts of this work. The other two paintings have fortunately survived: *The Feast of St. Gregory* is now located in the Pinacoteca of Bologna and *Christ in the House of Martha and Mary* is in the refectory of S. Michele in Bosco.

37. Corti, *el al, Principe, letterati e artisti nelle carte di Giorgio Vasari*, p. 56.
38. Barocchi, *Complimenti al Vasari*, p. 126.
39. The Boston Collector, Charles Giuliano, has graciously permitted the reproduction of Vasari's *Abraham with the Three Angels* for this essay. The drawing was purchased in 1960 from an art dealer in Newberry Slreet, Boston. For an elaborate study of this drawing see my forthcomingc article in *Master Drawings*. At a later date, Vasari completed another painting of *Abraham with the Three Angels* (1550) executed for the *gonfalone* of the Compagnia della Trinita of Arezzo (see Frey, *Der Literarische Nachlass Giorgio Vasris*, II, p. 885 for information on the commission). This painting remained *in situ* in the church of SS. Trinita in Arezzo till 1810 (see Corti, *Vasari*, p. 88). Today the painting is in the Museum of S. Salvi in Florence (see Serena Padovani and Silvia Meloni Trkulja, *Il Cenacolo di Andrea del Sarto a San Sanvi*, Florence, 1982, no. 9, pp. 29-30) who convincingly date the painting 1550 instead of 1573. For a drawing of *Abraham and the Three Angels* for the commission, see J.A. Gere, "The Larence-Phillips-Rosenback, Zuccaro Album," *Master Drawings*, VIII, Summer 1970, pp. 123-140, fig. 24b. In this drawing Vasari simplifies the compassion of his earlier versions; however, he elaborates on the treatment of the figures and their responses to the divine visitors.
40. This was the only painting returned to its location (in 1892), following the Napoleonic dispersion and suppression of Italian art works during the First Empire (see Barocchi, *Complementi al Vasari*, pp. 17-18 and 114).
41. C. Monbeig-Goguel, *Vasari et son temps*, Paris, 1972, note 190.
42. A. Emiliani, *La Pinacoteca di Bologna*, Bologna, 1967, p. 59.
43. Barocchi, in *Vasari Pittore*, pp. 16-17, figure A, *Project for a Decoration*, sustains that this drawing should be attributed to Cristofano Gherardi, one of the principal assistants to Vasari.
44. Vasari-Milanesi, V, p. 290.

45. See E. Gaudioso, "I lavori fernesiani a Castel Sant'Angelo, precisazioni e ipotesi," *Bolletino D'Arte*, I, 1976, pp. 30-32, and *Gli affreschi di Paolo III a Castel Sant'Angelo. Progetto ed esecuzione: 1543-1548*, Rome, 1986, for an elaborate study on the style of Cristofano Gherardi.

46. Kristina Hermann-Fiore, "Sui raporti tra l'opera artistica del Vasari e del Dürer," in *Atti del Convegno Il Vasari Storiografo e Artista*, Arezzo, 1974, pp. 701-715. See also Montague R. James, *The Apocalypse in Art*, London, 1931, and Frederick van der Meer, *Apocalypse*, London, 1978.

47. Mina Gregori, *Il paesaggio nella Pittura fra Cinque e Seicento a Firenze*, Florence, 1980. See A. Rubbiani, "Il convento oliventano di San Michele Bosco, sopra Bologna," *Archivo storico dell arte*, I, 1895, pp. 194-198, where he states that Vasari was probably indluenced by Antonia Bazzi's (*Il Sodoma*) vedute of the Monteolivetan monastaries (1503-1506), which were used as background decoration for a series of fresco paintings on the life of St. Benedict. These paintings were designed for the main cloister of the Monteoliveto Maggiore in Sienna. See Enzo Carli, *Le Storie di San Benedetto a Monteoliveto Maggiore*, Siena, 1980. Vasari had probably seen this fresco cycle (see Vasari-Milanesi, VI, pp. 383-384, for a discussion on the commission and description of the stories of St. Benedict).

48. The dates in parenthesis indicate the formation of said Monteolivetan monastery. See *Registri Olivetani* and *Familiarum tabulae* for compiled data on the origin and historical development of all the Monteolivetan monastaries.

49. See *Registri Olivetani, Familiarum tabulae, Chronicon Cancellariae* and *Necrologium* of the S. Michele in Bosco Archives.

50. Vasari-Milanesi, VII, p. 7, VI, p. 10, VIII, pp. 273-274, on Vasari's classical education with Giovanni Pollio Lappoli, known as Pollastra and his early travels with Francesco Salviati to Rome to draw all the works of antiquity.

51. St Gregory the Great became Pope in 590. He was the fourth and last of the traditional Latin Doctors of the Church. He was the creator of the *Gregorian Sacramentary* which is the standardization of the Roman Mass and fosterd the development of the liturgical music commonly known as *The Gregorian Chant*. See J.B. Galliccioli, "Gregory's Works," in J.P. Minge, *Patrologia latina*, LXXXV-LXXVIII.

52. Carli, *Le Storie di San Benedetto*, p. 7, and for the description of the Life of St. Benedict of Norcia, see pp. 162-180.

53. It is interesting to note that a copy of *The Gregorian Sacramentary*, dated 811 and preserved at Cambrai (MS 164), includes a Mass for the Feast of St. Gregory. Could it be possible that Serragli was familiar with such a type of manuscript? And, if so, could this be another reason for

the addition of *The Feast of St. Gregory* to the other Old Testament and New Testament suppers on the refectory wall?

54. In Christological and sacramental interpretations Abraham is associated with the Last Supper because Melchisedek, a preriguration of Christ (according to Hebrews 7), gave Abraham bread and wine (Genesis 14: 18-20 and Psalm 110: 4). See Gertrud Schiller, *Iconography of Christian Art*, vol. I, New York, 1971, p. 25. It is interesting to note that Vasari executed several small panel paintings with this same theme now located in the Museum Calvet in Avignon (with the most elaborate landscape and Mannerist treatment of the figures and drapery), in the Archicenobio in Camaldoni and in the Walters Art Gallery in Baltimore (which I believe to be a study done by Vasari).

55. David Mycoff, *The Life of Saint Mary Magdalene and of her Sister Saint Martha: A Medieval Biography*, Kalamazoo, 1989, p. 28. This annotated translation is one of the finest on the subject. See also Benedicta Ward, SLG, *Harlots of the Desert; A Study of Repentance in Early Monastic Sources*, Kalamazoo, 1987, for an eloquent discussion of Mary Magdalene as the archetypal penitent and lover of Christ.

56. The rare theme of Christ in the House of Martha and Mary was infrequently represented during the Renaissance but became common in the sixteenth and seventeenth centuries (see Schiller, *Iconography of Christian Art*, vol. I, pp. I58 - 59). Perhaps Vasari under the patronage of the Monteolivetan revived this subject. One of the best examples known to Vasari was Giovanni da Milano's fresco cycle of the life of Mary Magdalene dating from 1365 in the Cappella Rinuccini of S. Croce in Florence, which Vasari undoubtedly saw and studied since in the Bolognese painting the gesticulation of Christ and Martha, as well as the attentive position of Mary, imitate the composition of Giovanni da Milano. Another small Vasarian version of the same theme of Christ in the House of Martha and Mary, in the Bristol Collection at Ickworth has been attributed by Pillsbury to Vasari because of its similarity to the drawing (no. 647) in the Devonshire Collection in Chatsworth (see P. Pillsbury. "Three Unpublished Paintings by Giorgio Vasari," *The Burlington Magazine*, 1972, pp. 96-97). Corti argues against this attribution, suggesting it is the product of a Vasarian workshop (see Corti, *Vasari*, p. 62). For a study of the iconography of Mary Magdalene, see Marilena Mosco, *La Maddalena tra Sacro e Profano*, Milan, 1986, particularly pp. 97-101 on Christ in the house of Martha and Mary. See also Mycoff. *The Life of Saint Mary Magdalene and of her Sister Saint Martha*, p. 41, for a version of the reply of Mary Magdalene to her sister Martha - who is busy preparing the supper for Christ and his twelve apostles and requests help from Mary Magdalene who sits at the feet of Christ - "For it is written: "I sit in the

shadow of my beloved, and the fruit of his lips is sweet to my taste."

57. T. S. R. Boase, *Giorgio Vasari: The Man and the Book*, Princeton, 1979, p. 31.

58. Charity, Faith and Hope, the basis of Christian life, were referred to as "theological virtues" and identified as such by St. Paul (I Cor. 13: 13; I Thess. I: 3; Gal. 5: 5-6; Col. 1: 4-5) to contrast them with the "natural virtues" or "cardinal virtues" (Prudence. Temperance, Fortitude, and Justice) identified by Cicero in *De natura decorum*, III, xv, and in *De officiis*, I. xliiif., after his reading of Plato and Aristotle. Virtue from the Latin word *virtus* (manliness) and the Greek word *areté* (excellence) and ethical signification on the value of the soul and actions of people. During ancient times the virtues were four in number (Wisdom, Courage, Temperance, and Justice). Socrates began the discussion by identifying vinue with knowledge and holding that one could not know the good without likewise willing it. Plato (*Republic*, IV, 427-435) contributed an extensive analysis on the four virtues. Aristotle (*Nicomachean*, VI, 5; V, 1; III, 7 and 10) made the distinction between intellectual and moral virtues, relating Plato's four virtues to the theoretical (spiritual) life and practical (natural) life. During the Early Christian period and the Middle Ages the four natural virtues were thoroughly studied by the Church Fathers and Scholastics; for example, by St. Ambrose (*De officiis ministrorum*) who introduced the term "cardinal virtues," after reading Cicero's writings on Plato's classification; by St. Augustine (*De natura e gratia*) who maintained that love and the cardinal virtues of Plato were fundamental sources for the Christian life; and by St. Thomas Aquinas (*Summa theologica*, II, II) who studied their relations to each other and their relation to the concept of grace. On this topic see the excellent study by Jennifer O'Reilly, *Studies in The Iconography of The Virtues and Vices in the Middle Ages*, New York, 1988; Mary Daly, "Faith, Hope and Charity," in *Dictionary of the History of Ideas*, vol. IV, New York. 1973, pp. 209-212, for a discussion on the interrelation between the concepts of the theological virtues from Plato to the writings of the Church Fathers; and Helen F. North, "The Iconography of the Cardinal Virtues", in *Dictionary of the History of Ideas*, vol. IV. pp. 371 - 378, for a historical study on the four natural virtues.

Consider also that the writings of St. Gregory the Great on Faith, Charity and Hope in *Moralia* (*Expositio in librum Job sive moralium libri xxxv*) represented one of the most influential commentaries on the Bible in the sixth century as well as for the Monteolivetan order. See Jean Seznec, *The Survival of the Pagan Gods*, New York, 1961, p. 89, and O'Relliy, on Job as a prefiguration of Christ and of the Church as well as her discussion on St. Gregory tbe Great 's interpretation of Job as the prototype mediator in *Studies in The Iconography of The Virtues and Vices in the Middle Ages*, pp. 289-295, 298.

59. See H. M. Garth, *St. Mary Magdalene in Medieval Tradition*, Baltimore. 1950. St. Gregory the Great, *Homilies on the Gospels*, Hom. XXV, *Patrologia latina*, LXXVI, emphasizes the theme of love for the feast of St. Mary Magdalene during the week of Easter: "She [who] had previously been cold through sin was afterwards aflame with love." Knowing the historical and literary connections between Mary Magdalene and St. Gregory the Great, who wrote to the Romans about the moral and spiritual impact of her actions, it is still clearer why the abbot of the Monteolivetan monastery selected and commissioned Vasari to paint *Christ in the House of Martha and Mary* and *The Feast of St. Gregory* for their refectory.

60. St.Paul in I Corinthians 13.

61. See Schiller, Iconography of Christian Art, vol. II, p. 32.

62. *Ibid.*, p. 226. Probably Vasari was familiar with the reliefs restored by Luigi Capponi da Milano in 1470 of the altar of St. Gregory in S. Giorgio sul Celio in Rome.

63. Cross, in *The Oxford Dictionary of the Christian Church*, pp. 463 and 478, states that the history and theological significance of the *epiclesis* is still highly controversial.

64. See James Hall, *A History of Ideas and Images in Italian Art*, New York, 1983, p. 87. One of the earliest depictions of this theme (*Abraham and the Three Angels at Mamre*) and the use of the human figures to represent the Trinity, is illustrated in the mosaic cycles of the Early Christian church S. Maria Maggiore in Rome, which indubitably Vasari visited on his many trips to Rome.

65. J. M. Court, *Mystery and History in the Book of Revelations*, London, 1979.

66. Frey, *Der Literarische Nachlass Giorgio Vasaris*, I, Letter 60, pp. 135-137, and Ricordo 145, in Frey, *op. cit.*, II, pp. 861-862. Vasari was also commissioned to paint an altarpiece of *The Presentation in the Temple* (1544-1545) for the church of the S. Anna di Monteoliveto (S. Anna dei Lombardi) of the Monteoliveto monastery. See Frey, *op. cit.*, I, p. 144; de Castris, "Napoli 1544: Vasari e Monteoliveto," pp. 59-60; and, Corti, *Vasari*, p. 51, for a discussion of this painting and the two preparatory drawings (Cabinet des Dessins, Louvre, no. 2080, and Dijon Museum no. T42). For other alterpieces painted by Vasari during his Neapolitan sojourn, not discussed here, consult De Castris, "Napoli 1544: Vasari e Monteoliveto," pp. 86-88.

67. *Ibid.*, Letter 73, p. 155. See especially Letter 71, pp. 138-139, and Cod. 9

(43, c 4) from the Archivio Vasariano, Arezzo. This cordial letter of 27 December 1544 from Don Ippolito Olivetan in Rome addressed Giorgio Vasari in Naples as "Messer Giorgio mio quanto fratello." Interesting for us, Vasari uses the second page of this letter to record some data on the completed work and a tentative schedule for the distribution of the remaining work to be done. For example, Vasari wrote that in January "inposti le alje, rinitone dua," which I interpret to mean that the construction for the renovation of the refectory ceiling was laid out and plastered while two of the compartments were frescoed with allegorical figures of virtues and zodiac signs.

February: "finito diport' la manna et la ftorja del X (CriftO) e le due alje finite," by which I understand Vasari to mean that he has completed the painting of *The Fall of Manna with Moses and Aaron* and *Christ in the House of Simon* as well as two more compartments of the ceilings with virtues and zodiac signs.

March: "finito tutte le grottefche e le tauole," by which I understand Vasari to mean that all the ceiling decorations were completed with allegorical figures of virtues, zodiac signs, and grotteschi as well as the two "triptych" paintings for the walls above the altar and the doorway.

April: "refta finito ego cofa infiemj con la maefta del Generale," by which I think Vasari is referring to Ihe painting of the *Presentation of the Temple* commissioned to be placed above the main altar of the Church of Monteoliveto by the director of the Monteoliveto monastery, Fra Giammatteo d' Aversa. This painting is presently in the Museo di Capodimonte of Naples. See de Castris, "Napoli 1544: Vasari e Monteoliveto," pp. 59-88.

From these precious Vasarian notations further information can be drawn about the manner in which he assigned and paid for the work of his assistants. Towards the bottom of the page, Vasari wrote several initials with numerical data. Frey eloquently ascribes the initials to the names of Vasari's assistants, and the related numbers (*braccie*) to the amount of work painted by each artist for this commission. (I may add that probably these calculations helped Vasari distribute adequate payment to his assistants.) Then, according to Frey *R* stands for Raffaele delle Colle - 45 is for braccie; *C* is unidentified by Frey, but I think is probably Gian Battista (Bagnacavallo of Bolona) Cungi - 21; *G* for Giulo Manzoni - 24; *S* for Stefano Veltroni - 24; *G* for Gianpaulo - 12; and *G* also unidentified – 10 (but I think it may refer to the Spanish painter, Gaspare Becena). See also Alessandro del Vita, *Inventario e Regesto del Archivio Vasariano*, Arezzo, 1938, p. 70.

68.  Vasari-Milanesi, VI, pp. 228-229. See Capriglione, *Giorgio Vasari Pittare*,

pp. 48-51. This discusses the question regarding the identification of
the Spanish painter Pedro Ruviale (bom in Estramadura on 3 April
1511 and died in Rome 1582), who trained under Polidro da Caravaggio and assisted Vasari in Naples with a Spanish friend, Gaspare Be-
ceon (great confusion surrounds Ruviale's name and apprenticesltip
in Rome and Naples. At times he is referred to as Polidorino). Ruviale
also assisted Vasari in the *Sala dei Cento Giorni* (1546) in the Palazzo
della Cancelleria in Rome.

69. Frede, "Santa Maria di Monteoliveto," p. 516. See Seate Riedle, *Un-
dersuchungen zur Kunst Neaples in Reiseberichten von 1550-1750* (Diss.
Ludwig-Maximilianis Universität zu Munchen, 1977, pp. 64-71 on
Santa Maria di Monteoliveto), for an excellent discussion on the artistic commentaries written by visitors who travelled to Naples. See
also Enrico Sacco, Naples: *An Early Guide, 1616*, New York, 1991, p. 28,
who describes the garden and Monastery of Monteoliveto: "Opposite
to Poggio Reale is a beautiful garden with charming and delightful
fountains and playing waters, often visited in the summer, which belongs to the Olivetan Fathers." He continues: "the most beautiful Renaissance church in Naples was S. Anna dei Lombardi (Monteoliveto)
begun in 1411." (Unfortunately, this church was severely damaged
in the bombardments of 1943.) In his travel guide, Bacco records that
the Monteolivetan monastery housed approximately 120 monks (p.
53). See also Salvatore di Giacomo, *Napoli*, I, Bergamo, 1907, p. 92: "la
chiesa di Monteoliveto che'e davvero il museo piu folto, dei piu squis-
iti e piu delicati monumenti (*di Napoli*)." According to Pio Pecchai, *Le
Vite di Giorgio Vasari*, vol 3, Milan, 1944, p. 998, in the early twentieth
century, the refectory was transformed into the sacristy of the church;
hence, today the refectory is called the old sacristy (*sagrestia vecchia*).

70. Frede, "Santa Maria di Monteoliveto," p. 484.

71. Carlo Celano, *Notizie del bello del' antico e del curioso della città di Napoli*,
Naples, 1952, vol. II, p. 956.

72. *Ibid.*, p. 869.

73. Vasari's skepticism over the possibility of carrying out the commission due to the dark architectural setting, and his condescending attitude towards Neapolitan artists in his writings, created numerous
resentments on the part of Neapolitan writers. See Giusti and de Castris, *Pittura del Cinquecento a Napoli: 1510-1540 forastrieri e regnicoli*, pp.
60-76; 86-111; and 132-186, and Capriglione, *Giorgio Vasari Pittore*, pp.
35 - 38.

74. Vasari-Milanesi. VII, pp. 674-675. Vasari painted several simplified
versions of this theme for predella panels or small devotional panels,
such as the Pala of Camaldoli in the Church of SS. Donato e Ilariano at

the Monastery of Camaldoli. See Frey, *Der Literarische Nachlass Giorgio Vasaris*, I, pp. 107-108: Letter 15.XII. 1540 by Pietro Aretino in Venice to Vasari in Florence recalls a drawing for this theme of the Fall of Manna and admires it for three reasons: (1) the feeling of surprise and admiration expressed by the people seeing the miracle; (2) Moses's action of gratitude towards God, and (3) the treatment of certain figures gathering the manna: for example, the young woman in the foreground of the scene and the *ignudo* seen with his back towards the viewer. Pietro Aretino ends his letter stating that Vasari's style has surpassed Raphael's art: "*Raffaello disegno simili cose, non lo supera di tanto che ve ne haviate a dolere.*" A more elaborate representation but loosely painted is found in the Walters Art Gallery (Baltimore, Maryland). It has been attributed to a follower of the school of Vasari; however, I attribute it to Vasari on the basis of its theme and its stylistic qualities. And for the altarpiece in the church of S. Croce at Boscomarengo, Poppi, Vasari's assistant, repeated this theme as well as the story of Abraham meeting Melchisedek in 1569, thus reflecting Vasari's earlier conceptions on the subjects (see Barocchi, *Vasari Pittore*, p. 122).

75. de Castris, "Napoli 1544: Vasari e Monteoliveto," pp. 61-64, and Corti, *et al, Principe, letterati e artisti nelle carle di Giorgio Vasari*, p. 117. In the eighteenth century Vasari's oil paintings of *The Fall of Manna with Moses and Aaron* and *Christ in the House of Simon* were still *in situ*; however, these paintings were attributed to the school of Raphael. See Edward Wright, *Some observations made in travelling through France, Italy and other countries in the years 1720 and 1722*, 2 vols., London, 1764, I, p. 312: "And in the refectory, the gathering of Manna; and Mary Magdalene washing our Saviour's feet, of the school of Raphael."

76. The Amsterdam drawing and the Sotheby's drawing were first reproduced by de Castris, in "Napoli 1544: Vasari e Monteoliveto," figs. 8 and 5, respectively.

77. In representing a theme from the life of Moses, Vasari probably had in mind Botticelli's stories of Moses of 1482 in the Sistine Chapel in the Vatican and, of course, his teacher Marcillat's stories of Moses of the 1530s on the nave ceiling of the Cathedral of Arezzo (forthcoming article).

78. The texts from the Gospels relating to St. Mary Magdalene are the following:

> "Now when Jesus was in Bethany, in the house of Simon the Leper, there came unto him a woman having an alabaster box of very precious ointment, and poured it on his head, as he sat at meat." (Matthew 26: 6-8)
> "And being in Bethany in the house of Simon the Leper as he sat

at meat, there came a woman having an alabaster box or ointment of spikenard very precious; and she broke the box, and
poured it on his head." (Mark 14: 3)
"Then took Mary a pound of ointment of spikenard very costly
and anointed the feet of Jesus, and wiped his feet with her hair:
and the house was filled with the odour of the ointment." (John
12: 3)
"And, behold, a woman in the city, which was a sinner, when
she knew that Jesus sat at meal in the Pharisee's house, brought
an alabaster box or ointment, and stood at his feet behind him
weeping, and began to wash his feet with tears, and did wipe
them with the hairs of her head, and kissed his feet, and anointed them with the ointment." (Luke 7: 37-38). See also Mycoff,
*The Life of Saint Mary Magdalene and of her Sister Saint Martha*,
pp. 34-37.

79.  The ointment jar, an attribute of St. Mary Magdalene, also alludes to
the anointment of Christ's body at the Holy Sepulchre (Mark 16; 1).
See J. C. J. Metford, *Dictionary of Christian Lore and Legend*, London,
1982, p. 184.

80.  It is interesting to note that in these Gospel passages when referring
to the body of Christ allusion is made to his head or to his feet. In art
the anointing of Christ's head with oils is rare, the anointing of his
feet more common. The Gospels agree on two accounts about Christ's
interpretation of the woman's action: (1) Christ's criticism of those
who complained about the wasteful action of Mary Magdalene and
(2) on the prefiguration symbolism of the anointing which alludes to
the anointment of Christ for burial.

81.  Clearly one of the reasons for the selection of this passage by the Monteolivetan abbot of the Neapolitan monastery was to draw a parallel
between the sites for the monks while they dined in the refectory near
Vasari's painting. They would infer a similarity of ambience between
Christ having supper in a house on the Mount of Olives and their eating in the refectory - also located on a mount of olives-in Naples. This
is why the emblem of the Monteolivetan order contains the three hills,
with two olive branches and a cross

82.  One of the earliest representations of the Anointing occurs in the *Homilies* of St. Gregory of Nazianzus, a Greek manuscript of c. 867 in Paris
(Schiller, *Iconography of Christian Art*, vol. 2, p. 17). Vasari's source of
inspiration for this imagery is again Giovanni da Milano's fresco cycle
of the life of Mary Magdalene dating from 1365 in the Cappella Rinuccini of S. Croce in Florence, as it was for the scene of *Christ in the House
of Martha and Mary* for the refectory of S. Michele in Bosco. For a study

on the iconography of Mary Magdalene, see Mosco, *La Maddalena tra Sacro e Profano*, particularly pp. 92-94 on the Anointing.

83. Schiller, *Iconography of Christian Art*, vol. 1, p. 17, identifies (Luke 7: 33-50) not Mary Magdalene but Mary of Bethany, and Simon the Pharisee, not Judas Iscariot, as the protestor against the wastefulness of the precious ointment.

84. In designing the Solomonic column, Vasari obviously recalled Raphael's tapestry cartoon of *The Healing of the Lame Man* (1519) at the Victoria and Albert Museum in London and the tapestry in the Pinacoteca Vaticana in Rome (see John White and John Pope-Hennessy, "Raphael's Tapestries and their Cartoons," *Art Bulletin*, 40, 1958, pp. 193-221, 299-323). Many of Vasari's figure types, stances, and gestures in the drawings for *Christ in the House of Simon* are an assimilation of Raphael's figures represented in the cartoons, in particular, St. Paul Preaching in Athens, where the group of men in the left corner recalls Vasari's trio, also placed in the left corner. A thorough study of the impact of Raphael's art on Vasari's works is needed.

85. See notes 78 and 82.

86. Curiously, before we enter the refectory a Monteolivetan monk receives us by opening a window with a wheel motif (rose-window motif). A fortuitous Vasarian parallel of ceiling design and patron's conception? Probably Vasari's *Monteolivetan Monk* is a portrait of the abbot Don Giammateo d'Aversa.

87. A typical Neoplatonic conception of viewing the world in the sixteenth century. See Charles Trinkaus, "Marsilio Ficino and the Ideal of Human Autonomy," in Konrad Eisenbichler and Olga Zorzi Pugliese, *Ficino and Renaissance Neoplatonism*, Toronto, 1986, pp. 141 -153, and Stefano Caroti, *L'astrologia in Italia*, Rome, 1983, pp. 231-254.

88. See J. E. Cirlot, *A Dictionary of Symbols*, New York, 1962, pp. 65-66, and J. C. Cooper, *An Illustrated Encyclopaedia of Tradilional Symbols*, London, 1987, pp. 45-46.

89. Quoting Cirlot on Plato's *Timaeus*, where Plato comments on how the demiurge joins up the broken parts of the world-soul by means of the two sutures shaped like St. Andrew's cross. See Cirlot, *A Dictionary of Symbols*, pp. 65-66; and Cooper, *op. cit.*, pp. 45-46, and for the Heavenly City, the book of Revelation, 21, Cooper, *op. cit.*, pp. 75-76.

90. In my earlier studies on Vasari, The Paintings of the Casa Vasari , 1978 and 1985, pp. 83-92, 98-106, and in my subsequent publications, "Giorgio Vasari's *Chamber of Abraham*: A Religious Ceiling in the Aretine House," *Sixteenth Century Journal*, Fall, 1987, pp. 355-380; "Giorgio Vasari's Paintings of the Casa Vasari Arezzo," *Explorations in Renaissance Culture*, Spring 1985, pp. 53-73, and "The Emblematic Approaches in

the Paintings of Giorgio Vasari," *Emblematica* (forthcoming article), I discussed at length the iconographic sources for these personifications as well as their repetitive use in his decorative cycles. Furthermore, I pointed out not only the impact of emblematic sources such as Andrea Alciato, *Emblematum fibellus* (1536); Vincenzo Canari, *Imagini delli Dei de gli' Antichi* (1547), and Piero Valeriano, *Hieroglyphica sive De sacris Aegyptorum* (1556) on Vasari's imagery, but also the intellectual influence of the Humanists Pietro Aretino, Vincenzo Borghini. Annibale Caro, and Paolo Giovio on Vasari's iconography. See Daniel Russell, "Emblems and Hieroglyphics: Some Observations on the Beginnings and the Nature of Emblematic Forms," *Emblematica*, vol. II. 1986, pp. 227-260; R. A. Scorza, "Vincenzo Borgini and Invenzione: The Florentine Apparato of 1565," *Journal of the Warburg and Courtauld Institutes*, vol. 44, 1981, pp. 57-75; and Clare Robertson, "Annibal Caro as Iconographer: Sources and Method," *Journal of the Warburg and Courtauld Institutes*, vol. 45, 1982, pp. 160 -181. These learning experiences profited Vasari in such a manner that he developed a repetoire of iconographical images which he employed in most of his major decorative commissions, especially in the decoration of the Sala dei Cento Giomi in the Palazzo della Cancelleria (1546, Rome) and in the rooms of the Palazzo Vecchio (1565-1572, Florence), thereby anticipating the encyclopedic book of Cesare Ripa's *Iconologia* (1593). See Peter M. Daly, ed. *Andrea Alciato and the Emblem Tradition: Essays in Honor of Virginia Woods Callahan*, New York, 1989. For the stylistic attribution of these personifications to Vasari's assistants see de Castris, "Napoli 1544: Vasari e Monteolivelo," pp. 67-78, *passim*. For a comprehensive bibliography on iconographical symbolism from antiquity to the Renaissance, consult O'Reilly, *Studies in The Iconography of The Virlues and Vices in the Middle Ages*, pp. 450-465.

91. In the *Psychomachia*, an allegorical Latin poem written in the epic manner, Prudentius (348-410) drew from established traditions of allegorical interpretations of the Bible for his representations of virtues. These virtues are personified by women and men combating for the salvation of the human soul. See O'Reilly, *Studies in The Iconography of The Virtues and Vices*, pp. 1-59, for a sophisticated and elucidative discussion on Prudentius, *Psyehomachia*'s origins, content, and iconography of virtues and vices as well as for their survival and transformation from images of spiritual combat in the Middle Ages to moral guides in the Renaissance.

92. Marsilio Ficino, *The Book of Life*, translated by Charles Boer, Dallas, 1988; Konrad Eisenbichler and Olga Zorzi Pugliese, *Ficino and Renaissance Neoplatonism*, Toronto, 1986; and, G. Boas, "Ficino and the Gods

of the Zodiac," *Journal of lhe Warburg and Courtauld Institutes,* vol. 45. 1982. pp. 195 - 202.

93. See George Boas' translation of *The Hieroglyphics of Horapollo,* New York: Bolligen Series, XXIII, 1950, published by the Venetian printer Aldus Manutius in 1505.

94. This book was also printed in Venice by Aldus Manutius in 1499; however, knowledge of this text was available as early as 1467. See Mautizio Calvesi, *Il sogno di Polifilo prenestino,* Rome, 1980, pp. 15-19, and Linda Fierz-David, *The Dream of Poliphilo: The Soul in Love,* Dallas, 1987.

95. G. Semprini, *Pico della Mirandola: la vita e il pensiero,* Genoa, 1988, and Eugenio Garin, edited translation in Italian with notes, 2 vols., Florence, 1946.

96. George Sarton, *Appreciation of Ancient and Medieval Science Durjng The Renaissance: 1450-1600,* Philadelphia. 1955, pp. 161-162: "Copernicus' heliocentric astronomy was accepted without demur by Paul III (Alessandro Farnese, pope 1534-1549)." Perhaps under the impact of Copernicus, Pope Paul III collected the "Farnese globe" a sculpture of a constellation map including zodiac and planetary constellations. See Erwin Panofsky and Fritz Saxl, *La mythologie classique dans l' art medieval,* Paris, 1990, p. 17: "le globe Farnese e la plus celebre repcesentation astronomique classique qui nous soit parvenue." In this book Panofsky and Saxl illustrate an engraving of the eighteenth century after the Farnese globe (see fig. 6). Earlier maps of constellations were known before the Farnese globe; for example. Albrecht Dürer designed a *Celestial Map* with the calculations of Johannes Stabius, the astronomer, poet and historiographer to the emperor Maximilian, printed in 1515 in Venice. See Erwin Panofsky, *The Life and Art of Albrecht Dürer,* Princeton, 1955, pp. 175 and 192; Frederick Goodman, *Zodiac Signs,* London, 1990, p. 9, fig. 3: and Carmi, *L'astrologia in Italia,* pp. 292-297, for an excellent bibliography on the topics of constellations and astrology.

97. Jerry H. Bentley, *Politics and Culture in Renaissance Naples,* Princeton, 1987, pp. 283-287. According to Bentley "Neapolitan humanism developed along lines analogous to the pattern of civic humanism in central and northern Italy"; however, the disappearance of humanism in Naples was caused by the elimination of the royal court. See also Eric Cochrane, *Italy 1530-1630,* edited by Julius Kirshner, New York, 1988, *passim.*

98. See Bentley, *Politics and Culture in Renaissance Naples,* pp. 127-137, 176-194, and 246-252, on Pantano. For an insightful study on the history of astrology and its implications from ancient times to the Renaissance

in Italy, see Caroti, *L'astrologia in Italia*, pp. 244-245 on Pontano. See also E. Garin, *Lo zodiaco della vita: la polemica sulla astrologia dal Trecento al Cinquecento*, Rome, 1976. It is important to note that Michael Scot (1175-1234), a Scottish scholar, was a resident astrologer at the court of Frederick II. According to Dante in the *Inferno* (XX: 115-117), Scot "knew every trick of the magical arts," (see Caroti, *op. cit.*, pp. 127-132, for a discussion on astrology at the court of Frederick II). Michael Scot's *Liber introductorius* was an influential Medieval treatise on astrological matters during the Renaissance (see Caroti, *op. cit.*, pp. 133-140, and Lynn Thorndike, *Michael Scot*, London, 1965 for a biography on this significant Medieval astrologer.

99. Seznec, *The Survival of the Pagan Gods*, p. 98.
100. *Ibid.*, p. 98, and Aristotle, *Metaphysica*, I, II.
101. See Corti, *et al*, *Principi, letterati e artisti nelle carte di Giorgio Vasari, passim*, as well as Frey, *Der Literarische Nachlass Giorgio Vasaris*, I, II, and III, *passim*, for the extensive correspondence between the literati of the Cinquecento: Aretino, Caro, Bartoli, Borghini, Giovio, Don Miniato, and Vasari.
102. As prophesied by Isaiah (Is. 11:2) the Holy Spirit would bestow seven gifts on the Messiah: *sapientia* (wisdom), *intellectus* (understanding), *consillium* (counsel), *fortitudo* (strength), *scientia* (knowledge), *pietas* (piety), and *timor domini* (fear of God).
103. The number twelve for the fruits of the Holy Spirit is defended on theological grounds by St. Thomas Aquinas, *Summa theological*, II, I, q. 70, a. 3.
104. Isaiah 11:2-3. See O'Reilly, *Studies in the Iconography of The Virtues and Vices in the Middle Ages*, pp. 112-159; on their distinctive characteristics, pp. 199-205; on the impact of Cicero, *De inventione*, II, and Macrobius, *Commentariorum in Somnium Scipionis*, I, on the Medieval iconographical tradition of the cardinal virtues.
105. *Ibid.*, p. 130.
106. For an analysis of Charity as a theological virtue, see Daly, "Faith, Hope and Charity," in Dictionary of the History of Ideas, vol. IV, pp. 209-212, and for a discussion on Vasari's personification of Charity, see Cheney, *The Paintings of the Casa Vasari*, pp. 170-72. A beautiful drawing for this image can be seen in the Gabinetto dei Disegni e delle Dtampe at the Pinacoteca of Bologna (see Marzia Faietti, *Restauri alla collezione di disegni nella Pinacoteca Nozionale di Bologna*, Bologna, 1985, pp. 228-230, inv. 1613, on the recent restoralion on this drawing).

For the personifications of virtues the following standard iconographical books have been consulted in addition to those cited: Adolph Katzenellenbogen, *Allegories of the Virtues and Vices in Medieval Art from*

*Early Christian Times to the Thirteen Century*, New York, 1964; Emile Mâle, *L'art religieux du XIII siècle en France: étude sur l'iconographie du Moyen Age et ses sources d'inspiration*, Paris, 1910; Louis Reau, *Iconographie de l'art chrétien*, Paris, 1955; and Rosemond Tuve, *Allegorical Imagery: Some Medieval Books and Their Posterity*, Princeton, 1966.

107. Vasari's depiction of a man with his finger pointing to his lips alludes to the cardinal virtue of Prudence (see Macrobius, *Commentariorum in Somnium Scipionis, Libri* I, viii, 7, and Alciato, *Emblematum libellus* (I542), Emblem 11: "Wiseman keep your mouth closed with a finger and say little, if you want to teach such a virtue follow Harpocrates, the Egyptian god of wisdom (sapience)." Furthermore, Vasari's image is holding a bridle with bit and reins a symbol of restraint, endurance and obedience; therefore guiding the monks to show restraint and follow the monastic vows of poverty, chastity and obedience. (N.B. for Alciato. *Emblematum libellus*, I am consulting Peter Daly, *el al., Andreas Alciatus, Index Emblematicus*, 2 vols., Toronto, 1985.)

108. Vasari depicts two types of knowledge granted by the Holy Spirit: *ratio* or *intellectus* achieved for comprehending scientific investigations, and *providentia* for seeking inspiration to understanding spiritual knowledge (see Macrobius, *Commentariorum in Somnium Scipionis, Libri* I, viii, 7). Macrobius's work is a Neoplatonist commentary on the dream of Scipio from the sixth book of Cicero's *De republica*. In this commentary Macrobius examines the mystery of the soul and its destiny in view of Neoplatonism and the astronomical and mathematical sciences of the time.

109. The pious figure turns to contemplate the skull (mememto mori) while holding a large vase - perhaps an allusion to the penitent Mary Magdalene. Piety represents a gift from the Holy Spirit.

110. According to Macrobius, *Commentariorum in Somnium Scipionis, Libri* I, viii. 7, Poverty (*Parcitas*) is an aspect of Temperance, the cardinal virtue of abstinence and restraint (see North, "The Iconography of the Cardinal Virtues," *Dictionary of the History of Ideas*, vol. IV, pp. 371-378). Continence or Poverty manifests one of the fruits of the Holy Spirit. Poverty together with obedience and chastity represents one of the three vows taken by members of the monastic orders. Vasari portrays the personification of Poverty in a very inventive manner by first selecting a strong, emaciated old woman with bare feet and breasts, implying that she has received and given in life, and now, in her old age, she perseveres with dignity. The sense of emptiness can be seen in the vacuity of the basket and cornucopia which parallels the sagging breasts depleted of milk.

111. For Macrobius, *Commentariorum in Somnium Scipionis, Libri* I, viii, 7,

Goodness (*Bonta*) represents one of the fruits of the Holy Spirit. The lamb or *agnus* (Latin for pius) that rests on Goodness's lap alludes to her innocence. See T. H. White. *The Bestiary*, New York, 1954, p. 74, and William B. Clark and Meradith T. McMunn, ed., *Beasts and Birds of the Middle Ages: The Bestiary and its Legacy*, Philadelphia, 1989, pp. 156, 165, 169, and 171. It is interesting to observe how Vasari associated several animals with his personifications of virtues, such as Chastity (lamb), Fortitude and Strength (lion), Liberality (crow), Prudence (snake), Religion (dove), and Vigilance (crane). Influenced by his Humanist friends, Vasari knew about books and treatises on animals and their moral implications as stated in the Bible (Job 12: 7): "But ask now the beasts, and they shall teach thee," and also in the Bestiary, a Medieval comprehensive catalogue of animal images and their symbolic meaning, which was as popular in the Middle Ages as in the Renaissance (see T. H. White, *The Bestiary*, New York, 1954, *passim*, and James Hall, *A History of Ideas and Images in Italian Art*, New York, 1983, pp. 160-161). The Latin version of *Physiologus* (*The Naturalist*), an ancient text on animal lore, was popularized as a moral compendium of bestiary in the Middle Ages and Renaissance (see Clark and McMunn, ed., *Beasts and Birds of the Middle Ages*, pp. 2-5); also well known was Pliny, the Elder, *Naturalis historiae* (see Hall, *A History of Ideas and Images in Italian Art, passim*), as well as the emblematic text of Alciato, *Emblematum libellus*.

112. She holds a bundle of fasces signifying the strength that comes from unity and peace, while looking behind her at the military armor and broken fasces which symbolize discord and war. Vasari repeated this motif in many of his commissions. For an elaborate discussion on Vasari's personification of Concord, see Cheney, "Giorgio Vasari's *Chamber of Abraham*: A Religious Ceiling in the Areline House." pp. 355-380. A well preserved drawing of Concord can be found in the Staatliche Kunstsammlungen in Kassel (GS 9629), which clearly illustrates the iconography seen in the Monteolivetan painting. Concord expresses the reward obtained through the Holy Spirit.

113. The image of Instruction holds a mirror with her right hand, and a triangle with her left hand, while stepping on a book. Vasari's personification symbolizes the achievement of truth or perfect knowledge. In two ways instruction (knowledge) can be obtained: (1) through reflection on the supernatural world (moon, stars and planets) which is granted by divine intelligence and cannot be seen; and (2) knowledge can be acquired through efforts of learning about the natural and temporal world which can be measured and seen. The concept of measurability defines the limits and the boundaries of rectitude

while the concept of imagination or divine intelligence is undefinable. See James Hall, *Dictionary of Subjects and Symbols in Art*, p. 211, on the symbolism of the mirror as an attribute of Prudence; and Cooper, *An Illustrated Encyclopaedia of Traditional Symbols*, pp. 179-180, on the symbolism of the triangle as a sign of measurement. Instruction as Knowledge and Wisdom manifests the gifts of the Holy Spirit.

114. Vasari depicted a winged image of heavenly perfection, resting on a terrestrial globe, holding a candle, and looking al the divine light (Christ the light of the world). The lighted candle carried by Eternity alludes to the guidance required by the Christian to obtain eternal salvation or spiritual joy. Perhaps Vasari intended the personification of Eternity also to represent Hope. See George Ferguson, *Signs and Symbols in Christian Art*, New York, 1966, p. 162, on the candle as symbol of Christ.

115. Vasari painted Justice with all the attributes of good judgment - a book, scales, and Roman fasces, symbols of knowledge, impartiality, magisterial and judicial power, respectively. A favorite image for Vasari, since he repeated it many times in his decorative cycles: the Cornaro ceiling in Venice, Casa Vasari in Arezzo, Palazzo della Cancellcria in Rome, and Palazzo Vecchio in Florence. See Alciato, *Emblematum libellus* (1536), Emblem 27: "No one is to be injured by word or deed." For an interesting discussion on the two meanings of Justice - contemplation and action - and its historical development from the time of antiquity to the Renaissance, see Morris D. Forkosch, "Justice," in *Dictionary of the History of Ideas*, vol. II, pp. 652-658.

116. For a discussion of the personification of Liberality, see Cheney, *The Paintings of the Casa Vasari*, pp. 177-178. A fine drawing for this image can also be seen in the Gabinetto dei Disegni e delle Stampe at the Pinacoteca of Bologna (see Marzia Faietti, *Restauri alla collezione di disegni nella Pinacoteca Nazionale di Bologna*, p. 228-230, inv. 1615, on the recent restoration on this drawing).

117. Vasari depicts this virtue as a sixteenth-century warrior wearing armor and helmet, seated on a lion, and holding a Samsonic column, a visual combination of courage and strength of character as well as of physical power and endurance. Macrobius, *Commentariorum in Somnium Scipionis, Libri* I, viii, 7, alludes to *firmitas* (strength) as an aspect of Fortitude. See North, "The Iconography of the Cardinal Virtues," pp. 371-378. On the symbolism or the lion as courage, see White, *The Bestiary*, p. 7, and note 106.

118. Vasari's Vigilance holds a pine-tree branch in her right hand and a book and scepter in her left. It is interesting to note that the scepter rests on an awakened lion while a crane stands on top of the scepter.

The crane's stone can be seen at the feet of Vigilance. See Cooper, *An Illustrated Encyclopaedia of Traditional Symbols*, p. 44: Vigilance symbolizes "loyalty, goodness and good order in monastic me." And Alciato. *Emblematum libellus* (1542), Emblem 15: "Vigilance and Protection." For the symbolism of the crane as a sacred bird and a messenger of the gods, see White, *The Bestiary*, p. 110-112; William B. Clark and Meradith T. McMunn, ed., *Beasts and Birds of the Middle Ages, passim*; and L. Volkmann, "Hieroglyphic und Emblematik bei Giorgio Vasari," in *Werden und Wirken, ein Festgruss Karl W. Hiersemann zugesandt*, Leipzig, 1924, pp. 407-441, fig. 1, shows a crane as a symbol of vigilance from Piero Valeriano, Hieroglyphica sive De sacris Aegyptorum (1556). Although Valeriano's emblem book was printed later, Vasari and his Hunanist friends would have known about Valeriano's ideas. Obviously, I disagree with de Castris' interpretation that this personification represents Justice, see de Castris, "Napoli 1544: Vasari e Monteoliveto," p. 74, fig. 29.

119. Wisdom or *Sapientia* is one of the seven gifts of the Holy Spirit. See note 102. For a discussion on Vasari's personification of Wisdom, see Cheney, *The Paintings of the Casa Vasari*, p. 178. Vasari's image of Wisdom in the Neapolitan ceiling differs from the image painted in the Chamber of Fortune of the Casa Vasari. The Neapolitan image portrays a scholar consulting numerous opened texts. Some can be seen around him while others are placed on a lectern. These books allude to *liber mundi* and *liber vitae*, that is to say, to the book of life. Learning can be achieved through the spirit of wisdom, or through revelation (divine wisdom) or the wisdom of the scriptures. It is not by accident that Vasari painted the scholar's foot resting on a cube since the cube symbolizes perfection, stability, and immobility - and his hand pointing to the written words; both actions reinforce the idea that Truth can be obtained only through knowledge. See Cooper, *An Illustrated Encyclopaedia of Traditional Symbols*, pp. 24 and 48.

120. For an interpretation of Vasari 's personification of Fortitude, see Cheney, *The Paintings of the Casa Vasari*, p. 176. Fortitude, one of the cardinal virtues, was highly admired by Cicero, (*De inventione*, II, liii, and Macrobius, *Commentariorum in Somnium Scipionis, Libri* I, viii, 7). See North, "The Iconography of the Cardinal Virtues," pp. 371-378. Vasari portrays Fortitude wilh all the attributes of audacity, courage, endurance, and vigor (see also note 105).

121. Vasari's Providence holds a large horn of plenty with her left hand, and the keys with the right. Her attributes allude to her fidelity and prosperity as well as to the power of having access to the realms of the natural and divine goodness. See Hall, *Dictionary of Subjects and Symbols in Art*, p. 184, on the symbolism of keys in relation to Christ

delivering the keys of heaven to his apostle Peter.

122. This represent.ation of the Fear of God or Timidity strongly differs from the central personification of Eternity. In the center of the section, we see Vasari's depiction of eternal Hope while in the *ovato*, of human Hope or lack of it. The Vasarian image of Fear of God alludes to the individual desire for the soul to achieve salvation; however, the expression on her face suggests her uncertainty in achieving such a goal. Since the Fear of God is one of the gifts of the Holy Spiril, her state of anxiety is temporary and it can be eliminated by trusting or relying on divine Hope or Eternity. Thus the monks are taught that through the theological virtues redemption and salvation can be obtained. See Daly, "Faith, Hope and Charity," pp. 209-212. I disagree with de Castris, "Napoli 1544: Vasari e Monteoliveto." p. 72, fig. 26, who believes this is a personification of Hope because: (1) she does not carry any attributes, and (2) Vasari depicted the personification of Hope with her corresponding amibutes, anchor and hourglass, in the section of Faith in lhe same ceiling (see note 131).

123. Faith represents another image frequently depicled by Vasari. Her attributes combine the personification of Religion as well as Faith - cross, chalice and the Host. Redemption and salvation can be achieved through acts of faith. See Daly, "Faith, Hope and Charity," pp. 209 - 212.

124. Another fruit of the Holy Spirit is Peace. See Cheney, "Giorgio Vasari's *Chamber of Abraham*: A Religious Ceiling in the Aretine House," pp. 355-380, for the symbolism of Peace. A drawing by Vasari, *Peace Bearing an Olive Branch* (Graphische Sammlung Albertina, Vienna, inv. 462) which in the past was attributed to Perino del Vaga, represents a theme similar to that of the painting in Naples (see Corti, *et al, Principi, letterati e artisti nelle carte di Giorgio Vasari*, p. 114. And a second drawing on the theme of Peace, found in an American private collection, has also been attributed to Vasari by Monbeig-Goguel (see C. Monbeig-Goguel, "Giorgio Vasari et son temps," *Reveu de l' art*, no. XIV. 1971, p. 105-111). Both or these drawings have been related to Vasari's Apparato dei Sempiterni (1541-1542) for the Pietro Aretina comedy, *La Talanta* in Venice.

125. Vasari portrays a woman dressed in white with the habit of a monastic order -Dominican. A crown of thorns illustrates her victory over sin and her willingness to submit to pain in order to empathize with Christ's suffering. The crown of thorns and the rosary carried are both attributes of St. Catherine of Siena, one of most holy and influential saints of the fourteenth century. Obedience together with chastity and poverty represent the three vows taken by members of the monastic

orders.

126. In Pudicity Vasari repeats the symbol of the crane, as a protector of virtue, employed in Vigilance (see notes 111 and 118). See Cheney, "Giorgio Vasari's *Chamber of Abraham*: A Religious Ceiling in the Aletine House," pp. 355 - 380, for the symbolism of Modesty. In the Neapolitan ceiling Pudicity or Modesty refers to another fruit of the Holy Spirit.

127. Abundance or Joy also represents one of the twelve fruits of the Holy Spirit. The Neapolitan Abundance differs dramatically in style from the one in the Chamber of Fortune (see Cheney, *The Paintings of the Casa Vasari*, p. 172). At Monteoliveto Vasari depicted a sensual image of female beauty for the personification of Abundance or Joy. She stands in a *figura serpentinata* manner with a large basket of fruit. The British Museum owns a splendid drawing on this subject. We see in this work Vasari's mastery of *disegno* and *bella maniera*, thus treating a drawing as a product of *invenzione*.

128. Prudence is one of the four cardinal virtues (see North, "The Iconography of the Cardinal Virtues," pp. 371-378, and Cheney, *The Paintings of the Casa Vasari*, p, 180). The Monteolivetan Prudence surrounded with all her attributes of practical and speculative wisdom - mirror, serpent, key, Janus head - attends to her toilet. Her engaging attitude denotes her existence in the present. A superb drawing by Vasari on the allegory of Prudence (inv. 7777) exists in the Collection F. Lugt of the Institut Neerlandais in Paris. See C. Monbeig-Goguel and W. Vizthum, "Dessins inedits de Giorgio Vasari," *Reveu de l'art*, vol. II, 1968, p. 90, fig. 4, and Corti, *et al, Principi, letterati e artisti nelle carte di Giorgio Vasari*, p. 114, for another drawing of Prudence (13650F) at the Uffizi. Vasari's *disegno* differs from his painted image. The drawing illustrates an elaborate holder for the mirror and shows the inclusion of objects, such as the vanity table, comb, and a brush, not seen in the painting, and the presence of the serpent as a caution and wisdom. See Alciato, *Emblematum libellus* (1542), Emblem 18 on the Janus head, and Emblem 22 on the serpent: "The serpent protects the virgins." The word serpent derives from the Latin *serpens*, "because the animal creeps by secret approaches and not by open steps" (see White, *Bestiary*, p. 165. and note 106).

129. Patience, of course, denotes another fruit of the Holy Spirit. Patience with resignation holds her yoke, a symbol of obedience and servitude. Vasari describes the image or Patience as "il giogho al collo et il capo basso," (see Alessandro del Vita, *Lo Zibaldone di Giorgio Vasari*, Rome: Istituto Archeologico e Storia dell' Arte, 1938, p. 25, quoting Vasari). For Vasari's constant use of this image for other commissions, see

Cheney, *The Paintings of the Casa Vasari*, p. 178.

130. See Cheney, "Giorgio Vasari's *Chamber of Abraham*: A Religious Ceiling in the Aretine House," pp. 355-380, for a discussion on the symbolism of Purity, Chastity or Virginity. This personification together with obedience and poverty represents one of the three vows taken by members of the monastic orders. Chastity as a Christian virtue signifies the abstention from sexual relations since she is one the fruits of the Holy Spirit.

131. Hope forms part of the theological virtue threesome (see Daly, "Faith, Hope and Charity," pp. 209-212), Her attributes of the hourglass and anchor represent her safety and security. The hourglass, usually an attribute of Temperance, symbolizes the passage of life as well as the recurrence of life and death, the heavens and the earth (see Ferugson, *Signs and Symbols in Christian Art*, pp. 45 and 50). The depiction of the anchor recalls St. Paul's comments in Heb. 6: 18-19: "Hope is like an anchor for our lives...it enters in through the veil" See Hall, *Dictionary of Subjects and Symbols in Art*, p. 156, and Cheney, *The Paintings of the Casa Vasari*, pp. 92-98, for other Vasarian illustrations of Hope.

132. Vasari-Milanesi, VII, pp. 674-75.

133. See Edward Rosen, "Cosmology From Antiquity to 1850," in *Dictionary of the History of Ideas*, pp, 535-554, Frederick Goodman, *Zodiac Signs*, London, 1990, *passim*; Warren Kenton, *Astrology: The Celestial Mirror*, London, 1991, pp. 7-30; and, for an astrological study on S. Miniato al Monte, see Fred Gettings, *The Secret Zodiac: The Hidden An of Medieval Astrology*, London, 1987.

134. Garin, *L'eta nuova*, Naples, 1969, pp. 439-440.

135. *Ibid.,* pp. 256-290.

136. The *Farnese Globe* represents a Roman copy of a Greek original, where the images of the classical constellations correspond to Aratus's descriptions. The classical constellations of Aratus, Greek poet and astronomer, are best known from the images in the *Farnese Globe*, a huge celestial marble globe, which was part of the Farnese classical collection (perhaps moved to Naples in 1738 when the collection was transfered there; now in the National Archaeological Museum of Naples). See Jim Tester, *A History of Western Astrology*, p. 106; Jean Seznec, *The Survival of the Pagan Gods*, p. 38; and, Erwin Panofsky and Fritz Saxl, *La mythologie classique dans l' art mediéval*, p. 17.

One of the first Greek astronomers was Eudoxos of Cnidos (408-355 B.C.), a disbeliever of the stars' power on human lives, who wrote a book called *Phaenomena* (Things Appearing). Aratus (c. 315-240/239 B.C.) used this text as the basis for his poem of the same title for the marriage of Antigonos Gonatas, King of Macedonia. The *Phaenomena* surveys the constellations and circles of the heavens and the rising and setting of the stars. Aratus's focus is not on the position of the stars but on their meteorological significance (see Adolfo Kiessling, *Arati Phaenomena*, Berlin, 1964, for a Latin annotated version and explanation of the Greek text).

Aratus's poem was translated into Latin several times. One of the most noted Latin translators was Marcus Tullius Cicero (106-43 B.C.). Also Gaius Julius Hyginus (c. 64 B.C.-17 A.D.) translated and commented on Aratus's *Phaenomena*. This work influenced Hyginus's treatises, *Genelogiae* or *Fabulae* and *Poetica astronomica* or *Astronomiae*; however, his concern was with the illustrations and mythological interpretations of the constellations (see note 137). A tenth-century manuscript in the British Library (Harley MS647) shows Cicero's Latin translation below the illustrated constellalions: inside the outline of each constellation are extracts from Hyginus's treatise on the myths of the respective constellations (see T. S. Pattie, *Astrology*, London, 1980. pp. 16-22; and Raneed Katzenstein and Emilie Savage-Smith, *The Leiden Aratea: Ancient Constellations in a Medieval Manuscript*, Malibu, California, The J. Paul Getty Museum. 1988. pp. 11-20).

During the Renaissance the importance of Aratus's poem was such that a Greek copy of the *Phaenomena* was made in Italy in the fifteenth century for a member of the Medici family, whose arms appear in the border (currently this manuscript is in the British Library codified as Add MS 11866; see Pauie, *Astrology*, p. 16). Probably Vasari's awareness of the writings of Aratus and Hyginus was through his Humanist circle.

137. Vasari would have been familiar with these sources because he had worked for Pope Paul III and was aware of his Humanist court (see note 143). In regard to Dürer, Vasari had travelled to Venice during 1541-1542 to work for Pietro Aretino and surely he would have seen a print of Dürer's *Celestial Map* which had been published in 1515 in Venice. Two years later, Hyginus' *Astronomy* (1517) with woodcut illustrations of the constellations was also published in Venice. Gaius Julius Hyginus was a Spanish freedman of Augustus and a dear friend of Ovid. Most of his writings have been lost. He wrote commentaries on Virgil, treatises on agriculture, history, and archeology. Only two books have survived, one on astronomy, *Astronomiae*, and the other on mythology, *Genealogiae* or *Fabulae*. See M. C. Howatson, ed. *The Oxford Companion to Classical Literature*, Oxford, 1989, p. 291. Lucas Gauricus also published his astrological treatise in Venice. Moreover, since the time of Frederick II, The Neapolitan Court had been a center of astrological pursuit, especially with the writings of Michael Scot,

*Liber introductorius* (see note 93). When Vasari worked in Naples, he certainly became aware of this matter.

N.B. I identified Vasari's celestial images by consulting Hygus, *Astronomy* (Venice, 1517) and Albrecht Dürer's *Celestial Map*. It is interesting to note that Dürer's *Celestial Map* does not include the constellations of Canis, Anticanis, Argus, Lepus and Cetus, which are found in Hyginus's *Astronomy*. My claim is not that Vasari and the iconographers for the Neapolitan program would have consulted only these two sources; on the contrary, I have already pointed out that numerous printed texts and visual references could have innuenced them. The focus on these two sources reflects only the fact that they both were the paradigm of cosmological information at that time.

138. During the sixteenth century, astrologers composed many individual horoscopes for prominent popes, rulers and Humanists, such as Leo X, Julius II, and Sixtus V, Agostino Chigi, Pietro Bembo, Francis I, and Cosimo de Medici (see Caroti, *L' astrologia in Italia*, p. 240; James Hall, *A History of Ideas and Images in Italian Art*, pp. 255-256; and Seznec, *The Survival af the Pagan Gods*, pp. 76, 79-81). For the most recent studies on horoscopes, see Claudia Rousseau, "The Pageant of the Muses at the Medici Wedding of 1539 and the Decoration of the Salone dei Cinquecento," in *"All the world's a stage ... "* Art and Pageantry in the Renaissance and Baroque*, Papers in Art History from The Pennsyvania State University, vol. VI, Barbara Wisch and Susan S. Munsbower, eds., University Park, Pennsylvania, 1990, pp. 416 - 451, and Corinne Mandel, "Starry Leo: The Sun, and the Astrological Foundations of Sixtine Rome," *RACAR*, XVIII, 1991, pp. 17-39.

139. Appropriate for the *melieu* of Renaissance Neoplatonism, Vasari has created a theological and cosmological analogy between God the Creator (God the Maker or God the Architect) and himself - an artist who creates, invents, and imitates because he is in *enthos* (a Greek word for "filled with God"). See Milton Nam, *The Artist as Creator*, Baltimore, 1956, *passim*, and Nesca Robb, *Neoplatonism of the Italian Renaissance*, New York, 1968, *passim*.

140. Seznec, *The Survival of the Pagan Gods*, p. 50, for a discussion on astrotheosophy.

141. St. Thomas Aquinas, *Summa theologia*, III, 44, and Peter A. Berlocci. "Creation in Religion" in *Dictionary of the History of Ideas*, pp. 571 - 577. On a stylistic note, we see in this section only that masks depict portraits of artists. Although it is difficult to identify each portrait, it is a kind of signature on the part of the artists similar to what we saw in the refectory of S. Michele in Bosco - again a manifestation of *maniera humor* and *fama* on the part of the painters.

142. A fusion between the Pythagorean concept of the harmony in the cosmic world with the Christian idea of heaven is discussed for the first time by St. Ambrose, in *De bono mortis*, 12: 53. See Seznec, *The Survival of the Pagan Gods*, pp. 42-43.

143. George Boas, "Macrocosm and Microcosm," in *Dictionary of the History of Ideas*, pp. 126-131.

144. Jim Tester, *A History of Western Astrology*, p. 207, commenting on Ficino; Boas, "Ficino and the Gods of the Zodiac," pp. 195-201; and John Charles Nelson, "Platonism in the Renaissance." in *Dictionary of the History of Ideas*, pp. 509 - 515.

145. Here are the examples of the control of the zodiac signs over our bodies: the ram (Aries), the head; the Bull (Taurus), the neck; the twins (Gemini), the arms; the lion (Leo), the shoulders; the crab (Cancer), the breast; the maiden (Virgo) the entrails; the scales (Libra), the buttocks; the scorpion (Scorpio), the genitals; the centaur (Sagittarius), the thighs; the goat (Capricorn), the knees; the water bearer (Aquarius), the lower legs; and fish (Pisces), the feet, not included in this Vasarian compartment.

146. R. W. Hepburn, "Cosmic Fall," in *Dictionary of the History of Ideas*, pp. 504-507, for a discussion of the flood and the fall. See Tertullian, *De baptismo*, I, in Cross, *The Oxford Dictionary of the Christian Church*, pp. 1352-1353.

147. Carmi, *L'astrologia in Italia*, pp. 267-271, for an analysis of this topic.
    N.B. All works illustrated on the following pages are by Giorgio Vasari, unless otherwise noted.

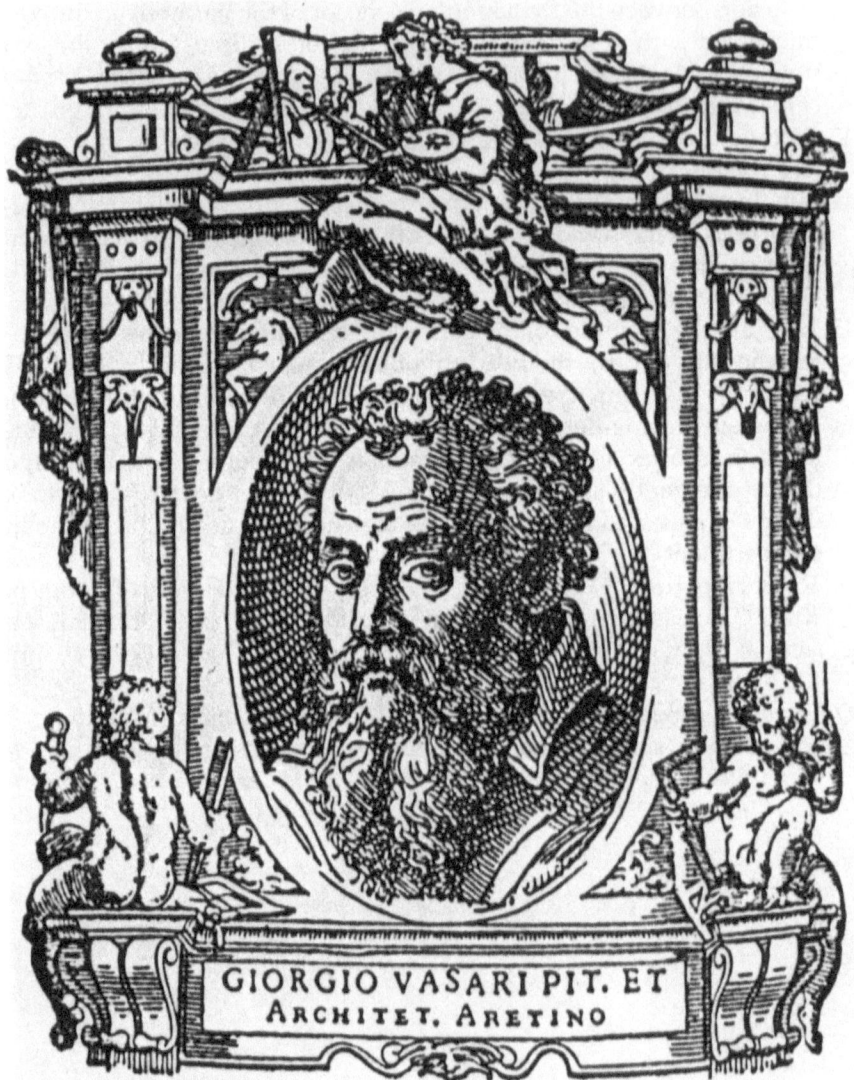

Fig. 1. Self Portrait. Woodcut from the *Vite*.

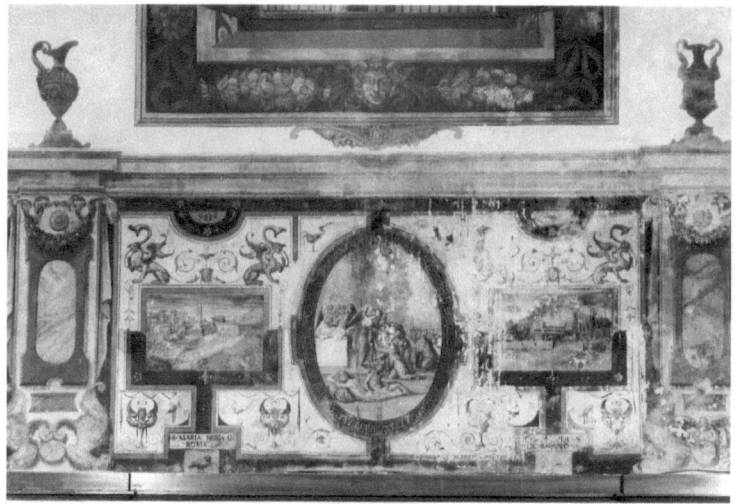

Fig. 2. San Michele in Bosco's Refectory (Bologna), 1539.

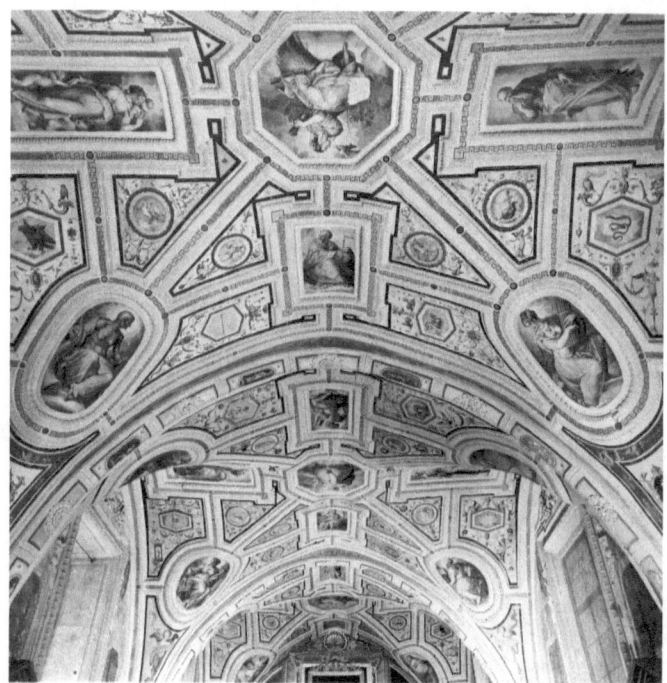

Fig. 3. Sta. Anna di Monteoliveto's Refectory (Naples), 1545.

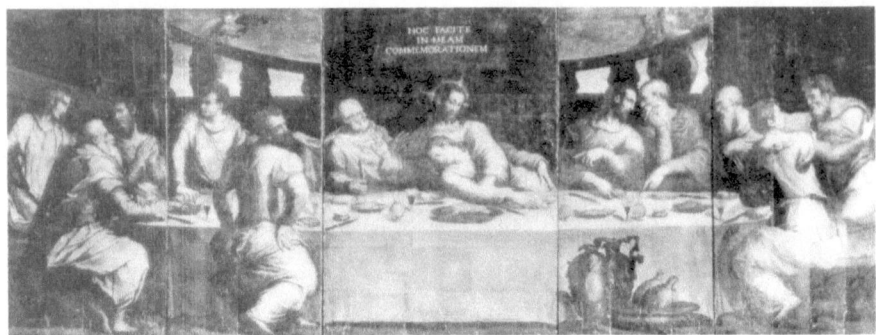

Fig. 4. *Last Supper* for the Murate's Refectory (Florence), 1540s.

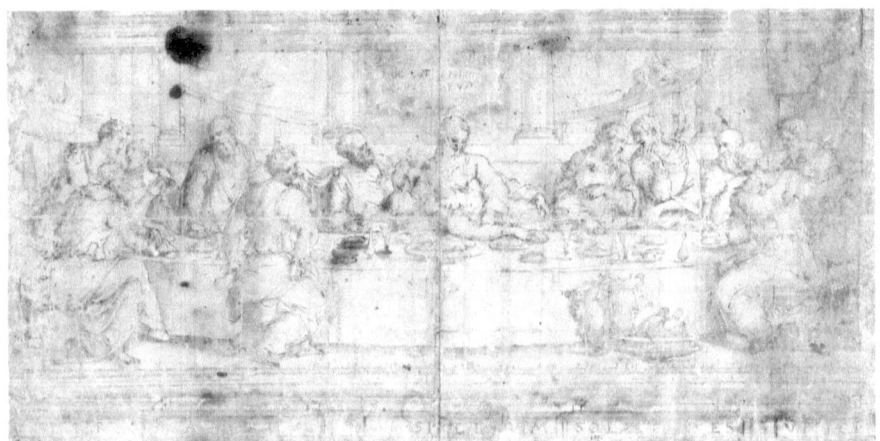

Fig. 5. Drawing of the above (Munich), 1540s.

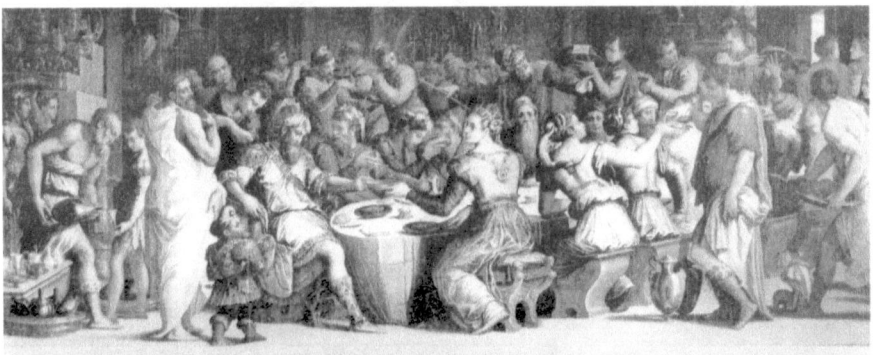

Fig. 6. *Esther and Ahsuerus Wedding*, Badia's Refectory (Arezzo).

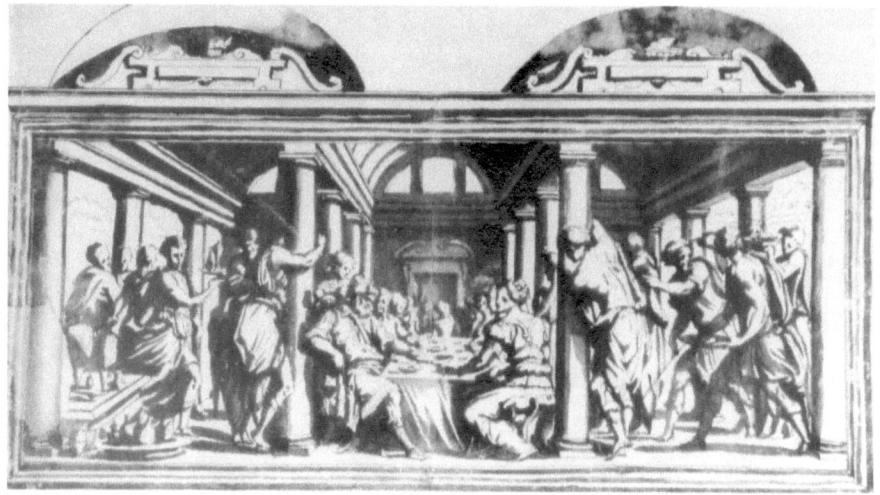

Fig. 7. Study of the above (Florence).

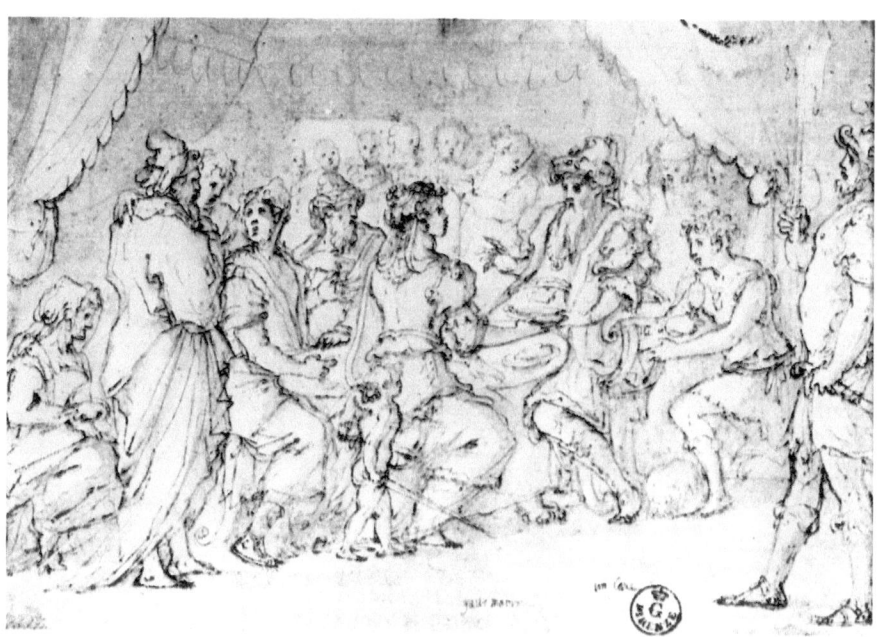

Fig. 8. Drawing of the above (Florence).

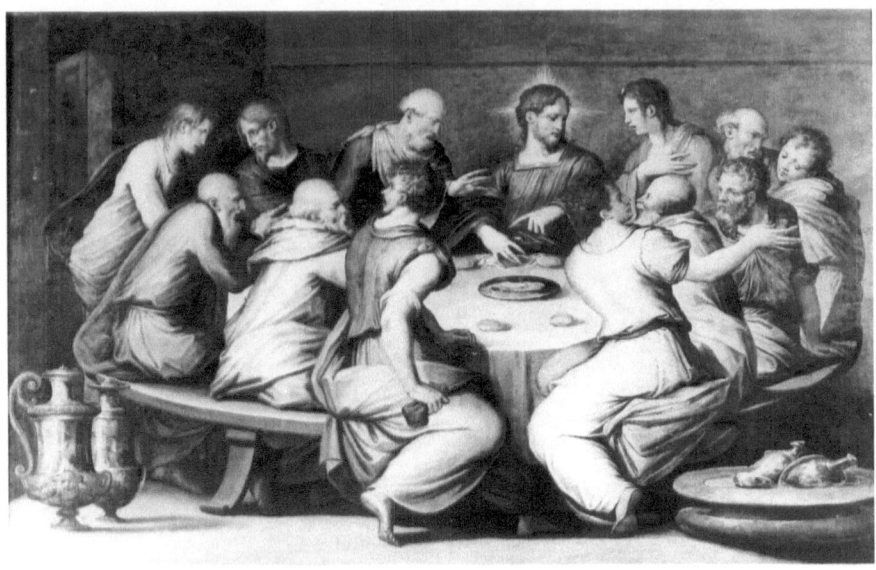

Fig. 9. *Last Supper*. Troyes, Musée des Beax-Arts et Archéologie.

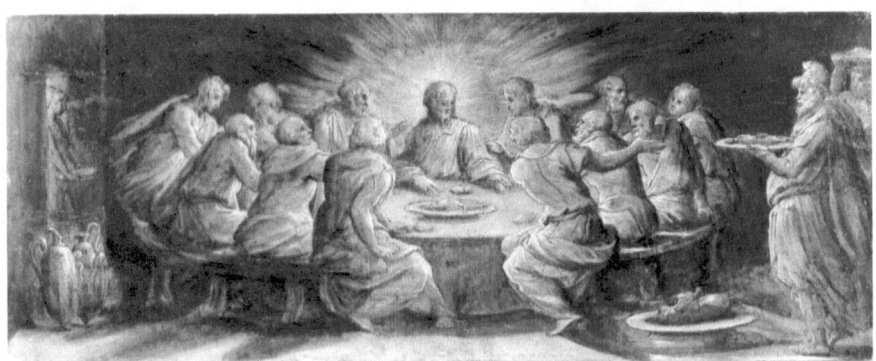

Fig. 10. *Last Supper*. Baltimore, Walters Art Gallery.

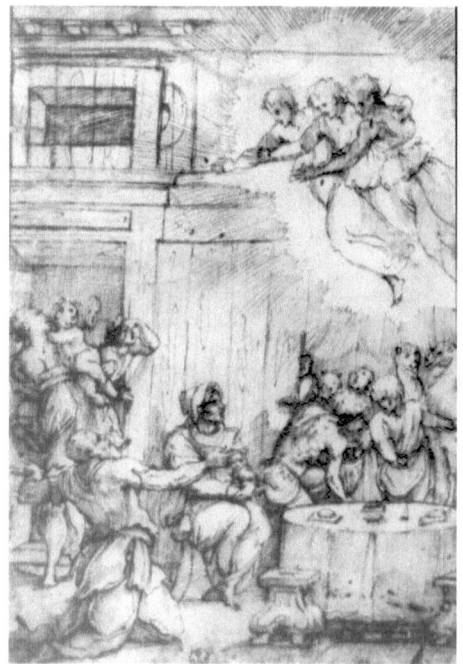

Fig. 11. Drawing I, *Abraham and The Three Angels*.

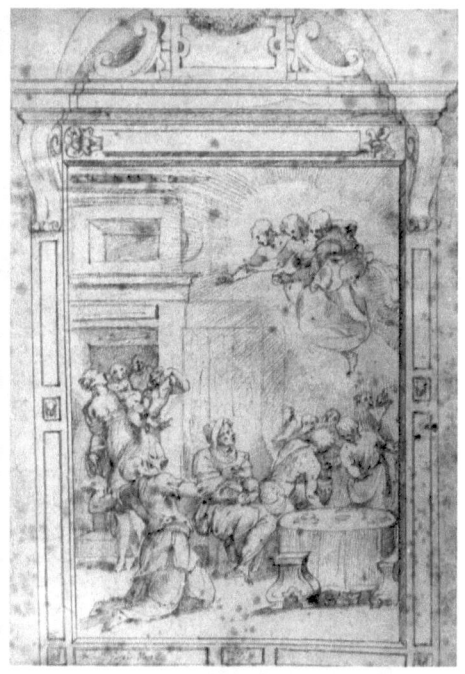

Fig. 12. Drawing II, *Abraham and The Three Angels* (Uffizi).

Fig. 13. Drawing III, *Abraham and The Three Angels* (Lille).

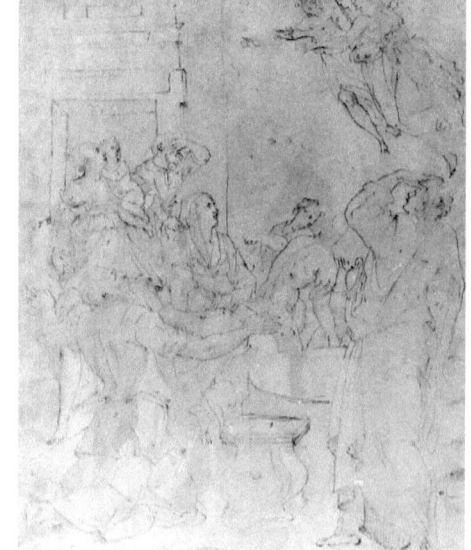

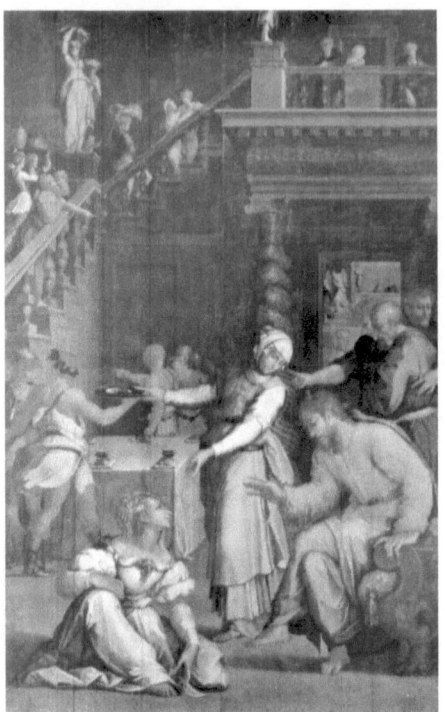

Fig. 14. *Christ in the House of Martha and Mary*. Bologna, San Michele in Bosco, Refectory.

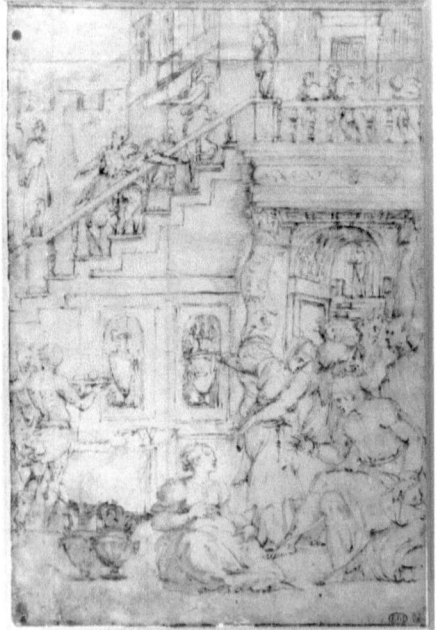

Fig. 15. Drawing for the above. Louvre, Cabinet des Dessins, N. R. F. 92.

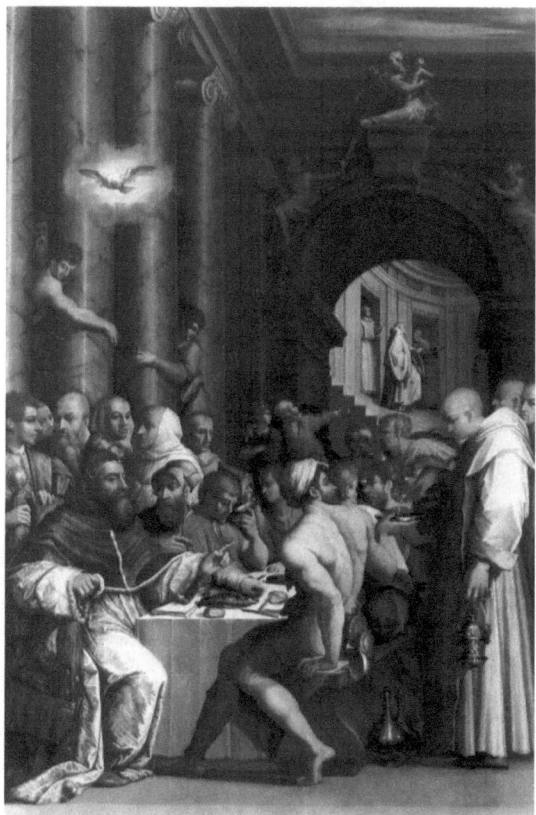

Fig. 16. *The Feast of St. Gregory.* Bologna, San Michele in Bosco, Refectory. Present location: Pinacoteca Nazionale, Inv. 534.

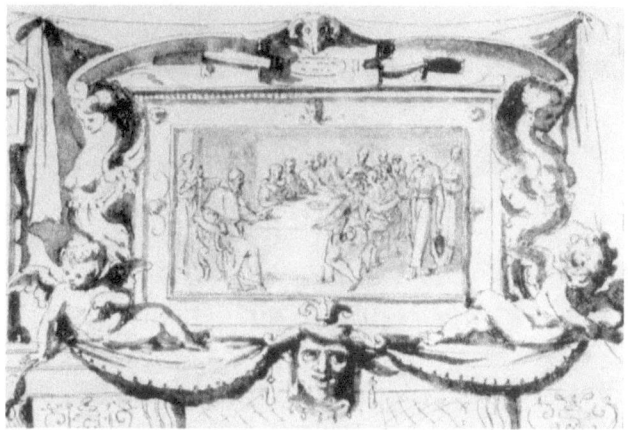

Fig. 17. Sketch for *The Feast of St. Gregory.* Florence, Galleria degli Uffizi, Gabinetto dei Disegni, N. 953E.

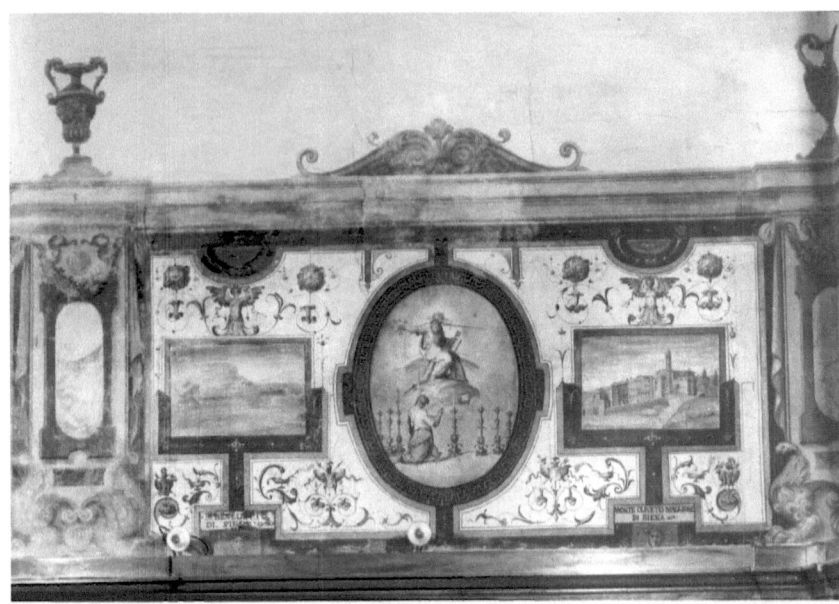

Fig. 18. *Vision of the Candlesticks*, Stories from the Apocalypse. Bologna, San Michele in Bosco, Refectory.

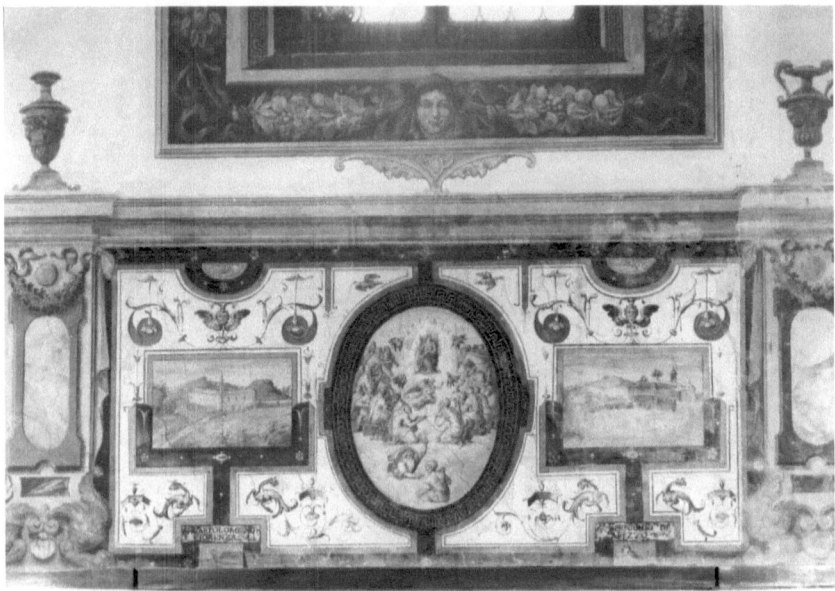

Fig. 19. *St. John with God and the Elders*, Stories from the Apocalypse. Bologna, San Michele in Bosco, Refectory.

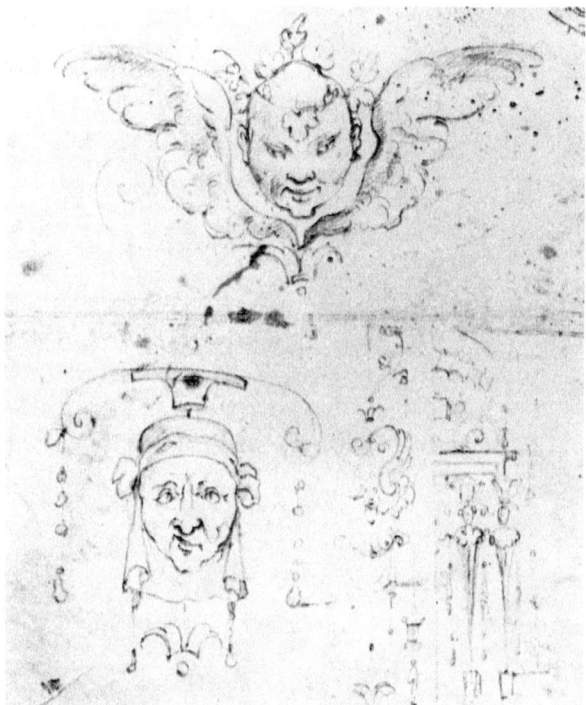

Fig. 20. Cristofano Gherardi, *Sketch for a Mask* (Self-portrait) , Florence, Galleria degli Uffizi, Gabinetto dei Disegni, N 93727.

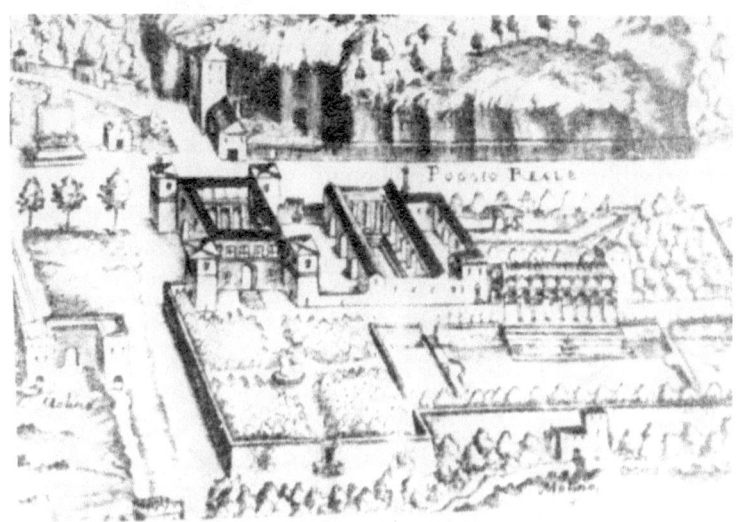

Fig. 21. *View Monte Oliveto*, Naples.

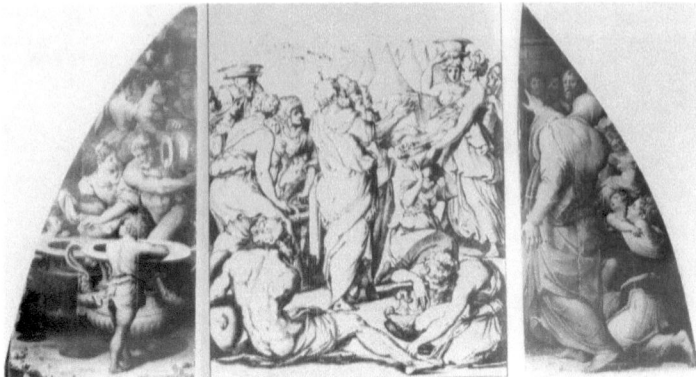

Fig. 22. Cheney's Reconstruction I of the *Fall of the Manna with Moses and Aaron* (reversing the image from the lithograph).

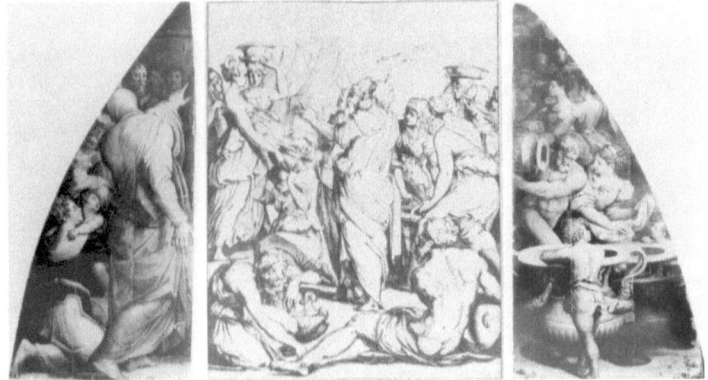

Fig. 23. Cheney's Reconstruction II of the *Fall of the Manna with Moses and Aaron* (without reversing the image).

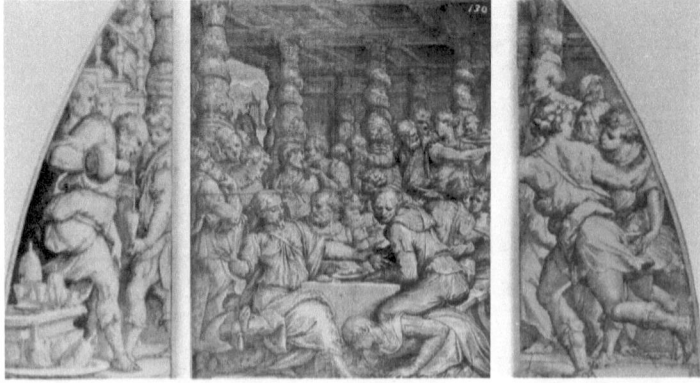

Fig. 24a. Cheney's Reconstruction I of *Christ in the House of Simon* based on the drawings from Amsterdam and Sotheby.

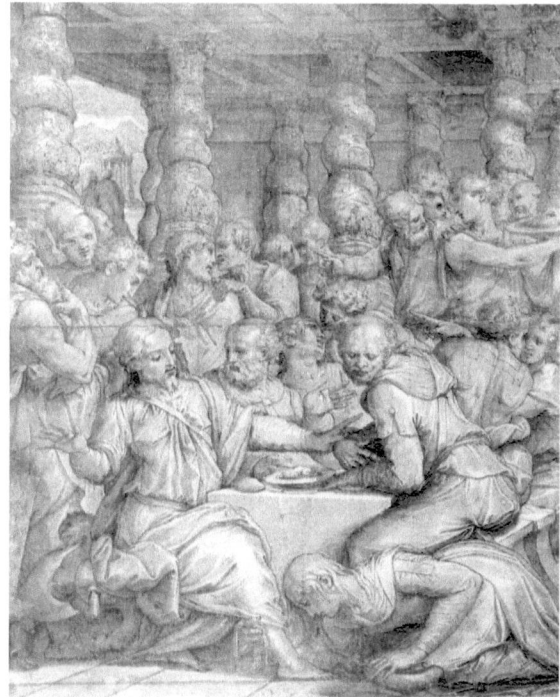

Fig. 24b. Drawing for
*Christ in the House of
Simon* (center).
Amsterdam, Rikjspren-
tenkabinet, N.1951.

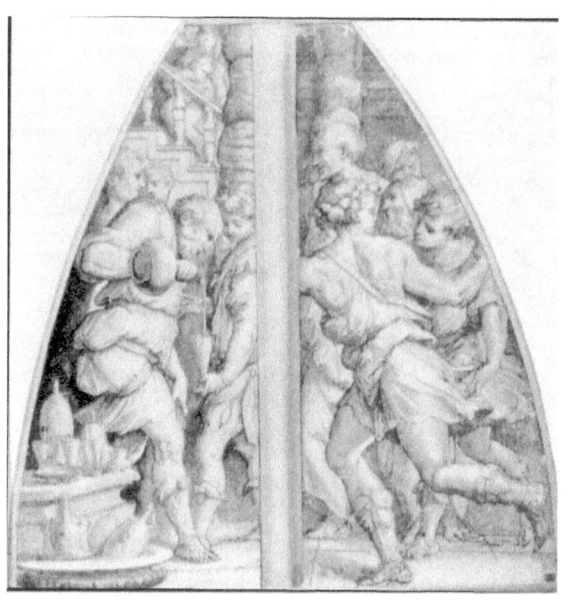

Fig. 24c. Drawings for
the side panels (left
and right). New York,
Sotheby, N. 144 (auc-
tion January 14, 1987).

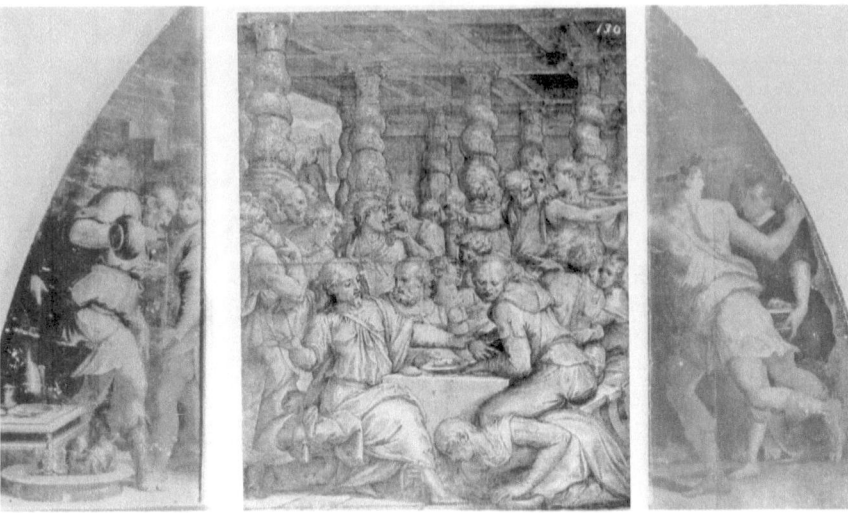

Fig. 25a. Cheney's Reconstruction II of *Christ in the House of Simon* based on the Amsterdam's drawing and Neapolitan panels.

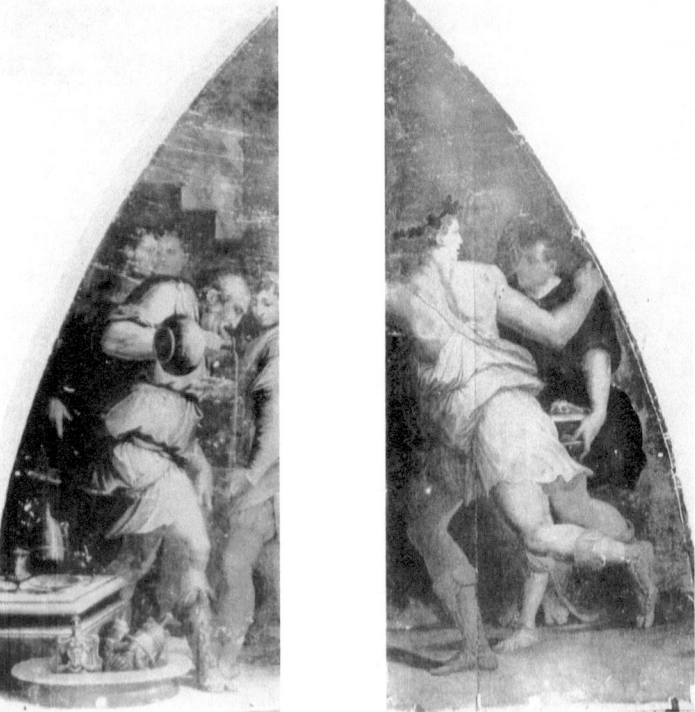

Fig. 25b and c. Side panels (left and right). Naples, Museo e Gallerie Nazionali di Capodimonte, Inv. 1076.

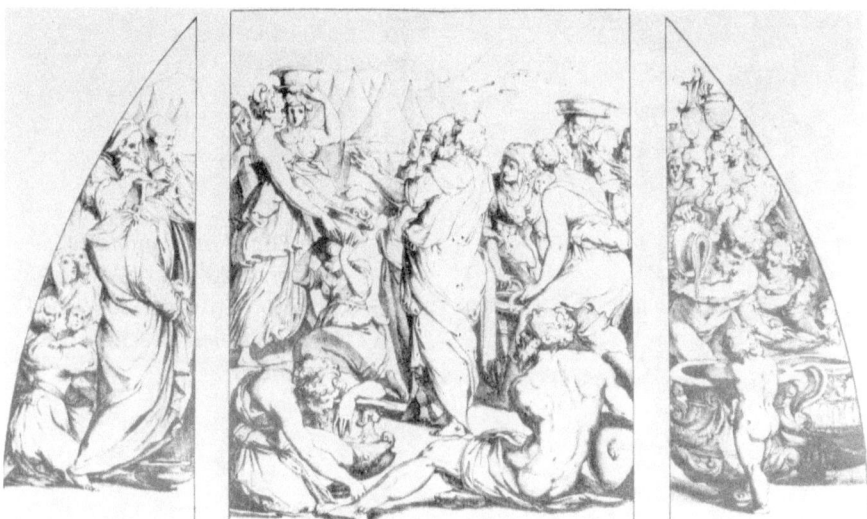

Fig. 26. D. Vivant-Denon, *The Fall of the Manna with Moses and Aaron.* Facsimile lithograph from *Monuments des arts du dessins chez les peuples tant anciens que modernes*, Ed. P. d'Amaury (Pineaux), Duval, Paris, 1829, III.

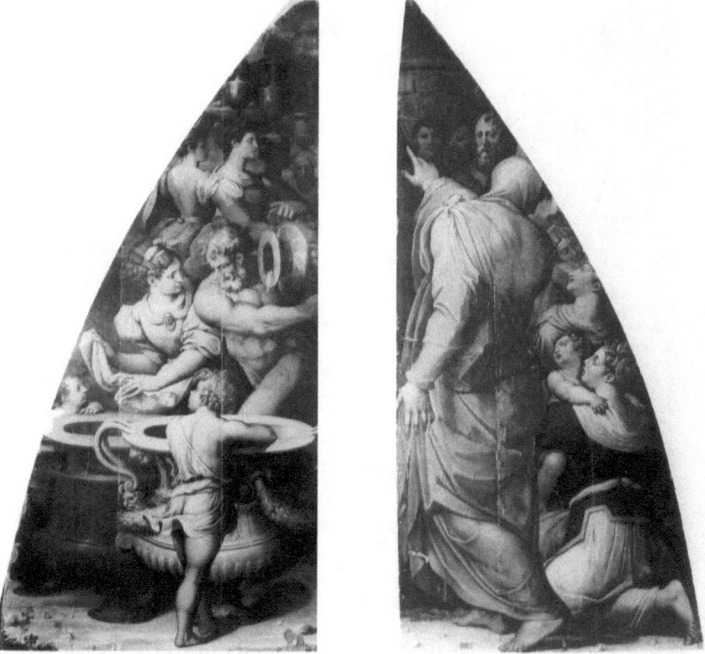

Fig. 27a and b. Left and Right wing panels for *The Fall of the Manna with Moses and Aaron*. Palermo, Museo Arcivescolive, Inv. 532 and 534.

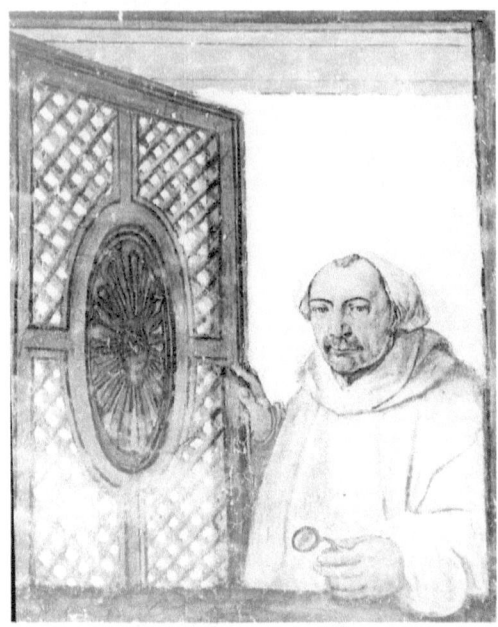

Fig. 28. *Don Giammateo d'Aversa,* Abbot of Monteoliveto. Entrance to Refectory. Naples, S. Anna dei Lombardi.

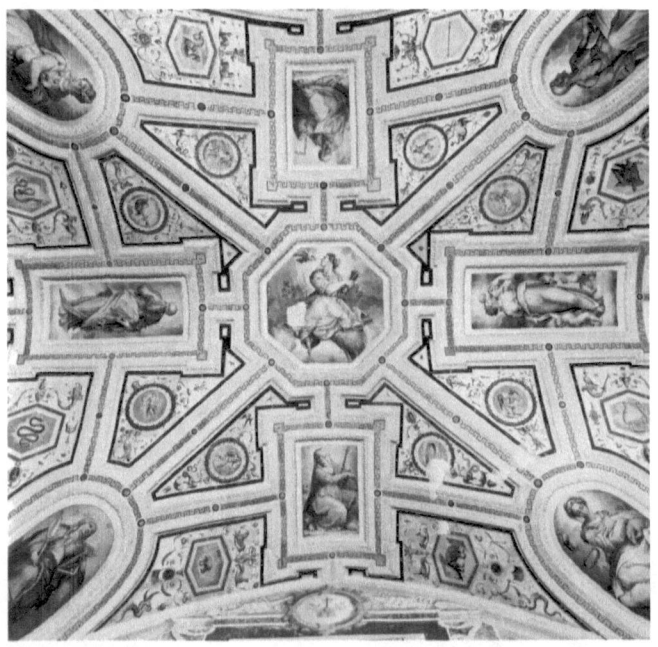

Fig. 29. *Religion* (detail). Naples, S. Anna dei Lombardi, Refectory of Monteoliveto.

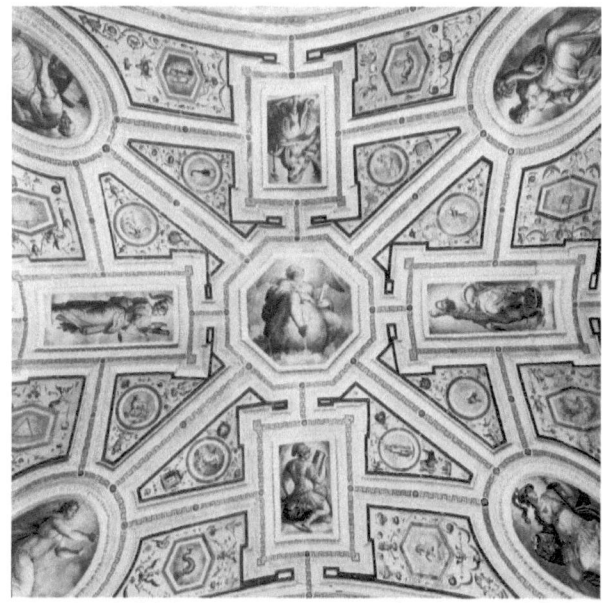

Fig. 30. *Eternity* (detail). Naples, S. Anna dei Lombardi, Refectory of Monteoliveto.

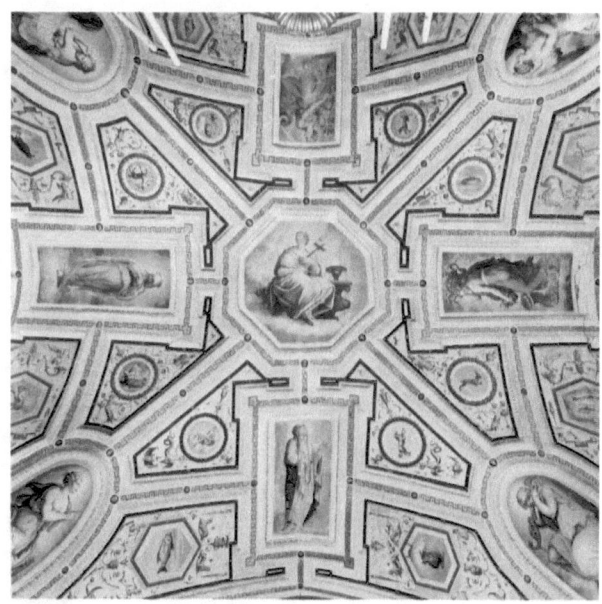

Fig. 31. *Faith* (detail). Naples, S. Anna dei Lombardi, Refectory of Monteoliveto.

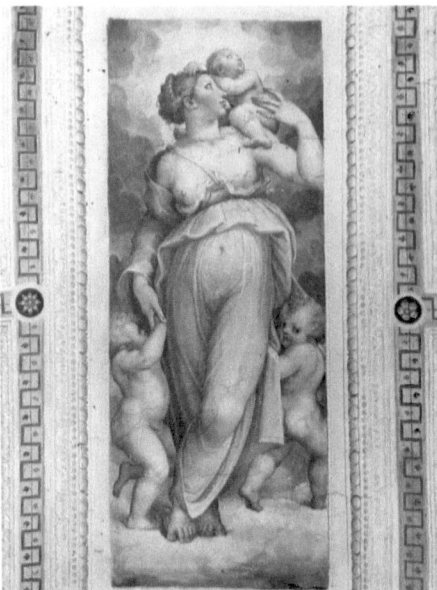

Fig. 32. *Charity* (detail).
Naples, S. Anna dei Lombardi,
Refectory of Monteoliveto.

Fig. 33. Drawing for *Charity*.
Bologna, Gabinetto dei Disegni e
delle Stampe, Inv. 1613.

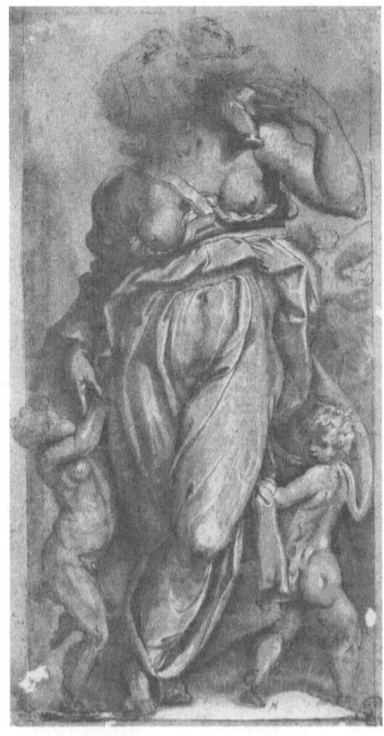

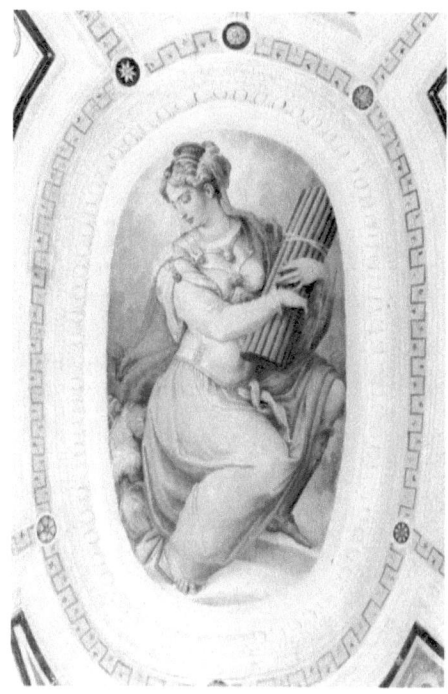

Fig. 34. *Concord* (detail).
Naples, S. Anna dei Lombardi,
Refectory of Monteoliveto.

Fig. 35. Drawing for *Concord*.
Kassel, Staatliche Kunstsammlungen, GS 9629.

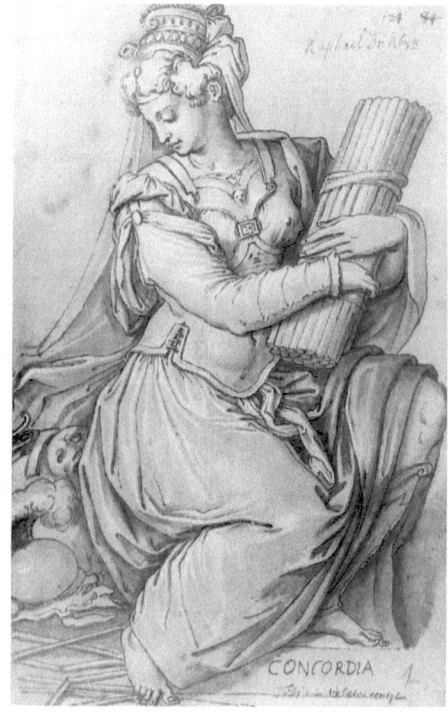

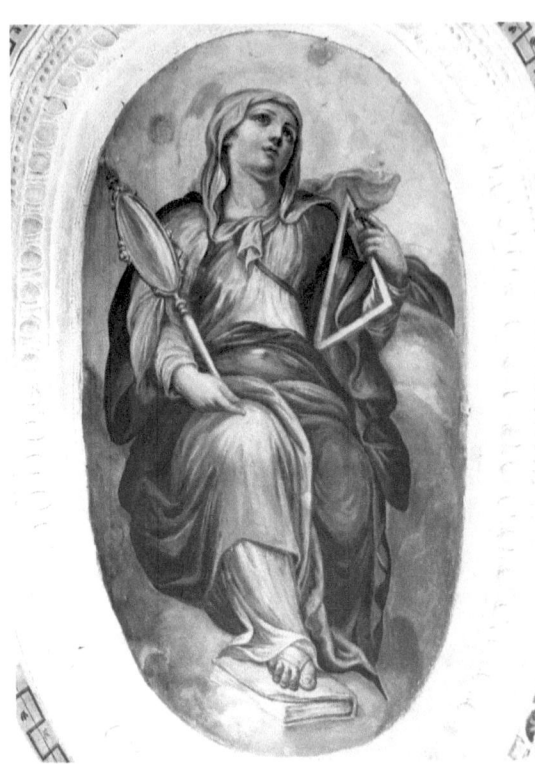

Fig. 36. *Instruction* (detail). Naples, S. Anna dei Lombardi, Refectory of Monteoliveto.

Fig. 37. *Justice* (detail). Naples, S. Anna dei Lombardi, Refectory of Monteoliveto.

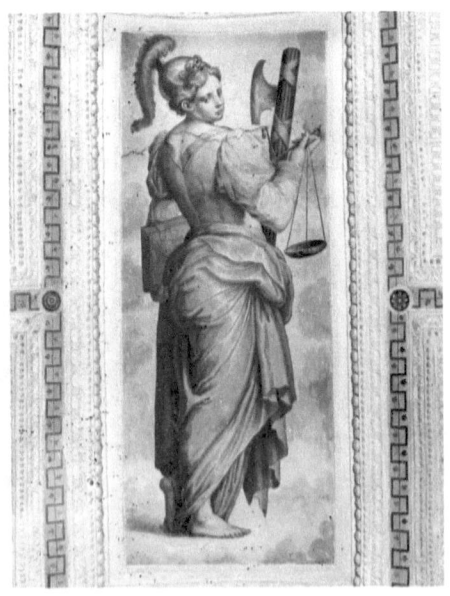

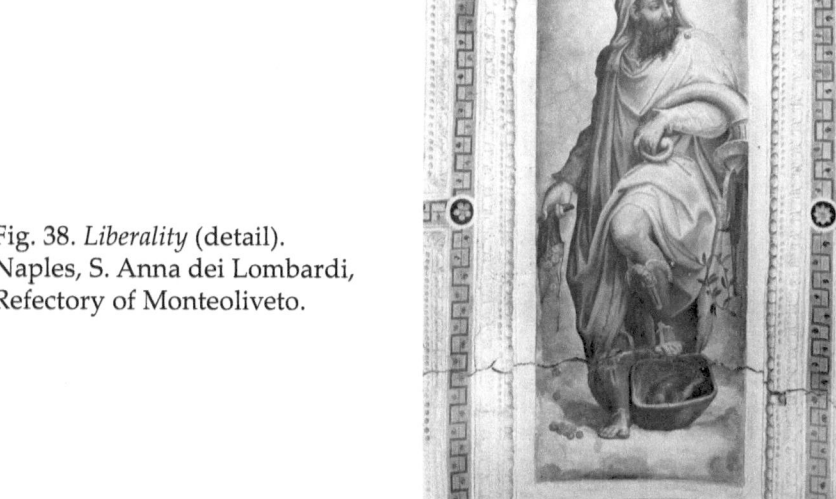

Fig. 38. *Liberality* (detail).
Naples, S. Anna dei Lombardi,
Refectory of Monteoliveto.

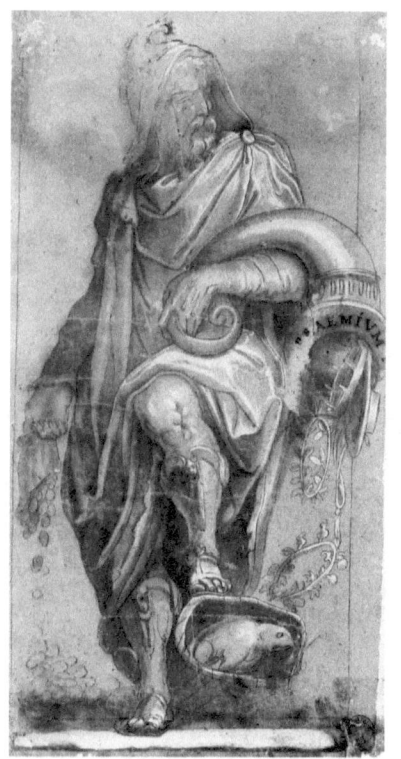

Fig. 39. Drawing for *Liberality*.
Bologna, Gabinetto dei Disegni
e delle Stampe, Inv. 1615.

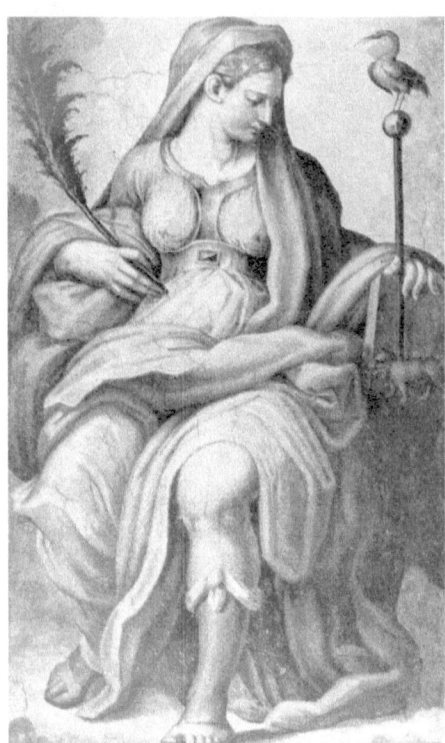

Fig. 40. *Vigilance* (detail).  Naples, S. Anna dei Lombardi, Refectory of Monteoliveto.

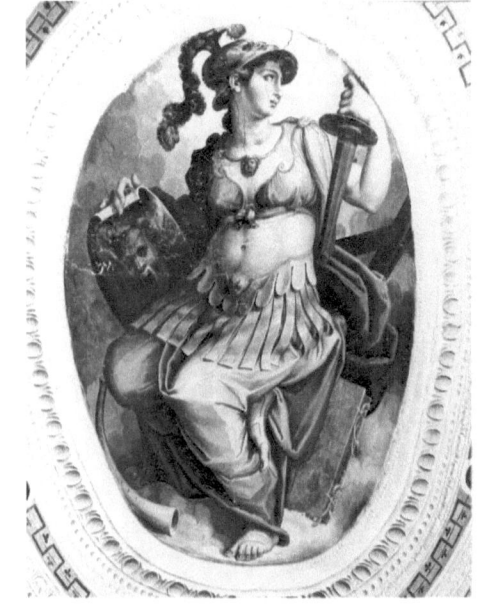

Fig. 41. *Fortitude* (detail).  Naples, S. Anna dei Lombardi, Refectory of Monteoliveto.

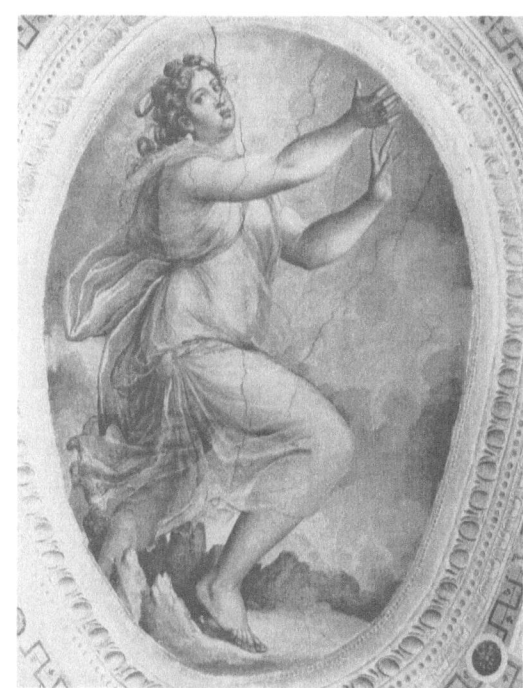

Fig. 42. *Fear of God* (detail). Naples, S. Anna dei Lombardi, Refectory of Monteoliveto.

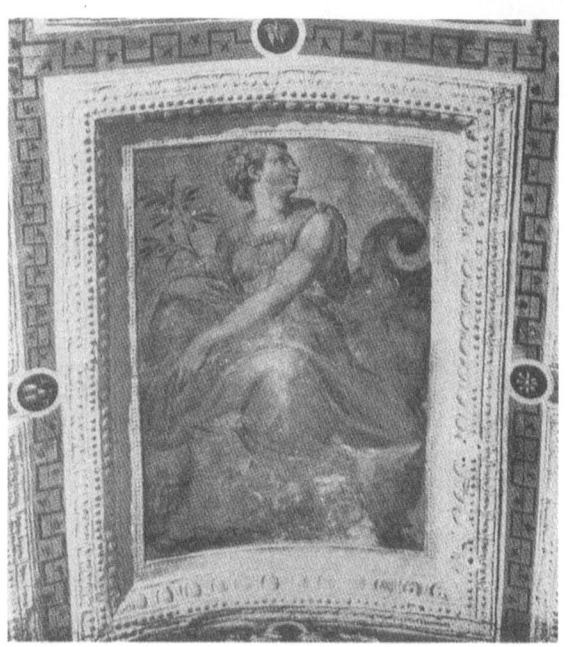

Fig. 43. *Peace* (detail). Naples, S. Anna dei Lombardi, Refectory of Monteoliveto.

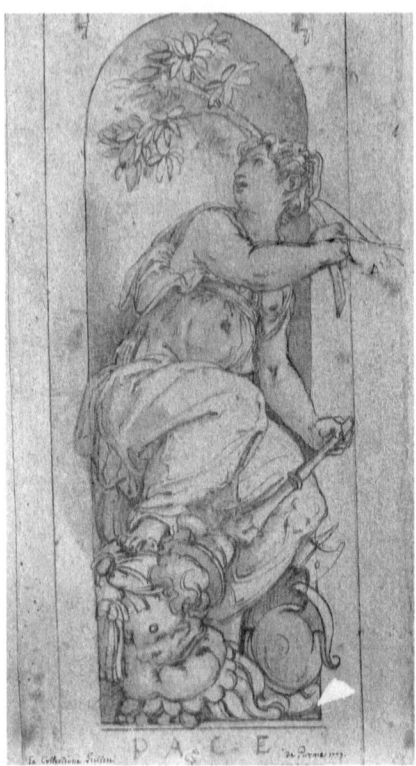

Fig. 44. Drawing for the *Peace*.
Vienna, Graphische Sammlung
Albertina, Inv. 462.

Fig. 45. *Obedience* (St. Catherine
of Siena) (detail). Naples,
S. Anna dei Lombardi,
Refectory of Monteoliveto.

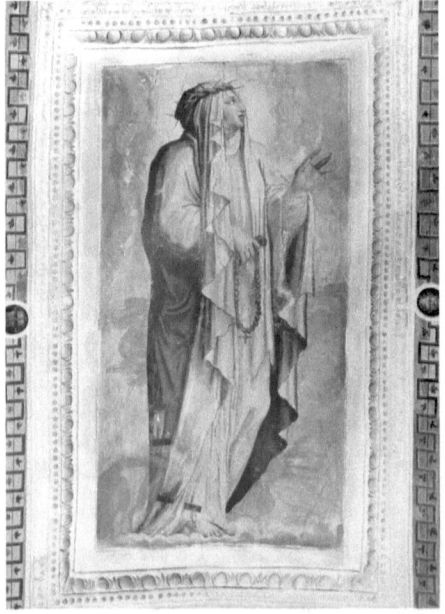

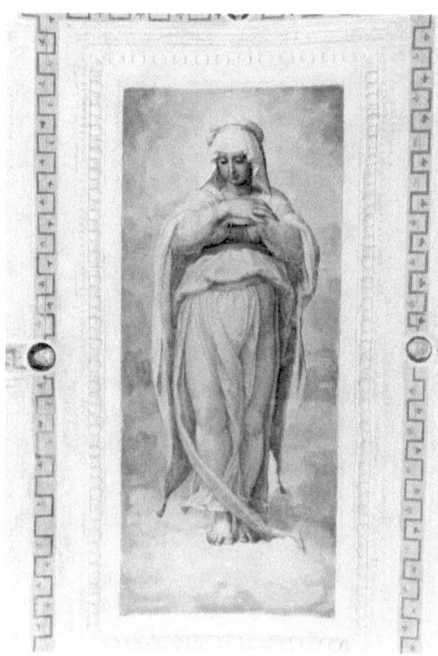

Fig. 46. *Pudicity or Modesty* (detail). Naples, S. Anna dei Lombardi, Refectory of Monteoliveto.

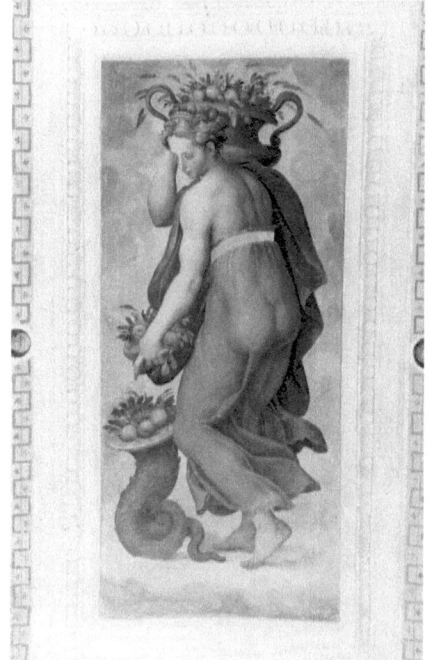

Fig. 47. *Abundance or Joy* (detail). Naples, S. Anna dei Lombardi, Refectory of Monteoliveto.

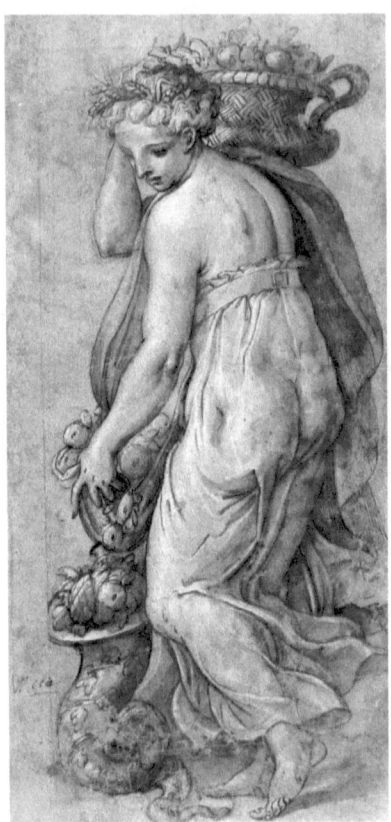

Fig. 48. Drawing for *Abundance*.
London, British Museum. (Photo:
courtsey of the Trustees of the
British Museum.

Fig. 49. *Prudence* (detail).
Naples, S. Anna dei Lombardi,
Refectory of Monteoliveto.

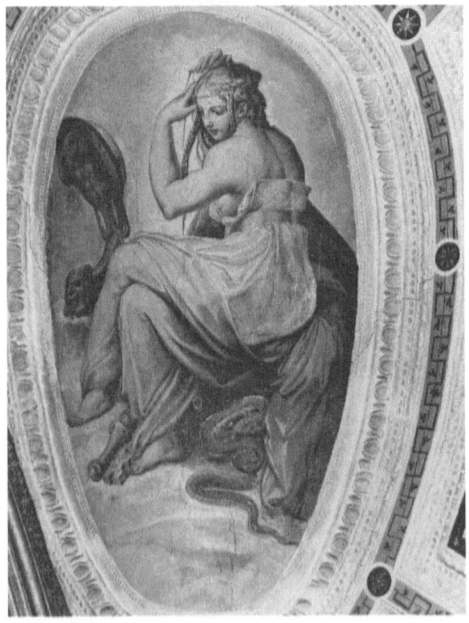

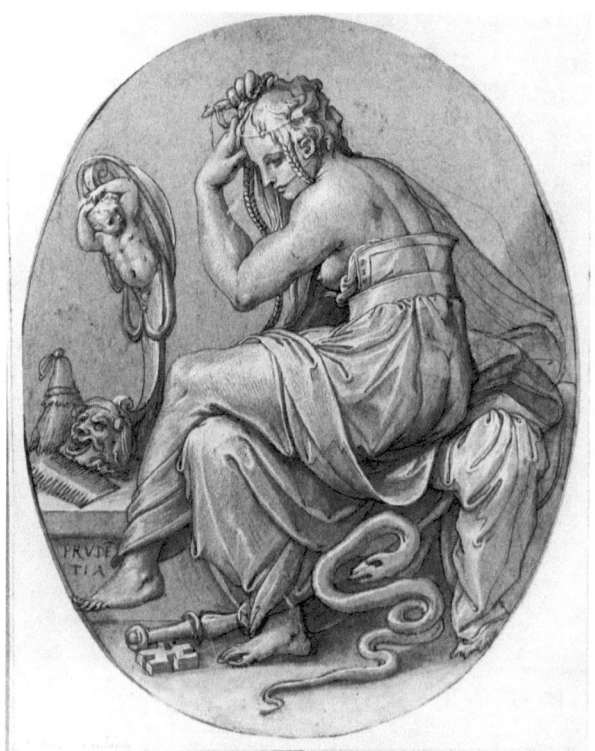

Fig. 50. Drawing
for *Prudence*. Paris,
Istitut Neerlandas,
Collection F. Lugt,
Inv. 7777.

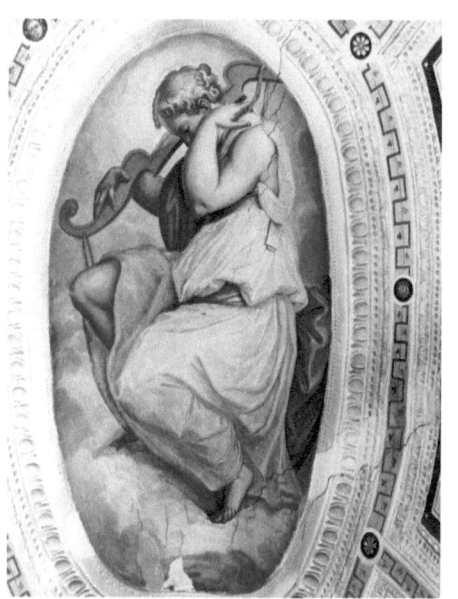

Fig. 51. *Patience* (detail). Naples,
S. Anna dei Lombardi, Refectory
of Monteoliveto.

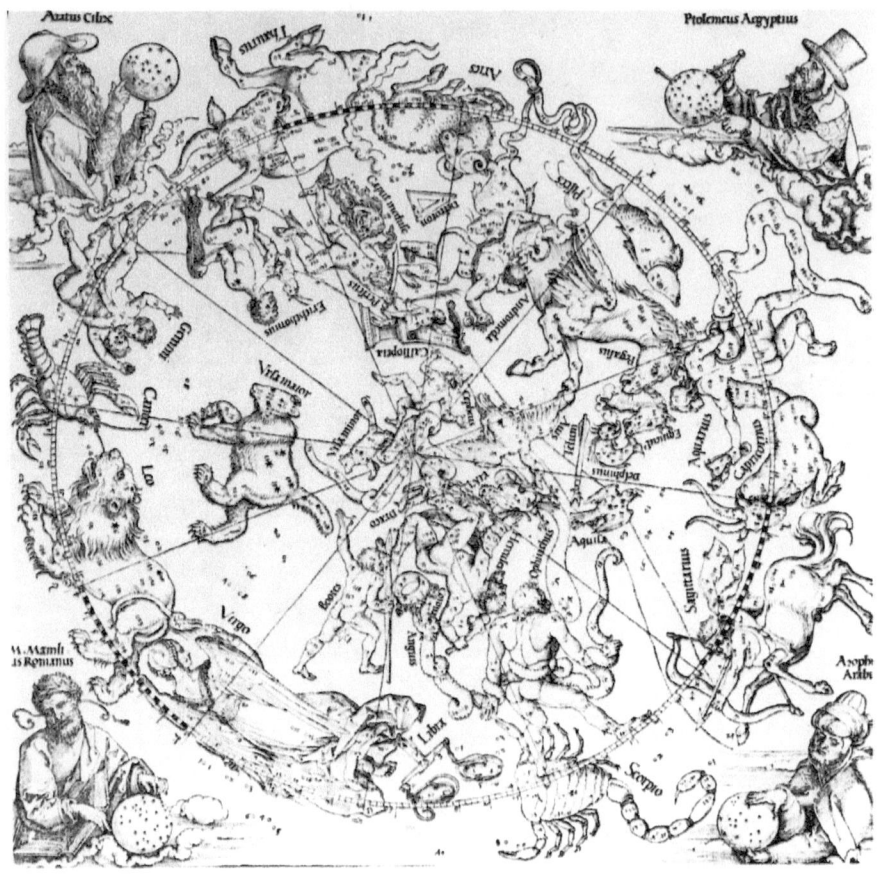

Fig. 52. Albrecht Durer, *Celestial Map*, 1515 (B. 151).  Woodcut engraving.

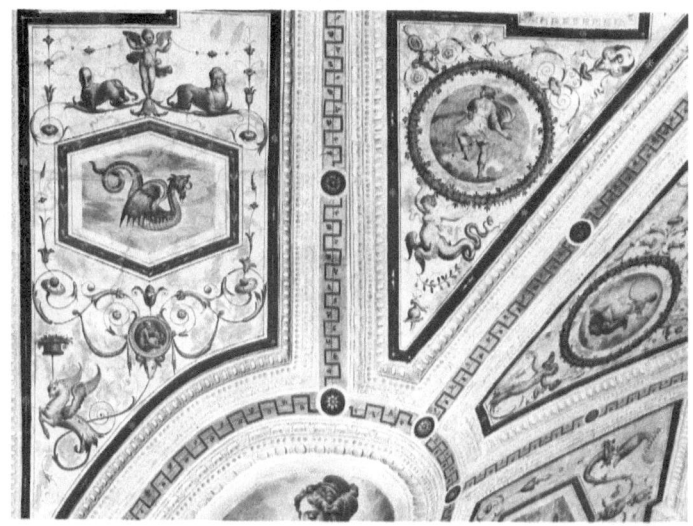

Fig. 53a. Giorgio Vasari, *Cepheus Constellation* (detail), Naples,
S. Anna dei Lombardi, Refectory of Monteoliveto.

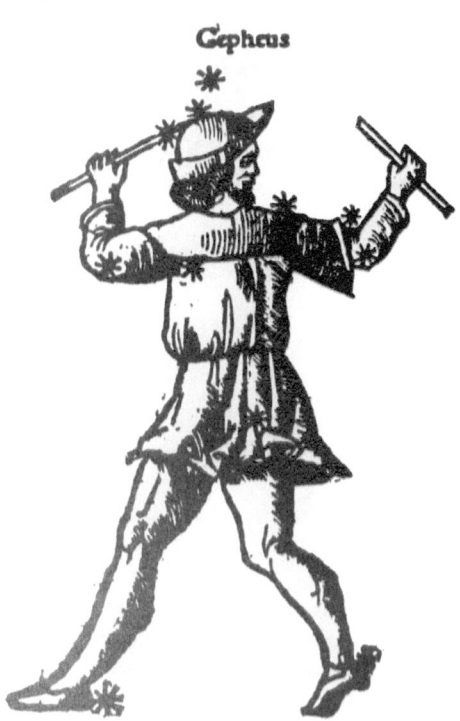

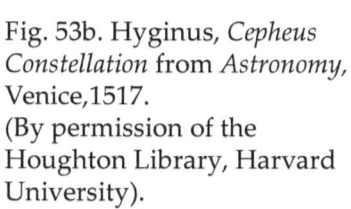

Fig. 53b. Hyginus, *Cepheus
Constellation* from *Astronomy*,
Venice,1517.
(By permission of the
Houghton Library, Harvard
University).

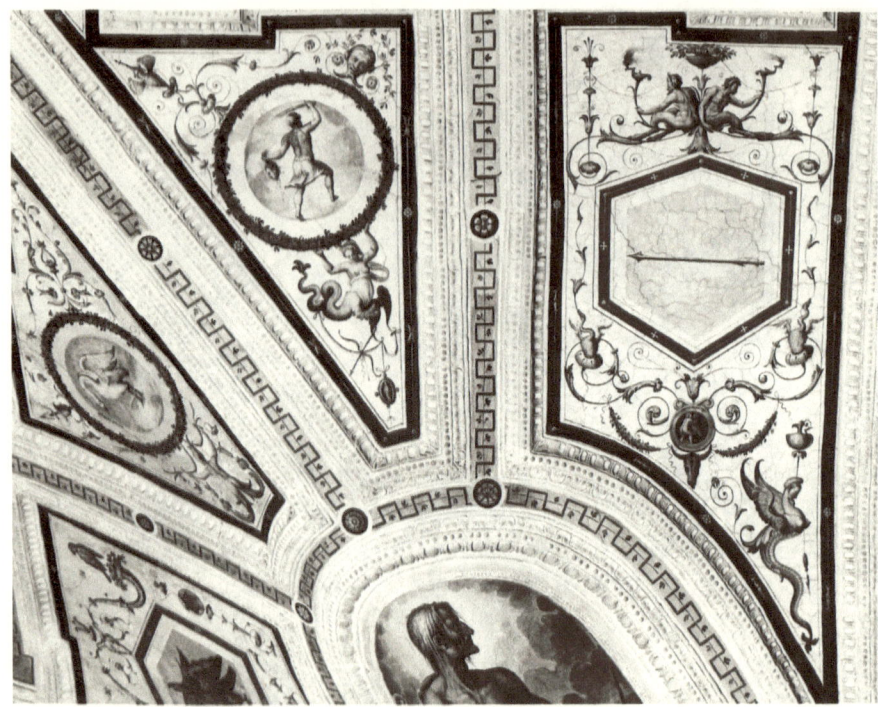

Fig. 54a. Giorgio Vasari, *Tetum or Sagitta Constellation* (detail), Naples, S. Anna dei Lombardi, Refectory of Monteoliveto.

Sagitta.

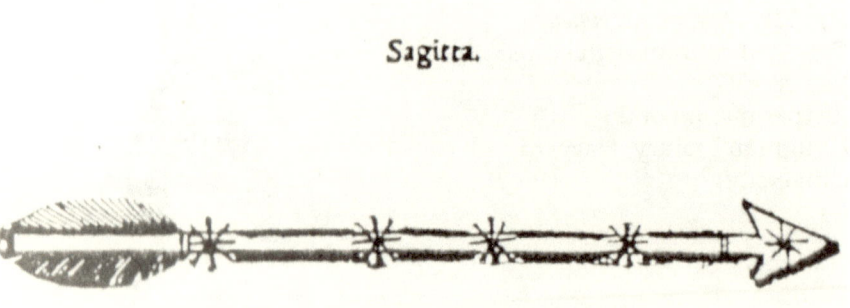

Fig. 54b. Hyginus, *Tetum or Sagitta Constellation* from *Astronomy*, Venice,1517. (By permission of the Houghton Library, Harvard University).

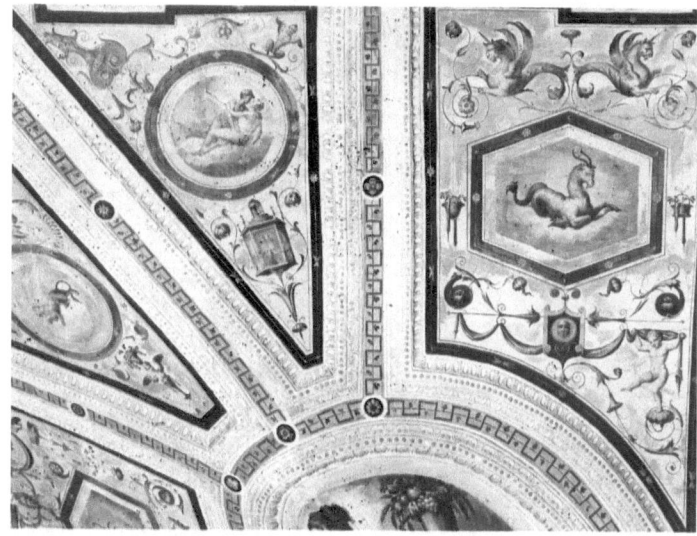

Fig. 55a. Giorgio Vasari, *Gemini* (detail), Naples, S. Anna dei Lombardi, Refectory of Monteoliveto.

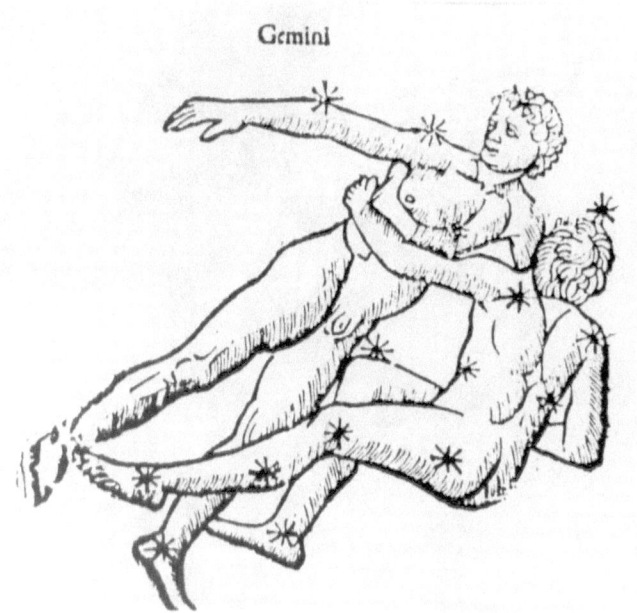

Fig. 55b. Hyginus, *Gemini* from *Astronomy*, Venice,1517.
(By permission of the Houghton Library, Harvard University).

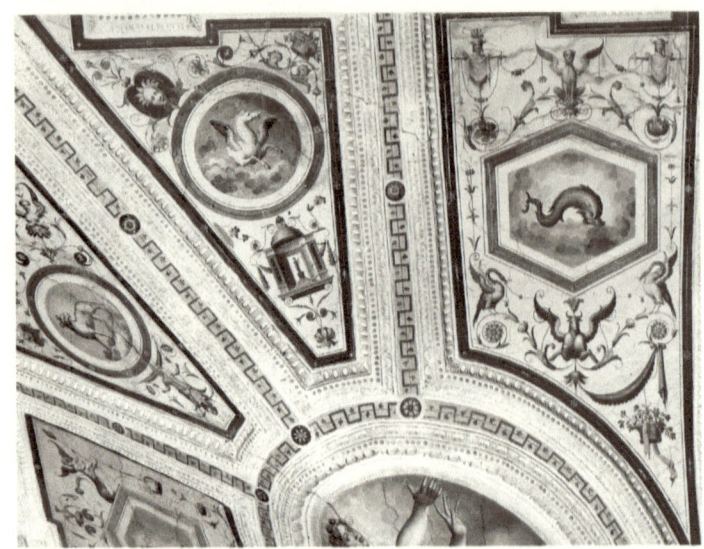

Fig. 56a. Giorgio Vasari, *Pegasus Constellation* (detail), Naples, S. Anna dei Lombardi, Refectory of Monteoliveto.

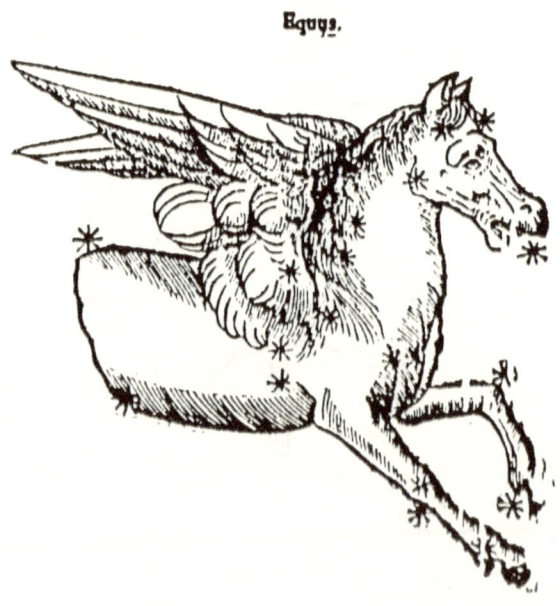

Fig. 56b. Hyginus, *Pegasus Constellation* from *Astronomy*, Venice, 1517. (By permission of the Houghton Library, Harvard University).

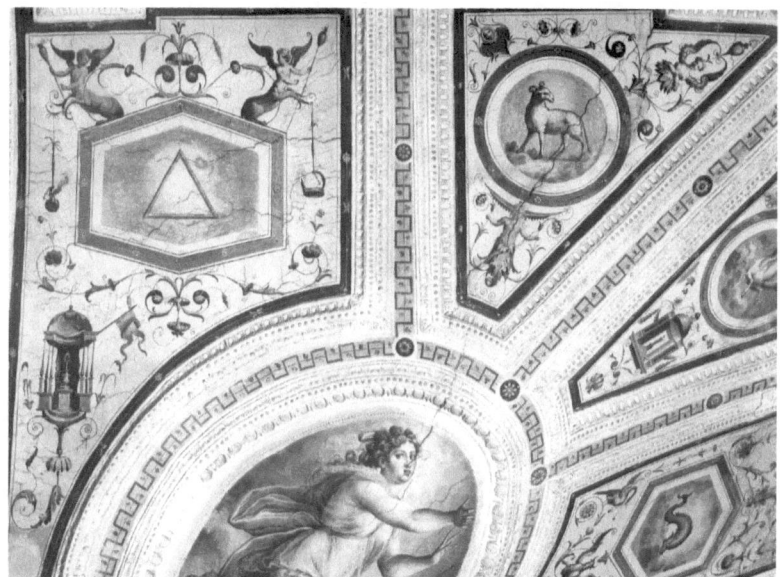

Fig. 57a. Giorgio Vasari, *Delthotons Constellation* (detail), Naples, S. Anna dei Lombardi, Refectory of Monteoliveto.

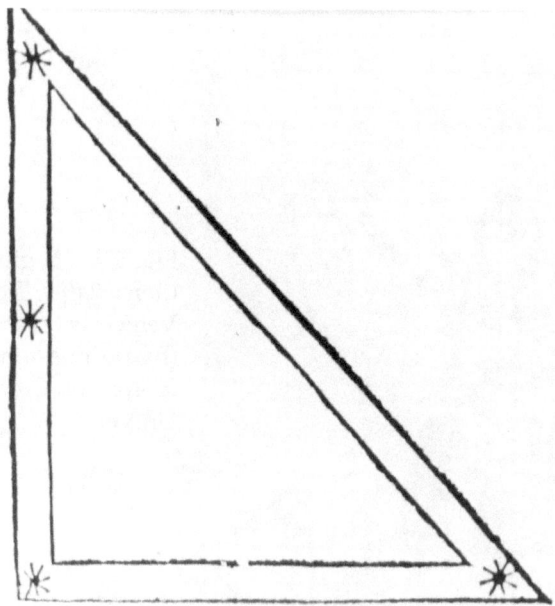

Fig. 57b. Hyginus, *Delthoton Constellation* from *Astronomy*, Venice, 1517. (By permission of the Houghton Library, Harvard University).

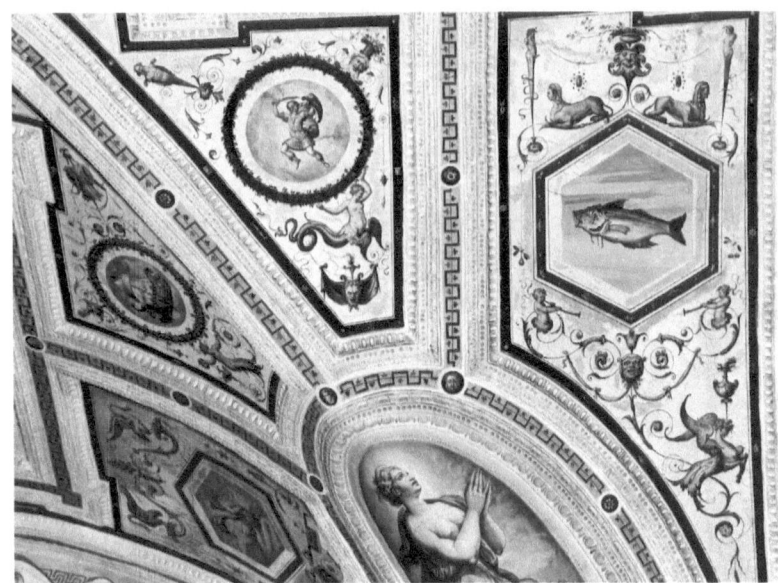

Fig. 58a. Giorgio Vasari, *Orion Constellation* (detail), Naples, S. Anna dei Lombardi, Refectory of Monteoliveto.

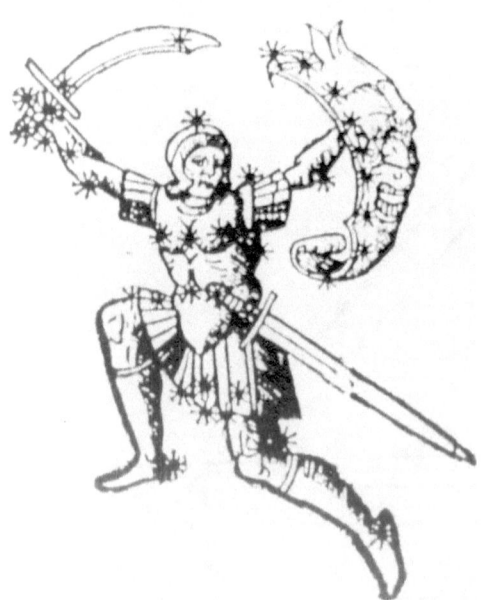

Fig. 58b. Hyginus, *Orion Constellation* from *Astronomy,* Venice,1517. (By permission of the Houghton Library, Harvard University).

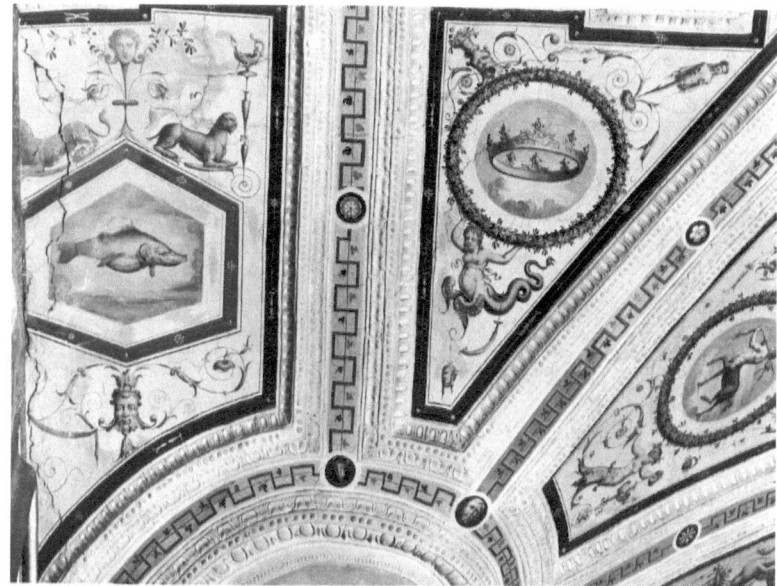

Fig. 59a. Giorgio Vasari, *Crown Constellation* (detail), Naples, S. Anna dei Lombardi, Refectory of Monteoliveto.

Fig. 59b. Hyginus, *Crown Constellation* from *Astronomy*, Venice,1517. (By permission of the Houghton Library, Harvard University).

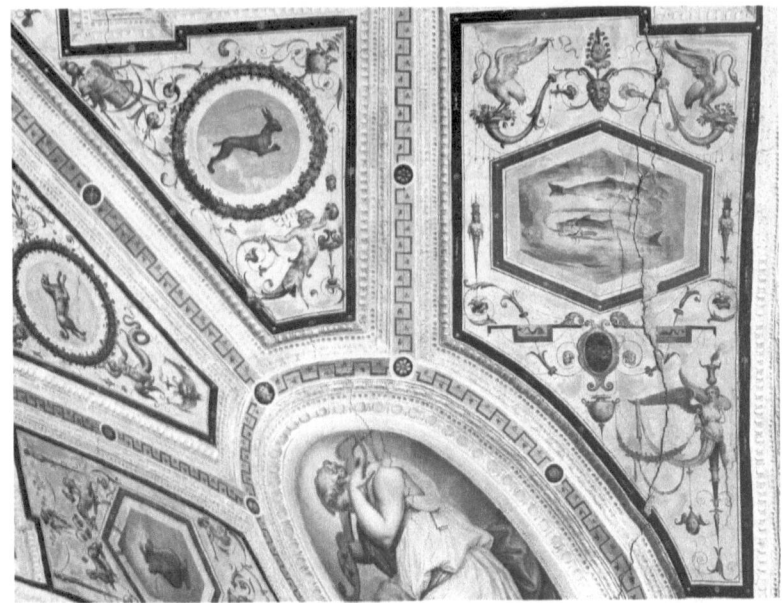

Fig. 60a. Giorgio Vasari, *Pisces* (detail), Naples, S. Anna dei Lombardi, Refectory of Monteoliveto.

Pisces.'

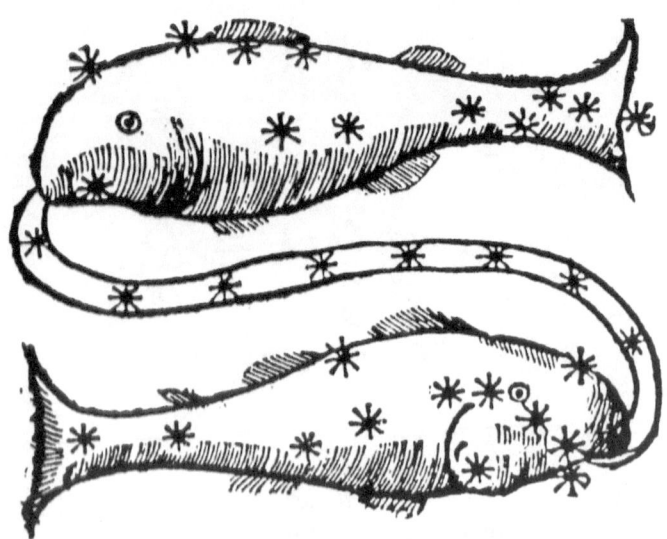

Fig. 60b. Hyginus, *Pisces* from *Astronomy*, Venice,1517.
(By permission of the Houghton Library, Harvard University).

# 6

# Giorgio Vasari's Sala Dei Cento Giorni: A Farnese Celebration

The Palazzo Della Cancelleria, or Chancery Palace, was built by Bregno da Montecavallo in 1483 on the ravine of the theater of Pompey for Sixtus IV's nephew, Cardinal Riario. Later, in 1535, the palace became the new residence of the Farnese family. At the suggestion of Paolo Giovio[1] and Bindo Altovito, Cardinal Alessandro Farnese (1520-1589) in March of 1546 commissioned Giorgio Vasari (Fig. 1) and his assistants to paint the great hall *al fresco*.[2] The purpose of the commission was to celebrate the life of Pope Paul III (Alessandro Farnese, 1468-1549), the cardinal's uncle, whom he greatly admired and after whom he was named. Two years earlier, Perino del Vaga had executed a commission honoring Pope Paul III as the new Alexander the Great in the Sala Paolina.[3] Later on, other commissions memorializing the Pontiff s accomplishments were executed by Francesco Salviati in the Sala dei Fasti Farnesiani (1552-58) (I. Cheney 791-820), and in numerous decorative cycles by Taddeo Zuccaro and his assistants - the Anticamera del Concilio and the Sala dei Fasti Farnesi (1560-66).[4] None of these commissions, however, so eloquently immortalizes the Farnese Pontiff's ecclesiastical and secular triumphs as do Vasari's decorative cycles in the Sala dei Cento Giorni (Figs. 2 and 3). The Sala dei Cento Giorni is a monumental commission honoring the temporal and spiritual powers of Pope Paul III Farnese.

In his notebook (*Lo Zibaldone*) and in the autobiographical section of his *Le Vite*, Vasari discussed the circumstances for this patronage, identified the personifications depicted, and explained the subject matter. In *Lo Zibaldone*, under the heading "Cose della Cancelleria 1545," Vasari first sketchily commented on some ideas concerning the program and the contract for this commission:

> I remember how on March 29, 1546, the Illustrious, most Reverend Monsignor, Cardinal Farnese, hired me to paint *al fresco* the second hall of the chancery in the Palazzo di San Giorgio. Four walls of this hall should represent historical events and tabernacles, friezes, and ornaments with various figures, according to my design shown to his most holy Reverend, in which we agreed that on the wall facing us, which is dark, will be depicted a story *dantur iura gentibus* [of the laws being given to the people]. All representatives from the Nations of the World come to the Pontiff in Rome for the peregrination and bring numerous tributes. In various areas of this wall and among the dignitaries stand Justice, Eloquence, Liberality, Industry, Merit, and Fecundity.
>
> The wall that faces the church shows the Pope commissioning the building of Saint Peter's. In its foreground Architecture, Sculpture, and Painting present to the Pontiff a ground-floor plan to be executed, where the representation of the Vatican, with seven putti representing the seven hills, holds all the honors. In this scene are Merit and Geometry and, above them, Providence and Wisdom. Another story depicts the Pope rewarding Virtue, who gives dignity to many poor people. On the steps Envy is bound, and within the tabernacles are Magnificence and Piety and, above them, Fame and Eternity. Below in the tabernacles are three virtues: Merit, Religion, and Abundance.
>
> On the third wall Concord, Peace, Victory, and Justice carry the Pope, illustrating the story of Peace created by the Pope and Christian princes. Fury is bound and the Temple of Janus is closed. Virtuous Love and Fortitude are depicted, as are Hilarity and Peace burning the arms of war. One of the tabernacles contains Charity and the other Concord.
>
> On the last wall are tabernacles with the three theological virtues. All of this work I promised to do in one hundred

days. He will pay me eight hundred and eight *scudi* on the tenth of July and will cover my expenses for two servants and a horse, as noted by the hand of Monsignor Giavio. The Bank of Montaguti has been ordered to pay me said amount.[5]

(del Vita 22-25)

In his autobiography, Vasari elaborates on the description of the commission, focusing on the depictions of ancient and contemporary portraits:

In that same year (1546) Cardinal Farnese proposed to paint the hall of the chancery in the palace of San Giorgio, and Monsignor Giovio, who wanted me to do this, got me to prepare designs, though they were never carried out. The Cardinal finally decided that the hall should be done *al fresco*, in a great hurry, by a certain date.

The room is more than a hundred *palmi* long, with a height and breadth of fifty. There is a large scene at the end of the first wall, and one side comprises two scenes of the second wall. Because there are windows along the third wall, only the upper portion has painted scenes. The fourth wall mirrors the first wall with a large scene. To avoid making a dado in the usual way for all the scenes, I tried a new device of steps up from the ground, with a scene in each; I placed figures along the steps until they reach the level of the scenes.

It would be tedious to describe the little details, so I will confine myself to a brief description of the main points. The scenes represent the achievements of Pope Paul III; each scene contains his portrait. The first central scene represents the dispatchers from Rome, with numerous nationalities and embassies and many portraits of people asking favors and offering tributes to the Pope. Large figures, placed above the doors of the Sala, stand on each side: Eloquence, above whom are two Victories holding the bust of Julius Caesar; and Justice, above whom two other Victories hold the bust of Alexander the Great. At this same level, in the middle, is the Pope's coat of arms, supported by Liberty and Merit.

On the principal wall is the Pope rewarding merit, bestowing awards, knighthoods, benefices, pensions, bishoprics, and cardinals' hats. Among those who receive them are Adoleto, Pole, Bembo, Contarino, Giovio, Buonarotto, and other great men, all likenesses. In a niche stands a Grace with a cornucopia full of honors, which she is pouring out. The Victories above her hold the bust of the emperor Trajan. Envy is there, consuming vipers and painfully bursting with spite. Above is the coat of arms of Cardinal Farnese, supported by Fame and Merit.

In another scene Pope Paul is represented as intent upon his buildings, especially Saint Peter's. Kneeling before the Pope, Painting, Sculpture, and Architecture receive a plan of Saint Peter's and orders to carry the commission out. Beside these figures a spirit points to his heart. Wealth and Plenty stand in a niche, with two figures holding the effigy of Vespasian. Religion stands in a niche separating two scenes; above her two Victories hold the bust of Numa Pompilius. The arms above are Cardinal San Giorgio's, who built the palace.

The other scenes opposite the dispatches of the court are Universal Peace in Christendom, achieved by this pope, with portraits of the emperor Charles V and Francis, King of France. Peace is burning arms, the Temple of Janus is closed, and Fury is chained. This scene is located between two niches containing Concord with two Victories above and the bust of the emperor Titus, and a Charity with numerous urchins. Two Victories above hold the bust of the emperor Augustus. Finally we see the arms of Charles V supported by Victories and Hilarity. The whole work is full of inscriptions and admirable mottoes, devised by Giovio.

(*Le Vite* 7: 678-81)

In his autobiography Vasari is very explicit in his description of this work and the circumstances surrounding its execution. He and his assistants - Battista Bagnacavallo of Bologna, Giovan Paolo del

Bargo, Bastiano Fiori, Fra Salvatore Foschi of Arezzo, and the Spaniards Bizzera and Roviale - completed the decorative cycles for this room in one hundred days, thereby giving the hall its name: the Sala dei Cento Giorni. At the time of its completion, the room was severely criticized by Michelangelo, Paolo Giovio, Annibale Caro, and even Vasari himself, who realized that he had sacrificed quality for the sake of time (del Vita 23). Vasari admitted that he had "committed an error in consigning the execution [of the frescoes] to my young assistants, for the sake of having them complete [the sala] more rapidly." (Vasari, *Le Vite* 7: 680),[6] Aware of the time spent on this cycle decoration, Michelangelo's comment on the artistic quality of the completed room was simply, "e' si conosce" (it is evident).[7] Paolo Giovio and Annibale Caro reported his displeasure over the portraits to Cardinal Farnese.[8]

Despite its stylistic shortcomings, Vasari's decorative cycle is important to mid-Cinquecento art in Rome, to the development of decorative cycles in honor of the Farnese family, and, in particular, to the iconography of Pope Paul III. Of equal importance is its use of emblemata and mottoes in narrative scenes. Giorgio Vasari informs us that Paolo Giovio, a humanist in the Farnese court, was mainly responsible for the selection of the iconography and Latin inscriptions, for the Farnese *imprese*, and for *invenzioni* the decorative program of the Sala.[9]

In this essay, I will first discuss how Vasari transformed the *camera picta* (painted room) into a theatrical setting, the painted walls of the room becoming illusionistic stages. Second, I will show how he established a formula for the decorative cycle with elaborate representations of narrative scenes (*istorie*) with Latin inscriptions, mottoes, coats of arms, personifications, and emblematic figures. Finally, I will explain how I interpret the Sala's iconography.[10] Although Vasari's contemporaries criticized its quality, the significance of this work rests on the meaning of the paintings.

Vasari illustrates the theatrical *frons scaenae* of antiquity in the Sala. In 1511 an illustrated version of Vitruvius's *Ten Books on Architecture* became very popular, and Vasari, who had received a humanistic training, was certainly familiar with Vitruvius's section on the theater.[11] Unlike their Greek counterparts, most Roman theaters were temporary wooden structures and only a few partially survived, such as the theater of Marcellus. The theater of Pompey, with its Portico of One Hundred Columns, was opened by Pompey in 55-52 BCE as the first Roman stone theater.[12] The porticoes contained trees and fountains and acted as a public gallery for painting and sculpture.

Vasari's interest in theatrical settings began to develop during his stay in Venice in 1541, when he was designing and painting stage settings for *La Talanta,* a comedy by his closest friend, Pietro Aretino.[13] His familiarity with the Venetian architect Sebastiano Serlio's theater design is evident in Serlio's *Second Book* of 1545. Years later, in 1565, Vasari translated the painted perspectival depiction of the Sala dei Cento Giorni into a fixed scene in the Salone dei Cinquecento of the Palazzo Vecchio in Florence. This portable theater could be disassembled, stored, and reassembled when needed during ceremonial festivities such as the entry of Johanna of Austria in Florence (Satkowski 107-12, Fig. 223). In 1570 Vasari carried further this concept of staging with the architectural structure of the Uffizi Gallery, thus creating an avenue as an ideal stage.

Vasari's awareness of ancient architectural history, his knowledge of present edifices, and his impresario techniques are evident in the Sala dei Cento Giorni. It is clear that the stage settings for the narrative in the frescoes reflect the affinity between the site of the palace and its theatrical function: Vasari knew that Pope Paul III's predecessor, Cardinal Riario (1478-86), who originally conceived of the Palazzo, held theatrical plays for the court of Rome, and that the Palazzo della Cancelleria rests on the ravine of the theater of Pompey. Thus Vasari set a stage for the unfolding of Giovio's iconographical apotheosis of the Pontiff, Paul III Farnese - a monument of Cinquecento illusionistic art and a sculpture gallery.[14]

Vasari gave his assistants drawings for the Sala, and they worked in an elaborate and fanciful manner. Although no large drawings have survived, several preparatory sketches dated 1546 are housed in the National Gallery of Ireland in Dublin, the Louvre Museum in Paris, the Biblioteca Reale in Turin, and the Uffizi in Florence.[15] The narrative takes place in a most unusual illusionistic space in which crowded figures are situated in painted architecture with trompe l'œil steps and stairways surrounded by simulated sculpture and decorated with an overabundance of allegorical motifs. The gesticulations, expressions, and movements of the figures are extravagant, exaggerated, and courtly, in the Maniera style of the mid-Cinquecento.

A few observations on the stage setting of the Sala dei Cento Giorni help us understand how Vasari's design reflects his assimilation of Roman and Venetian decorative schemes. The Sala dei Cento Giorni is rectangular, with a flat, wooden ceiling composed of sunken, coffered squares created by the intersection of wooden beams (Figs. 2 and 3). The end of each beam is supported by a volute, which rests on the upper part of the wall. The east wall contains six large windows in the lower zone and six small ones in the upper. The north and south walls contain one bay each, the west wall two. The wall decorations are geometric and architectonic. They are treated not as painted, two- dimensional surfaces, but rather as plastic, architectural structures in which the imagery and real space can expand and contract as one unit - in short, as a stage setting.

The walls are divided into two horizontal zones, each in turn divided into three vertical areas. The upper zone is treated as a frieze. At each right and left is a portrait bust of an ancient emperor, framed by winged *Ignudi,* or allegories of Victory. Above each bust is a Latin motto inscribed in a scroll. In the center of this upper zone, seated allegorical female figures, framed by the wooden corbels, present an escutcheon. They can be identified by the attributes they hold and the Latin inscriptions written on the scrolls at their feet. Variations of grotesque motifs embellish the overall decoration. For the treatment of this zone, Vasari was inspired by Perino del Vaga's decorative scheme in the Sala Paolina, 1544-45, of the Castel Sant'Angelo, Rome.[16] Vasari replaced Perino's *all'antica* standing emperors with bust portraits, and, between the allegorical female figures where Perino selected a *tondo* containing ancient histories, he placed an escutcheon containing the papal coat of arms.

The lower and upper zones are separated by two broken pediments located at the ends of the wall. The architrave between the two zones supports an elaborate mask and festoon motif. In the lower zone, two painted tabernacles support the broken pediments. The tabernacle motif contains an open area or niche in which a standing religious personification projects toward the viewer. This motif derives from Vasari's observations and studies of ancient tabernacles in religious temples, such as the Pantheon, as well as his visual knowledge of early sixteenth-century drawings or sketches from the interior of the Pantheon, such as Menicantonio's sketch of the *Interior of the Pantheon*, 1513 (*Sketchbook*), and Raphael's drawing, *Interior of the Pantheon*, 1510-1515.[17] This motif also derives from Vasari's observations, assimilation, and general knowledge of art works, such as the enthroned popes in Giulio Romano's Sala di Constantino, 1520s; Jacopo Sansovino's *Loggietta*, 1537; and Michelangelo's Medici Chapel, completed in 1534.

In the center portions of the lower zones, depictions of an *istoria* (dramatic narrative or dramatic scene)[18] are framed by Doric columns. The use of painted architecture or colonnades to frame or enclose a narrative scene was commonly understood in antiquity as a stage setting. This device was elaborated in the Quattrocento as a drama on the stage, for example in Francesco Cossa's and Cosmé Tura's *Salone dei Mesi*, 1470s, and Raphael's *The Healing of the Lame Man*, a tapestry cartoon, 1515-17. Finally, it was adopted in the Cinquecento as in Giulio Romano's Sala di Constantino, and in particular, Perino del Vaga's Sala Paolina.

The *istorie* depicted on the walls are filled with stylistic quotations from past and present art. The dado (*zoccolo* or *basamento*) has been transformed. Vasari tried to create a new device by using trompe l'œil steps that run from the center of the lower zone, where the narrative scene takes place, to the physical floor, creating the illusion that the viewer can step up and into the painted scene. His decorative scheme reflects an assimilation of Perino del Vaga's illusionistic steps in the frescoed doorways of the Sala Paolina and Michelangelo's staircase in the vestibule of the Biblioteca Laurenziana, 1524-34, Florence,[19] as well as Antonio Sangallo's and Sebastiano Serlio's studies of stage settings in the 1540s.[20]

Vasari's Sala as a *camera picta* with a continuous illusionistic "step up and into" motif is unprecedented in Cinquecento paintings. The trompe l'œil effect of the steps is not the only element in the Sala that alludes to a stage setting. The projected tabernacles with religious personifications, the *istorie* framed by architectural elements such as columns and niches, and the decorative frieze with busts *all'antica* and papal coats of arms reinforce the motif

Vasari placed a *didaskalia* (written explanation for the visual imagery), or stage cue, in the middle of each staircase, to assist the viewer with the meaning of the *istoria*. Furthermore, the numerous combinations of visual imagery (allegories, *all'antica* bust portraits, personifications, and *istorie*) with textual explanation (Latin inscriptions, mottoes, and *didaskalia*) created for the Sala decoration provide the viewer with an illustrated emblem book.[21] Obviously, in the Sala, the painter also made use of humanistic and emblematic traditions in his portrayal of the Farnese celebration. With the literary assistance of Paolo Giovio's and Annibale Caro's *invenzioni*, Vasari developed a manner of composing images as a compendium of visual iconography for a *camera picta* akin to Alciato's and Cartari's literary practices.[22] Thus Vasari has painted a play enacted in a theatrical setting.

Several letters Vasari wrote to his patron, Cardinal Farnese, attest to Giovio's *invenzioni*, and Antonio Francesco Doni's letter to Lelio Torelli (Bottari and Ticozzi 5: 37), the chief legal advisor to Duke Cosimo I, clearly demonstrates the source for the Sala's iconographical program. The description of the paintings in "Cose della Cancelleria, 1545," contained in Vasari's notebook, *Lo Zibaldone*, sheds further light on the analysis and meaning of the program.[23] The *istorie* in the Sala dei Cento Giorni emphasize the theme of papal supremacy along with themes of peace, temperance, prudence, and charity embodied in Paul III. The four scenes of the Sala dei Cento Giorni are *The Treaty of Nice* or *Universal Peace in Christendom* (Fig. 4), on the south wall; *Nations Paying Homage to Paul III* (Fig. 5), on the north wall; *Paul III's Supervision of the Rebuilding of Saint Peter's* (Fig. 6), and *Paul III Awarding Benefices* or *The Creation of Cardinals* (Fig. 7), both on the west wall; and *The Theological Virtues* or *Cardinal and Theological Virtues* (Fig. 8). on the east wall. The first two *istorie* - *The Treaty of Nice* and *Nations Paying Homage to Paul III* (south and north walls; Figs. 4 and 5) - are concerned with the secular or temporal powers of the Paul III, whereas *Paul III's Supervision of the Rebuilding of Saint Peter's*, *Paul III Awarding Benefices*, and *The Theological Virtues* (west and east walls; Figs. 6, 7, and 8) allude to the Pope's ecclesiastical authority and effectiveness. The four dramatic scenes depict events in the life of Pope Paul III, but only *The Treaty of Nice* (south wall; Fig. 4) relates to a precise historical event—commemorating the Pope's very important mediation between Charles V and Francis I in 1538.

It is obvious that the major theme is the glorification of Pope Paul III as a spiritual leader and humanistic ruler as written in the *didaskalia* on the steps of the walls:

> *The Treaty of Nice or Universal Peace in Christendom* (south wall; Fig. 4): *In pace optimae artes excoluntur, igenia ad frogem coalescunt; publicae privataeque opes augentur* (In peacetime, the best arts are cultivated; minds come together for useful purposes; public and private wealth are increased.)

> *Nations Paying Homage to Paul III* (north wall; Fig. 5): *Aureum saeculum condit qui recto aequabilique ordine cuncta dispensat* (He who dispenses all things justly and equitably founds a Golden Age.)

> *Paul III's Supervision of the Rebuilding of Saint Peter's* (west wall, bay I; Fig. 6): *Magnificentiae studium cum praeclara pietate coniunctum mortales coelo infert* (Zeal for great deeds joined with conspicuous piety carries mortals to heaven.)

> *Paul III Awarding Benefices* or *The Creation of Cardinals* (west wall, bay 2; Fig. 7): *In summa fortuna nihil praestantius quam benefici recte collati memoriam ad posteros extendisse* (At the height of good fortune nothing is more outstanding than to have extended to posterity the memory or a benefit rightly conferred.)

Aspects of this pontifical glorification include a comparison with previous rulers, especially Roman emperors such as Julius Caesar, Augustus, Pyrrhus, Numa Pompilius, Trajan, and Vespasian, as well as Alexander the Great of Greece. This parallelism establishes the ancestry of the Farnese family and its connection with ancient rulers. The inclusion or personifications of virtues, such as Charity, Religion, Faith, and Justice, refers to the divine gifts given to Pope Paul III so that he might act and guide in a Christian manner. The Latin inscriptions and mottoes associated with the imagery add another dimension to the iconography. The analogies between the contemporary Roman Pope and the ancient Roman emperors interconnect not only iconographically but stylistically as well. Vasari consciously copied gestures and actions from all'antica Roman emperors' statuary to illustrate this paragone. The text guides the audience just as the chorus in a Greek or Roman play informs the audience or the development of events.

Because of the fireplace, the south wall lacks the "step up and into motif (Fig. 4). The lower zone contains the narrative scene of The Treaty of Nice or Universal Peace in Christendom showing the signing or the treaty in a landscape with classical ruins, alluding to the ancient city of Rome. A Victory figure follows the papal cortege, energetically waving a flag. Prudence, holding the key to the Temple of Janus, and Peace, burning the arms of War, and Victory, bearing a pain of triumph, together carry the enthroned Pope, who holds a laurel branch. The Pontiff blesses Charles V and Francis I and the many soldiers, who are warmly embracing each other in a sign of armistice: this papal gesture obviously imitates the extended arm of the Roman emperor Marcus Aurelius in the bronze statue on the Campidoglio. In the background the Temple of Janus is being closed while in the foreground Fury, a nude male enchained by the actions of Discord and War, is depicted sitting on the arms of War. The scene is framed by tabernacles containing the figures of Concord (Concordia) and Charity (Caritas).[24] Latin inscriptions appear below Concord - Res parvas auget et insuperabiles reddit (She builds upon small things and restores the insurmountable) - and below Charity - Christianae virtutis perfectum specimen ostendit (She holds out a perfect example of Christian virtue).

In the center of the upper zone, above the istoria, two busts of Roman emperors bracket Charles V's coat of arms and are supported by seated figures of Felicity (Felicitas) and Hilarity (Hilaritas). Bust portraits crowned by Victory figures and honored by epitaphs or mottoes are located above each tabernacle. Vespasian, founder of the Temple of Peace, is portrayed above Concord with the inscription Templum pacis condidit (He built the Temple of Peace).[25] The bust of Augustus[26] above Charity, who closed the doors to the Temple of Janus, bears the inscription Ianum clausit (He closed the Temple of Janus). These Latin inscriptions allude to political interventions and astuteness in establishing universal peace, and thus the inscriptions bring to mind these same traits in Pope Paul III. Like the emperors, the Cinquecento Pope has achieved peace.

The *didaskalia* at the base of the main scene and the flanking tabernacles with personifications of Concord and Charity clarify the meaning of the *istoria*. *In pace optimae artes excoluntur, igenia ad frugem coalescunt; publicae privitaeque opes augentur* (In peacetime, the best arts are cultivated; minds come together for useful purposes; public and private wealth are increased): Pope Paul III strives to maintain these virtues with the aid of Constancy (*Constantia*) and Virtuous Love (*Amor*), represented by two painted statues that stand in niches on each side of the scene between the columns. Constancy is on the side of Concord, and Virtuous Love is close to the tabernacle of Charity. Each virtue needs the support of the other. As with the Roman ancestors, Pope Paul III's ability to maintain peace is achieved only with the help of Concord and Charity.[27]

On the opposite north wall, *Nations Paying Homage to Paul III*, or *Pope Paul III dispersing Goods* (Fig. 5), continues to illustrate the secular power of the Pope. His Holiness is accompanied by his two nephews - Cardinal Alessandro Farnese, Paul III's secretary of state, and Pier Luigi, a *gonfalonier* - and by his faithful secretary, Bartolomeo Guidaccioni. Surrounded by his entire court, he receives foreign dignitaries and accepts their tributes. The scene takes place in an audience hall. In the foreground, the Tiber is personified as a nude old man reclining on the steps. He is crowned with laurel and holds a cornucopia, and behind him two putti bear a wreath. This old figure on the trompe l'œil stairway may also personify Rome crowned by Romulus and Remus; the Lupa can be seen at his feet.[28] Several parallels are evident: the origin and power of ancient Rome, as embodied in the Tiber, parallel the origin of the papacy in Rome (*sedia apostolica*), the powers military and diplomatic of the Farnese family, and the power of the Christian Church. Paul III is the spiritual and temporal leader who extends his blessing to all Christendom.

Behind this group stands Mercury in a niche between two Doric columns. On the base of thee fore column is inscribed the word Industry (*Industria*). Still in the foreground, a group of people are deeply engaged in discourse. They are elegantly dressed in Mannerist costumes. Some of them are standing on the steps, and others are seated. Behind them and in between the Doric columns, Merit (*Merito*), represented as an old man holding a laurel crown, occupies a niche. The word "Merit" is inscribed on the base of the front column. In the middle ground, His Holiness is enthroned, surrounded by his court. Across from them and between the colonnades, a crowd with exotic animals - including giraffes, elephants, camels, monkeys, and parrots - comes to greet Pope Paul III. The middle ground is separated from the background by an archway through which a Madonna and Child are glimpsed with Faith and Hope. The landscape background shows a group of horsemen approaching the audience hall. The inclusion of religious imagery and an entourage creates an analogy between the homage paid by the Magi and shepherds and the homage given to the Pontiff by members of all nations.

The *didaskalia* interprets the scene: *Aureum seculum condit qui recto aequabelique ordine cuncta dispensa* (He who dispenses all things justly and equitably founds a Golden Age). Paul III has created a Golden Age in the papacy through his Eloquence (*Eloquentia*) and Justice (*Justitia*), personified in tabernacles that appear on either side of the scene. The inscriptions allude to virtues of a good ruler: Eloquence - *Segnes animos excitat iratos mulcet* (She awakens sluggish souls and soothes angry ones); Justice – *Maiestatis ac dictionis vim tuetur et fidem conciliat* (She safeguards the power of majesty and speech and brings about trust). Near Eloquence and the enthroned Pope, Mercury symbolizes Industry as well as the Pope's actions. The results of Paul III's industrious efforts were good leadership and great achievements. Next to the tabernacle of Justice, Merit, located in a niche opposite Mercury, observes the offering of exotic animals by Greeks, Latins, and Germans. Their offerings and good deeds are well regarded by the Pontiff. According to Julian Kliemann, the elephant and giraffe were not gifts that Paul III received during his reign, but were an allusion to the *paragone* between the Roman emperor, Julius Caesar, and the contemporary ruler, Pope Paul III ("La Sala" 121-23).[29]

In the center of the frieze the papal coat of arms of the Farnese family is presented by Liberality and Abundance (*Liberalitas* and *Copia*). These personifications are located between the bust portraits of two ancient emperors, Julius Caesar[30] and Alexander the Great,[31] both framed by Victory figures. The portrait of Julius Caesar, located above the tabernacle of Eloquence, is embellished with the Latin inscription, *Expedito vigore animi cuncta pervicit* (Through her ready force of mind, she has conquered everything). Another inscription, *Supra Garamantas et Indos protulit imperium* (He extended the Empire beyond the Garamantes and Indus), belongs with Alexander the Great, whose bust portrait is above the tabernacle of Justice. The words allude to the contemporary expansion of the empire by Pope Paul III and to past extensions by Alexander; Pope Paul's given name, Alessandro, provides another correspondence with the Macedonian ruler. In antiquity Plutarch's *De vitas impera* established the parallels between Julius Cesar and Alexander the Great. In the Cinquecento Giovio and Vasari made Paul III analogous to the ancient rulers who conquered the world with eloquence and justice.

Paolo Giovio's and Giorgio Vasari's iconographical apotheosis of Pope Paul III continues on the adjacent walls, where the iconography of the west wall emphasizes the ecclesiastical power of the Pope. This large wall is composed of two bays and in each one an *istoria* evolves: *Paul III's Supervision of the Rebuilding of Saint Peter's* (Fig. 6, bay I) and *Paul III Awarding Benefices* or *The Creation of Cardinals* (Fig. 7, bay 2). The Pope is honored for his diplomatic and temporal powers. In *Paul III's Supervision of the Rebuilding of Saint Peter's*, Paul III, as Moses or Peter dressed in Judaic clothes, comments on the architectural drawing presented to him by the liberal arts - Geometry, Painting, Sculpture, and Architecture (Fig. 6). They unfold a plan for the building of the basilica, as they receive orders to carry out the work. Saint Peter's is seen under construction in the background. The background also shows how, simultaneous to the building of Saint Peter's, other structures are demolished, such as the old mausoleum of Saint Andrew, the basilica of Constantine, and the presbytery of Rossellino. Others, according to Sangallo's new plan, are expanded, such as Bramante' s vaulting and bay systems. All of these reconstructions are under Michelangelo's architectural guidance. In the loggia behind the Pontiff, Antonio da Sangallo[32] and Michelangelo make recommendations while studying the architectural drawing. In niches between the Doric columns stand the painted sculptures of Magnificence (*Magnificentia*) and Sincerity (*Sinceritas*). The *didaskalia, Magnificentiae studium cum praeclara pierate coniunctum mortales coelo infert* (Zeal for great deeds joined with conspicuous piety carries mortals to heaven), expresses Paul's intention to expand Saint Peter's as the new Temple of Solomon.

The reclining old man on the steps personifies the Vatican with its attributes - keys, papal tiara, canopy, and books - surrounded by youths who crown the figure with laurel. This personification, depicted as a nude old man holding the keys of Saint Peter, is surrounded by seven putti, who stand for the seven hills of Rome. Vasari's personification of the Vatican derives from the personification of Rome or the River Tiber, a well-known Roman sculpture located in front of the Senate building at the Campidoglio.[33] The painted statue of Sincerity behind this figure alludes to the papal attitude towards the construction of the new house of Christendom.

In the tabernacles personifications frame the scene: Opulence (*Opulentia*) with her motto, *Optima cuique exercendae virtutis instrumentum* (For every good man, [Opulence is] an instrument for displaying virtue) on the right; Religion (*Religio*) with her inscription, *Deus hominis maximos facit* (God makes men great), on the left.[34] Above the tabernacle of Opulence, Marcus Agrippa is portrayed in a bust all'antica with his motto, *Ter cons Pantheon extruxit* (In his third consulship, he erected the Pantheon), Agrippa having been responsible for building the Pantheon. Parallels between Agrippa and Paw III are thus underscored: both were responsible for major religious constructions in Rome during their lifetimes; both rulers were concerned with the beautification of Rome.

Above the tabernacle of Religion is another bust *all'antica* of the second king of Rome, Numa Pompilius,[35] who spiritually led his Roman people, as the inscription states: *Ferocem victoris populum indicta Religione feliciter rexit* (Having imposed the conqueror's religion, he successfully ruled a ferocious people). Again, the Cinquecento Pope is being compared with a Roman ruler. In this instance, both figures were religious leaders. Pope Paul III is seen as continuing the ancient Roman tradition of improving the populous aesthetically and spiritually. The Pope is not only an architect of edifices but, like God, also a spiritual architect. Giovio's placement of the emblem and coat of arms for Cardinal Riario, the builder of the Palazzo della Cancelleria, and of the figures of Providence (*Providentia*) and Wisdom (*Sapientia*) are by deliberate design. By facing Numa Pompilius and looking down at Paul III, Providence furnishes guidance to the Pope, as she has done for Numa Pompilius and Cardinal Riario. Wisdom faces Agrippa, and below her is the personification of the Vatican.

Religion is the only personification placed between two bays. Religion faces the other scene, *Paul III Awarding Benefices or The Creation of Cardinals* (Fig. 7). This second bay of the west wall continues the ecclesiastical theme-the spiritual power of the Pope. The *didaskalia* on each side of the steps describes the meaning of the scene: *In summa Fortuna nihil praestantius quam benefici recte collati memoriam ad posteros extendisse* (At the height of good fortune nothing is more outstanding than to have extended to posterity the memory of a benefit rightly conferred). In a hypostyle hall the Pope is surrounded by prelates, poets, artists, and humanists, such as Giovio (profile with cane), Pole, Sadoleto, Bembo, Sangallo, and Michelangelo. The hypostyle columns represent the Temple of Solomon or the twisted Constantine columns. Figures interact between the columns while the Pontiff distributes awards, knighthoods, prebends, episcopates, and cardinals' hats. Vasari claimed to have drawn these portraits from life. Between the Doric columns, and framing the main scene, the niches contain figures of Virtue (*Virtus*) and Labor (*Labor*).

The tabernacle on the left of Religion contains the personification of Goodness or Benignity (*Benignitas*), scattering coins and carrying a cornucopia full of gifts. A globe at her feet, with her inscription *Vividae crescentique virtuti ianuam pandit* (She opens the door to bright and growing virtue), she opens the door to the flourishing of the papacy. Above this tabernacle in the broken pediment is the bust of Trajan,[36] with the inscription *Meritis honoribus quirites exornavit* (He adorned the Romans for their deserved honors). Trajan, like Paul, rewarded according to the merits, labors, and endeavors of his subjects. In the center of the frieze, crowning the scene below, Fame (*Fama*) and Eternity (*Eternitas*) embrace the coat of arms of Cardinal Farnese, Pope Paul III's nephew. The *didaskalia* on the steps and the personifications allude to the Pontiff s granting the benefit of the office to his grandson, an act of nepotism causing envy that was later combated by good deeds during the Pope's reign. This visual concept and the text on the steps explain the placement of Envy, the reclining female nude eating vipers. Vasari's image is clearly pre-figured by Alciato's emblem.[37] Envy's contorted pose, like Fury's on the south wall, derives from the Laocoön. Vasari creates an interesting visual and iconographical dichotomy between the actions of Envy and those of His Holiness. Captured and enchained by Virtue (in the above niche), Envy's movement is focused on a single hedonistic action: devouring snakes. Her behavior contrasts with the Pontiff s generous actions and with the *Ignudi*'s comportment. They assist him in the dispersal of the gifts: two of them share and hold the yoke, a traditional symbol of Patience, as the personification of Labor in the above niche; another *Ignudo* stands to look at an empty cornucopia, a symbol of giving, while his companion sits on a full one. To illustrate the strong message of the *didaskalia* and to interpret the personifications in the tabernacles (Religion and Goodness), Vasari intentionally depicted the vipers next to the horn of plenty, juxtaposing self-centeredness and benevolence.

The structure of the east wall is dominated by windows and a landscape of the Roman *campagna* (Fig. 8). A broken frieze with five small, alternating attic windows with festoons is decorated with numerous *all'antica* trophies and fanciful *grotteschi* - a Maniera conceit of a triumphal cortege. The broken frieze pattern continues, alternating large windows with "step up and into" motifs. The steps lead up to a circular loggia supported by classical columns and decorated with four niches containing full-length painted sculptures of the three cardinal virtues - Prudence, Temperance, Fortitude - and Patience as Justice. In turn, these virtues pair off and frame personifications of Hope and Faith seated on monumental pedestals. The personification of Hope is flanked by Prudence (*Prudentia*) and Temperance (*Temperantia*), with the inscription: *Alit animos et vividae virtutis nervos intendit* (She nourishes spirits and strains the sinews of vigorous virtue). The personification of Faith is accompanied by Patience (*Patientia*) and Fortitude (*Fortitudo*), with the inscription: *Sincera constantis animi puritate perficitur* (She is perfected through the genuine purity of a faithful heart). Unlike the other walls, the east wall portrays a landscape of the Roman *campagna*, which can be seen through the circular loggia. It also contains three *all'antica* bust portraits in the lower zone. In the center, the portrait of Pope Paul III is situated between Hope and Faith. To the left of Hope is a bust portrait of Pyrrhus,[38] and to the right of Faith, Titus.[39] Therefore, at each end of the east wall *all'antica* bust portraits of Pyrrhus and Titus are seen with the Pontiff in the center. These represent important leaders in the arts and the military in ancient Greece and Rome, further sources of emulation for the Pontiff as examples or visionary, compassionate, and skillful leadership.

The iconography of both east (*Cardinal and Theological Virtues*) and west (*Paul III Awarding Benefices* and *Paul III's Supervision of the Rebuilding of Saint Peter's*)[40] walls alludes to the ecclesiastical and spiritual power of the Pontiff as a vicar or Christ on earth (Figs. 6, 7, and 8). Spiritual leadership necessitates, at times, military and political astuteness. The virtues assist His Holiness in carrying out his office: cardinal virtues - Fortitude, Justice (Patience), Prudence, and Temperance; and theological virtues - Hope, Faith (east wall, Fig. 8), and Charity (south wall, Fig. 4).

The iconography of both east and west walls emphasizes the Pope's ecclesiastical power. The south and north walls' iconography focuses on his temporal power and specific events of his reign. The three reclining figures on the steps (Envy, the Vatican, and Rome) and one inside the scene (Fury) add cogency to the sense of drama of the *frons scaenae* and the meaning of the *didaskalia*. The Farnese Pontiff's spiritual and terrestrial successes, although challenged by adversaries' vain and megalomaniacal behavior (Envy), were accomplished through high-minded mediations and magnanimity (Vatican) on the part of the Pope, as well as through His Holiness's astute military and skillful political acumen. A return to the ancient *pax romana* thus established a Farnese Golden Age.

When visitors entered this hall, they were reminded in a dramatic manner or the activities of the Pope not only as a learned man and temporal ruler who promoted the artistic beautification of his city but also as a spiritual leader who expanded the Christian doctrine. As Pontiff, Paul III was an ambassador of Christ on earth; as keeper of justice and peace, he was the leader of Christianity. The Sala dei Cento Giorni attests to Vasari's ability to stage visually and textually the significance of the papacy in the Cinquecento. Giorgio Vasari honored and immortalized his patron family and himself in the dedicatory inscription below the personification of Religion in the west wall (Fig. 7): *Alexandro Farnesio Card. Vicecancellario iubente quum expediti operis picturam non ab re nata praceps occasio postularet Georgius Aretinus centesimo die ita manus absolvit ut properantem obsequendi necessitas iure excuset nisi mira celeritas augeat dignitatem. M.D. XLVI.* (At the command of Cardinal Alessandro Farnese, Vice Chancellor, because the sudden occasion required a painted work not already begun, Giorgio of Arezzo completed the work on the one hundredth day in such a manner that the obligation to obey would rightly have excused his haste were it not that his remarkable speed added dignity [to the work]. A.D. 1546).

## Notes

This article is a reprint from """Giorgio Vasari's  Sala dei Cento Giorni: A Farnese Celebration," *Exploration in Renaissance Culture,* Vol.  XXI (1995), 121-51.

This paper benefited from the suggestions of Professors Iris Cheney, University of Massachusetts Amherst, Gloria Fiero, University of Southwestern Louisiana, and Wolfram Prinz, Goethe University in Frankfurt/Main. Special thanks to Joseph J. Hughes of Southwest Missouri State University, and to Marco De Girolami, my nephew, for their generous assistance with the Latin translations, The ideas in this study were first presented at the South Central Renaissance Conference in 1987. I am grateful to the National Endowment for the Humanities and the University of Massachusetts Lowell for their grants to assist me in this research, and especially to Professor Tita French Baumlin for her constant assistance and invaluable comments.

1. See Robertson 252 n 12 for Giovio's comment on Vasari's artistry: *"un fattivo, espedito, manesco e resoluto pittore"* (an efficient, expeditious, handy, and energetic painter).
2. Today, the condition of the paintings is mediocre, even though they were restored in 1940 after a fire that same year, and other minimal interventions have been made since. See Ronchini 2:121-27 and Schiavo 151-65.
3. Gaudioso provides an excellent study of this commission. See also Harprath for a most informative iconographical discussion.

4. See Partridge's "Divinity," "Sala I," "Sala II," and "Vignola" on this commission .
5. In the *Zibaldone* on the verso of this folio, Ms. 4. C 7 Fil, there is a list with sketchy descriptions of the personifications in the Sala.. Vasari used most of their attributes, but in some instances he did not, as I will indicate here to the reader with bracketed writer's notes. Please note that a variety of animals are associated with the personifications' descriptions. Probably Giovio and Vasari were both familiar with Valeriano's *Hieroglyphica* (Venice, 1521) and Horapolo, *Hieroglyphica* (Venice 1543, illustrated edition), See Gonzàlez de Zàrate for the most recent translation from the Greek into Spanish of this emblematic book. My English translation of these sketchy notes is the first to appear:
Justice: with scepter of the stork and hippopotamus with ostrich's plumes-Julius Caesar [tenement]
Industry: caduceus, with Mercury's hat and wings, and the mirror and ermine-Pompeii [tenement]
Liberality: discarding jewels, coins, and the Lion - Alexander The Great Abundance: the horn of plenty and lots of ornaments-the eagle - Pyrrhus [see n 38]
Merit: royal crown, pontifical mantle, nude man below
Honor: laurel crown, spoils triumphs, peacock - the Tiber
For Peace: tied up Fury
Peace: burning the arms, holding an olive branch, dove with olive branch - Augustus- Trajan
Concord: broken rods and one unbroken bundle
Charity: children, fire, and pelican
Arnor [Virtuous Love]: arch, arrows, face and hand, male and female doves
Hilarity: Bacchus crowned with grapes and satyr, satyr with grapes
Beatitude: wings and the shape of an angel, a rainbow and a celestial arch [This image does not appear in the Sala decoration.]
For the building construction [of Saint Peter's]: the Vatican [personification]
Religion: bundle of palms, scales and the four books, the Holy Spirit, the keys - Numa Pompilius
Eternity: underneath the globe, lighted candle, the triangle - Deer
Fame: blowing one trumpet, holding the one on fire, a globe below Fame – Rhinoceros - Titus
Benignity: holding golden and silver rods, jewels and property - Marcus Agrippa
Courage: nude man with an open heart and sun rays surrounding the head - Lion [This personification does not appear in the Sala decoration]

For the benefaction of virtue: Envy drops dead

Merit: the horn of plenty full of dignity that showers the world - Stork

Abundance: apron with fruits that fill up a horn of plenty - Ant

Study/Knowledge: books, solitude, strength of soul, floating in the air - Horse

Virtue: nude woman with mouth open so that the heavens can fill her body with grace - Phoenix

Wisdom: the goddess Pallas [Minerva] with all the instruments of war, books and weapons - Unicorn

Faith: baptizing a young child, on the left holding a cross with all the other sacraments [This personification does not show the baptismal action.]

Patience: the yoke around her neck and head bent down - Dog

Hope: anchor, Noah's dove holding the olive branch and the supplicant hand turned to the sky

Prudence: beautifying herself at the sphere [mirror], with the serpent, keys, with Janus's head

Imprese [Impresa]: eight with lilies, the shell, the arrow

6. Translation from Vasri's autobiography: "As I have said, I did this as a young man without a thought except to serve this magnate, who wanted it done by a certain time, as I have said. Although I worked hard in the palling, and in making the cartoons, I confess that I was wrong to give the work to apprentices, to save time, for it would have been better to have toiled for a hundred months and to have done it myself. Even if I had not done as much as I desired for the cardinal's sake and my own honor, I should have had the satisfaction of having done it myself. But this mistake made me decide to finish everything myself, after my assistants did the preparatory work from my designs." (Vasari, *Le Vite* 7: 681). See also Bottari and Ticozzi 5:37 for the published letter of Antonfrancesco Doni, a Servile monk, to Lelio Torelli, a few months after the completion of this work, stating: "As I am in Rome...I want to tell you about something new and beautiful of which you may have heard, though you cannot have seen it: I refer to the *sala* of the most reverend and illustrious Cardinal Farnese which was painted last year by the most excellent artist, Giorgio Vasari of Arezzo." See also Frey 1: 177, for further discussion.

7. "Vuolsi che Michlangiolo, nel veder que' opera e nell'udire ch'era stata fatta in cento giorni, dicesse: e' si conosce." (Vasari, *Le Vite* 7: 680 n 1) .

8. See Frey I: 220-21 for the letter of May 10, 1548, from Annibale Caro in Rome to Giorgio Vasari in Florence. Sec Gombrich, *Heritage* 124-25 for an English translation of this letter.

9. In his insightful articles, Julian Kliemann has explained how Vasari's

depictions of the Farnese *imprese* reflect Giovio's descriptions in the *Dialogo delle'imprese militari e amorose* (126-27), and how his rendering of portraits and ancient busts alludes to Giovio's literary descriptions of famous portraits in his *Gli elogi degli uomini illustri*. See Kliemann, "La Sala" 121-23; Kliemann, "Il pensiero" 197-223; and Robertson, "Paolo Giovio" 224-33. For further study on the *imprese,* see Bregoli-Russo 6-7. For a discussion on the concepts of *impresa* and device, see also Giovio, *Dialogo*; Klein 124-50; Gombrich, *Symbolic* 160-80; and Russell, Emblem and Device.

10. In my studies of Vasari's decorative cycles, I demonstrated the importance of Paolo Giovio in the formulation of the program (L Cheney, Paintings). See also the significant studies of Jacobs; Kliemann, "Il pensiero" 197-223; Schröter, Robertson, "Paolo Giovio" 224-33; Robertson, "Il Grande Cardinale." Moreover, note Solari for a biographical study on the Farnese family. See also the well-known pioneering studies of Pastor and Steinmann. The recent exhibition catalogue (Schianchi and Spinosa) discusses the importance of the Farnese as collectors and patrons of the arts.

11. Vitruvius's books on architecture (c. 16-13 BCE) were first published with illustrations in 1511. See Morgan's translation (5: 137-54) for a discussion on Greek and Roman theaters. See also Blumenthal; Hartnoll 51-60; Kernodle; Nagler; and Strong.

12. The theater of Pompey no longer exists, and today in its place stands the Palazzo della Cancelleria. A model of Pompey's theater and portico now exists in the Museum of Roman Civilization in Rome.

13. Vasari arrived in Venice in December, 1541. By February 1542, he had completed the decorations for the *apparato* for *La Talanta* with the aid of three assistants: Cristoforo Gherardi, Battista. Cungi, and Bastiano Flori of Arezzo. For complete descriptions of the *apparato* in Vasari's letter written from Venice in 1542 to Ottavio de' Medici in Florence, sec: Vasari, *Le Vite* 6: 223-26, 7, 670-75; Frey 2: 111-16. See also L. Cheney, Painting 64-68, for a general discussion of this commission, and the forthcoming "Vasari and Venice."

14. Undoubtedly Vasari's Sala is a visual antecedent of Annibale Carraci's Farnese Gallery, 1597-1604, in the Palazzo Farnese, Rome, and reflects the stylistic assimilation of the decorations of Perino del Vaga in the Sala Paolina, 1544, in the Castel Sant' Angelo. See Dempsey 363-74; "Annibal Carraci" 269-311; and Pastoreau 431-55. See also n 3 for citations on the Sala Paolina.

15. See Jacobs, "A New Drawing" 371-74, for the Dublin drawing. Although Davis has objected to the attribution of this drawing to Vasari ("Letter," 292-93), I support Jacobs' interpretation. See also Monbeig-Goguel 168-

69 n 17 for the Louvre drawing RF 64 recto and verso; see Kliemann, "La Sala" 121-23 Fig. 141 for the Turin drawing inv. no. 15673, and 94 Fig. 143 for the Uffizi drawing 65 ORN. See also Barocchi 27-29, for another Uffizi drawing 6494F, a figure study for the *Universal Homage.*

16. See Gaudioso 186-87, and, in particular, Schröter 76-99, for comparative analyses of Perino's and Vasari's *sale.*

17. Domenico Antonio de Chiarellis, also known as Menicantonio, was *capomaestro* of the fabric of Saint Peter's and one of Bramante's assistants. See Wittkower 91-107, and, for illustrations of the interior of the Pantheon by both artists, 98.

18. I am using the term *istoria* in the Albertian manner. In his treatise *Oil Painting* Alberti states that an "*istoria* will move spectators when the men painted in the picture outwardly demonstrate their own feelings as clearly as possible" (Alberti, Grayson trans. 75). Alberti's concept of *istoria*, later assimilated in Vasari's literary and visual works, is deeply rooted in the Renaissance humanistic tradition. The humanists' tendency to incorporate literary and theological meanings in their writings influenced Vasari's creativity by fusing into his emblematic imagery the literary and visual traditions. See Alberti, Spencer translation, 23-28, for a discussion of the origin and impact of Alberti's *istoria.*

19. Folio 92 recto, Casa Buonarroti Museum, Florence, shows Michelangelo's three sketches for twin staircases, 1524. One, located in the lower pan of the folio, differs from the others because it illustrates twin staircases connected by an elliptical one. See Wittkower 11-72, and, in particular, 29 Fig. 20 for sketches of staircases. Michelangelo's influence on Vasari can be seen in the former's drawings for his Uffizi stage study 2191A. See Davis, "Giorgio Vasari" 94.

20. Both Cinquecento architects were concerned with reconciling Vitruvius's architectural descriptions with actual remains of ancient buildings. See Giovannoni for a discussion of Antonio Sangallo's large collection of ancient drawings at the Uffizi, and Thomson 118-21 for an account of Serlio's major architectural contributions toward the popularization of ancient Roman architecture in the Cinquecento. Serlio's *Libro Terzo* was published in March, 1540, in Venice. In 1541, Vasari went to visit his close compatriot Pietro Aretino in Venice. Undoubtedly, both were aware of Serlio's publication.

21. See Russell, "Alciati's Emblems," for an understanding of emblematic tradition in Cinquecento art and literature, and in particular, the importance of Andrea Alciato's *Emblematum libellus cum commentariis* (Lyon, 1531), since "it served as a manual to train readers in a particular approach to artistic artifacts" and "taught them to participate actively in the moralizing of visual arts" (549). See also Daly and Cal-

lahan, *Andreas Alciatus*; Daly, *Emblem Theory*: Saunders; and Russell, "Emblems and Hieroglyphics" for an interpretation of how Renaissance humanists employed hieroglyphic as a vehicle for "redefining the symbolic process [of] the context of Neoplatonic thought" (228). See also L. Cheney, "Emblematic Approaches," for Vasari's development of a visual emblematic book. An emblem is composed of *pictura, inscriptio,* and *subscriptio.* Like an emblem, a painting is composed of an image (*pictura*), with a title: (*inscriptio*), and it is based on a literary or historical text (*subscriptio*). Vasari accomplishes this *paragone* (parallel) in the Sala where the *pictura* of an emblem corresponds to the depiction of the *istoria*; the *inscriptio* becomes the head title of the personifications, and the *subscriptio* compares to the Latin *didaskalia* or honorific text.

22. See Robertson, "Annibale Caro," for an analysis of how Vasari acquired his knowledge of iconography and emblems through his study of the works of Annibale Caro. In *Le Vite* Vasari praises Annibale Caro - poet, translator of classical literature, and secretary to Cardinal Farnese - for his *invenzioni* "*cappriciose, ingeniose e lodevoli molto*" (115-29). See also Caro, *Lettere Familiari,* for Caro' s appraisal of Alciato's and Cartari's books as significant iconographical manuals. See also Giovio's *Dialogo* (1555), Vasari's prefaces from *Le Vite* (1568), and later Cesare Ripa, *Iconologia* (1603), for they concur that an *invenzione* or image should provide visual interest by showing beautiful elements, that its motto should be brief (two of three words or a line of verse) and that its meaning should be suggestively incomplete to intrigue or tease the viewer - in sum, a Maniera conceit.

23. See n 4.

24.. Vasari's personifications for this Sala are also visual quotations from earlier decorative commissions, in particular, the Monteoliveto refectory of Sant'Anna dei Lombardi, 1545, Naples. See L. Cheney, "Vasari and Naples," for a discussion of how Vasari develops a visual and emblematic encyclopedia of personifications.

25. See Graves 24 1-51 for an analysis of Vespasian's accomplishments.

26. Graves 37-61 (Figs. 50, 51) has an evaluation of Augustus's Roman propaganda by employing artistic and military devices, such as the Cup of Boscoreale, 20 BCE (Rothschild Collection, Paris), illustrating Augustus's Victory and Clemency. The cup's representation of Clemency resembles stylistically Vasari's depiction of *Creation of Cardinals* (west wall, bay 2).

27. Many of Vasari's personifications are visual quotations from his early commissions in Venice and Naples, and from his own house: in Arezzo. Vasari is creating a visual encyclopedia or dictionary of images. See L. Cheney, *Paintings* 59-83.

28. Vasari will employ again the motif of a reclining figure to symbolize the Arno River, or the personification of Florence, in two frontispieces. One is contained in his book on *L'Architettura di L. B. Alberti*, 1550, published in Florence by Lorenzo Torrentino (the same editor who published Vasari's first edition of *Le Vite*). The second appears in Cosimo Bartoli, *Del mondo di misurare*, 1564. See Corti 148 and Figs. 47a, b, c, d, respectively, for these frontispieces. Two studies presently exist for these frontispieces: a sketch (K.d.Z. 22-135) attributed to Vasari located in the Kupferstichkabinett, Staatliche: Museen Preussischer Kulturbesitz, Berlin, and a finished drawing (349 ORN) kept in the Gabinetto Disegni e Stampe, Uffizi.

29. See also Donati; and Vasari, *Le Vite* 4: 96 and 401, for comments on the collection of exotic animals kept by popes: "*tutti quegli animali che Papa Leone aveva: camaleone, i zibetti, le scimmie, i lioni, i liofanti et altri animali più stranieri.*" See also Bregoli-Russo who states, "it was the norm that animals be included in the imprese of famous men' (7).

30. Gaius Julius Caesar, 100-44 BCE. See Graves 11-46 for an appraisal of his accomplishments.

31. Alexander the Great (Alexander III of Macedon, 336-323 BCE), son of Philip II and Olympias of Epirus, second cousin to Pyrrhus, portrayed on the east wall of the Sala. See Weigall for an account of Alexander's life.

32. The inclusion of Antonio da Sangallo the Younger is honorific, since the architect died on September 29, 1546, while the fresco was being painted.

33. Vasari will again employ this motif of the reclining river god for the frontispiece of *Le Vite*.

34. It is interesting that the Turin drawing shows Concord in place of Religion. I speculate that this change for a stronger emblematic symbol was a Vasarian pentimento or oversight not consistent with Giovio's iconographical design. See n 5, "Cose della Cancelleria, 1545."

35. Numa Pompilius (715-673 BCE), legendary successor to Romulus as second king of Rome, had a peaceful reign, a Golden Age. He built palaces and temples as well as established many religious institutions and festivals, probably the reason Vasari placed his portrait above the tabernacle of Religion.

36. See n 5. Once again Vasari is the only source for the identification of this portrait. In the iconographical list Vasari writes the name of Trajan after Augustus. This portrait of Trajan is at the corner with the south wall on which the portrait of Augustus is punted. A Roman emperor, Trajan (Marcus Ulpius Traianus, 98-117 CE), devoted vast sums of money to the beautification of Rome . His numerous projects in the

Eternal City include the Forum where his Column commemorates his campaigns, new baths, and the foundation of the Biblioteca Ulpia. Pliny the Younger wrote a panegyric on Trajan's reign, which he described as memorable because of peace and prosperity. Probably Giovio and Vasari selected this ruler because of his artistic and humanitarian acts, which paralleled the Pontiffs. See Pliny, *Epistle* 10: 97.

37. See Alciato, Emblem LXXI, for Envy's depiction: "To represent Envy and its irritations, one paints a hag who eats vipers with constant pain in her eyes. She eagerly eats her own heart and holds in her hand a staff of thorns which prick her hands day and night."

38. See n 5 for Vasari's reference to the name of Pirro in the iconographical program for the Sala. See also Kliemann, "La Sala" 121-23, who attests to this portrait's identification of Pyrrhus, King of Epirus (319-272 BCE). This romantic Greek leader, a second cousin of Alexander the Great, desired to be the Alexander of the West and hoped to revive that famous empire. Plutarch honors Pyrrhus for his personal courage, brilliant tactics, skill as a commander, and impressive military experience, at the same time acknowledging his numerous misfortunes. Pyrrhus also developed a substantial art collection from the spoils of the conquered cities. See Plutarch, *Pyrrhus*, l.c. The Farneses' interest in Roman history and ancient rulers derives from their love of collecting ancient art, in particular, coins. Their coin collection of *uomini illustri* contained two coins with the portrait of Pyrrhus. See Schianchi and Spinosa 424-25 Figs. 205-6.

39. See n 5. Once again Vasari is the only source for the identification of this portrait. In his iconographical list, Vasari includes the name or Titus. The eldest son of the emperor Vespasian, Titus Flavius Vaspasianus (Roman emperor 79-81 CE) was famous for the capture of Jerusalem in 79 CE, commemorated by the Arc of Titus in the Roman Forum. Like Augustus, Trajan, and Vespasian, Titus was concerned with the urbanization and beautification of Rome. He completed the Colosseum (begun by his father Vespasian) and built the Baths of Titus. During his reign dreadful catastrophes occurred - the eruption of Mount Vesuvius, the three-day fire in Rome, and the outbreak of the plague. In *The Twelve Caesars*, an admiring Suetonius tells how Titus cured the plague by human and divine means He tried many medical remedies and made personal sacrifices - stripping his own mansions and public edifices to assist his homeless people and giving generous help to those who suffered (Graves 257). Probably Giovio and Vasari selected these two rulers because of their artistic and humanitarian acts, which paralleled the Pontiffs pursuits.

40. These images derive from previous conceits Vasari created in Venice

and Arezzo. I have demonstrated elsewhere how Vasari repeats images, thereby creating a decorative formula or emblematic inventory (L. Cheney, "Giorgio Vasari's Chamber").

## Works Cited

Alberti, Leon Battista. *On Painting*. Trans. Cecil Grayson. Baltimore: Penguin, 1991.

_____. *On Painting*. Trans. John R. Spencer. New Haven: Yale UP, 1966.

Alciato, Andrea. *Emblematum libellus cum commentariis* Venice, 1550.

"Annibal Carrache au Palais Farnèse." *Palais Farnèse* 1.1 (n.d.): 269-311.

Barocchi, Paola. *Vasari Pittore*. Milan; Club del Libro, 1964.

Bartoli, Cosimo. *Del mondo di misurare*. Venice: Francesco Franceschini, 1564.

Bregoli-Russo, Mauda. *L'impresa come ritratto del rinascimento*. Naples; Loffredo, 1990.

Blumenthal, Arthur R. *Theater Art of the Medici*. Hanover, NH; UP of New England, 1980.

Bottari, G. G., and S. Ticozzi. Raccolta di lettere, sulla pittura, scultura, et architettura scritte da' più celebri personaggi dei secoli XV, XVI, et XVII. Milan, 1822-25.

Caro, Annibale. *Lettere Familiari*. Ed. A. Greco. Florence: Sansoni, 1957.

Cartari, Vincenzo. *Imagine delli Dei de gl'Antichi*. Venice, 1550.

Cheney, Iris H. "Catalogue of preparatory drawings relating to the mid-sixteenth-century decorations in Palazzo Farnese." *Mélanges d'ecole française de Rome* 90 (1981): 791-820.

Cheney, Liana De Girolami. "Emblematic Approaches in the Paintings of Giorgio Vasari." *Emblematica* (forthcoming).

_____. "Giorgio Vasari's Chamber of Abraham: A Religious Ceiling in the Aretine House." Sixteenth Century Journal 18 (Fall 1987): 355-80.

_____. *The Paintings of The Casa Vasari*. Diss. Boston U, 1978. New York: Garland, 1985.

_____. "Vasari and Naples: The Monteoliveto Order." *Papers in Art History* 7 (1993): 10-48.

_____. "Vasari and Venice." *Papers in Art History* 13 (1996): (forthcoming).

Corti, Laura, ed. *Principi, letterati, e artisti nelle carte di Giorgio Vasari*. Florence: Edam, 1981.

Cossa, Francesco, and Cosmé Tura. *Salone dei Mesi*. Palazzo Schifanoia, Ferrara.

Daly, Peter M. *Emblem Theory; Recent German Contributions to the Character-*

*ization of the Emblem Genre.* Nendeln; KTO P, 1979.

Daly, Peter M., and Virginia W. Callahan. *Andreas Alciatus.* 2 vols. Toronto: U of Toronto P, 1985.

Davis, Charles. "A Letter to the Editor." *Master Drawings* 21 (1983): 292-93.

_____. "Giorgio Vasari." Corti. 94.

del Vita, Alessandro, ed. *Lo Zibaldone di Giorgio Vasari.* Arezzo: Tipografia Zelli, 1938.

Dempsey, Charles. "*Et nos cedamus amori*: Observations on the: Farnese Gallery." *Art Bulletin* 50 (1968): 363-74.

Donati, L. "La Giraffa." *Maso Finiguerra. Rivista della stampa incisa e del libro illustrato* 3 (1938): 247-68.

Frey, Karl. *Der literarische Nachlass Giorgio Vasaris.* Munich: Mueller, 1923.

Gaudioso. E. *Gli affreschi Paolo III a Castel Sant'Angelo, 1543-1548.* Rome: De Luca, 1981.

Giovannoni, C. *Antonio da Sangallo, il Giovane.* Florence: Sansoni, 1959.

Giovio, Paolo. *Dialogo dell'imprese militari et amorose.* 1555. Ed. M. L Doglio. Rome: Bulzoni, 1978.

_____. *Gli elogi degli uomini illustri.* Ed. R. Meregazzi. Rome: Straderini, 1972.

Gombrich, Ernst H. *The Heritage of Apelles.* New York: Cornell UP, 1976.

_____. *Symbolic Images.* London: Phaidon, 1972.

Gonzáles de Zárate:, J. M., ed. *Horapolo Hieroglyphica.* Trans. M. J. Garcia Soler. Madrid: Ediciones Akal, 1991.

Graves, Robert, trans. *Suetonius's The Twelve Caesars.* New York: Penguin, 1980.

Harprath, Richard. *Papst Paul III als Alexander der Grosse: Das Freskenprogramm der Sala Paolina in der Englesburg.* Berlin: de Gruyter, 1978.

Hartnoll, Phyllis. *The Concise History of Theatre.* New York: Abrams, 1968.

Jacobs, Fredrika Hermann. "A New Drawing by Vasari for the Sala dei Cento Giorni." *Master Drawings* 20 (1982): 371-74.

_____. *Studies in Patronage and the Iconography of Paul III.* Diss. U of Virginia, 1979.

Kernodle, George R. *From Art to Theatre: Form and Convention in the Renaissance.* Chicago; U of Chicago P, 1944.

Klein, Robert. *La Forme et I'ntelligible: Ecrits sur la Renaissance et l'art Moderne.* Paris: Gallimard, 1970.

Kliemann, Julian. "Il pensiero di Paolo Giovio nelle pitture eseguite sulle sue 'invenzione.'" *Atti del Convegno su Paolo Giovio: Il Rinascimento e la memoria.* Como: Presso la Società a Villa Gallia, 1985. 197-223.

_____. "La Sala dei Cento Giorni." Corti. 121 -23.

Menicantonio [Domenico Antonio de Chiarellis]. *Sketchbook.* Paul Mellon Collection.

National Gallery of Art, Washington, DC.

Michelangelo Buonarroti. Medici Chapel. San Lorenzo, Florence.

Monbeig-Goguel, Catherine. *Vasari et son Temps: Musée du Louvre, Inventaire Général des Dessins Italiens*. Paris: Editions des Musée Nationaux, 1972.

Morgan, Morris Hicky, trans. *Vitruvius: The Ten Books of Architecture*. New York: Dover, 1960.

Nagler, A. M. *Theatre Festivals of the Medici, 1539-1637*. New Haven: Yale: UP, 1964.

Partridge, L. W. "Divinity and Dynasty at Caprarola: Perfect History in the Room of Farnese Deeds." *Art Bulletin* 60 (1978): 494-530.

_____. "The Sala d'Ecole at Caprarola. Part I." *Art Bulletin* 53 (1971): 467-36.

_____. "The Sala d'Ecole: at Caprarola, Part II." *Art Bulletin* 54 (1972): 50-62.

_____. "Vignola and the Villa Farnese at Caprarola." *Art Bulletin* 52 (1970): 81-87.

Pastor, Ludwig Freiherren von. *Geschichte der Päpste*. Freiburg: n.p., 1909.

Pastoreau, M. "L'emblématique Farnèse." *Palais Farnèse* 1.2 (n.d.): 431-55.

Perino del Vaga. Sala Paolina. Castel Sant'Angelo, Rome.

Pliny the Younger. *Letters of the Younger Pliny*. London: Scott, 1900.

Plutarch. *Lives of the Noble Grecians and Romans*. Trans. John Dryden and Arthur Hugh Clough. New York: Modern Library, 1932.

Raphael. *Healing of the Lame Man*. Victoria and Albert Museum, London.

--. *Interior of the Pantheon*. Uffizi Gallery, Florence.

Ripa, Cesare. *Iconologia*. n.p., 1603 .

Robertson, Clare. "Annibale Caro as Iconographer: Sources and Method." *Journal of the Warburg and Courtauld Institutes* 45 (1982): 160-81.

_____. *"Il Grande Cardinale"*: Alessandro Farnese, Patron of the Arts. New Haven: Yale UP, 1991.

_____. "Paolo Giovio and the *'invenzioni'* for the Sala dei Cento Giorni." *Atti del Convegno su Paolo Giovio: Il Rinascimento e la memoria*. Como: Presso la Società a Villa Gallia, 1985. 224-33.

Romano, Giulio. Sala di Constantino. Vatican, Rome.

Ronchini, A. "Giorgio Vasari alla Corte del Cardinale Farnese." *Atti e Memorie delle R. Deputazione di Storia Patria per le Provincie Modensi et Parmensi* 2 (1864): 121-28.

Russell, Daniel. "Alciati's Emblems in Renaissance France." *Renaissance Quarterly* 34 (1981): 534-54.

_____. *The Emblem and Device in France*. Lexington: U of Kentucky P, 1985.

_____. "Emblems and Hieroglyphics: Some Observations on the Beginnings and the Nature of Emblematic Forms." *Emblematica* 2 (1986): 227-40.

Salviati, Francesco. Sala dei Fasti Farnesiani. Palazzo Farnese, Rome.

Sansovino, Jacopo. *Loggietta*. Piazza San Marco, Venice.

Satkowski, Leon. *Giorgio Vasari: Architect and Courier*. Princeton: Princeton UP, 1993.

Saunders, Alison. The Sixteenth Century French Emblem Book: A Decorative and Useful Genre. Geneva: Librairie Droz, 1988.

Schianchi, Lucia Fornari, and Nicola Spinosa, ed. *Farnese: Arte e Colleczionismo*. Milan: Electa, 1995.

Schiavo, Armando. *Il Palazzo della Cancelleria*. Rome: Staderini Editore, 1963.

Schröter, J. "Zur Inhaltsdeutung des Alexander Programms des Sala Paolina." *Römische Quartalschrift für christliche Altertumskunde und Kirchengeschichte* 75 (1980): 76--99.

Solari, Giovana R. *The House of Farnese; A Portrait of a Great Family of the Renaissance*. New York: Doubleday, 1968.

Steinmann, E. "Freskenzyklen der Spätrenaissance in Rom: I. Die Sala Farnese in der Cancelleria." *Monatshefte für Kunstwissenschaft* 3 (1910): 45-58.

Strong, Roy C. *Splendour at Court: Renaissance, Spectacle, and the Theater of Power*. Boston: Houghton, 1973.

Thomson, David. *Renaissance Architecture: Critics, Patrons, Luxury*. Manchester: Manchester UP,1993.

Vasari, Giorgio. *L'Architettura di L. B. Alberti*. Florence: Lorenzo Torrentino, 1550.

_____. Sala dei Cento Giorni. Palazzo della Cancelleria, Rome.

_____. *Le Vite de' più eccellenti pittori, scultori, et architetturi*. Ed. Gaetano Milanesi. Florence: Sansoni, 1970-74.

Weigall, A. *Alexander the Great*. New York: Linonia, 1933.

Wittkower, Rudolf. *Idea and Image: Studies in the Italian Renaissance*. London: Thames, 1978.

Zuccaro, Taddeo. Anticamera del Concilio. Villa Farnese, Caprarola.

_____. Sala. dei Fasti Farnesi. Villa Farnese, Caprarola.

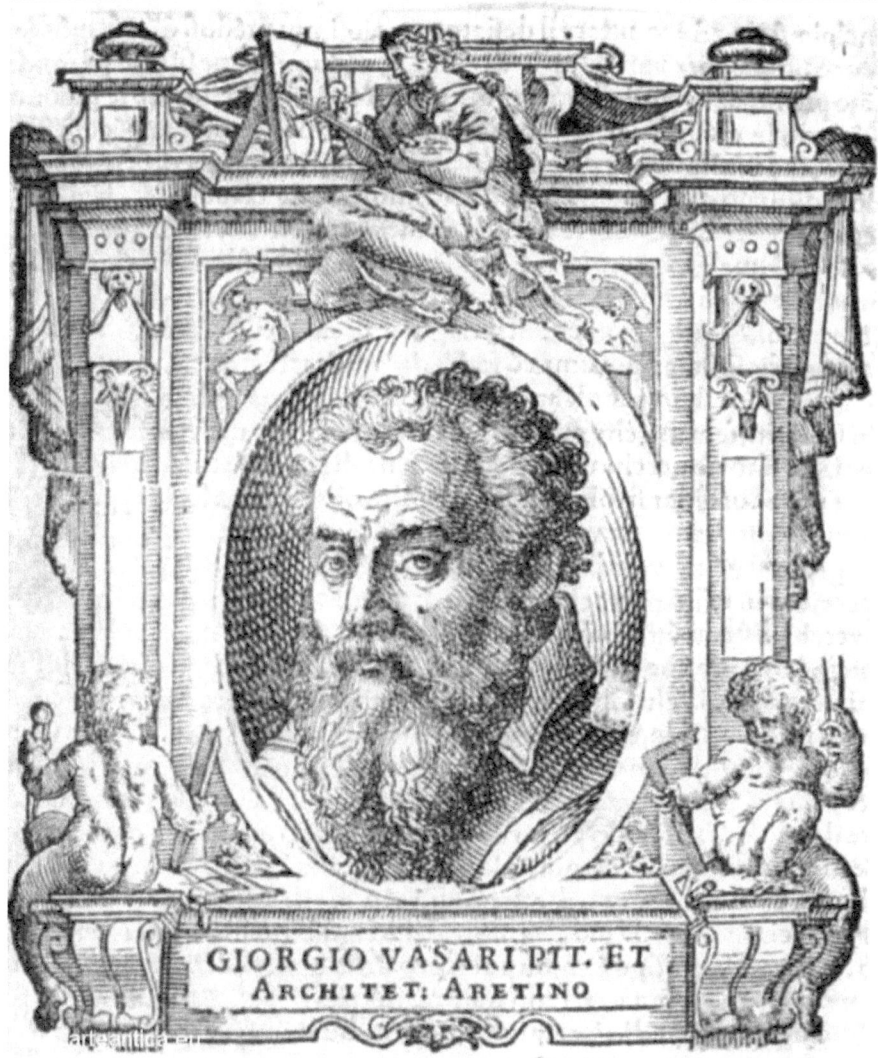

Fig. 1.   Giorgio Vasari, *Self Portrait*, 1568. Woodcut. Giorgio Vasari, *Le vite dei più eccellenti pittori, scultori ed architettori.*

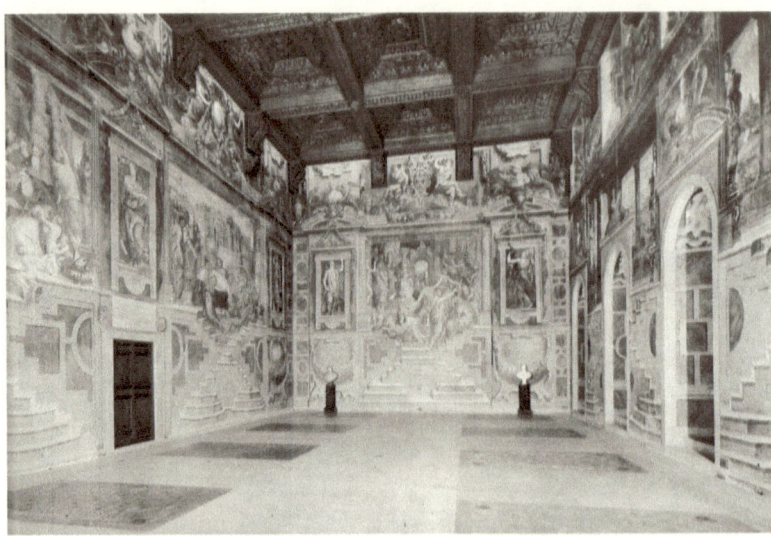

Fig. 2.   Giorgio Vasari, Sala dei Cento Giorni, 1546. Fresco. Entrance View. Rome, Palazzo della Cancelleria. Photo: Musei Vaticani, Archivio Fotografico.

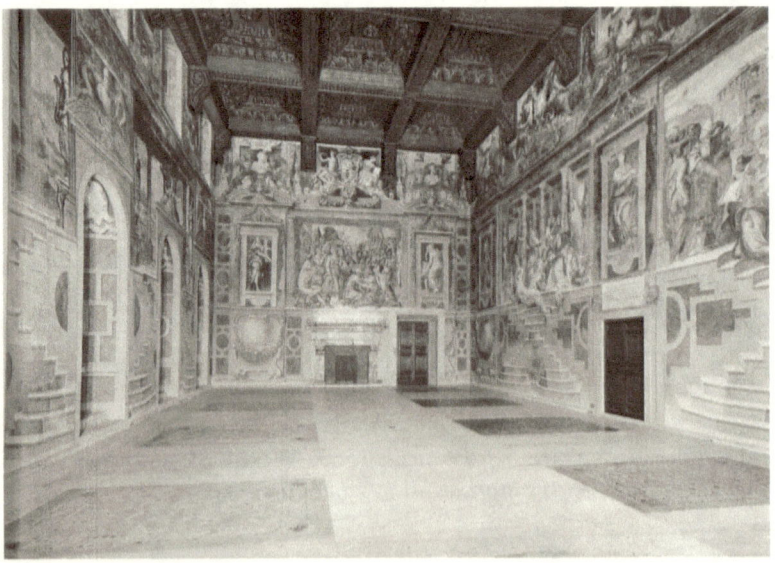

Fig. 3.   Giorgio Vasari, Sala dei Cento Giorni, 1546. Fresco. Exit View.   Rome, Palazzo della Cancelleria. Photo: Musei Vaticani, Archivio Fotografico.

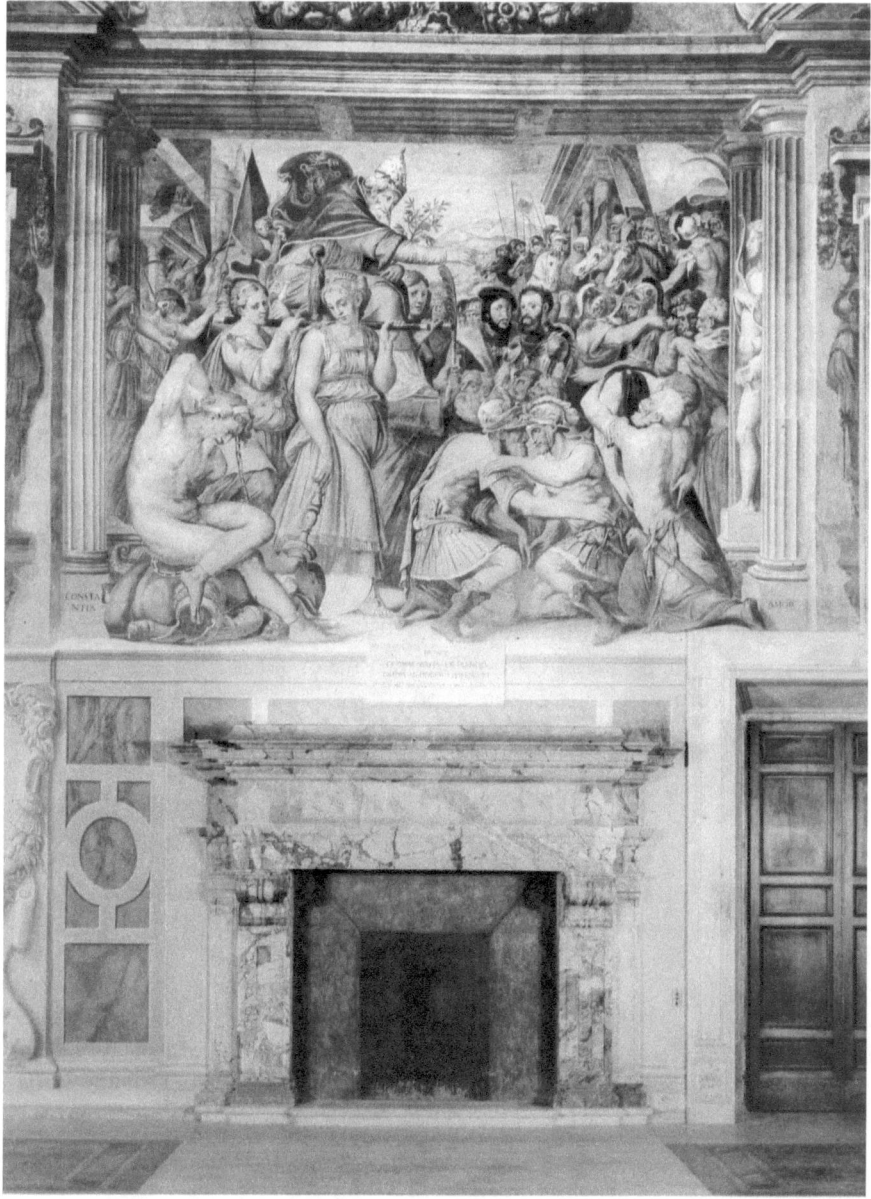

Fig. 4.   Giorgio Vasari, *The Treaty of Peace or Universal Peace in Christendum*, 1546. Fresco. South Wall. Rome, Palazzo della Cancelleria, Sala dei Cento Giorni. Photo: Musei Vaticani, Archivio Fotografico.

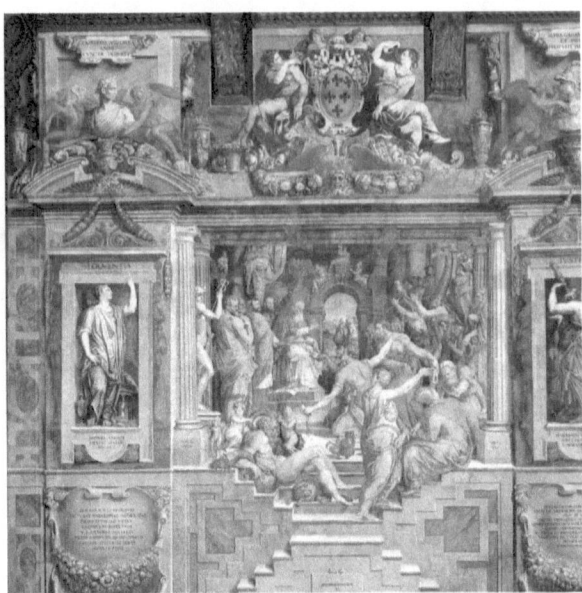

Fig. 5.   *Nations Paying Homage to Paul III,* 1546. Fresco.   North Wall. Rome, Palazzo della Cancelleria, Sala dei Cento Giorni. Photo:  Musei Vaticani, Archivio Fotografico.

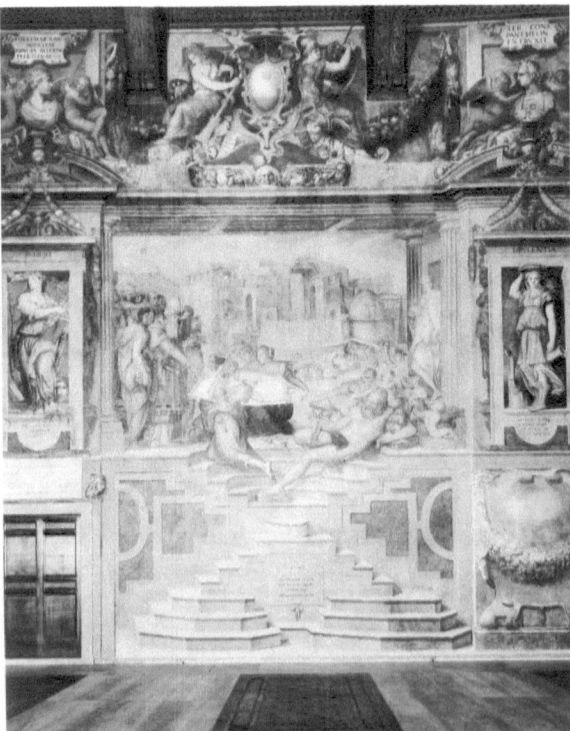

Fig. 6.   *Paul III's Supervision of the Rebuilding of Saint Peter's,* 1546. Fresco.  West Wall, Bay I. Rome, Palazzo della Cancelleria, Sala dei Cento Giorni. Photo:  Musei Vaticani, Archivio Fotografico.

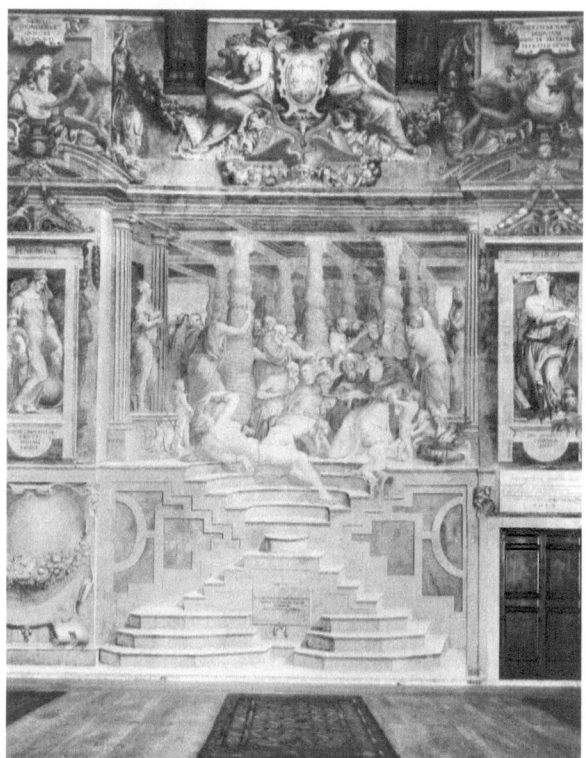

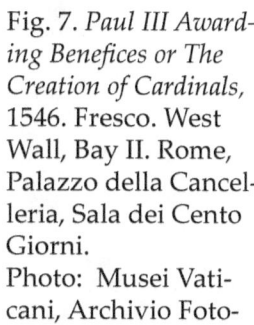

Fig. 7. *Paul III Awarding Benefices or The Creation of Cardinals,* 1546. Fresco. West Wall, Bay II. Rome, Palazzo della Cancelleria, Sala dei Cento Giorni.
Photo: Musei Vaticani, Archivio Fotografico.

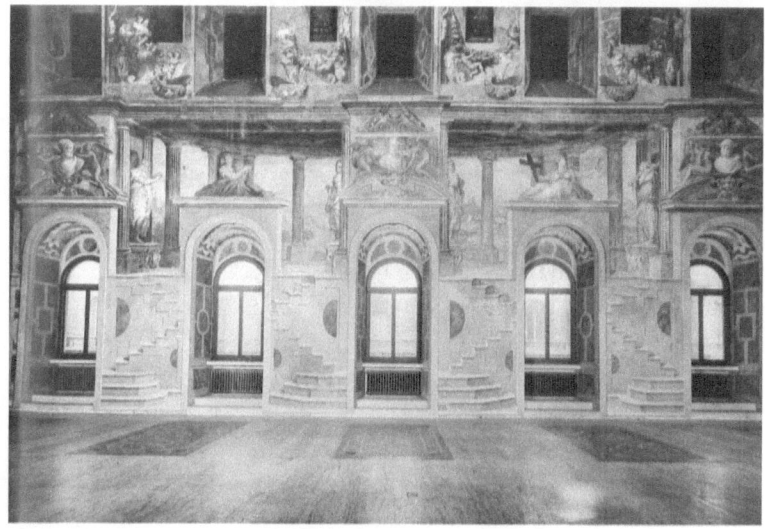

Fig. 8. *The Theological Virtues or Cardinal and Theological Virtues,* 1546. Fresco. East Wall. Rome, Palazzo della Cancelleria, Sala dei Cento Giorni. Photo: Musei Vaticani, Archivio Fotografico.

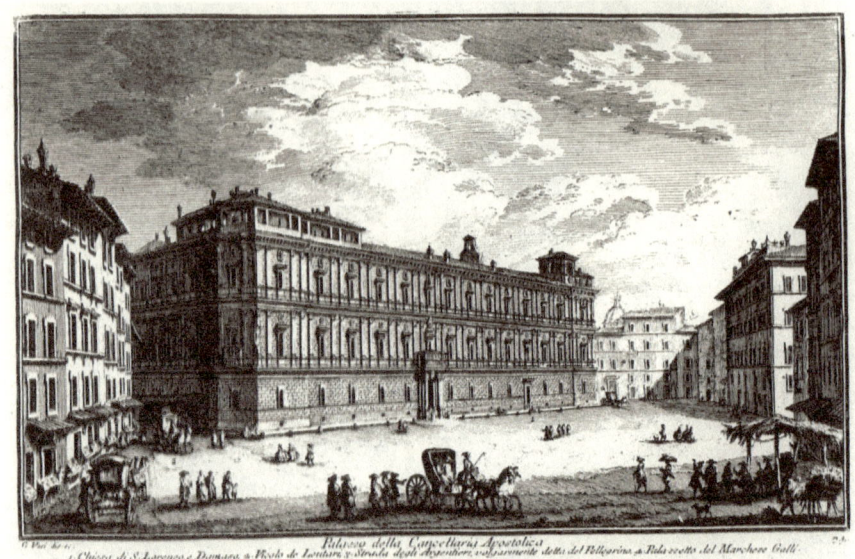

Fig. 9. *Palazzo della Cancelleria*, 1546, engraving

# 7

# Prefiguring Ripa:
# Vasari's Virtues in the Chamber of Fortune

*Vasari Adiuvat Ripa (Vasari Helps Ripa)*

Giorgio Vasari's importance in pioneering the codification of artistic and compositional elements within the emblematic tradition has long been overlooked. Yet his encyclopedic approach to the assimilation of the emblematic tradition establishes him as a forerunner of the iconographer, Cesare Ripa. Vasari's educational background and association with Renaissance humanists engendered his familiarity with the language and imagery of the emblematic tradition. This knowledge prompted him to appropriate and subsume some of these images in his work, anticipating Ripa's *figurazioni* or emblems in his 1593 *Iconologia*.[1] Vasari's paintings in the Casa Vasari at Arezzo, especially in the Chamber of Fortune (1548), a room in his home, best illustrate the connection that enables us to regard Vasari as Ripa's precursor. Vasari's referential approach to the emblematic tradition can particularly be seen in his depiction of the allegorical virtues in this chamber.

As Vasari recounts in his autobiography, his knowledge of emblems derives from his formal education in the classics with the humanists, Giovanni Pollastra and Pierio Valeriano; his contact with Andrea Alciato in 1540, when Vasari was painting the Refectory of San Michele in Bosco in Bologna; and his interactions with the humanists, Vincenzo Borghini, Annibale Caro, and Paolo Giovio, when Vasari was decorating the Sala dei Cento Giorni in Rome in

1546. As a consequence of his schooling and these contacts, Vasari became aware of the literary tradition associated with emblematic and mythographic sources such as Andrea Alciato's 1546 *Emblemata*, Francesco Colonna's 1499 *Hypnertomachia Poliphili*, Horopollo's *Hierogliphica* of 1505, and Pierio Valeriano's 1556 *Hieroglyphicae*. Mythological manuals also provided a vital source for Vasari's visual *concetti* (conceits); Boccaccio's *Geneologia de gli Dei* (1547), Natali Conti's *Mythologiae* (1551), Lilio Gregorio Giraldi's *De deis gentium* (1548), and Vincenzo Cartari's *Imagini delli Dei de gl' Antichi* (1556). Such compilations of medieval mythographies, hieroglyphs, and numismatic sources served as commonplace books for Cinquecento humanists and artists. These figurative encyclopedias or "dictionary-albums" allowed for easy consultation when time was lacking for reading primary texts. Since these manuals were so well known to Cinquecento artists and literati, humanists copied information directly from them without feeling need to credit their sources. Throughout the Renaissance, painters used these manuals as they assembled, assimilated, and adapted subjects from classical mythology into complex and allusive schemes.

In addition, the *Greek Anthology*, a series of anonymous Greek lyric and epigrammatic poems with a moral message, greatly influenced these sources, especially Alciato.[2] In 1494 Janus Lascaris, a renowned Hellenist, first published the *Greek Anthology* in Florence.[3] In 1522 Alciato translated it into Latin and assimilated its moral implications in his emblem book. Other literary and epigrammatic sources for Vasari's imagery and symbolism are Paolo Giovio's *Dialogo delle imprese militare el amorose* (1551) and the 1522 *Ragionamento delle Imprese* (Zimmermann; Caldwell) as well as Vincenzo Borghini's numerous letters and explanatory texts on programs of decorative cycles and literary subjects, published as *Discorsi* in 1584 (see Manni).

For sixteenth-century theorists the merit of the iconographical *invenzioni* (allegories, emblems, and *imprese*) lay in the artist's original and ingenious interpretation of a familiar myth or allegory (see Scorza). Vasari, in the prefaces to his *Vite*,[4] and Ripa, in his *Iconologia*, concur that the image should provide visual interest by showing beautiful elements and that its motto should be brief, containing two or three words or a line of verse left suggestively incomplete to intrigue or tease the audience - in sum, a Maniera conceit. In their writings both Vasari and Ripa strongly emphasize that an allegory (emblem) must visually and verbally assimilate its ancient sources. Such emblematic sources provided Vasari with an extensive repertoire of images that he collected and employed in the iconography of the Casa Vasari in Arezzo and expanded in such later commissions as the decorative cycles of the Palazzo Vecchio in Florence.[5]

Vasari's composition of images as a compendium of iconography for a decorative program was similar to the literary practices of Alciato, Valeriano, and Cartari and follows Giovio's advice on depicting an emblematic image or *impresa*. According to Giovio an *impresa* or badge must contain a figure and motto, its meaning should not be too obscure or too obvious, the imagery must be pleasant to look at, and the motto must be brief, inventive, and unambiguous.[6]

Later Ripa captured the symbolic meaning of an image by fusing the Cinquecento visual and literary traditions in his emblem book, *Iconologia*. He refers to the emblematic image as figurazione. In Ripa's *figurazione* or emblem of *Iconografia* (*Iconography*, Fig. 1), for example, a woman holds a square and other measuring devices, with a compass at her feet to assist in the drawing of natural forms (Ripa 2:432). The ruler in her right hand alludes to appraisal, as intelligence is needed for judging drawings. Ripa's description of iconography reveals his understanding of the concept of drawing and its meaning according to the Vasarian tradition. In his preface to the *Iconologia*, Ripa comments on the significance of the imagery and symbolism of Vasari 's *Sala dei Cento Giorni* of 1546 in Rome for his own literary and visual imagery, namely, the depictions of the allegorical figures, in particular, Merit (Ripa 2:467). Ripa also discusses the importance of Vasari's *Ragionamenti*, a manual for explaining paintings for the Palazzo Vecchio of 1565, in Florence.

Giorgio Vasari's *vita* or autobiography, his letters, and his *ricordi* remain the best and most complete source for dating and describing the paintings in the Casa Vasari.[7] Occasionally, however, he is vague about this matter, and his comments about the iconography are sketchy, perhaps even willfully cryptic. Nevertheless, Vasari is the inventor of an iconographical program depicted in the five decorated rooms. His ideas about subjects such as art, fame, fortune, history, culture, and religion are revealed here. Using allegorical themes and personifications, biblical and classical stories, or classical *istorie*, Vasari reveals his aesthetic interpretations of these concepts within a Cinquecento artistic and humanistic framework long before Ripa's *Iconologia*.

Between 1542 and 1554, Vasari painted the five rooms of the *piano nobile* of the Casa Vasari in Arezzo. The subjects depicted on their respective ceilings identify the chambers: Fame, Abraham, Apollo, Ceres, and Fortune. The rooms are painted in a variety of media: e.g., the Chamber of Abraham is in tempera, while the ceilings of the chambers of Fame and Apollo and the Corridor of Ceres are *al fresco*. The only room that has paintings on its ceiling in oils and walls *al fresco* is the Chamber of Fortune. In contrast to other rooms of the Casa Vasari, this Chamber portrays the Renaissance concept of the *camera picta*,[8] an illusionistic and secular decoration that achieved the status of a new art form by the end of the fifteenth century in Italy. Thus, in this chamber, Vasari fuses his Roman and Venetian artistic assimilations for painting decorative cycles. This room is the fictive studio of the painter.

The Chamber of Fortune, painted in 1548, reveals the most complex pictorial and iconographical program of all the rooms in the Casa Vasari (Cheney, "Giorgio Vasari's Painting"). The elaborateness of its style is matched by the complexity of the symbolism in the ceiling and the walls. Vasari describes the paintings in a general manner in his *vita*:

> On the ceiling, I did ... thirteen large pictures, containing the gods of heaven, four nude figures of the Seasons in the corners surrounding a large painting in the middle, that contains life-size figures of Virtue with Envy, under her feet, and Fortune, gripped by the hair, while she beats both. A circumstance that gave great pleasure then is that in going round the room Fortune at one place seems above Envy and Virtue, and at another Virtue is above Envy and Fortune, just as it is often the case in reality. On the sidewalls are Abundance, Liberality, Wisdom, Prudence, Strength, Honor, etc. and below them are stories of the ancient painters,

Apelles, Zeuxis, Parrhasius, Protogenes, with other details that I omit.

(Vasari-Milanesi II:93-107)

A drawing of the ceiling decoration at the Uffizi portrays the three themes: personifications in the *palco*, the four seasons, and the planetary gods.[9] The flat ceiling is segmented by a wooden framework that places the paintings in their separate compartments. Except for the central area or projected *palco*, all the painted areas are recessed within a wooden framework. The octagonal *palco* contains painted scenes of the personification of Envy, Fortune, and Virtue, around which are arrayed the Four Seasons depicting the Four Ages of Life and holding various seasonal garlands of flowers, fruits, and vegetables. Encircling the *palco* are eight rectangles containing paintings of the celestial rulers, recognizable from their attributes and zodiacal signs: Diana/Cancer; Apollo/Leo; Cupid/Taurus; Venus/Libra; Mercury/Gemini and Virgo; Mars/Aries and Scorpio; Saturn/Capricorn and Aquarius; and Jupiter/Sagittarius and Pisces. In each corner of the ceiling, within a sunken square, a flying *putto* carries Vasari's coat-of-arms. The wall decorations also consist of three themes, each of which is divided horizontally into an upper and lower zone. In the first section of the upper walls the personifications of Nature, Earth, Art, and Religion reside in landscapes and frame eight allegorical virtues residing in niches. The second section of the lower wall decoration is composed of *istorie*, classical stories associated with ancient artists, and fanciful and witty imagery.

This essay focuses only on the symbolism of the eight allegorical virtues - Wisdom, Prudence, Honor, Felicity, Patience, Justice, Fortitude, and Liberality - in the upper zone of the Chamber of Fortune in relation to Ripa's *figurazioni*.[10] The iconography of these virtues is connected with the meaning of the four personifications in the center of the upper zone of the walls - Nature as Diana or Artemis of Ephesus, Earth as Abundance (Copia), Art as Venus or Aphrodite, and Religion as Charity (Caritas) - all of which connect symbolically with the theme of the *palco*. Decorative curtains set off these four personifications standing on pedestals as simulated sculptures. The allegorical virtues compositionally bracket them.

Unlike the personifications that stand, these virtues sit or recline in adjacent enclosed niches. The personifications and allegorical virtues adhere to sixteenth-century iconographical and stylistic conventions. The allegorical virtues, in particular, are similar in composition to the allegorical virtues of the Refectory of Monteoliveto (1545) in Naples and the Sala dei Cento Giorni (1546) in Rome. In their portrayal, Vasari reveals the benefits they bestow to an artist who wishes to achieve a good, successful, and Christian life.

In the Chamber of Fortune, at the extremes of the upper zone of the north wall, the seated allegorical virtues of Wisdom and Prudence face Diana or Artemis of Ephesus, who stands in the center (Fig. 2). Behind Artemis, two landscapes represent a Roman harbor and a Roman hill of the Aventine. For Vasari, Artemis of Ephesus personifies Nature; he depicts her in accordance with Cartari's description, "dea della Natura tutta piena de poppe, per mostrare, che l'universo piglia nutrimento dalla virtu occulta della medesima" (the goddess of Nature filled with breasts to reveal that the universe obtains nutriment from the her occult virtue).[11] Vasari's visualization of Artemis of Ephesus derives as well from the ancient statue of Artemis of Ephesus, which he viewed in the Farnese classical collection of Naples in 1545. The lunar and solar deities depicted on the breastplate of the goddess, one holding a crab and the other carrying a symbol of the sun, likely represent the goddess Diana (Artemis) and her brother Apollo. The same deities appear directly above on the ceiling, suggesting a connection between the planetary deities of the ceiling and the deity of the wall decoration.

Behind the simulated sculpture of Artemis is a landscape with a flowering meadow and a seascape. According to Valeriano, Servius Tullius consecrated a temple to Artemis of Ephesus on the Aventine (68). Vasari's landscape contains an *all'antica* reconstruction of the Aventino, filled with personal *capricci*. The vegetation in the foreground of the landscape suggests late summer or early autumn. The seascape portrays a seashore suggesting Ostia Antica, the ancient Roman harbor. A few years later, Vasari repeated the Aretine theme of Art and Nature in his second home in Florence. In the Sala Vasari models enter the studio of Apelles to pose, thus assisting the artist in capturing natural forms and observations in his paintings. In the background of the *loggia*, a statue of Artemis of Ephesus stands in front of a capricious landscape, reminding the viewer that art is advanced by nature.

In the 1560s sculptor Benvenuto Cellini designed an emblem for the Accademia del Disegno in Florence employing an image of Artemis of Ephesus.[12] A diamond shape encloses a standing figure of Artemis of Ephesus holding two trumpets. A line drawn from one of them leads to Cellini's note: "La tromba della nostra Fama" (The trumpet of our Fame), alluding to signification of Nature for an artist. Surrounded by snakes and an ostrich, the winged goddess' torso is filled with breasts, symbolizing plentiful nature. A frieze with alphabetic letters is matched with hieroglyphic imagery, a parallelism between the word and the image. The frieze visually reinforces this concept with the depiction of the diamond-shaped imagery at the top of the page. Below the design is a lengthy text composed and signed by Cellini.

Cinquecento artists such as Vasari and Cellini drew the manifestations of nature through imitation or invention, thus the grasping of nature is associated with the concept of design (*disegno*) or art. In this connection between art and nature, Vasari assimilates emblematic tradition, especially Alciato's Emblem 98, *Ars Naturam Adiuvans* (Art Helps Nature, Fig. 3). Thus, nature helps an artist to create art and vice versa. Other iconographers have also illustrated emblems from this same Vasarian perspective. For example, Sambucus' emblem on Nature (*Physicae et Metaphysicae Differentia*) (Visser, passim), inspired by ancient hieroglyphs, personifies Nature in the image of Artemis of Ephesus, while Ripa's *figurazione* of *Invenzione* (Invention) depicts a woman holding a statue of Artemis of Ephesus, signifying that Nature represents the invention of all things, with the motto "Non Alivm De" (Art is none other than Nature or Art imitates Nature, Fig. 4).[13] Inventione wears a gold bracelet on her right hand, containing the motto, "Ad Operam" (For Work), alluding to the merits of the intellectual flow of ideas created by in invention.

In the Chamber Wisdom and Prudence frame Artemis of Ephesus. Although the fusion of Prudence and Wisdom was common in the period, Vasari portrays them separately and facing Nature (Fig. 2), According to classical tradition, "wisdom" derives from the Greek *sophia*, originally referring to the practical arts and then later viewed as knowledge and reason. Plato understood wisdom to be one of the chief virtues. For him, Wisdom was the faculty required for both scientific knowledge and practical experience. However, Aristotle distinguishes between speculative and practical wisdom, between *sophia* (wisdom) and *phronesis* (prudence). While practical wisdom (*phronesis*) relates to the conduct of life - behavior and moral conduct - by contrast, speculative wisdom (*sophia*) requires elements of intuitive reason. In assimilating the ideas of antiquity, Renaissance humanists emphasized the philosophical significance of wisdom. For example, Nicholas de Cusa defined wisdom as learned ignorance, whereas Marsilio Ficino elaborated on the concept through the Neoplatonic notion of reason and the manifestation of wisdom (*mens intellectus*), e.g., wisdom's control over ignorance (nature). In this light, wisdom incorporates a person's physical and metaphysical realms, since a human soul is composed of instincts (natural world) and reason or intellect (supernatural world - *mens*). In his portrayal, Vasari captures the Neoplatonic attributes of wisdom by depicting the dual realms of the virtue by facing the image with the personification of Nature and correlating with Prudence, located at the end of the wall.

Vasari's Wisdom (*Sapienza*) is an iconographical fusion of Knowledge (*Cognizione*) and Intelligence (*Intelligenza*) (see Ripa 3:38-43). Winged Wisdom, a symbol of solicitude, holds a book, suggesting her quest for knowledge (Fig. 2); a torch whose flame signifies the mind's ability to see the light of reason and to understand intellectual matters; and a sphere, alluding to Wisdom's attempt to comprehend the abstract laws of the universe in human terms. One of her feet is suspended in midair, a suggestion of detachment in her intellectual pursuits from earthly goods.[14] Wisdom rests comfortably and stably on a cube in her niche, unlike Felicity, who sits precariously on a wheel of Fortune residing in the opposite wall (Hall 86). Wisdom faces Nature, suggesting that the desire to comprehend the laws of nature requires knowledge, perseverance, strength, and stability and that these qualities are prerequisites for a creative mind and a successful artistic career. When Ripa later portrayed a figurazione of Knowledge (*Cognizione*, Fig. 5), he reflected Vasari's composition and meaning of Wisdom (Ripa 3,38).

On the other side of Nature is the allegorical virtue of Prudence (Fig. 2). Vasari's drawings and description of the *invenzione* of Prudence assist in the interpretation, "Prudenzia...aver la serpe et le chiavi di Jano" (to hold the serpent and the keys of Janus).[15] Instead, the Aretine Prudence portrays a Janus head and holds the key to the Janus temple. The Janus head implies that Prudence must look to the past as well as to the future before making a decision, namely to foresee and provide (*prevedere e provedere*).

Symbolically, the Aretine Prudence combines attributes from the Prudentia and Providenza, as revealed in Alciato's *Emblemata*,[16] Emblem 18, *Prudentes Problema*. Alciato notes Janus was the most ancient king of Italy, who supposedly was the wisest of all the monarchs of his age, knowing the past and foreseeing the future, which is why he is depicted with two faces. When Janus died, he was put among the gods and had a temple at Rome, which was opened in time of war. Alciato elaborates on the meaning of the emblem by citing the epigram:

> Janus, you who have been provided with two faces, to know the past and the future; and since you see what is offered, you can mock what has happened. Why have you been depicted with so many faces? Is it perhaps because a strong and wise man should be such that at the same time can see the presented and the future?[17]

As noted, the Aretine figure is identified as Prudence because she is portrayed with the Janus head holding a key. Her key is a symbol of peace, as seen in Cartari's emblem, where Janus is dosing the Temple of War with a key (*Imagini* 255). The key symbolizes as well the guidance needed to open the door to success and thus rise above the difficulties of life. When the key held by Prudence is associated with Cybele, the Earth goddess, Prudence's symbolism is connected with Good Fortune or Providence. Thus, Vasari's Prudence is a stylistic fusion of two images of Prudence and Providence and reveals a dual nature because it is also depicted holding a cornucopia and resting her foot on a globe, both attributes of Providence. The globe is a symbol of ubiquity and the cornucopia of plentitude as portrayed in Cartari's emblem, *Bonus*

*Eventus* or Felicity. In the Aretine imagery, the globe is barely visible because of heavy restoration. Vasari portrays Prudence with its dual nature to stress the difficulties encountered by a person on earth. Human beings must be prudent to achieve success in life. For Vasari, Prudence is a significant virtue for guiding and conducting a purposeful life. In a letter to his fellow artists, Vasari reminds them of this desirable quality and encourages them to acquire it (Bettarini-Barocchi 3:315).

Renaissance humanists and artists assimilated the ideas of antiquity, portraying in art the fusion of the personification of Wisdom with the medieval personification of Prudence (Tuve 246-47). But Vasari separates these virtues as independent qualities. Of all the virtues, Prudence is the dearest to the Renaissance humanists, so much so that Alciato represents ten emblems of this virtue in his book. Thus, it is not mere coincidence that Vasari's Prudence is an appropriation of Alciato's emblem.

Among the many of Vasari's drawings of Prudence is the beautiful 1545 depiction in the Collection F. Lugt of the Institut Neerlandais in Paris (inv. 7777). Vasari's *disegno* differs from his painted Aretine image. Surrounded with all her attributes of practical and speculative wisdom such as a mirror, a serpent, a key, and Janus' head, Prudence attends to her toilet. Her engaging attitude denotes her existence in the present. The drawing also reveals an elaborate holder for the mirror and shows a vanity table, a comb, and a brush, not seen in the painting, and a serpent as caution and wisdom, recalling Matthew 10:16. "Be prudent [wise] as serpents."[18] Inspired by the ancient traditions of Aristotle, the Neoplatonists, Plutarch, and Pliny the Elder, medieval treatises such as Vincent of Beauvais' *Speculum morale*, Thomas Aquinas' *Summa Theologia*, and the thirteenth-century *Somme le Roi* associated personifications of the virtues with a specific animals, e.g., a serpent with Prudence.[19] Proto-Renaissance examples studied by Vasari in which Prudence is depicted with a serpent are Nicola Pisano's *Prudence* on the pulpit of the baptistery in Pisa (13 10) and Giotto's *Prudence* portrayed in the Scrovegni or Arena Chapel in Padua (1305).

The Cinquecento imagery of Prudence is reflected in Ripa's *figurazione* for *Prudenza* (Prudence), depicting a woman with a Janus head holding a mirror and spear with a serpent.[20] Under the proliferation of meanings, the personifications and allegories also expand the repertoire of their attributes, e.g., Ripa's inclusion of a deer at the feet of Prudence, suggesting that the animal, like Prudence, ponders like a sage (Fig. 6).

In the Chamber of Fortune, across the room on the south wall, Aphrodite, goddess of Love, stands on a shell (Fig.7). Stylistically, this composition is a variation on the birth of Venus motif and the statue of the Medici Venus or Venus Belvedere at the Uffizi (see Nesselrath). Aphrodite is the sale figure on these walls who is portrayed in sculptural form, emphasizing her status in the room as the personification of Art. In the landscape behind her, Troy is destroyed at night by fire. Beneath this scene and the statue is a fireplace. In keeping with the Cinquecento theory of decorum, a scene of the legend of Croesus or the legend of Troy burning are obligatory. In accordance with this tradition, Vasari depicts a fire, supplemented by two mottoes, on the mantelpiece: "Ignem gladio ne fondito" (Thou shalt not poke a fire with a sword) and "Homo vapor est" (Man is smoke). Derived from a Pythagorean motto, the first motto also appears on Correggio's Camera di San Paolo's fireplace mantel, which Vasari may have seen during his trips to Northern Italy while collecting drawings and research material for his book on the artists' biographies. The second motto, "Man is smoke," recalls Psalms 144:4, "Man is no more than a puff of wind."[21] Both mottoes sound a cautionary notes of human frailty, *memento mori*, and the vagaries of chance. Surely Vasari's placement of Aphrodite as the personification of Art above the fireplace and before a burning landscape is no mere coincidence. Ripa, in agreement with Vasari, describes fire as an attribute of the personification of Art because "fire provides heat and light, which is manifested in the burning of things, and with the flickering of his flames renders partial light to the most obscure shadows of the night"[22] and elaborates with "the firing flame becomes a principal tool for the creation of artificial things: because in creating solidified or softened objects, the flame makes them able to be employed by the individual in numerous artistic activities."[23]

Purposely, Vasari arranges for the statue of Aphrodite to face the painting of Artemis of Ephesus.[24] The strong contrast between the attributes, elements, and composition of these two figures gives added cogency to their identification as Art and Nature. Vasari again underscores the significance for depictions of the realm of nature and the realm of art, focusing on the notion that the realm of art is superior to the realm of nature because it is, at once, fanciful and inventive.

For Vasari, an artist must experience nature but ultimately create art (Vasari-Milanesi 1:95-102). However, he also connects the symbolism of the realms of art and nature with the *palco*'s allusion by appropriating Alciato's connection between Nature and Fortune, e.g., Alciato's on Ars Naturam Adiuvans (Art Helps Nature), Emblem 98, explains how:

> Fortune stands upon an unstable sphere and Mercury sits on a solid cube: he presides over the arts, she over chance events. Art is made to counter the power of Fortune, but when Fortune is bad, she often requires the help of Art.[25]

Fortune's fickleness, the turning of her wheel, threatens the creation and judgment of art. Therefore, the Virtue is necessary for maintaining constancy, firmness, and perseverance in the creative process.[26] Because of the whimsical nature of Fortune, Alciato advises youth "to be industrious and learn good arts which bring with them much of use and great fortune" (Daly, *Andrea Alciatus* 37). Alciato also observes that Fortune's plans are unstable. Accordingly, the person who makes use of art is wise, and everyone should learn good art, which ensures that Fortune will ultimately be achieved. Alciato further says that Art helps Nature because of the guidance of Fortune and the liberal arts. But Art needs to control the power of Fortune to be efficacious because when Fortune is bad, it does not assist the other arts. Then, Art intervenes and provides a remedy for Fortune. Thus, bad Fortune necessitates the help of good Art; Art sets Fortune right.

Framing the limestone sculpture of Aphrodite, the personification of Art, are the two allegorical virtues of Honor and Felicity (*Felicità Publica*) (Fig. 7). Felicity or *Bonus Eventus* sits on a wheel holding a caduceus and a cornucopia. Vasari alludes to Cartari's description of the image of Felicity or *Bonus Eventus* (see Ripa 1:246). He describes this image as "Felicità...una donna vestita, con un corno di dovitia nella sinistra, et un caduceo di mercurio nella destra" (Felicity...a dressed woman, holding a horn of plenty with her left hand and a Mercury's caduceus with her right") (qtd. in Del Vita 9). The caduceus and the cornucopia symbolize the elements needed for happiness: The caduceus is a symbol of peace and industry, and the cornucopia contains the products of hard work. Ripa appropriates this type of imagery for his *figurazjone* of Felicity (Fig. 8). Vasari's Felicity sits precariously on the wheel of Fortune, which is a symbol of authority and good fortune (see Ripa 1:271-73). For the ancient Romans as well as for Vasari, Felicity is a personification of happiness, since she "symbolized a fortunate event and the happy issue of an enterprise" (De Tervarent 95).

Since the figure of Honor in the Chamber has suffered great physical deterioration, it is difficult to ascertain the attributes he holds (Fig. 7). Honor appears to be a female but is a male crowned with laurel and holding a crown of laurel and palms. For Vasari's *invenzione*, Honor is "Giovane armato all'antica...con corona di lauro e palme in mano" ("Young man, armed in a classical manner... with a crown of laurel and palms in hand") (qtd. in Del Vim 8). According to Alciato and later Ripa, Honor holds a laurel crown and represents a virtuous and honest person. A crown of laurel, an evergreen plant, is a symbol of nobility, immortality, Fame, and Glory whereas the palm is a symbol of Victory (Ripa 2:298). A basket of flowers is located next to Honor (this part in the fresco is severely damaged). Likely, the basket suggests another attribute of Honor, a cornucopia, a symbol of richness. The symbol of Honor holds a special meaning for Vasari. The image of Honor relates to the recognition which rewards a person's actions. The praise of these virtues and noble endeavors distinguishes a person (Vasari as an artist) from his peers (other contemporary artists). These awards and honors bestow fame and immortality upon a person.

On the west wall of the Chamber of Fortune the personification of Charity (*Caritas*/Religion) is flanked by the allegorical figures of Fortitude and Liberality (Fig. 9).[27] Behind her is a landscape depicting the Campo Vaccino and the Temple of Venere et Roma at the Roman *forae*. In his painting of Charity, Vasari depicts a bare-breasted statuesque figure holding a nursing child in one arm with two other children standing next to her. The beautiful drawing from the Pinacoteca of Bologna testifies to Vasari's artistic inventiveness.[28] According to Thomas Aquinas, the three children held by Charity symbolize aspects of Charity, including the theological virtues: Faith, Hope, and Love.[29] The female figure of Charity represents the unity of these three aspects and personifies Religion as well because Charity symbolizes the three theological virtues given to people by the love of God (*amor dei*). Her generosity and love for humankind, emulated by good Christians (*amor proximi*) are also important to her role as the personification of Religion.[30] Stylistically, the Aretine Charity refers to Vasari's earlier depiction of Charity in the Refectory of Monteoliveto. Thematically, Vasari employs a similar image of Charity in the Sala dei Cento Giorni. Clearly, his imagery anticipates Ripa's emblem in its depiction of a nursing woman, dressed *all'antica* and with three infants (Fig. 10).[31]

The landscape scenes flank each personification, the topography and stylistic composition of which are Vasarian inventions. The scenes adjoining Charity indicate by means of cloud formations two different times of day - morning and afternoon - and by means of the vegetation, two different seasons - spring and summer.[32] In the foreground of the Campo Vaccino, Vasari depicts a grotto where a man sits drawing his shadow in a partially illuminated area, alluding to the invention of *disegno* or painting. This, Vasari's favorite theme, is repeated in the lower portion of the opposite wall as part of the classical *istorie*, where a man, Gyges of Lydia, also is drawing his shadow. Years later, in a larger format, Vasari elaborated on the same imagery in the Sala Vasari of his Florentine home. The depiction of the grotto is Vasari's reference to the discovery of the Domus Aurea, the House of Nero, as well as to one of his stylistic *capricci*.

Next to the Charity is Fortitude (*Fortezza*, Fig. 9). Although the image in the Aretine house is indistinct, comparison with a similar painting from the Refectory reveals its proper attributes and its identification as Fortitude. The Aretine Fortitude is depicted as an armed woman with a Herculean body wearing a helmet and carrying a sword and a shield (Fig. 9). Subsequently, Ripa described this type of figure as an armed woman with a helmet, a sword, and a shield with a lion's head (1:129). But Vasari's shield contains the head of Medusa as having lion-like qualities. The attributes of Fortitude symbolize bodily strength and the generosity of the soul. Medusa represents a cardinal virtue. In the treatment of this figure, Vasari illustrates Valeriano's saying "Fortezza d'animo, e di corpo" (Mental and Physical Strengths) (*Hieroglyphica* 1:2; qtd. in Ripa 1:270).

Perhaps Fortitude also personifies Sagacity or Reason. Vasari describes Sagacity (Sagacità) as "Pallas with a shield with a Medusa and a lance."[33] He is also referring to Alciato's *Custodiendas Verginis, Emblemata* XXII (Alciato 124-125). The book at the feet of Fortitude (as the Monteoliveto counterpart) symbolizes the mental effort necessary to gain knowledge. The horn seen in the Monteoliveto figure is no longer recognizable in the Aretine image. Perhaps for Vasari Fortitude symbolizes the moral, mental, and physical efforts required of a person to live a purposeful and good life.

Liberality (Liberalità) sits on the other side of Charity (Fig. 9). Vasari's definition of Liberality as "una donna che versi un bacino pieno di danari e di gioie" ("a woman that discards from a full bag of money and jewelry") anticipates Ripa's later interpretation of Liberality as "una donna con un bacino voto da una mano et dall'altra una borsa aperta" (a woman that carries an empty purse in one hand and an open purse in the other hand).[34] The principal aspects of liberality are parsimony and generosity. The Aretine Liberality differs from the Monteoliveto conception of a man discarding the contents of a cornucopia and a purse. The Aretine Liberality holds a closed purse or bag with her right hand while opening and releasing the contents of another purse with the left.[35] Securing a purse represents industry, fortune, frugality, and avarice, while emptying one symbolizes generosity, charity and prodigality. As held by this Aretine figure, the two purses are parallel, suggesting a balance between saving and spending. This balance and the avoidance of the extremes of avarice and prodigality can be achieved only through strength of character. To suggest this, the Aretine figure is clad in a breastplate, symbolic of strength. She rests on a full cornucopia, representing the richness and fullness of life. Hence, for Vasari, Liberality is probably a personification of the noble nature of a generous individual who saves to procure the good life and gives according to his moral and material capabilities.

Located at the center of the east wall of the Chamber across from

Charity, Abundance (*Copia*), personifying Earth (Fig. 11), stands on a pedestal with her allegorical companions, Justice and Patience, reclining on plinths on each side of her. The cornucopia Abundance holds and the wooden barrel next to her are filled with fruit and flowers. On her head she carries a basket filled with various grains. Vasari describes this figure as Copia, "Un grembio di frutte che riempia un corno piena" (An apron with fruits that can fills a horn of plenty) (qtd. in Del Vita 24). For Cartari and later Ripa, Abundance represents not only the positive aspect of earth, but an absolute need in one's life as well. Through the attributes she carries (cornucopia, fruits, and grains), Abundance personifies the copiousness and richness of Earth.[36] Vasari's depiction of Abundance combines two of his early images, Opulentia from the Sala del Cento Giorni and Abondanza from the Refectory of Monteoliveto.[37] Ripa's *figurazione* or emblem depends on Vasari's *invenzione* of Abundance (Fig. 12).

Framing Earth are the virtues of Patience and Justice (Fig. 11). Their reclining positions are a further quotation from the figures in the Cornaro Palace (1541) in Venice and the Chamber of Abraham (1548) at Arezzo. With her yoke, Patience rests quietly. Vasari describes her as "Patientia...il giogho al collo et il capo basso" (Patience...the yoke on her neck and the head bent).[38] The yoke is a symbol of submission and compliance, as depicted in Ripa's *figurazione* of Patienza (Patience), Obedienza (Obedience) and Servitudine (Servitude).[39] In Vasari's painting, Patience's endurance in life is portrayed by her humble and austere appearance. Another attribute alluding to endurance and perseverance is the snail on Patience's shoulder-pad. This is why Patience is looking so intensely at the slow-moving animal. Later Ripa too attributes the snail to the allegory of Patience (Ripa 2:556). Vasari is likely noting that by acquiring the virtue of patience, a person can tolerate and even venture with tranquility through the adversity of life.

In the adjacent compartment, Justice, with her back to the viewer, holds a book and a sword with a terrestrial globe at her feet (Fig. 11).[40] The sword is a symbol of power and impartiality; the book signifies the codes on which her judgments are made; and the globe represents the universality of Justice's judgments (Cartari 242-43; Ripa 2:298-99). Justice, like Fortitude, is a cardinal virtue. Perhaps by depicting the figure of Justice as facing the heavens with her back to the viewer, Vasari is suggesting that God assists the judgment of Justice, which is essentially impartial. Ripa's imagery derives from Vasari while focusing on the Platonic allusion of Justice as eyewitness of all things. Hence, Ripa places a medallion containing a large eye on Justice's necklace (2:298).

Through his depiction of Charity and Abundance, Vasari implies that both goodness of heart (spiritual richness) and goodness of earth (natural richness) are essential for the welfare of his home and that Fortune has smiled kindly upon him in making it possible to achieve this. Vasari chooses to depict the personification of Charity and Abundance to affirm the Good Fortune in his life.[41] He portrays this meaning by demonstrating that continued Good Fortune depends on the necessary participation of Love/Charity supported by Fortitude and Liberality as well as the acquisition of material riches and wealth supplied by Abundance. However, Patience and Justice must control Abundance for the realization of Good Fortune.[42]

Vasari affirms here that the acquisition of knowledge and the desire to comprehend the laws of nature are aspirations of an artist's quest for inventing and imitating nature and creating art. Similar to Patience, Justice, and Fortitude, Knowledge requires perseverance, strength, and stability, whereas Felicity, Prudence and Liberality vacillate according to the wheel of Fortune. Symbolically, the eight allegorical figures personify the virtues necessary to achieve a good, productive, and Christian life. The message conveyed in the Chamber of Fortune is difficult to summarize in systematic fashion. Although Vasari's decorations contain theological, philosophical, historical, and didactic schema, the structure is not logical, contrary to the Sala dei Cento Giorni in Rome or the Sala dell'Udienza in Florence. The decoration of the chamber is not meant to display a specific mythological narrative or classicizing modes of expression, as in the Camera di San Paolo in Parma. In the Chamber of Fortune, a general underlying philosophy gives unity and meaning to the various allegories, personifications, and *istorie*. But this philosophy is a set of personal convictions influenced by Renaissance Neoplatonism and humanistic treatises rather than the result of systematic thought. Thus, in the Chamber of Fortune, iconographical relationship exists between the ceiling and the walls.

Their first obvious connection is schematic. On the ceiling are four personifications, four seasons, and eight planetary gods. On the walls are four dominant personifications, simulated as sculptures, and eight allegorical virtues.

The second connection between the ceiling and the upper walls relates to the *palco*'s symbolic structure with Fortune in the center and the confrontation of Art and Nature on the adjacent walls, clearly reflecting Alciato's emblematic imprint on Vasari's program. Vasari had the good fortune to acquire knowledge of the liberal arts through his artistic and literary studies and his personal and humanistic contacts. He surrounds the personification of Art with the allegories of Honor and Felicity, alluding to his artistic recognition. He accompanies the personification of Nature with the allegories of Wisdom and Prudence for the judgment needed to create his paintings. Vasari's artistic successes are realized by inventing and imitating art and dictated by his natural ability. Although his artistic achievements are directed by the power of Good Fortune, Vasari's fears of professional envy, jealousy, and slander are emphasized in the chamber's conception and design, particularly in instances in which the interference of Envy would cause bad Fortune or blind Fortune, as recorded in Catari's Felicity (*Bonus Eventus*), where Envy and Adulation blind Fortune, thus keeping her from performing good deeds (*Imagini* 254). Familiar with Cartari's view, however, Vasari is confident that Good Fortune is attained through the intensity of human effort (Abundance), moral strength (Charity), and artistic merits (Art). Therefore, he absorbs Alciato's motto, "Art Helps Nature," in the *palco* scene by uniting the symbolism of Fortune with the abutting walls and expressing the way his art has given him Good Fortune and made it possible for him to achieve recognition and fame as an artist.

The third connection between the ceiling and the upper walls relates to the astrological function of the planetary gods who control and grant benefits to Vasari. These benefits are personified on the walls of the Chamber of Fortune in levels. The first level is dominated by the four personifications treated as sculptures; the second by the seated and enthroned allegorical virtues; and the last by landscape scenes. The four personifications depicted as sculpture represent the gifts of the planetary gods: natural richness of the earth (Abundance), spiritual richness (Religion or Charity), Nature (Artemis of Ephesus), and Art (Aphrodite), The remaining eight allegories of virtues on the walls represent qualities a virtuous person needs to live a rich and happy life. These qualities are learned from the example of the planetary gods: Fortitude (Mars), Liberality (Mercury), Wisdom (Diana), Prudence (Apollo), Honor (Cupid), Justice (Jupiter), Patience (Saturn), and Happiness or Felicity (Venus). Furthermore, the four seasons control the elements of the universe such as fire, water, air and earth - elements portrayed in the form of landscapes on the chamber walls.

The fourth connection between the ceiling and the walls relates to the *palco* scene and the *istorie* in the lower portion of the walls. Here Vasari pays tribute to the art of painting, to famous antique masters, and to himself as a successful Cinquecento artist. These *istorie* comment on the criteria for judging painting: selection from nature (Zeuxis with Parrhasius), inventiveness (Gyges' *Outlining His Shadow*), imitation and realism (Protogenes' *Ialysus and His Dog*), portraiture (Apelles' *Alexander and Campaspe*), and narrative (Timanthes' *Sacrifice of Iphigenia*). Moreover, in the classical *istorie*, Vasari portrays the ancient painters' interpretations of art in relation to nature: to imitate nature (Gyges of Lydia, Parrhasius, Prorogenes) and to surpass it (Zeuxis, Apelles, and Timanthes).

In the Chamber of Fortune, the lower zone of the walls portrays ancient stories or classical *istorie* based on Pliny the Elder's account of the origin of drawing and painting and famous painters of antiquity (see Cheney, "Vasari's Depiction"). Although not apparent, there is a connection with the personifications and allegorical virtues depicted above them in the upper walls. Below the representation of Patience, Gyges of Lydia invents the art of drawing, alluding to the importance of diligence, labor, and patience in the invention of art. Below Abundance (*Copia*) appears the story of Zeuxis and Parrhasius, referring to the imitation or the copying of nature as well. On the west wall, three narrative scenes from renowned paintings of antiquity depict Apelles' *Alexander and Campaspe*, Protogenes' *Ialysus and His Dog*, and Timanthes' *Sacrifice of Iphigenia* below Fortitude, Charity, and Liberality, respectively. The three virtues' influences reveal a positive impact in each scene. For example, the ruler Alexander the Great and the painter Apelles demonstrate emotional fortitude and restraint in the presence of the beautiful Campaspe. Alexander displays his magnanimity and generosity as well when he gives his mistress to the painter. In the Protogenes' story, the painter reveals his artistic stamina and liberality of execution when he persists in depicting the foam from the dog's mouth. Timanthes' drama reflects the charity of the goddess Diana in saving the life of Iphigenia and the fortitude of Iphigenia in accepting her unjust sacrifice.

In other instances, the connection between the upper walls and the lower walls are not as literal but significant nonetheless. For example, below Prudence is the depiction of an artist drawing from the window, an ancient edifice, the Roman Pantheon. Here, Prudence is associated with artistic judgment or selectivity. Vasari singles out this virtue in his advice of living a discreet existence to artists in his *Vite* (Bettarini-Barocchi 3:3, 15). His unsystematic theory of art connects beauty with nature and nature with appreciation of ancient ideals or "rebirth." For example, Vasari's purpose in writing the *Vite* is to provide his fellow artists with an historical perspective and artistic guidance (see Prinz). These two significant issues are evident in his explanation of the concept of "rebirth"- a return to classical ideals that combine artistic progress and moral intention. Vasari's moral intention is related to the Cinquecento's spirit of history, which fulfills its purpose in making individuals prudent and showing them how to live: "Il che a proprio l'anima dell'istoria, e quello che invero insegna vivere e fa gli uomini prudenti" [The real spirit of history is that one that teaches men how to live and make them prudent] (Bettarini-Barocchi 3:3, 15). Thus, with the depiction of the virtues, Vasari reveals the hope that his fellow artists and humanists will honor his artistic and moral accomplishments. In the same manner, Ripa's goal is for the compendia of his *figurazioni* or emblems to provide artists with a dictionary of visual imagery.

In the Chamber of Fortune, Vasari's imagery contains theological, philosophical, historical, and didactic schema, revealing the influence of Renaissance Neoplatonism and the impact of the emblematic tradition. Vasari has the good fortune to acquire knowledge of the liberal arts through his artistic and literary studies and his personal and humanistic contacts. Thus, he accompanies the personification of Nature with the allegories of

Wisdom and Prudence for the judgment in creating his paintings. His artistic success is realized by inventing and imitating art and dictated by his natural ability (Cartari 254). Vasari absorbs Alciato's motto, "Art Helps Nature."

Using allegorical imagery, Vasari reveals his aesthetic understanding of concepts such as art, fame, fortune, history, culture, and religion within a Cinquecento artistic milieu, paving the way for Ripa's visual compendium. The heraldic and emblematic tradition of the sixteenth century augmented and further elaborated on the iconography of allegories and personifications. A collection of books and compendia of emblems and heraldry appeared in the Florentine and Venetian presses during the early sixteenth century, giving impetus to a new and complex visual iconology in art. Vasari's decorative cycles for his homes in Arezzo (1542-48) and Florence (1562-64), the Refectory of Monteoliveto in Naples (1545), the Sala dei Cento Giorni in the Palazzo della Cancelleria (1546) in Rome, and the decoration of the Palazzo Vecchio (1565-72) in Florence attest to the power of this emblematic tradition as well as to Vasari's contribution of the visual rendition on the formation of a pictorial album containing iconographical images.

At the conclusion of the sixteenth century, the fusion of Vasari's visual encyclopedia and the conventional emblematic approaches culminated in the publication of Ripa's *Iconologia*. Since its conception, Ripa's *figurazioni* assisted artists and humanists in the creation of allegories and personifications. The impact of Vasari's imagery on Ripa's emblems is best incorporated in one of Alciato's emblems, which appropriates and modifies Emblem 98, *Ars Naturam Adiuvans* (Art Helps Nature) to articulate the connection between Vasari and Ripa: "Vasari Adiuvat Ripam" (Vasari Helps Ripa).

## Notes

A version of this study was presented at the first Society for Renaissance Art History (SRAH) during the annual South-Central Renaissance Conference at Pepperdine University, Malibu, California in March 2005. I offer my gratitude to Profs. Norman Land of the University of Missouri at Columbia and Frances Malpezzi of Arkansas State University. Unless otherwise noted, translations throughout are the author's. All photographs are by the author. The Ministerio per i Bene e le Arrività Culturali, Soprintendenze della Toscana, granted permission to photograph the Chamber of Fortune at the Casa Vasari. The volumes by Alciato and Ripa are in the author's collection.

1. The first edit ion of *Iconologia* (1593) is sans illustrations. The revised 1603 edition contains woodcut illustrations based on the drawings of the Roman Maniera painter Giuseppe Cesari, called Cavalier d'Arpino. See the first scholarly study of Ripa by Mandowsky, "Ricerche" and Mandowsky's introduction to Garland's facsimile edition; see also Cheney, "Giuseppe Cesari d'Arpino." References to *Iconologia* in the essay are from the 1630 illustrated edition, which is based on the illustrated edition of 1603.

2. Russell defines the importance of Alciati's emblem book in Cinquecento art and literature: It "served as a manual to train readers in a particular approach to artistic artifacts. It taught them to participate actively in the moralizing of visual arts" ("Alciati's Emblems" 549).

3. This version is known as the Planudean text because a monk named Maximus Planudes assembled it at the end of the thirteenth century. See Daly, Alciato's Book of Emblems at www.mun.ca/alciato, based on Daly, *Andreas Alciatus*; *Emblem Theory*; and Russell, "Emblems and Hieroglyphics." For Russell, Renaissance humanists employed hieroglyphics as a vehicle for "redefining the symbolic process with the context of Neoplatonic thought" (232). See also Saunders. For Alciato's *Emblemata*, this study draws upon several editions dating from 1542 to 1577.

4. Unless otherwise noted, references are to the 1568 edition.

5. See the invaluable comparative study of Bettarini and Barocchi on the 1550 and 1568 editions of Vasari's, *Le vite de' più eccellenti architetti, pittore, et scultori,* hereafter referred to as Bettarini-Barocchi; see also Milanesi's edition of Vasari's work, hereafter cited as Vasari-Milanesi.

6. Vasari-Milanesi 8: 1-224; see also Draper. For Vasari's explanation of *invenzione, imitazione,* and *concetti,* see Vasari-Milanesi 2:93-107.

7. See Zimmermann's introduction to *Paolo Giovio.*

8. See Cheney, *Giorgio Vasari's Homes.* Paccioni explains the concept of *camera picta* in Mantegna's *Camera degli Sposi* of the 1470s in the Mantuan Ducal Palace.

9. A drawing of the ceiling of the Chamber of Fortune is at the Gabinetto Disegni e Stampe of the Galleria degli Uffizi (N 1617E) in Florence. Although distributed to Cristoforo Gherardi, an assistant of Vasari, it is probably a sketch drawn by Vasari for the ceiling of this chamber. For

a comparison of Vasari's celestial deities and Cartari's planetary gods in *Imagini delli Dei de gl'Antichi*, see Cheney, *The Paintings of the Casa Vasari* 160-70.

10. Personification is defined here as the embodiment of an abstract idea in the depiction of a human form, e.g., the personification of Nature in the depiction of Artemis of Ephesus. Allegory is the visual form alluding to a moral symbol - e.g., Janus' head alludes to a symbol of Prudence.

11. Cartari (65) states that during the reign of Leo X an antique medal of Adrian was discovered. For its illustration, see Cartari 298. This medal was the likely source of inspiration for Polidoro da Caravaggio's grotesque decoration in the Stanza dell Incendio. See also Sambucus, *De emblemate* (1564) and Ripa 2:507-508. All of these iconographers identify the depiction of Artemis as a symbol of Nature. All references to Cartari's *Imagini* in this essay are from the Bussagli and Bussagli edition.

12. Cellini's drawing is at the British Museum of London (No. 180.6.6.18).

13. See Ripa 2:348-49. Ripa is referring here to Valeriano's concept of invention in Book 40 of the *Hierogliphica*.

14. See Ripa 1: 116 for *Cognizione*; 2:3 45 for *Intelligenza*; 3:41 for *Sapienza*.

15. See Del Vita 25. In the Aretine Prudence, the serpent (Matthew 10:16) and the mirror (Italian Renaissance conception) are missing, but they are present in the painting and drawing for the Neapolitan Prudence.

16. See Alciato's series of emblems on Prudence (Lyon 1549): Emblem 19, *Prudens magis quam loquax* (The prudent man without eloquence); Emblem 22, *Custodiendas virgines* (Virgins must be protected well); Emblem 23, *Vino prudentiam augeri* (Prudence augments with wine); and the most popular, Emblem 20, *Maturandum* (The wise decisions should be implemented at the right time). In Renaissance art, this emblem - an anchor and a dolphin, coupled with the mono *Festina lente* (Make haste slowly) and maxim - is appropriated from the writings and descriptions of hieroglyphics by Franceso Colonna in *Hypnerotomachia Poliphili* (The Dream of Poliphilo or The Soul in Love), a book published by the Venetian printer Aldus Manutius in 1499. In turn, Aldus employs this motto as a seal for his printing press.

17. See Alciato 115, and Ripa 3:599 for Prudence.

18. See Alciato, Emblem 22, on the serpent: "The serpent protects the virgins." The word *serpent* derives from the Latin *serpens* "because the animal creeps by secret approaches and not by open steps."

19. Typically Prudence is depicted as a woman with a double or triple head, holding a mirror, a serpent or sieve, with Solomon at her feet. Sometimes, Prudence is portrayed carrying a compass as a sign of her measured judgment or a book alluding to the Scriptures and rarely with a dragon, a substitute for a serpent, to suggest the elusion of evil pursuers.

20. See Ripa 3:595 for Prudence, where he refers as well to Alciato's Emblem 20, *Maturandum* (The wise decisions should be implemented at the right time).

21. For the first citation of these Biblical and classical references, see Cheney, "The Paintings of the Casa Vasari" 174.

22. See Vasari-Milanesi 1:102. Vasari is describing a fire scene at night. Ripa comments on the effect of fire: "Il fuoco tanto di caldo e di luce, che si vede manifestamente ardere le cese, e quasi tremmolando nelle sue fiamme rendere in parte luminose le più oscure tenebre della notte." See Ripa 1:61-63, 77.

23. This continues: "La fiamma del fuoco si pone come instrumento principale delle case artificiose: perche consolidando 0 mollificando le materie, Ie fa habili ad essere adoperate dall'uomo in molti essercitii industriosi" (Ripa 1:63).

24. Vasari alludes to the traditional *paragone* debate regarding the superiority of painting over sculpture or vice versa. See Varchi.

25. For Alciato, Art is similar to Nature because Art produces works as Nature does, and Art is not similar to Nature because Art imitates Nature. See Daly, Emblem Theory 37; Alciato's emblem "Art Helps Nature" in *Emblemata* (Lyon, 1551). For variations of text and image, see also *Emblemata*'s editions from Lyon (1549), Paris (1561), and Frankfurt/Main (1567).

26. See Henkel and Schone 1552. The two emblems contain the mottoes: "Non obest virtuti sors" (Chance is not a hindrance to Virtue) and "Major quam cui possit Fortuna noceri" (Chance can do greater harm than what Fortune can do) allude to Ovid, *Metamorphoses* (6:195). The symbolism of instability is associated with Fortuna's wheel and constancy with Virtue's cube. In the first emblem, Virtue seated on a cube controls the spinning of the Wheel of Fortune. In the Vasarian *palco*, Virtue's control over Fortune is explicitly seen by Virtue's pulling the forelock of Fortune.

27. See Cheney, *The Paintings of the Casa Vasari* 170-82. Stylistically, the allegorical virtues in the chamber are part of Vasari's imagery as seen in the Cornaro ceiling (Venice, 1541-42), the refectory of Monteoliveto (Naples, 1544-45), and the Sala dei Cento Giorni (Rome, 1546). In addition, Vasari borrows from the Tarot card tradition for his concept of allegorical figures; see Cavendish, passim and Heninger, passim.

28. Vasari's Drawing of Charity is at the Bologna Gabinetto dei Disegni e delle Stampe (Inv. 1613).

29. *Summa Theologia*, sections IIa. IIae Q, XXIII a. 5. Other representations of Charity depict her as a garlanded woman offering a heart from a cornucopia (Giotto's *Charity* of 1305 at the Scrovegni Chapel in Pad-

ua) or drawing a sword as described in Prudentius' *Psychomachia*. See Burton, passim; Katzenellenbogen Figs. 8a-b; and Tuve.

30. Augustine stressed the importance of Charity as Religion. See Burnaby. Vasari's awareness of this meaning of Charity probably derives from Marsilio Ficino's Neoplatonic philosophy, which integrates Augustine's concept of Charity. See Ficino, *Opera omnia*, passim .

31. See Ripa 1:106. In Ripa's emblem, the flaming hair alludes to the passion of giving and teaching the Christian life: "Ignem veni mittere in terram, & quid volo, nisi ut ardeat?" (I came to earth to send out [spread] fire; what should I desire, if not that it should burn?). See Ripa 1:107; for Alciato's comment on Charity, see Emblemata 47.

32. See Panofsky passim, and Heninger passim for the iconography of the seasons and the elements.

33. Qtd. in Del Vita, 9; see Ripa 3:5-6 for the descriptions of Ragione (Reason).

34. See Del Vita 8 and 109, quoting Vasari, and Ripa 2:442. According to Hall (7, 256) the purse is an attribute of Mercury as the god of Commerce; or Judas Iscariot as a personification of Avarice; or Matthew as the tax collector. Also, the purse symbolizes the transience of earthly riches and personifies Vanity.

35. See Ripa 2:554 for the concept of impartiality, "mano destra ferrata... sinistra aperta" (right hand closed ... left hand open).

36. Cartari (300) describes Abundance as Copia: "la terra coltivata e quella che produce l'abbondama o Copia" (The cultivated earth is that one that produces abundance or copiousness). Also Ripa 1:9 describes Abundance as Copia: "e perche l'abbondanza si dice Copia, per mostrarla cosi la rappresentiamo che il braccio sinistro abbia come il destro la sua carica, e davvantaggio, essendo che parte di quelle spiche si spargono per la terra" (And why abundance is called copiousness, to show her in this manner, we represent her left and the right arms carrying a load and conveniently some of the branches are discarded on the ground).

37. See Cheney, "Giorgio Vasari's Sala dei Cento Giorni" and "Giorgio Vasari and Naples" for comparative imagery.

38. See Cheney, "Giorgio Vasari's Patience" and Del Vita 25, quoting Vasari.

39. See Ripa 2:255.56 for Patience, 2:520·21 for Obedience, and 3:62 for Servitude. See also Wittkower.

40. See Cheney "Giorgio Vasari's *Astrae*." See also Vasari's Drawing of Justice at the Teylerstiching Museum in Haarlem (N. K94).

41. From the time of Paul, Charity signifies the reciprocal love between God and humanity. Charity forms part of the Theological or Pauline

Virtues (See I Corinthians 13:13). For a historical discussion on Charity, see Katzenellenbogen 27·57; Wind; Freyhan; and O'Reilly 11 2-62.

42. See Cartari 252 for the image of Good Fortune holding a cornucopia, a symbol of Abundance or Copia. Amor, a symbol of Charity or Love, accompanies her. Also see Cartari's *The Goddess Nemesi* where Abundance appears with Fortune (241).

## Works Cited

Alciato, Andrea. *Emblemata*. Antwerp, 1577.

_____. *Emblemata*. Frankfurt/Main, 1567.

_____. *Emblemata*. Lyon, 1542.

_____. *Emblemata*. Lyon, 1549.

_____. *Emblemata*. Lyon, 155 1.

_____. *Emblemata*. Paris, 1561.

Aquinas, Thomas. *Summa Theologia*. New York: Benzinger Brothers, 1948.

Burnaby, J. *Amor Dei: A Study of the Religion of St. Augustine. The Hulsean Lectures for 1938*. London: Hodder & Stoughton, 1938.

Burton, Rosemary, ed. *Prudentius. Psychomachia: Commentary and Text*. Bryn Mawr: Bryn Mawr Commentaries, 1989.

Caldwell, Dorigen Sophie. *The Sixteenth-Century Italian Impresa in Theory and Practice*. New York: AMS P, 2004.

Cartari, Vincenzo. *Imagini delli Dei de gl'Antichi*. Eds. Marco Bussagli and Mario Bussagli. Genova: Nuovo Stile Regina Editrice, 1987.

Cavendish, Richard. *The Tarot*. New York: Crescent Books. 1986.

Cheney, Liana De Girolami. "Giorgio Vasari and Naples: The Monteoliveto Order." *Papers in Art History*. Vol. 5. Ed. Jeanne Chenault Porter and Susan Scott Munshower. University Park: Pennsylvania State UP, 1994. 48-126.

_____. "Giorgio Vasari's *Astrae*: Allegory of Justice." *Visual Resources* 19.4 (2003), 5-15.

_____. *Giorgio Vasari's Homes*. London: Peter Lang, 2005.

_____. "Giorgio Vasari's Paintings of the Casa Vasari Arezzo." *Explorations in Renaissance Culture* 11 (1985): 53-73.

_____. "Giorgio Vasari's Patience: The Measure of Time." *The Inspiration of Astronomical Phenomena*. Ed. Raymond E. White. Tempe, AZ: OTS Foundation Publishers, 2000. 13-23.

_____. "Giorgio Vasari's Sala dei Centro Giorni: A Farnese Celebration." *Explorations in Renaissance Culture* 21 (I995): 121-51.

_____. "Giuseppe Cesari d'Arpino and Cesare Ripa: ut pictura poesis." *In-*

*ternational Emblematic Conference*. Glasgow, Lanarkshire, UK. Summer 1990.

_____. *The Paintings of the Casa Vasari*. New York: Garland, 1985.

_____. "The Paintings of the Casa Vasari." Diss. Boston U, 1978.

_____. "Vasari's Depiction of Pliny's Histories." *Explorations in Renaissance Culture* 15 (1989): 97-121.

Daly, Peter M. *Alciato's Book of Emblems*. 26 Apr. 2005. Department of English at Memorial University of Newfoundland. <www.mun.ca/alciato>.

_____. *Andreas Alciatus*. 2 vols. Toronto: U of Toronto P, 1985.

_____. *Emblem Theory*. Nendeln: KTO Press, 1979.

Del Vita, Alessandro. *Lo Zibaldone di Giorgio Vasari*. Rome: Istituto Archeologico e Staria dell'Arte, 1938.

Draper, J L. "Vasari's Decoration in the Palazzo Vecchio: The Ragionamenti." Diss. U of North Carolina, 1973.

Ficino, Marsilio. *Opera omnia. Book I, Chapter IV*. Florence: Froben, 1489.

Freyhan, R. "The Evolution of the Caritas Figure in the Thirteenth and Fourteen Centuries." *Journal of the Warburg and Courtauld Institutes* 11 (1948): 68-86.

Hall, James. *Dictionary of Symbols and Symbols in Art*. New York: Harper and Row, 1974.

Heninger, S. K., Jr. *Touches of Sweet Harmony*. Malibu, CA: The Huntington Library, 1974.

Henkel, Arthur, and Albrecht Schone. *Emblemata*. Stuttgart/Metzler: Erg. Neuausg, 1967.

Katzenellenbogen, Adolf. *Allegories of the Virtues and Vices in Medieval Art from Early Christian Times to the Thirteenth Century*. New York: Harper and Row, 1964.

Mandowsky, Erna. Introduction. *Iconologia*. By Cesare Ripa. 1603. New York: Garland, 1970.7-10.

_____. "Ricerche Intorno alia Iconologia di Cesare Ripa." *Bibliofilia* 41 (1939): 7-27, 111-24, 204-35, 279-327.

Manni, Domencio Maria, ed. *Discorsi di Vincenzo Borghini*. 4 vols. Milan: Società tipografica de' Classici Italiani, 1808-1809.

Nesselrath, Arnold. "The Venus Belvedere: An Episode in Restoration." *Journal of the Warburg and Courtauld Institutes* 50 (1987): 205-14.

O'Reilly, Jennifer. *Studies in the Iconography of the Virtues and Vices in the Middle Ages*. New York: Garland, 1988.

Ovid. *Metamorphoses*. Trans. R. J. Tarrant. New York: Oxford UP, 2004.

Paccioni, G. *La Camera Picta di Andrea Mategna*. Milan: Edizione del Milione. 1960.

Panofsky, Erwin. *The Life and Art of Albrect Dürer*. Princeton: Princeton UP, 1971.

Price Zimmerman, T. C. *Paolo Giovio*. Princeton: Princeton UP, 2001.

Prinz, Wolfram. "I Ragionamenti del Vasari sullo sviluppo e Declino delle Arti." *Ill Vasari storiografo e artista: Atti del Congresso Internazionale nel IV centenario della sua morte*. Arena: Casa Vasari. 1974. 857-66.

Ripa, Cesare. *Iconologia*. Padua: Donate Pasquardi, 1630.

Russell, Daniel. "Alciati's Emblems in Renaissance France." *Renaissance Quarterly*, 34 (1981), 534-54.

_____. "Emblems and Hieroglyphics: Some Observations on the Beginnings and the Nature of Emblematic Forms." *Emblematica* 2 (1986): 227-40.

Sambucus, Johannes. *De emblemate*. Antwerp: Palatio, 1566.

Saunders, Alison. *The Sixteenth-Century French Emblem Book: A Decorative and Useful Genre*. Geneva: Drol, 1988.

Scorza, R. A. "Vincenzo Borghini and Invenzione: The Florentine Apparato of 1565." *Journal of the Warburg and Courtauld Institutes* 44 (1981): 57-75.

Tervarem, Guy de. *Attributs et symbols dans l'art profane, 1450-1600: Dictionnaire d'un langage perdu*. Geneva: Draz, 1958.

Tuve, Rosemund. "Notes on the Virtues and Vices. Part I: Two Fifteenth. Century Lines of Dependence on the Thirteenth and Twelfth Centuries." *Journal of the Warburg and Courtauld Institutes* 26.3-4 (1963): 264-303.

Valeriano, Pierio. *Hierogliphica*. Florence, 1625.

Varchi, Benedetto. *Due Lezzioni*. Florence: Lorenzo Torrentino. 1549.

Vasari. Giorgio. *Le Vite dei più eccellenti pittori, scultori, et architettori*. Ed. Gaetano Milanesi. Florence: Sansoni. 1906-10.

_____. *Le Vite dei più eccellenti pittori, scultori, et architettori*. Ed. Rosanna Bettarini and Paola Barochhi. Florence: Sansoni, 1971-86.

Visser, A. S. Q. *Joannes Sambucus and the Learned Image: The Use of the Emblem in Late-Renaissance Humanism*. London: Brill, Z005.

Wind, Edgar. "Charity: The Case History of a Pattern." *Journal of the Warburg and Courtauld Institutes* 1.4 (1938): 322-330.

Wittkower, Rudolf. "Chance, Time and Virtue." *Journal of the Warburg and Courtauld Institutes* 1.4 (1938): 313-21.

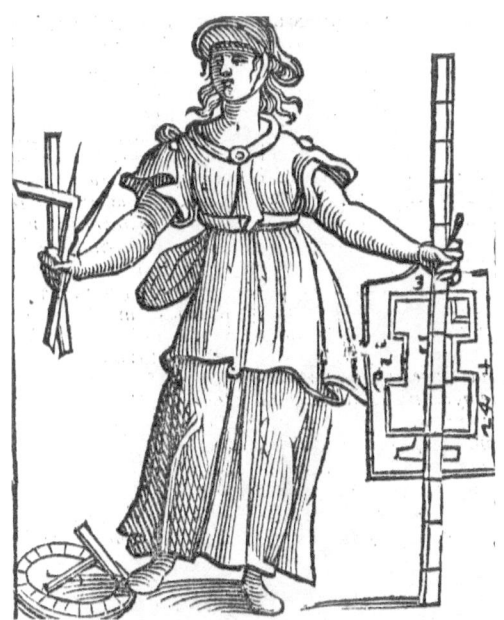

Fig. 1 Cesare Ripa, *Iconografia*, from *Iconologia*.

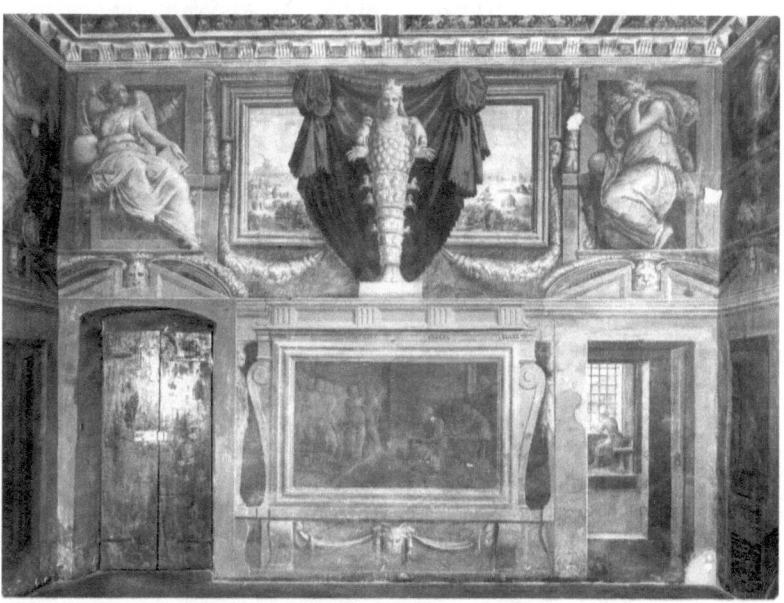

Fig. 2. Giorgio Vasari, *Wisdom, Artemis of Ephesus*, Prudence. North Wall, Chamber of Fortune, Casa Vasari, Arezzo.

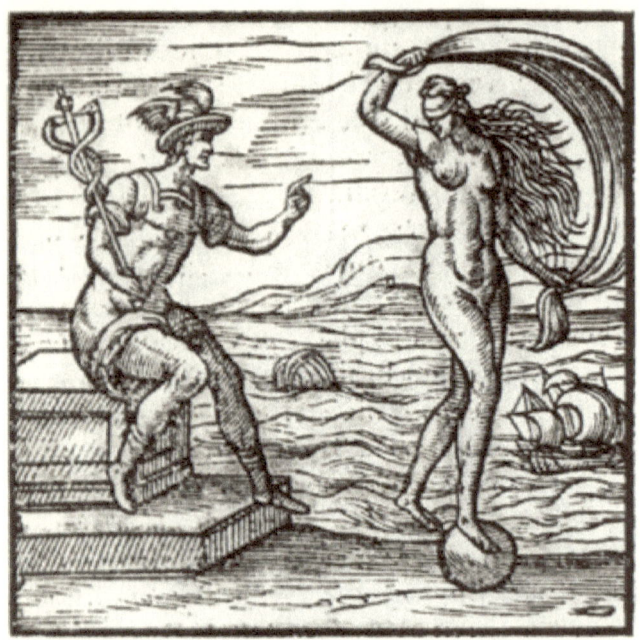

Fig. 3. Andrea Alciato, Emblem 98, *Ars Naturam Adiuvans*, from *Emblemata*.

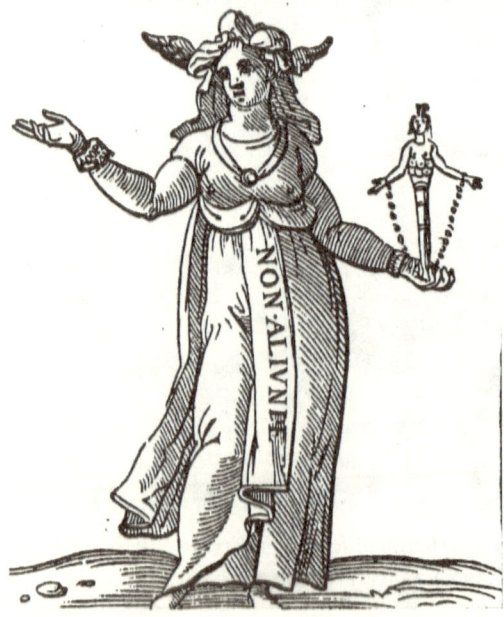

Fig.4. Cesare Ripa, *Inventione*, from *Iconologia*.

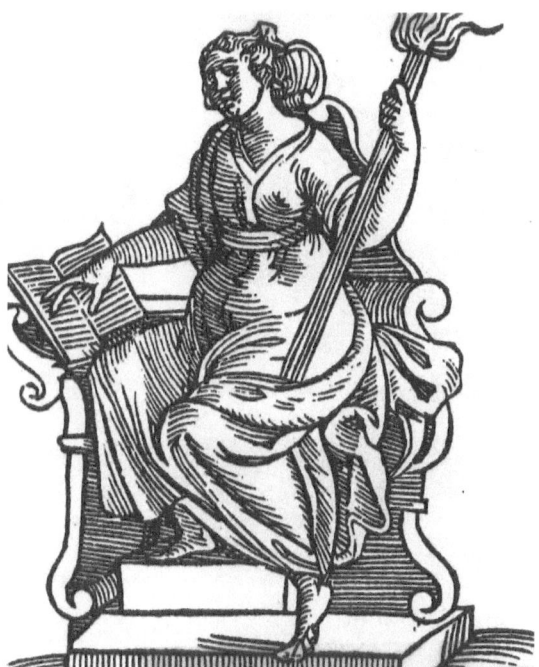

Fig. 5. Cesare Ripa, *Cognizione*, from *Iconologia*.

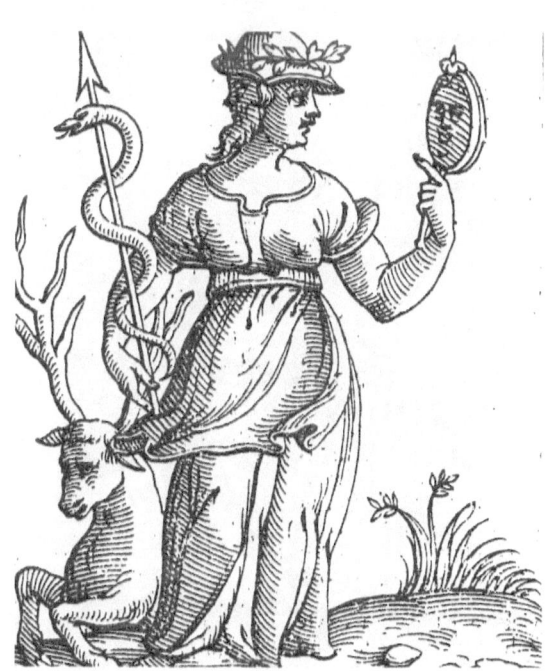

Fig. 6. Cesare Ripa, *Prudenzia*, from *Iconologia*.

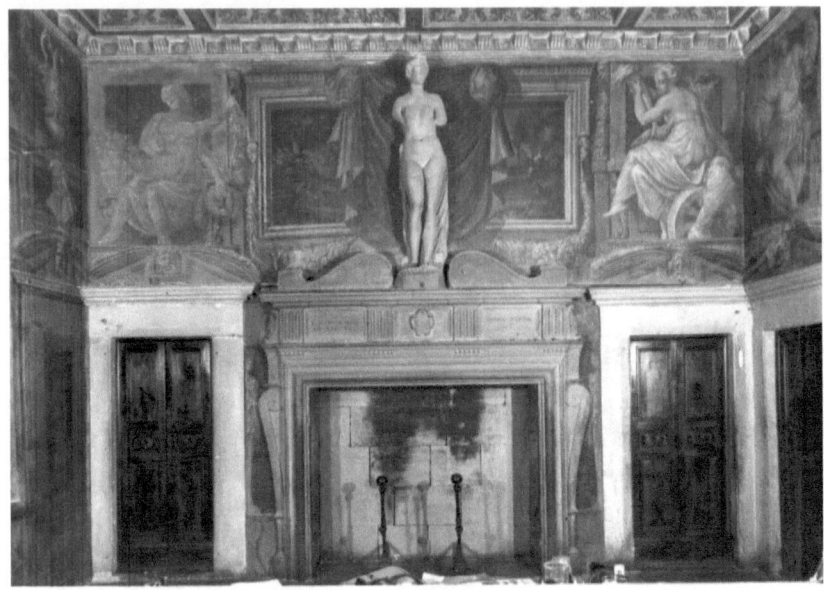

Fig. 7. Giorgio Vasari, *Honor, Venus, Felicity,* South Wall, Chamber of Fortune, Casa Vasari, Arezzo.

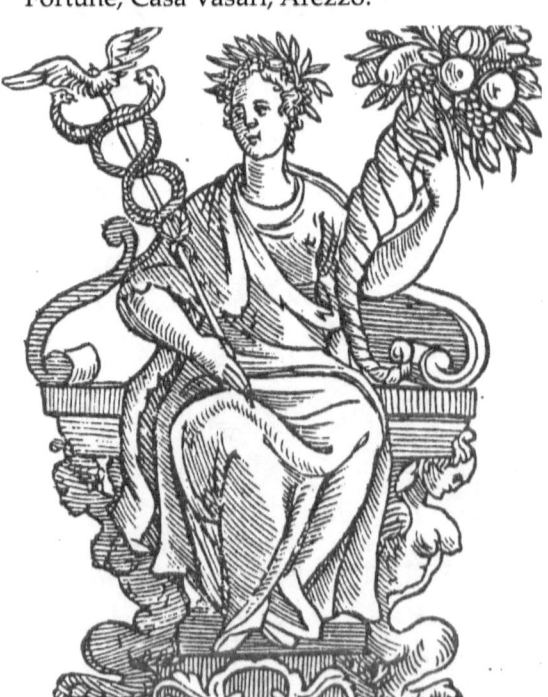

Fig. 8. Cesare Ripa, *Felicita or Buon Evento,* from *Iconologia.*

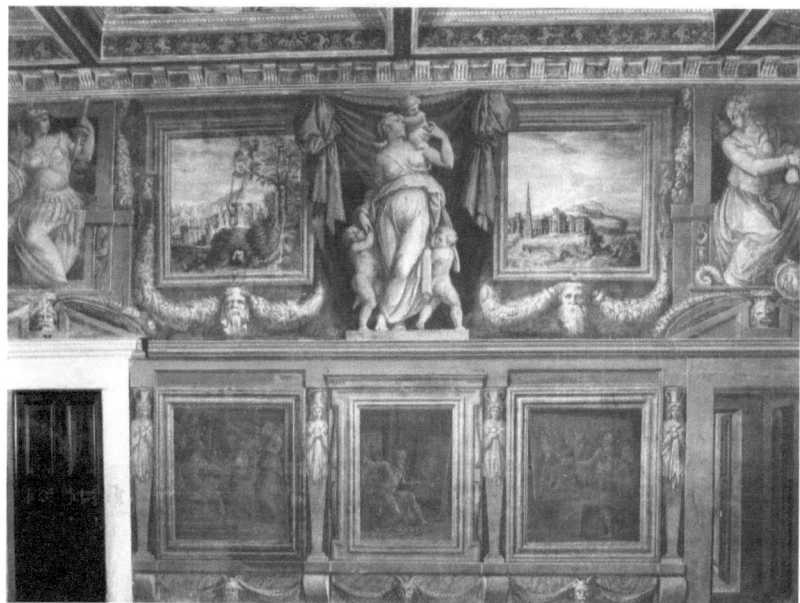

Fig. 9. Giorgio Vasari, *Fortitude, Charity, Liberality*, West Wall, Chamber of Fortune, Casa Vasari, Arezzo.

Fig. 10. Cesare Ripa, *Charity*, from *Iconologia*.

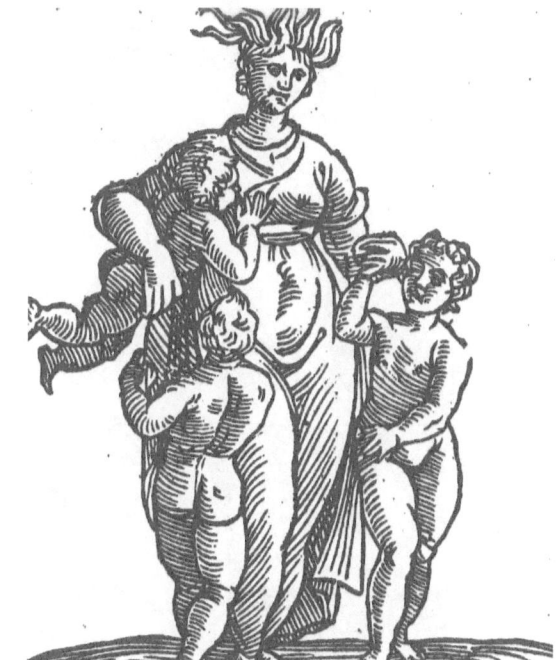

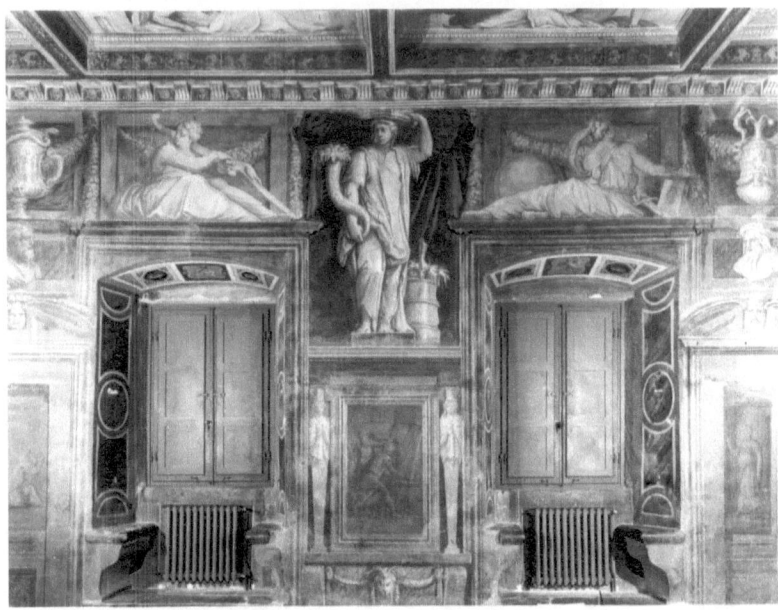

Fig. 11. Giorgio Vasari, *Patience, Abundance, Justice,* East Wall, Chamber of Fortune, Casa Vasari, Arezzo.

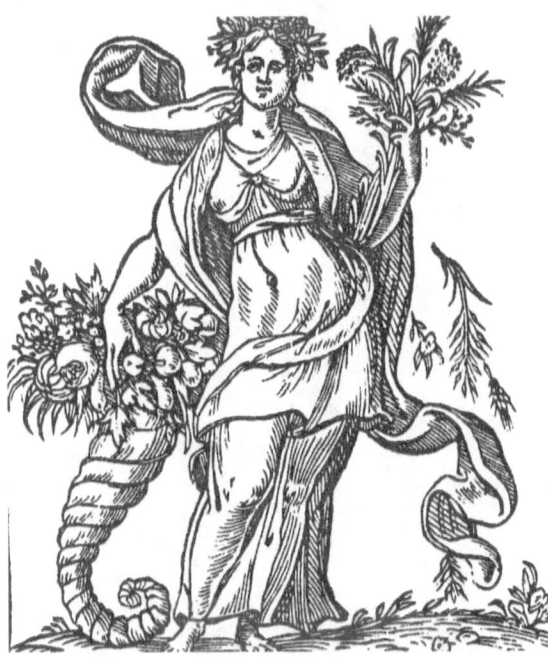

Fig. 12. Cesare Ripa, *Abbondanza,* from *Iconologia.*

# Part Two

## Moral and Religious Paintings

# 8

# Vasari's *Chamber of Abraham*: A Religious Painted Ceiling in the Casa Vasari in Arezzo

One indication of the Cinquecento artist's professional status was a new freedom to purchase, design, and decorate his own house. Vasari had established himself as a painter and writer by the 1540s, when he began work on a small house in Arezzo which still stands. His intellectual curiosity, enthusiasm, and artistic ability made it possible for him to develop a new attitude of patronage in art. The Casa Vasari represents a collection of works created to express in personal terms Vasari's love for his masters, his fascination with antiquity, and his delight in artistic virtuosity. He succeeded in building his house as an artistic monument to his own accomplishments. Among the ceilings of the Casa Vasari, only the *Chamber of Abraham* (1548) is religious in subject matter and the content of its representation referring to the blessing of parenthood attests to the function of this room as a nuptial chamber. As a good Christian of the sixteenth century, he painted the Old Testament scene of *God the Father blessing the seed of Abraham* accompanied by the depiction of Cardinal virtues (Temperance, Prudence, Fortitude, and Justice) and Christian virtues (Modesty, Chastity, Concord, and Peace), which are essential for the harmony of the soul and the honor of a Christian home.

One indication of wealth, fame, and professional status of the artist in the fifteenth and sixteenth centuries was his freedom to design and decorate his own house. Giorgio Vasari is a prime example of the artist as householder, and the paintings of the

Casa Vasari abundantly demonstrate his standing. The paintings express his concern for success, a fascination with the antique and a delight in artistic virtuosity that was common in the Cinquecento; for all this, the Casa Vasari is a unique museum of its time, which immortalizes a specific man as painter, writer, and historian.[1] The decorative program of this small private building stands as Vasari's monument to his own accomplishments, a personal, intimate, and original statement made in the late 1540s, when Vasari's public reputation as painter and writer was well established.[2]

The *piano nobile* or main floor of the Casa Vasari originally consisted of a kitchen, a chapel, and five rooms named for the subject matter depicted on their ceilings: the Chambers of Fame, Abraham, Fortune and Apollo, and the Corridor of Ceres.[3] Although no clear evidence exists concerning the designer of the Corridor, documents indicate that the other four rooms are by Vasari himself. He worked on them intermittently and somewhat haphazardly over a twelve-year period between 1542 and 1554.[4]

Of these four rooms, the most instructive for understanding Vasari's thoughts about religion is the Chamber of Abraham (1548). In this room Vasari includes many personal conceits; in both its iconography and its decorative scheme, however, this chamber also displays significant connections to various conventions rooted in both fifteenth-and sixteenth-century art. Among the ceilings of the Casa Vasari, only the Chamber of Abraham is religious in subject matter, and the content of its representation referring to the blessing of parenthood attests to the function of this room as a nuptial chamber (Fig. 1). Although Vasari never referred to the Chamber of Abraham as a bedroom, to this writer, the iconography, format, and Vasari's description of the ceiling suggest that this room was designed as a nuptial chamber. In the Chamber of Abraham, the central piece is a tondo; its contents show God bestowing the gift of a son, Isaac, upon Abraham. In the fifteenth century birth salvers were given as special gifts on the occasion of a newborn child, and the shape of the tondo echoes the shape of the circular birth salver.[5]

Vasari, as a good Christian of the sixteenth century, painted on the ceiling of his bedroom a religious subject with a message of God's blessing for the multiplication of humankind. The Old Testament scene accompanied by the New Testament depiction of cardinal and Christian virtues was intended to guide the householder, Vasari himself, in the pursuit of matrimonial bliss and sanctity. Unmarried at the time he completed this ceiling, he was not aware that he would wed a noblewoman of Arezzo, Nicolosa Bacci, in 1550, and that eventually he would leave no progeny.[6]

As the name implies, the main theme of this ceiling is the story of Abraham and Isaac. Unlike traditional Quattrocento and Cinquecento depictions of the sacrifice of Isaac, however, Vasari shows God the Father blessing the seed of Abraham. This blessing, after the attempted sacrifice of Isaac by Abraham, is described in Gen. 22:17: " I [God] will bless you [Abraham] abundantly and greatly multiply your descendants until they are numerous as the stars in the sky and the grains of sand on the seashore."[7] Vasari may have borrowed and varied the theme from the paintings of immediate predecessors: Peruzzi's *God blessing the seed of Noah* in the Sala di Eliodoro in the Vatican apartments, and Giulio Romano's *God blessing Isaac* in the Vatican Loggie (compare Figs. 2 and 3 with 1).[8]

Despite the information Vasari provides about the project, his description of the program and his explanation of its meaning are so sketchy and even cryptic that the iconography has yet to be adequately studied. This essay will attempt to interpret the meaning of the paintings in the Chamber of Abraham in the Casa Vasari, in the light of Vasari's ideas about a Christian life.

According to Vasari, the Chamber of Abraham was the second ceiling he painted. He began work in May of 1548 and finished the ceiling by the end of July of the same year (Fig. 3).[9] In speaking of the subject matter Vasari says: "In the carved wooden ceiling of a room, I did God blessing the seed of Abraham in a large roundel. In four squares about this I did Peace, Concord, Virtue, and Modesty."[10] His description is not entirely accurate, since the symmetrical composition of a circle within a square within a larger square places the allegorical figures in subsidiary framing rectangles on the central axes of the central tondo. The remainder of the outer frame is taken up by L-shaped fields in each corner, decorated in the manner of Roman *grotteschi*. Vasari probably first learned about this type of wooden ceiling with raised wooden cornices and framing elements in 1541, when he executed a series of scenographic paintings for Pietro Aretina in Venice.[11]

Vasari worked on five decorative cycles before or during the execution of the Casa Vasari. These include drawings for the *apparato* for *La Talanta* in 1541, ceiling paintings for the Cornaro Palace (also known as Corner-Spinelli Palace) in Venice in 1542, ceiling paintings for the Refectory of Monteoliveto in Naples in 1544-45, drawings for the Loggie of Pietro de Toledo in 1544-45, and wall paintings in the *Sala dei Cento Giorni* in the Palazzo della Cancelleria in Rome in 1546.

For Vasari the allegorical figures of Virtue (Chastity), Modesty, Peace, and Concord represent his personal interpretation of religious virtues *per se*, an interpretation he first began to develop in the Faith and Peace figures of the Cornaro Palace ceiling in 1542 (Fig. 5 and 9) and continued in the allegorical figures of Hope and Faith in the *Sala dei Cento Giorni* of 1546 (Figs. 6 and 10). The allegorical figures the Chamber of Abraham are viewed from below, posed in the same manner as those of the Cornaro Palace and the *Sala dei Cento Giorni* (compare Figs. 5 and 6 with 4, and Figs. 9 and 8). Vasari 's design for these allegories became a formula, or topos, repeatedly employed in his early decorative cycles, particularly evident in the Chamber of Abraham and the Chamber of Fortune in the Casa Vasari (Fig. 11). Furthermore, some of the attitudes and attributes of the Casa Vasari virtues are similar to those found in the Refectory of Monteoliveto, executed in 1544-45. The allegories of Chastity, Concord, Peace and Modesty in the Chamber of Abraham clearly resemble the allegories of Chastity, Peace, Concord and Modesty in the Refectory (compare Figs. 4, 8, 14, and 16 with 7, 12, 15 and 17).[12] Specifically, similarities between the two figures of Chastity can be seen in the type of the figure, its pose, and the placement of its hand around the vessel or vase. The composition of the Chamber of Abraham figure is simple, but Chastity has no wings and some Christian symbols have been introduced, such as the lily substituted for the unicorn, (compare Fig. 4 with Fig. 7).[13] The figure of Modesty in the Chamber of Abraham is drawn from the allegorical figures of Modesty and Humility in the Refectory in Naples (compare Figs. 17 and 18 with Fig. 16). The decorum and propriety of the Refectory's figures, like those of Modesty in the Casa Vasari, are represented in both paintings by the veiling and draping of the forms and by the downcast eyes.

Problems arise in interpreting the allegorical figures of the Chamber of Abraham, because of the discrepancy between the painted attributes of these figures and the attributes traditionally associated with these virtues. Vasari is of no help here, unfortunately, since he did not discuss the meaning of the four allegories. But from his other writings one can arrive at some understanding of his meaning. It appears that Vasari, following the Renaissance Neoplatonic tradition, fused pagan symbols with Christian motifs, intending a dual meaning. Yet the philosophical ramifications and complexity of this fusion are not directly dealt with in the pictorial image, but merely alluded to.

The dual meaning is particularly noticeable in the case of Chastity, who is portrayed with objects (the rose, myrtle, lily, and vase) having different associations in the classical and the Christian cultures (Fig. 4).[14] The attributes she holds seem to denote the Renaissance Neoplatonic concept of Venus - Virgo, or Love - Chastity. This dual meaning, based on Virgil's *Aeneid*, was applied by the Renaissance Neoplatonists to the Christian doctrine of chastity and love.[15] Virgil relates that Venus disguised herself as Diana, a virgin goddess, in order to appear as a "devotee of chastity."[16] In Vasari's Chastity one sees on the breastplate of her dress a female figure standing, perhaps on a shell, and holding a bow and arrow. She may well be Diana, a personification of Chastity, or Diana disguised as Venus standing on a shell, a personification of Love.

The lack of detail in the painting makes a more precise identification impossible. Vasari's Chastity also displays other Christian and pagan motifs associated with Venus - Virgo or Love - Chastity. She holds a classical vase with its base in the shape of a scalloped shell. The scalloped shell, of course, is commonly associated with the birth of Venus; it was also used in Christian art as a symbol of resurrection and of pilgrimage.[17] In the Cinquecento several writers, including Cartari and Valeriano, associated Venus with chastity or virginity, and Vasari's allegorical figure of Chastity likewise has attributes associated with chastity and virginity: she holds wilted white roses in one hand.[18]

For Concord in the Chamber of Abraham, Vasari employed the same attributes as those described in the *Sala dei Cento Giorni*, adding a centaur holding a torch in the medallion on the sleeve of her garment (Fig. 8).[19] The allegorical figure of Concord, like that of Chastity, also hints at Neoplatonic ideas, such as the concept of *concordia discors* or *discordia concors*.[20] This phrase embodies the idea that discord or strife severs the harmony of the universe, while concord re-establishes harmony. The idea of Concord can therefore legitimately be coupled with allegorical representations of Love, Faith, and Peace.[21] But representations of Concord may have the opposite meaning. If the Casa Vasari figure of Concord is viewed in relation to the adjacent Chastity, its im·plication is positive. The bound rods symbolize the union created by those who wish to live together in harmony. But in relation to the centaur, discord may be alluded to, as is also suggested by the broken rods: separated from the bundle, the strength of the rods is diminished, resulting in disharmony.

Next to the figure of Chastity is Peace (Fig. 14), whose representation in the *Sala dei Cento Giorni* Vasari described as " having an olive branch in hand."[22] The olive tree or olive branch was a symbol of peace for the Greeks as well as the Hebrews. According to Saint Augustine, olive trees symbolize the feast of Epiphany because "Abraham and Isaac and Jacob are the progenitors from whom the Jews drew their lineage, not as legitimate offspring of these trees, but as engrafted upon the olive tree of which Paul speaks (Rom. 11:24)."[23] Thus in the figure of Peace, as in the figures of Chastity and Concord, one observes again the fusion of pagan motifs with religious symbolism. The fact that the figure of Peace is located just below the tondo scene and has the same orientation is significant. Unlike the other figures in the ceiling, the figure of Peace relates directly to God blessing Isaac and Abraham, as if God is reassuring the Hebrew people both of His protection and of peace on earth.

The last allegorical figure in the ceiling of the Chamber of Abraham, the figure of Modesty, sheds light on the meaning of the program (Fig. 16). Modesty, seated across from Chastity, is easily identified because she is holding an open book displaying the Latin inscription *Modestia vestra nota sit omnibus hominibus* (Let your modesty be known to all humankind).[24] The symbolism of Modesty is based on well-established tradition, but shows an interesting variation on the customary portrayal. On the breastplate of her dress is the head of a weasel-like animal, probably an ermine. The veil, along with the ermine, indicates that Modesty possesses the attribute of candor.[25] Another innovation on the part of Vasari is the use of a female figure with an open book with an inscribed exhortation, which recalls the tablet held by the figure of Law (Lex) painted by Marcillat on the ceiling of the nave of the Cathedral in Arezzo (Fig. 19). The inscription in the book is divided between two pages, as are the inscriptions of the Ten Commandments on the tablets of Moses in the paintings of Raphael's *Disputa* and Marcillat's *Moses Proclaims the Law* and in the print of the emblem *Consilium* in Sambucus, *De Emblemate*, No. 30 (Fig. 20).[26]

In the ceiling of the Chamber of Abraham the four virtues of Modesty, Chastity, Peace, and Concord convey a Christian message. But this meaning derives in part from pagan iconography and is transformed into a Christian language encapsulated in the Latin inscription *Modestia vestra nota sit omnibus hominibus*, in turn quoted from a passage in Paul's Epistle to the Phillippians, where he stresses the importance of living a model life by imitating Jesus (a descendant of Abraham), and exhorts the congregation to bear gifts and receive greetings and benediction. According to Paul, in order to do this Christians must fill their "thoughts with all that is true, all that is noble, all that is just and pure, all that is lovable and gracious." Although achieving this is difficult and creates anxiety, Paul encourages Christians to request help from God the Father "in prayer and petition with thanksgiving. Then the peace of God will keep guard over their hearts."[27]

The decorative L-shaped fields, also a mixture of Christian and pagan symbolism, only indirectly relate to the subject of the central tondo scene (Fig. 1). The statues painted in each corner are pagan personifications of virtues, surrounded by other pagan decorative motifs. The objects each statue holds (water vessel, serpent, cornucopia, column, and rod) show that these figures symbolize the four seasons or the four elements of the universe.[28] It is likely that they also represent the four cardinal virtues of Temperance, Prudence, Fortitude, and Justice.[29]

In Medieval and Renaissance iconography the attributes of these four virtues changed frequently, so that an unequivocal identification is not always possible. Although Justice is usually depicted as a blindfolded female holding scales, Vasari's image is of a fully robed man holding a measuring rod (Fig. 16), suggesting that it represents judgment as well as justice.[30] Three syncretistic types were used by Vasari in many of his decorative projects in the early 15405, such as the *apparato* for *La Talanta* and the *loggie* for Pietro de Toledo and Tommaso Cambi. Artists of this time typically experimented with the attributes of such figures.[31]

The four cardinal virtues are based on the classical conception of the forces of the soul. Socrates and Cicero thought that the virtues of Temperance, Justice, Prudence, and Fortitude were essential to the life of a perfect human being.[32] Similar views were held by Christian theologians such as Ambrose and Alcuin, who considered the cardinal virtues to be the foundation of Christian life; they were special benefits of grace bestowed upon man by God through the Eucharist.[33] During the Middle Ages the cardinal virtues were associated with the four evangelists, the prophets, and particularly with King Solomon. In the Book of Proverbs, Solomon praised these virtues as intellectual gifts.[34] During the tenth and eleventh centuries, moreover, both the cardinal and the theological virtues were specifically associated with allegorical depictions of Humility, a clustering related to the special virtues attributed to Mary (*Virginitas, Sobrietas, Continentia,* and *Castitas*).[35]

Vasari was cognizant of these diverse classical and Christian sources and antecedents because of his association with learned ecclesiastical and humanistic circles. He was also aware that the cardinal virtues were considered a gift of God and that they were specifically associated with the Old Testament.[36] To illustrate this in the Chamber of Abraham, Vasari depicted, in the comers of the square wooden inner frame, *bucrania* and floral swags surrounding the *tondo*, along with the cardinal virtues in the outer corners, suggesting a purification rite with a sacrificial meaning - the sacrifice of Isaac (Gen. 22:1-19) or the sacrifice of the Mass (the crucifixion of Christ). Underlying these suggestions is the simplest and most literal meaning: God granting Abraham a son, Isaac. The *tondo* scene also prefigures Abraham's sacrifice of Isaac on Mount Moriah. A more complex interpretation is the conflict between life and death of Abraham's love for Isaac set against God's demand that Abraham take Isaac's life. On yet another level of meaning, the story of Abraham and Isaac foreshadows the central event of the New Testament: God bestows upon people His own son, Christ, only to have His life sacrificed on Mount Golgotha. The sacrifice of Isaac by Abraham is a traditional prefiguration of Christ's sacrifice. Through His resurrection, life transcends death.[37] These levels of meaning interact between the circle of life (the *tondo*) and the square of death (the *bucrania*). The symbolism within the circle states that Christian life transcends death through the cardinal virtues in the corners of the ceiling and the Christian virtues on the axes of the central scene.

Vasari followed a specific Christian program in the Chamber of Abraham. It is clear from the alternate placement of cardinal and Christian virtues in the painted frame that he intended the room to have a special meaning. Because cardinal virtues are gifts of grace, they may be logically related to the gift of God's blessing on Abraham.[38] Although Abraham is particularly associated with the moral virtue of obedience,[39] his life reflects his willingness to live by all the Christian virtues, chastity, concord, peace, and humility. For Vasari, Abraham was the exemplary figure of Christian faith, because of his obedience, and was thus appropriately surrounded by all the virtues.

In depicting a religious scene in this ceiling, Vasari has also expressed his wish for God to bless and protect his new home. The blessing of a house is consistent with Italian religious tradition. From early Christian times it has been the custom to bless the house during the feast of Epiphany. The rite of blessing involved a recital of the Magnificat and a sprinkling of holy water and incense in the rooms by a priest, saying the following prayer:

> Bless, O Lord, almighty God, this house, that therein be found good health, chastity, the power of spiritual victory, humility, goodness and meekness, the plenitude of the Law, and thanksgiving to God, the Father, Son, and Holy Spirit: and may this blessing remain on the house and on its inhabitants. Through Christ our Lord. Amen.[40]

Giorgio Vasari has translated the meaning of the blessing and prayer into pictorial imagery.[41] Reference to such a prayer makes more meaningful the placement of the Christian virtues on the ceiling. Modesty, for instance, stands for humility, goodness, and meekness; Chastity for purity, virginity, and chastity; Concord for the power of spiritual victory; Peace for good health and plenitude of the law; and in the center, the Blessing of God for thanksgiving. Traditionally, for no clear reason, the Chamber of Abraham was thought to be Vasari's bedroom. Perhaps this is one reason for the religious themes depicted on the ceiling: the blessing scene and the cardinal virtues from the Old Testament and the Christian virtues from the New Testament. According to Paul's teachings, the four Christian virtues are essential for the harmony of the soul and the honor of a Christian home.

## Notes

This article is a reprint from "Giorgio Vasari's Chamber of Abraham: A Religious Ceiling in the Aretine House," *Sixteenth Century Journal* (Fall 1987), 355–380.

1. For literature containing bibliography on the houses of Quattrocento and Cinquecento artists, see K. W. Forster and R. J. Tullle, "The Casa Pippi: Giulio Romano's House in Mantua," *Architectura* (1973): 104-30 n.2. A Cecchi, "Vasari e le Case degli Artisti," Cat. *Mostra di Giorgio Vasari: Principi, letterati e artisti nelle carte di Giorgio Vasari*, ed. Laura Corti, Margaret Daly Davis, Charles Davis, and Julian Kliemann (Florence: Edman, 1981), 35-7; and. Liana Cheney, *The Painting of the Casa Vasari* (New York: Garland Publishing, 1986).

2. The best and most complete source for the dating and description of the paintings in the Casa Vasari today is still Vasari's own comments from his autobiography, his letters, and *ricordi*. See Giorgio Vasari, *Le Vite dei più eccellenti Pittori, Scultori, el Architettori*, Florence, 1550 and 1568; K. Frey, *Der Literarische Nachlaas Giorgio Vasaris*, Vol. 1; Vol. 2. (Munich: Georg Muller, 1923, 1930); W. Kallab, Vasaristudien (Vienna: K. Graeser und Kie, 1908); A del Vita, *Il Carteggio di Giorgio Vasari* (Arezzo: Tipografia Zelli, 1923 and 1941); *Le Ricordanze di Giorgio Vasari* (Arezzo: Tipografia Zelli, 1938); *Lo Zibalone di Giorgio Vasari* (Arezzo: Tipografia Zelli, 1938); and J. Draper, *Vasari's Decoration in the Palazzo Vecchio: The Ragionamenti: translated with Introduction and Notes*. Unpublished Ph .D. dissertation, University of North Carolina, 1973.

3. L. Berti, *La casa del Vasari in Arezzo e il suo museo* (Rorence: Leo S. Olschki, 1955). 10. A. Cecchi, "La Casa del Vasari in Arezzo, *Il Vasari Storiografo e Artista*. Atti del Convegno internazionale nel IV centenario della morte, Firenze, 1976, 75-81. L. Cheney, *The Paintings of the Casa Vasari*, Fig. 120 for the placement of these rooms; and A. Cecchi, "Casa Vasari," 24-30.

4. K. Frey, *Der Literarische Nachlass Giorgio Vasaris*, 1:34lf; W. Kallab, *Vasaristudien*, 90 and 93-94; and, A. del Vita, *Inventario e Regesto dell'Archivio Vasariano* (Arezzo: Tipografia Zelli, 1938), 23, letter 21.

5. For a clear explanation of the tondo motif in Renaissance Art, see Moritz Hauptmann, *Der Tondo* (Frankfurt: V. Klostermann, 1936).

6. Vasari·Milanesi, *Le Vite*...1972, 7:690. At the beginning of 1549, Vasari went to Bologna to visit Cardinal del Monte (later Pope Julius Ill) who convinced Vasari to marry Nicolosa Bacci, of a noble Aretine family. In the same year, Vasari requested Vincenzo Borghini to arrange for his marriage. Judging from one of Borghini's letters to Vasari, dated Florence, September 10, 1549, Borghini was effective in making the nuptial arrangements. See A. del Vita, *Le Ricordanze di Giorgio Vasari*, 133, Letter 4:c.6 e7; and W. Kallab, *Vasaristudien*, 83.

7. *The New English Bible with the Apocrypha* (New York : Doubleday and Company, Inc., 1970), 22. See D. Gorce, *Traites sur L'Ancien Testament* (Namur: Quatrechemins, 1967); and Ambrose, "The Patriarchs," *The Fathers of the Church* (Washington, D.C.: Catholic University of America Press, 1972), 65:10-65 for the symbolism of Abraham and Isaac, respectively.

8. B. Davidson, *Marcantonio Raimondi: The Engravings of his Roman Period*, Unpublished Ph.D. dissertation, Harvard University, 1954, 126-27; K. Oberhuber, ed. *The Illustrated Bartsch: The Works of M. Raimondi and his school* (New York: McGraw Hill, 1978), 6:11-12, Figs. 3, 4 (London) 3c(5) (Vienna); and N. Dacos, *Le Loggie di Raffaello* (Rome: DeLuca Editore, 1977), 109-12.

9. A square room, 4,568 m. one each side. Vasari-Milanesi, 7:686. A del Vita, *Le Ricordanze di Giorgio Vasari*, 60, Letter 68. The ceiling of the Chamber of Abraham was probably finished by the end of July, 1548, when Vasari began painting the third room in his house, the Chamber of Fortune. Vasari-Milanesi, 7:685-86; and, A. del Vita, *Le Ricordanze di Giorgio Vasari*, 60-61, Letters 68 and 70.

10. Vasari-Milanesi, 7:686. Alessandro Cecchi has identified this scene as God blessing Abraham and Ishmael without stylistic and iconographical evidence. See Cecchi, "Casa Vasari," 25.

11. Called to Venice in 1541 by Pietro Aretino, Vasari was requested to do a series of scenographic paintings for an *apparato* commissioned by the Compagnia della Caza, named the Sempiterni. In this *apparato*

Aretino's comedy, *La Talanta*, was to be performed. For a complete description of these paintings, see Vasari-Milanesi, 6:222-23 and 670; K. Frey, *Der Literarische Nachlas Giorgio Vasaris*, 2:111-19; and, David McTavish, "Giorgio Vasari," Cat. *Mostra Da Tiziano al Greco* (Milan: Electa Editrice, 1981), 86.

12. Unfortunately, the ceiling of the Refectory of Monteoliveto has not been studied iconographically. It displays many interesting ideas of Vasari's which need to be investigated. The most recent article by Pierluigi Leone DeCastris, "Napoli 1544: Vasari e Monteoliveto," *Bolletino d'Arte* 12 (1981): 59-88, only discusses the stylistic sources for the Refectory.

13. Some of the Christian symbols for Virginity or Chastity are the white rose, the myrtle, a vessel or vase, the lily, and the unicorn. See M. Levi d'Ancona, *The Garden of the Renaissance* (Florence: Sansoni, 1967), 210, 238, 300, and 331. For a painting of the unicorn associated with Chastity, see *The Triumph of Chastity* by Francesco di Giorgio in the Berenson Collection at the Villa I Tatti.

14. *Rose*: Traditionally in ancient Rome, the rose was a symbol of victory, pride and love. It was the flower of Venus, goddess of love. In Christian iconography the white rose is a symbol of purity. According to Ambrose, the Virgin Mary was called the "rose without thorns" since she was free of original sin. See M. Levi d ' Ancona, *The Garden of the Renaissance*, 230-31.

*Lily*: The lily, a symbol of purity, represents the virginity of Mary in scenes of the Annunciation. See Petrus Berchorius, *Repertorium Morale*, 2:63; J. D. Migne, ed., *Patrologia Latina*, 23 (1865): 264; E. Panofsky, *The Iconography of Correggio's Camera di San Paolo* (London: The Warburg Institute, 1961), 53, m.l, for an elaborate discussion of the symbolism of the lily associated with the virginity of Mary. According to the Bible, because flowers signal the coming of spring their fragrance and beauty are a symbol of the Messianic kingdom (Isa. 35:1). And the death of flowers is symbolic of the transitoriness of life (Jacob 14:1 and James 1:10). It is also of interest that, according to the great seventeenth century iconographer Cesare Ripa, wilted flowers were associated with virginity; see C. Ripa, *Iconologia* (New York: Carland Publishing, 1970), 505. And in the Chamber of Abraham, Vasari has depicted Virtue or Chastity holding wilted flowers. It is important to note that Vasari was a conscious pictorial encyclopedist familiar with the Biblical and classical traditions, paving the way for Ripa who followed the Vasarian tradition by collecting ancient and contemporary ideas for his encyclopedic *Iconologia*.

See also E. Halg, *The Floral Symbolism of the Great Masters* (London: Thames and Hudson, 1913); and, R. Koch, "Flower Symbolism in the Portinari Altar," *Art Bulletin* 46 (1964): 70-77 for floral symbolism.

*Myrtle*: In Roman mythology myrtle was considered sacred to Venus and was a symbol of grace, sanity, victory (see P. Valeriano, *Hieroglyphica* [Lyon, 1602], 600, 421, and 445) and love (see Cicero's *Somnium Scipionis*), whereas in Christian iconography myrtle alludes to the Gentiles who were converted by Christ (Zech. 1:8).

*Vessel or Vase*: In Christian iconography the vase or vessel is associated with Temperance, one of the seven virtues. Stylistically, Vasari's vase makes reference to Cinquecento interpretation of antique vases, as it is decorated with garlands, a mask, and a skull motif. In addition, this vase contains myrtle leaves. In the Renaissance a vase containing plants or flowers was emblematic of virtue or grace (E. Wind, *Pagan Mysteries in the Renaissance* [New York: W.W. Norton and Company, 1968], 268 n.l). Thus all of these attributes may attest to the goodness of love, Venus, or to a Christian virtue, perhaps Chastity, Purity, or Virginity as ascribed to the Virgin Mary.

15. E. Wind, *Pagan Mysteries in the Renaissance*, 77, and E. Panofsky, *Studies in Iconology* (New York: Harper and Row Publishers, 1962), 157.

16. E. Wind, *Pagan Mysteries in the Renaissance*, 75. See, for example, the medal of Giovanna degli Albizzi with the Latin inscription from Virgil alluding to the Venus -Virgo concept: *Virginis os habitumque gerens et virginis arma* (Virgil 1:315).

17. J. Layer, *The Cradle of Venus in the Scallop: Studies of the Shell and its Influence on Humankind* (London: Phaidon, 1957).

18. V. Cartari, *Imagini delli Dei de gl'Antichi* (Austria: Akademische Druck Verlag Sanstalt Graz, 1963), (W. Koschatzky edition of V. Cartari, *Imagini . . .* [Padova, 1556]), 273; P. Valeriano, *Hieroglyphica* 4: C. Ripa restated this tradition in his book, *Iconologia* (Rome, 1603) 66-67, and 505.

19. A. del Vita, *Lo Zibaldone di Giorgio Vasari*, 24. Cartari described the image of Concord as a symbol of multiplicity and abundance (Y. Cartari, *Imagini delli Dei de gl'Antichi*, 169). Later Ripa elaborated the definition a bit more by describing the figure of Concord (Concordia) as a woman holding a bundle of rods, fastened tightly, and some single rods which are broken (C. Ripa, *Iconologia*, 81).

20. Pico della Mirandola, one of the most important Renaissance Neoplatonic philosophers, associated concord with discord (E. Wind, *Pagan*

*Mysteries in the Renaissance,* 71 and 78; and, E. Panofsky, *The Iconography of Correggio's Camera di San Paolo,* 57). In striving to reconcile pagan, Hebrew, and Christian theologies by showing that there are strong affinities among them, Pico della Mirandola developed a philosophy of tolerance which was based on a concept of hidden concordances, or principles of contradictions. These principles or laws of contradictions were personified by pagan gods who were called *dei ambigui* because of their dual nature. For instance, the cool Diana was the goddess of Chastity as well as the mad goddess of the Hunt. And Venus, the goddess of Concord, loved Mars, the god of Strife or Discord, And for the early formation of virtues and vices, such as concordia versus discordia, see Q. S. F. Tertullian, *De Spectaculis,* trans. T. R. Glover, (New York: Philosophical Library, Inc., 1931); Prudentius, *Psychomachia,* trans. H. I. Thomson, (Cambridge, Mass.: Harvard University Press, 1949), and Leo Spitzer, "Classical and Christian Ideas of World Harmony," *Traditio* 2 (1944):409-64.

21. Cartari associated Concord with Faith (V. Cartari, *Imagini dell Dei de gl'Antichi,* 169). In the moral tradition of Greece and Rome, Concord was associated with Peace. Seznec, *The Survival of the Pagan Gods,* 86). See E. Wind, Pagan Mysteries in the Rennaissance, 76, for the relationship between Concord and Constancy (Concordia e Constantia).

22. According to Cartari, Peace and Concord are one and the same thing. Both were adored by the ancients who desired a quiet and peaceful life (V. Cartari, *Imagini delli Dei de gl'Antichi,* 167-68, P. Valeriano, Hieroglyphica, 452, and M. Levi d'Ancona, *The Garden of the Renaissance,* 261-71). According to the Bible, since the time of Noah the olive tree was a symbol of peace (Gen. 8:11). The Hebrews called the olive tree a "tree full of richness" Judges 9:8-9).

23. Augustine commenting on Paul in "Sermons on the Liturgical Seasons," *The Fathers of the Church* Vol. 38 (Washington, D.C.: Catholic University of America Press, 1959), 69.

24. Paul's Epistle to the Philippians 4:125 in Biblia Sacra: Justa Vulgatum Clementinam (Rome: Typis Societatis S. Joannis Evang., 1956).

25. Modesty (*Pudicitia*) is traditionally portrayed as a veiled woman holding in her hand an ermine, a symbol of candor. The veiled head indicates that a chaste woman must despise her embellishment, just as the ermine preferred death to impurity. See C. Ripa, *Iconologia,* 420.

26. For Sambucus the motif of an open book is used to symbolize laws and a constitution by which one must abide, and implies the purification of religious practice. See A. Katzenellenbogen, *Allegories of the Virtues and Vices in Medieval Art* (New York: W. W. Norton and Company, 1964), 45.

27. See n. 24.

28. These tetrads refer to Pythagorean cosmology. The four basic qualities of hotness, dryness, coldness, and moistness are related to fire, earth, water, and air. See S. K. Heninger, *Touches of Sweet Harmony* (Berkeley, Calif.: University of California Press, 1974), 153-54 and 160-76, for an interesting discussion of Pythagorean cosmology. This cosmology was known in the Cinquecento and was associated with the theory of humors. Vasari repeatedly employed this symbolism in his decorative cycles, for example, the *Studiolo* in the Palazzo Vecchio, Florence.

29. The iconographic symbol for Temperance was usually a water vessel (a reminder of diluting water with wine); for Prudence, a serpent or a book (signifying wisdom) and a cornucopia (signifying richness); for Fortitude, a sword, column, or a figure with a Herculean body (signifying strength); and for Justice a pair of scales or a measuring rod (signifying impartiality). See A. Katzenellenbogen, *Allegories of the Virtues and Vice in Medieval Art*, 33 n.1; 45 n.2; 49 nn.1 and 2; 50 n.1; 51-52 n.8; and 56; E. Panofsky, *Studies in Iconology*, 157 n.97; R. Bernard, *La vertu*, (Paris, 1933-35); and, E. Male, *Gothic Image*, (New York: Harper and Row Publishers, 1958), 110, for a discussion of Ambrose's concept of the cardinal virtues as well as of Thomas Aquinas's position on the interconnection of moral virtues with cardinal virtues.

30. In later ioonographical traditions one sees this change; for example, Ripa's allegory of the Judge is represented by a man dressed in a long garment and holding a measuring rod, a symbol of power in the human realm. See C. Ripa, *Iconologia*, 186. Stylistically this figure recalls the portrayal of the evangelist or prophet of the Quattrocento, particularly, Donatello's *S. Mark* or *Jeremiah*.

31. In terms of stylistic sources there are many French and German medieval examples of representations of cardinal virtues. An Italian medieval example, probably known to Vasari, is Giovanni Pisano's Pisa pulpit (E. Panofsky, Studies in Iconology, 156-57). And the verso of Piero della Francesca's Urbino portraits is a Renaissance example known to Vasari .

32. A. Katzenellenbogen, *Allegories of the Virtues and Vices in Medieval Art*, 30 n.3.

33. Ibid.

34. A. Katzenellenbogen, *Allegories of the Virtues and Vices in Medieval Art*, 33, Proverb VIII, 12; "Ego sapientia habito in cosiglio;" Proverb VIII, 14: " Mea est prudentia, mea est fortitudo;" Proverb VIII, 16: "Per me principes imperant et potentes decernunt justitiuam."

35. This association was also interpreted as symbolizing Mary as the *Sede Sapientia*. See A. Katzenellenbogen, *Allegories of the Virtues and Vices in Medieval Art*, 33-34 n.2; and 52-53 n.l .

36. A. Katzenellenbogen, *Allegories of the Virtues and Vices in Medieval Art*, 45, Exodus 38:2. The four horns of Old Testament altars are related to the cardinal virtues. And according to Ambrose the beauty of the soul of Isaac is similar "to the beauty of the firstborn of a bull, his horns are those of a unicorn, with them he will push the nations." Ambrose, "The Patriarchs," *The Fathers of the Church*, 65:269f. A. W. Strado in the twelfth century manuscript, *Glossa Ordinaria*, relates the crown of thorns to the ram's horn; and the ram became Christ crucified. See E. Male, *Gothic Image*, 138 and 155.

37. The mountain in the landscape also suggests Mount Tabor, where the Ascension of Christ took place. In this farewell event, Christ reminded His disciples of His teachings, the observance of the Law and His eternal life (Matt. 28: 16-20). In the Old Testament, God offered his Son to guide mankind to achieve a good life. Furthermore, Vasari's depiction of Abraham's embrace of Isaac suggests the Christian motif of Abraham's bosom, a place of happiness where the just went after death to partake of the celestial banquet in heaven (Luke 16:22-23). And Abraham's "Sacrifice of Isaac" is a traditional typology for Christ's sacrifice.

38. The Old Testament has several examples of a moral virtue particularly associated with a virtuous man (Psalm 52:8): for instance, Patience with Job, Cleanliness with Moses, and Obedience with Abraham. See Petrus Berchorius, *Repertorium Morale*, 1:102; and, A. Katzenellenbogen, *Allegories of the Virtues and Vices in Medieval Art*, 57.

39. According to Migne, Abraham is associated with God-fearing Obedience (Abraham... oboediens in praeceptis) and the sacrifice of Isaac is symbolic of Abraham's obedience to God. See J. D. Migne, ed., *Patrologia Latina* Vol . 83, (1862), 133f and 103f; and, Vasari had seen depicted the association of virtues with the sacrifice of Abraham in Salviati's Sala della Udienza of Palazzo Vecchio, Florence.

40. F. X. Weiser, *Christian Feasts and Customs* (New York: Harcourt, Brace and Company, 1958), 141-49.

41. Vasari may have been familiar with this or other prayers used for the rite of blessing. See S. da Sabbio, *Predica del Vivere Christiano*, (Venice, 1536).

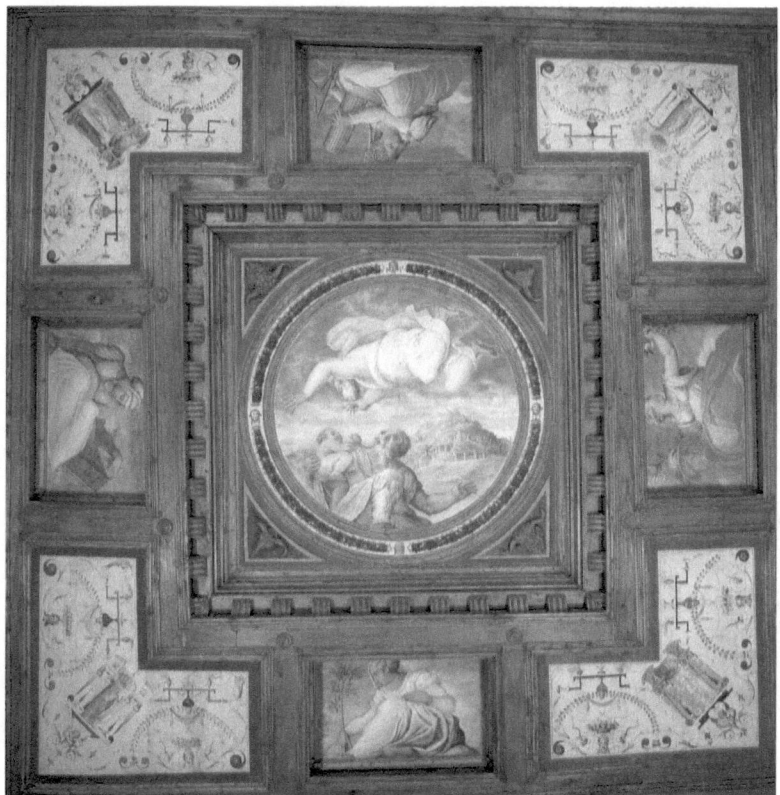

Fig. 1. Giorgio Vasari, *Chamber of Abraham*, 1548. View of the ceiling. Casa Vasari, Arezzo.

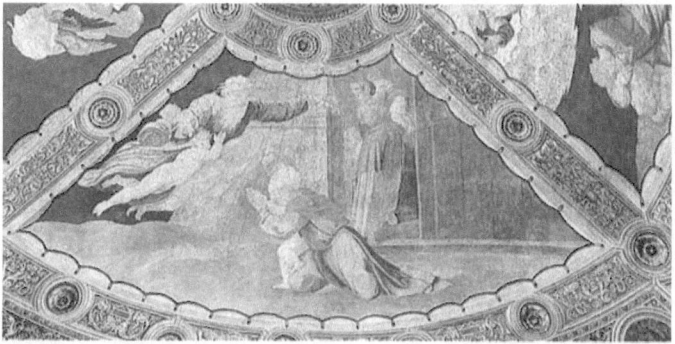

Fig. 2. Baldassare Peruzzi, *God blessing the Seed of Abraham*, det. 1508-12. Sala di Eliodoro, Vatican, Rome. Photo: Alinari.

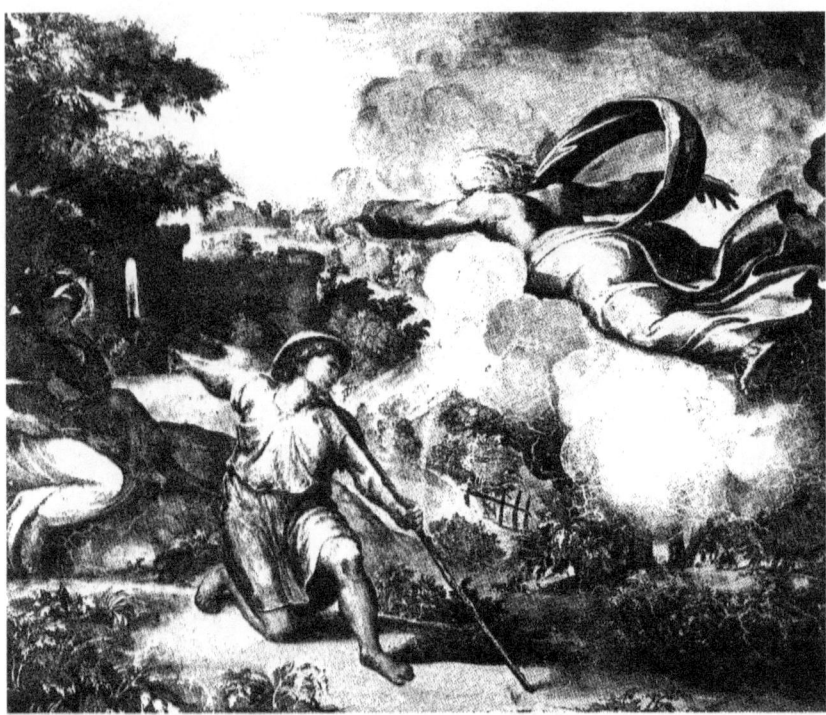

Fig. 3. Giulio Romano, *God Appearing to Isaac*, 1508-12, det. Vatican Loggie, Rome.

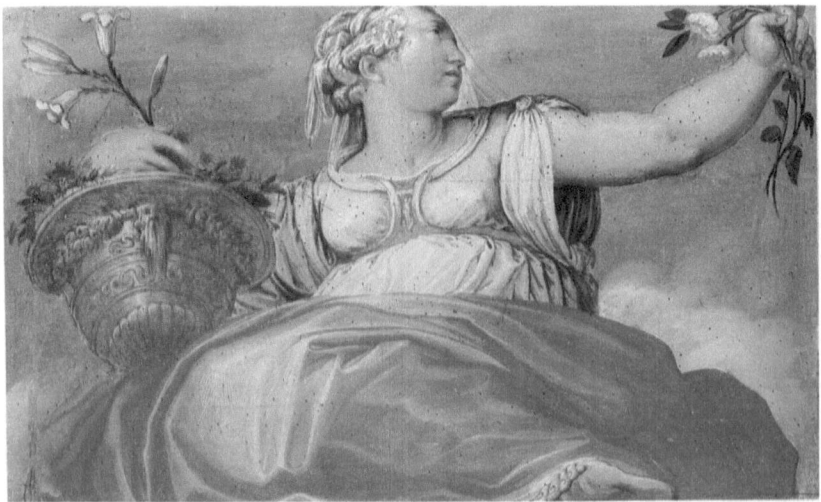

Fig. 4. Giorgio Vasari, *Virtue* (Chastity), 1548, det. Chamber of Abraham, Casa Vasari, Arezzo.

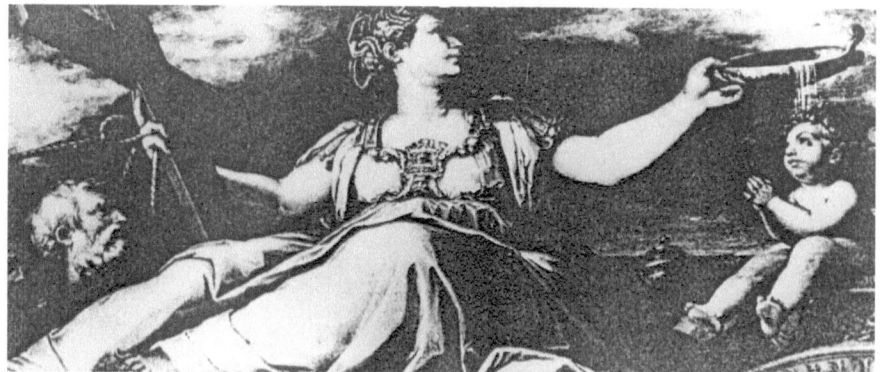

Fig. 5.  Giorgio Vasari, *Faith*, 1541-42, det. Cornaro Palace, Venice.
Photo: J. Schulz

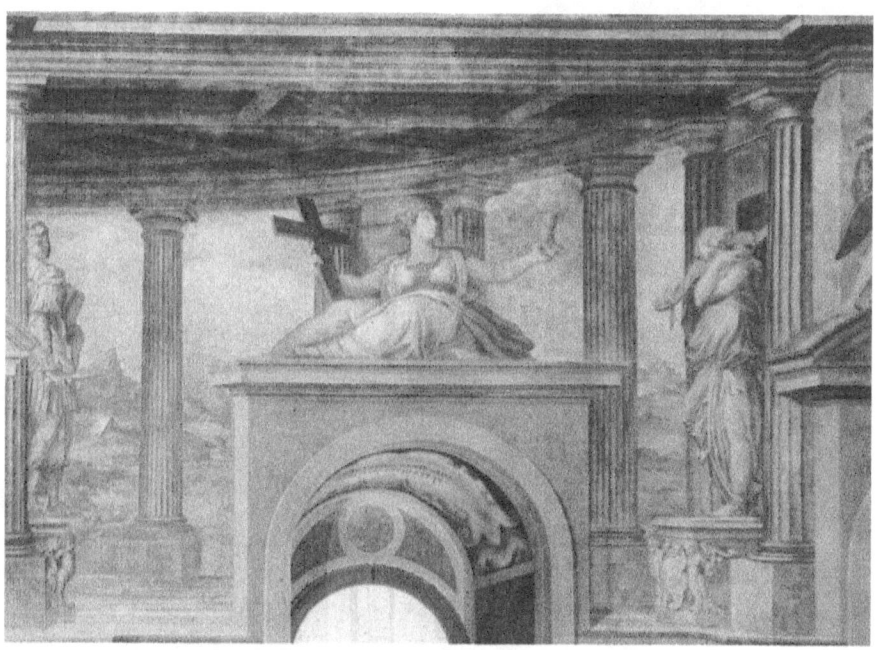

Fig. 6.  Giorgio Vasari, *Faith,* 1546, det. Sala dei Cento Giorni Palazzo della
Cancelleria, Rome. Photo: Rigamonti.

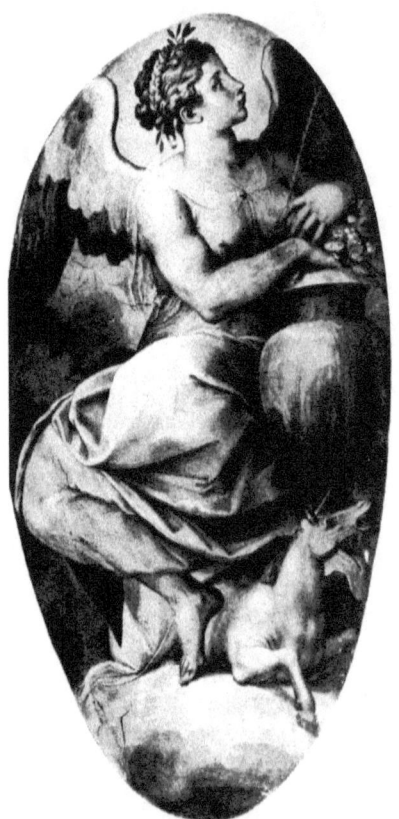

Fig. 7. Giorgio Vasari, *Chastity*, 1545, det. Refectory of Monteoliveto, (Sant'Anna dei Lombardi), Naples. Photo: Rigamonti

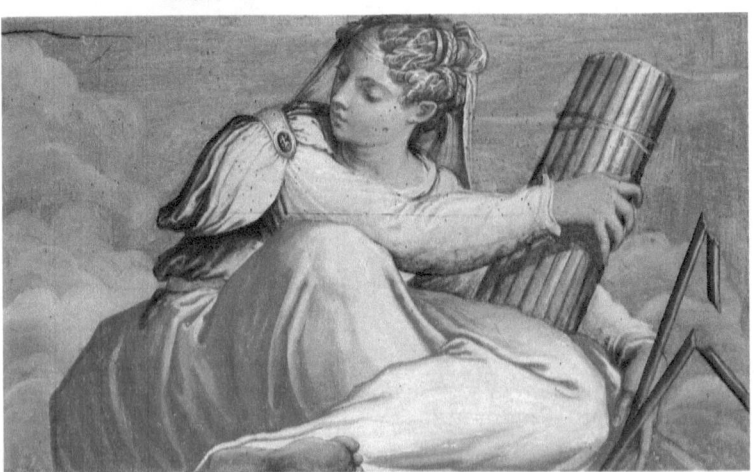

Fig. 8. Giorgio Vasari, *Concord*, 1548, det. Chamber of Abraham, Casa Vasari, Arezzo.

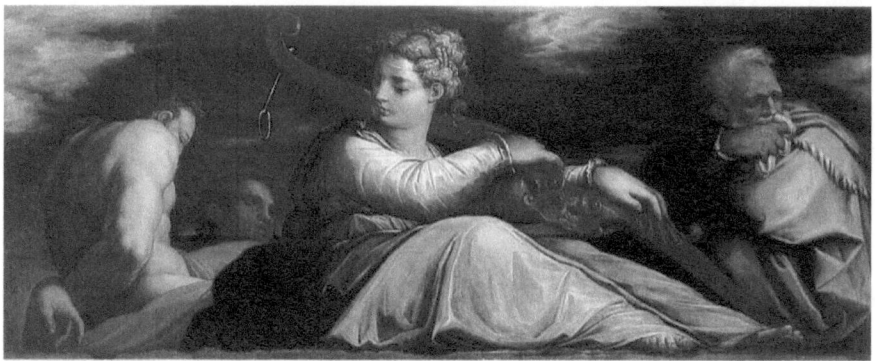

Fig. 9. Giorgio Vasari, *Peace*, 1541-42, det. Cornaro Palace, Venice. Photo: J. Schulz.

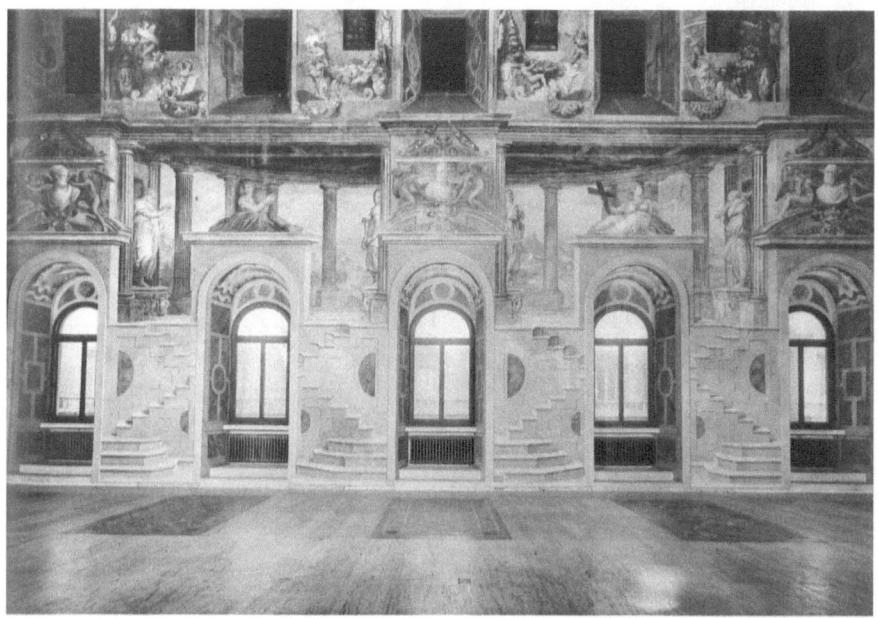

Fig. 10. Giorgio Vasari, *Hope and Faith*, 1546, det. Sala dei Centro Giorni, Palazzo della Cancelleria, Rome.

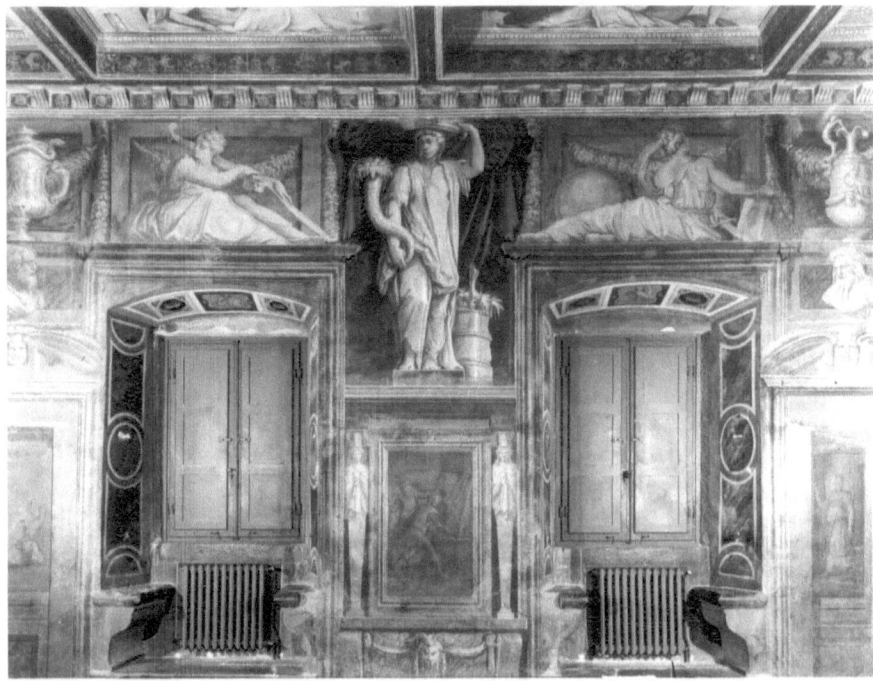

Fig. 11. Giorgio Vasari, *Peace and Justice*, 1548, det., east wall, Chamber of Fortune, Casa Vasari, Arezzo.

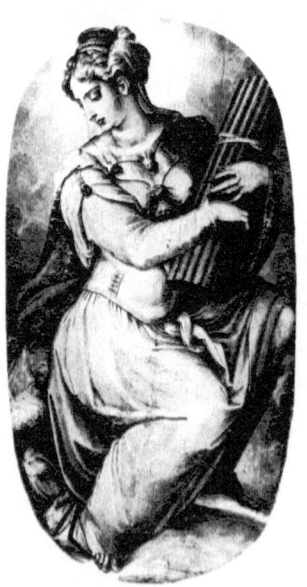

Fig. 12. Giorgio Vasari, *Concord*, 1545, det., Refectory of Monteoliveto (Sant'Anna dei Lombardi), Naples. Photo: Rigamonti

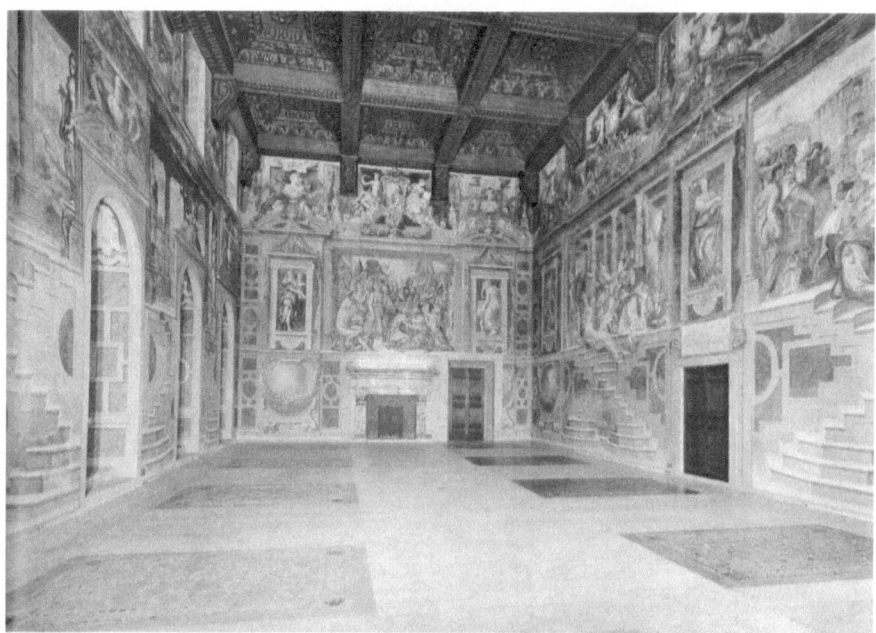

Fig. 13. Giorgio Vasari, *Universal Peace in Christendom*, 1546, det., Sala dei Cento Giorni, Palazzo della Cancelleria, Rome. Photo: Rigamonti.

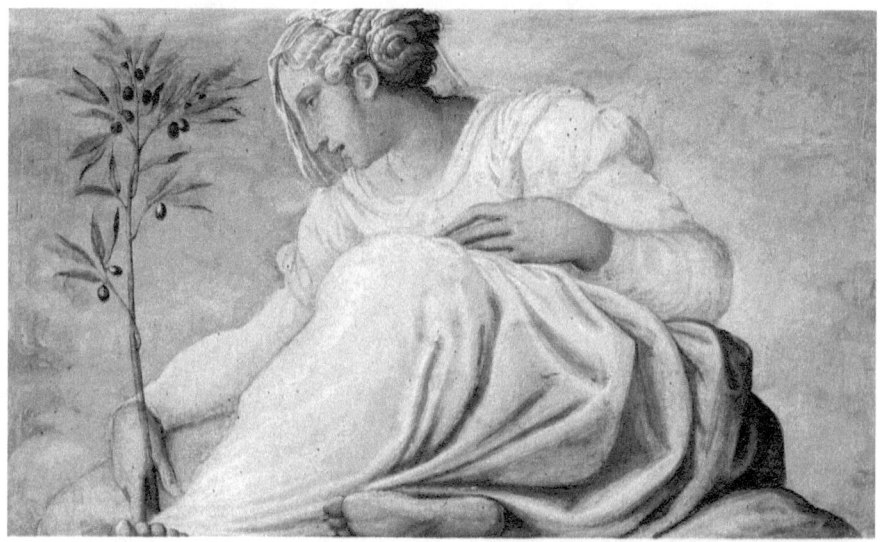

Fig. 14. Giorgio Vasari, *Peace*, 1548, det., Chamber of Abraham, Casa Vasari, Arezzo.

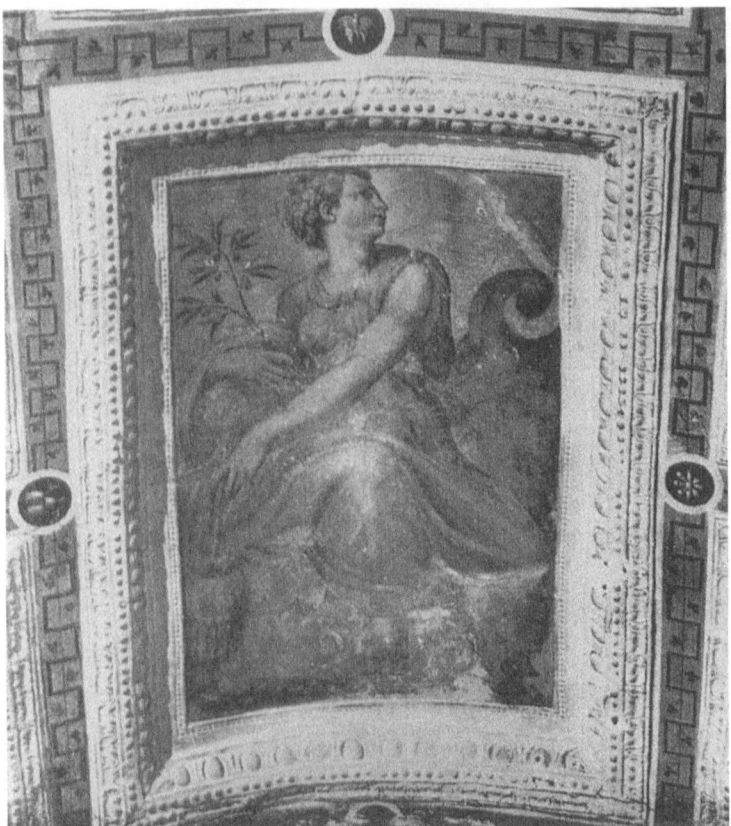

Fig. 15. Giorgio Vasari, *Peace*, 1545, det., Refectory of Monte-oliveto (Sant'Anna dei Lombardi), Naples. Photo: Rigamonti.

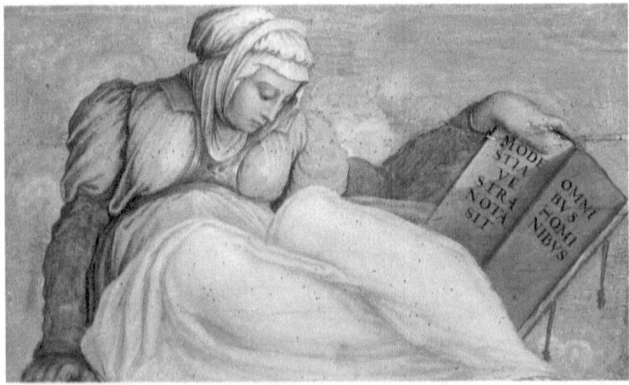

Fig. 16. Giorgio Vasari, *Modesty*, 1548, det.. Chamber of Abraham, Casa Vasari, Arezzo.

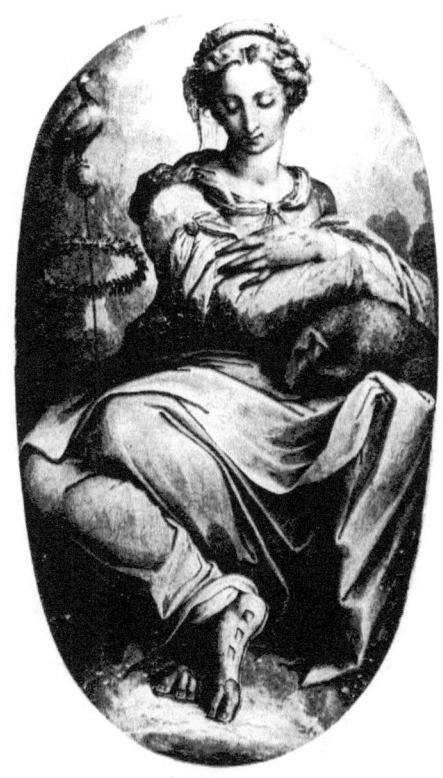

Fig. 17. Giorgio Vasari, *Modesty*, 1545, det., Refectory of Monteoliveto (Sant'Anna dei Lombardi), Naples.
Photo: Rigamonti.

Fig 18. Giorgio Vasari, Humility, 1545, det., Refectory of Monteoliveto (Sant'Anna dei Lombardi),Naples.
Photo: Rigamonti.

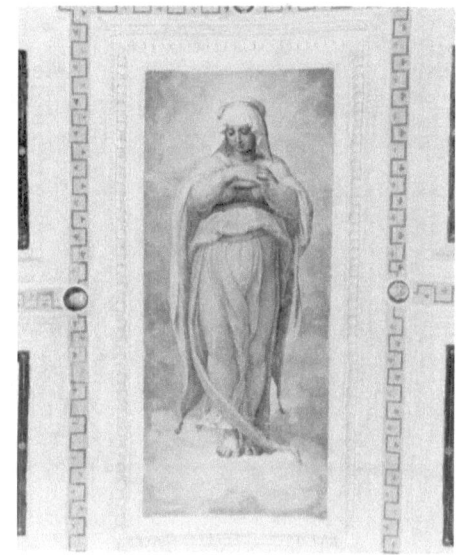

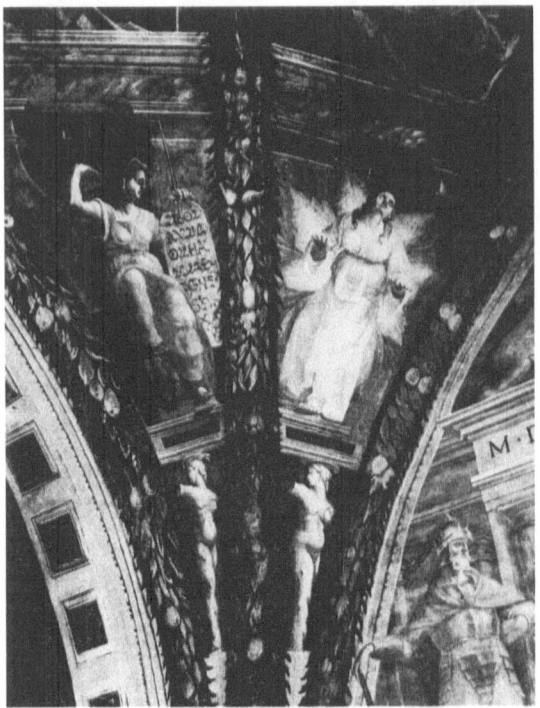

Fig. 19. Guglielmo Marcillat, *Law*, 1530, det., Nave, Cathedral of Arezzo, Arezzo. Photo: Gabinetto Fotografico Soprintendenza Beni Artistici Storici di Firenze.

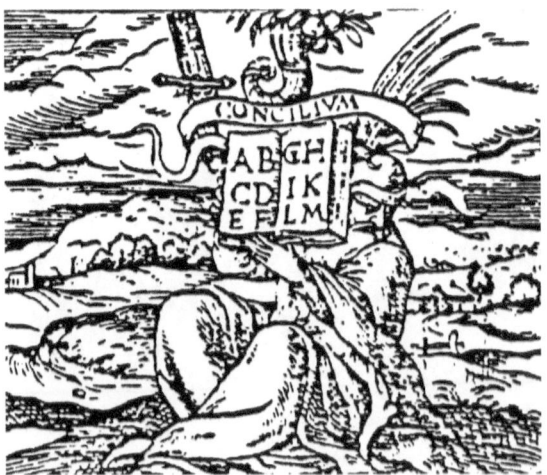

Fig. 20. Johannes Sambucus, *Consilium*, Emblem 30, *De Emblemate*, 1564 (Antwerp: Christopher Plantin).

# 9

# Giorgio Vasari's *Judith and Holofernes*: Athena or Aphrodite?[1]

*God has sent me to do things with thee at which the whole world
will be astonished.*
—Judith 11:16

The story of Judith and Holofernes has been a popular theme
for artists for many centuries, particularly, the sixteenth-century.
The story is taken from the Book of Judith from the Apocrypha:[2]
Nebuchadnezzar, who reigned over the Assyrians in Niveah, sent
his general, Holofernes, against the Jews, who had refused to help
him in his war against King Arphaxad of the Medes. Holofernes laid
siege to Bethulia, which blocked his route to Jerusalem and cut off
his water supply. Their chief priest, Ozia, persuaded its despairing
inhabitants to surrender. Judith, a beautiful and deeply religious
widow, arrives in Bethulia to assist her people and to present them
with a bold plan.

Abandoning her widow's sackcloth, Judith bathed and anointed
herself with rich perfume. She arranged her hair elaborately, tied it
with ribbons, and dressed in all her finery. She went with her maid,
Abra, to the enemy camp. She informed Holofernes that the Jews of
Bethulia had broken the laws of their God and were about to lose
His protection. She said she was his ally, and if he allowed her to
pray in private outside the camp every night she would help him
achieve victory over her people. Struck by her beauty and courage,
the Assyrian general agreed.

For three days and three nights, Judith prayed and ate the fruits and grains brought from her home. The next day, Holofernes invited her to have dinner with him. Trembling with passion, he ordered a feast for the two in which he consumed vast quantities of food and drank a great deal of wine.

After the banquet he lay sprawled on his bed, dead drunk. Taking advantage of this moment, alone in the tent with Holofernes, Judith quickly and cautiously reached for his sword. Drawing close to the bed, she gripped him by the hair, prayed for strength, and struck his neck twice with all her might and cut his head. Then wrapped it in the canopy of the couch, she hurried of the tent and gave the head to Abra, who put it in her food bag. The two women left the camp to pray, as they did every night, and walked through enemy lines back to Bethulia. There Judith stood on the city walls and showed the prized head of Holofernes to the Assyrians, who had already found his headless body and fled in terror when the Israelites attacked them. Judith sang a hymn of thanksgiving.

The Book of Judith became very popular in Jewish intellectual circles, as demonstrated by the elaboration of the midrashich literature from the Greek original writings. The tale's importance can be understood through the association with its midrasich literature and the struggle of the Hasnomeans against the Greeks and with the festival of Hanukkah by the Maccabes.[3]

Since biblical times and antiquity, an heroic parallelism was noted between Judas of Maccabeus, who had freed his Jewish people from the Greeks, and Judith, from the Assyrians. Judith was also affiliated with the Jewish heroes who had freed their people, including Samson, Jason, and David.[4] Her virtues of humility and heroism connected her with the founders of the Jewish nation, such as Moses and Aaron, and her name became identified with Israel.[5] Judith's trusts in Divine Providence and her willingness to be guided by God in order to save her people connects her with Abraham, whose faith and trust in God's demand for the sacrifice of his son, Isaac, made him a symbol of obedience to the Jewish people. Both figures became parental role models and mentors for their people–Abraham as father and Judith as mother.

In the visual arts, the story of Judith interested artists for many reasons and they interpreted it in a variety of ways. Through the centuries, the theme of Judith and Holofernes changed in terms of artistic representations, involving many different texts and voices, from the narrative or epic depiction to the single image. In the epic depiction the entire story from beginning to end was illustrated on one page, as seen in biblical texts of the Middle Ages, such as the Bible of Charles the Bald of 870, where the scenes of *Judith Departing Bethulia*, *Judith Before Holofernes* and *Judith Slaying Holofernes* were all depicted sequentially on one page.[6] During the Renaissance, this format changed to a selection from or fragment of the story: the decapitation (Donatello's *Judith and Holofernes*, 1456, in the Palazzo Vecchio, Florence, Fig. 1); placing the severed head in a sack or basket (Andrea Mantegna's drawing of *Judith and Her Slave* of 1491, Uffizi, Florence, Fig. 2; Correggio's *Judith* of 1512, Musée des Beaux-Arts, Strasbourg; Rosso's drawing of *Judith and Holofernes*, 1525, Los Angeles County Museum of Art; Parmigianino's etching of *Judith*, 1526, Rosenwald Collection, Washington, D.C.; and Paolo Veronese, *Judith*, 1570, Kunsthistorisches Museum, Vienna); standing on the severed head (Giorgione, *Judith*, 1504, Hermitage, Leningrad);[7] presenting the head to the viewer (Titian's *Judith* of 1516, Doria Pamphili Collection, Rome,[8] Lavinia Fontana's *Judith and Holofernes*, 1595, Museo Davia Bargellini, Bologna, and Hendrick Goltzius's engraving after Bartholomaeus Spranger, *Judith*, 1585 [B. III. 83.272]), and fondling the severed head (Lorenzo Sabatini's *Judith*, 1565, Carimonte Banca, Bologna).

The numerous visual interpretations can also be seen associated with the symbolic reference alluded to in the imagery of Judith. From the Middle Ages to the end of the sixteenth century, the story of Judith and Holofernes alluded to diametric concepts of virtue over vice: *virgo-virago, humilitas-superbi,; fortitudo-acedia, pudicita-libido* or *intellectus-luxuria,*[9] woman's beauty triumphant over a man's physical weakness; woman's mental strength over man's physical power; civic pride and patriotism over subjugation and domination. Throughout the Middle Ages, the portrayal of the spiritual combat between good and evil or the conflict between the virtues and vices was best illustrated in Prudentius' *Psychomachia*, whose enormous popularity rested on its illustrations as well inspirational text, since he was able to draw and compile in his manuscript the already established tradition of the allegorical interpretation of the Bible. Biblical commentaries and literary texts could best represent the human's spiritual conflict through abstract imagery such as personifications of virtues or vices–Judith as virtue and Holofernes as vice.

Since the Book of Judith was included in the canonical books of the Old Testament, the Christian typology of Judith became a prefiguration of Virgin Mary, as St. Bonaventura commented on the virtuous similarity between Mary and Judith for their fight against the Devil.[10] In part, this association can be found with the meaning of the name Bethulia or *betulah*, which in Hebrew means not only *virgin* but also an innocent and pure young woman.[11] In addition, the Hebrew word *betulah* was understood as *bêt éloah*, which meant the house of the Lord, that is the Temple in the Old Testament or the city of Jerusalem, a prototype in the New Testament for the Christian church. Judith not only represented Mary in that she is symbolically pure, but also prefigured her in the Bible. As Mary foreshadowed the Church and the New Testament, Judith, prefigured the synagogue and the Old Testament. Since the time of the Middle Ages, Judith as a symbol of virtue was considered a precedent for Mary, because she had defeated the villain, Holofernes, just as Mary had conquered the Devil, as illustrated in *Speculum humane salvationis*. [12] Judith in the Old Testament and Mary in the New Testament became the antitype of the victorious Church (*ecclesia*). This is best illustrated in *The Story of Judith and Lucifer's Fall* in the Pamplona Bible of 1200 Hamburg, where the two stories were paralleled.[13] The Devil fell at the exact moment that Judith offered the decapitate head of Holofernes to the Israelites of Bethulia.

Moreover, as all virtues were considered to be derived from the Church and all vices from the Devil, alluding to the conquest of virtue and vice, as Mary had conquered Satan with her chastity and humility, in the same manner that Judith had triumphed over Holofernes. His desire to conquer Bethulia, for personal gain of land and money, contrasted with Judith's charity. Although she stayed humble and chaste during her widowing, she sacrificed her chastity to save her people. Mary paralleled Judith's *humilitas* by accepting the incarnation and the sacrifice of her Son for the sake of Christianity.

Other allusions to Judith's virtue such as purity or humility are mentioned in the *Speculum virginum* from the twelfth century, where the figure of Judith is identified in the inscription *Humilitas* (Humility and Chastity) for her willingness to give up her household to save her people as she prayed for divine guidance.[14] In contrast, Holofernes symbolized *Superbia* (Pride and Avarice) for his wishes to conquer the Bethulia land and its richness.

During the Middle Ages, the importance of divine guidance during Judith's murderous action was constantly stressed in the biblical writings referring back to the Book of Judith. Of course, divine intervention can also be seen in other Hebrew stories, such as God's intervention during Abraham's sacrifice of Isaac and God's assistance in David's killing Goliath. All of them allude to God's guidance and protection for His chosen people. Thus, Judith became a personification of a multitude of virtues, such as chastity, obedience, prudence and fortitude, whose sword is an attribute that symbolized her adroitness.

In the Renaissance, it became popular to depict the story of Judith in a symbolic act rather than in epic narrative, selecting the aesthetic moment of suspension or "pregnant momement"[15] of the story when Judith, holding the sword high in the air, a symbolic gesture of victory, is about to strike Holofernes, as seen in Donatello's *Judith and Holofernes* of 1456 in Palazzo Vecchio, Florence (Fig. 1)[16] Ingeniously, Donatello departed from the artistic tradition not only by creating the aesthetic "pregnant moment," but also by narrating the epic story as a prolegomena to the execution in a series of reliefs at the base of the sculpture. The most important influences for Donatello's imagery were the Bible, Prudentius' *Psychomachia*, the Medici family as patrons, and the cultural history of Florence. Donatello adhered to the medieval symbolism of psychomachia–virtue (Judith) triumphing over vice (Holofernes)–as well as to the classical Renaissance tradition of Christianizing pagan myths–personifying the gods of antiquity Minerva as Wisdom or *Humilitas* in Judith and the Centaur as Ignorance or *Superbia* in Holofernes, as seen in Botticelli's *Minerva and The Centaur* of 1480 at the Uffizi. Using ancient statues and reliefs from the Medici collection for his monument, Donatello was promoting the artistic attitude of the Florentine and the Medici of the love for antiquity.[17]

Under the patronage of the Medici, Donatello raised the civic action and patriotism of Judith to another level of symbolism–she freed Bethulia as the Medici protected Florence. The Medici family presented a strong voice in the creation of Judith and Holofernes. Many of its motifs can be traced back to difficulties in the history of the family–their exile and their losses. The Medici struggle and survival paralleled the Florentine's endurance and victory in battles and wars. The general idea of virtue against vice or the strong of mind defeating the weak of heart became a metaphor for Florence's good government and civic patriotism.[18] This metaphor embraced other biblical images, such as David. Judith, like David, for the Florentine came to personify, heroism, freedom and the city of Florence.

Donatello introduced the perception of Judith as temptress who uses her feminine wiles to kill a man. He minimized the divine intervention and stressed instead the humanist and civic aspects of Judith's victory. The theme of a woman victorious over a man or killing a man, even an enemy, was disconcerting for the Hebrew people,[19] however, and for the Florentines as well. Paradoxically, although Judith heroically saved her people and their town, her heroism was not completely virtuous, because she had killed Holofernes through betrayal and seduction. However, virtuous and courageous Judith, like Mary, had trodden on evil–Judith's foot pressed on Holofernes' hand, Mary's on the serpent. Both had triumphed over vice.

Inspired by the medieval tradition, fifteenth and sixteenth century attributes focused on Judith's brutal action as symbols of justice and victory, as seen in Botticelli's diptych paintings of *Judith and Holofernes* of 1470-72 in the Uffizi; Andrea Mantegna's paintings and engravings of *Judith with the Head of Holofernes* of 1491 (Fig. 2), in the National Gallery of Art, Washington, D. C.; Michelangelo's *Judith and Holofernes*, 1509-11, a pendentive on the Sistine Chapel Ceiling, Vatican; Paolo Veronese's *Judith and Holofernes* of 1570 in the Musée des Beaux-Arts, Caen; and Lavinia Fontana's *Judith and Holofernes*, 1595, in the Oratorio del Ritiro di San Pellegrino, Bologna.

Michelangelo's pendentive in the Sistine Chapel Ceiling was coupled with the theme of *David and Goliath*. The moment selected by the artist is the flight from the camp after the decapitation. Her back to the viewer, Judith covers the severed head held on a platter by Abra, turning her face toward the open tent where Holofernes' body lies. By omitting the sword and its violent action, Michelangelo accentuates the completion of Judith's deed, and her fear rather than her heroic action.

By contrast, Giorgio Vasari's *Judith and Holofernes*, 1554, now in the Saint Louis Art Museum (Fig. 3), conceived Judith as an universal hero, or *heros-theos*, a term embodying all the characteristics and manifestations of *arete* and *virtù* associated with the pagan warrior and the Christian knight.[20] This association, grafted onto combined with the legendary story of Judith from the Apocrypha,[21] created a new image of Judith in sixteenth-century art.

According to Vasari's account books, he designed three versions of the story of Judith and Holofernes. The first version, now lost, was a small painting (one braccia or approximately twenty-five square inches) commissioned by Francesco Lioni, a Florentine merchant residing in Venice, and completed in 1541 when Vasari was visiting his friend Pietro Aretino, a satirist and virtuoso poet. Vasari describes this painting as "a Judith who cuts off the head of Holofernes while an old woman holds the severed head."[22]

Vasari's Saint Louis version was painted for Antonio Bracci of Florence in 1554.[23] In his *Ricordanze*, Vasari writes: "I remember that at the end of the year I finished one of those painted panels which shows a Judith who is cutting off the head of Holofernes, with life-size figures, which was given to Antonio Bracci. I requested a payment of twelve *scudi*."[24]

Only one drawing has survived of Vasari's third version of the Judith theme, located in the Graphic Farnesina Collection in Rome (Fig. 4). Its simplified composition, with soldiers, women, and children represented in the lower half of the work, suggested the connection of the painting this drawing with the Roman drawing.[25] The Roman pen-and-ink drawing with washes was recorded in a letter from Vincenzo Borghini in Poppiano to Vasari in Florence in 1564, in which he described it as "a sketch depicting Judith showing the head of Holofernes to her people."[26] A likely earlier drawing of 1561 is located in the Habich Kassel Collection.[27]

From Vasari's description of the Judith paintings and drawings, it is clear that the first or Lioni version was a conventional Quattrocento and Cinquecento depiction of the Judith story, showing Judith with her maid, Abra, as she places Holofernes' head in a sack or basket. Botticelli's painting of about 1470-72, in the Uffizi, is representative of the Quattrocento conception of Judith,[28] as is Mantegna's painting of 1491, in the National Gallery of Art, Washington, D.C., and his Uffizi and Dublin drawings of 1491,[29] and Michelangelo's Sistine Chapel Ceiling drawing and fresco of 1509-11.[30] Other similar treatments of the story include Parmigianino's etching of 1526 in the Rosenwald Collection, Philadelphia,[31] Lorenzo Sabatini's painting of 1565 in the Carimonte Banca, Bologna,[32] and Lavinia Fontana's painting of the 1595 in the Museo Davia Bargellini, Bologna.[33] In these examples, as in Vasari's depiction, her graceful physical beauty and fine clothes softened the image of Judith as a heroic and victorious woman. This new aesthetic quality–*pulcritudo* (beauty)– added to the imagery of Judith an implication of forgiveness, as physical beauty attested to spiritual beauty or innocence of the heart. In this manner, Judith's violent act was somehow excused as a necessary moral deed.[34] The moral tradition to hide a didactic meaning within a story and to explain human behavior was part of the antique culture and appropriated in Renaissance Neoplatonic philosophy.[35] By endowing mythological or historical characters with edifying meaning–Minerva as Prudence, Venus as Beauty– passions or comportments could be explained and understood.

In some Cinquecento representations of Judith and Holofernes– such as Barthel Beham's engravings of 1530, in the Rosenwald Collection, Washington, D.C.,[36] and Rosso Fiorentino's red chalk drawing of 1540 at the Los Angeles County Museum of Art (Fig 5)[37]–the image of Judith as a hero is even more disguised, if not completely negated, because she and her maid are portrayed naked. Judith's beautiful nude body and her feminine sexuality negate her heroic *virtù*. In these last Cinquecento examples, it is not Judith's *virtù* but her voluptuousness that has turned a moral act into a homicidal act; her sexuality leads the viewer to this interpretation.

The Cinquecento artists' desire to alter the meaning of Judith's story was also evident in Vasari's later versions, which were composed under the direction of Borghini's *invenzione*. In the first version, the Roman drawing ("a sketch depicting Judith showing the head of Holofernes to her people"),[38] Vasari represented a new image of Judith. This time she was not a voluptuous beauty but a victorious conqueror who presented the head of Holofernes to her Bethulian people and to his Assyrian soldiers. Perhaps Vasari's *invenzione* was meant to relate more closely to the familiar heroic or victorious representations of public heroes like David in his triumph over Goliath or even Perseus with the head of the Medusa.[39]

Vasari created a *publicly praised* Judith–someone whose significant acts were no longer confined to the private world of the home, the tent, or the bedroom. Vasari consciously embedded his Judith into a composition dependent on Raphael's tapestry cartoon depicting *Saint Paul Preaching to the Multitudes* of about 1515-20, now in the Victoria and Albert Museum, London. Vasari's Judith was not the Venus Pudica transformed into a vicious executioner by Albrecht Altdorfer, neither was she infected with a death-dealing sensuality, as seen in Bartholomeus Spranger's *Judith* (both engravings of about 1520-30 in the Rosenwald Collection, Washington, D.C.).

In the Cinquecento, depictions of Judith and Holofernes varied. Many emphasized female sexuality illustrated through the expressiveness of sheer beauty, both unclothed and clothed, as well as by the female virago and *pudica victrix* role.[40] In addition to the examples already cited here, other variations include Judith with the head of Holofernes, as in Barthel Beham's engraving of 1526 in the Rosenwald Collection, Washington, D.C., which shows a clothed, pregnant Judith holding the cut-off head–a most unusual depiction of the chaste Judith. Hans Beham's engraving of 1547, also in the Rosenwald Collection, Washington, D.C., depicted a nude Judith seated at a window contemplating the severed head of Holofernes. The Latin caption above her head states: "The Lord has taken away the head of Holofernes by the hand of Judith,"[41] as if her voluptuousness and beauty were the primary means of her heroic act. Perhaps the most astonishing representation of Judith was Barthel Beham's engraving of 1525, also in the Rosenwald Collection, Washington, D.C., showing a nude, sensuous, angry Judith seated on the naked body of Holofernes holding a sword and his severed head.[42] In these later examples, Judith's sexuality became as alluring as her violence, repulsive. Her virago figure as a Mannerist conceit combined the sensuality of the female body with the assumed heroic *virtú* of the male figure.[43]

In these representations, there was a clear connection between the association of the female sexuality with the depiction of her body or clothing. In the Renaissance, according to Anne Hollander, "the compartmentalized conception of feminine nudity came from perceiving women's bodies in relation to a visually compelling style of dress," or the powerful suggestion of removed clothing, which gave the nude image its erotic force as well as its power.[44] This sexual paradox of dressed or undressed female body representations in sixteenth-century paintings were generated from the classical and mythological response to female beauty and action, as invested in Athena (Minerva) wearing a military armor over a flowing *himatia* veiling her feminine body and representing a heroic male body. By contrast, Aphrodite (Venus) can be seen undressed or nude, alluding to female revilement and the power of seduction through sight, while Athena's power of seduction was through action. These representations of Judith, obviously combined the classical mythological tradition with Renaissance religious interpretation of a heroine.

Consistent with Cinquecento artists's desire to find new ways of interpreting old themes, Vasari presented an inventive conception of Judith in the Saint Louis painting. His figure appears as a Mannerist *concetto* (conceit) that combined the sensuality of the beautiful female body (Aphrodite-Venus) with the assumed heroic *virtú* implied by women endowed with the male trait of heroism (Athena-Minerva). Vasari's *concetto* was based on his adroitness on fusing classical mythology with Judeo-Christian iconography, as promoted in Renaissance Neoplatonic philosophy.[45] This intellectual ability was manifested in the visual representations of Vasari's paintings, as in *Judith and Holofernes*. His image of Judith was unlike most of the faithful, conservative, and passive virago representations of the Quattrocento or Cinquecento depictions, for he portrayed Judith as a beautiful, strong woman in an active male role. The ambiguity of male/female imagery in Vasari's Judith was unsurpassed in his century.

Vasari selected to depict the most dramatic moment in the story of Judith–when the young widow from Bethulia, beautifully dressed, enters the tent of the drunk Holofernes. She seized him by the hair with her right hand, wielding a sword in her left to strike and sever his head. Furthermore, Judith, as paradigm of a hero, is paradoxically portrayed by Vasari as Aphrodite-Venus with feminine qualities such as beauty and sensuality—aesthetic elements highly admired by Maniera painters—and as an Athena-Minerva figure as well, empowered with manly attributes. Judith's attire evokes both eroticism and prudishness. A decorated and mainly cuirass of classical armor articulating the parts of upper body, like the late armors worn by military men, evokes sexual allure. In contrast, Judith's long skirt and triple girdle of chastity with an elaborate metal belt denote her modesty.[46] The arrangement of her braided hair, with a scarf intertwined through its tresses, created a helmet shape as well as a veiled beret, again alluding to a defined Vasarian depiction of Judith in an ambivalent sexual role, through her attire as well as through her action.[47]

In this new, complex interpretation, Vasari transformed Judith's female sexuality, endowing it with the potency of a male hero, and she manifested a desexualized valor that transcends gender. Vasari's figure combined the images of Athena-Minerva and possibly even Hercules, incorporating their symbolic associations with the virtues of courage, fortitude, and wisdom. Hiss Judith as Athena, in her valiant purposefulness devoid of what Elena Ciletti called "feminine wiles,"[48] stood for the Maniera concept of *virtù*- -under the guidance of Fortune, the imitation and assimilation of ancient moral actions and good deeds for humankind and God.[49]

Vasari's conception of Judith as a universal hero, or *heros-theos*, was unprecedented in the art of the Cinquecento and derived much from his familiarity with types of Roman sarcophagi, such as the Amazonomachy Sarcophagus of 230, in the Museo Pio Clementino in the Vatican (Fig. 6), and the Amazonomachy Sarcophagus of 3rd century in the Archeological Museum of Thessalonica, Greece (Fig. 7).[50] The depiction of a heroic Judith has its roots in part in Vasari's knowledge of the legendary Amazons, and from his familiarity with such works as the Medicean sarcophagus depicting an Amazonomachy of 180-190 A.D.[51] *Amazon* is a Greek for the powerful woman with one breast from Cappadocia, which, perhaps significantly, was also the birthplace of Holofernes. According to the legend, Amazons amputated their breasts to facilitate physical mobility as well as self-protection during battle.[52] The ancient Amazon and the biblical Judith embodied female beauty and heroism. Judith's heroism is an example of a Christian Amazon or *virago*.

In "Virgo et Virago," Margaret King defines *virago* as a "female military hero who achieves equivalence, or indeed eminence, in the world by becoming not a greater woman, but, as it were, a man (vir)."[53] Judith's physical and spiritual beauty represented both a threat and a lure for Holofernes because like the Amazons, she chose to defy, even deny, her own sexuality (widowhood). Furthermore, she risked a permanent blemish (loss of her chastity) in order to dispatch the enemy of her people.[54] Dismemberment is a form of both disintegration and reintegration in the action of Judith, where the mutilation or decapitation occurred as a moral sacrifice in defense of Bethulia, as well as her spiritual sacrifice to offer her sexual services to Holofernes in order to save her people. (Judith, then, becomes a prefiguration of Christ.

The bond between the ancient Amazon and the biblical Judith was deeper than imagined. Like the Amazon, Judith yielded to physical dismemberment for heroic reasons.[55] Both were symbols of fortitude and human strength, and both were triumphant liberators. Judith was especially valiant because she was a widow acting alone. Both surfaced out of a mythical tradition in order to explain sources of conflict and tension in the social order and human condition of their respective patriarchal society–Athens and Bethulia.

According to William Blake Tyrrell, the Greek mythical culture for categorizing male and female roles depended on three mythmaking motivations as well as sexual conflicts: one focused on the male, as a symbol for culture, superiority and normality; the second, for the opposite, the female, which denoted whatever is not valued by men–nature, inferiority, chaos, and abnormality; and the third, the feminine, combined a mediation between male/female and culture/nature.[56] For the mythical tradition, the feminine fused positive aspects of female nature such as physical and mental strength that were similar to male culture and valued by men, such as courage, astuteness and heroism. However, the negative aspects of the female nature–of course, similar to men but not viewed as such in the mythical culture–such as her seduction and self-gratifying sexuality, were feared by men because of her potential to destroy them.

Vasari sought to visualize these iconographical implications by searching for antique representations of male/female heroes as well as Quattrocento or Cinquecento interpretations or sources for a seductress Herculean Judith. In Antonio Pollaiuolo's *Hercules and the Hydra* of about 1460-75, now at the Uffizi, he found an image that he greatly admired for its vitality: "Truly a marvelous thing, particularly the serpent, the coloring of which is so vividly done, and so appropriately, that it is impossible that anything could be more lively."[57] Hercules served as a pagan guardian of Florence, just as David served as a Christian guardian.

Another Hercules known to Vasari was Caraglio's 1525 engraving after Rosso's drawing of *Hercules Fighting Cacus*, in the Bibliothèque Nationale, Paris, (Fig. 8). The biographer of the *Lives* admired this work because "the print revealed an energetic response to the Roman and pagan artistic milieu."[58] Vasari's knowledge of classical literature and his immersion in Florentine and Roman humanism provided him with a subtle understanding of the myth of Hercules, whose very name meant force.[59] In Euripides's *Alcesti*, Herakles force was described as mute and within himself.[60] Euripides commented on how Herakles achieved this force by speaking to his vigorous arm.[61] The power of Hercules was concentrated in the arm of the hero.

In the Saint Louis painting, Vasari invested the force of Hercules in his Judith as she looked toward her left hand, which pulls Holofernes' hair, while in her right hand she courageously held the deadly weapon. The beautifully exposed nude arm of Vasari's *Judith* can be compared to the nude leg in Giorgione's *Judith* of 1504, in the Hermitage, Leningrad, in both cases alluding to the old notion of strength.[62]

While looking at her arm, Judith gazes at the image on the medallion on her cuirass in which stands the figure of Athena, holding her lance and shield. The wise war goddess protected heroes like Hercules by helping then outwit their enemies. By depicting Athena-Minerva on Judith's cuirass, Vasari implied that wisdom and power will assist the woman in her heroic act.[63]   A classical source for Vasari's image of Minerva  was found in the Hellenistic bronze of the third century BCE discovered in Arezzo in 1541 (now in the Museo Archeologico of Arezzo, Fig. 9). Vasari likely was familiar with the Roman copy of the first century found in the Museo Archeologico in Florence, which was even known to Botticelli, who drew it in 1480.[64] Other possible Renaissance sources include coins, gems, and Tarot cards depicting *Philosophia* or Athena, for example, Mantegna's Tarot card of *Athena* or *Philosophia*, 1490, in the British Museum, London, and drawings, such as Mantegna's *Judith and Her Slave*, 1491, now at the Uffizi, which Vasari owned (Fig. 2).[65]

Traditionally, Vasari's depiction of Judith seen from the back has been associated with Michelangelo's *Libyan Sibyl* of 1509-11, on the Sistine Chapel Ceiling, both artists appropriating the imagery from the Torso Belvedere.[66] However, the most obvious source of inspiration for the entire composition of the Saint Louis painting was Rosso's *Moses Defending the Daughters of Jethro*, about 1523-24, at the Uffizi (Fig. 10).[67] It is not by  mere accident that Vasari assimilated Rosso's Herculean Moses for the representation of Judith.  From his early career onward, Vasari sought Rosso's advice and assistance, so once again in the Saint Louis Judith, Vasari relies on his teacher's art to create a new and powerful image.

Vasari's familiarity with traditional Renaissance representations of Judith, associating her with Florentine civic humanism, with moral implications of Neoplatonism, as well as with the medieval *psychomachia* and classical mythmaking, assisted him in creating a Judith who expressed the very meaning of the word "Jewess." The heroine symbolized Israel's faith and spirit.  For Vasari, Judith was a strong and resourceful individual as well as womanly, beautiful, and sensual.

In the Saint Louis painting, Vasari also intended to make an emblematic analogy between Judith and Moses, both whom had the task of freeing their people, and both of whom struggled to abide by the law of God.  These two Old Testament figures believed in God's commitment to the Jewish people and in their own ability to achieve victory and freedom for God's chosen people.

Vasari composed an image of Judith that combines two conceits.

When the Vasari *Judith* is viewed in the role of Athena, Hercules, and Moses, she personifies fortitude, courage, wisdom and freedom. In this instance, Vasari allows Judith to adopt a male model of moral and physical strength. However, Vasari's Judith does not discard Aphrodite or associations with idealized female beauty or with the chastity of the virgin-widow and even with charity–the gift of the widow who wills to sacrifice her body and her honor for the sake of her people. As a result, the Vasari's Judith personifies a Mannerist *psychomachia* of a heroine-goddess–Athena-Aphrodite.[68] A finely-tuned paradox revealing a quintessential Mannerist conceit.[69] Thus, Vasari's various depictions of Judith and his reliance on ancient and contemporary sources to work out this evolving image created a new iconography in representing the story of Judith in Cinquecento art.

## Notes

1. This article is based on "Giorgio Vasari's *Judith*: Athena or Aphrodite," *Fifteenth Century Studies Journal*, Vol 25 (2000), 154-92. A research grant from the University of Massachusetts Lowell made this study possible. It greatly benefited from the numerous comments and observations of Profs. Jane Aiken, Virginia Technology University; Yael Even, University of Missouri at Saint Louis; and William C. McDonald, University of Virginia.

2. I have relied on the Oxford Bible and its commentaries in considering the theme. This book was originally written in Hebrew, but only the fourth-century Greek versions have survived. In the Christian Church, it was known to Clement of Rome, and this version was also consulted in the Renaissance. It is not the intent of this presentation to discuss historical, philosophical, theological or archeological controversies related to the book of Judith. See M. Jack Suggs, Katharine Doob Sakenfeld, and James R. Mueller, ed., *The Oxford Study Bible: Revised English Bible with the Apocrypha* (London/New York: Oxford University Press, 1992), 1071-86. See also Bruce Metzer, ed. *The Oxford Annotated Apocrypha* (New York: Oxford University Press, 1977) and JCJ. Metford, *Dictionary of Christian Lore and Legend* (London: Thames & Hudson, 1983), 151-52.

3. Gabrielle Sed-Rajna, *The Hebrew Bible* (New York: Rizzoli, 1987), 148.

4   Mira Friedman, "The Metamorphoses of Judith," in *Jewish Art*, 5, 12-23 (1986): 231, for an informative study on the early representations of the story of Judith.

5.  Ibid., 225.
6.  See also the Catalan Bibles of Rhoda Ripoll and Arsenal Bible (ms 11639 and ms 2626 in the British Museum, London) and the Jerusalem Bible (from the Rothschild Miscellany, MS. 180, Jerusalem, Israel Museum of 1470-80 in Ferrara).
7.  Serena Romano, "Giuditta e il Fondaco dei Tedeschi," in *Giorgione la cultura veneta tra '400 e '500: Mito, Allegoria, Analisis iconologica* (Rome: De Luca, 1981), 103-25, for an excellent iconographic study on the story of Judith, particularly as it relates to the Venetian depictions of Judith in Giorgione, Titian and Catena, and the relationship of the Venetian Judith as a symbol of Justice.
8.  Paul Jonnides, "Titian's *Judith* and its context: The Iconography of Decapitation," presents a discussion on the concept of the trencher or plate symbol of offering and trophy, and the correlation between the image and iconography of Judith with Salome.
9.  Jennifer O'Reilly, *Studies in the Iconography of the Virtues and Vices* (London: Garland Publishing, Inc. 1988), 10. This study on Prudentius' *Pyschomachia* explains the medieval cultural framework and imagery of good and evil. Throughout the middle ages, the enormous popularity of Prudentius' work rested in its illustrations as well inspiration.
10. F. L. Cross, *The Oxford Dictionary of the Christian Church* (Oxford: Oxford University Press, 1983), 186.
11. Friedman, "The Metamorphoses of Judith," 225.
12. See the miniature of *Mary Conquers the Devil and Judith Decapitates Holofernes* in *Le Miroir de l'humanine Salvation*, Chapter XXX, MS. 40, fol. 30 verso, Newberry Library, Chicago, and another version in MS. Fr. 139, Musée Condé, Chantilly. See also Figs. 9 and 11 of Judith as *Humilitas* in Herrade de Landsberg, *Speculum Virginum* sec. 12, Zwettl MS. 180, fol. 45 (MS. 44 Arundel fol. 34, British Museum Library, London) and Judith and Mary in *Speculum Humanae Salvationis*, sec. 14 (no location cited), in Serena Romano, "Giuditta di Leningrado," in *Giorgione la cultura veneta tra '400 e '500: Mito, Allegoria, Analisis iconologica* (Rome: De Luca 1981), 103-104.
13. Collection L.E.K. Fürst von Oettingen Wallersterin. MS. I. 2, lat. 4, 15, fol. 168r. See illustration Fig. 11 in Friedman, "The Metamorphoses of Judith," 233.
14. Adolf Katzenellenbogen, *Allegories of the Virtues and Vices in Medieval Art* (New York: W. W. Norton & Company, 1964), 57, and R. Tuve, "Notes on the Virtues and Vices," *Journal of the Warburg Institute* (1964), 44-72. See *Speculum virginum*, twelfth-century manuscript (MS. Arundel 44, fol. 34v, British Museum Library, London), for an illustration of the scene.
15. Marvin Levich, ed. *Aesthetics and the Philosophy of Criticism* (New York:

Random House, 1963), 31, for a discussion of theory of painting in Gotthold Ephraim Lessing's *Laocoön*. In a painting, the "pregnant moment" is experienced by perceiving in a single instance the coexisting visual elements of the composition thus easily apprehending what preceded and what follows.

16. H. W. Janson, *The Sculpture of Donatello* (Princeton: Princeton University Press, 1957), 198-296. Other Florentine Renaissance sculptors also represented Judith, such as Ghiberti's Judith of 1450 in the left-hand area of the East Doors of the Baptistery and Antonio Pollaioulo's *Judith*, 1455, in the Detroit Institute of Art. What is unusual about Pollaioulo's bronze statue is that the figure of Holofernes was omitted and Judith stood holding a sword in her raised arm. See Samuel Sachs II and Edmund P. Pillsbury, ed., *Italian Renaissance Sculpture in the Time of Donatello* (Detroit: Detroit Institute of Art, 1985), 99-201.

17. Other visual sources for classical reference may have been sarcophagi reliefs depicting bacchanals, such as the *Frenzied Maenad*, stucco relief, first century A. D. in the Basilica Sotterranea di Porta Maggiore. See Friedman, "The Metamorphoses of Judith," p. 246, nn. 78 and 79, Fig. 30.

18. Christine Sperling, "Donatello's Bronze *David* and the Demands of the Medici politics," *The Burlington Magazine* 134 (April 1992), for variations on these ideas, see Yael Even, "The Loggia dei Lanzi," *Woman's Art Journal* (Spring/Summer 1991), 10-14; Yael Even, "Mantegna's Uffizi Judith: The Masculination of the female Hero," *Konsthistorisk Tidsskrift* 61 (December 1992), 1-13; Mary Garrad, *Artemisa Gentileschi* (Princeton: Princeton University Press, 1989), 285-297; and, James Vanderkam, ed., *No One Spoke Ill of Her: Essays on Judith* (Atlanta, GA: Scholars Press, 1992).

19. Suggs, et al., *The Oxford Bible*, Book of Judith 13:16, 1083: "The Lord has struck him down by a woman's hand." To be struck down by a woman's hand was the ultimate disgrace for a warrior.

20. Here, I am using Pindar's meaning of hero and god or hero-god. See Pindar, *Third Neman*, 22, cited in Yves Bonnefoy, ed., *Greek and Egyptian Mythology* (Chicago: University of Chicago Press, 1992), 180.

21. See n. 2.

22. "Apresso si mando a detto Francesco Lioni un quadro di un bracchio per ogni verso. Drentovi una mezza figura, che era una Judit, che aveva tagliato la testa a Oloferne; e drentovi una vecchia, che teneva la testa del morto tagliata." Karl Frey, "Le Ricordanze di Giorgio Vasari," in *Der Literarische Nachlass Giorgio Vasari*, 3 vols. (Munich, 1930), 2, App., 858.

23. Giorgio Vasari's *Judith and Holofernes* (oil on panel, cm 108 x 80 or 42 1/2 x 31 1/2 in.), was acquired by the Saint Louis Art Museum in 1982 (inv. 12.1982). The museum purchased it through Colnaghi in London,

which obtained it from a private collector in England. Antonio Bracci was a Florentine for whom Vasari had previously painted two portraits (locations unknown), and later in 1557 a *Cupid and Psyche* in the Gemäldegalerie Staatliche Museen, Berlin. He is listed among Vasari's correspondents, and when the artist and his family moved from Arezzo to Florence early in 1555, Vasari likely delivered *Judith and Holofernes* to him. See D. Colnaghi, *Italian Paintings: 1550-1780* (London: P. & D. Colnaghi & Co. Ltd, 1976), entry 1. See Nora W. Desloge and Laura Lewis Mieyer, "Italian Paintings and Sculpture," *Saint Louis Art Museum Bulletin* (Winter 1988), 43-45.

24. "Riccordo, come al fine dell anno (1554) fini un di que quadri bozati; che vera dentro una Judit, che tagliava la testa a Oloferne, grande quanto il naturale, che si dono a messer Antonio Bracchi. Mando a donar argenti per 12 scudi." Frey, "Ricordanze," App., 871, and Alessandro del Vita, *Il Libro delle Ricordanze di Giorgio Vasari* (Rome, 1938), Carta 21, 73.

25. See Vincenzo Borghini 's letters to Giorgio Vasari of August 14 and 17, 1564, quoted in Frey, "Ricordanze," 100-102 and 105-6. In the first letter, Borghini described the biblical subject to Vasari: "In questa fara l'historia di Giudit che e semplice e piana; et queste historie bisogna che favellino senza lingua et esprimino quel fatto che segui il meglio et più naturalmente che si puo." See also Alessandro Cecchi, "Vasari, Naldini e la 'Giuditta'," *Paragone*, 28 (1977), 100-107, Figs. 61-64. The Farnesina drawing is located in the Istituto Nazionale per la Grafica, inv. FC12419, Rome.

26. Frey, "Le Ricordanze." See Borghini to Vasari, August 3, 1564, 89-90. "Vi ricordo quel poco di schizzo di Judit, che mostra la testa d'Oloferne al popolo." According to Borghini, Vasari executed this drawing to assist his fellow artist, Battista Naldini, in executing a painting on the same subject commissioned by the Prior of Arezzo.

27. See Cecchi, "Vasari, Naldini e la 'Giuditta'", 100-103, Fig. 61, for the Vasari's drawing in the Habich Kassel Collection.

28. See Elena Ciletti, "Patriarchal Ideology in the Renaissance Iconography of Judith," in *Refiguring Woman: Perspectives on Gender and the Italian Renaissance*, ed. Marilyn Migiel and Juliana Schiesari (Ithaca: Cornell University Press, 1991), 35-70.

29. See Yael Even, "Mantegna's Uffizi *Judith:*," 8-20. In his collection, Vasari had a drawing of Mantegna, *Judith and Her Slave* of 1491 (now at the Uffizi); it is unclear, however, whether the Uffizi drawing is the same one. See Licia Ragghianti Collobi, *Il Libro de' Disegni del Vasari* (Florence: Vallecchi, 1974), 84, Fig. 232, for a discussion of the drawing attribution. In his *Il Libro de' Disegni*, Vasari commented on a Mantegna's *Judith and Her Slave*: "Nel nostro libro e in un mezzo foglio reale un disegno di

mano d'Andrea finito di chiaroscuro, nel quale è una Judit che mette nella tasca d'una schiava mora la testa di Oloferne, fatto d'un chiaroscuro non piú usato, avendo egli lasciato il foglio bianco, che serve per il lume della biacca tanto nettamente, che visi veggono i capegli sfilati e le altre sottigliezze." See also Jane Martineau, ed., *Andrea Mantegna* (Milan: Olivetti/Electa, 1992), 435-44.

30. I believe that the drawing of *Judith and Holofernes* of 1509-11 (FD1036, in the Collección de Dibujos Italianos, Museo del Prado, Madrid), is likely a Michelangelo's study for the fresco painting. See Mira Friedman, "The Metamorphoses of Judith," 225-46.
31. H. Diane Russell with Bernadine Barnes, *Eve/Ave: Woman in the Renaissance and Baroque Prints* (Washington, D.C.: National Gallery of Art, 1990), 63.
32. M. Scolaro, *Carimonte. La raccolta d'arte* (Bolonga: Carimonte Banca, Spa, 1993), 24. Sabatini depicted a brutal and erotic scene where the Holofernes dismembered body can be viewed through the canopy of the tent while Judith triumphantly gazed at the viewer. With her right hand, she held the sword erect as a banner, while caressing the soft beard of the severed head with her left. The objects of victory–helmet, cut-off head, sword–were placed on a table in the tent as trophies and still-life decorations of success. The apprehension of the barbaric and voyeuristic depiction of the scene parallels contemporary Surrealist paintings.
33. Maria Teresa Cantaro, *Lavinia Fontana bolognese: "pittora singolare" 1552-1614* (Milan: Jandi Sapi Editori, 1989), 197 and Vera Fortunati, *Lavinia Fontana: 1552-1614* (Milan: Electa, 1994), 204-5.
34. Edgar Wind, *Pagan Mysteries in the Renaissance* (New York: W. W. Norton & Company, 1958), 73, for a discussion of the Neoplatonic definition of Love (*Pulchritudo-Amor-Voluptas or Castitas-Pulchritudo-Amor*): "Love is Passion aroused by Beauty" or "Beauty is Love combined with Chastity."
35. Jean Seznec, *The Survival of the Pagan Gods* (Princeton: Princeton University Press, 1972), 86.
36. Russell with Barnes, *Eve/Ave*, 64-66.
37. Eugene Carroll, *Rosso Fiorentino: Drawings, Prints, and Decorative Arts* (Washington, D. C.: National Gallery of Art, 1988), 364.
38. Frey, "Le Ricordanze." See Borghini to Vasari, August 3, 1564, 89-90. "Vi ricordo quel poco di schizzo di Judit, che mostra la testa d'Oloferne al popolo."
39. See Yael Even, "The Loggia dei Lanzi: A Showcase of Female Subjugation," *Woman's Art Journal* 12 (Spring/Summer 1991), 10-14.
40. The purpose of this paper is not to survey or focus on the Renaissance models of virago and *pudica victrix* images as seen in heroines such as

Artemisia, Diana, Lucretia, Agatha, Mary Magdalene, or the Virgin Mary.. or female warriors of the Western lore. Future study needs to be done on this subject. See Margaret L. King, "Virgo et Virago," *Women of the Renaissance* (Chicago: University of Chicago, 1991).

41. Quoted in Russell with Barnes, *Eve/Ave,* 68.
42. See ibid., 67.
43. I am using the term conceit here, or *concetto,* in the Panofskian manner. See Erwin Panofsky, *Idea: A Concept in Art Theory* (Columbia: University of South Carolina Press, 1968).
44. Anne Hollander, *Seeing Through Clothes* (Berkeley, CA: University of California Press, 1993), 215. See also the following chapters on "Nudity," 83-156, and on "Undress," 157-236, and Jonathan Sawday, *The Body Emblazoned: Dissecting and the Human Body in Renaissance Culture* (London: Routledge, 1995), 16-22, for a discussion on the unity of the body and soul and the revelation of the struggle for the body to house the desire of the soul.
45. Liana De Girolami Cheney, *Botticelli's Neoplanotic Images* (Potomac Park, MD: Scripta Humanistica, 1993), 27-33.
46. Hollander, *Seeing Through Clothes,* 214-16, 266 and 472, and Nora W. Desloge, "Italian Paintings and Sculpture," 44.
47. For a discussion of the symbolism of hair in biblical times see Veda Cobb-Stevens, "Speech, Gesture and Women's Hair in the Gospel of Luke and First Corinthians," in *The Symbolism of Vanitas in the Arts, Literature, and Music,* ed. Liana De Girolami Cheney (New York/London: The Edwin Mellen Press, 1989), 315-51, and Liana De Girolami Cheney, "Locks, Tresses, and Manes in Pre-Raphaelite and Victorian Paintings," in *Pre-Raphaelitism and Medievalism in the Arts* (New York/London: The Edwin Mellen Press, 1992), 159-93.
48. Ciletti, "Patriarchal Ideology," 52.
49. See Mario Bonfantini, ed. *Opere di Niccolò Machiavelli* (Milan: Riccardo Riccardi, 1963), 497-508. "Non ci può essere utile imitazione degli esempi antichi senza adeguata preparazione morale; e ancora, la *virtù* di un uomo siffatto non potrà farsi valere senza la opportuna occasione, che `e dalla *fortuna.*"
50. See Phyllis Pray Bober and Ruth Rubinstein, *Renaissance Artists and Antique Sculpture* (New York: Oxford University Press, 1986), 186, no. 153, and 175-80, nos. 139-141.
51. William Blake Tyrrell, *Amazons: A Study in Athenian Mythmaking* (Baltimore, MD: The Johns Hopkins University Press, 1984), xv. See Bober and Rubinstein, 177, no. 140.
52. No ancient images represent the Amazons without a breast. This is because of a sense of decorum, the horror of a woman without a breast, or

is it because of the Greek aesthetic concept of the idealized. See Liana De Girolami Cheney, "The Cult of Saint Agatha," *Woman's Art Journal*, XVII (Spring/Summer, 1996), 3-10, and Mareily Yalom, *A History of the Breast* (New York: Alfred A. Knopf, 1997).

53. Margaret L. King, "Virgo et Virago," *Women of the Renaissance* (Chicago: University of Chicago, 1991), 192.

54. Giual Sissa, *Greek Virginity*, trans. Arthur Goldhammer (Cambridge: Harvard University Press, 1990), 87-104. Sexuality and virginity were compatible in ancient times only if sexual activity remained secret. In the case Judith talked to her people and asked them not to interfere, but to trust her actions.

55. Caroline Walker Bynum, *The Resurrection of the Body in Western Christianity, 200-1336* (New York: Columbia University, 1995), for a discussion on this topic.

56. Tyrrell, *Amazons: A Study in Athenian Mythmaking*, xv. This scholar eloquently explains Greek mythmaking through sexual polarization.

57. Gaetano Milanesi, *Le opere di Giorgio Vasari: con nuove annotazioni e commenti*, 9 vols. (Florence 1878-85), 3, 294 (to be noted in this text as *Vasari-Milanesi*). When reversing Pollaiuolo's image, it is obvious that Vasari assimilated the Herculean act, which must have fascinated him because he also employed it in other later paintings, such as the warrior figure in the fresco of the Sala Regia, Rome. See Philipp Fehl, "Vasari's Extirpation of the Huguenots," *Gazette des Beaux-Arts* 84 (1974), 257-83. Furthermore, in his *Libro de' Disegni*, Vasari collected several drawings on this theme by artists such as Bartolomeo Ammannati, Baccio Bandinelli and Domenico Beccafumi. See Collobi, *Il Libro de' Disegni*, 282, 235, and 231, respectively, for illustrations of these images. In addition, Vasari provided drawings for Cristofano Gherardi for his painting on the Hercules theme in the Palazzo Vecchio (see Paola Barocchi, *Complementi al Vasari Pittore* (Florence: Leo S. Olschki Editore, 1964), 269-79.

58. Vasari-Milanesi, 1878, 5:424, and Carroll, *Rosso Fiorentino*, 75-86.

59. Bonnefoy, ed., *Greek and Egyptian Mythology*, 181.

60. Richard Lattimore, trans., *"Alcesti," Euripides* I, ed. David Grene and Richard Lattimore (Chicago: University of Chicago Press, 1955), 52.

61. Lattimore, *"Alcesti,"* 40-41.

62. Hollander, *Seeing Through Clothes*, 216.

63. In previous paintings, to symbolize strength and audacity, Vasari decorated personifications of Fortitude and Courage with military cuirasses like the one seen on Judith. See Liana De Girolami Cheney, "Vasari and Naples: The Monteoliveto Order," *Papers in Art History by Pennsylvania University Press* 5 (1994), 48-126.

64. Botticelli's drawing of *Minerva* is located at the Uffizi, inv. 201E.
65. See nn. 10 and 25. Furthermore, the association of Judith with Athena was emphasized by the fact that they both act as wise women whose skillful and persuasive powers orchestrated freedom for their people. For example, Athena assisted the Greeks in conquering the Trojans by suggesting the offer of a gift–the horse. Similarly, Judith helped the Israelites overcome the Assyrians by offering her body. Because of their moral and deliberate actions Athena and Judith personified wisdom or illustrate the emblem of *Philosophia*. It is interesting to note that Vasari's image anticipates Cesare Ripa's emblem on *Philosophia*. See Cesare Ripa, *Iconologia* (Padua, 1618), 126.
66. Liana De Girolami Cheney, "Giorgio Vasari and Antiquity," paper delivered at the International Society for the Classical Tradition, Boston University, March 8-10, 1995. In this presentation (and forthcoming article), I discussed here the impact of the Torso Belvedere in Vasari's work, in particular in the personification of the arts that frame the artist's portraits in the *Vite* of 1568. Of note, the Torso Belvedere came from the antique collection of Vasari. See Francis Haskell and Nicholas Penny, *Taste and the Antique* (London: Yale University Press, 1981), 312.
67. In the depiction of the figure with the exposed breast, the Roman type of Amazonomachy sarcophagi likely influenced Rosso's imagery.
68. Sissa, *Greek Virginity*, 73-86, and Edgar Wind, *Pagan Mysteries in the Renaissance* (New York: Oxford University Press, 1980), 75, 200, and 203 for the concept of *venus-virgo*.
69. Vasari's ambiguous *desexualization* of Judith manifests the Italian Maniera style as well as his assimilation of the Quattrocento and Cinquecento conventions of Donatello, Botticelli, Mantegna, Michelangelo, Parmigianino, Rosso, Titian, and later Lavinia Fontana, and Veronese. Furthermore, Vasari's new *psychomachia* of Judith, in which the virile and violent act dominated the scene, anticipated the representations of Judith in Phillippe Galle's engraving of 1610 (after Maerten van Hemmskerck) for the book *The Fatal Power of Women*, 1610. See also the representation on this topic by Michelangelo Caravaggio, Artemisia Gentileschi, Fedele Galizia, and Elizabetta Sirani during the Baroque period.

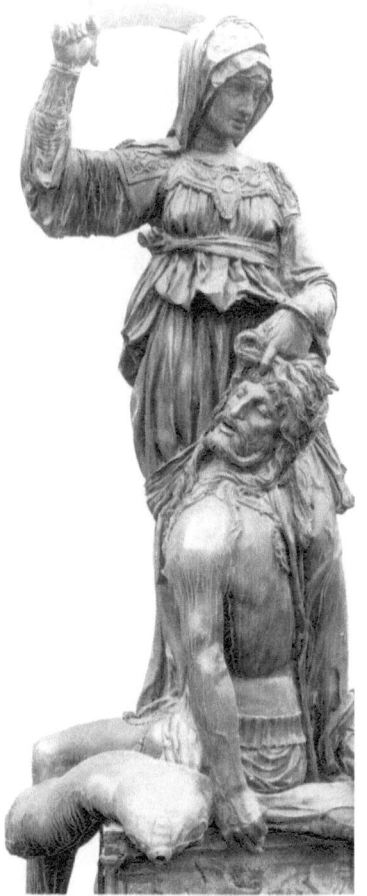

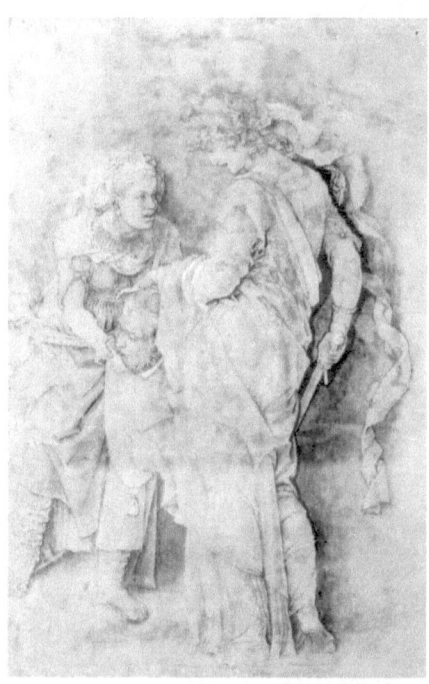

Fig. 1 Donatello, *Judith and Holofernes*, 1456. Bronze. Palazzo Vecchio, Florence.

Fig. 2  Andrea Mantegna, *Judith and Her Slave*, 1491. Drawing. Gabinetto dei Disegni e delle Stampe, Galleria degli Uffizi, Florence. Photo: Gabinetto dei Disegni e delle Stampe, Galleria degli Uffizi, Florence.

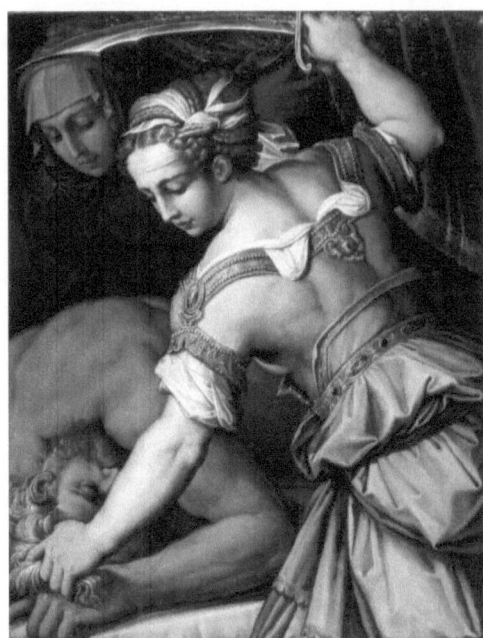

Fig. 3 Giorgio Vasari, *Judith and Holofernes*, 1554. Oil painting. Saint Louis Art Museum, Saint Louis, MO. Photo: Friends Fund and funds given in honor of Betty Greenfield Grossman. Saint Louis Art Museum, Saint Louis, MO.

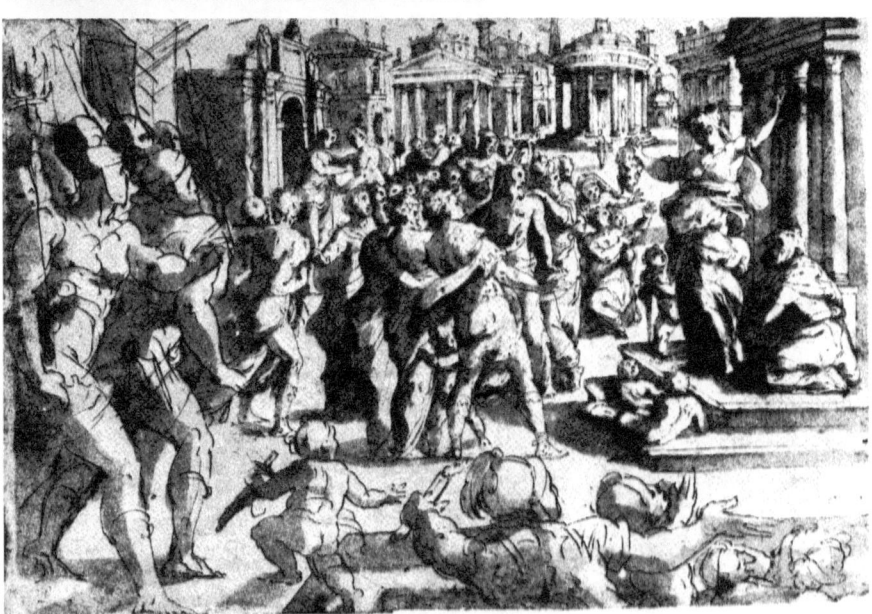

Fig. 4 Giorgio Vasari, *Judith and Holofernes*, 1564. Drawing, inv. FC12419. Istituto Nazionale per la Grafica, La Farnesina, Rome. Photo: Istituto Nazionale per la Grafica, La Farnesina, Rome.

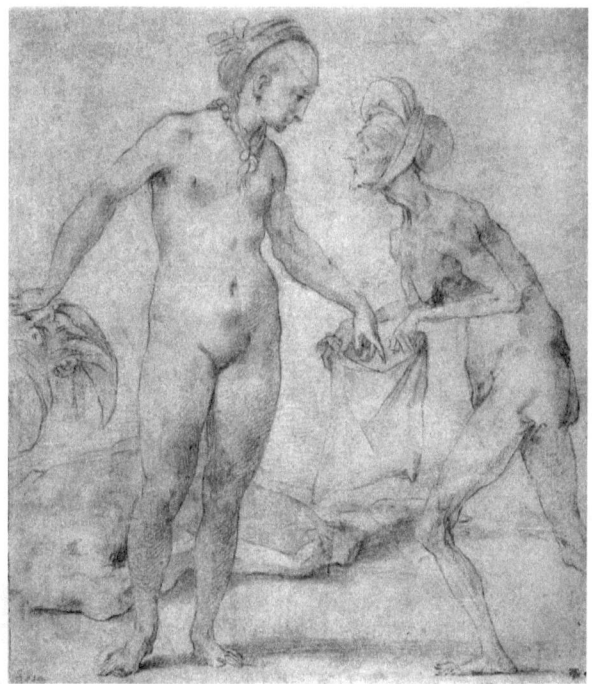

Fig. 5 Rosso Fiorentino, *Judith and Holofernes*, 1525. Drawing, LACM.M 77.13 Los Angeles County Museum of Art, Los Angeles, CA. Photo: Dalzell Hatfield Memorial Fund, Los Angeles County Museum of Art, Los Angeles, CA/Art Resource/NY.

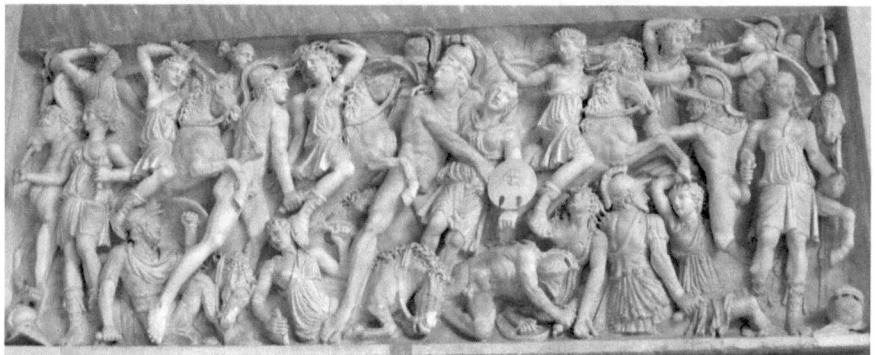

Fig .6.   Amazonomachy Sarcophagus, 230. Marble. Museo Pio Clementino, Vatican Museums. Photo: Sailko, GNU Free Documentation License.

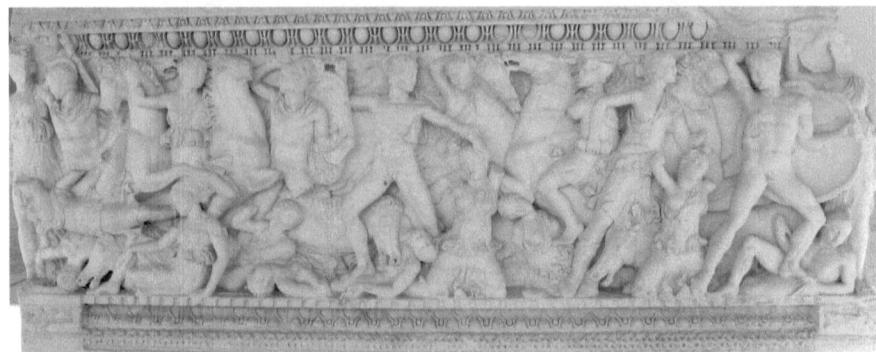

Fig. 7.    Amazonomachy Sarcophagus, 3rd century, inv. 1235, Archeological Museum Thessalonica, Greece.

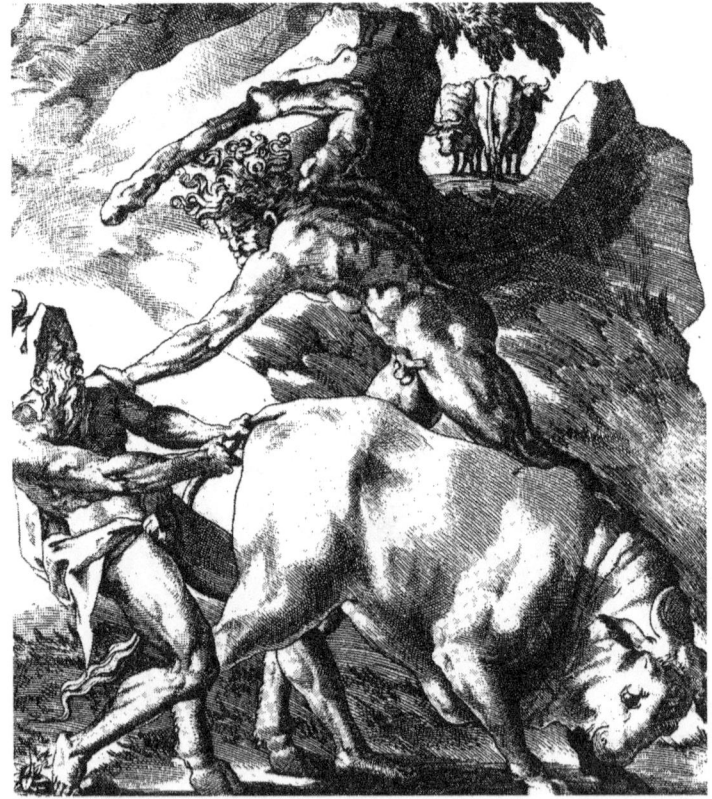

Fig. 8.    Giovanni Jaccopo Caraglio, *Hercules Fighting Cacus,* 1525. Engraving after Rosso's drawing.   Vol. Eb 6b Réserve. Bibliothèque Nationale, Paris. Photo: Bibliothèque Nationale, Paris.

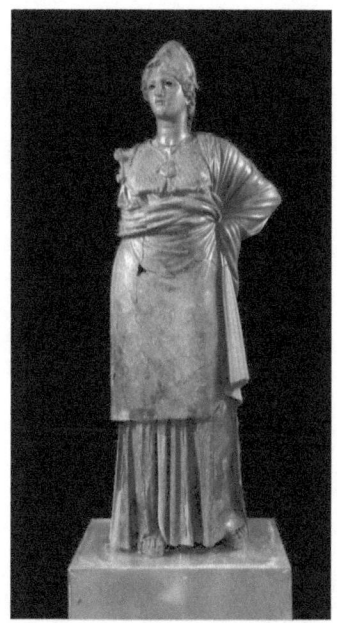

Fig. 9.    *Athena-Minerva* of Arezzo,
Hellenistic, 3rd Century BCE, bronze.
Museo Archeologico, Arezzo.

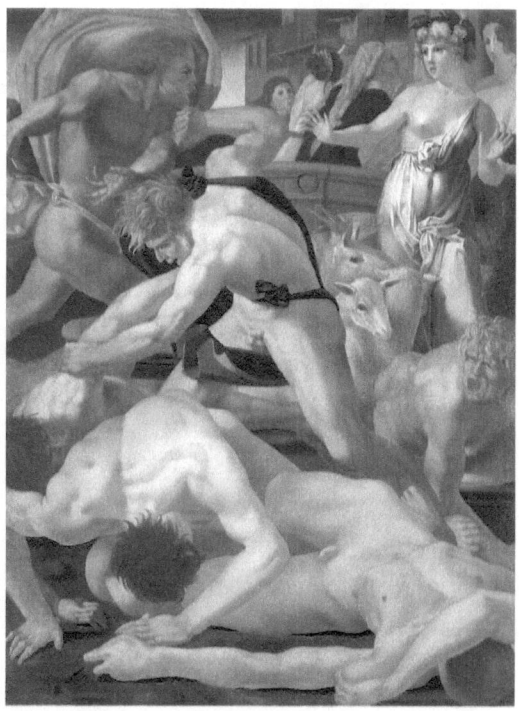

Fig. 10. Rosso Fiorentino, *Moses Defending the Daughters of Jethro*, 1523-24.
Oil painting. Galleria degli Uffizi, Florence. Photo: Art Resource/NY.

# 10

# Giorgio Vasari's *Saint Luke*:
# A Patron of Painting and *Disegno*

*The academy is worthy by virtue of the judgment and esteem in which they hold* disegno.[1]

Giorgio Vasari, *Vite* This essay considers one aspect of Giorgio Vasari's notion of *disegno* (drawing),[2] focusing on the iconography of the academy's chapter house, the Cappella degli Artisti (Chapel of the Artists) in the church of Santissima Annunziata in Florence (Figs. 1 and 2). This essays centers on the integration of the fine arts, poetry, and music with the principle of *disegno*, as illustrated in a religious painting, *Saint Luke Painting the Virgin* of 1562, in the chapel.

## Cappella degli Artisti, The Academy Chapter House

In 1562, the sculptor and monk Giovan Angelo Montorsoli (1506-1563) bequeathed a funeral chapel in the church of Santissima Annunziata to the Compagnia di San Luca, a confraternity, in the hope that his gift would reactivate an interest in pious and charitable works in the artistic community. With Montorsoli's gift of his chapel (which is also his tomb) to indigent artists for their burial and to Florentine artists for their meeting place, the time seemed appropriate to revive the deteriorating Compagnia di San Luca. From Montorsoli's idea, Vasari claims, the concept of an academy for artists developed. The first ceremony occurred in 1562 to pay tribute to the painter Jacopo Pontormo, whose remains were taken from the first cloister of Santissima Annunziata, carried in a torchlight procession around the piazza, and buried in the new shrine in the chapter house, the Chapel of the Artists, also called the Chapel of Saint Luke or the Chapel of Santissima Trinità.[3]

To decorate this special chapel, Montorsoli consulted with the Servite theologian Michelangelo Naldini, who collaborated on the iconographical program, orchestrating the selection and compositional arrangement of the biblical sculptures and paintings. The Chapel of the Artists contains sculptures and paintings executed by Cinquecento Florentine artists who were members of the academy between 1562 and 1575.[4]   Eleven of the sculptures portray holy fathers from the Old Testament, among them, *Abraham* carved by Stoldo Lorenzi, *Melchisedek* by Francesco Cammilliani, *Joshua* by Vincenzo Danti, *David* by Gian Francesco Lottini, *Solomon* by Giovanni Battista Casali(?), and *Moses* by Montorsoli and Matino Montanin. And from the New Testament there are statues of the four evangelists: *Luke* by Vincenzo Danti, *John* by Giovanni Battista Casali, *Mark* by Giuseppe Corsali, and *Matthew* by Michelangelo Nacherini or Necherino(?), with the addition of *Saint Paul* by Montorsoli and Matino Montanin and *Saint Peter* by Domenico Poggini. The only earthly figure is the portrait of the founder of academy, *Cosimo I de' Medici* by Vincenzo Danti and Zanobi Lastricati.

The paintings depict narrative scenes associated with biblical themes but focusing on the creation of art: Santi di Tito's *Solomon Constructing the Temple of Jerusalem*, honoring the art of architecture; Vasari's *Saint Luke Painting the Virgin*, symbolizing the invention of painting through the divine guidance of the Virgin Mary. The last painting, Alessandro Allori's *Holy Trinity*, presents the supreme creations of the Trinity: God creating his Son, Christ transforming his death in resurrection, and the Holy Spirit providing illumination for the understanding of creativity.

The Counter-Reformation iconography for the sculptures and the paintings is well elaborated and clearly discussed by Zygmunt Wazbinski in *L'Accademia Medicea del Disegno a Firenze nel Cinquecento*.[5] The focus on the study at hand is to further analyze the *Saint Luke Painting the Virgin* in terms of Renaissance Neoplatonic associations of *furor divinus* and *furor poeticus*.

## Marble Plaque

In the Cappella degli Artisti, the crypt is below the chapel. On the floor of the chapel, in its center, there is a square marble plaque or epitaph, which lauds the fusion of the arts and the goals of the artists of the academy (Fig. 3). Montorsoli, with the assistance of the academy members, composed the design for the plaque. It contains a complex iconographical program. The composition is a square format framing two receding ovals. Each corner of the square contains a skull that grips two crossed bones, indicating a sepulchral site.[6]

An ornamental ribbon flows through the bucrania [explain this term], uniting the four corners with a Pauline inscription: "Mortui sumus, et vita nostra ascondita est cum Cristo in Deo" ("We are dead, and our life is [now] hidden with Christ in God").[7] As if descending or ascending from earth to heaven, in Neoplatonic terms, the next format is an oval composition surrounded by a rim enclosing a second Latin inscription: "Floreat semper velin vita morte" ("May it flourish always whether in life or death"), alluding to the spiritual and secular triumph of the soul and the human achievements of deceased members, in particular, these Florentine artists. The word "floreat" alludes to blooming or flowering, connecting the accomplishments of the artists with their place of origin, "Florentia" or Florence.[8] Thus, the buried Florentine artists will achieve resurrection through God.

The last layer, oval in shape as well, contains a cornucopia of art symbols. The center of the oval holds a metal mirror, framed by an hourglass and a burning lamp. An hourglass marks temporal time while a lamp sustains time.[9] Both objects allude to the individual life in its transitoriness as well as to the recurrences of life and death—the metaphorical ascent to heaven and descent to earth. The metaphor of the flame in constant flux alludes to the spiral movement, up and down, from earth to heaven. The running sand of the hourglass signifies as well a changeable state. The mirror absorbs the reflection of both measuring devices, paradoxically combining the temporal with the everlasting moment. The instruments of the arts–architecture (square and compass), painting (brushes and drawing tools), and sculpture (chisels and hammers)–that surround the mirror honor the artists who created these art forms with their tools and are now immortalized for their accomplishments, or *exemplum virtutis*.[10] Other honorific decorations are festoons and ribbons that embrace the instrument of the arts, while garlands hang from the measuring devices.

Because of its reflective surface, the mirror or *speculum* symbolizes wisdom and knowledge. In Neoplatonic terms, the mirror is called "the symbol of symbolism itself";[11] it conveys cosmological meaning as the image of the microcosm reflecting the macrocosm, meaning that individual essences reflect the Divine Being and vice versa. The souls of the deceased artists are reflected in the mirror as it contemplates the Divine; it transforms and purifies. Reciprocally, the mirror reflects a celestial world or an intellectual world symbolizing the manifestations of the creative mind, that is, the minds of the deceased artists. For humanists, the human mind is a mirror that has the capacity to transform the tangible world into an image and an idea; an artist perceives nature and interprets the world like a mirror that absorbs and reflects the natural and divine creation.[12]

The mirror, then, is another tool for artists. It assists reflecting both the self, as in portraiture, and the natural world. The mirror, like art, reveals an imitation of nature. In the mirror, the image of reality is reversed, while in art the created image is a reflection or revelation of the artist's mind. The eyes of the artist, as the windows of the mind, then, capture the world and reflect that world in their creation.[13] In the *Vite,* Vasari comments on the power of the eyes when looking and judging a work of art, and he claims that "gli occhi [son la] miglior guida e giudice" ("the eyes are the best guide and judge").[14] He embues his concept of seeing with a moral overtone when he writes: "La facilità del buono [è] quando si guarda, non è aspra a gli occhi" ("the ability in perceiving beauty is when the eyes perceive it without harshness").[15]

The triangular formations composed by the instruments of the arts create an illusory spatial movement and connect with the mirror shape at another level. The illusion of descending or ascending is repeated as well as the concept of "what is above is as what is below."[16] The mirror, like the hourglass and the burning lamp, reflects the soul from those artists who are below in the sepulcher and are ascending into the divine world.

Montorsoli epitomizes the Vasarian arts of *disegno* in portraying the instruments of architecture, painting, and sculpture. However, Montorsoli is alluding to another *paragone* related to materials: the slab of marble and the mirror of metal—marble being, perhaps, the superior material for accomplished artists, but metal being the training material employed by many artists in their earlier careers, including Vasari. Montorsoli is also expressing Duke Cosimo's special interest in metals and his planning for building a private foundry in Florence.

Moreover, the symbolism of the metal is significant in that it alludes to the planetary elements of the underworld as well as to the heavens. The cosmic energy associated with metal contrasts with the frozen aspect of marble. The volatile aspect of the metal when connected with fire (the burning lamp in the plaque) contrasts with the cold and permanent material of marble Thus, this marble plaque, with bucrania and instruments of the arts, is a *memento mori*, alluding to the eternal life of the arts and the memory of the artists, thanks to the foundation of the academy.

Along the lower sections of the chapel's walls, below the statuary, still-life paintings are inserted above or beside the artworks, in honor of the members of the academy. The still-life paintings contain a series of emblematic references: books with a crown attest to the intellectual commitment of Duke Cosimo I to the academy; painters' palettes, architectural surveying instruments, and sculptural tools connect with the member's professional endeavors; and musical instruments, such as a lyre, allude to the sister arts of music and poetry. The inclusion of the lyre with a garland acknowledges the parallel between artistic *élan vital* and *furor poeticus*.

## Saint Luke Painting the Virgin

In the Chapel of the Artists, above the altar, hangs Vasari's *Saint Luke Painting the Virgin* of 1562–65 (Figs. 4 and 5).[17] It reveals the new role of the painter as an inventor, not a technician, and a professional member of an academy. As an inventor or creator, the artist experiences *furor divinus* through *furor poeticus* expressed in *disegno*. The drawing becomes the source for the expression to be articulated in painting, sculpture, or architecture.

Vasari portrays himself as Saint Luke. In an elegant studio, the patron saint of painters is drawing a portrait of the Madonna and Child. In a cloud, carried by angels, the Madonna holding her Child in her arm appears in the artist's atelier to commission a family portrait. In the artist's studio, the Madonna and Child are models for the artist's composition. The holy group also advises the artist on how to compose the portrait painting; the Madonna actively participates, instructing the artist on how to paint her. Her action of pointing is mimed by her Son, whom she holds in her arms. Although the artist is comfortably seated at an easel, holding a palette, a brush, and a maulstick, he is attentively following the instructions provided by the holy group.

Vasari plays with a spatial illusion of viewing. As the viewer looks at the entire painting, two images are perceived: a semi-profile of the Madonna and Child and a frontal view of their painted image on the canvas. The artists and the onlookers standing on the right side of the painter can see both the Madonna and Child and their painted images at the same frontal level. The drawing or painting on the easel differs from the holy group: the Madonna and Child are seen from the front and are not instructing (Figs. 4 and 5). The two onlookers, the aging Montorsoli and the dead Martino di Bartolomeo Montanini, are experiencing the event in a different manner. Montorsoli, with his arms crossed in reverence, admires the beauty of the Madonna and Child, while the young Montanini admires the painter's rendering on the easel. Amusingly, the bull next to Saint Luke is lifting his head as if to compare the actual image with the painted image. The bull's winged plumage decorated with many eyes, like a peacock's,[18] suggests the multiplicity of ways in which to look at, observe, and judge a work of art. By use of these images of the bull, the onlookers, the artist, and the Virgin Mary, Vasari is showing the levels of perception by which the viewer may see and judge a work of art. First is a simple look, "veduta dell'occhio" ("eye's gaze"): the casual manner in which the bull sees the painting. Another aspect of looking is through the analysis of an object. Vasari refers to this aspect of seeing as "giudizio dell'occhio" ("the judgment of the eye"): the way the onlookers observe the unfinished painting. The last observation on how to perceive is through "la facilità del buono" ("the ability to see excellence"): the artist's evaluation of the work of art by means of good judgment of what constitutes excellence of *disegno*. The Virgin Mary's gaze is guided by a divine intellect and perfect judgment; thus, it is a perfect viewing.

The instruments of the artist's trade are visible in the foreground of the painting: a box with brushes, an artist's palette, and a small glass bottle. Next to Saint Luke sits a large and lively bull with peacock wings decorated with eyes, resting his paw on a book. The animal is the traditional attribute of the evangelist as well the patron of the artists as indicated by the Academy's emblem (Fig. 6). In the foreground, Vasari places on a parallel line the attributes of the painter with the attribute of the evangelist, revealing that the process of creating a painting by artists is equal to the writing of the gospel by the evangelist; both creative processes are guided by divine inspiration. The unusual depiction of peacock wings on the bull relates to the multiple actions of seeing or perceiving by the artist and viewer. It is the function of the artist to observe nature and re-create what he sees; it is the function of the viewer to observe or gaze at what the artist has created.

The architecture of the studio is Mannerist in proportion. Decorations with *all'antica* elements appear on the doors, such as pedimental designs with insertions of garlands, and putti holding funerary urns.[19] The painter's stool is also decorated with classical funerary motifs. The elaborate design of the room alludes to the concept of artistic excellence or virtù, "virtutum omnium vas" ("the cups of all virtues"), as well as to the artistic mind.[20] Further expressing Vasari's fascination with the antique, he places between the door pediments a garlanded roundel with a bust of Minerva, the patron of the arts, including metalwork.[21] The smiling image is also looking at the scene, but from another perspective, from top down. The pagan virgin, Minerva, gazes at the depiction of the Christian virgin, Mary. It is no accident that Vasari places the image of Minerva on the same axial line as the portrait of the Virgin Mary; both Minerva and the Virgin Mary reside in the studio of the artist and inspire his *disegno*, the Virgin Mary serving as an incarnate model for Saint Luke's portrayal.

Vasari makes another parallel between the creative powers of artists and the ancient gods, in particular, the goddess Minerva.

Her name originally meant "thought"; Ovid calls her the "Goddess of a Thousand Works." Minerva is a multitalented goddess of wisdom, poetry, music, medicine, arts and crafts (especially wool), science, commerce, and war. More generally, she is considered the patroness of intellect and learning. In Roman times, Minerva was celebrated as the patroness of artisans during the *Quinquatrus*, the artisans' holiday, from March 19 to 23. Her temple on the Aventine Hill was considered to be a center for craft guilds.

In the Vasari's painting, the first adjacent room depicts a setting that is less grand.  It is a workshop and not a studio.  An artist can be seen making a mold out of a clump of clay. His working clothes contrast with the painter's elegant attire.[22] In the second adjacent room, a young assistant grinds color pigments for the master.  A predella panel located below the mural painting is now missing.[23]

In the painting of Saint Luke there are numerous subtle classical references not only depicted in the architectural design but also in the portrayal of pagan gods and myths, e.g., in the portrait bust of Minerva, in the peacock plumage associated with Juno's sacred bird, and in the numerous painted eyes on the peacock's plumage, which are reminiscent of Argus, the mythological monster with watchful eyes.

Vasari parallels God's act of creating the world with the artist's creation of beauty; for him, God is an artist who studies conscientiously and persistently.  For Vasari, artistic success stems from divine inspiration, innate talent, and diligent labor:

> Now the material in which God worked to fashion the first man was a lump of clay, and this was not without reason; for the Divine Architect of time and of nature, being wholly perfect, wanted to show how to create by a process of removing from, and adding to, material that was imperfect in the same way that good sculptors and painters do when, by adding and taking away, they bring their rough models and sketches to the final perfection for which they are striving.[24]

By the sixteenth century, artists, including Vasari, were asserting that their work was the result of divine inspiration and that they were creative geniuses.  The artists claimed that they worked like God; they did not just imitate nature, but they created a *new* nature (they surpassed nature) and a new beauty through inspired contact with God. These radical ideas had enormous repercussions on the roles of the artist and on art in the sixteenth century. In his artists' biographies, Vasari comments on the intellectual and scientific ability of artists by emphasizing their interest in mathematics, perspective, proportion, and anatomy, as manifested in the art of *disegno*.

Vasari's conception of artistic creativity is related to his theory of painting. He considers two alternatives for achieving artistic creativity for a painter: by imitation (*imitazione*) and by invention (*invenzione*). Imitation is the exercise of copying art as a method of learning, whereas invention is a means for conceiving artistic ideas. Imitation guides and teaches the artist in composing and creating perfection. For Vasari, imitation draws from two different sources: copying from nature (*copia dal vero*) and selecting from one's own work (*imitare se stessi*). He emphasizes the notion that copying from nature is important for the artist in order to learn to create forms that are alive. It also facilitates the artist's ability to draw, so that eventually the artist may draw anything from memory without the aid of a model. Hence, an artist demonstrates the manner in which the arts surpass nature when he copies or quotes from his own work.

The manifestation of *disegno* in the painting refers in part to a previous work by Vasari: the depiction of Fine Arts for his house at Arezzo, in particular, the personification of Painting, who is drawing a portrait of Dante (Fig. 7). This painting appears on the ceiling of the Chamber of Fame of 1542 in Vasari's Aretine home. Here, Vasari emphasizes how drawing is an invention. He continues to express his artistic theory of *disegno* through the action of imitation in another room of the Casa Vasari, the Chamber of Fortune of 1548.[25] In the lower section of the north wall, where themes on ancient painters are illustrated, there is a depiction of Zeuxis in his studio selecting parts of the most beautiful women for his painting of Helen (or Venus, Fig. 8). Zeuxis as well as Vasari attempts to surpass nature through the process of selection and judgment. And in the *Sala Vasari* for his house in Florence, Vasari once again repeats the same theme in his depiction of Apelles the artist (always with the features of Vasari, Figs. 9 and 4, 8 and 10). In his studio, Apelles is painting a nude portrait of Juno/Diana (the personification of power/the personification of nature, Figs. 10 and 11). In his studio, Apelles is outlining or drawing his shadow or portrait; in this way, Vasari reflects on the supremacy of creativity.

The fusion of artistic goals is compared with the fusion of the secular aims of the academy as well as its spiritual tradition. As a painter, creator, and artistic leader, Vasari is imitating and impersonating ancient painters, like Apelles and Zeuxis; holy artists, like the evangelist Saint Luke; and the Christian creator, through the Virgin Marry.

In *Saint Luke's Painting the Virgin*, Vasari also expresses his theory of *disegno*—drawing as the principle of art. The concepts of imitation (*copia dal vero*) and judgment (*giudizio*) are clearly expressed. Vasari portrays Saint Luke receiving divine inspiration. The evangelist is inspired and guided by the Madonna and Child. The artist imitates nature (*copia dal vero*) as he draws from life: the Madonna and Child are his models.

The artist also invents and surpasses nature by imitating himself or quoting himself from previous works (*imitarsi se stessi*). Examples are Vasari's images of the artist working in his studio: *Zeuxis Painting Helen of Troy, Apelles Painting Diana, Saint Luke Painting the Virgin* (Figs. 7, 9 and 4). In all of these paintings, Vasari alludes to the notion of judgment (*giudizio*), an essential quality for the deification of art as well as for the fame of the artist. The act of judgment is expressed in the faces, gestures, and expressions. Hence, when Vasari paints an artist in his studio—as in the paintings of Zeuxis, Apelles, and Saint Luke—he includes not only the onlookers who analyze and admire the artist at work, but also considers the various aspects of perception from the viewer's or artist's perspective (*veduta dall'occhio*).

In *Saint Luke Painting Virgin*, Vasari visualizes and reveals the aims of the Accademia del Disegno. The establishment of the Accademia del Disegno was the result of artistic necessity to foment the aims of the arts through the principle of *disegno* in Florence, including fostering the Cinquecento theories of art. Through *furor divinus* (from God) and *furor poeticus* (*disegno*), Vasari conceives and actualizes his vision for an academy of art.

## Short History of the Accademia

The Accademia del Disegno, founded in Florence in 1562, was the first formal academy of art and served as a model for later artist academies.  Its place in the history of art includes the history of artistic ideas, the merits  of artists' accomplishments, and an investigation of various art theories. Many books and articles have been published on the subject of the *accademia*,[26] but only Zygmunt Wazbinski's study focuses on the iconography of the architectural residence of the academy, the Chapel of the Artists (Cappella degli Artisti), also known as the Chapel of Saint Luke or the Chapel of the Holy Trinity (Santissima Trinità), which is located in the second cloister of the church of Santissima Annunziata in Florence (Fig. 2).

In the development of the Accademia, an important forerunner was a school administered by Bertoldo di Giovanni, in the Giardini di San Marco in Florence, with the support of Lorenzo de' Medici. This fifteenth-century institution was the first to have the essential characteristics of an academy: erudite, learned training, which no longer consisted only of manual help for the master. The young artist now also participated with the master artist in the completion of the artwork, as well as in the discussions about its creation. This new academy ignored the economic aspect of art as well as the restrictions imposed by the guilds. Its main political connection resided with the Medici court.  In the sixteenth century, the Florentine sculptor Baccio Bandinelli would form another such academy in Rome, "in luogo detto Belvedere" ("located in the Belvedere gardens").  At the same time, a group of artists in Florence, mostly sculptors, was organizing a center for discussions on art theory and practice.

However, the first real academy of art in Florence was Vasari's Accademia del Disegno. Two important socio-economic events contributed to the establishment of the Accademia: the weakening of the *arti* or guilds, and the cessation of the confraternity of artists. Vasari proposed an academy of art or confraternity of Saint Luke as a new system of organization intended to free artists from corporate guild sanctions. He intended to provide for the best Florentine artists an art center with a common purpose: the art of drawing (*disegno*). Vasari requested the protection of the grand Duke of Tuscany to ensure support for the academy.  As a result of Vasari's appeal, the guilds—the Medici and Speziali for painters, the Fab-bricanti for sculptors, and the Compagnia di San Luca, the artists' confraternity—were suspended and subordinated to the new Accademia del Disegno.

The members of the academia met on their patron saint's day, the Feast of Saint Luke, in October of 1562, at the chapter house of the second cloister in the church of Santissima Annunziata, which they called the Chapel of the Artists, dedicated to the Holy Trinity. Its regulations were supported and managed by Cosimo I de' Medici, duke of Tuscany. In 1562, in making Duke Cosimo I head of the organization, the guilds had no juridical power over the academy's members, painters, sculptors, and architects. Although originally founded for painters, the company was not an exclusive craft society, like the minor guilds. Early membership lists included the names of tailors and cheesemakers, alongside those of artisans such as those more traditionally associated with an artist's workshop. These men and women presumably had personal reasons for their devotion to Saint Luke, but the openness of the company/academy later allowed painters and sculptors to associate in an organization that ignored the craft demarcation lines established by the Florentine guilds.

The Accademia del Disegno was a professional association where artists met and discussed their work. It was a landmark in the struggle for artistic independence and a dignified position in Florentine society. Throughout the Middle Ages, artists had worked for a guild that regulated their private lives and their working conditions. Artists were treated as skilled craftsmen and worked like tradesmen. During the late fifteenth century, mainly in Florence, artists attempted to break away from the guilds. They rejected manual status and began to claim equality of rank with poets, musicians, intellectuals, and scientists. Vasari's *Vite* is a triumphant anecdotal record of the artist's new status in the Cinquecento.

The leading figures in the organization of the Accademia del Disegno were Duke Cosimo I, the courtly patron and lover of art, who approved the regulations; Vasari himself; and Vincenzo Borghini, the eminent humanist, historian, and scholar, and prior of the Hospital of the Innocents. Vasari's and Borghini's characterization of the academy most likely "predates the explicit incorporation of *disegno* and grew fundamentally from their view of the visual arts as an area of practice straddling manual and intellectual labor."[27] In the *Selva di notizie*, an important theoretical statement rediscovered by Paola Barocchi, Borghini maintains that painting and sculpture occupy a middle position in the hierarchical system of the cultural values he sketched out, neither very low, like the mechanical trades, nor very high, like "civil and speculative" practices.[28] Borghini's speech ends the debates on the supremacy of one art over another and encourages its members to maintain the goals of the Accademia as an "accademia di fare e non di ragionare" ("academy for doing, not for chattering").[29]

Borghini's speech originates from the bitter disputes caused by Benvenuto Cellini over the placement of the figure of Sculpture on Michelangelo's catafalque designed by the members of the academy. Michelangelo's tomb was originally intended for the Medici church of San Lorenzo, but it was finally located in the Church of Santa Croce. Other, similar debates about the arts were provoked by Benedetto Varchi's discussions on the *paragone* or the superiority of one art to another, especially in regard to painting and sculpture.[30]

Vasari's energetic nature found kindred spirits in two equally productive Florentines. Duke Cosimo I appreciated this busy artist who was constantly active in the transformation of the former republican city of Florence into a wealthy duchy that would eventually expand and become the grand duchy of Tuscany. No one in Florence could match the rapidity with which Vasari completed grand projects. In 1546, Vasari took pride in completing the decorations of the *salone* in the Palazzo della Cancelleria of Rome in one hundred days, prompting Michelangelo to say, *"e si vede"!* ("and it shows!").

Borghini enjoyed an exceptionally high and powerful position in Florence during the second half of the sixteenth century. He was equally interested in the formulation of the academy. Borghini was a close friend of Vasari's and an important figure in Cosimo's court, as well as in Florentine religious circles. Like Vasari, he loved the arts and was a prolific writer of discourses and letters (many not published until after his death).[31] Also like Vasari, Borghini collected drawings by admired painters. Vasari even dipped into his own collection of drawings to enrich that of his friend, and it was likely Vasari who introduced Borghini to the idea of collecting drawings. Just as Vasari framed his own collected drawings,[32] Borghini annotated his with epitaphs in Latin and Greek, in the same way he embellished his own writings.

With words and phrases from the classic languages, Borghini combined his interest in art with his historical and literary interests, supplying iconographic programs for projects executed by Vasari, among them, the iconography for the program in the Sala dei Cento Giorni at the Palazzo della Cancelleria in Rome. The most famous of these extensive projects was the *apparato* for the wedding of Francesco de' Medici to Giovanna of Austria in 1565.[33] Borghini also provided artistic programs for the frescoes in the Palazzo Vecchio, in particular, the Salone dei Cinquecento.

Vasari credits the formation of the academy for artists to Duke Cosimo's literary and artistic interest in bringing together all artists concerned with *disegno*; there was also his desire to meet formally to carry out good deeds for the community and to teach promising young students. For Vasari, the institution of the academy represented an opportunity to effectuate his belief in the importance of an artist's training and education. *Disegno*, a quality and facility, was the crucial difference separating the Accademia from the guilds.

### Vasari's Neoplatonic Notion of *Disegno*

For Vasari, the main purpose of the Accademia was to emphasize the concept of *disegno*. The *Vite* or biographies of the artists of 1550 to 1568 are filled with reminders to the reader of the rewards that come to an artist with *disegno*.[34] *Disegno*, Vasari claims, is "[una] cava di molte cose un giudizio universale, simile a una forma ovvera idea di tutte le cose della natura" ("a cave of many things, a universal judgment, similar to a form whose idea reveals all things of nature").[35]

In the second edition of the *Vite* published in 1568, Vasari further explains what he means by *disegno* and why it rules artistic creativity:

Seeing that Design, the parent of our three arts, Architecture, Sculpture, and Painting, having its origin in the intellect, draws out from many single things a general judgment, it is like a form or idea of all the objects in nature . . . afterwards, when expressed by the hands, it is called Design. We may conclude that Design is not other than a visible expression and declaration of our inner conception and of that which others have imagined and given form to in their ideas.[36]

Vasari goes on to observe that in the arts:

The chief use [of *disegno*] is in Architecture because its designs are composed only of lines, which so far as the architect is concerned, are nothing else than the beginning and the end of his art . . . In Sculpture, drawing [*disegno*] is of service in the case of all the profiles, because in going round from view to view the sculptor uses it when he wishes to delineate the forms which please him best, or which he intends to bring out in every dimension . . . In Painting, the lines of *disegno* are of service in many ways, but especially in outlining every figure, because when they are well drawn and made correct and in proportion, the shadows and lights that are then added give the strongest relief to the lines of the figure, and the result is all excellence and perfection.[37]

In his *Vita*, in particular, Vasari writes that from his earliest years his father directed his study "in the right way . . . particularly in design."[38] He notes that as a youth in 1531, he and his artistic companion, Francesco Salviati, worked hard at copying works of art while in Rome. One of the constant subjects to which Vasari refers in the *Vite* and in his *Libro de' Disegni* is his collection of drawings.[39] This album formed a virtual history of drawings from Cimabue's time to his own, and its content revealed the interdependence between drawing and the creation of the other visual arts.

In his writings, Vasari means that *disegno* is more than simply the physical act of drawing or the planning process of composing. In theory, *disegno* is the cognitive faculty that makes the practice of painting, sculpture, and architecture possible.[40] Artists associate because of a common artistic quest instead of gathering together because they work with particular materials. Vasari's interpretation of the term *disegno* encompasses the larger notion that drawing is a principal artistic element, together with invention and color, in the composition of a work of art. Vasari's notion of *disegno* reflected Venetian art critic Paolo Pini's understanding of the term, and Milanese art critic Giovanni Paolo Lomazzo's awareness of *disegno* as the basis for all works of art. Thus, Vasari understood *disegno* to be the element linking painting to sculpture and architecture. In his writing of the *Vite*, Vasari found in *disegno* the artistic concept linking artists, students, and amateurs of the visual arts. For example, in the *vita* of Torrigiano, he describes the artistic gatherings of collectors and young artists in the garden of Lorenzo the Magnificent, or the so called the *Giardini di San Marco*, as a "school and academy for painters and sculptors and all others who study *disegno*."[41] And later, in 1562, Vasari would employ the word in the name of the new academy–the Accademia del Disegno.

Perhaps no word appeals to Vasari as much as *disegno* because it encompasses the visual element common in all that is beautiful in art. From Neoplatonic Renaissance aesthetics, Vasari appropriated his theory of beauty, in particular, from Marsilio Ficino's *Commentary on Plato's "Symposium" about Love*. Vasari absorbed two of Ficino's notions. The first was his definition of beauty "as the splendor of *divine goodness* present everywhere" — personal beauty expresses an interior moral good. The second definition considers beauty "as a process of ascent from the sensual cognition of earthly beauty to the apprehension of the immortal ideal of beauty itself."[42] In Vasari's aesthetics (from the Greek *aisthesis*, meaning "sensation"), physical beauty becomes the creation of a beautiful image from the combination of arranged parts of a body commensurately and proportionately arranged as a whole. Vasari visually represents this *concetto* on the creation of physical beauty in connection with the concept of *disegno*. This notion of beauty is conveyed in two paintings of the same subject and their corresponding drawings: *Saint Luke Painting the Virgin*, where the figure of the Virgin Mary personifies divine beauty.[43]

Vasari's aesthetic is concerned with the beautiful in art and in nature. His philosophy of art depends on the poetical and philosophical traditions of the Quattrocento and Cinquecento. He emphasizes beauty as a human creation that possesses symmetry and proportion of form. Following the Neoplatonic theory of beauty that encompasses divine and human creativity revealed in *disegno*, Vasari understands beauty as a divine creation. He writes: "God fashioned the first forms of painting and sculpture in the sublime grace of created things."[44] God is the "Architect of Design," according to Vasari's Neoplatonic theory of art. This concept had been expressed earlier in medieval imagery, in which God is portrayed as the architect of the universe.

Vasari parallels God's act of creating the world with the artist's creation of beauty, and God is described as an artist who studies conscientiously and persistently. For Vasari, artistic success stems from divine inspiration, innate talent, and hard work or "diligent labor":

> Now the material in which God worked to fashion the first man was a lump of clay, and this was not without reason; for the Divine Architect of time and of nature, being wholly perfect, wanted to show how to create by a process of removing from, and adding to, material that was imperfect in the same way that good sculptors and painters do when, by adding and taking away, they bring their rough models and sketches to the final perfection for which they are striving.[45]

Through divine inspiration, Vasari comments on the intellectual and scientific ability of artists by emphasizing their interest in mathematics, perspective, proportion, and anatomy. By the sixteenth century, artists were claiming that their work was the result of divine inspiration and that they were creative geniuses [this and following repeats earlier statement]. Artists thought that they worked in a manner similar to God's; they did not merely imitate nature but instead created a new nature and a new beauty through inspired contact with God. These ideas had enormous repercussions on the roles of the artist and on art in the sixteenth century.[46]

Vasari's explanation of artistic creativity is fundamentally based on the Italian Renaissance tradition that considers creativity to be present in any human activity. Vasari envisions two stages in artistic creation. The first concerns what the painting, sculpture, or building will look like; God provides this idea to the artist through "divine rapture or *furor divinus*."[47] The artist executes his intentions, his skilled hand obeying his brain. The skilled draftsmanship or *disegno* that Vasari values so highly is the promise that the ideal will become visually concrete through *furor poeticus*. The stress on the imaginative and intellectual effort involved in art, which is what Vasari usually means by invention, is part of the artist's rejection of the manual status of the medieval craftsman or artisan.

Vasari relates the concept of *furor poeticus* to the creative visual arts:

> Many painters achieve in the first *disegno* of their work, as though guided by an inspirational fire, a certain measure of boldness; but afterwards, in finishing it, the boldness vanishes.[48]

In Cinquecento art, the model for the pictorial representation of *furor poeticus* was Raphael's drawing of *Poetry* of 1510, on the ceiling of the Stanza della Segnatura in Rome. Some years after Raphael's rendering, this concept became so popular that Andrea Alciato and Cesare Ripa even wrote an emblematic entry for it in their books, and Vasari painted a personification of Poetry with the Fine Arts in the Chamber of Fame in his house of Arezzo, and the personifications of Poetry and Music in the *Sala Vasari* at his Florentine home. The addition of the Poetry and Music to the realm of the Fine Arts is most revealing, since it alludes to the Renaissance Neoplatonic concept of *furor poeticus*, poetic inspiration. In the Chamber of Fame and *Sala Vasari*, the concept of *furor poeticus* is manifested not only by the depiction of Poetry and Music but also by the fact that all the Fine Arts are creating particular art forms.

## NOTES

This is a reprint from *Giorgio Vasari's Sacred and Profane Art* (London: Peter Lang Publisher, 2007).

1. Giorgio Vasari, *Le vite dei più eccellenti pittori, scultori, et architettori,* edited by Rosanna Bettarini and Paola Barocchi (Florence: Sansoni, 1976–97), constitutes the most accurate study of the 1550 and 1568 editions of the *Vite,* here cited as Bettarini-Barocchi. See also Giorgio Vasari, *Le vite de' più eccelenti Pittori, Scultori, et Architettori,* edited by Gaetano Milanesi (G. C. Sansoni, 1970–74), here cited as Vasari Milanesi.

2. I interpret Vasari's *disegno* to mean drawing, and I employ the word "design" to mean a compositional arrangement in a work of art. For the original version of Vasari's *Vite,* beside the Cinquecento editions, I also consulted Gaston Du C. de Vere's 1912 translation of the 1568 edition, with an introduction by Kenneth Clark (New York: Harry N. Abrams, Inc., 1979), 503, here cited as Vasari-de Vere. Also, Giorgio Vasari, *The Lives of the Most Excellent Painters, Sculptors, and Architects,* translated by George Bull (Baltimore: Penguin Books, 1965 and revised edition, 1971).

3. The chapel has gone through numerous transformations since it was built, through the Napoleonic interventions, followed by the damaging flood of 1966. The present restoration is with the goal of returning it to its original form of the Cinquecento.

4. Zygmunt Wazbinski, *L'Accademia Medicea del Disegno a Firenze nel Cinquecento: Idea e Istituzione,* 2 vols. (Florence: Leo S. Olschki, 1987), I, 111–12.

5. Ibid., 120–54.

6  Traditionally, the depiction of a skull alludes to the symbolism of physical death. The crossbones refer to Saint Andrew's cross, a symbol of nature quartered under the influence of the spirit. Skull and crossbones refer to the *speculum humane vitae* or representations of death. See Jean Chevalier and Alain Gheerbrant, *A Dictionary of Symbols* (London: Blackwell, 1994), 888.

7. Saint Paul's epistle to the Colossians.

8. Liana De Girolami Cheney, "Giorgio Vasari's *Last Judgment*: A Neoplatonic Vision," in *Neoplatonism and the Arts,* edited by Liana De Girolami Cheney and John Hendrix (London/New York: Edwin Mellen, 2002), 242, for the symbolism of the lily and its association with the city of Florence.

9. For Pierio Valeriano, the burning lamp signifies the illuminated intellect, a gift of God, and immortality; see his *Hieroglyphica sive De sacris Aegyptorum* (Basel: Oporinum, 1556), Book XLVI, Chapters V and IX. For Cesare Ripa, the hourglass alludes to the consummation and destruction caused by time, as in the case of Father Time; see his *Iconologia* (Rome: Gio. Gigliotti, 1593/1603), 483.

10. Wazbinski, *Accademia,* I, 116.

11. Chevalier and Gheerbrant, *A Dictionary of Symbols*, 660. See also Sabine Melchior-Bonnet, *The Mirror: A History* (London: Routledge, 2002), 101.

12. Giannozo Manetti, *De Dignitate et Excellentia Hominis* (Basel: Oporinum 1582), LI, 121. See also Melchior-Bonnet, *The Mirror*, 127.

13. Mark Pendergast, *Mirror: A History of Human Love* (New York: Basic Books, 2003), 55, for Plato's discussion of the mirror as a reflection of the world and the eye's vision as a mirror's reflection. For Plato, to know oneself means that the soul must see through the eyes a reflection of the self. Melchior-Bonnet, 105, citing Plato's *Phaedrus*, 235d.

14. Bettarini-Barocchi, Proemio, II, 8. In the *vita* of Uccello, Vasari also mentions the eye as the judge of [something missing here—"seeing"?] ing, "veduta dell'occhio" and "giudizio dell'occhio." Ibid., Text I, 62. Vasari's analysis of perception is consistent with the Albertian tradition.

15. Ibid., Text II, 399, on the *vita* of Desiderio da Settignano.

16. Chevalier and Gheerbrant, *A Dictionary of Symbols*, 658.

17. A preparatory drawing for the painting is at the Prado Museum in Madrid. For a history on the imagery and symbolism of Saint Luke Painting the Virgin, see I. Howard Marshall, *Luke: Historian and Theologian* (Downers Grove, Illinois: Paternoster Publication, 2006) and Giordana Mariani Canova, ed. *Luca evangelista. Parola e imagine tra Oriente e Occidente* (Padua: Il Poligrafo, 2011).

18. Vasari was inspired by the legend of Argus. In order to give immortality to her faithful servant Argus, Hera transferred his eyes onto the tail of the bird that was sacred to her, the peacock. See Vasari-Milanesi, VIII, 74, referring to Argus's transformation into a peacock. See also Vincenzo Cartari, *Imagini delli Dei degl'Antichi*, edited by Walter Koschatzky (Vienna: Akademische Druck Verlagsanstalt Graz, 1963), 98, for an explanation of how Juno (Hera) inherited the peacock as her attribute.

19. Wazbinski, *Accademia*, I, 130, n.112.

20. Ibid., 30.

21. Ibid., 130, n.115. Vasari is likely connecting Minerva's patronage of the arts and metals with Montorsoli's composed metal mirror on the floor's central platform of the chapel.

22. With the construction of the rooms and in the attire's design, is Vasari indirectly alluding to the *paragone* between the superiority of painting over sculpture? For Leonardo, painting was superior because, in its creation, only the intellectual faculty was required. But for Michelangelo, sculpture was superior because of the physical effort involved in the process of creation.

23. Ridolfo Siviero, *Accademia dell'Arte del Disgeno* (Florence: Giunti, 1979), fig. 32.

24. Bettarini-Barocchi, I, 1–5.

25. Liana De Girolami Cheney, "Giorgio Vasari's Paintings of the Casa Vasari Arezzo," *Explorations in Renaissance Culture* (Spring 1985), 53–73.
26. Bendetto Varchi, *Due Lezioni* (Florence: Giunti, 1547); Federico Zuccaro, *Scritti d'Arte* (Florence, 1604), edited by D. Heikamp (Florence: Leo S. Olschiki, 1961); Nicholas Pevsner, *Academies of Art: Past and Present* (Cambridge: Cambridge University Press, 1940); Charles Dempsey, "Some Observations on the Education of Artists in Florence and Bologna during the Later Sixteenth Century," *Art Bulletin* (1980), 552–69; Carl Goldstein, "Vasari and the Florentine Accademia del Disegno," *Zeitschrifit für Kunstgeschichte* (1975), 145–52; M. A. Jack, "The Academy del Disegno in Late Renaissance Florence," *Sixteenth-Century Journal* (1976), 3–20; Siviero, pp. 13–43, figs. 32 and 40; Anthony Hughes, "An Academy of Doing," *Oxford Journal* (1986), 25–25; Zygmunt Wazbinski, "La Cappella dei Medici e l'origine dell'Accademia del Disegno," in *Firenze e la Toscana dei Medici nell'Europa dell 500* (Florence: Leo S. Olschki, 1983), vol. I, 54–69; Wazbinski, *L'Accademia Medicea*, II, 235–67; Anton W. A. Boschloo, ed., *Academies: Between Renaissance and Romanticism of Art* (Leiden: SDU Uitgevereij, 1989), 14–32; Rick Scorza, "Borghini and the Florentine Academy," in *Italian Academies of the Sixteenth Century* (London: The Warburg Institute, 1995), 137–52; and "Borghini and Florentine Academies," in D. S. Chambers and F. Quiviger, eds., *Italian Academies of the Sixteenth Century* (London: The Warburg Institute, 1991), 137–52.
27. Scorza, "Borghini," 149.
28. Paola Barrochi, "Una *Selva di notizie* di Vincenzo Borghini," edited by Paola Barocchi, *Un Augurio a Raffaele Mattioli* (Florence: G. S. Sansoni, 1970), 87–91.
29. Scorza, 149, citing Lornzoni's *Carteggio*, n. 32, no. viii, 12, 14.
30. Leatrice Mendelsohn, *Paragoni: Benedetto Varchi's Due Lezzioni and Cinquecento Art Theory* (Ann Arbor, MI: UMI Research Press, 1982), 3–15.
31. Daniela Francalanci, Franca Pellegirini, and Eliana Carrara, eds., *Il Carteggio di Vincenzo Borghini* (Florence: Studio Per Edizioni Scelte, 2001), 37–38.
32. Vasari was a collector. His collection of drawings was chosen to illustrate the styles of the artists whose lives he has writing. In part he inherited a collection of drawings from a descendant of Lorenzo Ghiberti in 1528. One of the great prizes Vasari refers to constantly in *Vite* is his *Libro de' Disegni*, a collection of drawings that formed a virtual history of art from Cimabue's time to his own. B. Degenhart, "Zur Graphologie der Handzeichnungen," *Kunst-geschichtliches Jahrbuch der Bibliotheca Hertziana* (1937), 34–48: B. Degenhart and A. Schmitt, A. "Methoden Vasaris bei den Gestaltung seines "Libro," in *Studien zur toskanischen Kunst, Festschrift fur L. H. Heydenreich* (Munich: Georg Müller, 1964); L. Collobi–

Ragghianti, *Vasari Libro dei Disegni* (Milan: Archittetura, 1973); L. Collobi–Ragghianti, *Il Libro de Disegni del Vasari* (Florence: Vallecchi Edition, 1974); and Per Bjurström, *Italian Drawings from the Collection of Giorgio Vasari* (Stockholm: Nationalmuseum, 2001).

33. Giorgio Vasari, "Descrizione dell'apparato fatto in Firenze per le nozze dell'Illustrissimo ed Eccelentissima Regina Giorvanna d'Austria," in Vasari-Milanesi, VIII, 227–51; see also James M. Saslow, *The Medici Wedding of 1598: Florentine Festival as "Theatrum Mundi"* (London: Yale University Press, 1996), for an elaborate discussion on wedding *feste.*

34. Vasari-de Vere, III, 269-71. In 1531, while in Rome with Cardinal Ippolito de Medici, the youthful Vasari and his companion Francesco Salviati worked diligently in the self-training process of learning to draw by copying antique statues. Years later, in his letter to the Academicians of Designers, Painters, and Architects, Vasari thanks them for their artistic achievement, in particular, in the art of drawing.

35. Vasari-Milanesi, I, 168.

36. Ibid., II, 93–107.

37. Ibid., II, 93–107.

38. Vasari-de Vere, *Vite*, III, 222.

39. See nn. 32.

40. Erwin Panofsky, *Idea: A Concept in Art Theory,* translated by Joseph S. Peake (Columbia: University of South Carolina Press, 1968), 60–63; and Moshe Barasch, "Zuccari: The Theory of Disegno," in *Theories of Art: From Plato to Winckelmann* (New York: New York University Press, 1985), 25–34.

41. Goldstein, "Vasari and the Florentine Accademia del Disegno," 145–52.

42. Liana De Girolami Cheney, "Giorgio Vasari's Theory of Feminine Beauty," in *Concepts of Beauty in Renaissance Art* (London: Ashgate/Scolar Press, 1997), 180–90.

43. Edgar Wind, *Pagan Mysteries in the Renaissance* (New York: W. W. Norton and Company, Inc., 1968), 71 and 252, fig. 56.

44. Bettarini-Barocchi, I, 1–5.

45. Ibid.

46. Ibid.

47. Ficino, *Meditations on the Soul,* 70, on poetic frenzy.

48. Vasari-Milanesi, V, 260.

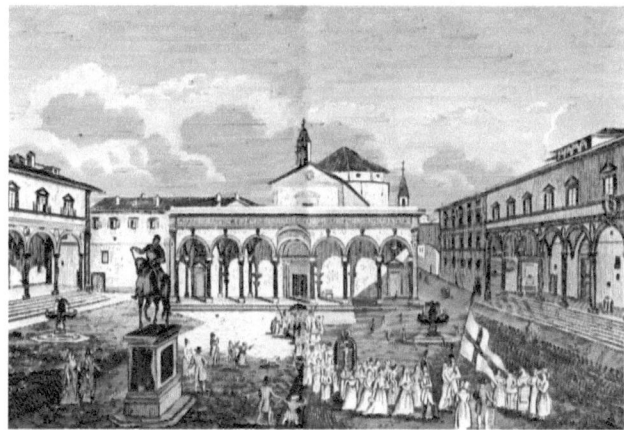

Fig. 1. Anonymous engraver, *Funeral Procession*, 16th century, SS Annunziata, Florence.

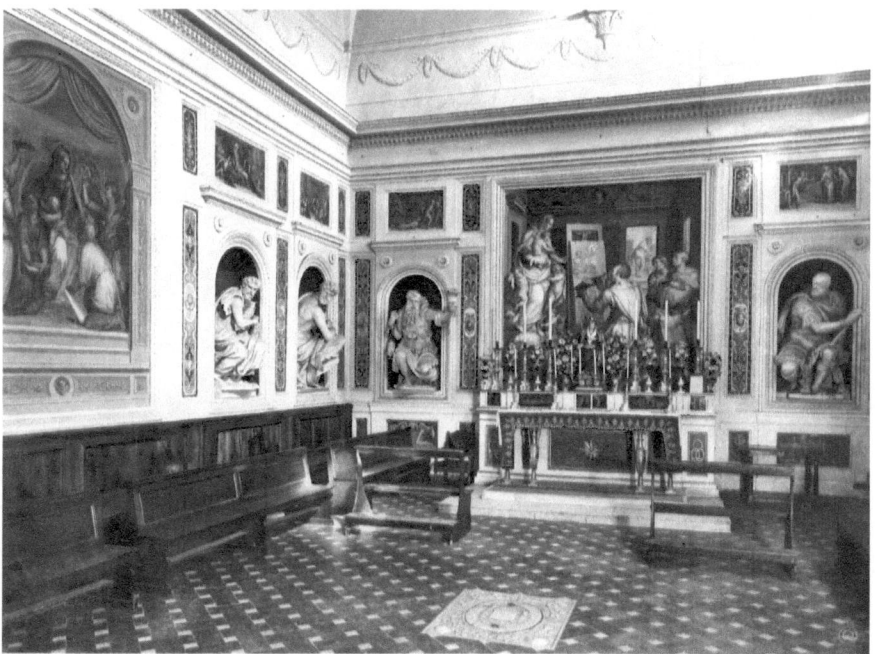

Fig. 2. Chapel of the Artists, 1560-62, SS Annunziata, Florence.

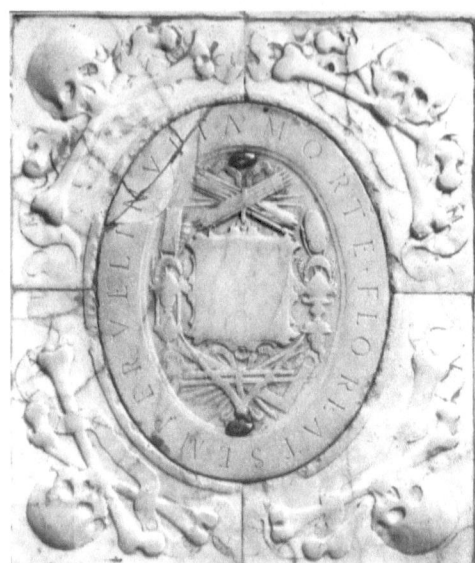

Fig. 3. Giovan Angelo Montorsoli, 1562, Plaque, pavement, Chapter of the Artists, SS Annunziata, Florence.

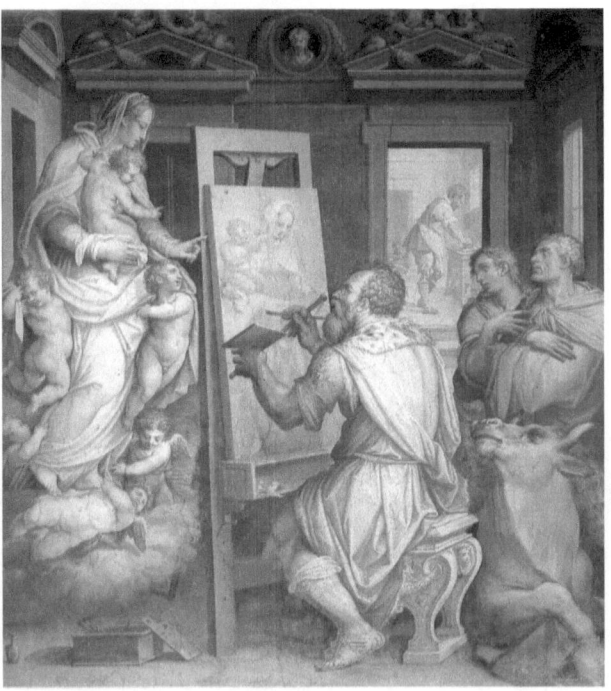

Fig. 4. Giorgio Vasari, *Saint Luke Painting the Virgin*, 1562. Chapter of the Artists, SS Annunziata, Florence. Photo: Art Resource/NY.

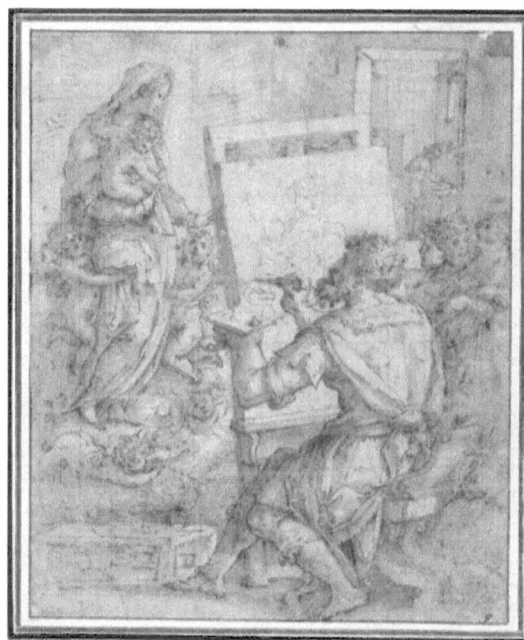

Fig. 5. Giorgio Vasari, *Saint Luke Painting the Virgin*, 1561, drawing. Museo del Prado, Madrid. Photo: Museo del Prado, Madrid.

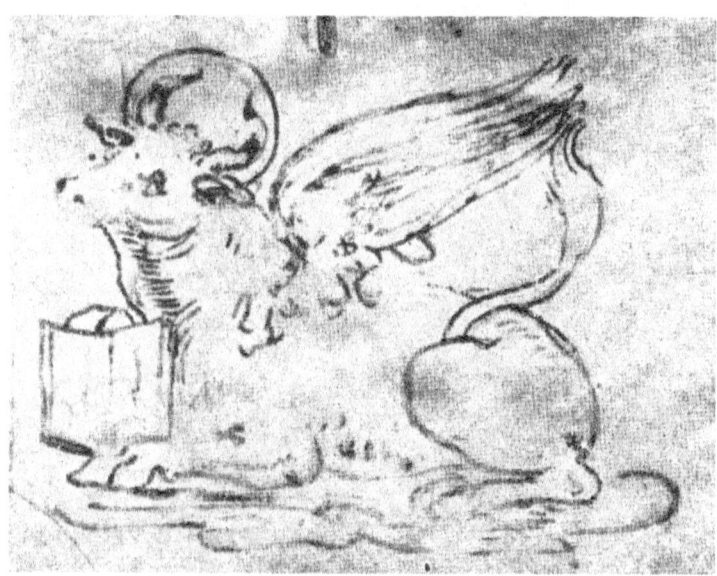

Fig. 6. Emblem of the Academy, *The Bull*, 1560s, drawing.

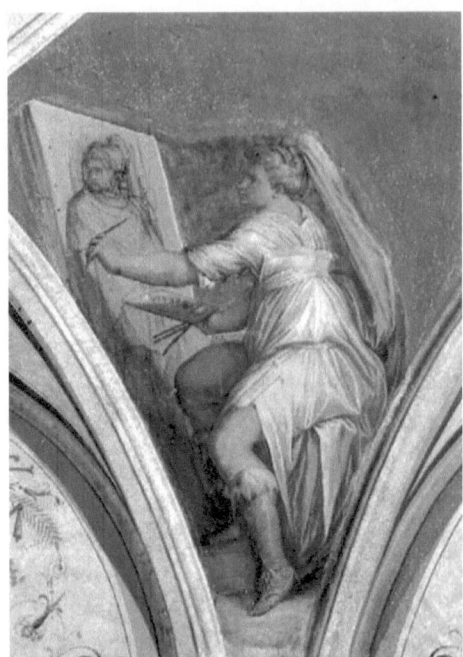

Fig. 7. Giorgio Vasari, *Allegory of Painting*, 1542. Chamber of Fame, Casa Vasari.

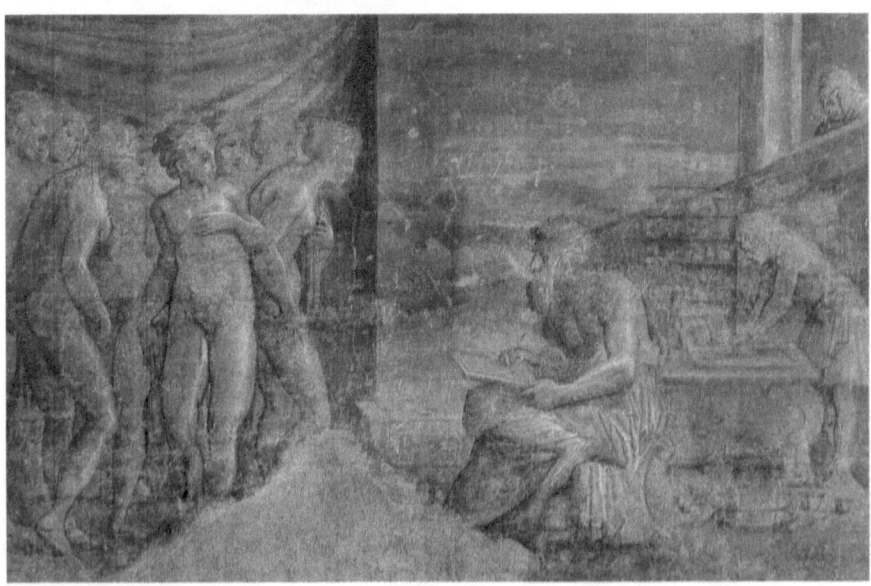

Fig. 8. Giorgio Vasari, *Zeuxis Painting Helen of Troy*, 1548, Chamber of Fortune, Casa Vasari, Arezzo.

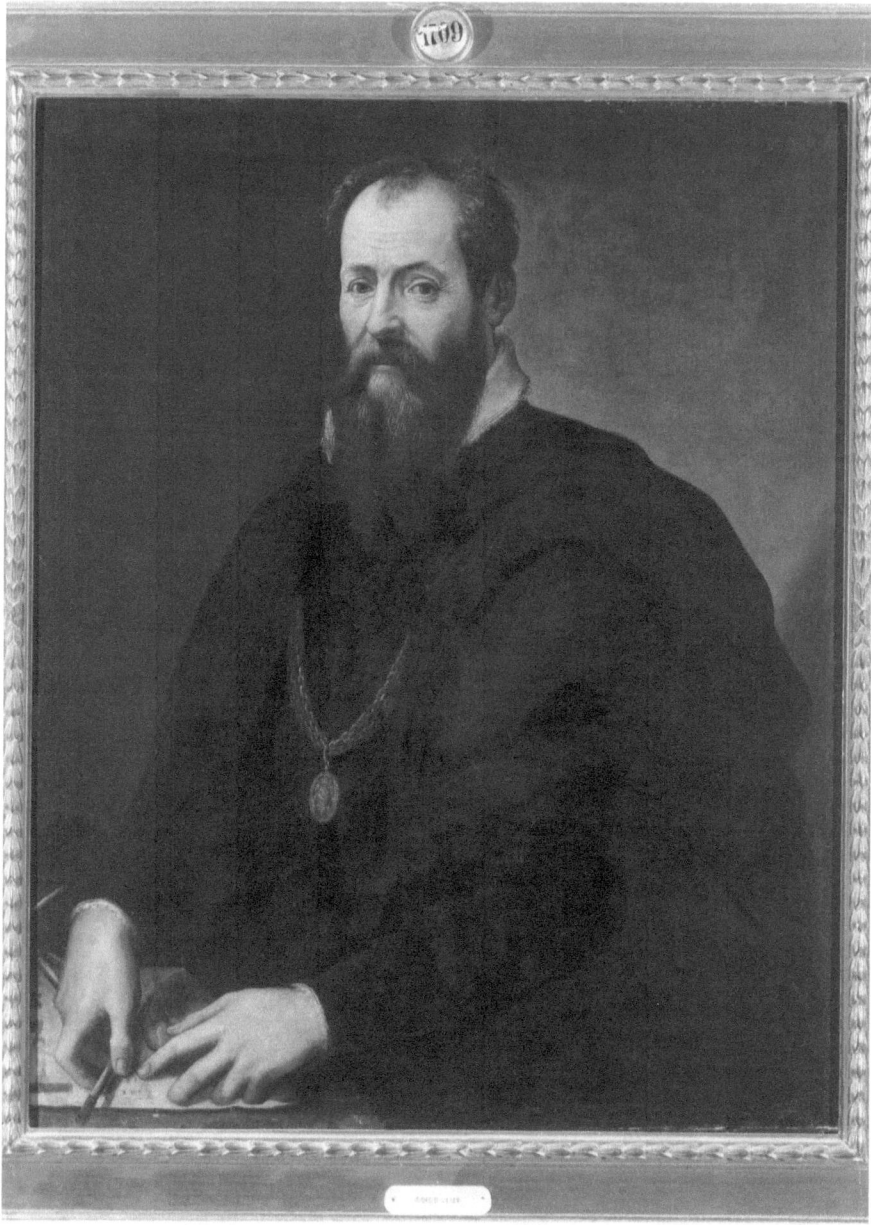

Fig. 9. Giorgio Vasari, *Self-Portrait*, 1550-56. Galleria degli Uffizi.
Photo: Scala/Art Resource, NY.

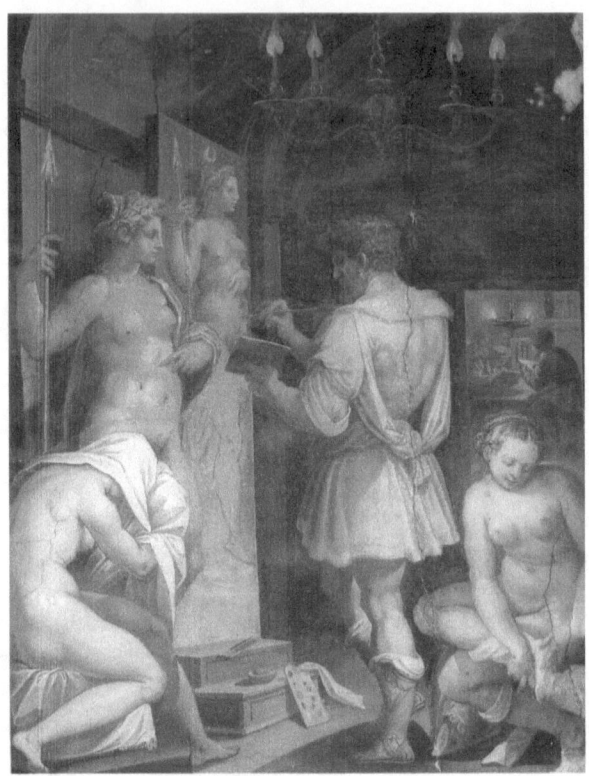

Fig. 10. Giorgio Vasari, *Apelles Painting Juno/Diana*, 1561. Sala, Casa Vasari, Florence. Photo: Art Resource, NY.

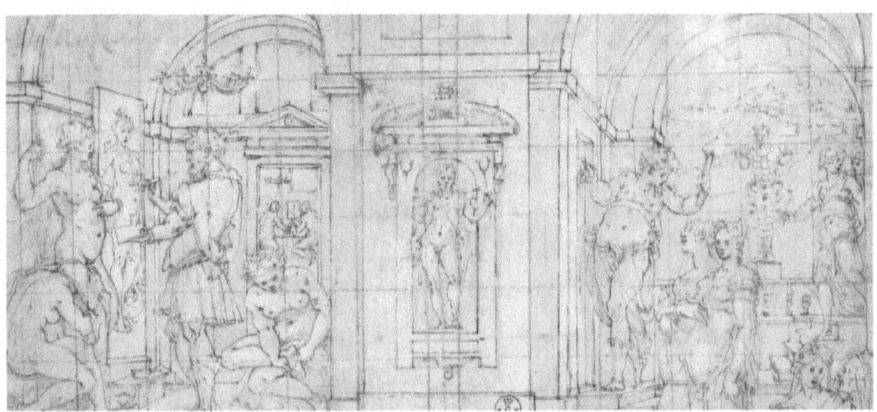

Fig. 11. Giorgio Vasari, *Apelles' Studio*, 1561, drawing. Gabinetto di Disegni e delle Stampe, Galleria degli Uffizi, Florence. Photo: Gabinetto di Disegni e delle Stampe, Galleria degli Uffizi, Florence.

# 11

# Giorgio Vasari's *Madonna of the Rosary*

*For Ettore Mosé Lombroso De Girolami, M.D.\**

In 1572, Giorgio Vasari depicted *The Madonna of the Rosary* for the private chapel of the Capponi family in the church of Santa Maria Novella, Florence (Fig. 1). In his *Ricordanze*, he explained the commission and documents the assistance of Jacopo Zucchi in the completion of the painting.[1] This essay analyzes Vasari's religious symbolism of the rosary in this altarpiece as a reflection of the Tridentine Reform in Florence.

The chapel and altar were a bequest of Camilla Capponi. According to her will of August 4, 1568, she wished not only to have a chapel and altar with a panel painting of the Madonna of the Rosary, but also to have a mass said every morning for her soul. Following her wishes, her inheritors contacted Angelo Malatesti, Prior of Santa Maria Novella and executor of Capponi's will, and Giorgio Vasari. The chapel was completed six months after Capponi's death. At the end of 1569, Vasari records his completion of the painting and the receipt of two hundred florins from Malatesti.[2] The installation of the painting in the chapel occurred in May 1570, as recorded in the church inventory.[3]

The original chapel consists of an altar with the *Madonna of the Rosary* and a tondo of angels dispersing roses. Marcia Halls has explained that the tondo still exists and is visible in the Capitolo del Nocentino behind the refectory of Santa Maria Novella.[4] It is unclear, however, how the tondo was meant t be placed in the chapel. Although Vasari claimed that the tondo was placed above the painting, the window above the altar prevented this. It may be that originally the tondo was designed to accompany the painting, but then its size prevented its placement above the altar or perhaps it was part of another commission.

Another uncertain account reported by Hall is that at some point ownership of the chapel passed from the Capponi family to the Compagnia del Rosario, a confraternity. In her will, Camilla Capponi did not mention the confraternity, and at one time the coat of arms of the Capponi family was on the altar and window of the chapel, proving that the chapel was originally owned by the Capponi family. Records reveal that until 1906, the Capponi altar was located on the left side of the nave, covering the precious work of Masaccio's *Trinity* of 1427.[5] The altar was moved into the chapel located to the right transept of the church, where it is presently on view.

Vasari's *Madonna of the Rosary* is composed of two parts: a heavenly realm and an earthly realm; the Madonna's mantle unites the two. In the heavenly realm, God the Father appears from heaven holding a globe. Accompanying him is the Holy Spirit in the shape of a dove. Large and small angels appear in the sky carrying a large rosary containing blue and red beads that encircle large medallions portraying the mysteries of the rosary. Two small angels crown the Madonna, while two large angels hold above the Madonna's head another crown composed of the central part of the rosary. Other angels hold open the mantle of the Madonna. With her blue mantle, the large Madonna of Mercy carrying Christ stands on a sarcophagus (likely alluding to Camilla Capponi's tomb). The Madonna extends her hand to Saint Dominic, who gratefully kisses it in thanks for providing love and protection for devotees. The Madonna's mantle engulfs and embraces people from all aspects of life: poor and rich, women and men, old and young, and holy figures. There are seven haloed figures, e.g., on the right side of the painting there is a Dominican monk, perhaps a portrait of the prior of Santa Maria Novella, distributing rosaries to the faithful; Catherine of Siena in a nun's habit, holding a crucifix and rosary; and a crowned Elizabeth of Hungary, a patron of charity and sorrow, gazing at Catherine's crucifix. Depicted on the left side of the painting are Carlo Borromeo, Archbishop of Milan, and Dominican holy figures, such as Peter Martyr, Vincent Ferrer, and Dominic, who is kissing the Madonna's hand. In front of this scene, in poor condition, two large figures complete Vasari's original composition: the personification of Charity and Carlo Borromeo, Archbishop of Milan.

On the right side of the painting is the personification of Charity, clothed with the colors of the Roman Catholic church, yellow and blue, and embracing small children while providing them with a rosary. The medallion that adorns the personification depicts a figure of Charity as well, confirming her identification with that theological virtue. The child who Charity holds in her arms makes a gesture of victory or blessing with his small fingers, while holding a cluster of rosaries in his other hand. The pose of the Christ Child parallels the small child's gesture of triumph; heaven and earth are celebrating the victory of praying and reaping the benefits of charity.

The personification of Charity turns to gaze at an elegant Florentine noble lady, perhaps the deceased Camilla Capponi, who stands behind Catherine of Siena and Elizabeth of Hungary. She points to herself as if requesting a rosary from the Dominican monk who is dispersing the holy treasure. Her placement near Saint Catherine, Saint Elizabeth, and the personification of Charity is not accidental; Vasari is comparing Camilla's charitable actions with those of the female saints. Saint Catherine, a member of the Dominican Tertiary Order, honors charity and prayer, as reflected in her writings in the *Dialogue* or *Treatise on Divine Providence*.[6] Saint Elizabeth of Hungary was a princess who dedicated her life to providing alms for the poor. Roses became her attribute: on a secret errand of mercy, she was threatened with death by her non-Christian husband if she continued to give bread to the poor. At the moment of discovery, the bread she was carrying was transformed into roses.

On the right of the scene, the clerical figure kneeling and gazing at the Madonna is Carlo Borromeo, Archbishop of Milan. Of a noble Florentine family, son of Magherita de' Medici and nephew of Pope Pius IV, Angelo de' Medici, Borromeo was appointed to his clerical role as archbishop of Milan in 1566, after the death of his uncle. Borromeo was an active participant in the religious reforms in the Roman Catholic Church and a strong advocate for praying to the Virgin Mary. No doubt these actions reflected his role as archbishop of the cathedral of Milan, as well as his architectural guidance in its renovation. The cathedral of Milan is dedicated to the Virgin Mary, depicted in a fifty-foot-high golden statue, *La Madonnina* (The Little Madonna), placed on the highest of the cathedral's spires.

In the scene, there are numerous portraits of Florentine dignitaries who are not easy to identify. For example, the young female figure behind Borromeo may be a portrait of his mother, Margherita de' Medici, when she was young.

In consultation with his humanist and prelate friend Vincenzo Borghini, Vasari painted the iconography of the rosary with its fifteen mysteries. He composed a giant rosary that crowns the Madonna. The mysteries of the rosary depicted in the medallions framed by the rosary beads relate to the life of Mary and the Passion of Christ.[7] The mysteries are composed of three parts: the Joyful Mysteries, the Sorrowful Mysteries, and the Glorious Mysteries. Each cluster of mysteries in turn reveals five scenes from the New Testament. The Joyful Mysteries are composed of the following: 1) *The Annunciation* The Angel Gabriel is sent from God to Nazareth, a town in Galilee. Coming to Mary, he says, "Hail, favored one! The Lord is with you" (Luke 1:26–28);   2) *The Visitation* Mary travels to the house of Zechariah and greets Elizabeth, who is pregnant. When Elizabeth hears Mary's greeting, the infant leaps in her womb, and Elizabeth, filled with the Holy Spirit, cries out and says, "Most blessed are you among women, and blessed is the fruit of your womb" (Luke 1:39–45); 3) *The Birth of Our Lord* Mary gives birth to her firstborn son. She wraps him in swaddling clothes and lays him in a manger. Suddenly there is a multitude of the heavenly host praising God, saying: "Glory to God in the highest and on earth, peace to those on whom his favor rests" (Luke 2:1–20); 4) *The Presentation in the Temple* Mary and Joseph take the baby Jesus to the Temple to present him to the Lord. At the Temple, Simeon and Anna come forward, give thanks to God, and speak about Jesus to all who are present (Luke 2:22–38); 5) *The Finding of the Child Jesus in the Temple* The boy Jesus remains behind in Jerusalem, but his parents do not know this. After three days pass, they find him in the Temple, sitting in the midst of the teachers, listening to them and asking them questions (Luke 2:41–50).

The second set of mysteries, the Sorrowful Mysteries, also contain five scenes: 1) *The Agony in the Garden* Jesus travels to Gethsemane to pray: "My Father, if it is possible, let this cup pass from me; yet, not as I will, but as you will" (Matthew 26:36–46); 2) *The Scourging at the Pillar* The chief priests hold a council with the elders and the scribes. They bind Christ, lead him away, and hand him over to Pilate, who, wishing to satisfy the crowd, has Christ scourged and hands him over to be crucified (Mark 15:1–16); 3) *The Crowning with Thorns* Soldiers strip Christ's clothes off and throw a scarlet military cloak on him. They weave a crown out of thorns and place it on his head and put a reed in his right hand. Kneeling before him, they mock him, saying, "Hail, King of the Jews!" (Matthew 27:27–31); 4) *The Carrying of the Cross* Weak from being beaten, Christ is unable to carry his cross to Golgotha alone; Simon, a Cyrenian, helps him (Mark 15:20–22); 5) *The Crucifixion* When the procession comes to Golgotha (The Place of the Skull), they crucify Christ and two criminals, one on his right, the other on his left. Christ proclaims, "Father, forgive them, for they know not what they do" (Luke 23:33-46).

The third group of Mysteries, the Glorious Mysteries, consists of five scenes as well: 1) *The Resurrection*  Mary Magdalene and the Mary Martha arrive to see the tomb. An angel appears to them and says, "Do not be afraid! I know that you are seeking Christ the Crucified. He is not here, for he has been raised, just as he said" (Matthew 28:1–10); 2) *The Ascension of Our Lord* Christ blesses his disciples and then is taken up into heaven (Luke 24:44-53); 3) *The Descent of the Holy Spirit* Christ comes and stands in the midst of his disciples and says to them, "Peace be with you. Receive the Holy Spirit" (John 14:15–21); 4) *The Assumption of Our Lady into Heaven* "For if we believe that Christ died and rose, so too will God, through Christ bring with him those who are asleep. Thus we shall always be with the Lord" (1 Thessalonians 4:14–17). Finally the Immaculate Virgin, preserved free from all stain of original sin, when the course of her earthly life was finished, was taken up body and soul into heavenly glory; 5) *The Coronation of the Blessed*

*Virgin Mary* "A great sign appears in the sky, a woman clothed with the sun, with the moon under her feet, an on her head a crown of twelve stars" (Revelation 12:1).

Vasari's visual sources for this original composition derive from at least three sources, one of which is the Tree of Life or Tree of Jesse, e.g., Taddeo Gaddi's *Tree of Life* of 1360, in the Refectory of Santa Croce (Fig 2), where there is a depiction of a wooden trellis or branches where inscriptions and figures allude to biblical events.

The second source is the subject of the Madonna of Mercy, e.g., Bernardo Daddi, *Madonna of Mercy* of 1342, Bigallo Oratory, in Florence (Fig. 3); Piero della Francesca's *Pala Montefeltro* of 1492, at San Sepolcro (Fig. 4); Rosso Fiorentino's *Madonna of Mercy* of 1525, a drawing now in the Louvre; and Vasari's banner of the *Madonna of Mercy* of 1560 for the Aretine Fraternità of Santa Maria. Vasari's banner, which is painted with oils on silk, is conserved at the Museo Diocesano of Arezzo.[8] In these types of imagery, a colossal figure of the Madonna is portrayed opening her mantle to engulf and protect the fervent parishioners or devotees.

Vasari's third visual source is likely Lorenzo Lotto's *Madonna of the Rosary* of 1539 (Fig. )  In this type of depiction, the fifteen mysteries of the rosary are represented in medallions hanging on a wooden trellis or on branches of a robust tree. The medallions replace the inscriptions or biblical figures contained in the Tree of Life. They depict the rosary's fifteen mysteries on the wooden trellis that alludes to the symbol of the vine and the legend of the True Cross. The rose vine and the rose motif, however, symbolize the *hortus conclusus* (enclosed garden or perfumed garden) of Solomon's *Song of Songs* or *Canticles* (4:12–15).[9]

After his trip to Venice, Lotto depicted this complicated altarpiece in the Marche for the church of San Domenico at Cingoli.[10] The Confraternity of the Rosary commissioned this visually and iconographically complex altarpiece. In consultation with the confraternity, Lotto incorporated a combination of narrative medallions depicting the fifteen scenes from the lives of Christ and the Virgin. He also included images of the principal Dominican saints, such as Dominic, Vincent Ferrer, Catherine of Siena, and Peter Martyr. These holy figure are also incorporated in German prints celebrating the cult of the Madonna of the Rosary, e.g., Wolf Traut's woodcut of 1510, *The Virgin of the Rosary* in the *Freudenreich, hurt rich und glorious Mary Rosary*.[11] Peter Humfrey and Esperança Camara have also suggested Alberto Castellano's *Rosario della gloriosa Vergine Maria* as a literary source for Lotto's painting. (Figs. [12] In his altarpiece, however, Lotto includes Mary Magdalene with her ointment jar, and Saint Exuperantius, the patron saint of Cingoli, holding a model of the city.

Lotto's composition is divided in two parts. In an open landscape, framed by two horizontal walls, a bushy tree with large branches supports a wooden trellis of roses and medallions, containing the mysteries of the rosary. The mysteries are displayed in three semicircles, acting as a triple crown for Mary: the row closest to the seated Madonna displays the Joyful Mysteries, the next row displays the Sorrowful Mysteries, and the top row displays the Glorious Mysteries. In front of the hedge of roses there is a second parapet, in front of which there is a stepped stone platform.

At one level, there is a stone throne, which is covered with an oriental cloth of honor, where the Madonna is seated. She awards a rosary to San Dominic with one hand and with the other she holds Christ, who is reaching for Saint Exuperantius's gift, a model of the city. In front of the second level of the platform, six saints in a *sacra conversazione* (holy conversation) are gathered. Lotto composes a grouping of three figures on each side of the platform, while in the center reside small angels and John the Baptist. They are placed around a large open barrel containing white rose petals. The angels disperse rose petals to the viewer and saints. Lotto depicts a gentle wind, causing the rose petals to float and scatter as well as catch on the trellis. In this manner, the artist cleverly decorates the entire scene with pink and white petals, alluding to joy, love, and blessings.[13] John the Baptist not only points to the Christ Child, recognizing his significance as a divine creator, but points as well to the throne's edge, where the artist's signature is visible, a human creator.

Allegorically, the scatter rose petals along with the pine trellis perfume the interior space of the painting where the religious scene takes place as well as the exterior space where spectators reside.[14] Angelic putti playfully toss the rose petals at viewers as well at the holy group. Iconographically, the perfume of the roses is associated with the grace and virtue of Mary as mean to purify the terrestrial realm.[15] Lotto is revealing the Dominican religious iconography on the senses, in particular, the sense of smell and sight when praying the rosary as well as other prayers as the *Ave Maria* or *Pater Noster*.[16] For the Dominican, the purpose of creating a perfumed environment is to evoke a spiritual well being in the faithful as well as to efficaciously engage the devotee to immerse in the act of praying, particularly, the rosary.

In his altarpiece, Lotto symbolically combines the themes of holy conversation and heavenly garden with the depiction of the rosary's mysteries. Vasari emulates Lotto's manner of combining several religious themes in one by combining the same theme of holy conversation with the depiction of the rosary, but he adds the theme of charity and mercy and the theme of salvation, following Tridentine spiritual aims.[17] Vasari's scene is not in a specified earthly place; it does not take place in an enclosed garden or open landscape as in Lotto's altarpiece. Vasari's imagery is didactic, again following Tridentine teaching on love and charity. He creates a vision on the benefits of praying the rosary in order to achieve eternal salvation.

Through his friend the humanist Vincenzo Borghini (1515–1580), Vasari was aware of the recent Milanese publication of Bartolomeo Scalvo's *Meditazioni del Rosario: Della Glorissima Maria Vergine*, which was dedicated to Cardinal Borromeo on April 20, 1569 (Figs. 9 and 10). This text contains a frontispiece with images of the mysteries, as well as a decorated page on Mary as preacher of the rosary. Scalvo's dedication to Borromeo suggests both his support for Borromeo's recent establishment of the Confraternity of the Rosary in the Milan cathedral and his awareness of the conflict between the cardinal and the Milanese Dominicans. The Dominicans objected to the creation of another confraternity of the rosary because they were already sponsoring two confraternities of the rosary in Milan, in the churches of Sant' Eustorgio and Santa Maria della Rosa.[18] Vasari's foreground composition relates to Scalvo's woodcut in the text of the *Madonna of the Rosary*.

Marcia Hall has suggested that in placing the Capponi chapel on the funerary fresco of Masaccio's *Trinity* of 1427, Vasari was paraphrasing certain motifs in that painting, e.g., the presence of the Trinity, God the Father appearing with the Holy Spirit, and

Mary's action of interceding on behalf of humankind.[19] Another such paraphrasing is the imagery of apparition or vision: Mary and her heavenly court appear to the faithful consoling them and guiding them to pray the rosary, as well as blessing them for performing acts of charity in the manner of the exemplary Camilla Capponi. Furthermore, in placing a rosary medallion depicting the Coronation of the Virgin above the celestial crown of the Madonna, Vasari is emphasizing the very moment of Mary's glorification. Thus, for the devotee Camilla, eternal salvation has been achieved by praying the rosary to the Mother of Mercy or the Mother of God.

After the completion of the altarpiece, the humanist and art critic Rafaello Borghini (1537–1588) commented favorably on the painting's artistic merits and iconographical content in *Il Riposo* (1584), but he criticized the size of the Madonna: "Ogni cosa mi soddista, fuorché quella donna...la quale a un braccio, che poco più grande che fosse, sarebbe disdicevole a un gigante" ("I am satisfied with everything, except the Madonna...whose arm, which is larger than normal, resembles a giant's").[20]  Obviously, Borghini is not equating the Madonna of the Rosary with the Madonna of Mercy. For Vasari, *The Madonna of the Rosary* embodies his religious fervor with the acceptance of a complex spiritual manifestation of the Counter Reformation in Florence.

During the Baroque period, the Bolognese painter, Guido Reni, assimilates the visual message of the paintings of Lotto and Vasari in the *Madonna of the Rosary* of 1596-98 (the Basilica della Madonna di San Luca in Bologna, Fig. 11). In this painting, Reni purposefully separates the upper part of the painting with the lower part of the painting through the depiction of steps. He divides the heavenly realm from the natural realm.  In the upper part of the painting, Reni depicts a celestial vision of a Christ child guided by his mother, Mary, donating a rosary to San Dominic. The holy figures appear in large puffy clouds surrounded by angelic putti.  In the lower part, Reni emphasizes the mysteries of the rosary by depicting a special vignette on the steps. Here, a golden chalice is filled with symbolic branches such as rose branches (love), pine branches (suffering and forgiveness) and palm branches (martyrdom and salvation). These branches hold medallions with narrative scenes according to the mysteries of the rosary, e.g., on the left of the chalice, the rose branches contain medallions with Joyful Mysteries; on the center of the chalice, the pine branches display medallions with the Sorrowful Mysteries; and on the right of the chalice, the palm branches are decorated with the Glorious Mysteries. The handles of the chalice are in the shape of morning angels, emphasizing the signification of the chalice as a symbol of the Eucharist and salvation.

Unlike Lotto and Vasari, whose painting of the *Madonna of the Rosary* is composed frontally and in the shape of a hanging rosary (Figs 1, 8 and 12), Reni creates two separate scenes within the composition, both alluding to the miraculous powers of the rosary. In the upper part of the painting, the spatial construction of the scene is in profile. Reni depicts a private experience for San Dominic receiving a rosary from the celestial apparition of Madonna and Child. In the lower part, however, the scene is frontal (Fig. 14). Reni is visually calling attention of the viewer, to the single large chalice, and its symbolic contents of branches and medallions. He purposely engages the viewer to look up and observe the miracle experienced by San Dominic. Then, to look down and observe the chalice, where a personal religious experience may occur, thus paralleling the miraculous event up above. These didactic paintings of Lotto, Vasari and Reni pay homage to the miraculous efficacy of the rosary, reflecting the ongoing teaching of the Counter-Reformation tradition.

## Notes

\* I dedicate this essay to my beloved father, Ettore De Girolami, M.D., who, although born of Jewish faith, placed his faith in the Madonna, The Virgin Mary, throughout his life.

1. Karl Frey *Der literarische Nachlass Giorgio Vasaris* (Munich: George Müller, 1930), II, 881, Ricordo 348. See also Marcia B. Hall, *Renovation and Counter-Reformation: Vasari and Duke Cosimo in Santa Maria Novella and Santa Croce, 1565-1577* (Oxford: Warburg Studies/Clarendon Press, 1979), for a study on Vasari's artistic interactions in Santa Maria Novella.
2. ASF Notarile Antecosimiano, N184 (1568), fos. 108ff, and AFS Conv. Suopp. 102, vol. 90, fos.35v-36r, dated March 20, 1568, and recorded as "Debitori e Creitori Segnato A a.c.151."

3. AFS Conv. Suopp. 102, vol. 90, fos. 35v-36r, dated March 20, 1568, and recorded as "Debitori e Creitori Segnato A a.c.153."

4. Hall, *Renovation and Counter-Reformation*, 114-17

5. Walter Paatz, *Die Kirchen von Florenz* (S. Maria Novella) (Frankfurt: Vittorio Kostermann, 1952-53), III, 795, n. 219.

6. Leslie J. Walker, trans. Douglas J. Potter, "Dedicated to the Sacred Heart of Jesus Christ," in *The Catholic Encyclopedia* (New York: Robert Appleton Company, 1911), Vol. XIII.

7. Herbert Thurston and Andrew J. Shipman, "The Rosary," in Remy Lafort, D.D. ed., *The Catholic Encyclopedia* (New York: Robert Appleton Company, 1912), Volume XIII.

8. Laura Corti, *Vasari* (Florence: Cantini, 1989), 120.

9. In Christian terms, Solomon's *Song of Songs* is considered an allegory of the relationship between Christ and the Church or Christ and the individual believer. In the Jewish tradition, *The Song of Songs* is an allegorical representation of the relationship between God and Israel as husband and wife. In the *Song of Songs*, the characters are a woman and a man. This poem suggests the amorous transfer from courtship to marriage. Duane A. Garrett, *Song of Songs. Word Biblical Commentary* (Nashville: Nelson, 2004), 15. 23B.

10. Peter Humfrey, *Lorenzo Lotto* (London: Yale University Press, 1997), 129-31, fig. 131. There church is dedicated as well to San Niccolò.

11. Humfrey, *Lorenzo Lotto*, 131 and fig. 132, and Bernard J. H. Aikema, "La pala di Cingoli," *Lorenzo Lotto*, ed. P. Zampetti and V. Sgarbi (Trevisio: Atti del Convegno a Cingoli, 1981), pp. 443-45.

12. Esperança Camara, *Pictures and Prayers*, Ph.D. diss., The John Hopkins University, Maryland, 2002, for recent bibliography on the symbolism of the rosary. See also, Winston Allen, *Stories of the Rose, the Making of the Rosary in the Middle Ages* (University Park, PA: Pennsylvania University Press, 1997); R. J. M. Olson, "The Rosary and its Iconography," *Arte Cristiana*, 86 (1998), 253-76.

13. Camara, *Pictures and Prayers*, 91, n. 161, for the symbolism of petals as gifts of the Holy Spirit during Pentecost, as representing Christ's blood (red petals) or the joy of Mary (white petals). See also Katherine Powers, "Musical Images for Devotions: Bendetto Coda's Altarpiece for the Rosary," in K. A. McIver, *Art and Music in the Early Modern Period* (London: Ashgate, 2003), pp .27-43. Rose petals could be compared to musical notes.

14. François Quiviger, "Fleurs éparpillés dans deux tableaux du Cinquecento vénetien. Essai d'iconographie olfactive," *Flore du paradis*, ed. Paulette Choné and Bénédicte Gaulard (Glasgow: Galsgow Emblem Studies, 2004) Vol. 9, 160-62.

15. Alberto da Castello, *Rosario della gloriosa vergine Maria* (Venice: V. della Serena & Compagni, 1541), fol. 40, states, "la suavita del odore cioè Maaria Vergine la quale per le eccelentissime virtue gratie fu odorifera al eterno Dio e a gli angeli e a gli huomen" ("the gentle smell of the Virgin Mary, who reflects virtue and grace, was odoriferous [pleasant odor] to the Eternal God, to the angels and to the individuals").

16. Quiviger, "Fleurs éparpillés dans deux tableaux du Cinquecento vénetien, 160.

17. Geoffrey W. Bromiley, *Historical Theology* (Grand Rapids, MI: W. B. Eerdmans Publishing, Company, 1978), 283-88.

18. Camara, *Pictures and Prayers*, 114, n. 61.

19. Hall, *Renovation and Counter-Reformation*, 114-17.

20. Rafaello Borghini, *Il Riposo* (1584), ed., Lloyd H. Ellis, Jr. (Toronto: University of Toronto Press, 2008), pp. 96 and 625. "Non mi pare che si possa se non molto lodar l'invenzione" ("I doubt that one cannot do anything else, but highly praise the invention"). In this context, Borghini reviews the history of the rosary and its function.

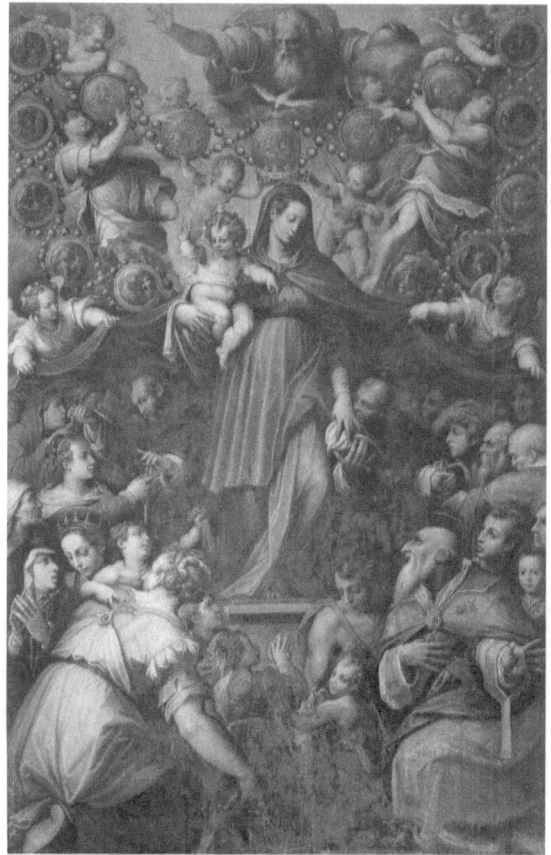

Fig. 1 Giorgio Vasari, *Madonna of the Rosary*, 1572. Capponi Chapel, Santa Maria Novella, Florence.

Fig. 2. Taddeo Gaddi, *Tree of Life*, 1360, Refectory, Santa Croce, Florence.

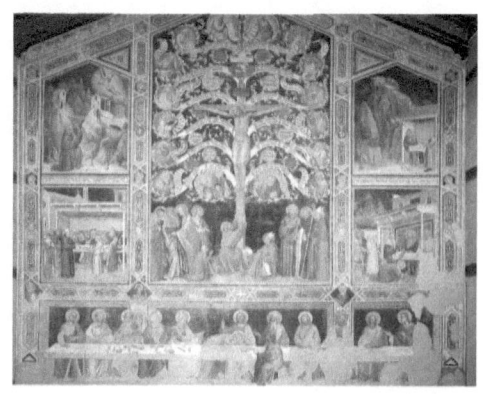

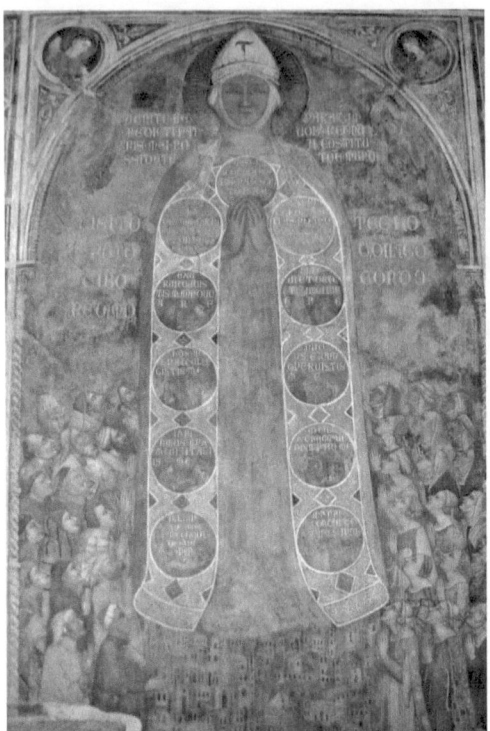

Fig. 3. Bernardo Daddi,
*Madonna of Mercy*, 1342.
Bigallo Oratory, Florence.

Fig. 4. Piero della Francesca, *Madonna of
Mercy*, Pala Montefeltro, 1492.
San Sepolcro, Tuscany.

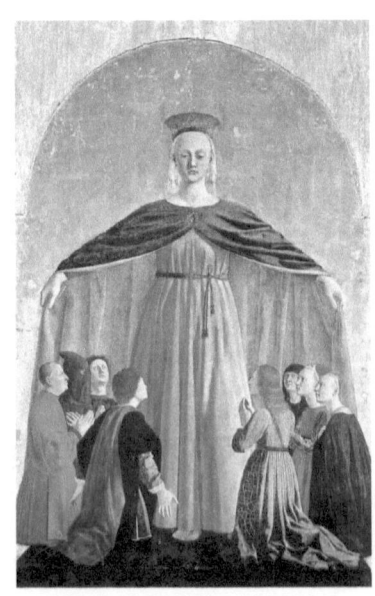

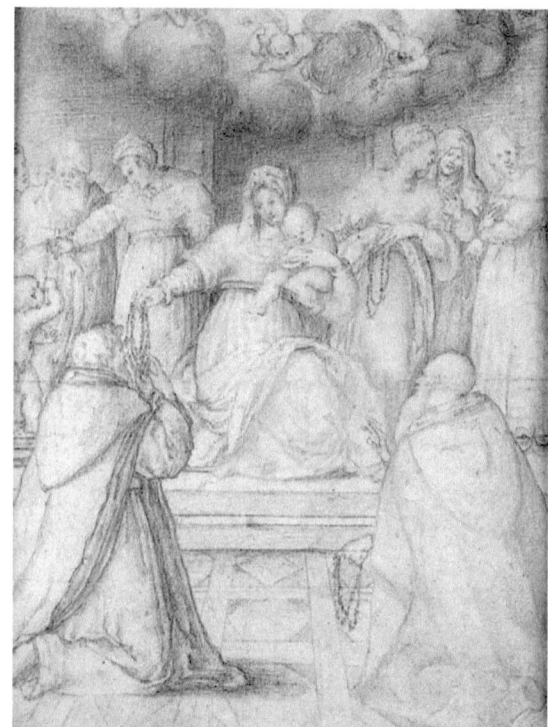

Fig. 5.  Rosso Fiorentino, *Madonna of the Rosary*, 1525, drawing. Christie's Sales 2414/Lot 680, 2002.

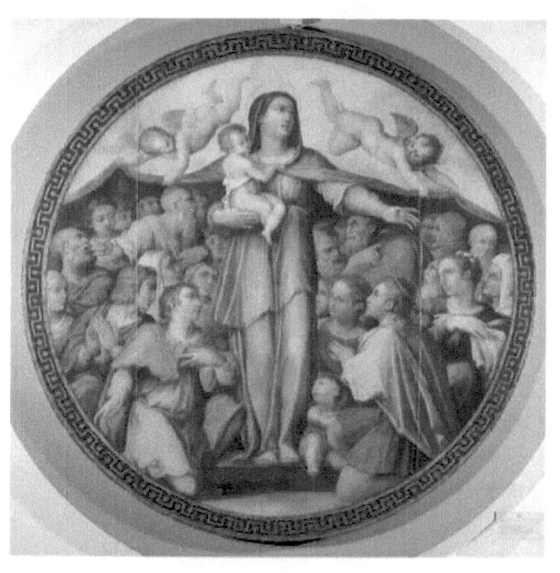

Fig. 6. Giorgio Vasari, *Madonna of Mercy*, 1560, banner. Museo Diocesano, Arezzo.

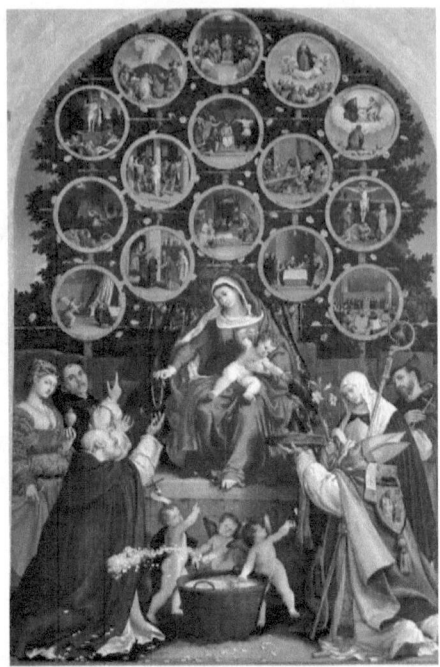

Fig. 7. Lorenzo Lotto, *Madonna of the Rosary*, 1539. San Domenico, Cingoli.

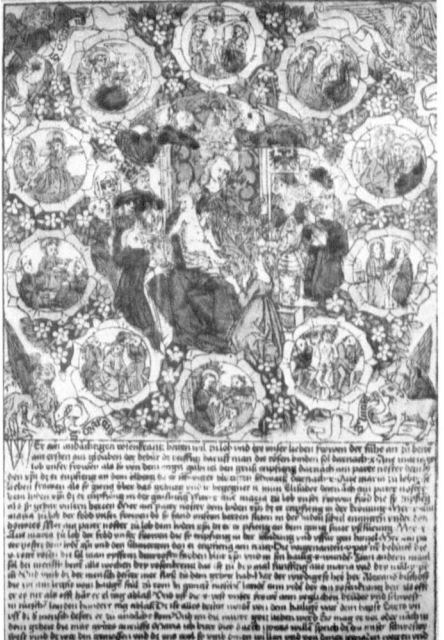

Fig. 8. Wolf Traut, *The Virgin of the Rosary*, 1510, woodcut in *Freudenreich, hurt rich und glorious Mary Rosary.*

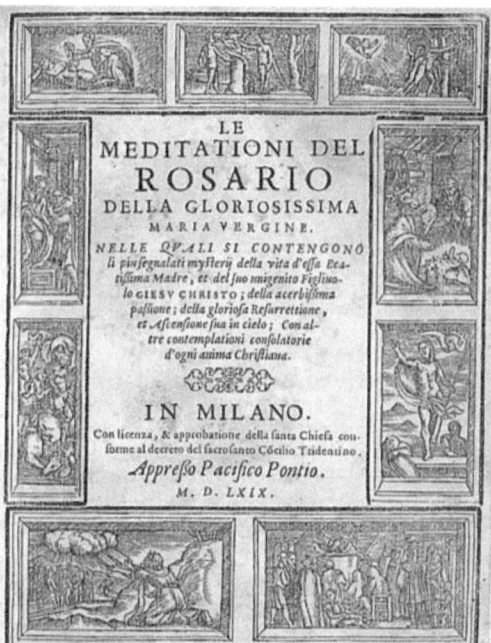

Fig. 9. Bartolomeo Scalvo, *Meditazioni del Rosario: Della Gloriosa Maria Vergine*, 1569, Milan: Pacifico Pontio.

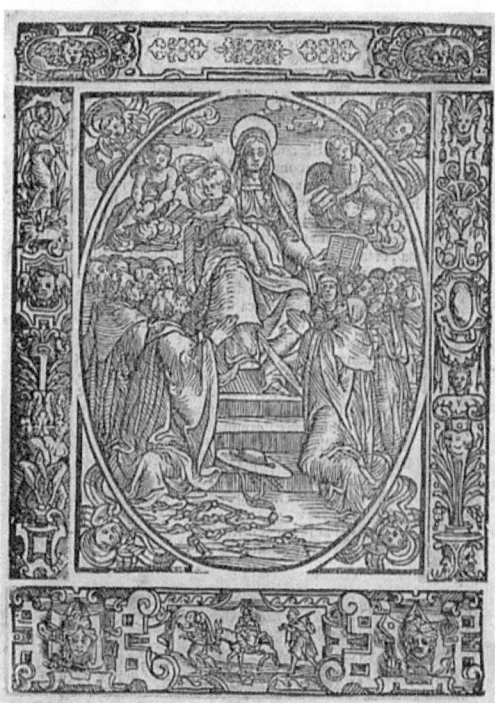

Fig. 10. Bartolomeo Scalvo, Frontispiece, *Meditazioni del Rosario: Della Gloriosa Maria Vergine*, 1569, Milan: Pacifico Pontio.

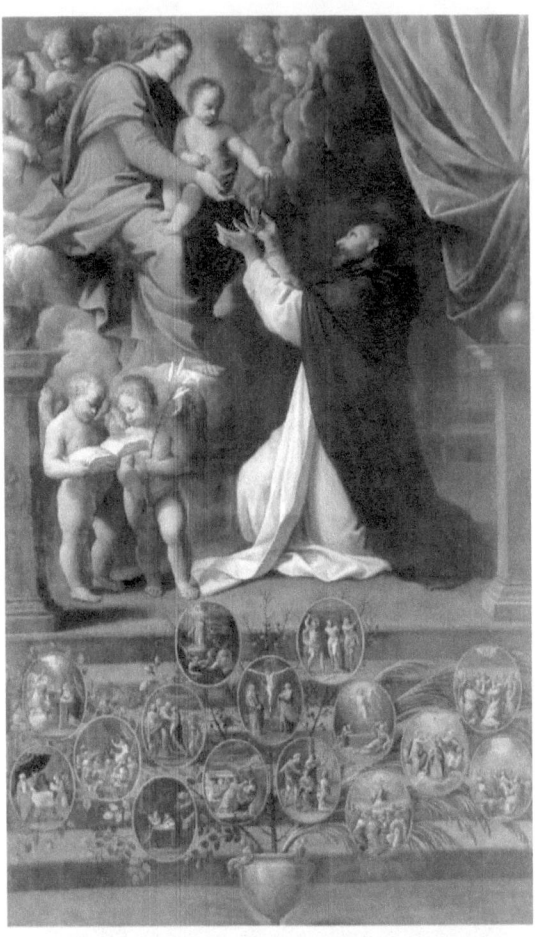

Fig. 11. Guido Reni, *Madonna of the Rosary*, 1596. Basilica della Madonna di San Luca, Bologna.

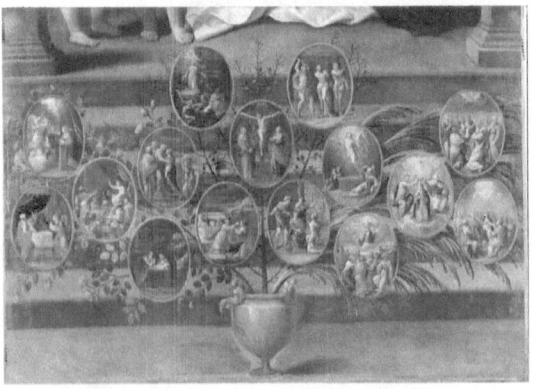

Fig 12. Guido Reni, *Madonna of the Rosary*, det., 1596. Basilica della Madonna di San Luca, Bologna.

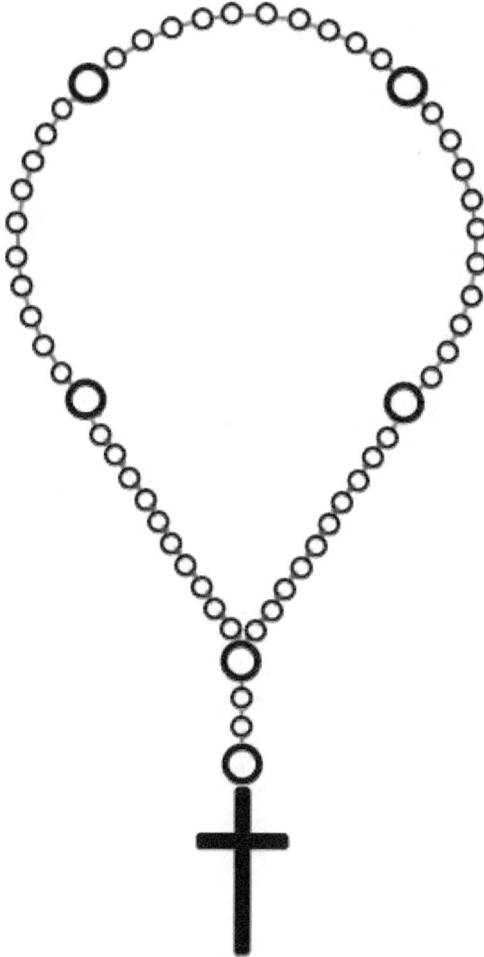

Fig. 13. Cheney's reconstruction of a hanging rosary.

# 12

# Giorgio Vasari's *Patience*:
# The Measure of Time[1]

This essay discusses three points in relation to Giorgio Vasari's *Patience*, a personification of measuring time: (1) how sixteenth-century artists in Italy, in particular, Giorgio Vasari, employs emblem books for personification of aesthetic, moral and philosophical concepts, in particular, Andrea Alciato's *Emblematum libellus cum commentarii*, Achille Bocchi's *Symbolica Questionae* and in Renaissance numismatic imagery; (2) how Vasari uses the technology of the period–the astrolabe, the water clock and the armillary sphere–to personify moral aims, such as Patience, a personification of time and temperance; and (3) how Vasari's paintings and writings clearly embody these humanistic issues, reflecting the cultural milieu of the time as exemplified in his painted versions of *Patience* of 1530 and 1554.

In his writings, particularly in the prefaces of the *Vite*,[2] Vasari emphasizes that an allegory (emblem) must visually and verbally assimilate its ancient sources. Moreover, in the *Ragionamenti*, Giorgio Vasari stresses that in a painting "everything must have meaning" (*"tutto ha da aver significato"*)."[3]

Such emblematic sources provide Vasari with an extensive repertoire of images, which he collected and used in the iconography of his early paintings, and which he repeated and expanded on in his visual repertoire in such subsequent commissions as his paintings of the Palazzo Vecchio in Florence.[4] For example, the personification of Patience was painted earlier by Vasari in the decorative cycles, such as the Cornaro Palace in Venice, Vasari's house in Arezzo, and the refectory of Monteoliveto in Naples, and later in panel paintings such as *Patience* at the Pitti Palace in Florence.

The word "patience" derives from the Latin *patiens*, meaning enduring. Vasari depicts two types of Patience incorporating classical and medieval texts. The first type, an earlier depiction of Patience from 1530-1548, excludes the concept of measurability, focusing on the traditional notion of viewing the image Patience as a symbol of Humility, Obedience and Servitude, for example the *Cornaro Patience*. In 1542, Giovanni Cornaro commissions Michele Sanmichele to enlarge and renovate his palace, known as Corner-Spinelli Palace, on the Grand Canal, and Vasari to decorate the ceiling of the main hall. Vasari describes this commission in the *Ricordanze:* "On April 8, 1542, [I executed] nine large paintings for the main hall of Giovanni Cornaro's palace on the Grand Canal. In the center of the ceiling is Charity crowned with her angels, around her, in four paintings are Faith, Hope, Justice and Patience, all accompanied by various figures" (Fig. 1).[5] The ceiling is eventually dismantled. (Today the pictures are no longer *in situ*.)

In the *Cornaro Patience*, the reclining figure is barefooted and turns her back to the viewer. Two men are bound on her right, while a pensive Michelangelesque Jeremiah sits at her left. Patience carries a yoke, a symbol of her perseverance.[6] With her yoke, Patience rests quietly. In his writings, Vasari describes the personification of Patientia as "il giogho al collo et il capo basso" ("The yoke placed on her neck, and bending her head").[7] The yoke, a symbol of the virtues of Obedience and Servitude,[8] emphasizes her endurance in life, along with her humble and austere appearance. The yoke refers to a selfless willingness to surrender autonomy and to devote oneself to a goal that demands great self-abnegation. In Alciato's *Emblematum*, Emblem 34 (Fig. 2) contains the motto, *Bear and forbear.* The picture depicts a bull being separated from three cows by a man with a club. There is a landscape in the background. The epigram explains the image:

Sad fortune must be endured by the man suffering it, and a too happy fortune is often to be feared. Epictetus used to say *bear and forbear.* It is fitting to endure much, and to keep one's hands from illicit things.  Thus the bull with its right knee tethered suffers the command of its master; thus it abstains from the pregnant cows.[9]

In *Symbolic Questionaes*, Achille Bocchi, a Bolognese emblematists, visually matches the representation of Patience in Emblem 109 (Fig. 3) with the description of the personification of Patience in Pompeo Vizani's apparatus for Julius III's entry into Bologna on September 24, 1541.[10] In Bocchi's emblem, Patience carries a helmet and a trophy decorated with garlands, bucrania and plums, and there is a yoke around her neck.  A chain hanging from heaven is attached to her yoke, alluding to *omnia duri* –the individual should surrender and endure willingly all difficult things.  Bocchi's emblem is associated with honest labor or victory resulting from hard work. The Old Testament figure Job is an example of the virtue of patience because he bore his troubles with fortitude and perseverance.  The bending of one's head under the yoke alludes to the virtue of Humility.

In his depiction of *Cornaro Patience*, Vasari notes that by acquiring the virtue of patience, an individual can tolerate life's adversities, even venture with tranquility. According to Christian instruction, the individual can achieve this virtue through the blessings of the Holy Spirit, since Patience is one of the Holy Gifts.

In 1548, Vasari repeats the compositional motif of Patience that is previously found in the ceiling of the Cornaro Palace on the east wall of the Chamber of Fortune at his house in Arezzo (Fig. 4).[11] Here, Vasari portrays a simplified version of Patience, a reclining figure and barefooted, embracing a yoke. Patience turns her head toward her shoulder to examine the decoration of her attire.  A medal ornament on her shoulder pad contains an image of a snail, a symbol of perseverance and endurance through vicissitudes of life. The cautious and slow movement of the snail alludes to the saying, "snail's pace."[12] The snail motif alludes to the stamina that Patience must acquire in order to undergo the mutations and transformations of time in the cycle of life.[13] Vasari's *Patience* presage Cesare Ripa's emblem of Patience in the *Iconologia*. The seventeenth-century Roman emblematist, Ripa, also associates the snail with the personification of Patience, in that the snail remains inside her conch for long periods of time.[14]

Enthusiastic about this image of Patience, Vasari in 1545 repeats her again in the frescoed ceiling of the Refectory of Monteoliveto in Naples (Fig. 5).[15] This depiction, however, is seated, not reclining. The attributes that the *Neapolitan Patience* carry continue with the traditional emblematic tradition of Patience's depiction, such as the yoke and reins. Vasari visually comments on an established tradition for the imagery and symbolism of Patience. For example, Valeriano's emblem in *Hieroglyphica* consists simply of a yoke and the motto *Suave*, alluding to the virtues of sufferance and tolerance.[16] Valeriano's motto derives, in turn, from Virgil's writings (*Aeneid*, V, 710). Years later, Ripa appropriates Valeriano's emblem in his emblem of Patience (*Patientia*) by adding the motto *Suave* to the portrayal of a seated figure with a yoke placed on her shoulder and holding manhandles or reins (Fig. 6).

In the second version of the representation of Patience, Vasari adds another meaning to the personification of Patience, the measurement of time, as seen in the *Patience* of 1551-52 at Pitti Palace in Florence (Fig. 7). In October 1551, Bernardetto Minerbetti, bishop of Arezzo, writes to Vasari, to ask him to paint a personification of Patience for his *impresa*.[17] On November 14th, Vasari replies with an elaborate description of the painting, suggesting its design for an emblematic medal.  After examining several ancient hieroglyphs, coins and statues ("perche nessuno rovescio antico ne negli eroglifi ne statue se n'è trovate"),[18] Vasari consults with Michelangelo for the creation of this new *invenzione* on the subject, since no previous images of it exists ("giudichiamo, che la fussi virtù propria, et non ne facessino memoria").[19]  Vasari execute several drawings for this commission, but because Michelangelo, could not come to an agreement on the iconography, Vasari decides to send along with his drawing a lengthy explanation on the symbolism to the bishop.[20] The drawing now is at the Cabinet des Dessins at the Musée du Louvre (Inv. 1660, Fig. 8).[21]

There are essential points in Vasari's description of *Patience* (Fig. 7). He notes that Patience should be of a standing figure,  of a middle age female, she should be neither completely dressed nor totally undressed (to show the balance between Richness and Poverty). She should have her left foot chained in order not to affect the other nobler parts of the body.  Her arms  should be loose to show her ability to free herself from the enchained position if she wishes. The chain should be attached to a stone. With her folded arms on her chest, Patience should gently await the passing of time for the droppings of water to consume the stone, where she is enchained. The droppings of water should flow from a clepsydra, an ancient clock, used by orators during their speeches.[22] Vasari writes, "I portrayed the clepsydra next to Patience's shoulder, where she looks intensely at how long the droppings of water will take to dissolve the stone where the chain is forged. The motto placed on the stone should be "Diuturna Tollerantia" ("Daily Tolerance")," as it appears in the Louvre drawing (Fig. 8). Vasari continues explaining how the *impresa* should be designed on the medal. "The clepsydra should stand alone on one side of the medal, and on the other side, these should be another fantasy or Patience as previously described ("per impresa, facci fare l'eclissidera sola…ò rovescio di medaglia ò altre fantasie, come la stà")."[23]

Bishop Minerbetti and Annibale Caro, Vasari's friend and adviser in humanist questions, highly praised Vasari's drawings of Patience.[24] Minerbetti is so pleased with Vasari's *invenzione* that he allowed Ercole II Duke of Ferrara to borrow the conceit for the duke's emblem  on *Patience*.[25]  In 1554,  Pompeo Leoni strikes the medal for the duke with the Vasarian conceit in mind and with the motto borrowed from Gelli's *Device, Mottoes and Imprese*, a saying *Superanda omnis fortuna ferendo est*  ("You must win each fortune with patience" or "Through Patience the individual stands above the powers of Fortuna"  (Fig. 9).[26]  The impact of Vasari's image, in particular the clepsydra associated with the personification of Patience, is reflected in Alberti Battisti's engraving, *Fortitudo and Patientia* of 1554, as well as Francesco Salviati's painting, *Patience* of 1554 based on Vasari's drawings (Fig. 9).[27] In both visual representations, the clepsydra is placed next to Patience, alluding to the measurement and passing of time.

In the Pitti painting, Vasari follows his earlier description, but in addition, he elaborates on the original drawing. For example, in the painting, which has darkened over time, the motto, "Diuturna Tollerantia," is not visible (Figs. 7 and 8). He places an armillary sphere above the water clock (water-thief) and creates a composition in a rocky landscape. From studying Leoni's medal, however, it becomes easier to study Vasari's darkened painting, which depicts a standing, bare-breasted woman, with crossed arms, is resigned to her faith with her  left ankle is enchained. She looks at the water clock that drips steadily drops of water onto a square stone surface. An armillary sphere rests above the clepsydra.  The foreground landscape depicts a cluster of wild flowers and a turtle. This scene is representative of a rocky landscape.

In comparing the previous depictions of *Patience* with the *Pitti Patience*,  Vasari, in order to emphasize the aspect of passing of time, substitutes the yoke for the chain, the hourglass for the water clock, and the snail for the turtle. He connects the symbolism of the turtle with the concept of time, a connection that originates in Egypt. For the Egyptians, the tortoise, as a creature of the waters, is lunar in its symbolism, typifying the powers of time.[28] It represents steady persistence. There are well known fables of the hare and the tortoise and of Zeno's paradox of the race between Achilles and the tortoise.  Moreover, the Egyptian association of measuring time is recorded by Heron of Alexandria, who writes about the various mechanical devices of this type during the first century, including the clepsydra.[29] Years later, the clepsydra took on other geometric forms, such as a straight-sided shape. The development of the clepsydra from siphon to water clock as a means of determining an interval of time during ancient times is sketched by Volker Aschoff in *Geschichte der Nachrichtentechnik* (Figs. 12 and 13).[30]

Vasari's knowledge of clepsydra derives from his studies of Vitruvius.  In *De architectura* IX.8.2-15, Vitruvius explains the regulating mechanism of water clock, also called "winter clocks," that exists during his lifetime.[31] An example of Vitruvius' *horologium* originated in the Tower of the Winds erected by Andronicus of Kyrson in the first century BCE in Athens.  Each of the eight sides of the tower, approximately 13 meters high, has a sundial, with the water clock inside the tower, moving other astronomical mechanisms and keeping time for a day.

Vasari's inclusion of the clepsydra in connection with Patience alludes to another aspect of this virtue, her temperance or moderation, as he describe his invention and the motto, "Diuturna Tollerantia."[32]  In Roman times, the judicial authorities limit the court speeches by adding a bridle or *frenum* to the outpouring of the water in the clepsydra.[33] As a consequence of this signification, the Renaissance employed the bridle in iconographical representations of the cardinal virtue Temperance. In contrast to the *Cornaro Patience* (Fig. 1), in the *Pitti Patience* (Fig. 11), Vasari replaces the bridle with a metal chain. Both items restrain the quick movements of Patience or time and ensures the continuous, slow and gradual passing of time.

Vasari includes other objects of time in his painting such as the armillary sphere placed above the clepsydra. Whereas the water clock symbolizes the measuring of terrestrial time, the armillary sphere alludes to the marking of celestial time. Unlike the armillary sphere, the water clock is used mostly at night or on overcast days. Vasari portraying this functional aspect of the clepsydra by depicting the scene in a landscape and in the early evening, where the terrestrial and celestial measuring of time can be accomplished.

In the *Pitti Patience*, Vasari's armillary sphere contains the celestial sphere, with its various coordinates in relation to earth at the center, as well as the zodiacal band.[34] By placing these two measuring devices together, he continues the convention of considering the clepsydra to be a horoscopic vase. Since the time of Macrobius, the measuring of the quantity of water flowing from a clepsydra assisted in understanding the rising of the signs of the zodiac.[35] The armillary sphere is an instrument employed by astrologers to accurately measure the planets and constellations, as represented in the woodcut on Ptolemy, the Greek-Egyptian astronomer of Alexandria (Fig. 9).[36] However. the precision achieved by this instrument to accurately measure the universe cannot compare to Patience's immeasurable spirit and goodness.

In the *Pitti Patience*, Vasari combines the iconographical tradition of symbolic meaning concerning the association of Patience as an emblem of endurance and temperance with his own stylistic evolution. At the same time, he also makes specific substitutions in the attributes of Patience in order to add another level of signification, the slow passing of time. Vasari associates the aspect of endurance with the concept of time by surrounding Patience with technical measurements on the flow of time. His familiarity with the language and imagery of the allegoric, emblematic, hieroglyphic and visual traditions prompts him to create a new vocabulary in art–an encyclopedia of images and symbols. This visual dictionary demonstrates not only the assimilation of the emblematic tradition in Italian paintings of the sixteenth century, but also the integration of scientific knowledge in the arts. Vasari wishes to demonstrate that art can visualize science as well. For him, the intellectual goal of an artist is similar to that of a scientist. Both artist and scientist create and invent–the painter in composing visual images and the scientist in articulating experimental constructions.

Correspondingly, art and science in the Renaissance embody the Humanistic and Neoplatonic traditions, as well as the emblematic in unveiling a *clavis interpretandi* in a mysterious story filled with hieroglyphs and enigmatic actions, with a secret purpose. Thus, the image requires a decoding of the riddles at many levels for achieving an understanding and interpreting the meaning of the universe.

Marsilio Ficino observes that "things that are visible are the mirror of those things which are invisible [and] all the world objects have a signification."[37] His comments parallel Andrea Alciato's concept that the universe is a forest of symbols.[38] Vasari's *Patience*, visually manifest Alciatio's conceit as well as conveying Ficino's Neoplatonic view on the depicting the meaning of an idea with actual forms to provide a moral and efficacious message. In Vasari's painting, Alciato's didactic function of the emblem or image is manifested through the depiction of scientific and technical devices, such as the clepsydra and the armillary sphere in association with the image of Patience. For example, in the painting, the clepsydra and armillalry sphere  symbolize the measuring of terrestrial and celestial time, respectively. Their association with Patience, however, further reminds the viewer to slowly, carefully and wisely measure the vicissitudes of life. In Renaissance Neoplatonic terms, for Vasari and his time, the role of Patience parallels the role of the Angel of Time, who observes the flowing of time from the past to the present and on into the future, similar to the flowing of one physical form– the dropping of water in the clepsydra–into another as renewal of life, the divine cosmic transformations recorded with the armillary sphere.

# Notes

This article is a reprint of "The Inspiration of Astronomical Phenomena," in Raymond E. White, ed., *Memorie: Journal of the Italian Astronomical Society* (2001-2002), 112-21.

1. A shorter version of this essay was published as "Giorgio Vasari's Patience: Astronomical Symbol of Time," in *The Inspiration of Astronomical Phenomena*," ed. Raymond E. White, *Memorie: Journal of the Italian Astronomical Society* (2001-2002), 112-121.
2. Giorgio Vasari, *Le Vite dei più eccellenti pittori, scultori, et architettori* (1550, 1568), ed. Gaetano Milanesi (Florence: G. C. Sansoni, 1970-74), 115-29. All succeeding references to this text will be noted as Vasari-Milanesi.
3. Vasari-Milanesi, VIII, 87, "io mi preparava per l'invenzione di questa sala nel leggere le storie antiche e moderne di questa città."
4. Vasari-Milanesi, VIII, 1-224. For Vasari's explanation of *invenzione, imitazione* and *concetti*, see Vasari-Milanesi, II, 93-107.
5. Vasari-Milanesi, VII, 671, Alessandro del Vita, *Lo Zibaldone di Giorgio Vasari* (Arezzo: Tipografia Zelli, 1938), 39, quoting Vasari.
6. Vincenzo Cartari's *Imagine delli Dei degl'Antichi* (Venice, 1547), ed. Walter Koschatzky (Graz: Akademisch Druk, 1963), 242–43, and Cesare Ripa, *Iconologia* (Padua, 1618), ed. by Piero Buscaroli (Milan: Tea Edition, 1992), 339.
7. del Vita, *Lo Zibaldone di Giorgio Vasari*, 25, quoting Vasari.
8. Ripa, *Iconologia*, 317-404.
9. For Emblem 34, see Andrea Alciato, *Emblematum libellus cum commentarii* (Lyon, 1546), Andrea Alciato, *Emblematum libellus* (Basel, 1529), Italian ed. and trans. by Guilliame Roville as *Diverse impresse accommodate a diverse moralita con versi che i loro significati dichiarono tratte da gli Emblemi dell' Alciato* (Lyon, 1549), and Peter M. Daly, ed. *Andreas Alciatus' Index Emblematicum* (Toronto: University of Toronto Press, 1985), 2 vols., Vol 1, Emblem 34.
10. Elizabeth See Watson, *Achille Bocchi and the Emblem Book as Symbolic Form* (Cambridge: Cambridge University Press, 1993), 53.
11. Liana De Girolami Cheney, *The Paintings of the Casa Vasari* (New York: Garland Publishing, 1985), 46, Fig. 408.
12. Hans Biedermann, *Dictionary of symbolism: Cultural Icons and The Meaning Behind Them*, trans. By James Hulbert (New York: Meridian Books, 1994), 310.
13. Pierio Valeriano, *Hieroglyphicae* (Venice 1575), 359-60. Valeriano also discusses the snail as a symbol of Temperance. Jean Chevalier and Alain Gheerbrandt, *A Dictionary of Symbols* (London: Blackwell, 1994), 390-91.

14. Ripa, *Iconologia,* 339.
15. Liana De Girolami Cheney, "Vasari and Naples: The Monteoliveto Order." *Papers in Art History,* The Pennsylvania State University, Vol. V (1994), 48-126.
16. Valeriano, *Hieroglyphicae,* 31.
17. On April 4, 1551, from Arezzo Bernardetto Minerbetti, Bishop of Arezzo, writes to Vasari regarding the commission for a painted image of Patience. See Karl Frey, *Giorgio Vasari der Literarische Nachlass* (New York: Georg Olms Verlag, 1982), Vol. 1, 307 and p. 313. See also a letter from Florence date November 14, 1551, "A Monsignore Minerbetti Vezcovo d' Arezzo, sopra la *Pattentia* in the Biblioteca Riccardiana, MS 2354, Vol. 31-32. See Julian Kleimann, "La Pazienza," in *Giorgio Vasari,* ed. Charles Davis (Florence: Edam, 1981), pp. 130-33, for a reproduction of Minerbetti's letter as well as illustrations of other images of Patience by an unknown Ferarrese painter. This painting contains the same inscription as Leoni's medal and is now in the Galleria Estense in Modena.
18. Frey, *Giorgio Vasari der Literarische Nachlass,* 313.
19. Ibid., 313.
20. Rudolph Wittkower, *Allegory and the Migration of Symbols* (London: Thames and Hudson, 1977), 108-112, describes the complexity of this commission and dates the painting later, between 1553-54, according to Minerbetti's letters. See also G. de Tervarent, *Attributs et Symboles dans l'Art, 1450-1600* (Geneva: Droz, 1997), 27, Fig. 37, for Prospero Sugari's *Patience,* representing her enchained to a clepsydra. Sugari (1516-1584), also known as Spani, executes this relief in marble, presently located in warehouse of the Galleria Estense in Modena.
21. Catherine Monbeig-Goguel, *Dessins Italians du Musée du Louvre: Vasari et Son Temps* (Paris: Éditions des Musées Nationaux, 1972), 210, Fig. 315.
22. Clepsydra is used in Egypt 2000 BCE. This measuring instrument is then introduced into Greece and later from there into Rome. The clepsydra or water clock is also invented to mark the overcast days. It is much more consistent than sundials or shadow clocks because it does not rely on a changing factor. Water drips from the top basins to the bottom basin and the hours are marked off by marks. See Macrobius, *Commentary on the Dream of Scipio,* especially Book II, Chapter XV. Translated by W. H. Stahl (New York 1952); Martianus Capella, *The Marriage of Philology and Mercury,* Book VIII. Translated in W. Stahl, R. Johnson, & E. Burge, *Martianus Capella and the Seven Liberal Arts,* 2 vols. (New York: 1971-1977); and J. U. Powell, The Simile of the Clepsydra in Empedocle," in *The Classical Quarterly,* Vol. 17, No. 3/4 (Jul. - Oct., 1923), 172-74.
23. I have translated the Italian text which reads:

Una femmina ritta, di mezza età, ne tutta vestita ne tutta spogli-
ata, accio tenga fra la Ricchezza e la Povertà il mezzo, sia incate-
nata per il pie manco per offender meno la parte più nobile, sendo
in libertà sua il potere con le mani schiolte scatenarsi et partirsi a
posta sua. Haviamo messo la catena à quel sasso; et lei cortese,
con le braccia mostra segno di non voler partire, fin chel'tempo
non consuma con le gocciole dell'acqua la pietra, dove ella è in-
catenata: la quale à goccia à goccia escie della eclissidera, oriuolo
antico, che serviva à gl'oratori mentre oravano. Cosi risterettasi
nelle spalle, mirando fisamente quanto gli bisogna spettare che si
consumi la durezza del sasso, tollera et spetta...Il motto mi pare
che stia molto bene et à proposito nel sasso: "Diuturna tollerantia." See Frey, *Giorgio Vasari der Literarische Nachlass*, 313.

24. In another letter from Bishop Minerbetti in Arezzo to Vasari in Rome
dated November 28, 155, he profusely thanks Vasari in this manner:
Ho trovata la mia Patienza di vostra mano, cosi ben disegnata
che è si vede ben, che veramente la patisce; et se io trovassi che
le pintassi cosi viva in una tela di tre braccio, io contentere esso
si bene, come io ne resteri contentissimo. La mi piace in summa
tanto "("I have received my "Patience" painted by you, so well
design, it reveals clearly that she is suffering. Will it be possible
for you to paint the same on a three braccia canvas. It would be
please me a great deal and I would remain very gratified." See
Frey, *Giorgio Vasari der Literarische Nachlass*, 317.

25. Wittkower, *Allegory and the Migration of Symbols*, 109, Figs. 158 and 159.
He explains how Minerbetti offers Vasari's drawing to Duke Ercole II.

26. The medal is in the British Museum of London and another version is in
the Museo Nazionale of Florence.

27. Wittkower, *Allegory and the Migration of Symbols*, 112. Fig. 161. Battisti's
engraving represents an earthly Fortitude embracing her attribute, the
column, while looking down to Patience, who stands and points to the
stars. A clepsydra is located next to Patience as her attribute. See also
Luisa Mortari, *Francesco Salviati* (Rome: Leonardo De Luca, 1982), 667,
Entry 35, and p. 121, for an illustration, in which the standing figure
of Patience rests on the clepsydra while caressing her long tresses. Salviati's painting, also titled "Artemisia Piange Mausolo," is located at the
Galleria delgi Uffizi in Florence, Inv. 1528.

28. For J. C. Cooper's *Symbolic and Mythological Animals*, the tortoise or turtle
is not distinguished in the sixteenth century.

29. An early Egyptian clepsydra of conical shape is at the Harvard Semitic
Museum, Cambridge, MA.

30. The sketch is based on Gerhard Dohrn-van Rossum's study of Vitruvi-

us, *De architectura.* See Gerhard Dohrn-van Rossum, *The History of the Hour* (Chicago: University of Chicago, 1996), 22 and 26. In the second century BCE, the Syrian astronomer, Andronikos Kyrrestes, composes *The Tower of the Winds* in the Athenian agora (*plaka*). He conceives it as a type of clepsydra, sundial and *horologium.* A top of the octagonal tower, there is a frieze depicting the eight wind gods: Boreas (N), Kaikias (NE), Apeliotes (E), Euros (SE), Notos (S), Lips (SW), Zepyhros (W), and Skiron (NW). Below the frieze, there are nine sundials and inside a water clock carrying water running down from the Acropolis to the agora (Fig. 13). See also Stephen C. McCluskey, *Astronomies and Cultures in Early Medieval Europe* (Cambridge: Cambridge University Press, 1998), 111-12, for a discussion of ancient clepsydra. For example, Macrobious describes the clepsydra as a bronze vessel with a very small opening near the bottom, with no indication of an attachment pointer to measure the flow of time. The more sophisticated analemma used in some ancient clepsydras are to account for the varying lengths of seasonal hours. See Macrobious, *Commentari in Sommium Scipionis,* ed. C. E. Lutz (Leiden, 1962-65), 2 vols. pp. I. 21, II. 22. In the Middle Ages, Gerbert of Aurillas (945-1003), later Pope Sylvester II (999-1003), while residing in Ravenna, constructed a water clock. See McCluskey, *Astronomies and Cultures in Early Medieval Europe,* 175-76. Gerbert of Aurillas is also credited with introducing demonstrational armillary spheres into medieval Christian Europe. It is assumed that he acquires knowledge of this instrument through Islamic Spain. Gerbert's correspondence reveals that he employs at least two types of spherical models, both equipped with sighting tubes for alignment with the heavens. See Sacrobosco, *De Sphaera,* especially Chapter II. Translated in L. Thorndike, *The Sphere of Sacrobosco and its Commentators* (Chicago: University of Chicago Press, 1949); D. Price, "A Collection of Armillary Spheres and Other Antique Scientific Instruments," *Annals of Science* 10 ( 1956), 172-187, and O. Pedersen, "'In quest of Sacrobosco'," *Journal for the History of Astronomy* 16 (1985), 175-221.

31. Dohrn-van Rossum, *The History of the Hour,* 25-28. See also Alfred W. Crosby, *The Measure of Reality: Antification and Western Society: 1250-1600* (London: Cambridge University Press, 1998), 75-93.

32. de Tervarent, *Attributs et Symboles dans l'Art, 1450-1600,* 419, and Jean Chevalier and Alain Gheerbrant, *A Dictionary of Symbols,* trans. John Buchana-Brown (London: Blackwell, 1994), 978.

33. Dohrn-van Rossum, *The History of the Hour,* 223-24.

34. In the Renaissance, there are hundreds of extant manuscript copies of Sacrobosco's *De sphaera,* where the armillary sphere is illustrated. Surviving armillary spheres from the sixteenth century reveal that the

instrument is often constructed from precious material as a work of art for princely collections. These types of armillaries are decorative and not functional. They display a variety of forms and feature: star-pointers like an astrolabe, a mechanical drive to simulate the rotation of the heavens and circles to represent the orbits of the planets. Their forms varies as well, from sculptural shape to small armillaries "sur-mounting decorated celestial globes and astronomical clocks, even finger-rings which opened out to become spheres." See J. Bennett & D. Bertoloni Meli, *Sphaera Mundi: Astronomy Books in the Whipple Museum 1478-1600* (Cambridge: Cambridge University Press, 1994), 14-15, 32-44, 65, and F. Johnson, "Astronomical text-books in the sixteenth century," in E. Underwood, ed., *Science, Medicine and History* (Oxford: Oxford University Press, 1953), Vol. I, 285-302.

35. McCluskey, *Astronomies and Cultures in Early Medieval Europe*, 111, citing Macrobius' *Sommnium Scipionis*, I. 21, II. 22.
36. E. Schön, *Celestial Sphere* (Germany, 1515), representing astronomers measuring the sky with their devices, including the armillary sphere.
37. Patricia Castelli, *Il Lume del Sole: Marsilio Ficino Medico dell'Anima* (Florence: Opus Libri, 1984), 11-24, for a discussion on the meaning of symbols and images
38. Peter M. Daly, *Word and Emblem* (Toronto: University of Toronto, 1998), 73-121, on the literature in the light of the emblem in Andrea Alciatio's emblems.

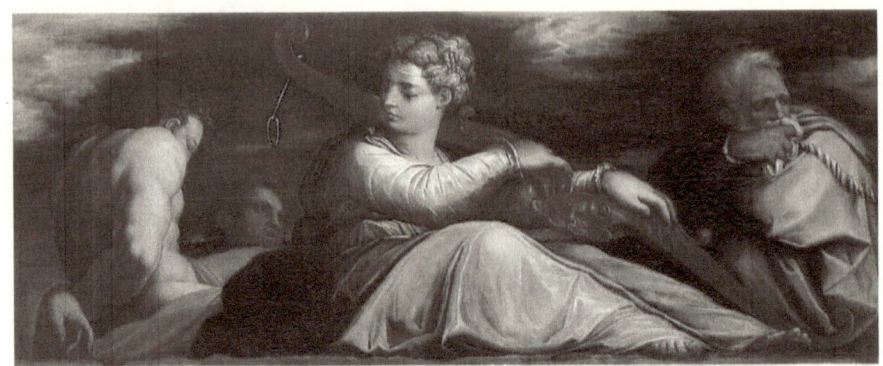

Fig. 1. Giorgio Vasari, *Patience*, 1542, Cornaro Ceiling, Venice.
Photo: Art Resource, NY.

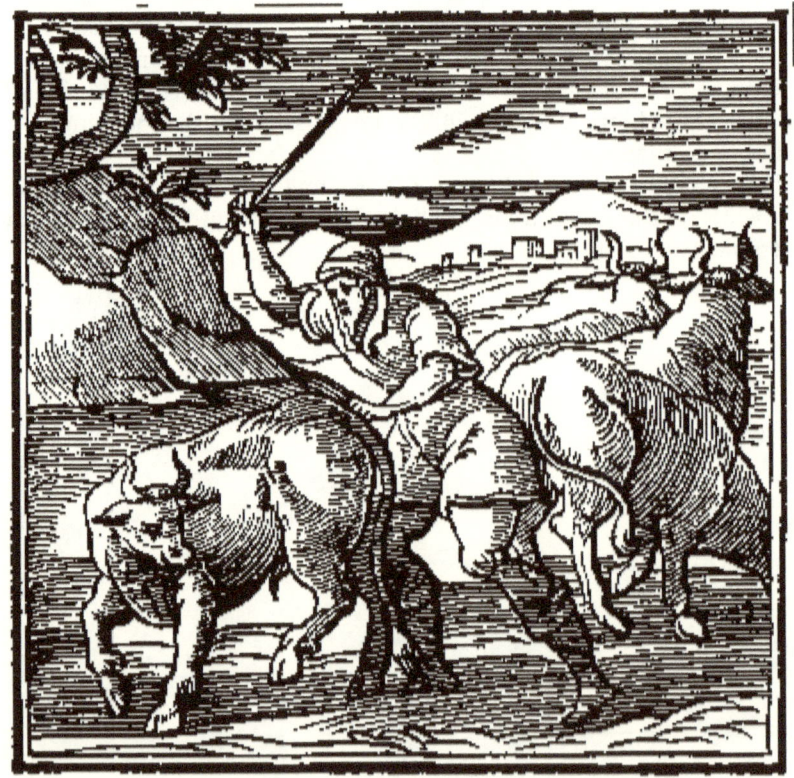

Fig. 2. Andrea Alciato, Emblem 34, *Bear and Forbear*, from
*Emblematum Liber*, Lyon 1546

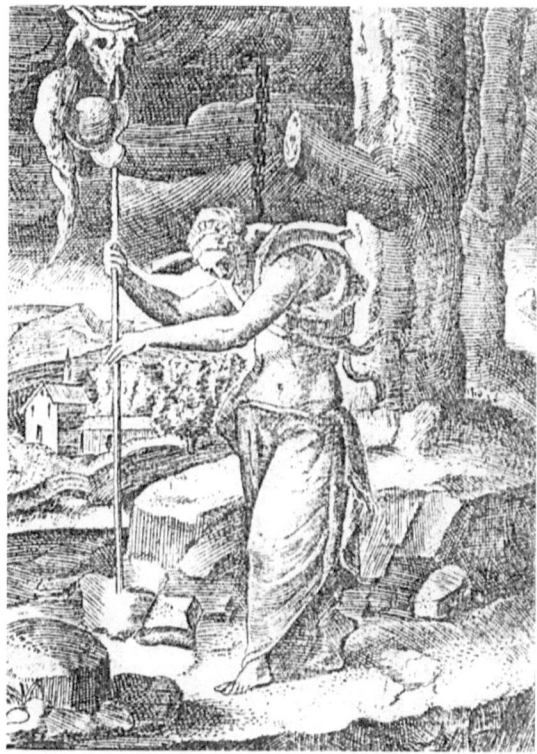

Fig. 3. Achille Bocci, Emblem 109, *Patience*, from *Symbolic Questionaes*, Bologna 1555.

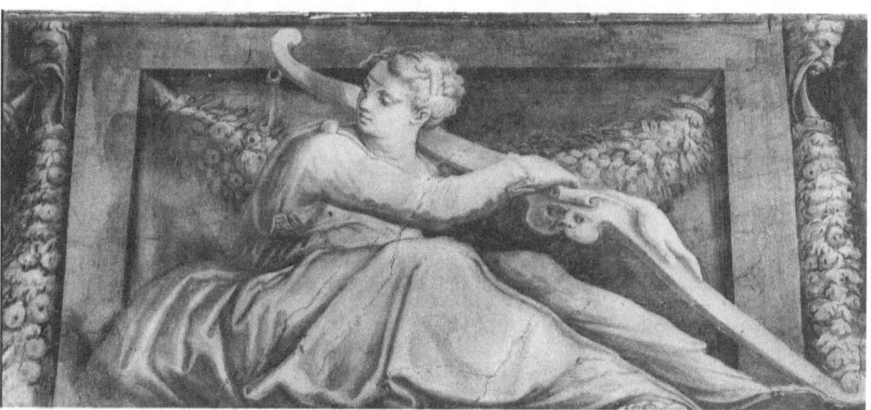

Fig, 4. Giorgio Vasari, *Patience*, 1548, Chamber of Fortune, Casa Vasari, Arezzo.

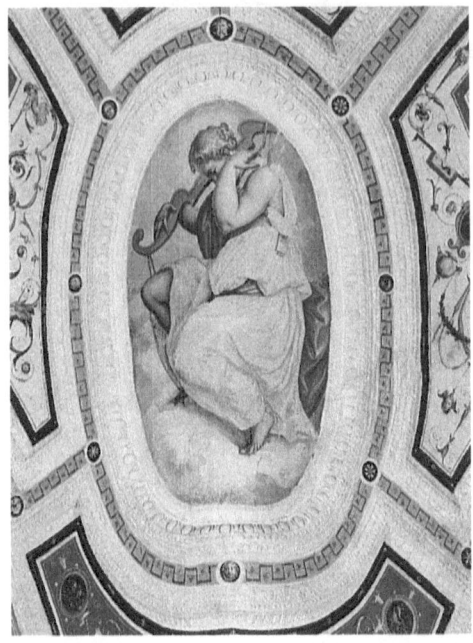

Fig, 5. Giorgio Vasari, *Patience*, 1545, Monteoliveto (Sant'Anna dei Lombardi), Naples.

Fig. 6a. Cesare Ripa, *Patience (Suave), Iconologia,* 1603.

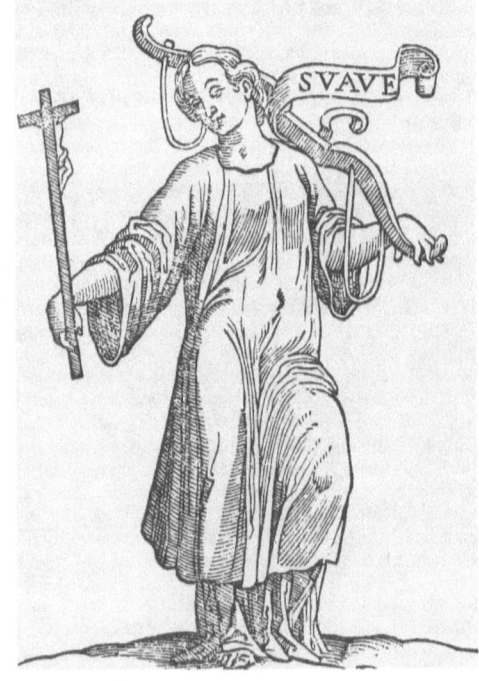

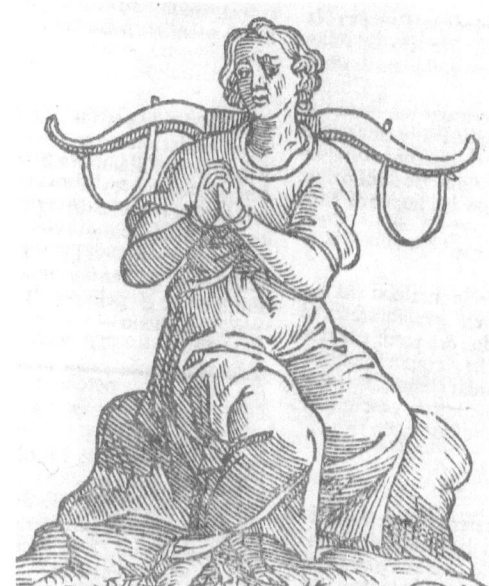

Fig. 6b. Cesare Ripa, *Patience, Iconologia*, 1603.

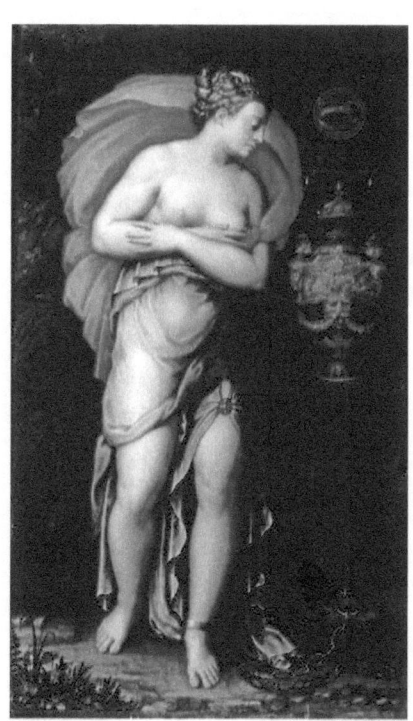

Fig 7. Giorgio Vasari, *Patience*, 1551, Palazzo Pitti, Florence.

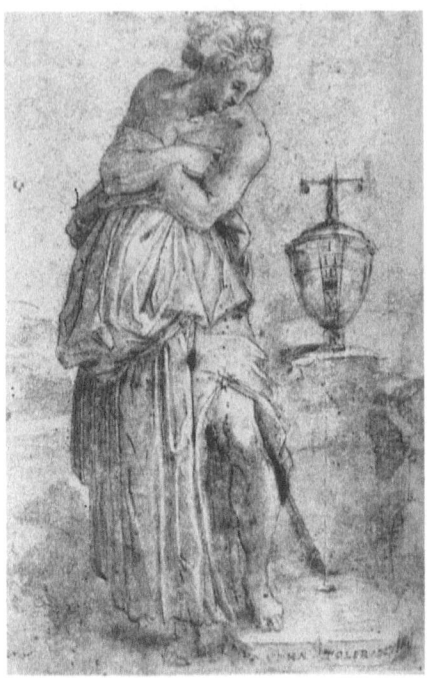

Fig. 8. Giorgio Vasari, *Patience*, 1551, drawing. Musée du Louvre (Inv. 1660). Photo: Réunion des Musées Nationaux, Paris

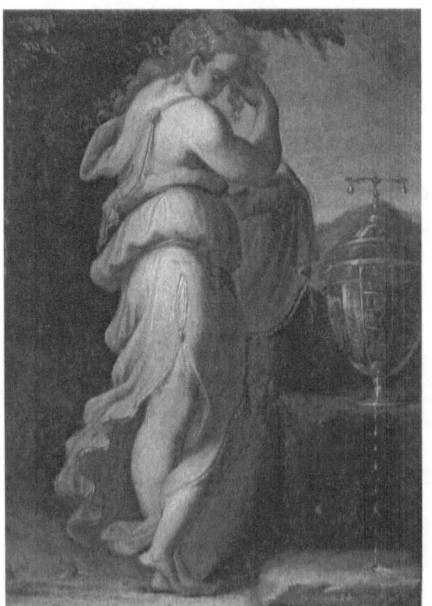

Fig. 9. Giorgio Vasari/Francesco Salviati, *Patience* 1551, Galleria degli Uffizi, Florence.

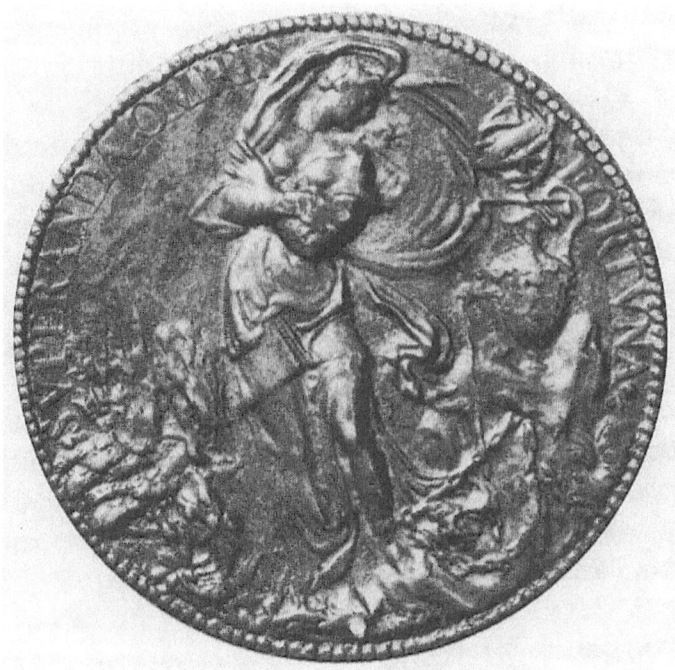

Fig. 10. Pompeo Leoni, *Patience*, 1554, reverse medal for
Ercole II d'Este, British Museum, London.

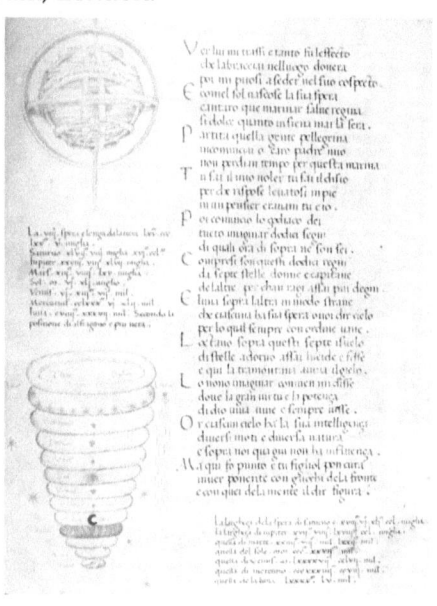

Fig. 11. Volke Aschoff, *Clepsydra*,
in *Geschichte der Nachrichtentechnik*.

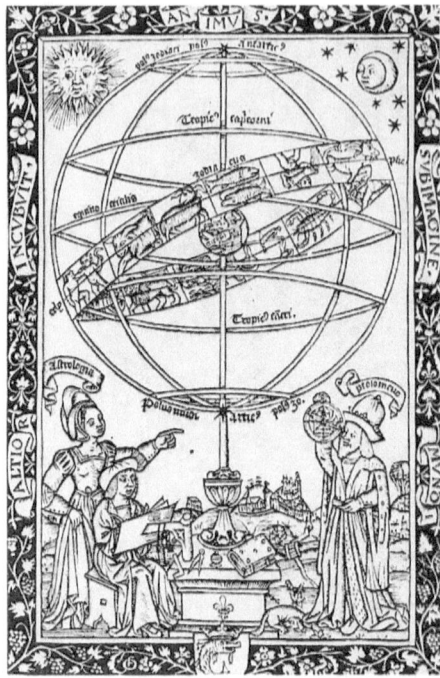

Fig. 12. E. Schön, *Armillary in Celestial Sphere* (Germany, 1515).

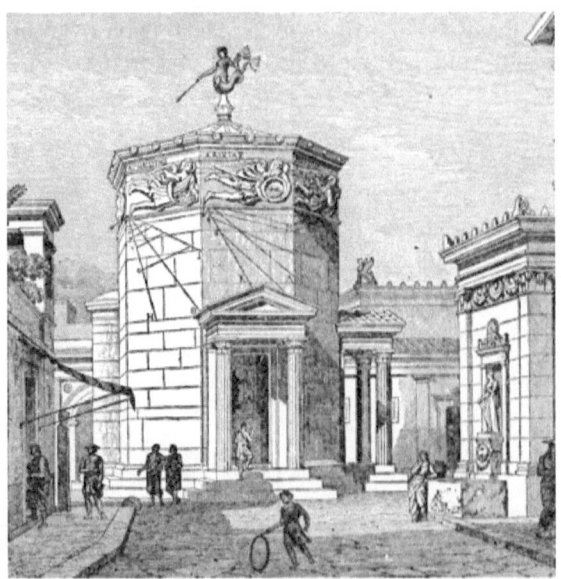

Fig. 13. Andronikos Kyrrestes, *The Tower of Winds*, second century BCE, Athens. Photo: author from a 17th-century unknown print.

# Amore e Baci:
# Giorgio Vasari's Poems to
# Nicolosa Bacci[1]

In 1550, Giorgio Vasari (1511-1574) wedded Nicolosa Bacci (1536-1583), after they moved into a house built and decorated by Vasari. This essay discusses Vasari's expressed love for Nicolosa in both painting and poetry. Two examples of the latter are analyzed. Although the exact date of their composition is uncertain, these poems were likely composed when Vasari was working in Rome, and Nicolosa, whom he affectionately called Cosina resided in Arezzo. Because so little is known about Vasari's marital relationship, the two poems are very important in that they display aspects of Vasari's personality not easily seen when considering only his work as courtier-artist. The poems convey Vasari's loneliness, his sentimental nature and his nostalgia for not having children with her.[2] But beyond that, they also reflect his concern for success, wealth and recognition as well as the longing for marital bliss.

Giorgio Vasari, author of *Le vite de' più eccellenti architetti, pittore, et scultori*,[3] viewed himself as a *uomo buono et docto in buone lettere*. He was one of the most important cultural figures in Italy during the mid-sixteenth century, having achieved prominence as an art critic, historian, aesthetician, architect and painter. In many respects, he was an exemplary case of Castiglione's *renaissance man* (courtier-artist). One indication of the professional status of an artist in the Cinquecento was the freedom to purchase, design and decorate his own house. In 1542, Vasari began to construct and decorate (al fresco, in oils and on tempera) his house in Borgo San Vito at Arezzo. The paintings in the Casa Vasari represent a collection of works of art created by Vasari to express his love for his masters, antiquity and art. The message conveyed is personal, intimate and original–an artistic monument to Vasari's own accomplishments as an artist and as a man.

Unmarried at this time, Vasari was encouraged by his friends, Pietro Aretino, Paolo Giovio, Vincenzo Borghini and Cardinal del Monte (later Pope Julius III), to seek a noble Aretine spouse. At the beginning of 1549, Vasari went to Bologna to visit Cardinal del Monte, who convinced him to marry Nicolosa Bacci, daughter of a well-to-do Aretine family. In that same year, he requested Vincenzo Borghini, a Humanist and close friend, to make the nuptial arrangement.

The Bacci family, a noble and apothecarian family of Arezzo, had contributed for generations to the patronage of the arts in this city. For example, among their most prestigious commissions was a Piero della Francesca painting of the Legend of the True Cross in the choir of the Church of San Francesco in 1452.[4]

In January 1550, Vasari wedded Nicolosa Bacci. Following their marriage, he continued decorating their Aretine house by painting *al fresco* the dining room ceiling. This room is named the Chamber of Apollo because Vasari painted Apollo surrounded by the nine muses, which he portrayed with the physiognomy of Nicolosa (Fig. 1 and 2).

On the ceiling of the Chamber of Apollo, the depicted court of the muses with Apollo reveal a Vasarian *concetto* (conceit). The crowned Apollo becomes an allusion to Vasari's literary and artistic accomplishments, while the muses surrounding the god attest to the favorable influence of the function of their sphere on the artist's life. For Vasari, the intervention of the dual nature of Apollo–at once, divine and human–guides his artistic pursuits, and the complex activities of the Muses becomes a vehicle of inspiration and emulation for the pursuit of his erudition. He achieves this, in this chamber, by creating a personal, familial ambience by including his wife, Nicolosa Bacci, in the realm of the muses and depicting them in the likeness of her portrait, and by representing an Apollonian-Orphic allusion to the harmony and power of love.

Nicolosa Bacci, personified as Euterpe (Fig. 2), the muse of wind instruments, resides between Terpsichore, the muse of dance, who stares at the viewer coquettishly, and Polyhymnia, the muse of singing or mimicry, with the scarf around her face and neck, symbolizing the care and protection of her throat for her singing. Across from the room, Euterpe sees Clio, the muse of history, and Uranaia, the muse of astronomy. Euterpe turns her head, glancing at Thalia, the muse of comedy, and Melpomene, the muse of tragedy, both on the adjacent wall. Thus, looking at Melpomene, yet attired like Clio, the muse of history, Euterpe draws attention to the connection between tragedy, history and music.

The prominent position of her portrait suggests that Cosina is special and presides over the others. This emphasis, along with similarities of physiognomy and attire between the muses, creates a further suggestion that this is a courtly gathering: the lady of the house is surrounded by the attendants of Apollo. He with his music and poetry, inspires the muses' cultural activities. Cosina informs their dining guests about the erudition of the Vasarian family. In his writings, in particular *I Ragionamenti*, Vasari explains the meaning of Euterpe's name to her ability "for delighting in what others appreciated," thus, as his wife, Cosina, delights him and his guests in this chamber or dining room.

Vasari always honors Cosina by depicting her as a muse or a saint. Although Cosina's image is idealized as a muse, her portrayal is nonetheless similar to Vasari's 1569 portrait of her in the *sala* of his Florentine house, Vasari's second home. In here, Vasari portrays Cosina as a beautiful woman who enters the studio of the ancient painter Apelles to be considered as a model for the painting of Diana. Years later, in 1570, Vasari depicts Mary Magdalena with the charming physiognomy of Cosina for their memorial family chapel in the Church of La Pieve in Arezzo, now transferred in the Badia of Santissime Fiore e Lucilla in Arezzo.[5]

Vasari's affection for his wife is demonstrated not only by his depiction of her in his houses, but most of all, by the poems he penned for her. This is one of the few instances where Vasari reveals his feelings of love for a woman.[6] Two important changes had occurred in Vasari's life by the time he completed this room. One was the publication of the first edition of the *Vite* (1550); the other was his marriage, commemorated by the portrait of his wife. From this time on, Vasari was recognized as an accomplished writer, historian, and artist.

Thus, Vasari expressed his love for Nicolosa in painting and poetry. Two examples of the latter are presented here. Today, the two poems are found in a collection of "Poesie di Giorgio Vasari" in the Biblioteca Riccardiana of Florence (M 2948, p. 3032). The date of their composition is uncertain. Between 1557 to 1573 Vasari traveled extensively throughout Italy, spending lengthy periods of time in Florence and Rome, decorating the rooms of Duke Cosimo I in the Palazzo Vecchio in Florence, painting the Sala Regia, a Vatican chapel, in Rome, and traveling throughout Italy, collecting and preparing more material for the second edition of the *Vite.*. One line of the longer of the poems, "By coming where you are [Arezzo/ sic], or you to Rome," clearly shows that Vasari was in Rome when he wrote this to Nicolosa, affectionately called Cosina.

Because so little is known about Vasari's marital relationship, the two poems are very important, displaying aspects of Vasari's personality not easily seen when considering only his work as a painter. The poems convey Vasari's loneliness, his sentimental nature, his nostalgia for not having children with her. Moreover, one realizes the measure of Vasari's concern for success, wealth and recognition, overriding his prospect for marital bliss.

The Italian Cinquecento tradition for lyrical poetry, in particular, from love poems from a man to a woman, is extensive. (Also love poems from a woman to a man can be found in Vittoria Colonna, Barbara Torelli, Gaspara Stampa and Veronica Franco; however, this is not the focus of this presentation.) Coleman I need to explain this here!

The Cinquecento lyrical poetical convention originates in the Trecento with the Tuscan poets such as Petrarca, Dante and Boccaccio, who wrote poems to their *donna amata* (loved lady) Laura, Beatrice and Fiammetta, respectively. This tradition was carried in the Quattrocento by poets and benevolent rulers, such as Poliziano's poems to an unknown lady and Lorenzo de Medici's love poems to Lucrezia Donati. In the Cinquecento, too, poets and artists expressed their sentiment in verse. Examples include Pietro Bembo to Maria Savorgnan, Tarquato Tasso to Lucrezia Bendidio, and Michelangelo to Vittoria Colonna.

Although in Italian Cinquecento, there are numerous love poems from men of letters or the arts to unknown loved women, usually unidentified because the women were married or were involved with other men, or the women were imaginary, one rarely finds poems from a poet to his wife, with the exception of Ludovico Ariosto's poems to his much loved wife, Alessandra Benucci. She was the widow of Tito Strozzi and secretly married Ariosto in 1528. In sonnet 17, Ariosto agonizes because he is unable to see her, misses her love and beauty. With passion and pain, he recalls the pleasure of their bond. Even more exceptional, at this time is to find poems from a painter to his wife, as in the case of Giorgio Vasari to his wife Nicolosa Bacci.

Vasari composed two love poems. One poem is short, containing 3 stanze and entitled "Giorgio Vasari to his Consort or Wife" and the second is a long poem or *capitolo* of 73 uninterrupted lines addressed to "Madonna Nicolosa Bacci." The capitolo was a new poetical genre of provincial quality used for salutary effects. In *Capitoli*, Francesco Berni invented this lyrical form to achieve monochromatic effects and personal references. Using the capitolo as a colloquial form of writing, Cinquecento writers were establishing a fragile link with Dante's *Divina commedia*. Vasari was attempting to imitate this new literary style; however, both of his poems are colloquial, regional and direct, with limited allegorical references. Their uniqueness rely on the fact that they are painter's poems pining over his wife.

Traditionally most love poems deal with suffering and pain for not seeing the beloved, for recalling their brief bliss together and for their wishes to reunite soon. In these poems, the physical elements and connecting body parts, such as eye, heart, lips, tears, face are mentioned and connected to the five senses–sight, touch, smell, taste and hearing–in order to accentuate and express through them a psychological state of mind and the emotional condition of the lover. Interestingly, the senses of sight and touch are predominantly stresses. The physical humor or emotional or psychological implication such as passion (*furor* or *ardor*), pain (*dolor*), lover (*amor*), suffering, lamenting and crying (*pathos*) are strongly present.

Vasari, familiar with these literary appropriations, integrates these physiological and psychological components in his love poems. However, what is distinctive is the explicit expression for the consummation of love and the continuation of the species as noted in Vasari's poems. This is so because Vasari's poems are to his wife, a married woman, and not imaginary love of the woman of another man.

Vasari's poems can be seen as composed of a revelation about his feelings and personal relation with his wife, his praises for his wife's behavior and accomplishments, and his professional hopes and aspirations. When Vasari reveals his state of mind to his wife he comments on his love, loneliness and suffering. In the poems, Vasari stresses the importance of their marital relation, remarking that they are husband and wife in this manner: "Consorte cara (Dear wife) or "il tuo marito (your husband)."

In the second poem, Vasari opens his heart to Cosina, blaming fortune for their separation.

> Rolling its mortals high and low.
> Never did man proceed to make a plan
> That Fortune, with its contrary aim,
> Did not then spoil it for him. (Second Poem)

In both poems, Vasari declares his love, longing and desire for a prompt reunion.

> Only one hope and one desire are mine:
> that I come back as soon as possible to you. (First Poem)
> By staying so far from you, resolves
> To wish you near me while you are on earth.
> To rest this weary mind of mine...
> And quit my ardent longing,
> Dear wife, in this blind world,
> Nor is it any use to grieve or rage... (Second Poem)

Vasari also comments on the joy upon receiving her messages and finding solace in reading them.

> If you are grieved by my long absences,
> Dear wife, I am very bit as grieved as you...
> My life find solace in your messages. (First Poem)

Furthermore, Vasari's familiarity with Dante's *Divina commedia*, in particular *Il Paradiso*, is evident when he states in his second poem: "blinds my eyes so they see nothing else [but you/sic]." This verse relates to Dante's verse on blindness when he saw Beatrice in Paradise, Canto XXX.

The second aspect of the poems demonstrates Vasari's respect and praise for Cosina, acknowledging her spiritual and physical beauty as well as for her virtue in doing labors and good deeds in the community. He states:

No one esteems and values more than I your great nobility
and faith...
And continue to do good works as you are doing:
So, pleasing God, you'll please me even more.
(Second Poem)

He commends Cosina for being patient and compassionate. He also reiterates his fidelity and faithfulness to her.

This is a promise, never to be absent from my heart...
Now what can it tell you of my other pleasures?
I have nothing but my work... (Second Poem)

The third aspect in analyzing Vasari's poems is his revelation about his need for familial continuation and fame. He confides in Cosina his desires for immortality and wish to have children. The distance imposed by his work causes him emptiness and loneliness. He apologizes and justifies his separation because he wants to be a good provider as well as fulfilling his desire for fame. It is due to his ambition and work that he has to be away from her. Vasari is anxious about their constant distance that causes them to be childless life and expresses his desire for a family in order to continue his name, and to transmit his fame and his immortality.

I dreamed, I would despair of having progeny. (First Poem)
What will it vial me after many years to have
Children by you, and not be there to teach them...
I know well that my vain destiny

Of acquiring ever for me fame and wealth
Keeps me far from your side, dear consort...
But that desire for glory deep in my heart,
The wish to make us both immortal here on earth...
I will still live some years, and I hope that you will see
Your husband numbered among his followers. (Second Poem)

Once again Vasari demonstrates his inventiveness and artistic creativity by fusing ancient, allegorical and artistic traditions of *ut pictura poesis* in his art. Like the ancient painter, Apelles, who depicted the chaste goddess Diana, Vasari painted the most beautiful image of a chaste woman in his house, his wife Cosina. Similar to Apollo, god of harmony and love, who chanted and honored the muses, Vasari, too, immortalizes his wife, Cosina, but in painting, by depicting the muses with Cosina's portrait and in poetry by chanting poems in her honor. Vasari has imitated Ariosto's marital poetry and love poetry tradition. The Aretine painter reveals explicitly in painting and poetry his intimate feelings about love–a man's love for his wife, unprecedented in the Cinquecento artistic tradition.

### Giorgio Vasari a Sua Consorte

Se nel mio starti lontano a te dispiace,
Consorte cara, a me dispiace e duole,
Che non si leva o colca in nel ciel sole
ch'io posi quest' affletta anima in pace.

Ardo tal' or qual' accesa fornace,
M'agghiaccia ancor in bocca le parole,
Divento come fredda neve al sole
E nel fonte d'Epiro intinta face.
Pur vivo di speranza e di disio
Di venir presto a te; or la mia vita
si parce d'ambasciate e di parole.

Se la speranza mia e tua, Ch'in Dio
Non fussi tal che me porgessi aiuta,
Dispererei di noi non lasciar prole.

## Giorgio Vasari to His Wife

If you are grieved by my long absences,
Dear  wife, I'm every bit as grieved as you.
May the sun never rise or set in heaven
Until my troubled spirit finds surcease.
Though I may burn like leaping furnace flames,
Still my words turn to ice on my ardent lips;
I turn to snow under the sun's hot rays,
Extinguished in Epirus' chill springs.
Only one hope and one desire are mine:
that I come back as soon as possible to you,
my life find solace in your messages.
If all my trust and yours, reposed in God,
Prove not to be the firm support I dreamed,
I would despair of having progeny.

## Capitolo a Madonna Nicolosa Bacci
## Sua Consorte

Per dar riposo alla mia mente stanca
E dare aiuto ai caldi mia sospiri,
Poi che la lena al cor e al corpo manca,
Nacqui per sopportar doglie e martiri,
Consorte cara, in questo cieco mondo,
Ne val ch'io seco mi dolga o m'adiri;
Per che chi ël fece, come vedi, tondo,
Non gli fe' basa per che non fermassi
Rotando I suoi' mortali in alto e in fondo.
Nessun si mosse mai che non andassi
Per far un suo disegno e la fortuna
Con contrario suo far non gliel guastassi
Si che colui che assai cose raguna
Di ricchezze, muraglie e possessioni,
E'un'ombra cieca al sciemo della luna!
Per che le nostre vane openioni,
Che fan disegni perperpetuarsi
Quaggi, che non son nostre abitazioni,

Color che pensier fanno in Dio fermarsi
E da lui riconoscano ogni bene
A quelli il Paradiso debba darsi.
Certo ch'io mertar debbo queste pene
Ch'io patisco, ogni giorno in questa corte,
Che chi fa ben, quasi mal sempre gli viene (sic).
Conosco ben che la mia vana sorte,
Per acquistar più fama a più ricchezze,
Mi tien lontan da te, cara consorte.
Non e chi più de me stimi ed apprezze
La nobiltà tua e la tuo fede (sic),
E ch'ogni altro mio ben odi e disprezze;
Ma quello onor che drento al cor mi siede,
De lasciarti immortal con meco in terra,
Fa che nel mio occhio é cieco e piti non vede.
Or se l'animo mio, ch'in ver trop'erra
Di starti sí lontano, é risoluto
Volerti appresso fin che star‡ in terra,

Conoscendo che il tempo ch'ho perduto
In cose vane mai pi˘ si racquista,
Ne creder ch'in ch'ha fame sia pasciuto.
Or, poi che chiara io ho dal ciel la vista,
E chel mio mal conosco e la tuo voglia,
Vo' lasciar questa vita amara c tn-sta.
Caverb te di pensier e me di doglia (sic)
Col venir io costh o tu a Roma:
Questo 'e un si, ch'al cor mal piú si spoglia.
Che il portar ogni di si grave soma
Di pensier, di fatiche, e non sapere
Per ch'io lo facci, il cervel mio si doma.
Che mi varrk dopo molt'anni avere
Figli di te e non poter mostrarli
e vertli che ci fanno uomin tenere?
Che vartia lor, s'io potessi lassarli
Ricchezze e non avessin altro intorno
Clie gente che studiassino in rubarli?
Per'o riposerati infin ch'io tomo,

Ne ti dar passion, ch'io ti prometto
Esser costi di carnovale il giorno.
Or per dirti, qua altro mio diletto
Non ho che 'l mio lavor, e la mia fine
Pensa a far ch'ogni cosa sia perfetto.
Certo che mi parria star sulle spine,
Se la dolcezza del gran vecchio mio
Qual pasce noi di cose alte e divine,
Chi non ha voglia o d'imparar desio
Specchisi pure in lui, che vedr'a poi
Di quanto ben ci abbi dotato Iddio.
Che se la bonta sua 'l mantiene a noi
Vivo qualch'anno, ho speranza vedrai
Il tuo marito fra i seguaci suoi.
Or mentre in questo tempo, che tu stai
Da me lontana, attendi a darti pace
E seguita il far ben che tu fai,
Ch'a Dio piacendo a me molto piú piace.

### Giorgio Vasari to Madonna Nicolosa Bacci His Wife

To rest this weary mind of mine
And quit my ardent longing,
Since my heart and body lack their strength,
I was born to bear torment and pain,
Dear wife, in this blind world,
Nor is it any use to grieve or rage;
Since as you know, the one who made it round
Gave it no base so that it would not stop
Rolling its mortals high and low,
Never did man proceed to make a plan
That fortune, with its contrary aim,
Did not then spoil it for him,
So that the man who lays up quantities
Of riches, buildings and possessions,
Is a blind shadow at the moon's waning.
Therefore our designs are truly vain
If we think to perpetuate ourselves

Here below, where we do not really dwell;
Those who turn their thoughts to God
And recognize that all good comes from Him
Deserve to have Paradise as their reward.
Certainly I must deserve these pains
I suffer every day here in this court,
For the man who does good almost always gets back evil.
I know well that mv vain destiny
Of acquiring ever for me fame and wealth
Keeps me far from your side, dear consort.
No one esteems and values more than I
Your great nobility and faith,
And loathes and despises all his other goods.
But that desire for glory deep in my heart,
T'he wish to make us both immortal here on earth,
Blinds my eyes so they see nothing else.
Now if my spirit that in truth errs grievously

By staying so far from you, resolves
To wish you near me while you are on earth,
Knowing full well the time that I have lost
In meaningless pursuits will never be given back,
And not believing a hungry man is ever satisfied,
Now that I have a clear view from the heavens,
And know my weakness and your wish.
I long to leave this bitter sad existence.
I will disburden you of care, myself of pain,
By coming where you are, or you to Rome:
This is a promise, never to be absent from my heart,
Since carrying so heavy a burden every day
Of thoughts, of toll, not knowing why
I am doing it, quite overpowers my brain,
What will it avail me after many years to have
Children by you, and not be there to teach them
The virtues that make men of us?
What good to them if I could leave them rich
If all they have around them
Are people intent on robbing them?

However, try to be tranquil until I return,
Do not be agitated, for I promise faithfully
To be with you on the Day of Carnival.
Now what can I tell you of my other pleasures?
I have nothing but my work; my aim
Is one thing only, and that is perfection.
True it is I seem to be on tenterhooks,
If the sweetness of that old man of mine
Who nourishes us with high and heavenly things,
Whoever has no wish or no desire to learn,
Let him reflect on him and he will see
With how much good God has endowed us.
If only he continues to bestow his bounty on us
I will still live some years, and I hope that you will see
Your husband numbered among his followers.
Now while in this period when you
Are far away from me, try to wait patiently
And continue to do good works as you are doing:
So, pleasing God, you'll please me even more.

## Notes

1. Liana  De Girolami Cheney, "Amore e Baci: Giorgio Vasari's Poems to Nicolsa Bacci," *Italian Culture* (Hamilton, Canada: The Symposium Press, Ltd., 1987), 44-51. With gratitude to Ruth Feldman for assisting in the Italian translation.  See also, Liana De Girolami Cheney, *The Paintings of the Casa Vasari* (New York: Garland Publishing, 1985).
2. Although in his poems Vasari longs for children with Cosina, he already has two children, Anton Francesco (1539) and Alessandra (1540) with Maddalena Bacci. In 1567, Anton Francesco resides with Cosina and Vasari in their second house, the Florentine home in Borgo Santa Croce. See Archivio di Stato di Firence, Notarile Antecosimiano, 3940, notary Camillo Calderini of Arezzo, Doc. 4: 12 May 1541, states that Maddalena Bacci, daughter of Francesco Bacci and sister of Nicolosa Bacci, is the mother of Anton Francesco and Alessandra, the first children of Giorgio Vasari.  In 1541, Francesco Bacci contracts an arranged marriage for Maddalena with Bernardo Scamisci. In 1542, she dies of an epidemic illness. In 1548, Francesco Bacci reassumes marriage arrangements for her second daughter Nicolosa with Giorgio Vasaari. The marriage occurs in

1549. See Nicoletta Lepri and Antonio Palesati, *Fuori dalla Corte* (Arezo: Le Balze, 2003), 8–18, for these documents regarding the paternity of Giorgio Vasari, including wills and baptismal records in the Archivio di Stato di Firenze, Archivio di Stato di Arezzo and Archivio dell'Opera del Duomo.

There is conflicting information regarding these found documents on the birth record of Anton Francesco. Some documents claim that Maddalena Bacci born Anton Francesco in 1539, while others claim that Isabella Mora born him on August 22, 1547. This date also refers to the child's baptism executed by Vincenzo Borghini, a closed friend of Vasari and Director of the Hospital of the Innocents in Florence. See Archivio Storico dell' Instituto degli Innocenti, Balie e Bambini serie 16.41 e Balie e Bambini dell'anno 1565 all'anno 1568, duplicated in Lepri and Palesati, *Fuori dalla Corte*, 79. Furthermore, the documentation is unclear as to whether it was an actual a baptism or a baptismal renewal (a Communion or a Confirmation, a sacrament considered as a baptismal vow, usually administered 7 years after baptism). If it was a baptism, why the name of the defunct natural mother, Maddalena Bacci, is not recorded? And why the name of Isabella Mora, assistant/nursemaid residing in the Vasari's household in Florence, is recorded? Anton Francesco resided for some time with Cosina and Vasari in the Florentine home, and maybe in the Arezzo home as well. Does this record suggest that Isabella was the natural mother and not Maddalena? Or that Isabella attended the religious event in lieu of Cosina, the natural aunt? Was it improper for Cosina to have recorded her name as caregiver for the child?

Sketchy documentation on Alessandra reveals that she marries Paesano Canelli di Lucignano and has two children Giovanni and Margarita. See Lepri and Palesati, *Fuori dalla Corte*, 14.

3. Giorgio Vasari, *Le vite...* ed., Gaetano Milanesi (Florence: G.C. Sansoni, 1970–1974), hereafter cited as Vasari-Milanesi.

4. Vasari-Milanesi, VII, 690. The Bacci family was a noble and apothecarian family in Arezzo, who had contributed for generations to the patronage of the arts in the city. Among their most prestigious commissions is Piero della Francesca's paintings of the *Legend of the True Cross* in the choir of the Church of San Francesco in c.1452. A. del Vita, *Le Ricordanze di Giorgio Vasari* (Rome: R. Istituto Archeologico e Storia dell'Arte, 1938), 133, Letter IV; W. Kallab, *Vasaristudien* (Vienna: K. Graeser and Kie, 1908), 83; K Frey, *Der literarische Nachlass Giorgio Vasaris*, Vol I (Munich, 1923), 228, 233 and 242. For the correspondence on the marriage between Giorgio Vasari and Cosina Bacci; see A del Vita, *Inventorio e Regesto delli Archivio Vasariano* (Arezzo, 1938), 86, 133; K. Frey, *Der literarische Nachlass Giorgio Vasaris*, Vol. I (Munich, 1923), 228, 233 and 242; and T. S. Boase, *Giorgio Vasari: The Man and the Book* (Princeton: Princeton University Press, 1979), 41-42.

5. Liana De Girolami Cheney, *The Paintings of the Casa Vasari*, 153-54. See F.H. Jacobs, "Vasari's Vison of the History of Painting: frescoes in the Casa Vasari, Florence," *Art Bulletin*, Vol 66 (October, 1984), 399-416, for a discussion on the iconography of the *sala* of Florence; and C.A. Isermeyer, "Die Capella Vasaris un der Hochaltar in der Pieve von Arezzo," *Festschrift fur Carl Georg Heise* (Berlin, 1950), 137-53, for a history on Vasari's burial chapel. Originally, Vasari's burial altarpiece was designed and placed in the Romanesque church of the Pieve in Arezzo. Vasari had strong affection for this old church since he was instructed in early childhood and his forefathers were buried there (Vasari-Milanesi, I, 474-76). In 1865, the Pieve was again restored to its Romanesque style, Vasari's burial altarpiece was dismantled, and rebuilt in the Badia of SS. Fiore e Lucilla by the efforts of the Confraternity of S. Maria della Misericordia. Vasari and his wife were buried in the Pieve but its placement is unknown. See Ugo Viviani, "La Tomba di Giorgio Vasari," *Il Vasari*, VI (1924), 1-16, for a clear documentation on the burial of Giorgio Vasari.

6. Today, the two poems are found in a collection of "Poesie di Giorgio Vasari" in the Biblioteca Riccardiana of Florence (M 2948, 3032). See Pio Pecchiai, *Le Opere di Giorgio Vasari*, III (Milan, 1928-1931), 989, 992 and 1028. Luckily, he published for the first time the two poems together in Italian. Pecchiai does not see merit in studying the long poem due to the difficulty in understanding its meaning. To our knowledge the longer poem has never been translated into English. And we have translated the shorter poem with a fresher, more modern style than its first translation into English as found in the English edition of Einar Rud's *Vasari's Life and Lives: The First Art Historian*, ed. Liana De Girolami Cheney, (Washington, DC: New Academia Publishers, 2011).

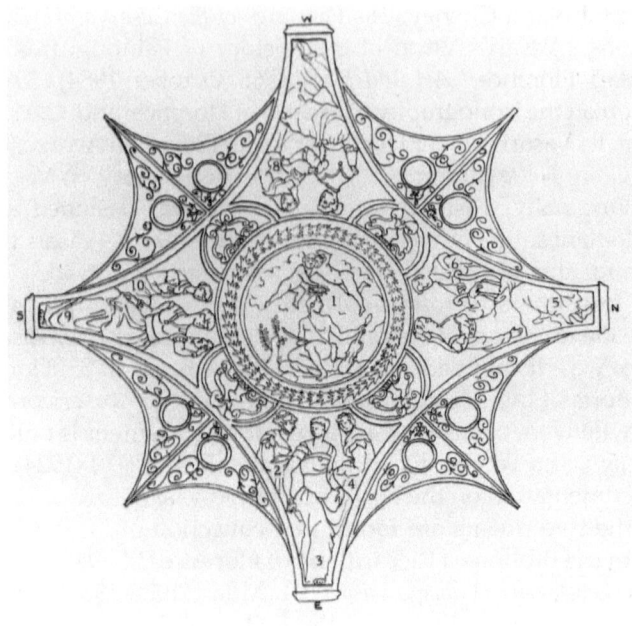

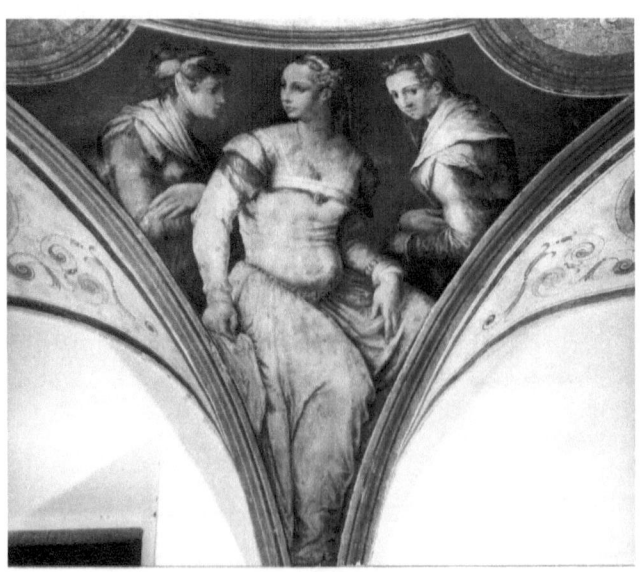

# Selected Bibliography

P. R. Ackroyd, ed., *The Cambridge History of the Bible*, Cambridge: Cambridge University Press, 1963-70.

Thomas Acquinas, *Treatise on the Virtues*, trans. John A. Oesterle, Notre Dame, IN: University of Notre Dame, 1966.

Leon Battisti Alberti, *De re aedificatoria*, Florence: Giuntina, 1550.

_____, *De re aedificatoria* (Florence, 1488), Italian trans. F. Borsi, *L'Architettura*, 2 vols, Milan: Il Polifilo, 1966.

_____, *On Painting*, trans. J. R. Spencer, New Haven: Yale University Press, 1996.

_____, *On Painting*, trans. Cecil Crayson, London: Penguin Books, 1991.

Andrea Alciato, *Emblemata*, Augsburg: Steyner, 1531.

_____, *Emblemata*, Paris: Wechel, 1534, 1536 and 1542.

_____, *Emblemata*, Venice: Aldus, 1546.

_____, *Emblemata*, Lyon: Roville–Bonhomme, 1547, 1548, 1549 and 1551.

_____, *Emblemata*, Paris: Ruelle, 1562.

_____, *Emblemata*, Frankfurt/Main: Feyerabend, 1567.

_____, *Emblematum libellus cum commentaries*, ed. Claude Mignault, Antwerp: Plantin, 1577.

_____, *Emblematum libellus cum commentaries*, ed. Claude Mignault, New York: Garland Publishing, Inc., 1976.

Linda Alcoff, "Cultural Feminism versus Post-Structuralism: The Identity Crisis in Feminist Theory," *Signs* 13 (1988), pp. 405–36.

Thomas W. Allen, *Commentary on the Homeric Hymns*, London: Macmillan, 1904.

_____, and E. E. Sikes, *Commentary on the Homeric Hymns*, Cambridge: Cambridge University Press, 2003.

Hein-Th.Schulze Altcapenberg, *Sandro Botticelli: Pittore della Divina Commedia*, Milan: Skira, 2000.

Ambrose, "The Patriarchs," in *The Fathers of the Church*, Washington, DC: Catholic University of America Press, 1960, LXV.

W. Amelug, *Die Skulpturen des Vaticanischen Museum*, Berlin: G. Grote, 1903.

Sydney Anglo, *Macchiavelli*, London: Paladin, 1969.

Apollodorous, *Library and Epitome*, ed. James George Frazer, New York: Crown Publishers, 1969.

Pietro Aretino, *I Ragionamenti*, Milan: dall'Oglio, 1534.

John Arthos, *Dante, Michelangelo and Milton*, London: Routledge & Kegan Paul, 1963.

Elena Parma Armani, *Perin del Vaga*, Genoa: Sagep, 1986.

G. B. Armenini, *De' veri precetti della pittura,*Milan: dall' Oglio, 1587.

W. Arondeus, *Giorgio Vasari*, Amsterdam: Nederlandsche Kenrboekeris, 1946.

Apostolos N. Athanassakis, ed. *The Orphic Hymn*, Atlanta GA: Scholars Press, 1977.

Charles Avery, "Benvenuto Cellini's Bronze Portrait of Bindo Altovito," *Connoisseur* (1978), pp. 71–72.

Augustine, "Sermons on the Liturgical Seasons," in *The Fathers of the Church*, Washington, DC: Catholic University of America Press, 1959, XXXVIII.

_____, "Treatise on Various Subjects," in *The Fathers of the Church*, Washington, DC: Catholic University of America Press, 1965, XLI.

R. Bacou and C. Monbeig–Goguel, *Giorgio Vasari: Dessinatoeur et Collectionneur*, Paris: Cabinet des Dessins, Louvre, 1965.

_____, "Giorgio Vasari: *Prudenza*," *Revue de l'Art* (1968), pp. 88–92.

U. Baldini, *Palazzo Vecchio e i Quartieri Monumentali*, Florence: Leo S. Olschki, 1950.

_____, *Catalogo della Mostra Vasariana*, Florence: Leo S. Olschki, 1952.

_____, "La deposizione di Giorgio Vasari per il Cardinale Ippolito de'Medici," *Revista d'Arte* (1952), pp. 195–205.

_____, *Mostra dei Bozzetti delle Gallerie di Firenze*, Florence: Leo S. Olschki, 1952.

F. Baldinucci, *Notizie dei professori del disegno da Cimabue in qua*, Florence: Giunti, 1681–1728.

F. Baldinucci and F. Ranalli, *Notizie dei professori del disegno da Cimabue in qua*, Florence: Giunti, 1854–1847.

Cesare Balbo, *Vita di Dante*, Turin: Libro Mania, 1839–1856.

Moshe Barasch, "Zuccari: The Theory of *Disegno*," in *Theories of Art: From Plato to Winckelmann*, New York: New York University Press, 1985, pp. 25-34.

Michele Barbi, *Della fortuna di Dante nel secolo XVI*, Pisa: Nistri, 1890.

Piero Bargellini, ed., *Santa Reparata: La Cattedrale Risorta*, Florence: Bonechi, 1970.

Paola Barocchi, "Sul Vasari Pittore," in *Studi Vasariani*, Florence. G. C. Sansoni, 1952, pp. 186–91.

_____, "Il Vasari Pittore," *Rinascimento* (1956), pp. 187–212.

_____, "Il Vasari Architetto," *Atti dell' Accademia Pontaniana* (1956–1957), pp. 34–39.

_____, ed., *Trattati d'Arte del Cinquecento fra Manierismo e Controriforma*, Bari: G. Laterza, 1960–1962.

_____, "Complementi al Vasari Pittore," in *Atti dell'Academia Toscana di Scienze e Lettere*, Florence: Leo S. Olschki, 1963, pp. 253–309.

_____, *Mostra di disegni dei fondatori dell'Accademia delle arti del disegno nel IV centario della fondazione*, Florence: Leo S. Olschki, 1963.

_____, *Mostra di disegni del Vasari e della sua cerchia*, Florence: Leo S. Olschki, 1964.

_____, *Vasari Pittore*, Milan: Club del Libro, 1964.

_____, "Appunti su Francesco Morandini," *Mitteilungen des Kunsthistorischen Institutes in Florenz* (1964), pp. 1–32.

_____, "Itinerario di Giovambattista Naldini," *Arte Antica e Moderna* (1965), pp. 3–47.

_____, "Una Selva di Notizie di Vicenzo Borghini," in *Un Augurio a Raffaello Mattioli*, Florence: Leo S. Olschki, 1970, pp. 87–172.

_____, *Scritti d'Arte del Cinquecento*, Milan/Naples: Ulrico Hoepli, 1971.

_____, "Le postille di Del Migliore alle *Vite*," in *Il Vasari Storiografo e Artista*, Florence: Istituto di Studi sul Rinascimento, 1976, pp. 439–49.

_____, *Studi Vasariani*, Turin: Einaudi, 1984.

_____, "Michelangelo tra le due relazione delle *Vite* vasariane (1550-1568)," in *Studi Vasariani*, Turin: Einuadi, 1984, pp. 35–42.

Paul Barolsky, *Michelangelo's Nose: A Myth and its Maker*, University Park, PA: Pennsylvania State University Press, 1990.

_____, *Why Mona Lisa Smiles and Other Tales*, University Park, PA: Pennsylvania State University Press, 1991.

_____, *Giotto's Father and the Family of Vasari's 'Lives'*, University Park, PA: Pennsylvania State University Press, 1992.

Cosimo Bartoli, *Ragionamenti accademici di Cosimo Bartoli gentil'huomo et Accademico Fiorentino sopra alcuni luoghi difficili di Dante, con alcune invetioni et significati*, Venice: Francesco de Franceschi, 1567.

A. Bartsch, *Le peintre graveur illustre*, Vienna: Akademische Druck Verlagsanstalt Graz, 1802–1821.

K. Barzman, "The Florentine Accademia del Disegno: Liberal Education and the Renaissance Artist," in A. Boschloo ed., *Academies of Art Between Renaissance and Romanticism, Leid Kunsthistorisch Jaarboek* (1996–97), pp. 14–32

E. Battisti, "Il concetto d'imitazione nel cinquecento italiano," in *Rinascimento e Barocco*, Turin: Edam, 1960, pp. 175–215.

Baxter, Paola Tinagli "Giorgio Vasari's Ragionamenti." PhD dissertation, University of Edinburgh, 1988.

Mary Beagon, *Roman Nature: The Thought of Pliny the Elder*, Oxford: Clarendon Press, 1992.

J. Bean and F. Stampfle, *Drawings from New York Collections: I. Italian Drawings*. New York: The Metropolitan Museum and the Pierpont Morgan Library, 1956.

G. Becatti, "Raphael and Antiquity," in *The Complete Works of Raphael*, New York: Reynald and Company, 1969, pp. 523–26.

N. Bemporad, "Il restauro del corridoio Vasariano a Firenze," *Architetti* (1953), pp. 45–50.

_____, "Gli Uffizi e la Scala Buonalentina,"*Architettura* (1968), pp. 610–19.

_____, "Considerazioni sul fabbricato degli Uffizi," in *Il Vasari Storiografo e Artista*, Florence: Istituto di Studi sul Rinascimento, 1976, pp. 225–53.

J. Bennett & D. Bertoloni Meli, *Sphaera Mundi: Astronomy Books in the Whipple Museum 1478–1600*, Cambridge: Cambridge University Press, 1994.

P. Berchorius, *Repertorium Morale*, Cologne: J. W. Huisch, 1700.

B. Berenson, *Drawings of the Florentine Painters*, Chicago: University of Chicago Press, 1962.

_____, *The Italian Pictures of the Renaissance*, New York: Phaidon, 1968.

Daniel Beresniak and Michel Random, *I simboli: il Drago*, Rome: Edizione Mediterranee, 1987.

P. Bergellini, *Scoperta di Palazzo Vecchio*, Florence: Vallecchi, 1968.

Thomas G. Bergin, *Dante*, New York: The Orion Press, 1964.

I. Bergstrom, *Revival of Antique Illusionistic Wall Painting in Renaissance Art*, Gothenburg: Goteborg University, 1957.

Hans Bidermann, *Dictionary of Symbolism*, New York: Meridian Books, 1989.

Per Bjurström, *Italian Drawings from the Collection of Giorgio Vasari*, Stockholm: Nationalmuseum, 2001.

R. Bernard, *La vertu*, Paris: Gallimard Editions, 1933–1935.

S. J. Berner, "The Florentine Patriciate in the Transition from Republic to Principato: 1530–1610," PhD dissertation, University of California at Berkeley, 1969.

_____, "Florentine Society in the late Sixteenth and early Seventeenth Centures," *Studies in the Renaissance* (1971), pp. 203–46

R. Berner, *Myth and Religion in European Painting: 1270–1700*, New York: George Braziller, 1973.

L. Berti, *La casa del Vasari in Arezzo e il suo Museo*, Florence: Salimbeni, 1955.

_____, *Mostra del Pontormo e del Primo Manierismo Fiorentino*, Florence: Leo S. Olschki, 1965.

_____, *Il Principe dello Studiolo: Francesco dei Medici e la fine del Rinascimento Fiorentino*, Florence: Edam, 1967.

_____, *Il Primato del Disegno*, Florence: Centro Di, 1980.

R. Bettarini and P. Barocchi, ed. *Giorgio Vasari Vite de' più eccellenti Pittori, Scultori e Architettori nelle redazioni del 1550 e 1568*, Florence: G. C. Sansoni, 1966–1990.

Guido Biagi, *Le illustrazioni alla Divina Comedia di Giovanni Stradano 1587*, Florence: Fratelli    Alinari, 1892 and 1893 editions.

J. Bialostocki, "The Renaissance Concept of Nature and Antiquity," in *Acts of the XX International Congress of the History of Art*, Princeton: Princeton University Press, 1968, pp. 19–30.

*Biblia Sacra: Juxta Volgatum Clementinam*, Rome: Typis Societatis S. Joannis Evang, 1956.

A. F. Blunt, "Illusionistic Decoration in Central Italian Paintings," *Journal of the Royal Society of the Arts* (1959), pp. 309–25.

_____, *Artistic Theory in Italy: 1450–1600*, New York: Oxford University Press, 1968.

T. S. R. Boase, *Giorgio Vasari: The Man and the Book*, Princeton: Princeton University Press, 1979.

P. Bober, *Drawings after the Antique by Amico Aspertini*, London: The Warburg Institute, 1957.

G. Boccaccio, *Della geneologia de gli dei di M. Giovanni Boccaccio*, Italian trans. Gioseppe Betussi da Bassano, Venice: F. Lorenzini da Turino, 1564.

_____, *Genealogie Decorum Gentilium Libri*, ed. Vincenzo Romano. Bari: Gius. Laterza e Figli, 1951.

Achille Bocchi, *Symbolica Quaestiones*, Bologna: Novae Academiae, 1555.

Francesco Bocchi, *Le bellezze della città di Firenze* (1587), ed. M. Giovanni Cinelli, Florence: Giovanni Gugliantini, 1677.

F. Bocchi, *Le Bellezze della città di Fiorenza, dove a pieno di pittura, di scultura, di sacri tempii, di palazzi i piu notabili artifizie e piu preziosi si contengono*, Florence: Giunti, 1591.

H. Bodmer, "Le note marginali di Agostino Carracci nella edizione del Vasari nel 1568," *Il Vasari* (1939), pp. 89–127.

A. M. Severinus Boetius, *De consolatione philosophiae*, ed. S. Thomas. P. I, Nuremberg: Anton Koberger, 1476.

F. Bologna and R. Causa, *Fontainebleau e la Maniera Italiana*, Florence: Salimbeni, 1952.

W. Bombe, "Giorgio Vasari Hauser in Florenz und Arezzo," *Belvedere* (1928), pp. 58–62.

R. Borghini, *Il Riposo*, ed. Mario Rosci, Milan: Edizione Labor, 1967.

V. Borghini, *Discorsi di Monsignore Don Vincenzio Borghini*, Florence: Giunti, 1584.

_____, *Carteggio Artistico Inedito di D. Vincenzo Borghini*, ed. A. Lorenzoni, Florence: S.. B. Seeber, 1912.

K. Borinski, *Die Antike in Poetik und Kunsttheorie von Ausgang des klassichen Altertums bis auf Goethe und Wilhelm von Humboldt*, Leipzig: K. F. Koehler, 1914–1924.

Franco Borsi and Stefano Borsi, *Leon Battista Alberti*, Bologna: Giunti, 1990.

E. Borsook, "Art and Politics at the Medici Court. The Funeral of Cosimo I de' Medici," *Mitteilungen des Kunsthistorischen Institutes in Florenz* (1965), pp. 31–54.

G. Bottari, *Vite de' più eccelenti pittori, scultori e architetti, scritte da Giorgio Vasari, pittore e architetto aretino, corrette da molti errori e illustrate con note*, Rome: de Rossi, 1759–1760.

_____, ed. *Raccolta di lettere sulla pittura, scultura ed architettura*, Milan: Giovanni Silvestri, 1822–1825.

Anton W. A. Boschloo, ed. *Academies: Between Renaissance and Romanticism of Art*, Leiden: SDU Uitgevereij, 1989.

J. Bosquet, *Mannerism*, New York: George Braziller, 1964.

R. Bragard, *Musical Instruments in Art and History*, New York: Viking Press, 1968.

Horst Bredekamp, *The Lure of Antiquity and the Cult of the Machine*, Princeton: Markus Wiener Publishers, 1995.

G. Briganti, *Italian Mannerism*, trans. Margaret Kunzle, Princeton: Van Nostrand, 1962.

A. M. Brizio, "Rileggendo Vasari," *Emporium* (1939), pp. 123–130.

G. Bruno, *Spazio della bestia trionfante*, Venice: Giunti, 1584.

M. Bucci, *Lo Studiolo di Francesco I*, Florence: Leo S. Olschki, 1965.

A. Buchner, *Musical Instruments*, New York: Crown Publishers, 1973,

_____, *Musical Instruments Through the Ages*, London: Phaidon, 1975.

Wallis Budge, *Magia egizie*, Rome: Newton, 1980.

F. A. W. Budge, *Amulets and Talismans*, New York: University Books, Inc., 1961.

J. Burckhardt, *The Civilization of the Renaissance in Italy*, New York: Harper and Row Publishers, 1958.

J. Burnaby, "Amor Dei: A study of the Religion of St. Augustine," London: : Lee Warner, 1938, pp. 132–35.

P. Calamandrei, "Sulle relazioni tra Giorgio Vasari e Benvenuto Cellini," in *Studi Vasariani*, Florence: G. C. Sansoni, 1952, pp. 195–214.

Antonio Caleca, Andrea Del Grosso and Margherita Melaini, eds., *La topografia artistica di Giorgio Vasari*. Poggio a Caiano: CB Edizioni, 2007.

J. Camacetti, *Tratti dai protocolli dei notai Aretini conservati nell'archivio notarile Antecosimiano di Firenze del R. Archivio di Stato di Firenze*, Florence: Leo S. Olschki, 1934.

M. G. Camerani, *Mostra documentaria e iconografica di Palazzo Vecchio,* Florence: Salimbeni, 1957.

Piero Guelfi Camajani, *Dizionario Araldico,* Florence: Arnaldo Forni, 1940.

Malcolm Campbell, "Il ritratto del Duca Alessandro de' Medici di Giorgio Vasari: contesto e significato," *Arezzo Convegno di Studi* (Florence), pp. 339–61.

Caterina Caneva, ed. *Painters by Painters,* Wisbech, England: National Academy of Design, 1988.

Martianus Capella, *The Marriage of Philology and Mercury,* trans. W. Stahl, R. Johnson and E. Burge, New York: Columbia University Press, 1971-1977.

_____, *The Berlin Commentary on Martianus Capella's De Nuptiis Philologiae et Mercurii,* Book I and II, ed. Haijo Jan Westra, Tanja Kupke, Benjamin Garstad, Leiden: Brill Academic Publishers, 1994–1998.

_____, *Martianus Capella and the Seven Liberal Arts,* trans. W. Stahl, R. Johnson, and E. Burge, 2 vols, New York: Columbia University Press, 1971–1977.

R. W. Carden, *The Life of Giorgio Vasari,* London: Lee Warner, 1910.

Annibale Caro, *Lettere Familiari,* ed. Aulo Greco, Florence: G. C. Sansoni, 1957–1961.

Stefano Caroti, *L'astrologia in Italia,* Rome: Newton Compton, 1983.

E. A. Carroll, "Lappoli, Alfani, Vasari, and Rosso Fiorentino," *Art Bulletin* (1967), pp. 297–304.

Vincenzo Cartari, *Imagini delli Dei de gl'Antichi,* Venice: Marcolini, 1556.

_____, *Imagini delli Dei de gl'Antichi,* Venice: Vincenzo Valgrisi, 1571

_____, *Imagini delli Dei de gl'Antichi,* Venice: Francesco Ziletti, 1587.

_____, *Imagini delli Dei de gl'Antichi,* Venice: Il Tomasini, 1647

_____, *Imagini delli Dei de gl'Antichi,* Walter Koschatzky, ed. Vienna: Akademische Druck Verlagsanstalt Graz, 1963.

_____, *Imagini delli Dei de gl'Antichi,* Stephen Orgel, ed. New York: Garland Publishing, Inc., 1976.

_____, *Imagini delli Dei de gl'Antichi,* Ginetta Auzzas, ed. Vicenza; Neri Pozza, 1996.

Maurizio Dardano, "La progressione tematica nella prosa del Vasri," in *Storia della lingua e stroria dell'arte in Italia: dissimmetrie e intersezioni,* eds., Vittorio Casaleand Paolo D'Achille, Florence: Cesati, 2004, pp. 331-47.

David Cast, "Reading Vasari again: history and philosophy," Word and Image (1993), pp. 29–38.

C. Casati, *Leone Leoni d' Arezzo scultore e Giovanni Paolo Lomazzo pittore Milanese,* Milan: Ulrico Hoepli, 1884.

E. Cassirer, *The Individual and the Cosmos in Renaissance Philosophy,* New York: Harper and Row Publishers, 1963.

D. Cast, *The Calumny of Apelles*, New Haven:  Yale University Press, 1981.

Patricia Castelli, *Il Lume del Sole: Marsilio Ficino Medico dell'Anima*, Florence: Opus Libri, 1984.

Baldassare Castiglione, *Il cortegiano*, Venice: Aldus, 1528.

———, *The Book of the Courtier*, trans. George Bull, Baltimore, MD:  Penguin Books, 1967.

Anne Caubet, ed., *L'Emire du Temp: Mythes et Creations*, Paris: Musée du Louvre, 2000.

R. Causa, *Mostra documentaria e iconografica di Palazzo Vecchio*, Florence: Salimbeni, 1957.

C. J. Cavallucci, *Notizie Storiche intorno alla R. Accademia delle Arti del Disegno in Firenze*, Florence: G. C. Sansoni, 1873.

Richard Cavendish, *The Tarot*, New York: Crescent Books, 1986.

Alessandro Cecchi, *La case del Vasari a Firenze*," in Laura Corti, ed., *Giorgio Vasari:  Principe, letterati e artisti nelle Carte di Giorgio Vasari*, Florence: Edam Editrice, pp. 37–43

———, "Le case Vasari in Arezzo e Firenze," in R. P. Ciardi, ed., *Case di Artisti in Toscana*, Florence: Amilcare Pizzi, 1998, pp. 30–77;

B. Cellini, *I trattati dell'oreficeria e della scultura, i discorsi e i ricordi intorno all'arte, le lettere e suppliche, le poesie*, Florence: Valente Panizzij and Marco Peri, 1568.

Federico Chabod, *Machiavelli and the Renaissance*, New York: Harper and Row Publishers, 1965.

D. S. Chambers, *Patrons and Artists in the Italian Renaissance*, Columbia: University of South Carolina Press, 1971.

D. S. Chambers and F. Quiviger, *Italian Academies of the Sixteenth Century*, London: The Warburg Institute, 1995.

M. Chappel, "Cigoli, Galileo and Invidia," *Art Bulletin* (1975), pp. 91–98.

André Chastel, "Vasari et la legend Mediceenne:  L'école du Jardin de Saint–Marc," *Studi Vasariani*, Florence:  G. C. Sansoni, 1952, pp. 159–72.

———, *The Golden Age of the Renaissance: 1460–1500*, London: Thames and Hudson, 1965.

———, *Studios and Styles of the Italian Renaissance*, New York:  Odyssey Books, 1966,

———, "Vasari en son temps et aujourd'hui," *Oeil* (1967), pp. 10–17.

———, *Art et humanisme a Florence au temps de Laurent de Magnifique*, Paris: Gallimard Editions, 1968.

———, *Ficin et l'art*, Geneva: Droz, 1954.

———, *Marsile Ficin et L'Art*, Geneva: Droz, 1996.

Iris Cheney, "Francesco Salviati," PhD dissertation, New York University, 1963.

———, "Vasari and Procaccini by Barocchi. Review," *Art Bulletin* (1965), pp. 302–303.

Liana De Girolami Cheney, "The Paintings of the Casa Vasari," PhD dissertation, Boston University, 1978.

_____, *The Paintings of the Casa Vasari*, New York: Garland Publishing, Inc. 1985.

_____, "Giorgio Vasari's Paintings of the Casa Vasari Arezzo," *Explorations in Renaissance Culture* (Spring 1985), pp. 53–73.

_____, "Giorgio Vasari's Chamber of Abraham: A Religious Ceiling in the Aretine House," *Sixteenth Century Journal* (Fall 1987), pp. 355–80.

_____, "Amore e baci: Giorgio Vasari's Poems to Nicolosa Bacci," in *Italian Culture*, Hamilton, Canada: The Symposium Press, 1988, pp. 43–53.

_____,"Vasari's Depiction of Pliny's Histories," *Explorations in Renaissance Culture* (December 1989), pp. 97–120.

_____,"Giorgio Vasari and Naples: The Monteoliveto Order," in *Parthenope's Splendor: Art of the Golden Age in Naples*, eds. J. C. Porter and S. S Monshower, *Papers in Art History, The Pennsylvania State University,* (1994), pp. 48–126.

_____,"Giorgio Vasari's Sala dei Cento Giorni: A Farnese Celebration," *Exploration in Renaissance Culture* (1995), pp. 121–51.

_____,"Vasari's Pictorial Musing on the Muses: The Chamber of Apollo of the Casa Vasari," *Studies in Iconography* (Spring 1994), pp. 135–77.

_____,"Giorgio Vasari's Theory of Feminine Beauty," in *Concepts of Beauty in Renaissance Art,* London: Ashgate/Scolar Press (Spring 1997), pp. 180–90.

_____,"Giorgio Vasari's Andromeda: Transformations of an Ancient Myth," *Discoveries* (Fall 1998), pp. 2–5.

_____, "Giorgio Vasari's "The Toilet of Venus: Neoplatonic Notion of Female Beauty," in *Neoplatonism and Western Aesthetics*, ed. Aphrodite Alexandrakis, New York: State University of New York Press, 2000, pp. 99–113.

_____, "Giorgio Vasari's Planetary Gods in the Chamber of Fortune," in *The Inspiration of Astronomical Phenomena*, ed. Raymond E. White, Temple, AZ: University of Arizona Press, 2000, pp. 25–35.

_____, "Giorgio Vasari's Visual Interpretation of Ancient Lost Paintings," in *Lost Works of Art*, ed. Deborah Mauskopf Deliyannis, *Visual Resources Association Journal*, Los Angeles: Getty Publications, 2000, pp. 229–58.

_____, "Giorgio Vasari's *Judith*: Athena or Aphrodite," *Fifteenth Century Studies Journal* (2000), pp. 154–92.

_____, "Giorgio Vasari's Patience: Astronomical Symbol of Time," in *The Inspiration of Astronomical Phenomena*," ed. Raymond E. White,

*Memorie: Journal of the Italian Astronomical Society* (2001–2002), pp. 112–21.

_____, "Giorgio Vasari's and Niccolo Machiavelli's Medicean Emblems of War and Peace in the *Portrait of Duke Alessandro de' Medici*," in *Artful Armies, Beautiful Battles*, ed. Pia Cuneo, Leiden: Brill, 2001, pp. 107–31.

_____, "Giorgio Vasari's *Calliope*," *Discovery Journal* (2001), pp. 4–8.

_____, "Giorgio Vasari's Venetian Decorative Cycle: The *apparato* for Aretino's La Talanta," *Exploration in Renaissance Culture* (Winter 2002), pp. 239–85.

_____ and John Hendrix, ed. *Neoplatonism and the Arts*, New York/ London: Edwin Mellen Press, 2002.

_____, "Giorgio Vasari's *Last Judgment*: A Neoplatonic Vision," in *Neoplatonism and the Arts*, eds. Liana De Girolami Cheney and John Hendrix, New York: Edwin Mellen Press, 2002, pp. 227–49.

_____, "Giorgio Vasari's Allegory of Avarice," *SECAC Journal* (2002), pp. 1–15.

_____, "Giorgio Vasari's *Scrittorio of Calliope*: A Neoplatonic *ut pictura poesis*," in *Neoplatonism and the Arts*, eds. Liana De Girolami Cheney and John Hendrix, New York: Edwin Mellen Press, 2002, pp. 214–27.

_____, Dante's *Inferno*: Renaissance Illustrations," *Italian Culture* (Fall 1998), pp. 35–90.

_____, "Giorgio Vasari's Astrae: Allegory of Justice," in *Depiction of Images*, ed. Jan de Jong, London: Taylor and Francis Publishers, *Visual Resources* (2003), pp. 5–15.

_____, "*Giorgio* Vasari's Venetian Decorative Cycle II: The Cornaro Ceiling," *Exploration in Renaissance Culture* (Summer 2003), pp. 23–59

_____, "Giorgio Vasari's Neoplatonic Cosmology: The Planets," in Liana De Girolami Cheney and John Hendrix, eds., *Neoplatonic Aesthetics: Music, Literature and the Visual Arts*, London: Peter Lang, 2003, pp. 227–49.

_____, "Giorgio Vasari's Studio, Diligenza ed Amorevole Fatica," in *Reading Vasari*, eds. A. Barriualt, et.al, London: Philip Wilson, 2005, pp. 259-76.

_____, "Giorgio Vasari's *Iconology* and Cesare Ripa's *Iconology*: The Chamber of Fortune's Allegorical Figures in the Casa Vasari," in *Exploration in Renaissance Culture* (Fall 2008).

_____, ed., *Readings in Italian Mannerism*, London: Peter Lang, 1993 and rev. 2004.

_____, *The Homes of Giorgio Vasari*, New York: Peter Lang, 2006.

_____, *Giorgio Vasari's Teachers: Sacred and Profane Art*. London: Peter Lang, 2007.

_____, *Giorgio Vasari's Prefaces: Art and Theory*. New York/London: Peter Lang, 2011.

_____, *Le Dimore di Giorgio Vasari*, New York: Peter Lang, 2011.

_____, ed., *Giorgio Vasari's Life and Lives by Eniar Rud*, Washington, DC, New Academia, 2011.

_____, "*Il Corridoio Vasariano*: A Resplendent Passage to Medici and Vasari's Grandeur," in Paul Emmons, John Hendrix, Jane Lomholt, eds. *The Cultural Role of Architecture*. Abingdon, UK: Taylor and Francis/Routledge, pp. 26-36.

_____, Joanna Wolanska and Joseph Grabski, eds., *Giorgio Vasari: Pennello, pluma e ardore*, Krakow: *Artibus et Historiae, Special Edition*, 2011.

Jean Chevalier and Alain Gheerbrant, *A Dictionary of Symbols*, London: Basil Blackwell Ltd, 1994.

A. Chiapelli, "L'opere di giorgio Vasari scrittore e il suo significato civile," *Il Vasari* (1939), pp. 129–38.

P. V. Chiaroni, "Il Vasari e l'architetto Fra Ristoro da Campi construttore della Chiesa di S. Maria Novella in Firenze," in *Studi Vasariani*, Florence: G. C. Sansoni, 1952, pp. 140–46.

Alan Chung, et. al., *Raphael, Cellini and A Renaissance Banker*, Milan: Mondadori Electa, 2003.

S. J. A. Churchill, *Bibliografia Vasariana*, Florence: Salimbeini, 1912.

R. P. Ciardi, ed., *Case di Artisti in Toscana*, Florence: Amilcare Pizzi, 1998.

Cicero (Marcus Tullius), *De Oratore*, trans. E.W. Sutton, Cambridge: Harvard University Press, 1942.

_____, *De inventione*, trans. H.M. Hubbell, Cambridge: Harvard University Press, 1949.

_____, *Somnium Scipionis*, ed. F. H. Rockwood, Norman: University of Oklahoma Press, 1966.

_____, *The Nature of the Gods*, trans. by Horace C. P. McGregor, Baltimore: Penguin *Books*, 1972.

G. Cinelli, *Le Bellezze della Città di Firenze*, Pistoia: Fortunati. 1677.

J. E. Cirlot, *Dictionary of Symbols*, New York: Philosophical Library, 1962.

John R. Clark, "The Manuscript Tradition of Marsilio Ficino's *De vita libri tres*," *Manuscripta* 27 (1983), pp. 158–64.

Kenneth Clark, *Landscape into Art*, Boston: Beacon Press, 1969.

_____, *The Drawings by Sandro Botticelli For Dante's Divine Comedy: After the Originals in the Berlin Museum and Vatican*, New York: Harper & Row, Publishers, 1976.

N. Leopoldo Speliakos Clark, "Artists' Home in Sixteenth Century Italy," PhD dissertation, Johns Hopkins University, 1980.

R. S. Clements, "Michelangelo on Effort and Rapidity in Art," *Journal of the Warburg and Courtauld Institutes* (1954), pp. 310–20.

_____, *Michelangelo's Theory of Art*, New York, 1961.

G. Clovio, *Farnese Hours*, New York: George Braziller, 1976.

Eric Cochrane, *Historians and Historiography in The Italian Renaissance*, Chicago: The University of Chicago Press, 1985.

D. Coffin, *The Villa d'Este at Tivoli*, Princeton: Princeton University Press, 1960.

_____, *History of Landscape Architecture*, Washington, DC: Dumbarton Oaks, 1971.

_____, *The Italian Garden*, Washington, DC: Dumbarton Oaks, 1972.

A. Colasanti, "Il memoriale di Baccio Bandinelli," *Repertorium für Kunstwissenschaft* (1945), pp. 406–43.

_____, *Volte e Soffitti Italiani*, Milan: Ulrico Hoepli, 1923.

Michael W. Cole, *Cellini and the Principles of Sculptures*, Cambridge: Cambridge University Press, 2002.

L. Collobi–Ragghianti, *Vasari Libro dei Disegni*, Milan: Archittetura, 1973.

_____, *Il Libro de Disegni del Vasari*, Florence: Vallecchi Edition, 1974.

F. Colonna, *Hypnerotomachia Poliphili*, Venice: Aldus, 1499

_____, *Hypnerotomachia Poliphili*, New York: Garland Publishing, Inc. 1976.

_____, *Hypnerotomachia Poliphili*, ed. Joscelyn Godwin, London: Thames and Hudson, 1999.

Natale Comes (Conti), *Mythologiae*, Venice: Marcolini, 1567.

Claudia Conforti, *Vasari Architetto*, Milan: Electa, 1993.

A. Conti, "La casa dell'artista," in *Storia dell'Arte Italiana*, Turin: Edam, 1979, pp. 205–208.

C. Conti, *La Prima Reggia di Cosimo I de' Medici*, Florence: G. C. Sansoni, 1893.

J. Coolidge, "Villa Giulia: A study of Central Italian Architecture in the mid–Sixteenth Century," *Art Bulletin* (1943), pp. 177–25.

J. C. Cooper, *An Illustrated Encyclopedia of Traditional Symbols*. London: Thames and Hudson, 1978.

J. C. Cooper, *Symbolic and Mythological Animals*, London: Aquarian Press, 1992.

G. F. Cope, *Symbolism in the Bible and the Church*, London: Thames and Hudson, 1959.

Laura Corti, *et al*, *Giorgio Vasari: Principe, letterati e artisti nelle Carte di Giorgio Vasari*, Florence: Edam Editrice, 1981.

C. C. Coulter, "The Geneology of the Gods," *Vassar Medieval Studies* (1923), pp. 317–41.

Janet Cox-Rearick, *Dynasty and Destiny in Medici Art: Pontormo, Leo X, and The Two Cosimos*, Princeton: Princeton University Press, 1984.

B. Croce, *Teoria e Storia della Storiografia*, Bari: G. Laterza, 1920.Press, 1985.

_____, *Emblem Theory*, Nendeln: KTO Press, 1979.

_____, *The literature in the Light of the Emblem*, Toronto: University of Toronto Press, 1979.

P. D'Ancona, "Le rappresentazioni allegoriche delle arti liberali," *L'Arte* (1902), pp. 13, 221–27, 269–89 and 370–85.

M. Levi D'Ancona, *The Garden of the Renaissance*, Florence: Leo S. Olschki, 1967.

E. Darragon, *Manierisme en crise*, Rome: Edizioni dell'Elefante, 1983.

C. R. Dati, *Vite dei Pittori Antichi*, Padua: Tipografia della Minerva, 1821.

B. F. Davidson, "Vasari's Deposition in Arezzo," *Art Bulletin* (1954), pp. 228–31.

_____, "Marcantonio Raimondi: The Engravings of his Roman Period," PhD dissertation, Harvard University, 1954.

_____, "Decoration of the Sala Regia under Pope Paul III," *Art Bulletin* (1976), pp. 417–30.

C. Davis, "Per l'attivita Romana del Vasari nel 1553: Incisioni degli Affreschi di Villa Altoviti e la Fontanalia di Villa Giulia," *Mitteilungen des Kunsthistorischen Institutes in Florenz* (1979), pp. 197–223.

_____, "New frescoes by Vasari: 'colore' and 'invenzione' in mid 16th century Florentine painting," *Pantheon* (1980), pp. 153–57.

_____, "Frescoes by Vasari for Sforza Almeni, 'coppiere' to Duke Cosimo I," *Mitteilungen des Kunsthistorischen Institutes in Florenz* (1980), pp. 127–99.

Charles T. Davis, *Dante's Italy and Other Essays*, Philadelphia: University of Pennsylvania Press, 1984.

B. De Campos–Redig, *Raffaello nelle Stanze*, Milan: Aldo Garzanti, 1965.

P. L. De Castris, "Napoli 1544: Vasari e Monteoliveto," *Bolletino d'Arte* (1981), pp. 59–88.

A. De Franciscis, *Guide to the National Archeological Museum of Naples*, Naples: Di Mauro Edition, 1968.

B. Degenhart, "Zur Graphologie der Handzeichnungen," *Kunstgeschichtliches Jahrbuch der Bibliotheca Hertziana* (1937), pp. 34–48.

_____, and A. Schmitt, A. "Methoden Vasaris bei den Gestaltung seines "Libro," in *Studien zur toskanischen Kunst, Festschrift fur L. H. Heydenreich*, Munich: Georg Müller, 1964.

Joseph Jay Deiss, *Captains of Fortune*, New York: Thomas Crowell, 1967.

Elly Dekker and Peter van der Korgt, *Globes from the Western World*, London: Zwemmer, 1993.

Alessandro Del Vita, *Il Carteggio di Giorgio Vasari*, Arezzo: Tipografia Zelli, 1923.

_____, *Guida di Arezzo*, Arezzo: Società Tipografica Aretina, 1923.

_____, "Un parere di Michelangelo sul Vasari," *Il Vasari* (1928), pp. 5–10.

_____, "Uno specchio Vasariano," *Dedalo* (1929), pp. 42–49.

_____, *La Casa Vasari*, Rome: R. Istituto Archeologico e Storia dell'Arte, 1938,

_____, *Inventario e Regesto dell'Archivio Vasariano*, Arezzo: Tipograffia Zelli, 1938.

_____, *Le Ricordanze di Giorgio Vasari*, Rome: R. Istituto Archeologico e Storia dell'Arte, 1938.

_____, *Lo Zibaldone di Giorgio Vasari*, Rome: R. Istituto Archeologico e Storia dell'Arte, 1938.

_____, *Il Carteggio di Giorgio Vasari*, Arezzo: Tipografia Zelli, 1941.

_____, *Bibliografia degli scritti di Allessandro del Vita: 1910–1943*, Arezzo: Tipografia Zelli, 1943.

_____, "Vasari Uomo," in *Studi Vasariani*, Florence: G. C. Sansoni, 1952, pp. 215–21.

_____, *Rapporti e Contrasti tra Artisti nel Rinascimento*, Città di Castello: Tipografia Unione Arti Grafiche, 1958.

_____, "Aspetti vari e minori dell'attivita del Vasari," *Il Vasari* (1960), pp. 107–29.

_____, "Giorgio Vasari e la Cupola di San Pietro," *Il Vasari* (1961), pp. 25–29.

John G. Demaray, "Dante and the Book of the Cosmos," *Transactions* (1987), pp. 1–61.

C. Dempsey, "The Textual Sources of Poussin's Marine Venus in Philadelphia," *Journal of the Warburg and Courtauld Institutes* (1966), pp. 438–42.

_____, "Some observations on the education of artists in Florence and Bologna during late sixteenth century," *Art Bulletin* (1980), pp. 552–56.

_____, "Some Observations of the Education of Artists in Florence and Bologna during the Late Sixteenth Century," *Art Bulletin* (1980), pp. 552–69.

V. De Ruvo, "La concezione estetica di Giorgio Vasari," in *Studi Vasariani*, Florence: G. C. Sansoni, 1952, pp. 47–56.

C. De Salas, "Un exemplaire des vies de Vasari annote par le Greco," *Gazette des Beaux–Arts* (1967), pp. 176–80.

G. De Tervarent, "Veritas and Justitia Triumphant," *Journal of the Warburg and Courtauld Institutes* (1944), pp. 95–101.

_____, *Attributes et symboles dans l'art profane: 1450–1600*, Geneva: Droz, 1958.

Charles De Tolnay, *Michelangelo: Sistine Ceiling*, Princeton: Princeton University Press, 1945.

_____, "Zur interpretation der Vasari für flitlen über die blocke des Julius grabe," *Zeitschrift Kunstgeschichte* (1966), pp. 315–17.

G. Degli Azzi, *Documenti su opere d'arte e pittori aretini*, Arezzo: Typografia Zelli, 1934.

E. Dhanens, *Jean Boulogne:   Douai 1529–Florence 1608*, Brussels: Jarrolds, 1965.

Gabriella Di Cagno, *The Cathedral, The Baptistery and The Campanile*, Florence: La Mandragora, 1997.

Gerhard Dohrn-van Rossum, *The History of the Hour*, Chicago: University of Chicago, 1996.

L. Dolce, *Dialogo della Pittura*, Venice: Marcolini, 1557.

_____, *Dialogo della Pittura*, trans. M. Roskill, New York: New York University Press, 1968.

M. Donati, "Dell'attivita di Guglielmo di Marcillat nel Palazzo Vaticano," *Rendiconti Pontefica Accademia d'Archeologia* (1949–1951) pp. 25–26 and 267–76.

A. Doren, "Fortuna in Mittelater und in der Ranaissance," *Vortrage der Bibliothek Warburg* (1922–1924), pp. 71–144.

M. D'Orsi and M. Terenzi, *Castel Sant'Angelo: The Mausoleum of Hadrian*, Rome: Tipografia Terenzi, 1970.

James David Draper, *Bertoldo di Giovanni: Sculptor of the Medici Household*, Columbia, MO: University of South Carolina Press, 1992.

J. L. Draper, "Vasari's Decoration in the Palazzo Vecchio. The Ragionamenti: Translated with an Introduction and Notes," PhD dissertation, University of North Carolina, 1973.

*Drawings and Prints of the First Maniera:  1515–1535*, Providence:  Rhode Island School of Design, 1973.

Lois Drewer, "Margaret of Antioch the Demon-Slayer, East and West: The Iconography of the Predella of the Boston Mystic Marriage of St. Catherine," *Gesta*  32 (1993), pp. 11–20.

P. Dreyer, *Dantes Divina Commedia mit den Illustrationen von Sandro Botticelli*, Berlin: G. Grote, 1986.

E. Droulers, *Dictionnaire des attributes, allegories, emblemes et symbols*, Turnhout: Brepols, 1949.

C. Dumont, *Francesco Salviati au Palais Sacchetti de Rome et la decoration murale italienne (1520–1560)*, Geneva: Droz, 1973.

A. Ellenius, "Reminder of a Young Gentlemen," in *Idea and Form*, Uppsala: University Press, 1959, pp. 108–126.

L. D. Ettlinger, "Diana von Ephesus," *Reallexikon zur Deutschen Kunstgeschichte*, Stuttgart: Erg. Neuausg, 1954.

_____, "Muses and Liberal Arts. Two miniatures from Herrard of Landsberg's 'Hortus Deliciarum'," *Essay in the History of Art Presented to Rudolf Wittkower* (1967) London: Phaidon, 1967, pp. 29–36.

M. Falciai, *Arezzo: la sua storia e i suoi monumenti*, Florence: Francesco Lumachi, 1910.

_____, *Arezzo*, Arezzo: Tipografia Federigo Scheggi, 1926.

P. Fanfani, *Le pitture del Quartiere di Papa Leone in Palazzo Vecchio*, Florence: G. C. Sansoni, 1861.

E. Fantorri, *Nuova guida ovvero descrizione storico artistico critira della città e contorni di Firenze*, Florence: Gonelli, 1842.

Elena Fasano, *L'Italia moderna e la Toscana dei principi: discussioni e recerche storiche*, Grassina: Le Monnier, 2008.

R. Favero, ed., *Giorgio Vasari: La vita de' più eccellenti architettori*, Padua: Biblioteca dell'Imagine, 1984.

P. Fehl, Vasari's Extripation of the Huguenots, *Gazette des Beaux–Arts* (1974), pp. 257–83.

_____, "Stradanus and Vasari in the Palazzo Vecchio," in    *Il Vasari Storiografo e Artista*, Florence: Istituto di Studi sul Rinascimento, 1976, pp. 207–25.

Fenech Kroke, Antonella, *Giorgio Vasari: La fabrique de l'Allégorie, culture et Fonction de la Personnification au Cinquecento*. Florence: Olschki, 2011.

P. N. Ferri, *Catalogo raissuntivo della raccolta di disegni antichi e moderni, posseduti dalla R. Galleria degli Uffizi di Firenze*, Rome: Biblioteca d'Arte, 1890.

Marsilio Ficino, *Opera omnia*, Basel: Oporinum, 1563.

_____, *De vita coelitus comparanda* (Florence, 1489), reprinted in 2 vols. as *Opera omnia* (Basel: Oporinum, 1576), reprinted as *Opera omnia*, Turin: Bottega d'Erasmo, 1965.

_____, *Commentary on Plato's Symposium*, trans. S. R. Jane, Columbia: University of Missouri, 1944.

_____, *The Book of Life*, trans. Charles Boer, Dallas: Irving, 1980.

_____, *Three Books on Life*, trans. Carol V. Kaske and John R. Clark, Tempe, AZ: Medieval and Renaissance Texts and Studies, 1998.

_____, *Commentary on Plato's Symposium on Love*, ed. and trans. by Jayne Sears, Dallas, TX: Spring Publications, Inc., 1985.

_____, *Meditation on the Soul: Selected Letters of Marsilio Ficino*,    t r a n s . and ed. Clement Salaman, Rochester, VT: Inner Traditions,    1997.

_____, *Ficino's Il Libro dell"Amore*, ed. Sandra Niccoli, Florence: Leo    S. Olschki, 1987.

*The Figure in Mannerist and Baroque Drawings*, Storrs: University of Connecticut, 1967.

A. Filarete, *Filarete Tractact über die Baukunst*, trans. W. von Oettingen, Vienna: K. Graeser and Kie, 1890.

_____, *Filarette's Treatise on Architecture*, trans. John R. Spencer, New Haven: Yale University Press, 1965.

Zirka Z. Filipczak, *Hot Dry Men; Cold Wet Women: Theory of Humors in Western European Art*, New York: The American Federation of the Arts, 1997.

F. Flora, "Giorgio Vasari scrittore e storico delle Arti," *Il Vasari* (1957), pp. 1–17 and 65–74.

R. Foerster, "Die Verleumdung des Apelles in der Renaissance," *Jahrbuch der königlich preussischen Kunstsammlungen* (1887), pp. 29–31 and 89–90.

_____, "Studien zu Mantegna und den Bilder in Studierzimmer der Isabella Gonzaga," *Jahrbuch der königlich preussischen Kunstsammlungen* (1901), pp. 78–80.

R. Forichon, "La chapelle de Leon X et le Tesoretto du Palais Vieux," *Revue de l'art ancien et modern* (1909), pp. 307–12.

A. Forlani, *Mostra del disegno Italiano di cinque secoli*, Florence: Leo S. Olschki, 1961.

_____, "Disegni del Vasari e della sua cerchia," *Il Vasari* (1963), pp. 178–82.

_____, "Disegni dei fondatori dell'Accademia dell Arti del Disegno," *Il Vasari* (1963), pp. 41–44.

A. Forti, "L'Opera di Giorgio Vasari nella Fabbrica degli Uffizi," *Bolletino degli Ingenieri* (1971), vols. 11 and 12.

K. W. Forster, "Metaphors of Rule. Political Ideology and History in the Portraits of Cosimo I de' Medici," *Mitteilungen des Kunsthistorischen Institutes in Florenz* (1971), pp. 65–104.

_____ and R. J. Tuttle, "The Casa Pippi: Giulio Romano's House in Mantua," *Architectura* (1973), pp. 104–30.

T. Fossati, "I ritratti del Museo Giovio e un particolare quello di Cristoforo Colombo," *Periodico della Societa Storica Comense* (1803), pp. 33–34.

M. Fossi, "Richerche documentari sulla Chiesa di S. Maria dell'Umiltà di Pistoia," in *Il Vasari Storiografo e Artista*, Florence: Istituto di Studi sul Rinascimento, 1976, pp. 127–43.

Daniela Francalanci, Franca Pellegirini and Eliana Carrara, ed. *Il Carteggio di Vincenzo Borghini*, Florence: Studio Per Edizioni Scelte, 2001.

G. Franciosi, *Guida d'Arezzo*, Bergamo: Istituto Italiano d'Arti Grafiche, 1909.

Thomas Frangenberg, "Bartoli, Giaumbullari and the Prefaces to Vasari's *Lives* (1550)," in the *Journal of the Warburg and Courtauld Institutes*, Vol. 65 (2002), pp. 224-58.

_____, "The Art of Taling about Sculpture: Vasari, Borhini and Bocchi," *Journal of the Warburg and Courtauld Institutes*, Vol. 58 (1995), pp. 115-31.

S. Freedberg, *Parmigianino*, Cambridge: Harvard University Press, 1950.

_____, *Andrea del Sarto*, Cambridge: Harvard University Press, 1963.

_____, "Observations on the Painting of the Maniera," *Art Bulletin* (1965), pp. 187–197.

_____, *Painting of the High Renaissance in Rome and Florence*, New York: Harper and Row Publishers, 1971.

_____, *Painting in Italy: 1500–1600*, Baltimore:  Penguin Books, 1975.

Karl Frey, ed., *Il Codice Magliabecchiano*, Berlin:  G. Grote, 1892.

_____, ed., *Der literarische Nachlass Giorgio Vasaris* I, Munich: George Müller, 1923.

_____, ed., *Der literarische Nachlass Giorgio Vasaris* II, Munich: George Müller, 1930.

H.M. Frey, ed., *Neue Briefe von Giorgio Vasari* III, Munich:  August Hopfer, 1940.

R. Freyhan, "The Evolution of the Caritas Figure in the Thirteenth and Fourteenth Centuries," *Journal of the Warburg and Courtauld Institutes* (1948), pp. 68–86.

W. F. Friedlaender, *Mannerism and anti–Mannerism in Italian Paintings*, New York: Columbia University Press, 1957.

C. Frommel, *Die Farnesina und Peruzzi*, Berlin: G. Grote, 1961.

C. L. Fromme, "Der Palazzo Zuccari und die Institutgebäude," *Max–Plank–Geselleschaft, Berichte und Mitteilungen* III (1991), pp. 36–51.

A. Frova, *L'Arte di Roma e del mondo Romano*, Turin: Edam. 1961.

Galileo Galilei, *Dialogue Concerning the Two Chief World Systems, Ptolemaic and Copernican*, Florence: Giovanni Batista Landini, 1632, trans. S. Drake, Berkeley: University of California Press, 1967.

C. Gamba, *Disegni della R. Galleria degli Uffizi: Disegni dei Maestri Tosco–Romani del secolo XVI*, Florence: G. C. Sansoni, 1912–1932.

G. Gamba, *Fantasie e bizzarrie di artisti estratte dalle Vite di Giorgio Vasari*, Venice: Premiate Officina Grafiche Carlo Ferrani, 1839.

A. Gambuti, "Storia e critica dell'architettura nella storiografia Vasariana," in *Il Vasari: Storiografo e Artista*, Florence: Istituto di Studi sul Rinascimento, 1976, pp. 83–93.

G. F. Gamurrini, *Le Opere di Giorgio Vasari in Arezzo*, Arezzo: Scheggi, 1911.

F. Gandolfo and Mario Salmi, *Arezzo nelle due edizioni delle 'Vite' del Vasari*, Arezzo: Administrazione Provinciale di Arezzo, 1974.

Eugenio Garin, "Le 'elezioni" e il problema dell'astrologia," in *L'eta nuova*, Milan/Naples: Ulrico Hoepli. 1969, pp. 256–90.

Eugenio Garin, *Lo ziodiaco della vita: la polemica sull'astrologia dal Trecento al Cinquecento*, Bari: G. Laterza 1976.

Mary D. Garrard, "Artemisia Gentileschi's Self–Portrait as the Allegory of Painting," *Art Bulletin* (1980), pp. 97–112.

A. Gatti, *San Michele in Bosco di Bologna*, Bologna: Chiara Lubic, 1896.

F. Gaudioso, *Gli Affreschi di Paolo III: A Castel Sant'Angelo: 1543–1548*, Rome: De Luca Editore, 1981.

L. Gauricus, *Opera omnia*, Basel: Oporinum, 1575.

C. Gausti, *Giorgio Vasari*, Florence: F. C. Barbera, Bianchi, 1855.

G. Gaye, *Carteggio inedito d'artisti dei secoli XIV, XV, XVI*, Florence:  Molini, 1960.

J. W. Gaye, *Carteggio inedito d'artisti dei secoli XIV, XV, XVI*, Florence: Molini, 1939–1940.

Jacopo Gelli, *Divise, Motti e Imprese di Famiglie e Personaggi Italiani*, Milan: Ulrico Hoepli, 1976, reprint from Rome: Antonio Baldo, 1534.

J. A. Gere, *Taddeo Zuccaro*, Chicago: University of Chicago Press, 1969.

P. Giambullari, *Apparato et feste nelle nozze del Illustrissimo Signor Duca di Firenze et della Duchessa sua consorte, con le sue Stanze, Madriali, Comedia, et Intermedii in quelle recitati*, Florence: Giuntina, 1539.

F. Gibbons, *Dosso and Battista Dossi*, Princeton: Princeton University Press, 1968.

O. H. Giglioli, " Il Vasari e Palazzo Vecchio," *Il Marzocco* (1911), pp. 8–12.

C. E. Gilbert, "Antique Frameworks for Renaissance Art Theory: Alberti and Pino," *Marsyas* (1946), pp. 87–96.

F. Gilbert, "The Renaissance Interest in History," *Art, Science and History in the Renaissance*, Baltimore: Penguin Books, 1967, pp. 373–87.

R. Gilles, *Les symbolisme dans l'art religieux*, Paris: Mercure de France, 1943.

Carlos Gilly, *Magic, Alchemy and Science, XV-XII: The influence of Hermes Trismegistus*, Florence: Centro Di, 2002.

P. Ginori–Conti, *L'apparato per le nozze di Francesco de' Medici e di Giovanna d'Austria*, Florence: Leo S. Olschki, 1936.

Paolo Giovio, *Elogia virorum doctorum*, Florence: Giuntina, 1546.

_____, *Dialogo delle imprese militari et amorose di Monsignor Giovio, Vescovo di Nocera, con un regionamento di Messer Lodovico Domenichi nel medesimo soggetto*, Lyon: Roviglio, 1559.

_____, *Opere*, Rome: Istituto Poligrafico dello Stato, 1958–1972.

_____, *Paolo Giovio, Dialogo dell'Imprese Military e Amorose*, ed. by Maria Luisa Doglio, Rome: Bulzoni, 1978.

_____, *Paolo Giovio, Dialoghi et descriptions*, ed. E. Travi e M. Penco, Rome: Bulzoni, 1984.

_____, *Paolo Giovio, Elogia virorum illustrium*, ed. R. Meregazzi, Rome: Bulzoni, 1987.

_____, *Paolo Giovio*, ed. Sonia Maffei, Pisa: Scuola Normale Superiore, 1999.

Lillio Gregorio Giraldi, *De Deis Gentium*, Basel: Oporinum, 1548.

Corrado Gizzi, *Botticelli e Dante*, Milan: Electa, 1990.

_____, ed. *Signorelli e Dante*, Milan: Electa 1991.

_____, ed., *Federico Zuccari e Dante*, Milan: Electa, 1993.

_____, ed., *Giovanni Stradano e Dante*, Milan: Electa, 1994.

_____, *Dante Istoriato*, Milan: Skira, 1999.

D. Gnoli, "La demolizioni in Roma: Palazzo Altoviti," *Archivio Storico dell'Arte*, (1888), pp. 202–10.

D. Gorce, *Traites sur l'Ancien Testament*, Namur: De Lezenaar, 1967.

M. Goering and P. Gazzola, "Giorgio Vasari," *Thieme–Becker: Allegemeines Lexikon der bildenden Künstler*, Leipzig: E. A. Seeman Verlag, 1940, XXXV.

_____, *Mostra del Cinquecento Toscano*, Florence: G. C. Sansoni, 1940.

C. Goldstein, "Vasari and the Florentine Accademia del Disegno," *Zeitschrift für Kunstgeschichte* (1975), pp. 145–52.

L. M. Golson, "Serlio, Primaticcio and the Architectural Grotto," *Gazette des Beaux–Arts* (1971), pp. 95–108.

E. H. Gombrich, "Vasari's *Lives* and Cicero's *Brutus*," *Journal of the Warburg and Courtauld Institutes* (1960), pp. 309–11.

_____, "Style all'antica. The Renaissance and Mannerism," in *Studies in Western Art*, Princeton: Princeton University Press, 1963, pp. 122–27.

_____, *Norm and Form*, New York: Paidon, 1966.

_____, *Symbolic Images*, New York: Phaidon, 1972.

_____, *Giulio Romano*, Milan: Electa, 1989.

F. A. Gragg, *An Italian Portrait Gallery*, Boston: Chapman and Grimes Publishers, 1935.

Monica Grasso, "Le storie di Cerere e il ciclo dei mesi," in Maria S. Sconci, ed. *La volta vasariana di Palazzo Venezia restaurata*, Rome: Retable Cultura, 2003, pp. 47–63.

Peter Green, *The Poems of Catullus: A Bilingual Edition*, Berkley: University of California Press, 2006.

Michael Greenhalgh, "Pliny,Vitruvius and the Interpretation of Ancient Architecture," *Gazette des Beaux–Arts* (1974), pp. 297–304.

_____, *The Classical Tradition in Art*, New York: Harper and Row, Publishers, 1978.

M. Gregori, *Il paesaggio nella pittura fra Cinque e Seicento a Firenze*, Florence: T.A.P. Grafiche, 1974.

Pierre Grimal, *The Dictionary of Classical Mythology*, London: Blackwell, 1990.

Cesare Guasti, *La Cupola di Santa Maria del Fiore*, Florence: Forni 1996.

Francesco Maria Guazzo, *Malleus Maleficarum*, New York: Dover Publications, The Montague Summers Edition, 1988.

P. Guicciardini, *Il ritratto Vasariano di Luigi Guicciardini*, Florence: G. C. Sansoni, 1942.

W. K. C. Guthrie, *Orpheus and Greek Religion*, New York: Norton 1966.

J. R. Hale, *Artists and Warfare in the Renaissance*, London: Yale University Press, 1990.

E. Halg, *The Floral Symbolism of the Great Masters*, London: Phaidon, 1913.

J. Hall, *Dictionary of Symbols in Art*, New York: Harper and Row Publishers, 1974.

M. B. Hall, "Tramezzo in S. Croce, Florence, and Domenico Veneziano's Fresco," *Burlington Magazine* (1970), pp. 797–99.

_____, "Operation at Vasari's Workshop and the Designs for S. Maria Novella and S. Croce," *Burlington Magazine* (1973), pp. 204–09.

N. G. L. Hammond and H. H. Scullard, *The Oxford Classical Dictionary*, New York: Oxford University Press, 1970.

A. M. Harmon, trans. *Lucian's Slander*, Cambridge, MA: Harvard University Press, 2003.

F. Hartt, "Gonzaga Symbols in the Palazzo del Te," *Journal of the Warburg and Courtauld Institutes* (1950), pp. 151–10.

_____, *Giulio Romano*, New Haven: Yale University Press, 1958.

_____, "Power of the Individual in Mannerist Art. Renaissance and Mannerism," in *Studies in Western Art*, Princeton: Princeton University Press, 1963, pp. 222–28.

_____, "Art and Freedom in Quattrocento Florence," in *Essays in Memory of Karl Lehmann*, New York: Harper and Row Publishers, 1965, pp. 114–31.

_____, *The History of Italian Renaissance*, New York: Harry N. Abrams, Inc, 1969.

Francis Haskell and Nicholas Penny, *The Taste and the Antique*, London: Yale University Press, 1982.

A. Hauser, *Mannerism*, New York: Knoff, 1965.

d. Heikamp, "Appunti in margine alla 'Vita di Baccio Bandinelli' del Vasari," *Paragone* (1959), pp. 51–62.

_____, "A Florence la maison de Vasari," *Oeil* (1960), pp. 2–10.

_____, "Zur geschichte der Uffizien Tribuna und der Kunstschraüke in Florenz und Deutschland," *Zeitschrift fur Kunstgeschichte Jahrgang* (1963), pp. 2–10.

_____, "Federico Zuccari a Firenze 1575–1579: Federico e la sua casa," *Paragone* (1967), pp. 3–34.

_____, "Le case di Federico Zuccari a Firenze," *Dialoghi d istoria dell'arte* III (1996), pp. 4–31.

_____, "L'istituto Germanico e la Casa Zuccari a Firenze," in *Magnifizenza all Corte dei Medici*, Milan: Electa, 1997, pp. 416–25.

Klaus Heitman, *Fortuna und Virtus: eine Studie zu Petracas Lebensweisheit*, Köln: Boehlau, 1958.

Julius S. Held, "The Early Appreciation of Drawings," in *Studies in Western Art*, Princeton: Princeton University Press, 1963, pp. 72–95.

S. K, Heninger, Jr., *Touches of Sweet Harmony*, California: The Huntington Library, 1974.

Arthur Henkel and Albrecht Schone, *Emblemata: Handbuch zur Sinnbild Kunst des XVI und XVII Jahrhunderts*, Stuttgart/Metzler: Erg. Neuausg, 1967.

K. Hermann–Fiore, "Die Fresken Federico Zuccari in seinem römischen

Kunstlerhaus," *Römisches Jahrbuch für Kunstgeschichte* (1979), pp. 35–112.

Hesiod, *Theogony,* trans. Dorothea Wender, Baltimore: Penguin Books, 1976.

L. H. Heydenreich and W. Lotz, *Architecture in Italy: 1400–1600*, Baltimore: Penguin Books, 1974.

H. Hildebrandt, "Carlo Carlone. Alexander der Gross übergibt Pankaste an Apelles. Neue Beiträge zur Archäologie und Kunstgeschichte Schwabens," in *Festschrift Julius Baum*, Stuttgart: Erg. Neuausg, 1952, pp. 55–65.

Arthur M. Hind, *Early Italian Engraving: A Critical Catalogue*, New York: Dover Publications, 1938.

R. P. Hinks, *Myths and Allegory in Ancient Art*, London: The Warburg Institute, 1939.

M. Hirst, "The Chigi Chapel in S. Maria della Pace," *Journal of the Warburg and Courtauld Institutes* (1960), pp. 161–85.

_____, "Salviati Illustrateur de 'Vidus Vidus'," *Revue de l'Art* (1969), pp. 19–29.

C. Hohler, "The Badge of St. James," in *The Scallop: Studies of a shell and its influences on humankind*, London: Phaidon, 1967, pp. 23-33.

R. T. Holbrook, *Portraits of Dante: from Giotto to Raphael*, London: Phaidon, 1911.

Charles Hope, ed., *Benvenuto Cellini: Autobiography*, New York: St. Martin's Press, 1983.

_____, "*Le Vite* vsariane: un esempio di autore multiplo," in *L'autore multiplo*, ed., A. Santoni, Pisa: Scuola Normale e Superiore, 2004, pp. 59-74

_____, "Can You Trust Vasari," *New York Review of Books,* 42, no. 15, 1985.

Horopollo, *Hierogliphica,* Venice, Aldus, 1505.

*The Hieroglyphics of Horapollo*, ed. and trans. George Boas, New York: Bolligen Series, 1950.

Horapollo, *Hieroglyphica*, ed. J. M. González de Zárate, Madrid: Akal, 1991.

S. Houlet, *Les combats des vertus et des vices; les psychomachies dans l'art*, Paris: Nouvelles Editions Latines, 1969.

M. C. Howatson, ed., *The Oxford Companion to Classical Literature*, Oxford: Oxford University Press, 1989.

E. Howe, "Architecture in Vasari's *Massacre of the Huguenots,*" *Journal of the Warburg and Courtauld Institutes* (1976), pp. 258–61.

Anthony Hughes, "An Academy of Doing," *Oxford Journal* (1986), pp. 25–25.

H. Huntley, "Portraits by Vasari," *Gazette des Beaux–Arts* (1947), pp. 23–26.

E. Hüttinger, ed., *Case d'artista. Dal Rinascimento ad oggi*, Turin: Umberto Allemandi, 1992.

Jacob Isager, *Pliny on Art and Society*, London: Routledge, 1991.

C. A. Isermeyer, "Die Capella Vasaris un der Hochaltar in der Pieve von Arezzo," in *Festschrift für Carl Georg Heise*, Berlin: G. Grote, 1950, pp. 33–37.

_____, "Il Vasari e il restauro delle chiesi medievali," *Studi Vasariani*, Florence: G. C. Sansoni, 1952, pp. 229–36.

*Italian Drawings from the Collection of Janos Scholz*, New Haven: Yale University Press, 1964.

Erik Iverson, *The Obelisks of Rome*, Copenhagen: GAD Publishers, 1968.

J. Jacquetand E. Konigson, *Les Fêtes dela Renaissance*, Paris: Mercure de France, 1975.

M. A. Jack, "The Academy del Disegno in Late Renaissance Florence," *Sixteenth Century Journal* (1976), pp. 3–20.

Philip Jacks, *The Vasari and Spinelli Families: Provenance of an Archive*, New Haven: Yale University Press, 1994.

_____, ed., *Vasari's Florence: Artists and Literati at the Medicean Court*, London: Cambridge University Press, 1998.

Fredrika H. Jacobs, "New drawing by Vasari for the Sala dei Cento Giorni," *Master Drawings* (1982), pp. 371–74.

_____, "Vasari's Vision of the History of Painting: Frescoes in the Casa Vasari, Florence," *Art Bulletin* (1984), pp. 399–416.

_____, *Defining the Renaissance Virtuosa: Women Artists and the Language of Art History and Criticism*, Cambridge, MA: Cambridge University Press, 1997.

Rachel Jacopff, ed., *The Cambridge Companion to Dante*, New York: Cambridge University Press, 1993

H. W. Janson, A 'memento mori' among early Italian Prints," *Journal of the Warburg and Courtauld Institutes* (1939–1940), pp. 243–47.

———. *The History of Art*, Englewood Cliffs: Prentice–Hall, Inc., 1974.

*The Jerusalem Bible*, New York: Doubleday and Co., 1971.

F. Johnson, "Astronomical text-books in the sixteenth century," in E. Underwood, ed., *Science, Medicine and History* (Oxford: Oxford University Press, 1953, Vol. I, pp. 285-302.

S. Jones, *The sculptures of the Palazzo dei Conservatori*, Oxford: Oxford University Press, 1926.

Constance Jordan, *Renaissance Feminism: Literary Tests and Political Models*, Ithaca, NY: Cornell University Press, 1990.

W. Kallab, *Vasaristudien*, Vienna: K. Graeser and Kie 1908.

Carol V. Kaske, "Marsilio Ficino and the Twelve Gods of the Zodiac," *Journal of the Warburg and Courtauld Institutes*, 45 (1982), pp. 195–202.

A. Katzenellenbogen, *The Sculptural Programs of Chartres Cathedral*, New York: W.W. Norton &Company, Inc., 1959.

_____, *Allegories of the Virtues and Vices in Medieval Art*, New York: W.W. Norton & Company, Inc., 1964.

Hans-Martin Kaulbach and Reinhart Schleier, *Der Welt Lauf: Allegorische Graphikserien des Manerismus*, Stuttgart: Gerard Hatje, 1997.

W. Kayser, *The Grotesque in Art and Literature*, New York: Harper and Row Publishers, 1963.

W. Kemp, "Disegno: Beiträge zur Geschichte des Begriffes zwischen 1547 und 1607," *Marburger Jahrbuch für Kunstwissenschaft* (1974), pp. 219–40.

William Kerrigan and Gordon Braden, "The Neoplatonic Individual of Marsilio Ficino," in *The Idea of Renaissance*, Baltimore: Johns Hopkins University Press, 1989, pp. 101–15.

Margaret L. King, *The Woman of the Renaissance*, Chicago: University Press of Chicago, 1991.

Robin Kirkpatrick, *Dante: The Divine Comedy*, New York: Cambridge University Press, 1987.

E. Kirschbaum, *Lexicon der christlichen Ikonographie*, Frieburg: Herder Roma, 1968–1972.

C. W. Kirwin, "Vasari's tondo of Cosimo I with his architectects, engineers and sculptors in the Palazzo Vecchio. Typology an Re–Identification of Portraits," *Mitteilungen des Kunsthistorischen Institutes in Florenz* (1971), pp. 105–22.

D. Klein, *St. Lukas als Maler der Maria*, Berlin: G. Grote, 1933.

R. Klein, *La forme et l'intelligible*, Paris: Gallimard Editions, 1970.

R. Klein and H. Zerner, *Italian Art: 1500–1600*, Englewood Cliffs: Prentice-Hall, Inc., 1966.

Julian Kliemann, "Zeichnugsfragmente aus der werkstatt Vasaris und ein unbekanntes programm Vincenzio Borghinis *Inventioni per Pitture Fatte*," *Jahrbuch der Berliner Museen* (1978), pp. 157–208.

_____, "Il pensiero di Paolo Giovio nelle pitture eseguite sulle sue 'invenzioni'," *Atti del Convegno su Paolo Giovio: Il Rinascimento e la memoria*, Como: Presso la Società a Villa Gallia, 1985, pp. 197–223.

R. Koch, " Flower Symbolism in the Portinari Altar," *Art Bulletin* (1964), pp. 70–77.

W. Korte, *Der Palazzo Zuccari in Rom*, Leipzig: K .F. Koehler, 1935.

Michiaki Koshikawa, "Apelles's Stories and the Paragone Debate: A Re-Reading of the Frescoes in the Casa Vasari in Florence," *Artibus et Historiae* (2001), pp. 17–25.

A. Cyryll Korvin Krasinski *Microcosmo e Macrocosmo nella storia delle religioni*, Milan: Rusconi, 1973.

Dorothy M. Kosinsky, *Orpheus in the Nineteeth-Century Symbolism*, Ann Arbor: University Microfilms, Inc., 1989.

Alice Kramer, "Giorgio Vasari," PhD dissertation, Columbia University, New York, 1990.

_____, Review, *Vasari's Florence: Artists and Literati at the Medicean Court*, 2000, ed., P. Jacks, in *Sixteenth Century Journal*, XXXI/2, pp. 500-502.

_____, Review, comparing Introductions by D. Ekserdjian and K. Clark to two 1999, editions of Vasari's *Lives*, in *Sixteenth Century Journal*, XXX/1, pp. 234-37.

_____, Review, P. L. Rubin, *Giorgio Vasari: Art and History*, in *Sixteenth Century Journal*, 1996, XXVII/3, pp. 973-975.

R. Krautheimer, "The tragic and comic scene in the Renaissance. The Baltimore and Urbino Panels," *Gazette des Beaux–Arts* (1958), pp. 327–46.

Ernest Kris and Otto Kurz, *Die Legende vom Kunstler*, Vienna: Kunstverlag Anton Schroll, 1934, trans. A. Laing and L. M. Newman, *Legend, Myth and Magic in the Image of the Artist*, London: Yale University Press, 1979.

P. Kristaller, *Die Tarocchi. Graphische Gesellschaft*, Berlin: G. B. Teubner, 1910.

Paul Oskar Kristeller, "Humanist Learning in the Italian Renaissance," in Paul Oskar Kristeller, *Renaissance Thought II: Papers on Humanism and the Arts* (New York: Harper and Row, Publishers, 1965, pp. 93-117.

Antonella Fenech Kroke, *Giorgio Vasari: La Fabrique de l'Allégorie*. Florence: Leo S. Olschki, 2011.

Thomas Kuhn, *Structure of Scientific Revolutions*, Chicago: University of Chicago, 1997.

K. Kunstle, *Ikonographie der chirstlichen Kunst*, Frieburg: Breisgau Herder, 1926–1928.

O. Kurz, "Il libro dei disegni di Giorgio Vasari," *Old Master Drawings* (1937), pp. 1–10.

_____, "Il libro dei disegni di Giorgio Vasari," *Old Master Drawings* (1937), pp. 32–43.

_____, "Il libro dei disegni di Giorgio Vasari," in *Studi Vasariani*, Florence: G. C. Sansoni, 1952, pp. 225–28.

_____, *Legend, Myth and Magic in the Image of the Artist*, New Haven: Yale University Press, 1979.

Andrew Ladis, Carolyn Wood and William U. Eiland, *The Craft of Art*, Athens, GA: University of Georgia Press, 1995.

_____, *Victims & Villains in Vasari's "Lives,"* Chapel Hill, NC: The University of North Carolina Press, 2008.

Pietro Lampetti, *Lorenzo Lotto nelle Marche*, Florence: Centro Di, 1981.

L. Landucci, *Giorgio Vasari a Venezia*, Venice: Premiate Officina Grafiche Carlo Ferrani, 1911.

_____, "Giorgio Vasari a Venezia." in *Atti del Reale Instituto Veneto di Scienze, Letter e Arti*. Venezia I (1911–1912), pp. 167–76.

K. Langedijk, *The Portraits of the Medici: 15th-18th Centuries*, Florence: Leo S. Olschki 1981-87.

E. Lavignino, *Il Palazzo della Cancelleria*, Rome: Studi Vaticani, 1940.

_____, "Vasari Works Ruined by the Fire in Palazzo of della Cancelleria," Rome: R. Istituto Archeologico e Storia dell'Arte, 1940, pp. 14–20.

J. Laver, "The cradle of Venus," in *The Scallop: Studies of the shell and its influence on humankind*, London: Phaidon Press, 1957, pp. 34–42.

Irving Lavin, "Sources of and Meaning of Renaissance Portrait Bust," *Art Quarterly* (1971), pp. 207–15.

_____, *Santa Maria del Fiore*, Rome: Donzelli, 1997.

M. Lawrence, "The Birth of Venus in Roman Art," in *Essays in the History of Art Presented to Rudolf Wittkower*, London: Phaidon, 1967.

R. Lee, *Ut Pictura Poesis: Humanist Theory of Painting*, New York: W.W. Norton and Company, Inc., 1967.

Huigen Leefland and Ger Luijten, *Hendrick Goltzius: Drawings, Prints and Paintings*. Amsterdam: Waaders Publishers, 2003.

Mary F. Lefkowitz and Maureen Fant, *Women in Greece and Rome*, Toronto: Samuel-Stevens, 1977.

Roland Le Mollé, *Giorgio Vasari et le vocabulaire de la critique d'art dans les Vite*, Grenoble: Ellug, 1988.

Wolfgang Liebenwein, *Studiolo*, Ferrara: Edizioni Panini, 1977.

Emilio Lledó, ed. *Los Cinco Sentidos y El Arte*, Madrid: Museo del Prado, 1995.

A. Lensi, *Palazzo Vecchio*, Milan: Silvana, 1929.

Nicoletta Lepri and Antonio Palesati, *Fuori dalla Corte*, Arezo: Le Balze, 2003.

Leonardo, *On Painting*, ed. Martin Kemp, London: Yale University Press, 1989.

J. A. Levenson, *Early Italian Engravings from the National Gallery of Art*, Washington, DC: National Gallery of Art Publications, 1973.

Paolo Liverani, "Il Cortile delle Statue in Belvedere," in Vinzenz Brinkmann, ed. *Il Torso del Belvedere: da Aiace a Rodin*, Rome: Musei Vaticani, 1999, pp. 12–20.

M. Levey, *Painting at Court*, London: Weidenfeld and Nicholson, 1971.

_____, *High Renaissance*, Baltimore: Penguin Books, 1975.

H. Levin, *The Myth of the Golden Age in the Renaissance*, London: Weidenfeld and Nicholson, 1969.

R. B. Levinson, *A Plato Reader*, Boston: Houghton Mifflin Company, 1967.

M. J. Liebman, "Giorgio Vasari on Relief," *Acta Historiae Artium* (1981), pp. 281–86.

Ronald Lightbown, *Botticelli, Life and Work*, 2 vols, Berkeley, CA: University of California Press, 1978.

F. Lippmann, *The Seven Planets*, London: Macmillan, 1895.

Livy (Titus Livius), *The History of Rome and Its Foundations*, trans. Aubrey de Selincourt, Baltimore: Penguin Books, 1965.

G. P. Lomazzo, *Tratto dell' arte della pittura, scultura et architettura*, Milan: Paolo Gottardo Pontio, 1584.

_____, *Nei Grotteschi*, Milan: Paolo Gottardo Pontio, 1587.

_____, *Ideal del tempio della pittura*, Milan: Paolo Gottardo Pontio, 1590.

R. Longhi, *Il Correggio nella Camera di San Paolo*, Milan: Silvana Editoriale d'Arte, 1972.

W. Lotz, "Architecture in the later Sixteenth Century," *College Art Journal* (1958), pp. 129–59.

_____, "Mannerism in Architecture: Changing Aspects. Renaissance and Mannerism," in *Studies in Western Art*, Princeton: Princeton University Press, 1963, pp. 239–46.

Cristina Acidini Luchinat, "Federico Zuccari e la cupola del Fiore, "*Paragone* XL (1989), pp. 33–47

_____, "Per le pitture della Cupola di Santa Maria del Fiore," *Labyrintos* 13/16 (1988-98), pp. 153–75.

_____, "La pittura fiorentina di corte alla fine del Cinquecento," in *Magnificenza alla Corte dei Medici: Arte a Firenze alla fine del Cinquecento*, Milan: Electa, 1997, pp. 370–76.

_____, and Timonthy Verdon, ed., *The Rediscovery of The Last Judgment*, Florence: La Tipolito, 1997.

_____, *La Cupola di Santa Maria del Fiore*, Rome: Libreria dello Stato, 1995.

_____, *Il Battistero e il Duomo di Firenze*, Milan: Electa, 1994.

Helen M. Luke, *Dark Wood to White Rose: Journey and Transformation in Dante's Divine      Comedy*, New York: Parabola Books, 1989.

Marvin Lunenfield, "Most Brutal Madness: Warfare in the Works of Machiavelli and Leonardo," in *Politics, Religion, and Diplomacy in Early Modern Europe: Essays in Honor of Dr. Lamar Jensne*, ed. Malcolm R. Thorp and Arthur J. Slavin, Kirksville, MO: Truman State University Press, 1994, pp. 25-35.

E. MacDougall, "The Sleeping Nymph: Origins of a Humanist Fountain Type," *Art Bulletin* (1975), pp. 357–66.

N. Machiavelli, *The Prince and the Discourses*, trans. Luigi Ricci, New York: Random House, 1950.

_____, *History of Florence and of the Affairs of Italy*, ed. Felix Gilbert, New York: Harper and Row Publishers, 1960.

_____, *Opere*, ed. Mario Bonfantini, Milan: Riccardo Ricciardi, 1963.

_____, *The Prince*, ed. Christian Gauss, New York: Harper and Row Publishers, 1952.

_____, *Prince*, trans. George Bull, Baltimore, MD: Penguin Books, 1961.

_____, *Il Principe*, ed. Francesco Costero, Milan:  Il Polifilo, 1987.

_____, *The Art of War*, Florence: Giuntina, 1521.

_____, *The Chief Works and Others*, trans. Allan Gilbert, Durham, NC: Duke University Press, 1965.

_____, *Il Principe*, ed. Francesco Costero, Milan: Sonzogno, 1879.

_____, *Niccolò Machiavelli's The Art of War*, ed. and trans. Peter  Bondanella and Mark Musa, Baltimore, MD: Penguin Books, 1995.

Ian MacLean, *The Renaissance Notion of Woman: A Study in the Fortunes of Scholasticism and Medical Science in European Intellectual Life*, Cambridge: Cambridge University Press, 1980.

L. Maclehose and G. B.  Brown, *Vasari on Technique*, New York:  Dover Publications, Inc., 1960.

Macrobius, *Commentary on the Dream of Scipio*, trans. W. H. Stahl. New York:  Columbia University Press, 1952.

_____, *Commentari in Sommium Scipionis*, ed. C. E. Lutz (Leiden: SDU Uitgevereij, 1962-65.

A. M. Maetzke, *Restauri nella Casa del Vasari*, Arezzo: Soprintendeza ai Beni Culturali, 1977.

_____, *Arte nell'Aretino:  Dipinti e Sculture Restaurati dal XIII al XVIII secolo*, Florence: Leo S. Olschki, 1979.

Sonia Maffei, ed. Paolo Giovio: Scritti d'Arte, Pisa: Scuola Normale Superiore, 1999.

D. Mahon, *Studies in Seicento Art and Theory*, London: Phaidon, 1947.

F. Malagussi–Valeri, *La chiesa e il convento di San Michele in Bosco*, Bologna: Università delgi Studi, 1895.

E. Male, *L'art religieux de la fin du moyen âge in France*, Paris: Gallimard Editions, 1949.

_____, *L'art religieux da la fin du XVIe siécle, du XVIIe siécle et du XVIIIe siécle*, Paris: Gallimard Editions, 1951.

Thomas Malthus, An *Essay on the Principle of Population*, London: Printed for J. Johnson, St. Paul's Church-Yard, 1789.

Corinne Mandel, "Starry Leo: The Sun, and the Astrological Foundations of Sixtine Rome," *RACAR* (1991), pp. 17–39.

John Manning, *The Emblem*. London: Reaktion Books, 2002.

Giannozo Manetti, *De Dignitate et Excellentia Hominis*, Basel: Oporinum 1582.

Renzo Manetti, *Desiderium Sapientiae*, Florence: La Giuntina, 1996

_____, *Le Porte Celesti: Segreti dell' architettura sacra*, Florence: Aletheia, 1999.

A. Marabottini, *Polidoro da Caravaggio*, Rome: Edizione dell' Elefante, 1969.

_____, *Le case romane con facciate, graffite e dipinti*, Rome. Edizione dell' Elefante, 1960.

Elizabeth McGrath, "Il senso nostro: the Medici Allegory Applied to Vasari's Mythological Frescoes in the Palazzo Vecchio," in *Giorgio Vasari tra decorazione ambientale e storiografia artistica,* ed., Gian Garlo Garfagni, Florence: Olschki, 1985, pp 117-34.

L. Marcucci, *Mostra d'arte sacra della diocesi e delle provincie di Arezzo dal secolo XI ald XVIII,* Florence: Salimbeni, 1950.

S. Marcuse. *A Survey of Musical Instruments,* New York: Harper and Row Publishers, 1975.

Raymond van Marle, *Iconografie de l'art profane au moyen–âge et a la Renaissance,* Hague: Martinus Nijhoff, 1932.

J. R. Martin, *The Farnese Gallery,* Princeton: Princeton University Press, 1965.

Steven Marx, "Shakespeare's Pacifism," *Renaissance Quarterly* 45 (1992), pp. 49–55.

Jean Michel Massing, *La Calomnie d'apelle et son iconographie: du texte à l'image,* Strasbourg: Presses Universitaires 1990.

*Master Drawings of the Italian Renaissance,* Detroit: Detroit Institute of Arts, 1960.

Stephen C. McCluskey, *Astronomies and Cultures in Early Medieval Europe,* Cambridge: Cambridge University Press, 1998.

E. McGrath, "The Painted Decorations of Rubens' House," *Journal of the Warburg and Courtauld Institutes* (1978), pp. 245–77.

D. McTavish, "Giorgio Vasari," in *Da Tiziano a El Greco: per la storia del Manierismo a Venezia, 1540–1590,* Milan: Electra Editrice, 1981, pp. 86–87.

Sabine Melchior-Bonnet, *The Mirror: A History,* London: Routledge, 2002.

P. Meller, "La Capella Brancacci: Problemi Ritrattistici ed Iconografici," *Acropoli* (1961–962), pp. 186–27 and 273–12.

L. Mendelsohn, *Paragoni: Benedetto Varchi Due Lezzioni and Cinquecento Art Theory,* Ann Arbor: UMI Research Press, 1982.

J. C. J. Metford, *Dictionary of Christian Lore and Legend,* London: Thames and Hudson, 1983.

Marilyn Migiel and Juliana Schiesari, *Refiguring Woman: Perspectives on Gender and the        Italian Renaissance,* Ithaca, NY: Cornell University Press, 1991.

J. D. Migne, ed., *Patrologia Latina,* Paris: Garnier, 1800–1881, XVI, XXXIII and LXXXIII.

G. Milanesi, *Capricci e aneddoti di artisti descritti da Giorgio Vasari estratti dalle Vite,* Florence: G. C. Sansoni, 1859.

_____, ed., *Le vite de' più eccellenti Pittori, Scultori, et Architettori,* Florence: G. C. Sansoni, 1878–1895.

_____, ed., *Le vite de' più eccellenti Pittori, Scultori, et Architettori,* Florence: G. C. Sansoni, 1906–1910.

_____, ed., *Le vite de' più eccellenti Pittori, Scultori, et Architettori*, Florence: G. C. Sansoni, 1970–1974.

James V. Mirollo, *Mannerism and Renaissance Poetry*, New Haven: Yale University Press, 1984.

B. Mitchell, "The Patron of Art in Giorgio Vasari's Lives," PhD dissertation, Indiana University, 1975.

C. Monbeig–Goguel, "Giorgio Vasari et son temps," *Revue de l'Art* (1968), pp. 89–93.

_____, *Vasari et son temps: Inventaire General des dessins Italiens du Musée du Louvre*, Paris: Editions des Musée Nationaux, 1972.

C. Monbeig–Goguel and W. Vitzthum, "Dessins inedits de de Giorgio Vasari," *Revue de l'Art* (1971), pp. 105–11.

A. Mongan and P. J. Sachs, *Drawings in the Fogg Museum of Art*, Cambridge: Harvard University Press, 1946.

J. Montague, *The World of Medieval and Renaissance Musical Instruments*, New York: Viking Press, 1977.

Mark P. O. Morford and Robert J. Lenardon, *Classical Mythology*, New York: Longman, 1995.

F. L. Moore, "Contributions to the study of Villa Giulia," *Römisches Jahrbuch für Kunstgeschichtes* (1969), pp. 171–94.

Thomas Moore, *The Planets Within: The Astrological Psychology of Marisilio Ficino*, Hudson, NY: Lindsfarne Press, 1990.

Guido Morozzi, *Santa Reparata: The Ancient Cathedral of Florence*, Florence: Bonechi, 1987.

Luisa Mortai, *Francesco Salviati*, Rome: Leonardo De Luca, 1982.

A. Moschetti, *Giorgio Vasari*, Turin: Paravia Editore, 1935.

Ugo Muccini, *Il Salone dei Cinquecento in Palazzo Vecchio*, Florence: Le Lettere, 1991.

_____, *Palazzo Vecchio*, Florence: Le Lettere, 1997.

_____ and Alessandro Cecchi, *The Appartments of Cosimo in Palazzo Vecchio*, Florence: Le Lettere, 1990.

E. Müntz, Le Musée des portraits de Paul Jove. *Memoires de l'Academia des Inscriptions et Belles Lettres*, Paris: Imprimerie Nationale, 1911.

P. Murray, *The Architecture of the Italian Renaissance*, New York: Schocken Books, 1968.

A. M. Nagler, *Theatric Festivals of the Medici*, trans. George Hickenlooper, New Haven, CT: Yale University Press, 1964.

Milton Nam, *The Artist as Creator*, Baltimore: Penguin Books, 1956.

C. Naselli, "Aspetti della lingua e della cultura del Vasari," in *Studi Vasariani*, Florence: G. C. Sansoni, 1952, pp. 111–16.

Eugene Paul Nassar, *Illustrations to Dante's Inferno*, London: Associated University Press, 1994.

Katrin Naumann, "Die Ausstattung der Sala del Camino in Giorgio Vasaris Künstlerhaus in Arezzo," Thesis, Institut für Kunstgeschichte, Freien Universität Berlin, 2004.

U. Nebbia, *La casa degli Omenoni in Milano*, Milan: Mondadori, 1963.

G. Nencioni, "Sullo stile del Vasari scrittore," in *Studi Vasariani*, Florence: G. C. Sansoni, 1952, pp. 116–29,

Solange de Maille Nesle, *Astrology: History, Symbols and Signs*, Rochester, VT: Inner Traditions International, 1985.

Arnold Nesselrath, "Venus Belvedere: An Episode In Restoration," *Journal of the Warburg and Courtauld Institutes* (1987), pp. 205–14.

*The New English Bible with the Apocrypha*, Washington, DC: Catholic University of America 1970.

A. Noach, "Tomb of Paul III and Point of Vasari," *Burlington* Magazine (1956), pp. 376–80.

A. Nocenti, *Cenni storici sulla Accademia delle Arti del Disegno*, Florence: Leo S. Olschki 1963.

_____, *Mostra documentaria e iconografica dell'Accademia delle Arti del Disegno*, Florence: Leo S. Olschki, 1963.

Serena Nocentini, "Casa Vasari ad Arezzo: Passato, Presente e Futuri," Tesi in Museografia e Museologia, Università delgi Studi, Siena, 2004.

F. Nordstrom, "The Crown of Life and The Crowns of Vanity," in *Idea and Form*, Uppsala: University Press, 1959, pp. 27–37.

*Nota de' quadri che sono esposti per la Festi di S. Luca degli Accademici del Disegno, nella loro Capella posta nel Chiostro del Monasterio de' Padri della S. Nunziata di Firenze, l'Anno 1706.* 1706, 1715, 1724, 1727, 1729, Florence: SS. Annunziata, 1706–1729,

A. Nova, "Chronology of the Del Monte Chapel in S. Pietro in Montorio in Rome," *Art Bulletin* (1984), pp. 50–54.

K. Oberhuber, ed., *The Illustrated Bartsch: The Works of M. Raimondi and his school*, New York: Abaris Books, 1978.

L. Olschki, "L'Accademia Florentina del Disegno nella Storia delle Arti e delle Scienze," *Nuova Antologia* (1926), pp. 470 –80.

A. E. Oppe, *Raphael*, New York: Praeger Publishers, 1970.

S. Orgel, ed., *The Renaissance and the Gods*, New York: Garland Publishing, Inc., 1976.

G. L. Orlandi, *Il Palazzo Vecchio di Firenze*, Florence: Martello–Giunti Editors, 1977.

Jennifer O'Reilly, *Studies in the Iconography of the Virtues and Vices in the Middle Ages*, New York: Garland Publishing, Inc., 1988.

Ovid (Obvidius Naso, Publius), *Amores*, trans. G. Lee, New York: Viking Press, 1968.

_____, *Metamorphoses*, trans. F. J. Miller, New York: G.P. Putnam's Sons, 1911.

_____, *Metamorphoses*, trans. Raphael Regius, New York: Garland Publishing, Inc., 1976.

_____, *Ovidio metamorphoseos volgare*, Venice: Aldus, 1501 and 1531.

W. Paatz, *Die Kirchen von Florenz*, Frankfut am Main: V. Klostermann, 1940–54.

Hilmar M. Pabel, "The Peaceful People of Christ: the Irenic Ecclesiology of Erasmus of Rotterdam," in *Erasmus's Vision of the Church*, ed. Hilmar M. Pabel, Kirksville, MO: Truman State University Press 1995, pp. 57–63

G. Pacchioni, *La Camera Picta di Andrea Mantegna*, Milan: Edizione del Milione, 1960.

Thomas A. Pallen, *Vasari on Theatre*, Carbondale, ILL: Southern University Press, 1999.

R. Palluchini, *La giovinezza del Tintoretto*, Milan: Daria Guaranti, 1950.

R. Pallucchini, *Da Tiziano a El Greco: per la storia del Manierismo a Venezia, 1540–1590*, Milan: Electa Editrice, 1981.

Robert Panichi, *La Tecnica dell'arte negli sritti di Giorgio Vasari*, Florence: Alinea, 1991.

E. Panofsky, *Idea: A Concept in Art Theory*, trans. Joseph S. Peake, Columbia: University of South Carolina Press, 1924–1958.

_____, "Das erste Blatt aus dem 'libro' Giorio Vasaris eine Studie über die Beurteilung der Gotik in der italienischen Renaissance; mit einem Exkurs über zwei Fassadenprojekte Domenico Beccafumis, " *Staedel Jahrbuch* (1930), pp. 25–72.

_____, "Herkules am Scheidewege und andere antike Bildstoffe in der neueren Kunst," *Studien der Bibliothek Warburg*, Leipzig. K. F. Koehler, 1930, pp. 26–32.

_____, *Meaning of the Visual Arts*, New York: Doubleday and Company, Inc., 1955.

_____, "Introducing Benignus Campus," *Gazette des Beaux–Arts* (1959), pp. 257–70.

_____, *The Iconography of Correggio's Camera di San Paolo*, London: The Warburg Institute, 1961.

_____, *Studies in Iconology*, New York: Harper and Row Publishers, 1962.

_____, "Et Arcadia Ego," *Philosphy and History*, New York: Harper and Row Publishers, 1963, pp. 233–55.

_____, *Renaissance and Renascences*, New York: Harper and Row Publishers, 1969.

_____, *Problems in Titian*. New York: New York University, 1969.

_____, *The Life and Art of Albrect Dürer*, Princeton: Princeton University Press, 1971.

_____, and Fritz Saxl, *La mythologie classique dans l'art medieval*,    P a r i s: Gerard Monfort, 1990.

K. T. Parker, *Catalogue of the Collection of Drawings in the Ashmolean Museum*, Oxford: Oxford University Press, 1952.

L. W. Partridge, "Vignola and the Villa Farnese," *Art Bulletin* (1971), pp. 467–86.

_____, "The Sala d'Ercole in the Villa Farnese at Caprarola," *Art Bulletin* (1971), pp. 50–63.

U. Pasqui, *Nuova guida di Arezzo e de suoi dintorni*, Arezzo: Tipografia Bellotti, 1882.

U. Pasque and U. Viviani, *Guida illustrata, storica, artistica e commerciale di Arezzo e dintorni*, Arezzo: Ugo Viviani, 1925.

H. R. Patch, *The tradition of the goddess of Fortune in Medieval Philosophy and Literature*, Northampton, MA: Smith College Studies in Medieval Languages, 1922.

J. Paul, *Der Palazzo Vecchio in Florenz, ursprung und bedeutung seinar Form*, Florence: Leo S. Olschki, 1969.

A. Paolucci and A. M. Maetzke, *La Casa del Vasari in Arezzo*, Firenze: Casa di Risparmio, 1988.

Émile Passignat, "Vasari e I Ragionamenti in Palazzo Vecchio," in *Reverse engineering un nuovo approccioallo studio dei grandi cicli rinascimentali*, ed., E. Passignant and Antonio Pinelli, Rome: Carocci, 2007, pp. 115-28.

O. Pedersen, 'In quest of Sacrobosco', *Journal for the History of Astronomy* 16 (1985), pp. 175–221.

Mark Pendergast, *Mirror: A History of Human Love*, New York: Basic Books, 2003.

A. M. Petrioli, *Mostra di disegni Vasariani: Carri Trionfali e Costumi per la Genealogia degli Dei*, Florence: Leo S. Olschki, 1966.

A. Petrucci, *Panorama della Incisione Italiana: Il Cinquecento*, Rome: Carlo Bestetti Edizioni d'Arte, 1960.

N. Pevsner, "The Architecture of Mannerism," *The Mint*, London: Routledge and Sons, Ltd, 1936, pp. 111–38.

_____, *Academies of Art Past and Present*, Cambridge: Cambridge University Press, 1940 and 1946.

_____ and O. Grautoff, "Manerismus und Protobarock," in *Barockmalerei in dem Römanischen Landern*, Postadm: Wildpark, 1928, pp. 48–81.

Philosstratus, the Elder, *Imagines*, trans. Arthur Fairbanks, Cambridge: Harvard University Press, 1931.

Giovanni Pico Della Mirandola, *In astrologiam*, ed. E. Garin, Florence: Valecchi, 1946–1952.

_____, *Opera omnia*, Basel: Oporinum, 1575.

A. Pigler, *Barockthemen*, Budapest/Berlin:B. G. Teubner, 1956.

Elizabeth Pilliod, "Representation, Misrepresentations, and Non-

Representations: Vasari and His Competitors," in *Vasar's Florence, ed.* Philip Jacks, Cambridge, UK: Cambridge Press, 1998, pp. 30-52.

E. Pillsbury, "Drawings by Vasari and Vincenzo Borghini for the "Apparato" in Florence in 1565," *Master Drawings* (1967), pp. 281–83.

_____, "Three Unpublished Paintings by Giorgio Vasari," *Burlington Magazine* (1970), pp. 94–101.

_____, "Review of Catherine Monbeig–Goguel 'Vasari et son temps'," *Master Drawings* (1973), pp. 171–75.

_____, "Sala Grande drawings by Vasari and his workshop. Some documents and new attributions, *Master Drawings* (1976), pp. 127–46.

_____ and J. Caldwell, *Sixteenth Century Italian Drawings: Form and Function*, New Haven: Yale University Press, 1974.

M. Pittaluga, *L'Incisione Italiana nel Cinquecento*, Milan: Ulrico Hoepli, 1928.

Hanna Fenichel Pitkin, *Fortune Is a Woman: Gender and Politics in the Thought of Niccolo Machiavelli*, Berkeley, CA: University California Press, 1984.

Plato, *The Collected Dialogues of Plato: Republic*, ed. Edith Hamilton, Princeton: Princeton University, 1971, pp. 575–845.

Pliny (Plinius Secundus, C), *Naturalis Historiae*, XXXV, trans. H. Rackham, Cambridge: Harvard University Press, 1938–1962.

_____, *The Elder Pliny's Chapters on the History of Art*, trans. K. Jex–Blake and E. Sellers, New York: Macmillan, 1968.

_____, *Gaio Plinio Secondo, Storia Naturale*, trans. and notes, A. Corso, et.al, Turin: Giulio Einaudi, 1988.

_____, Plinio il Vecchio, *Storia delle Arti Antiche*, ed. Maurizio Harari and Silvio Ferri, Milan: Biblioteca Universale Rizzoli, 2000.

Plutarch (Plutarchus), *Makers of Rome: Nine Lives of Plutarch*, trans. Jan Scott–Kilvert, Baltimore: Penguin Books, 1965.

G. Poggi, "Il Vasari e Palazzo Vecchio," *Il Vasari* (1936–1937), pp. 43–48.

_____, "Il Vasari e Palazzo Vecchio," *Il Vasari* (1942–1943), pp. 49–54.

_____, "Studiolo di Francesco I nel Palazzo Vecchio in Firenze," *Il Vasari* (1942–1944), pp. 86–91.

Graham Pollard, *Renaissance Medals from the Samuel H. Kress Collection at the National Gallery of Art*, London: Thames and Hudson, 1967

Giovanni Pollastra, *Opera della Diva et Seraphical Catherine da Siena*, Siena: Gigli, 1505.

J. Pope–Hennessy, *Raphael*, New York: New York University Press, 1970.

_____, *Paradiso: The Illuminations of Dante's Divine Comedy by Giovanni di Paolo*, New York: Random House, 1993.

Arthur Ewart Popham, *Catalogue of Drawings in the Collection formed by Sir Thomas Philipps*, London: Thames and Hudson, 1935.

_____, "Drawings from the collection of Giorgio Vasari," *British Museum Quarterly* (1936), pp. 153–55.

E. Popham and J. Wilde, *The Italian Drawings of the XV and XVI Centuries in the Collection of his Majesty the King at Windsor Castle*, London: Phaidon, 1949.

Avigdor W. G. Posèq, *Caravaggio and the Antique*, London: Avon Books, 1998.

Mario Pozzi, *Lingua e cultura del Cinquecento: Dolce, Aretino, Machiavelli, Guicciardini, Sarpi e Borghini*, Padua: Liviana Editrice, 1975.

———, "Borghini e la lingua volgare," in *Fra lo 'spedale' e il principe: Vincenzio Borghini filologia e invenzione nella Firenze di Cosimo I*, ed., Gustavo Bertoli and Riccardo Drusi, Padua: Poligrafo, 2005, pp. 177-202.

M. Praetorius, *Syntagma Musicum*, ed., W. Gurlitt. Kassel: Bärenreiter, 1954.

M. Praz, *Studies in Seventeenth Century Imagery*, London: Phaidon, 1941. Reissued in Rome; Editiozni di Storia e Letteratura, 1964-74.

D. Price, "A Collection of Armillary Spheres and Other Antique Scientific Instruments," *Annals of Science* 10 (1956), pp. 172–87.

W. Prinz, "La seconda edizione del Vasari e la comparsa di 'vite' artistiche con ritrati," *Il Vasari* (1963), pp. 1–14.

———, "Una ristampa delle vite," *Il Vasari* (1963), pp. 116–20.

———, "Vasari's Sammlung von Kunstlerbildnissen," *Mitteilungen des Kunsthistorischen Institutes in Florenz* (1966), pp. 8–40.

———, "I ragionamenti del Vasari sullo sviluppo e declino delle arti," in *Il Vasari: Storiografo e Artista*, Florence: Istituto di Studi sul Rinascimento, 1976, pp. 857–67.

Ugo Procacci, *La Casa Buonarroti a Firenze*, Milan: Electa, 1965.

Prudentius, *Psychomachia*, trans. H. I. Thomson, Cambridge: Harvard University Press, 1949.

T. Puttfarken, "Golden Age and Justice in Sixteenth–Century Florentine Political Thought and Imagery: Observations on Three Pictures," *Journal of the Warburg and Courtauld Institutes* (1980), pp. 130–49.

Ricardo J. Quinones, *Foundation Sacrifice in Dante's Commedia*, Philadelphia: The Pennsylvania University Press, 1994.

Quintilian (Quintilianus, Marcus Fabius), *De istitution oratore*, ed. F. H. Colson, Cambridge: Cambridge University Press, 1924.

B. Radice, *Who's Who in the Ancient World*, Baltimore: Penquin Books, 1973.

C. L. Ragghianti, "Il Valore dell'Opera di Giorgio Vasari," *Rendiconti Reale Accademia Nazionale dei Lincei* (1933), pp. 758–26.

———, ed., *Le vite de' più eccellenti Pittori, Scultori ed Architettori di Giorgio Vasari*, Milan: Rizzoli, 1942–1949.

A. F. Ram and M. Rastrelli, *Serie degli uomini i piu illustri nella pittura, scultura, e architettura con i loro elogi e ritratti*, Florence: Stamperia di Domenico Marzi e Compagni, 1763–1769.

W. R. Rearick, *The Age of Veronese,* Cambridge, MA: Cambridge University Press, 1989.

L. Reau, *Iconographie del 'art Chrétien,* Paris: Presses universitaries de France, 1955–1959.

T. Reynolds, "The Accademia del Disegno in Florence. Its Formation and Early Years," PhD dissertation, New York: Columbia University, 1974.

I. Rica, "Giovan Paolo del Borgo," *Il Vasari* (1939), pp. 39–42.

Corrado Ricci, *Ultimo Rifugio di Dante Alighieri,* Milan: Treves, 1891.

_____, *La Divina Commedia di Dante Alighieri nell'arte del Cinquecento,* Milan: Treves, 1908.

C. Ricci, "Giorgio Vasari," *Nuova Antologia di Lettere, Arti e Scienze* (1911), pp. 353–60.

M. Rinehart, "A Drawing by Vasari for the Studiolo of Francesco I," *Burlington Magazine* (1964), pp. 74–76.

Cesare, Ripa, *Iconologia,* Rome: Gio. Gigliotti, 1593.

_____, *Iconologia,* Rome: Gio Gigliotti, 1603.

_____, *Iconologia,* ed. Pietro Paolo Tozzi, Padua: Lorenzo Pasquati, 1611.

_____, *Iconologia,* ed. Nicolo Pezzana, Venice: Il Tomasini, 1645.

_____, *Iconologia,* ed. Erna Mandowsky, New York: George Olms Verlag, 1970.

_____, Iconologia, ed. Edward A. Maser, New York: Dover Publications, Inc., 1971.

_____, Iconologia, ed. Stephen Orgel, New York: Garland Publishing, Inc., 1976.

G. Ristori, *Nuova guida della cittá di Arezzo,* Florence: Tipografia M. Cellini e Compagnia, 1871.

Nesca Robb, *Neoplatonism of the Italian Renaissance,* New York: Octagon Books, 1968.

K. Robert, *Die antiken Sarcophag–Reliefs,* Berlin: G. Grote 1897.

A. Ronchini, "Giorgio Vasari alla Corte del Cardinale Farnese," in Atti e Memorie delle RR. *Deputazione di Storia patria per le Provincie Modensi et Parmensi* (1864), pp. 122–27.

R. Rosenblum, "The Origin of Painting: A Problem in the Iconography of Romantic Classicism," *Art Bulletin* (1957), pp. 189–90.

E. E. Rosenthal, "The House of Andrea Mantegna in Mantua," *Gazette des Beaux–Arts* (1962), pp. 327–48.

Mark W. Roskill, *Dolce's Aretino and Venetian Art Theory of the Cinquecento,* Toronto:    University of Toronto Press, 2000.

J. Ross, *The Florentine Palaces and their Stories,* London:  J. M. Dent & Company, 1905.

A. Rossi, ed., *Le Vite de' più eccellenti Pittori, Scultori, ed Architettori di Giorgio Vasari,* Milan:  Club del Libro, 1962–1966.

Marco Rossi, ed., *La Gerusalemme Celeste*, Milan: Publicatione della Università Cattolica, 1983.

C. Roth, *The Last Florentine Republic: 1527–1530*, London: Methuen and Company, 1925.

J. Rouchette, *La Renaissance que nous a léguée Vasari*, Paris: Societe d'Edition, 1959.

———, "La Domestication de l'esoterisme dans l'ouevre de Vasari," *Archivio di Filosofia* (1960), pp. 345–70.

L. Rovelli, *L'opera storica ed artistica di Paolo Giovio – il suo museo dei ritratti*, Como: Azienda Autonoma Soggiorno Turismo, 1928.

———, *Paolo Giovio nelle storia e nel'arte: 1522–1552*, Como: Azienda Autonoma Soggiorno Turismo, 1952.

D. B. Rowland, *Mannerism–Style and Mood*, New Haven: Yale University Press, 1964.

A. Rubbiani, "Il convento Olivetano di San Michele in Bosco sopra Bologna," *Archivo Storico dell'Arte* (1895), pp. 196–98.

Patricia Rubin, *Giorgio Vasari: Art and History*, London: Yale University Press, 1995.

———, "Seductions of Antiquity," in *Manifestations of Venus: Art and Sexuality*, eds. Caroline Arscott and Katie Scott, Manchester: University of Mancester, 2000, pp. 24–38.

N. Rubinstein, "Vasari's Painting of the Foundation of Florence in the Palazzo Vecchio," *Essays in the History of Architecture Presented to Rudolf Wittkower*, New York: Phaidon, 1967, pp. 64–74.

Enair Rud, *Vasari's Life and Lives*, London: Thames and Hudson, 1963.

Marco Ruffini, *Le imprese del drago*, Rome: Bulzoni, 2005.

J. Rusconi, "Le Studio de Francois Ier de Medicis," *Les Arts* (1911), pp. 1–7.

Daniel Russell, "Alciati's Emblem in Renaissance France," *Renaissance Quarterly* (1981), pp. 534–54.

Daniel Russell, "Emblems and Hieroglyphics: Some Observations on the Beginnings and the Nature of Emblematic Forms," *Emblematica* (1986), pp. 227–40.

Claudia Russo, "The pageant of the Muse at the Medici Wedding of 1539 and the Decoration of the Salone dei Cinquecento," in *Theatrical Spectacle and Spectacular Theatre*, eds. B. Wisch and Susan S. Munshower (University Park: Pennsylvania State University, 1990), pp. 416–57,

Stefano Nicolini da Sabbio, *L'anno del Signore*, Venice: Giovannantonio e fratelli, 1536.

Sacrobosco, *De Sphaera*, trans L. Thorndike, *The Sphere of Sacrobosco and its Commentators*, Chicago: University of Chicago Press, 1949.

Mario Salmi, "La Mostra Vasariana," in *Studi Vasariani*, Florence: G. C. Sansoni, 1952, pp. 259–61.

Johannes Sambucus, *De emblemata*, Antwerp: Christopher Palatin, 1566.

E. Santarelli, *Catalogue della raccolta di disegni autografi antichi e moderni*, Florence: G. C. Sansoni, 1870.

M. Santoro, *Fortuna, Ragione e Prudenza nella vita letteraria del Cinquecento*, Naples: Liguori, 1967.

James M. Saslow, *The Medici Wedding of 1589*, London: Yale University Press, 1996.

Leon Satkowski, *Giorgio Vasari: Architect and Courtier*, Princeton: Princeton University Press, 1993

Alison Saunders, *The Sixteenth Century French Emblem Book. A Decorative and Useful Genre*, Geneva: Droz, 1988.

F. Saxl, "Probleme der Planetenkinderbilder," *Kunstchronik und Kunstmarkt* (1918–1919), pp. 10–12.

_____, "Antike Gotter in der spatrenaissance: ein Freskenzyklus un ein Discorso des Jacopo Zucchi," in *Studien der Bibliothek Warburg*, Leipzig. K. F. Koehler, 1927, VIII.

_____, *La Fede Astrologica di Agostino Chigi*, Rome: Reale Accademia d'Italia, 1934.

_____, "Veritas Filia Femporis," in *Philosophy and History*, New York: Harper and Row Publishers, 1963, pp. 197–223.

_____, "The Revival of Late Antique Astrology," in *A Heritage of Image*, Baltimore: Penguin Books, 1970, pp. 27–42.

Paolo Scarpi, ed. *Pimandres*, Venice: Marsilio, 1987.

S. Schaefer, "The Studiolo of Francesco I de' Medici in the Palazzo Vecchio," PhD dissertation, Bryn Mawr College, 1976.

_____, "The *Studiolo* of Francis I de' Medici: A checklist of the known Drawings," *Master Drawings* (1982), pp. 125–30.

Stephen K. Scher, ed. *The Currency of Fame: Portrait Medals of the Renaissance*, New York: Harry N. Abrams, Inc., 1994.

A. Schiavo, *Il Palazzo della Cancelleria*, Rome: Staderini, 1975.

A. Schiavo, "Venditti, Sul Refettorio di Monteoliveto a Napoli," in *Il Vasari: Storiografo e Artista*, Florence: Istituto di Studi sul Rinascimento, 1976, pp. 30–40.

J. von Schlosser, "Giustos Fresken in Padua un die Vorläufer der Stanza della Segnatura," *Jahrbuch der Kunst, Sammlungen des Allerhochsten Kaiserhauses* (1896), pp. 13–100.

_____, *Die Kunstliteratur*, Vienna: Kunstverlag Anton Schroll, 1924.

_____, *La Letteratura Artistica*, trans. Filippo Rossi, Florence: Leo S. Olschki, 1964 and 1977.

L. Schorn and e. Foerster, *Giorgio Vasari: Leben der ausgeezeichnetsten Maler, Bildhauer und Architekten*, Stuttgart: Erg. Neuausg, 1832–1849.

J. Schulz, "Vasari at Venice," *Burlington Magazine* (1961), pp. 500–11.

_____, "Pinturicchio and the Revival of Antiquity," *Journal of the Warburg and Courtauld Institutes* (1962), pp. 35–55.

_____, *Venetian Painted Ceilings of the Renaissance*, Berkeley: University of California Press, 1968.

G. Schurr, "Giorgio Vasari Painter and Collector," *Connoisseur* (1961), pp. 112–15.

Rick Scorza, "Borghini and the Florentine Academy," in *Italian Academies of the Sixteenth Century*, London: The Warburg Institute, 1995, pp. 137-52.

U. Scoti–Bertinelli, "Giorgio Vasari Scrittore," *Annali Reale Scuola Normale Superiore di Pisa* (1905), pp.1–33.

Joan W. Scott, "Deconstructing Equality-versus-Difference: Or, the Uses of Poststructuralist Theory for Feminism," *Feminist Studies* 14 (1988), pp. 33–50.

_____,"Multiculturalism and the Politics of Identity," *October* 61 (1992), pp. 12–19.

Elizabeth Sears, *The Ages of Man: A Medieval Interpretation of the Life Cycle*, Princeton: Princeton University Press, 1986.

Maria Selene Sconci, *La volta vasariana di Palazo Venezia restaurata*, Roma: Palazzo Venezia, 2003.

A. Secchi, "La Casa del Vasari in Arezzo," in *Il Vasari: Storiografo e Artista*, Florence: Istituto di Studi sul Rinascimento, 1976, pp. 75–83.

O. Seemann, O. *The Mythology of Greece and Rome with Special Reference to its Use in Art*, ed. G.H. Bianchi, London: Marcus Ward and Company, 1877.

G. Semprini, *Pico della Mirandola: la vita e il pensiero*, Genoa: Fratelli Melita, 1988.

Seneca, *Moral Essays: De Providentia, De Costantia, De Ira, De Clementia*, trans. John W. Basore Cambridge, MA: Harvard University Press, 1998.

Jean Seznec, "La Mascarade des Dieux a Florence en 1565," *Melanges d'Archeologie et d'Histoire* (1935), pp. 224–43.

_____, *The Survival of the Pagan Gods*, trans. Barbara F. Sessions, New York: Harper and Row Publishers, 1961.

_____, *Survival of the Pagan Gods*, 2nd. ed. Paris: Gallimard Editions, 1980.

J. Shearman, "Maniera as an Aesthetic Ideal," in *Studies in Western Art*, Princeton: Princeton University Press, 1963, pp. 200–21.

_____, *Mannerism*, Baltimore: Penguin Books, 1967.

Valerie Shrimplin, *Sun Symbolism and Cosmology in Michelangelo's Last Judgment*, Kirksville, MO: Truman State University Press, 2000.

A. Siebenhuner and L. H. Heydenreich, "Die Klosterkirche von S. Francesco al Bosco," *Mitteilungen des Kunsthistorischen Institutes in Florenz* (1939–1940), pp. 183–96 and 367–401.

C. Signorini, *Guida illustrata Arezzo, città e provincia*, Arezzo: Ettore Sinatti, 1904.

G. Sinibaldi, *Il Palazzo Vecchio de Firenze*, Roma: La Libreria dello Stato, 1934.

Ridolfo Siviero, *Accademia del Arti del Disgeno*, Florence: Giunti, 1979.

G. Smith, "Bronzino's Allegory of Happiness," *Art Bulletin* (1984), pp. 390–98.

Craig Hugh Smyth, *Mannerism and Maniera: With and Introduction by Elizabeth Cropper*, Vienna: IRSA, 1992.

_____, *Mannerism and Maniera*, New York: J. G. Augustin, 1963.

_____, "Sunken Courts of the Villa Giulia and the Villa Imperiale," *Marsyas* (1964), pp. 304–13.

_____, *Bronzino as a Draughtsman*, New York: J.C. Augustin, 1971.

George S. Snyder, *Maps of the Heavens*, New York: Abbeville Press, 1984.

Barbette Stanley Spaeth, *The Roman Goddess Ceres*, Austin, TX: The University of Texas, 1996.

Laura Speranza and Alessandra Baroni, *Guida: Casa Vasari*, Arezzo: Le Balze, 1999.

L. Spezzaferro, "La casa di Rafaello," in *Via Giulia*, Rome: Il Segnalibro, 1973, pp. 256–70.

L. Spitzer, "Classical and Christian Ideas of World Harmony," *Traditio* (194), pp. 409–64.

F. Stampfle, "A Ceiling Design by Vasari," *Master Drawings* (1968), pp. 266–71.

Randolph Starn, "Reinventing Heroes in Renaissance Italy," *Journal of Interdisciplinary History* 17 (1986), pp. 67–84.

W. Stechow, "Apollo and Daphne," *Studien de Bibliothek Warburg* (1932), pp. 28–42

_____, "Altarpiece by Vasari at the University of Wisconsin," *Art Quarterly*. (1939), pp. 178–84.

L. D. Steefel, "A Neglected Shadow in Poussin's *Et Arcadia Ego*," *Art Bulletin* (1975), pp. 99–101.

C. von Stegmann and H von Geymuller, *Die Architektur der Renaissance in Toskana*, Munich: Georg Müller, 1885–1904, IX.

E. Steinmann, "Zur Publication des Vasariarchivs," *Cicerone* (1910), pp. 286–10.

_____, "Freskenzyklen der Spätrenaissance in Rome," *Monatschrift für Kunstwissenschaft* (1910), pp. 45–58.

C. Stephanus, *Dictionarium historicum, geographicum, Poeticum*, New York: Garland Publishing, Inc., 1976.

R. Stilwell, et al. *Princeton Encyclopedia of Classical Sites*, Princeton: Princeton University Press, 1976.

Carl Brandon Strehlke, ed. *Pontormo, Bronzino and the Medici,* University Park, PA: The        Pennsylvania State University Press, 2004.

Roy Strong, *Art and Power: Renaissance Festivals, 1450-1650,* London: The Boydell Press,        1984.

David Summers, "Maniera and Movement:  Figura Serpentinata," *Art Quarterly* (1972), pp. 269–301.

_____, "Contrapposto:  Style and Meaning in Renaissance Art," *Art Bulletin* (1977), pp. 336–61.

_____, *Michelangelo and the Language of Art,* Princeton: Princeton University Press, 1981.

_____, *The Judgment of Sense: Renaissance Naturalism and the Rise of Aesthetics,* Cambridge: Cambridge University Press, 1987.

D. Sutton, "Mannerism:  The Art of Permanent Ambiguity," *Apollo* (1965), pp. 222–27.

M. Tafuri, *L'Architettura del Manierismo nel Cinquecento Europeo,* Rome: Fratelli Alinari, 1966.

_____, *L'Architettura dell'Umanismo,* Bari: G. Laterza, 1969.

_____, et al. *Florentine Palaces,* Florence: Salimbeni, 1972.

M. Tanner, "Chance and Coincidence in Titian's Diana and Actaeon," *Art Bulletin* (1974), pp. 535–50.

U. Tavanti, *Arezzo in una giornata,* Arezzo: Tipografia Aretina, 1928.

Charles H. Taylor and Patricia Finely, *Images of the Journey in Dante's Divine Comedy,* London:  Yale University Press, 1997.

Jim Tester, *A History of Western Astrology,* New York: Ballantine Books, 1987.

Tertullian (Tertullianus, Quintus S. F.), *De Spectaculis,* trans. T. R. Glover, New York:  G.P. Putnam's Sons, 1931.

Gum Thiem, "Vasaris Entwurfe für die Gemalde in der Sala Grande des Palazzo Vecchio zu Florenz," *Zeitschrift für Kunstgeschichte* (1960), pp. 97–135.

_____, "Neuentdeckte Zeichnungen Vasaris und Naldinis für die Sala Grande des Palazzo Vecchio in Florenz," *Zeitschrift für Kunstgeschichte* (1968), pp. 143–50.

_____, "Neue funde zu Vasaris Dekorationem im Palazzo Vecchio, in *Il Vasari: Storiografo e Artista,* Florence: Istituto di Studi sul Rinascimento, 1976, pp. 267–75.

H. Thiersch, *Artemis Ephesia,* Berlin:  G. Grote, 1935.

H. Thode, *Die Antike in dem Stichen,* Leipzig: K. F. Koehler, 1881.

Leslie Thomson, ed., *Fortune: "All is but fortune,"* Washington, DC: The Folger Shakespeare Library, 2000.

Malcolm R. Thorp and Arthur J. Slavin, eds. *Politics, Religion, and Diplomacy in Early Modern Europe: Essays in Honor of Dr. Lamar Jensne,* Kirksville, MO: Truman State University Press 1994.

C. Tiberi, " Il Vasari Restauratore," in *Il Vasari: Storiografo e Artista*, Florence: Istituto di Studi sul Rinascimento, 1976, pp. 365–75.

Lisa Tickner, "Feminism, Art History and the Sexual Differences," *Genders* 3 (1988), pp. 92–128.

Paola Bakter Tinagli Baxter, "Rileggendo i "ragionamenti," in *Giorgio Vasari tra decorazione ambientale e storiografia artistica*, ed., Gian Carlo Garfagnini, Florence: Olschki, 1985, pp. 83-93.

H. Tintelnot, *Baroktheater und Barocke Kunst*, Berlin: G. Grote, 1939.

Maria Foss Todorow, *Il Duomo di Firenze*, Florence: Plistampa, 1999.

Stéphane Toussaint, *De L'enfer a la coupole: Dante, Brunelleschi et Ficin*, Florence: L'Erma, 1997.

Marco Treves, "Maniera: The History of a Word," *Marsyas* (1941), pp. 69–89.

Richard C. Trexel and M. E. Lewis, "Two Captains and Three Kings: New Light on the Medici Chapel," *Studies in Medieval and Renaissance History* (1981), pp. 93–117.

G. Turnbull, *A Treatise on Ancient Painting*, Chicago: Adler Publishers, 1975.

Alice K. Turner, *The History of Hell*, New York: Harcourt Brace & Company, 1993.

Nicholas Turner, *Florentine Drawings of the Sixteenth Century*, London: Phaidon, 1986.

R. A. Turner, *The Vision of Landscape in Renaissance Italy*, Princeton: Princeton University Press, 1966.

R. Tuve, "Notes on the Virtues and Vices," *Journal of the Warburg and Courtauld Institutes* (1963), pp. 246–52.

Pierio Valeriano, *Hierogphyphica sive De sacris Aegyptorum*, Basel: Oporinum, 1556.

_____, *Hierogphyphica sive De sacris Aegyptorum*, Basel: Thoma Guarinum, 1575.

_____, *I Ieroglifici overo commentarii delle occulte significationi de gli Egittij & altre Nationi*, Venice: Gio. Battista Combi, 1625.

_____, *Hieroglyphica sive De sacris Aegyptorum*, trans. I. de Montlyard, New York: Garland Publishing, Inc., 1976.

Valerius Maximus, *Memorabilia*, Venice: Marcolini, 1534.

B. Varchi, *Due Lezioni*, Florence: Giuntina, 1549.

Giorgio Vasari, 1550. *Le vite de' più eccellenti Pittori, Scultori, et Architettori*, Florence: Lorenzo Torrentino, 1550.

_____, *Le vite de' più eccellenti Pittori, Scultori, et Architettori*, Florence: F. Giunti, 1568.

_____, *I Ragionamenti*, Florence: F. Giunti, 1588.

_____, *Le vite... ed.*, Gaetano Milanesi, Florence: G. C. Sansoni, 1878–1885.

_____, *Le vite*...ed., Gaetano Milanesi, Florence: G. C. Sansoni, 1906–1910.

_____, *Le vite*...ed., Karl Frey, Munich. Georg Müller, 1911.

_____, Le vite... *Lives of Seventy of the Most Eminent Painters, Sculptors and Architects* by Giorgio Vasari, ed., and trans., Mrs. Jonathan Fostemr London: H. G. Bohn, 1855-850

_____, *Le vite...Lives of Seventy of the Most Eminent Painters, Sculptors and Architects* by Giorgio Vasari, ed., and annotade, E. H. and E. W. Blashfiled and A. A. Hopkins, New York: Charles Scribner's Sons, 1902.

_____, Le vite... *Lives of Seventy of the Most Eminent Painters, Sculptors and Architects* by Giorgio Vasari, ed., and trans., Mrs. Jonathan Foster, 5 vols., London: George Bell & Sons, 1902-1907.

_____, *Le vite*....trans., 1912, Guston Du C de Vere, New York: Harry N. Abrams, Inc. Publishers, 1979.

_____, *Le vite*...trans., William Gaunt, London: Macmillan, 1927.

_____, *Le vite*... ed., Pio Peccahai, Milan: Sonzogno, 1918–1930.

_____, *Le vite*...ed., C. L. Ragghianti, Milan. Electa, 1945.

_____, *Le vite*...Luigi Grassi, Paola della Pergola, Giovanni Previtali, 8 vols., Milan: Edizione per il Club del Libro, 1962.

_____, *Le vite*...ed., Aldo Rossi, Milan: Club del Libro, 1962–1966.

_____, *Le vite*... ed., Gaetano Milanesi, Florence: G.C. Sansoni, 1970–1974 (noted in this book as Vasari–Milanesi).

_____, *Le vite*...eds., Carlo Ludovico Ragghianti, Licia Ragghianti Collobi, 4 vols., Milan: Rizzoli, 1971-78.

_____, *Le vite*... ed., Rossana Bettarini and Paola Barocchi. Florence: G. C. Sansoni, 1966–2002 (noted in this book as Bettarini–Barocchi).

_____, *Lives of Seventy of the Most Eminent Painters, Sculptors and Architects*, eds. E. H. and E. W. Blashfiled, New York: Charles Scribner's Sons, 1986.

_____, *Le vite*...(1550), ed., Luciano Bellosi, aldo Rossi, Giovanni Previtali, Turin: Einaudi, 1986.

_____, *Vasari: Le vite*, ed. Maurizio Marini, Rome: Newton, 1991.

_____, *Lives of the Painter, Sculptors, and Architects*, trans., Gaston Du C. de Vere, 2 vols., New York: Knopf, 1996.

C. L. Vegas, "Il Vasari e Michelangelo Architetto," in *Studi Vasariani*, Florence: G.C. Sansoni, 1952, pp. 73–77.

A. Venditti, "Sul Refettorio di Monteoliveto a Napoli," in *Il Vasari: Storiografo e Artista*, Florence: Istituto di Studi sul Rinascimento, 1976, pp. 33–40.

A. Venturi, *Storia dell'Arte Italiana*, Milan: Ulrico Hoepli, 1906, IV.

_____, *Storia dell'Arte Italiana*, Milan: Ulrico Hoepli, 1933, IX.

L. Venturi, "La critica di Giorgio Vasari," in *Studi Vasariani*, Florence: G. C. Sansoni, 1952, pp. 29–46.

_____, *History of Art Criticism*, New York: Dutton and Company, 1964.

E. Verheyen, "Eros et Anteros," *Gazette des Beaux–Arts* (1965), pp. 321–40.

_____, *The Paintings in the 'studiolo' of Isabella d'Este at Mantua*, New York: University Press, 1971.

Laura Vestra "Love and Beauty in Ficino and Plotinus," in Konrad Eisenbichler and Olga Zorzi Pugliese, ed. *Ficino and Renaissance Neoplatonism*, Toronto: Dovehouse Editions, 1986, pp. 177-90.

Claudia Cieri Via, ed. *Le Favole Antique*, Rome: Bagatto Libri, 1996.

F. Viatte, "Two Studies by Naldini for the Deposition in S. Simone, Florence," *Master Drawings* (1967), pp. 384–86.

_____, "A propos de Vasari historien et collectionneur," *Musée du Louvre* (1979), pp. 273–79.

*Vitruvius's De architectura: The Ten Books on Architecture*, ed. Morris H. Morgan, New York: Dover, 1960.

W. Vitzthum, "Review of Paola Barocchi, 'Vasari Pittore;' 'Complementi al Vasari Pittore;' 'Mostra di disegni del Vasari e della sua cerchia'," *Master Drawings* (1965), pp. 54–56.

D. Vivian, *Giorgio Vasari*, Arezzo: Tipografia I. Beucci, 1934.

A. Vivian–Fiorini, "Giorgio Vasari, artista del legno," *Il Vasari* (1940), pp. 40–45.

R. Viviani della Robbia, "Note e Notizie sul Cenacolo del Vasari per il Monastero delle Murate de Firenze," in *Studi Vasariani*, Florence: G. C. Sansoni, 1952, pp. 221–24.

L. Volkmann, "Hieroglyphic und Emblematik bei Giorgio Vasari," *Werden und Wirken, ein Festgruss Karl W. Hiersemann zugesandt*, Leipzig: K. F. Koehler, 1924, pp. 204–19.

_____, "Eine Melancolia des Vasari," *Zeitschrift für bildende Kunst* (1929), pp. 119–26.

Caterina Volpi, *Le immagini delgi dèi di Vincenzo Cartari*. Rome: Luca, 1996.

H. Voss, *Die Malerei der Spätrenaissance in Rom und Florenz*, Berlin: G. Grote 1920.

A. E. Waite, *The Holy Kabbalah*, New York: University Books, Inc., 1964.

D. P. Walker, *Musical Humanism in the 16th and Early 17th Centuries*, London: Macmillan, 1992.

D. P. Walker, *Spiritual and Demonic Magic: From Ficino to Campanella*, University Park, PA: The Pennsylvania State University press, 2000.

Aby Warburg, *Die Ernewerung der beidnischem Antike*, Leipzig: K. F. Koehler, 1932.

_____, "Italienische Kunst und internationale Astrologie im Palazzo Schifanoia zu Ferrara," in *Gesammelte Schriften*, Leipzig: K. F. Koehler, 1932, pp. 459–481.

_____, "Eine Astronomische Himmelsdarstellung in der alten Sakristei von San Lorenzo in Florenz," in *Gesammelte Schriften*, Leipzig: K. F. Koehler, 1932, pp. 169–72.

P. Ward–Jackson, "Vasari the Critic," *Apollo* (1963), pp. 454–59.

John Warden, *Orpheus: The Metamorphoses of a Myth*, Toronto: Toronto University Press, 1982.

James Wasserman, *Art and Symbols: Images of Power and Wisdom*, Rochester, VT: Destiny Books, 1993.

Barbara Watts, "Sandro Botticelli's Illustrations for *Inferno* VIII and IX: Narrative revision and the Role of Manuscript Tradition," *Word and Image*, pp. 149–73.

_____, "Drawings for Dante's Inferno: Narrative, Structure, and Manuscript Design," *Artibus et Historiae* XVI (1995), pp. 163–201.

Elizabeth See Watson, *Achille Bocchi and the Emblem Book as Symbolic Form*, Cambridge: Cambridge University Press, 1993.

Z. Wazbinski, "Le idée de l'historie dans la premiere et la second edition des vies de Vasari," in *Il Vasari: Storiografo e Artista*, Florence: Istituto di Studi sul Rinascimento, 1976, pp. 1–27.

_____, *L'Accademia Medicea del Disegno a Firenze Nel Cinquecento*, Florence: Leo S. Olschki, 1987.

_____, "La Capella dei Medici e l'origine dell''Academia del Disegno," in *Firenze e la Toscana dei Medici nell'Europa dell 500*, Florence: Leo S. Olschki, 1983, I, pp. 54-69.

J. C. Webster, *The Labors of the Months*, Evanston, ILL: New Western, 1938.

F. Weege, *Das golden Haus des Nero*, Berlin, G. Grote, 1913.

G. Weise, *Il Manierismo*, Florence: Leo S. Olschki, 1971.

R. Weise, *The Renaissance Discovery of Classical Antiquity*, Oxford: Basil Blackwell, 1969.

F. Weiser, *Christian Feasts and Customs*, New York: Harcourt, Brace and Company, 1958.

Philip P. Wiener, ed. *Dictionary of the History of Ideas*, New York: Scribner's Sons, 1974.

Richard H. Wilkinson, *Symbol and Magic in Spiritual Art*, London: Thames and Hudson, 1994.

Robert Williams, *Art, Theory and Culture in Sixteenth–Century Italy*, Cambridge: Cambridge Unviersity Press, 1997.

E. Wind, "Platonic Justice: designed by Raphael," *Journal of the Warburg Institute* (1937–1938), pp. 69–70.

_____, "The Four Elements in Raphael's Stanza della Segnatura," *Journal of the Warburg and Courtauld Institutes* (1938), pp. 75–79.

_____, "Charity: The Case History of a Pattern," *Journal of the Warburg and Courtauld Institutes* (1940), pp. 322–31.

_____, *Bellini's Feast of the Gods*, Cambridge: Harvard University Press, 1948.

_____, "Platonic Tyranny and the Renaissance Fortuna," *Essay in Honor of Erwin Panofsky*, London: Macmillan, 1961, pp. 491–96.

_____, *Pagan Mysteries in the Renaissance*, New York: W.W. Norton and Company, Inc., 1968.

_____, *Giorgione's Tempesta*, Oxford: Clarendon Press, 1969.

M. Winner, "Die Quellen der Pictura–Allegorien in gemalten Bildergalerien des 17 Jahrhunderts zu Antwerpen," PhD dissertation, University of Cologne, 1957.

_____, Federskizzen von Benvenuto Cellini," *Zeitschrift für Kunstgeschichte* (1968), pp. 283–304.

_____, *Mostra di disegni dei fondatori dell'Accademia delle arti del disegno nel IV centario della fondazione*, Florence: Leo S. Olschki, 1974.

_____, "Poussin Selbstbildnis im Louvre als kunsttheoretische Allegorie," *Römanisches Jahrbuch für Kunstgeschichte* (1983), pp. 417–48.

M. Winner, "Gemalte Kunsttheorie," *Jarburch der Berliner Museen* (1962), pp. 180–81.

E. Winternitz, "Archeologia Musicale del Rinascimento nel Parnaso di Raffaello," *Rendiconti Pontefica Accademia d'Archeologia* (1952–9154), pp. 359–88.

_____, "Lira da braccio," *Die Musik in Geschichte und Gegenwart*, Kassel: Bärenreiter–Verlag, 1960, VIII.

_____, *Musical Symbolism and Their Symbolism in Western Art*, London: Thames and Hudson, 1967.

_____, *Leonardo da Vinci as a Musician*, New Haven: Yale University Press, 1976.

B. Wisch and S. S. Munshower, eds., *All the world's a stage...": Art and Pageantry in the Renaissance and Baroque*, University Park, PA: Pennsylvania State University Press, 1990.

R. Wittkower, "Chance, Time and Virtue," *Journal of the Warburg and Courtauld Institutes* (1937–1938), pp. 313–21.

_____. "Patience and Change: The Story of a Political Emblem," *Journal of the Warburg and Courtauld Institutes* (1937–1938), pp. 171–77.

_____, "Eagle and Serpent: A Study in the Migration of Symbols," *Journal of the Warburg and Courtauld Institutes* (1938–1939), pp. 293–25.

_____, *The Divine Michelangelo: The Florentine Academy's Homage on His Death in 1564*, London: Phaidon, 1964.

_____, *Allegory and the Migration of Symbols*, London: Thames and Hudson, 1977.

R. Wittkower and Margot Wittkower, *Born Under Saturn*, New York: W.W. Norton and Company, Inc., 1969.

Diane Wolfthal, ed., *Peace and Negotiations: Strategies for Coexistence in the Middle Ages and the Renaissance*, Turnhout: Brepols Publishers, 2000.

Joanne Woodall, "Wtewael's Perseus and Andromeda," in Caroline Arscott and Katie Scott, eds. *Manifestations of Venus: Art and Sexuality,* Manchester: Manchester University Press, 2000, pp. 41–68.

Joanna Woods-Marsden, *Renaissance Self-Portraiture: The Visual construction of Identity and the Social Status of the Artist,* London: Yale University Press, 1998,

A. Wurtenburg, *Mannerism,* trans. Michael Heron, New York: Holt, Rinehart and Winston, 1963.

A. Wyatt, "Le 'libro dei disegni' du Vasari," *Gazette des Beaux–Arts* (1859), pp. 338–51.

E. S. Yuen, "Illusionistic Mural Decorations of the Early Renaissance in Rome," PhD dissertation, New York University, 1972.

Raffaella Maria Zaccaria, Il carteggio Vasari: metodologia di inventariazione e prospettiva di ricerca," *Richerche storice* 38, no. I (2008), pp. 5-21.

Gerardo Zampaglione, *The Idea of Peace in Antiquity,* Indiana: Notre Dame Press, 1973.

P. Zampetti, *Lorenzo Lotto nelle Marche. Il suo tempo, il suo influsso,* Florence: Centro Di, 1981.

H. Zerner, *The School of Fontainebleau,* New York: Harry N. Abrams, 1969,

_____, "Review of Bettarini and Barocchi editions of the *Vite,*" *Art Bulletin* (1972), pp. 355–57.

E. Zinner, *Astronomie,* Munich: Verlagkal Albert Freiburg, 1951.

Herbert Zschelletzschky, *Die "Drei gottlosen Maler," von Nürnberg: Sebald Beham, Barthel        Beham, und George Pencz. Historischsche Grundlagen und ikonologische Problem ihere        Graphik,* Leipzig: K. F. Koehler, 1975.

Federico Zuccaro, *Scritti d'Arte,* Florence, Giuntina, 1604, ed. D. Heikamp, Florence: Leo S. Olschiki, 1961.

G. Zucchini, "San Michele in Bosco di Bologna," *Archiginmasio* (1943), pp. 51–56.

_____," Il Vasari a Bologna," in *Studi Vasariani,* Florence: G. C. Sansoni, 1952, pp. 153–58.

M. J. Zucker, "Vasari and Parri Spinelli: A study of renaissance and modern attitudes toward a personality of artists," *Gazette des Beaux–Arts* (1979), pp. 199–206.

Stefano Zuffi, ed. *Il Ritratto,* Milan: Electa, 2000.

I. L. Zupnick, *The Age of Vasari: A Loan Exhibition,* Binghamton: Notre Dame College, 1974.